FD-302 (Rev. 5-8-10)

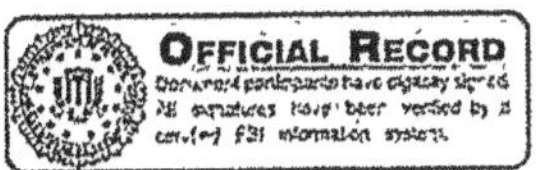

FEDERAL BUREAU OF INVESTIGATION

Date of entry 12/16/2012

[redacted] date of birth [redacted] of [redacted] [redacted] Sandy Hook, Connecticut, 06482, was interviewed at his residence. After being advised of the identity of the interviewing Agents and the nature of the interview, [redacted] provided the following information: b6 -6 b7C -6

[redacted] knew that the Lanza's were divorced. [redacted] [redacted] knew Adam Lanza. b6 -5, 6 b7C -5, 6

[redacted] never really saw the Lanza's. [redacted] [redacted] did not see or hear anything unusual on 12/14/2012. b6 -6 b7C -6

Investigation on 12/14/2012 at Sandy Hook, Connecticut, United States (In Person)

File # 4-NH-2619946 Date drafted 12/16/2012

by [redacted] b6 -1 b7C -1

4-NH-2619946 Serial 32

knew divorced

knew son (20)
-never really saw Lanzas

-did not see anything

b6 -5,
b7C -5,

FD-302 (Rev. 5-8-10)

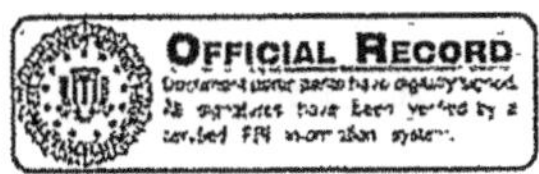

FEDERAL BUREAU OF INVESTIGATION

Date of entry 12/17/2012

[redacted] date of birth (DOB) [redacted] residence address [redacted] [redacted] Texas, cellular telephone number [redacted] was interviewed telephonically. After being advised of the identity of the interviewing Agent and the nature of the interview, [redacted] provided the following information: b6 -6 b7C -6

[redacted] b6 -6 b7C -6

At the news of the shooting, he began doing his own research of the [redacted] who he thought from the news was the shooter. b6 -2 b7C -2

He looked up [redacted] Facebook account and noticed that [redacted] had changed his Facebook avatar on 12/08/12. The new photo was of a male wearing all black clothes and sunglasses. [redacted] found this suspicious because that was similar to what the shooter in CT was wearing. b6 -2, 6 b7C -2, 6

There were a number of posts on [redacted] Facebook page by [redacted] [redacted] The comments said, "Looks like you're dressed like and assassin." [redacted] thought he was referencing a violent video game. [redacted] also made reference to [redacted] wearing a trench coat. [redacted] thought this was similar to the "trench coat mafia" and the Columbine HS shooters. [redacted] final post said, "This can only turn out awesome." b6 -2, 5, 6 b7C -2, 5, 6

[redacted] "read between the lines" and believed [redacted] may have had advance knowledge of the shootings. [redacted] could not access [redacted] Facebook account, it had been locked out. b6 -5, 6 b7C -5, 6

[redacted] later found out that the shooter was not [redacted] but [redacted] [redacted] ADAM LANZA, thus nullifying his thought that [redacted] had prior knowledge. b6 -2, 5, 6 b7C -2, 5, 6

Investigation on 12/14/2012 at Houston, Texas, United States (Phone)

File # 4-NH-2619946 Date drafted 12/17/2012

by [redacted] b6 -1 b7C -1

4-NH-2619946 Serial 33

FD-302 (Rev. 5-8-10)

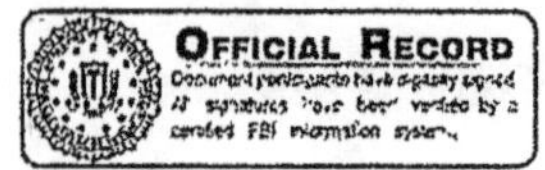

FEDERAL BUREAU OF INVESTIGATION

Date of entry 12/17/2012

[redacted] home telephone number [redacted] residence address [redacted] Sandy Hook, Connecticut, was interviewed at her residence by Special Agent (SA) [redacted] and SA [redacted] After being advised of the identities of the interviewing Agents and the nature of the interview, [redacted] provided the following information: b6 -1, b7C -1,

[redacted] father, [redacted] received a threatening phone call. SA [redacted] examined the caller ID for the home telephone number, [redacted] which showed calls on 12/16/2012, at 12:14pm, 12:16pm, and 12:20pm, from telephone number 646-843-7000, ICALLED INC. [redacted] stated her father, [redacted] answered the first call and an unknown male said in substance, "I'm Adam Lanza, I'm going to kill you." [redacted] argued with the caller and ended the call. The unknown male called the second time and called [redacted] a "faggot." [redacted] hung up on the caller on the third call. b6 b7C

SA [redacted] then called [redacted] stated the caller on the first call stated, "I'm Adam Lanza and you are going to be dead." After arguing with the caller, the caller stated, "No, I'm really going to kill you." [redacted] stated the caller did not have a noticeable accent. b6 -1, b7C -1,

Investigation on 12/16/2012 at Sandy Hook, Connecticut, United States (In Person, Phone)

File # 4-NH-2619946 Date drafted 12/17/2012

by [redacted] b6 b7C

This document contains neither recommendations nor conclusions of the FBI. It is the property of the FBI and is loaned to your agency; it and its contents are not to be distributed outside your agency.

4-NH-2619946 Serial 34

16/12

646-843-7000

I call inc

12:20 pm

12:14 , 16 , 12:20

b6 -7
b7C -7

answered

Adam Lanza , I'm going to kill you

→ argument , ended call

1st call 2nd call 3rd call hang up

yell yell

home phone called

phone

I'm AL and you are going to be dead

no accent (foreign)

– no I'm really going to kill you

FD-302 (Rev. 5-8-10)

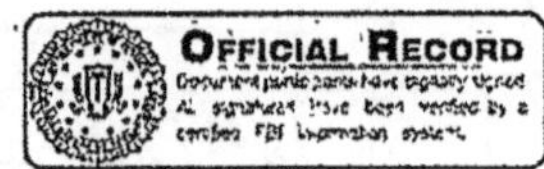

FEDERAL BUREAU OF INVESTIGATION

Date of entry 12/17/2012

[REDACTED] date of birth [REDACTED] residence address [REDACTED] Sandy Hook, Connecticut, was interviewed at his residence. Also present during the interview was [REDACTED] date of birth [REDACTED] After being advised of the identities of the interviewing Agents and the nature of the interview, [REDACTED] and [REDACTED] provided the following information: b6 - b7C

[REDACTED] and [REDACTED] have lived at [REDACTED] for the past [REDACTED] years. [REDACTED] b6 -5, b7C -

[REDACTED] and [REDACTED] didn't know the LANZA family. They never had any interaction with the anyone in the LANZA family. [REDACTED] and [REDACTED] never saw any children at 36 Yogananda Street. The only activity they saw at 36 Yogananda Street was a lady arriving and departing in an automobile. b6 - b7C

On December 14, 2012, [REDACTED] was at home in the morning between 8:00am and 9:00am. She then left her residence and returned home around 9:30am. [REDACTED] left home early in the morning and returned home at noon on December 14, 2012. b6 b7C

[REDACTED] b6 b7

[REDACTED] mentioned that he witnessed, four to five years ago, a kid dressed in all black walk up Yogananda Street to the bus stop and turned around and walked away. [REDACTED] didn't know who the kid was or where he came from. b6 b7

Investigation on 12/14/2012 at Sandy Hook, Connecticut, United States (In Person)

File # 4-NH-2619946 Date drafted 12/17/2012

by [REDACTED] b6 b7

4-NH-2619946 Serial 35

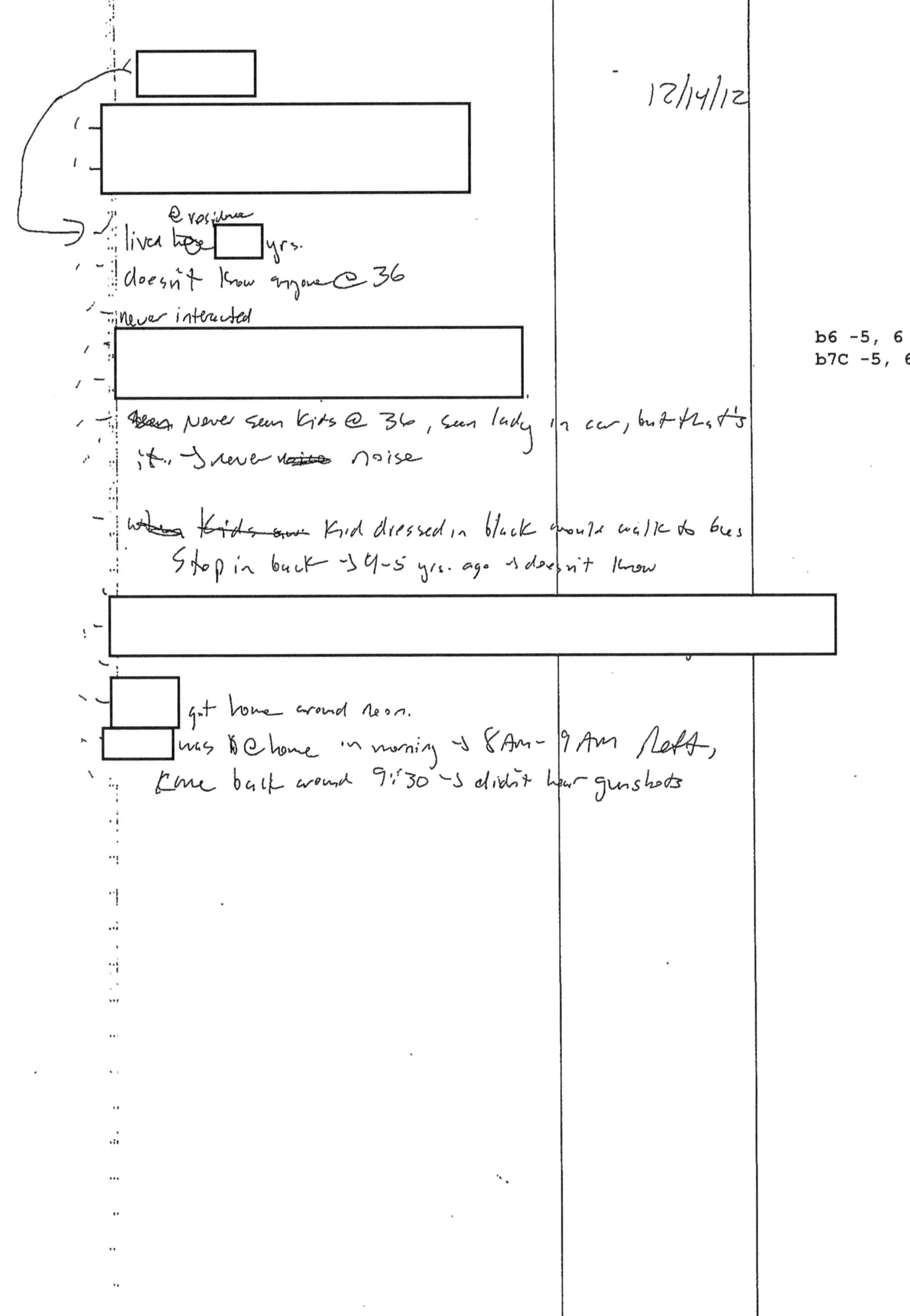

12/14/12

lived ~~here~~ @ residence [redacted] yrs.
doesn't know anyone @ 36
never interacted

~~Never~~ Never seen Kids @ 36, seen lady in car, but that's it. → never ~~noise~~ noise

~~When Kids gone~~ Kid dressed in black would walk to bus Stop in back → 4-5 yrs. ago → doesn't know

[redacted] got home around noon.
[redacted] was @ home in morning → 8AM - 9AM left, came back around 9:30 → didn't hear gunshots

b6 -5, 6
b7C -5, 6

FD-302 (Rev. 5-8-10)

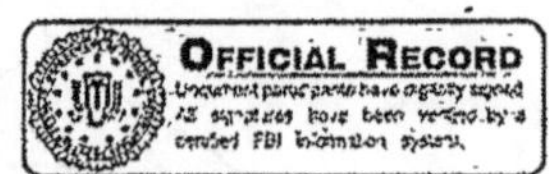

FEDERAL BUREAU OF INVESTIGATION

Date of entry 12/17/2012

Special Agent (SA) [redacted] and SA [redacted] attempted to interview [redacted] on 12/16/2012 at 5:10pm at his residence [redacted] Sandy Hook, Connecticut, telephone number [redacted] No one answered the door and no one answered the home telephone, which could be heard ringing in the house. There was no way to leave a voicemail.

b6 -1,
b7C -1,

Investigation on 12/16/2012 at Sandy Hook, Connecticut, United States (In Person, Phone)

File # 4-NH-2619946 Date drafted 12/17/2012

by [redacted]

b6
b7C

4-NH-2619946 Serial 26

12/14/12

Sandy Hook

5:10pm No answer, left voicemail

b6 -5
b7C -5

FD-302 (Rev. 5-8-10)

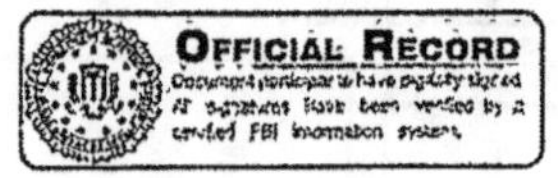

FEDERAL BUREAU OF INVESTIGATION

Date of entry 12/17/2012

[redacted] date of birth (DOB) [redacted] residence address [redacted] [redacted] was interviewed in the driveway of his residence. After being advised of the identities of the interviewing Agents and the nature of the interview, [redacted] provided the following information: b6 b7C

[redacted] advised that he did not know the LANZA family. He never heard other neighbors speak about the LANZA family. [redacted] did not observe any suspicious activity in his neighborhood over the past few weeks. The neighborhood has always been very quiet. b6 b7C

On the morning of December 14, 2012, [redacted] was at work [redacted] b6 -5, b7C -5,

[redacted] advised [redacted] b6 -6, b7C -6

[redacted] advised that he would be willing to cooperate further as it was deemed necessary. b6 -6 b7C -

Investigation on 12/14/2012 at Sandy Hook, Connecticut, United States (In Person)

File # 4-NH-2619946 Date drafted 12/17/2012

by [redacted] b6 b7C

4-NH-2619946 Serial 37

- Did not know the Lazas
- been
- nothing in the past few weeks that was suspicious
- who was in
- quiet neighborhood
- never met Lazas
- " heard anything about the

b6 -5, 6
b7C -5, 6

b6 -6, 7
b7C -6, 7

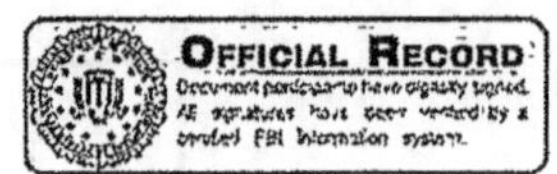

FEDERAL BUREAU OF INVESTIGATION

Date of entry 12/17/2012

[redacted] date of birth (DOB) [redacted] residence address [redacted] Newtown, Connecticut, was interviewed at her residence. After being advised of the identities of the interviewing Agents and the nature of the interview [redacted] provided the following information: b6 b7C

On December 16, 2012, an unidentified male left a voice message on [redacted] answering machine at approximately 9:00am. The voicemail stated, "this is ADAM LANZA, I'm going to kill you. hahaha." [redacted] accidentally erased the voicemail message. [redacted] did not receive any other threatening phone calls on December 16th. b6 b7C

[redacted] advised [redacted] b6 b7C

[redacted] b6 b7C

[redacted] advised that she would be willing to cooperate further as it was deemed necessary. b6 b7C

Investigation on 12/16/2012 at Newtown, Connecticut, United States (In Person)

File # 4-NH-2619946 Date drafted 12/17/2012

by [redacted] b6 b7C

4-NH-2619946 Serial 3

: one call on land line

not have caller ID

d [illegible] call came via

: voice mail

lish, clear - american accent

This is Adam Lanza I'm

g to kill you ha ha

:identaly erased.

other calls or hang-ups

gital answering service (V-Tech)

: +

b6 -7
b7C -7

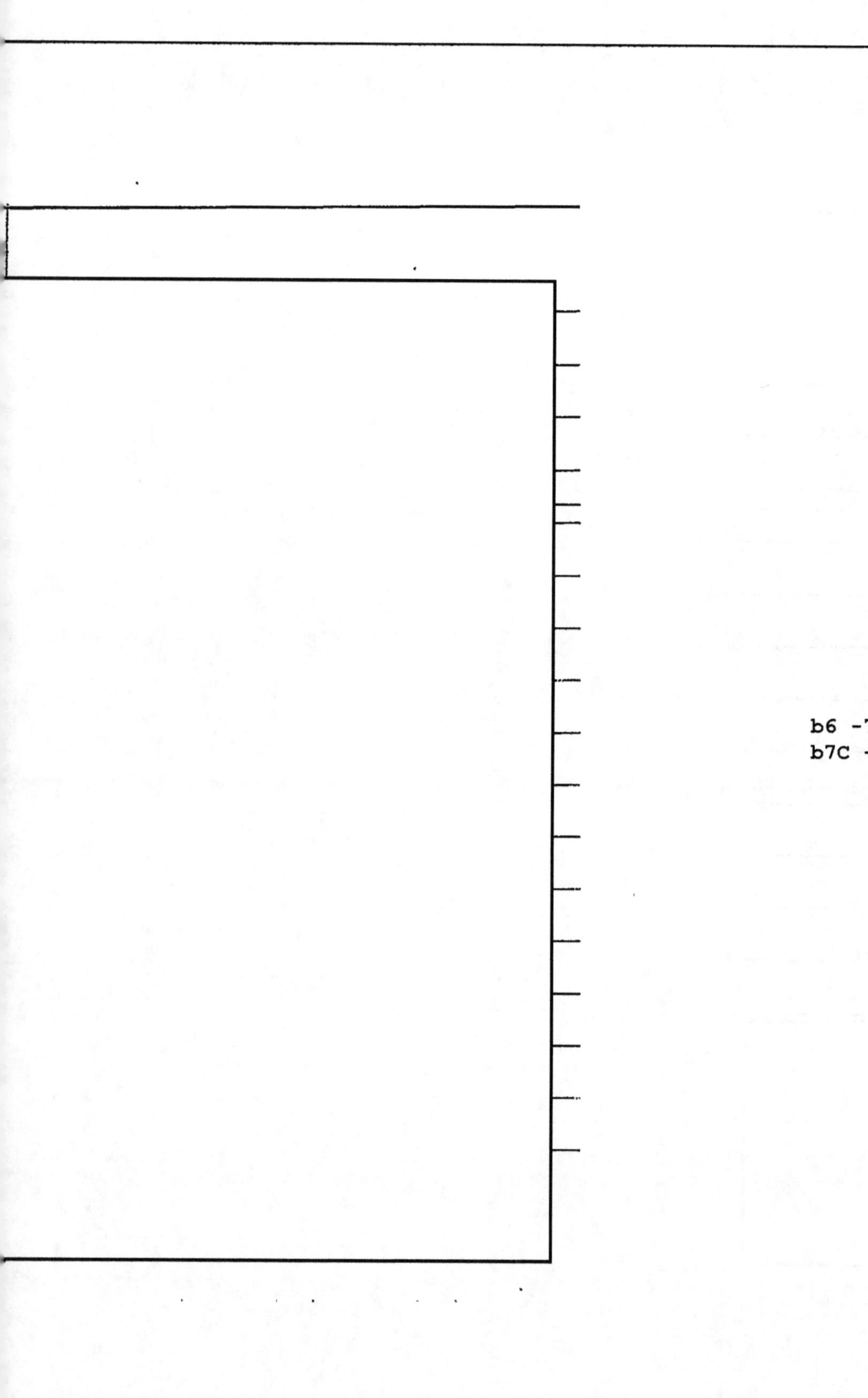

b6 -7
b7C -7

b6 -7
b7C -7

FD-302 (Rev. 5-8-10)

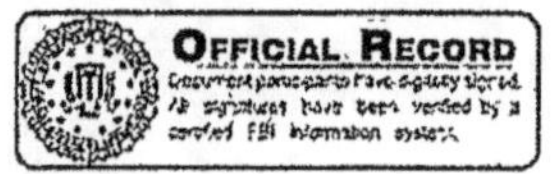

FEDERAL BUREAU OF INVESTIGATION

Date of entry 12/17/2012

[redacted] date of birth [redacted] residence address [redacted] [redacted] Newtown, Connecticut, home telephone number [redacted] was interviewed at his residence. Also present during the interview were [redacted] children, [redacted] date of birth [redacted] and [redacted] date of birth [redacted] After being advised of the identities of the interviewing Agents and the nature of the interview, the [redacted] family provided the following information: b6 - b7C

The [redacted] family received a threatening telephone call between 9:00am and 10:00am on December 16, 2012. [redacted] a friend of [redacted] answered the telephone. The caller identified himself as ADAM LANZA and said "I'm going to kill you." b6 - b7C

The [redacted] family received additional telephone calls on their residence land line. The unidentified male left two threatening voice messages. Administrative note: [redacted] consented to the Agents recording the voice messages left by the unidentified caller. SA [redacted] recorded the voice messages with his Federal Bureau of Investigation (FBI) issued Blackberry. The recording will be preserved and maintained in the case file. b6 -1, b7C -1,

[redacted] answered the telephone twice and spoke to the unidentified caller. The caller threatened to kill [redacted] family. [redacted] asked the caller some questions and the caller was responsive. b6 - b7C

The [redacted] family received more than five threatening telephone calls on December 16, 2012. The caller spoke English. Each time, the caller identified himself as ADAM LANZA. b6 -7 b7C -

[redacted] advised that he would be willing to cooperate further as it was deemed necessary. b6 -7 b7C -

Investigation on 12/16/2012 at Newtown, Connecticut, United States (In Person)

File # 4-NH-2619946 Date drafted 12/17/2012

by [redacted] b6 b7C

4-NH-2619946 Serial 39

b6 -7
b7C -7

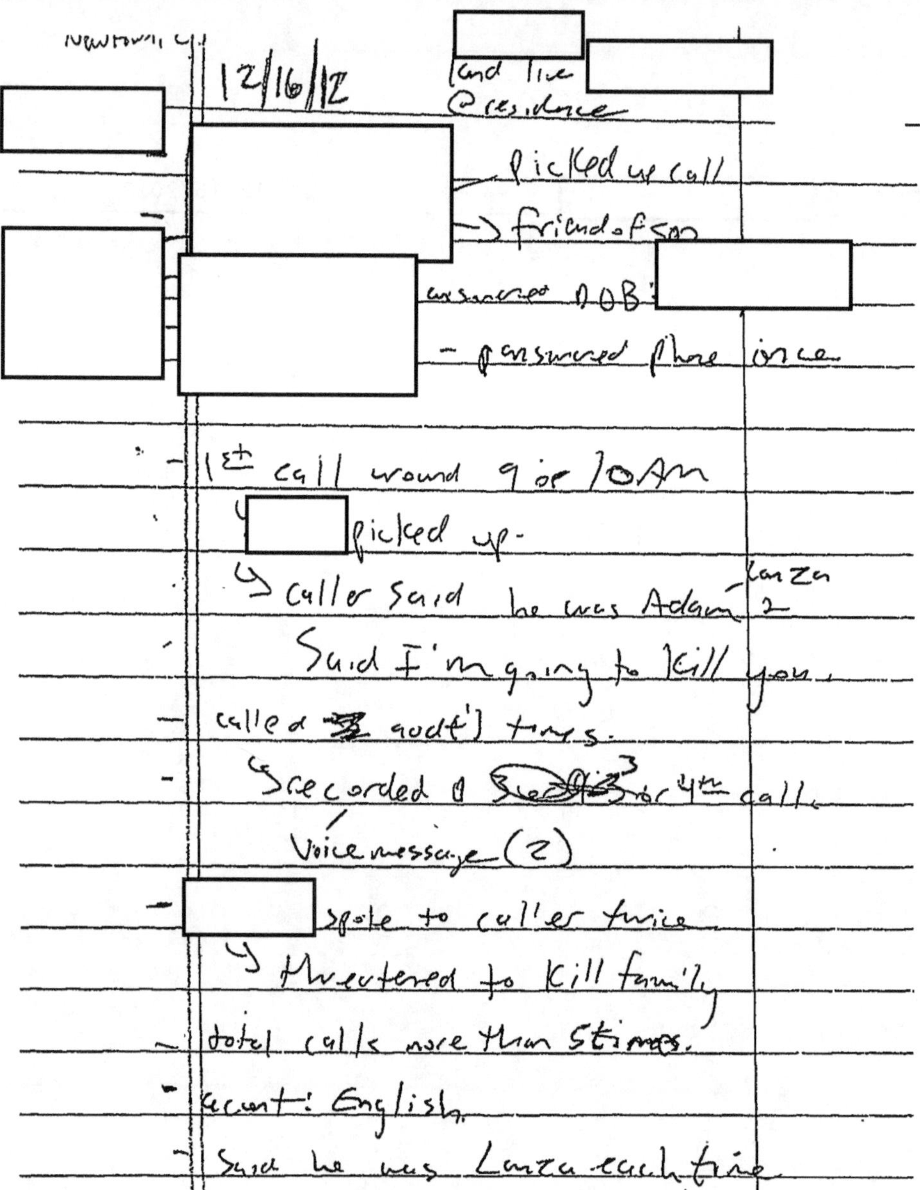

Newtown
12/16/12
land line
@residence
picked up call
friend of son
answered DOB
answered phone once
- 1st call around 9 or 10AM
picked up-
caller said he was Adam Lanza 2
Said I'm going to kill you.
- called addt'l times.
- recorded 3rd or 4th call.
Voice message (2)
- spoke to caller twice
threatened to kill family
- total calls more than 5 times.
- accent: English.
- Said he was Lanza each time
- Consented to taking voice message -

b6 -7
b7C -7

FD-1057 (Rev. 5-8-10)

UNCLASSIFIED

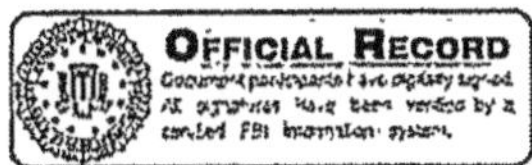

FEDERAL BUREAU OF INVESTIGATION

Electronic Communication

Title: (U) Request to interview [redacted] **Date:** 12/18/2012

To: [redacted]

From: NEW HAVEN
NH-7
Contact: [redacted]

b6 -1, 6
b7C -1, 6

Approved By: [redacted]

Drafted By: [redacted]

Case ID #: 4-NH-2619946 (U) UNSUB(S)
Sandy Hook Elementary School
12 Dickinson St, Sandy Hook, CT-Victim
Firearms Act.
OO:NH

Synopsis: (U) Lead to interview [redacted] for the Newtown, CT school system.

b6 -6
b7C -6

[redacted]

b7E -1

Details:

At 9:40 AM on 14 December 2012, initial call-in to Newtown emergency services (911) was received from Sandy Hook Elementary School in Newtown, Connecticut, that shots had been fired within the school. The gunman, Adam P. Lanza, (DOB:04/22/1992) shot out the windows at the front of the elementary school in order to gain access. Two law enforcement officers arrived during the shooting, at which time the suspect ducked into a classroom and shot himself. The shooter attended the school as a child, but no other relationship between Adam P. Lanza and Sandy Hook Elementary School has been established. There were a total of 28 dead, 20 children and 8 adults (seven at the school, including the gunman, and his mother at their 36 Yogananda Street residence).

UNCLASSIFIED

4-NH-2619946 Serial 40

Title: (U) Request to interview [redacted] b6 b7C
Re: 4-NH-2619946, 12/18/2012

In connection with the investigation into the attack on the Sandy Hook Elementary School on 12/14/2012, Connecticut State Police is requesting FBI assistance in interviewing [redacted] former [redacted] [redacted] for the Newtown, CT school system. [redacted] has been interviewed by numerous media outlets and claims extensive knowledge of the suspect, Adam Lanza. [redacted] b6 -6 b7C -

[redacted] b6 - b7C b7E

♦♦

FD-302 (Rev. 5-8-10)

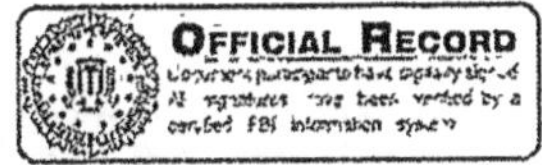

FEDERAL BUREAU OF INVESTIGATION

Date of entry 12/18/2012

On December 17, 2012, [redacted] was contacted at his place of employment, [redacted] After being advised of the identity of the Agent, [redacted] was served with Federal Grand Jury subpoena number [redacted] issued by the United States District Court for the District of CT.

b3 -1
b6 -5
b7C -5

Investigation on 12/18/2012 at New London, Connecticut, United States (, Other (Subpoena Service))

File # 4-NH-2619946 Date drafted 12/18/2012

by [redacted]

b6 -1
b7C -1

4-NH-2619946 Serial 41

AO 110 (Rev. 06/09) Subpoena to Testify Before a Grand Jury

UNITED STATES DISTRICT COURT

for the

District of Connecticut

SUBPOENA TO TESTIFY BEFORE A GRAND JURY

To:

b

YOU ARE COMMANDED to appear in this United States district court at the time, date, and place shown below to testify before the court's grand jury. When you arrive, you must remain at the court until the judge or a court officer allows you to leave.

Place: United States Courthouse 141 Church Street New Haven, CT 06510	Date and Time:

You must also bring with you the following documents, electronically stored information, or objects *(blank if not applicable)*:

b3 -

Date: ______________ *CLERK OF COURT*

December 15, 2012

Signature of Clerk or Deputy Clerk

The name, address, e-mail, and telephone number of the United States attorney, or assistant United States attorney, who requests this subpoena, are:

AUSA
1000 Lafayette Blvd, 10th Floor
Bridgeport, CT 06604

Personal appearance is not required if documents are provided on or before the appearance date to: FBI S/A
600 State St.
New Haven CT 06510

b6 -1, 4
b7C -1, 4

PROOF OF SERVICE

This subpoena for *(name of individual or organization)*
was received by me on *(date)* 12/15/12

☑ I served the subpoena by delivering a copy to the named person as follows:

on *(date)* 12/17/12 ; or

O I returned the subpoena unexecuted because:

b3 -1
b6 -5
b7C -

I declare under penalty of perjury that this information is true.

Date: 12/17/12

Special Agent
Printed name and title

b6 -1
b7C -

2 Union Plaza, Ste. 301, New London, CT 06320
Server's address

Additional information regarding attempted service, etc:

FD-302 (Rev. 5-8-10)

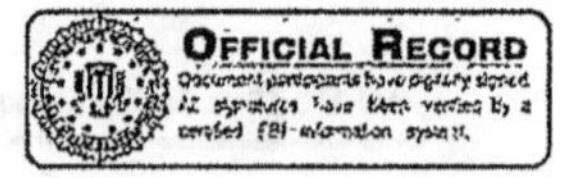

FEDERAL BUREAU OF INVESTIGATION

Date of entry 12/18/2012

On December 17, 2012, Special Agent (SA) [redacted] served [redacted] [redacted] Federal Grand Jury subpoena number [redacted] issued by the United States District Court for the District of Connecticut, via FedEx.

b3
b6
b7C

Investigation on 12/18/2012 at New London, Connecticut, United States (, Other (Subpoena Service))

File # 4-NH-2619946 Date drafted 12/18/2012

by [redacted]

b6
b7C

This document contains neither recommendations nor conclusions of the FBI. It is the property of the FBI and is loaned to your agency; it and its contents are not to be distributed outside your agency.

4-NH-2619946 Serial 42

AO 110 (Rev. 06/09) Subpoena to Testify Before a Grand Jury

UNITED STATES DISTRICT COURT

for the

District of Connecticut

SUBPOENA TO TESTIFY BEFORE A GRAND JURY

To:

b3 -1

to appear in this United States district court at the time, date, and place shown below to testify before the court's grand jury. When you arrive, you must remain at the court until the judge or a court officer allows you to leave.

Place: United States Courthouse 141 Church Street New Haven, CT 06510	Date and Time:

You must also bring with you the following documents, electronically stored information, or objects *(blank if not applicable)*:

b3 -1

Date: December 15, 2012

CLERK OF COURT

Signature of Clerk or Deputy Clerk

The name, address, e-mail, and telephone number of the United States attorney, or assistant United States attorney, who requests this subpoena, are:

AUSA
157 Church St., 23rd floor
New Haven, CT 06510

Personal appearance is not required if documents are provided on or before the appearance date to: FBI S/A
600 State St.
New Haven CT 06510

b3 -1
b6 -1, 4
b7C -1, 4

PROOF OF SERVICE

This subpoena for *(name of individual or organization)* ______
was received by me on *(date)* 12/15/12 .

☑ I served the subpoena by delivering a copy to the named person as follows: ______
______ via Fed Ex
______ on *(date)* 12/17/12 ; or

☐ I returned the subpoena unexecuted because: ______

I declare under penalty of perjury that this information is true.

Date: 12/17/12

Server's signature

______ Special Agent
Printed name and title

2 Union Plaza, Ste. 301, New London CT 06320
Server's address

Additional information regarding attempted service, etc:

b6
b7C

FD-302 (Rev. 5-8-10)

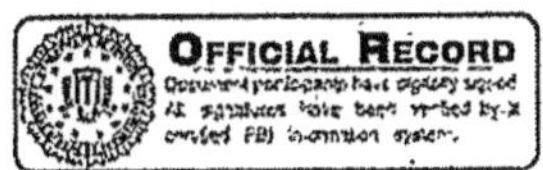

FEDERAL BUREAU OF INVESTIGATION

Date of entry 12/18/2012

On December 17, 2012, Special Agent (SA) [redacted] served [redacted] [redacted] Federal Grand Jury subpoena number [redacted] issued by the United States District Court for the District of Connecticut, via FedEx.

b3 -1
b6 -1
b7C -1

Investigation on 12/18/2012 at New London, Connecticut, United States (, Other (Subpoena Service))

File # 4-NH-2619946 Date drafted 12/18/2012

by [redacted]

b6 -1
b7C -1

4-NH-2619946 Serial 43

AO 110 (Rev. 06/09) Subpoena to Testify Before a Grand Jury

UNITED STATES DISTRICT COURT

for the

District of Connecticut

SUBPOENA TO TESTIFY BEFORE A GRAND JURY

To:

b3

YOU ARE COMMANDED to appear in this United States district court at the time, date, and place shown below to testify before the court's grand jury. When you arrive, you must remain at the court until the judge or a court officer allows you to leave.

Place: United States Courthouse 141 Church Street New Haven, CT 06510	Date and Time:

You must also bring with you the following documents, electronically stored information, or objects *(blank if not applicable)*:

b3 -1

Date: December 15, 2012

CLERK OF COURT

Signature of Clerk or Deputy Clerk

The name, address, e-mail, and telephone number of the United States attorney, or assistant United States attorney, who requests this subpoena, are:

AUSA
157 Church St., 23rd floor
New Haven, CT 06510

Personal appearance is not required if documents are provided on or before the appearance date to: FBI S/A
600 State St.
New Haven CT 06510

b3 -1
b6 -1
b7C -

PROOF OF SERVICE

This subpoena for *(name of individual or organization)* __________
was received by me on *(date)* 12/15/12 .

☑ I served the subpoena by delivering a copy to the named person as follows: __________
__________ via Fed Ex
on *(date)* 12/17/12 ; or

☐ I returned the subpoena unexecuted because: __________

b3 -1

I declare under penalty of perjury that this information is true.

Date: 12/17/12

b6 -1
b7C -

__________ Special Agent
Printed name and title

2 Union Plaza, Ste. 301, New London, CT 06320
Server's address

Additional information regarding attempted service, etc:

FD-302 (Rev. 5-8-10)

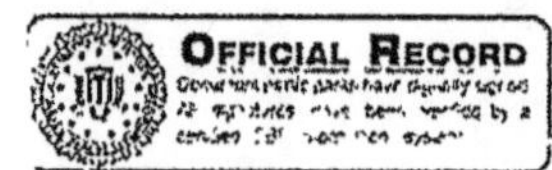

FEDERAL BUREAU OF INVESTIGATION

Date of entry 12/18/2012

[REDACTED] (PROTECT IDENTIY), [REDACTED] [REDACTED] telephone number [REDACTED] contacted the Newtown Command Post anonymously with information. A search of data bases revealed the above information being connected to the telephone number on which the anonymous call was made. Writer then telephonically contacted [REDACTED] After being advised of the identity of the interviewing Agent and the nature of the interview, [REDACTED] provided the following information: b6 - b7C b7D

[REDACTED] confirmed his identity and address and provided his date of birth as [REDACTED] b6 b7C b7D

[REDACTED]

[REDACTED] b6 -5 b7C - b7D -

[REDACTED] b6 -5, b7C -5, b7D -1

Investigation on 12/16/2012 at Newtown, Connecticut, United States (Phone)

File # 4-NH-2619946 Date drafted 12/18/2012

by [REDACTED] b6 b7C

4-NH-2619946 Serial 44

b6 -6
b7C -6
b7D -1

b6 -5, 6
b7C -5, 6
b7D -1

b6 -5, 6
b7C -5, 6
b7D -1

advised

b6 -5, 6
b7C -5, 6
b7D -1

advised that he would be willing to cooperate further as it was deemed necessary.

FD-1057 (Rev. 5-8-10)

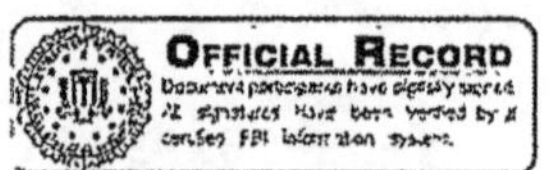

UNCLASSIFIED

FEDERAL BUREAU OF INVESTIGATION

Electronic Communication

Title: (U) [redacted] **Date:** 12/18/2012

From: NEW HAVEN
NH-3
Contact: [redacted] b6 -1, 2 b7C -1,

Approved By: [redacted]

Drafted By: [redacted]

Case ID #: 4-NH-2619946 (U) UNSUB(S)
Sandy Hook Elementary School
12 Dickinson St, Sandy Hook, CT-Victim
Firearms Act.
OO:NH

Synopsis: (U) To document Amtrak train ticket information related to [redacted] in the case file.

[redacted] b6 -2 b7C -2 b7E -1

Enclosure(s): Enclosed are the following items:
1. (U) Amtrak Tickets for [redacted]

Details:

On 12/17/2012, [redacted] Amtrak Police Department, Rail Security Team, NJTTF, telephone [redacted] advised that [redacted]

[redacted] b6 -2, b7C -2,

♦♦

UNCLASSIFIED

4-NH-2619946 Serial 45

FD-302 (Rev. 5-8-10)

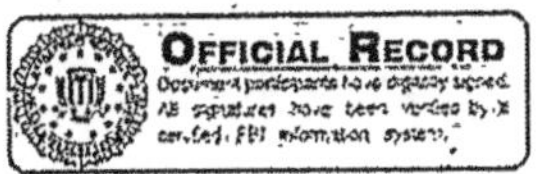

FEDERAL BUREAU OF INVESTIGATION

Date of entry 12/17/2012

The following are the results of a neighborhood canvass conducted in conjunction with captioned investigation. The canvass occurred on December 14, 2012. The addresses covered in this summary of the canvass were homes number [redacted] and [redacted] Newtown, Connecticut: b6 -5, 6 b7C -5, 6

[redacted]: [redacted] date of birth [redacted] and [redacted] date of birth [redacted] would not know any of the residents at 36 Yogananda Street even if they saw pictures of them. The [redacted] have lived in their home since [redacted]. They did not see or hear anything unusual in their neighborhood for the past several days, including today. b6 -6 b7C -6

[redacted] frequently walks the neighborhood and has noticed that the residents of 36 Yogananda Street always have many empty bottles of bottled water out on the street in their recycling when it is collected each week. She never saw anyone outside house number thirty-six on her walks. b6 -6 b7C -6

The telephone number for the [redacted] home is [redacted] b6 -6 b7C -6

[redacted]: There was no response to Agents knocking on the door and ringing the doorbell of this address. It appeared that there was no one home. b6 -5 b7C -5

Investigation on 12/14/2012 at Newtown, Connecticut, United States (In Person)

File # 4-NH-2619946 Date drafted 12/18/2012

by [redacted] b6 -1 b7C -1

4-NH-2619946 Serial 46

FD-302 (Rev. 5-8-10)

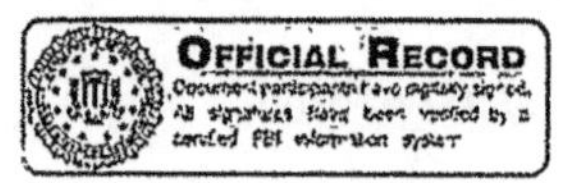

FEDERAL BUREAU OF INVESTIGATION

Date of entry 12/17/2012

[redacted] male, date of birth [redacted] was interviewed at his residence, located at [redacted] Sandy Hook, Connecticut, by the undersigned agents. Also interviewed was [redacted] female, date of birth [redacted] Their home telephone number is [redacted] and [redacted] cellular telephone number is [redacted] After being advised of the identities of the interviewing Agents and the nature of the interview, [redacted] and [redacted] provided the following information:

b6 b7C

[redacted] and [redacted] have lived in this house for approximately [redacted] years. [redacted]

b6 b7C

Neither [redacted] nor [redacted] knew NANCY LANZA (NANCY) very well. [redacted] NANCY never made an effort to introduce herself to [redacted] and [redacted] and [redacted] had heard [redacted] that the couple living at 36 Yogananda Street were getting a divorce. They did not know NANCY's former husband well, either.

b6 b7C

[redacted] and [redacted] weren't even sure of NANCY's last name until they heard it mentioned on news reports earlier today. They thought that NANCY had one son, but learned through the news reports that she had another son living in another State. [redacted] and [redacted] were unaware of the violence that had been inflicted upon NANCY until they heard about it on the news.

b6 b7C

At approximately 10:00 a.m. today, while [redacted] was at work, the Newtown Police Department told [redacted] she had to evacuate her residence immediately. [redacted] did as she was instructed by the police, and only returned to her home in the early evening. [redacted] date of birth [redacted] residing at [redacted] was with [redacted] when this happened, but has since returned to his residence. Neither [redacted] nor [redacted] thought that [redacted] would know any more about the LANZA family than they did.

b6 -5, b7C -5

Investigation on 12/14/2012 at Sandy Hook, Connecticut, United States (In Person)

File # 4-NH-2619946 Date drafted 12/17/2012

by [redacted]

b6 b7C

4-NH-2619946 Serial 47

FD-302 (Rev. 5-8-10)

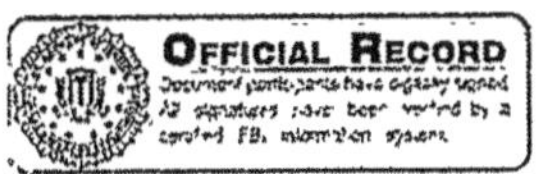

FEDERAL BUREAU OF INVESTIGATION

Date of entry 12/17/2012

[redacted] date of birth (DOB) [redacted] residence address [redacted] telephone number [redacted] was interviewed telephonically. After being advised of the identity of the interviewing Agent and the nature of the interview, [redacted] provided the following information: b6 -6 b7C -6

[redacted] advised that [redacted] stated on his Facebook page that ADAM LANZA and [redacted] were his heroes. [redacted] thought that [redacted] was friends with the LANZA brothers on Facebook. [redacted] also observed a Facebook conversation between [redacted] and another individual on Facebook. In the conversation [redacted] told the individual that he was moving to Canada and that if everything would have worked out, they would have made a lot of money. [redacted] was not certain if those statements were related to the LANZA brothers. [redacted] eventually removed those comments from his Facebook wall. [redacted] also had a picture of [redacted] on his Facebook page. [redacted] thought that [redacted] lived in Connecticut at one time, but she was not certain. [redacted] has never met [redacted] in person, but she believed that he currently resided in Indiana. b6 -5, 6 b7C -5, 6

[redacted] advised that she would be willing to cooperate further as it was deemed necessary. b6 -6 b7C -6

Investigation on 12/15/2012 at Bridgeport, Connecticut, United States (In Person)

File # 4-NH-2619946 Date drafted 12/17/2012

by [redacted] b6 -1 b7C -1

4-NH-2619946 Serial 48

12/15/12
Telephonic

[redacted] [redacted]

[redacted] FA - Concerns

[redacted] states that Lanzas are heroes

Am thought that Lanza's were friends w/ [redacted] b6 -5, b7C -5

FB conversation b/t [redacted] & friend - "Move to Canada, if everything worked out, they would have ~~gotten paid~~ made a lot of $. → Lanzas?

[redacted] removed those comments from FB wall

Thought that [redacted] lived in CT @ some time

never met in person, but believes live in Indiana

FD-302 (Rev. 5-8-10)

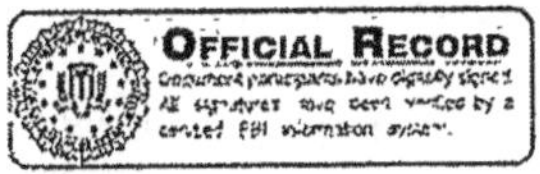

FEDERAL BUREAU OF INVESTIGATION

Date of entry 12/18/2012

[redacted] date of birth (DOB) [redacted] SSN: [redacted] Cell: [redacted] was interviewed at [redacted] After being advised of the identity of the interviewing Agent and the nature of the interview, [redacted] provided the following information: b6 -6 b7C -6

[redacted] b6 -5, 6 b7C -5, 6

[redacted] went to the Worcester rifle range to shoot Adam's two rifles. [redacted]

[redacted] Adam's schooling which began at Sandy Hook Elementary School for grades K-4th. Adam then moved onto Newtown Middle School for grades 5th-7th. Around 7th grade Adam moved to St. Mary's Catholic School. Once completing middle school Adam moved onto Newtown High School where he completed 9th grade and then Nancy [redacted] thought it was best to remove Adam from school and home school him through graduation. Around Adam's 6th grade he was diagnosed with Asperger's and a great deal of school and societal stresses started to present and was the reason why he moved to St. Mary's Catholic School. [redacted] Adam was bullied, but not excessively, for his social awkwardness and his physical gate, both results of his disease. Adam continued in school until his 9th grade year when stresses over papers, classes, pressure from grades and b6 -6 b7C -6

Investigation on 12/14/2012 at [redacted] United States (In Person) b6 -1, 6

File # 4-NH-2619946 Date drafted 12/18/2012 b7C -1, 6

by [redacted]

4-NH-2619946 Serial 49

b6
b7C

dealing with his disease he finally was removed from school. Adam never completely accepted that he had a disease and therefore never took any of his medication he was prescribed. [redacted] Adam was in complete denial of his disease from diagnosis and therefore was not on disability because of this denial.

b6
b7C

[redacted] Adam was a member of the tech club, but never was able to maintain any of the relationship he established there. [redacted] Adam [redacted] never had got in trouble in school or with the police [redacted] nor [redacted] demonstrate any violent tendencies as far as [redacted] knew when it came to harming animals, or getting into fights. [redacted]

b6 -5,
b7C -5,

November 2012 Nancy [redacted] to chip in for buying Adam a computer or parts for a computer for Adam to build himself. [redacted] summarizes the reason why Nancy wanted to do this as Adam has become a shut in and he hasn't gone anywhere in 3 months, his battery in his car is dead because it's been sitting there so long. [redacted] could tell that Nancy was worried about Adam.

b6 -
b7C

Adam's hobbies would vary over the course of time since he would find one interest and then not care about it every few months. Some of Adam's hobbies included building computers, online gaming, and writing, poetry, hiking, and shooting. Some of the walks [redacted] Adam would take would be around Sandy Hook Elementary School [redacted] Adam [redacted] loved this school and liked to visit. [redacted] took Adam to the range once or twice [redacted] only knew of Adam having two rifles, one black single barrel shotgun and one black large caliber rifle. [redacted] never knew that Adam owned any pistols or any other rifles, but does remember Nancy taking Adam to pistol safety courses so he could fire a pistol at the local range. [redacted] did not know how or why Adam became involved in firearms as a hobby.

b6
b7C

[redacted] never knew Adam to have any interest in social media such as Facebook, Myspace, forums, or anything of the same. [redacted] gave the one email address he knew of Adam's as blarvink@gmail.com. [redacted] also stated that this blarvink user name was what Adam used on all of his online gaming community account. [redacted] believed Adam played mostly fantasy role playing games, but couldn't remember any of their names.

b6
b7C

Adam had a cell phone but would never use it. [redacted] would attempt to call him on it, but it would only go to voice mail so he would mainly just email Adam when he would try to reach him. The number [redacted] had for Adam in

b6
b7C

b6 -6
b7C -6

his cell phone was 203-364-9879.

Nancy would take care of all of Adam's needs. She would shop for him, cook him food, do his laundry, and other household choirs. However, she never cleaned his room, nor was allowed in his room. Adam's room was his personal space that no one else was allowed into. [redacted] also mentioned that Adam would sometimes sleep on the floor, or sleep without pillows and some other strange behaviors [redacted] and Nancy just accepted as part of the disease [redacted] said Adam never appreciated what Nancy did for him.

b6 -6
b7C -6

FD-302 (Rev. 5-8-10)

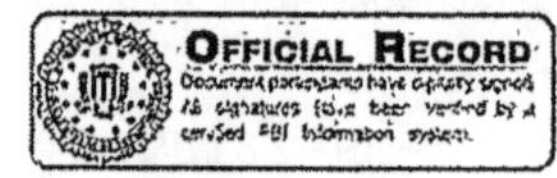

FEDERAL BUREAU OF INVESTIGATION

Date of entry 12/18/2012

[redacted] date of birth (DOB) [redacted] residing at [redacted] Cell [redacted] was interviewed at [redacted] on 12/14/2012. After being advised of the identity of the interviewing Agent and the nature of the interview, [redacted] provided the following information: b6 b7C

On 12/14/2012 [redacted] left his residence for work, [redacted] at approximately 8:50am. [redacted] purchased coffee at a Dunkin Donuts at [redacted] with his Bank of America Credit Card and arrived at his office at approximately 9:45am. b6 - b7C

[redacted]

b6 -5, b7C -5

Investigation on 12/14/2012 at [redacted] United States (In Person)

File # 4-NH-2619946 Date drafted 12/18/2012 b6 -1 b7C -

by [redacted]

4-NH-2619946 Serial 50

b6 -6
b7C -6

b6 -6
b7C -6

b6 -5, 6
b7C -5, 6

ADAM was diagnosed with Ashberger's Syndrome, a form of autism, in approximately the 8th grade. He left high school in either the 9th or 10th grade, and essentially became a "recluse", shutting himself in his bedroom, playing video games all day. He attended a few courses at Western Connecticut State University, but never attended full time. [redacted] b6 -6 b7C -6

[redacted] stated that ADAM has no friends, no associates, no girlfriend, but is very "computer savvy", and spends most of his time on his computer. At some point ADAM worked briefly at a computer repair shop in Newtown, but never held any other job, including summer work while still in school. b6 -6 b7C -6

[redacted] ADAM became very interested in firearms, and at one point considered joining the military. ADAM enjoyed target shooting, [redacted] ADAM and NANCY owned at least four guns; a black AR-15 semi-automatic b6 -6 b7C -6

 b6 b7C

.223 rifle, a Lee Enfield .308 rifle, a "semi-automatic" shotgun and a .45cal pistol [redacted] believed all the weapons had been legally purchased by NANCY, and were registered in her name, but that ADAM actually owned the AR-15, and that all the weapons were kept in a gun safe in ADAM's bedroom closet. b6 b7C

[redacted] advised that ADAM had taken an NRA safety certification course that allowed him to fire the .45cal pistol at the Danbury range, and that to his knowledge ADAM was able to purchase all his ammunition legally. b6 b7C

[redacted] advised that ADAM and NANCY had a "close relationship", and as he had no outside friends, she became the only person ADAM would talk to. Although ADAM spent the majority of his time playing video games, they were non-violent games. His favorite was Super Mario Brothers. Although he often became frustrated at not being able to "express himself", ADAM never became violent. He never used drugs or alcohol, and actually "hated the thought of it". [redacted] could provide no explanation or motive for ADAM's actions. b6 b7C

[redacted] b6 b7C

FD-302 (Rev. 5-8-10)

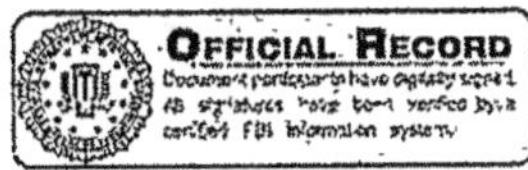

FEDERAL BUREAU OF INVESTIGATION

Date of entry 12/17/2012

[redacted] date of birth (DOB) [redacted] residence address [redacted] Sandy Hook, Connecticut, was interviewed at his residence. Also present at the interview was [redacted] [redacted] DOB [redacted] After being advised of the identities of the interviewing Agents and the nature of the interview, [redacted] and [redacted] provided the following information: b6 -6 b7C -6

[redacted] and [redacted] advised they did not know the residents who lived at 36 Yogananda Street, Sandy Hook, Connecticut. [redacted] and [redacted] moved to their current residence in [redacted] Since that time, they have not had any interactions with the family residing at 36 Yogananda Street. b6 -6 b7C -6

[redacted] and [redacted] were not home on the morning of December 14, 2012. They did not notice any suspicious activity in their neighborhood within the past few weeks. b6 -6 b7C -6

[redacted] b6 -5, 6 b7C -5, 6

[redacted] and [redacted] advised that they would be willing to cooperate further as it was deemed necessary. b6 -6 b7C -6

Investigation on 12/14/2012 at Sandy Hook, Connecticut, United States (In Person)

File # 4-NH-2619946 Date drafted 12/17/2012

by [redacted] b6 -1 b7C -1

4-NH-2619946 , Serial 51

- was @ work in
- she was not @ home

Dont know the family
moved here
did not here when they moved in

- mostly out of the ordinary
- never met Mrs [illegible]

b6 -5, 6
b7C -5, 6

FD-1057 (Rev. 5-8-10)

UNCLASSIFIED

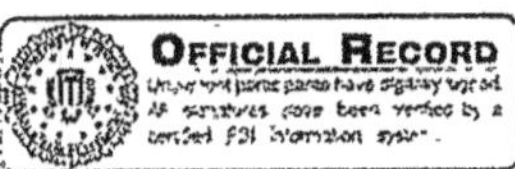

FEDERAL BUREAU OF INVESTIGATION

Electronic Communication

Title: (U) [redacted] Information

Date: 12/17/2012

From: NEW HAVEN
NH-3
Contact: [redacted]

b6 -1, 2
b7C -1, 2

Approved By: [redacted]

Drafted By: [redacted]

Case ID #: 4-NH-2619946

(U) UNSUB(S)
Sandy Hook Elementary School
12 Dickinson St, Sandy Hook, CT-Victim
Firearms Act.
OO:NH

Synopsis: (U) To document [redacted] information in case file.

b6 -2
b7C -2

[redacted]

b7E -1

Details:

On 12/14/2012, [redacted] [redacted] telephone number [redacted] advised [redacted]

b6 -2
b7C -2

♦♦

UNCLASSIFIED

4-NH-2619946 Serial 52

FD-1057 (Rev. 5-8-10)

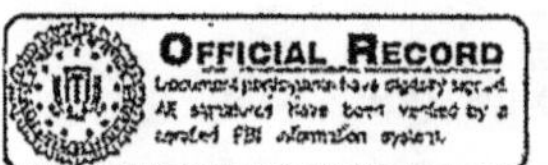

UNCLASSIFIED

FEDERAL BUREAU OF INVESTIGATION

Electronic Communication

Title: (U) [redacted] Information **Date:** 12/17/2012

From: NEW HAVEN
NH-3
Contact: [redacted] b6 -1, 2 b7C -1, 2

Approved By: [redacted]

Drafted By: [redacted]

Case ID #: 4-NH-2619946 (U) UNSUB(S)
Sandy Hook Elementary School
12 Dickinson St, Sandy Hook, CT-Victim
Firearms Act.
OO:NH

Synopsis: (U) To document [redacted] information in the case file. b6 -2 b7C -2

[redacted] b7E -1

Details:

On 12/14/2012, writer met with [redacted] provided the below listed [redacted] information [redacted] b6 -2, b7C -2

[redacted] b6 -2 b7C -2

UNCLASSIFIED

4-NH-2619946 Serial 53

Title: (U) [redacted] Information b6 -2 b7C -2
Re: 4-NH-2619946, 12/17/2012

[redacted] b6 -2 b7C -2

[redacted] advised that [redacted] b6 -2, 6 b7C -2, 6
records associated with [redacted] could be released with a subpoena requesting this information.

♦♦

FD-1057 (Rev. 5-8-10)

UNCLASSIFIED

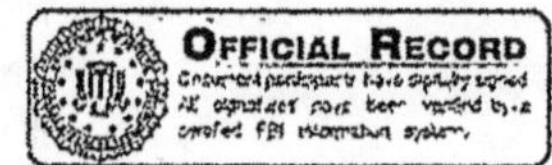

FEDERAL BUREAU OF INVESTIGATION

Electronic Communication

Title: (U) Agency Checks

Date: 12/17/2012

From: NEW HAVEN
NH-3
Contact: [redacted]

Approved By: [redacted]

Drafted By: [redacted]

b6 -1
b7C -

Case ID #: 4-NH-2619946

(U) UNSUB(S)
Sandy Hook Elementary School
12 Dickinson St, Sandy Hook, CT-Victim
Firearms Act.
OO:NH

Synopsis: (U) To document agency checks in case file.

[redacted] b7E -

Details:

(U) NJTTF reports [redacted]

[redacted] b7E -3

UNCLASSIFIED

4-NH-2619946 Seria

Title: (U) Agency Checks
Re: 4-NH-2619946, 12/17/2012

b7E -3

Title: (U) Agency Checks
Re: 4-NH-2619946, 12/17/2012

b7E -3

♦♦

FD-1036 (Rev. 10-16-2009)

UNCLASSIFIED

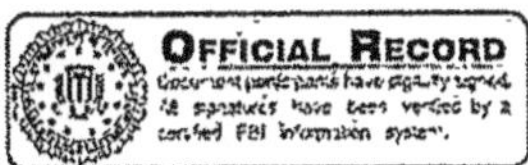

FEDERAL BUREAU OF INVESTIGATION

Import Form

Form Type: OTHER **Date:** 12/17/2012

Title: (U) 12/15/12 Preservation letter to [redacted] b3 -1 b7E -6

Approved By: [redacted]

Drafted By: [redacted] b6 -1 b7C -1

Case ID #: 4-NH-2619946 (U) UNSUB(S)
Sandy Hook Elementary School
12 Dickinson St, Sandy Hook, CT-Victim
Firearms Act.
OO:NH

Synopsis: (U) 12/15/12 Preservation letter to [redacted]

[redacted] b3 -1 b6 -2 b7C -2 b7E -6

♦♦

UNCLASSIFIED

4-NH-2619946 Serial 55

FAX TRANSMISSION

United States Attorney
Connecticut
157 Church St., 23rd floor
New Haven, Connecticut 06510

To ATTN:		b3 -1 b7E -6
Fax		
From	Assistant United States Attorney	**Voice**
Fax		b6 -4 b7C -4
Date	December 15, 2012	**Pages** 3, including this page
Subject	Preservation letter under 18 U.S.C. § 2703(f)	

U.S. Department of Justice

United States Attorney
Connecticut

157 Church St., 23rd floor
New Haven, Connecticut 06510

PHONE: 203.821.3796
FAX: 203.773.5373

December 15, 2012

b3 -1
b7E -6

Re: Request for Preservation of Records

Dear

Pursuant to Title 18, United States Code, Section 2703(f), this letter is a formal request for the preservation of all stored communications, records, and other evidence in your possession regarding the following screen names pending further legal process:

b3 -1
b6 -2
b7C -2
b7E -6

I request that you not disclose the existence of this request to the subscriber or any other person, other than as necessary to comply with this request. If compliance with this request might result in a permanent or temporary termination of service to or otherwise alert any user of as to your actions to preserve the information described below, please contact me as soon as possible and before taking action. b3 -1 b7E -6

I request that you preserve, for a period of 90 days, the information described below currently in your possession in a form that includes the complete record. This request applies only retrospectively. It does not in any way obligate you to capture and preserve new information that arises after the date of this request. This request applies to the following items, whether in electronic or other form, including information stored on backup media, if available:

b3 -1
b7E -6

b3
b7E

If you have questions regarding this request, please call me at

Sincerely,

David B. Fein
UNITED STATES ATTORNEY

b6
b7C

Assistant United States Attorney

FD-1036 (Rev. 10-16-2009)

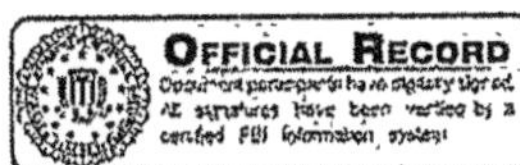

UNCLASSIFIED

FEDERAL BUREAU OF INVESTIGATION

Import Form

Form Type: OTHER

Date: 12/17/2012

Title: (U) 12/15/12 Preservation letter to [redacted] b3 -1 b7E -6

Approved By: [redacted] b6 -1 b7C -1

Drafted By: [redacted]

Case ID #: 4-NH-2619946 (U) UNSUB(S)
Sandy Hook Elementary School
12 Dickinson St, Sandy Hook, CT-Victim
Firearms Act.
OO:NH

Synopsis: (U) 12/15/12 Preservation letter to [redacted]

[redacted] b3 -1 b6 -2 b7C -2 b7E -6

♦♦

UNCLASSIFIED

4-NH-2619946 Serial 56

U.S. Department of Justice

United States Attorney
District of Connecticut

1000 Lafayette Boulevard, 10th Floor
Bridgeport, Connecticut 06604

(203) 696-3000
Fax (203) 579-5550

December 15, 2012

VIA FACSIMILE

b3 -1
b7E -6

Re: Preservation Letter

Dear Sir or Madam:

You are hereby requested to preserve, under the provisions of Title 18, United States Code, Section 2703(f)(1), all communications, records, and other evidence in your possession including records stored on backup media, associated with

b3 -1
b6 -2
b7C -2
b7E -6

You are requested not to disclose the existence of this request or its contents to the subscribers or to any other person; other than as necessary to comply with this request. If compliance with this request might result in a permanent or temporary termination of service or otherwise might alert any user of as to your actions to preserve the information described below, please contact me as soon as possible before taking action.

b3 -1
b7E -6

I request that you preserve, for a period of 90 days, the information described below currently in your possession in a form that includes the complete record. This request applies only retrospectively. It does not in any way obligate you to capture and preserve new information that arises after the date of this request. This request applies to the following items, whether in electronic or other form, including information stored on backup media if available:

b3 -1
b7E -6

If you have questions regarding this request, please call me at Thank you for your assistance in this matter.

Very truly yours,

DAVID B. FEIN
UNITED STATES ATTORNEY

b6 -4
b7C -4

ASSISTANT UNITED STATES ATTORNEY

FD-1036 (Rev. 10-16-2009)

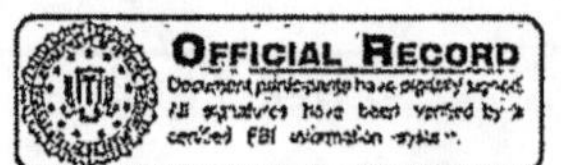

UNCLASSIFIED

FEDERAL BUREAU OF INVESTIGATION

Import Form

Form Type: OTHER **Date:** 12/17/2012

Title: (U) 12/14/12 Preservation letter to [redacted]

Approved By: [redacted]

Drafted By: [redacted]

b3 -1
b6 -1
b7C -1
b7E -6

Case ID #: 4-NH-2619946 (U) UNSUB(S)
Sandy Hook Elementary School
12 Dickinson St, Sandy Hook, CT-Victim
Firearms Act.
OO:NH

Synopsis: (U) A 12/14/12 preservation letter to [redacted] prior to legal process: [redacted]

b3 -
b7E

♦♦

UNCLASSIFIED

4-NH-2619946 Serial 57

FAX TRANSMISSION

United States Attorney
Connecticut
157 Church St., 23rd floor
New Haven, Connecticut 06510

To			b3 -1
Fax			b7E -6
From	Assistant United States Attorney	**Voice**	b6 -4
Fax			b7C -4
Date	December 14, 2012	**Pages**	3, including this page
Subject	Preservation letter under 18 U.S.C. § 2703(f)		

U.S. Department of Justice

United States Attorney
Connecticut

157 Church St., 23rd floor
New Haven, Connecticut 06510

PHONE: 203.821.3796
FAX: 203.773.5373

December 14, 2012

b3 -1
b7E -6

Re: Request for Preservation of Records

Dea

Pursuant to Title 18, United States Code, Section 2703(f), this letter is a formal request for the preservation of all stored communications, records, and other evidence in your possession regarding the following

I request that you not disclose the existence of this request to the subscriber or any other person, other than as necessary to comply with this request. If compliance with this request might result in a permanent or temporary termination of service to or otherwise alert any user of as to your actions to preserve the information described below, please contact me as soon as possible and before taking action.

b3 -
b7E

I request that you preserve, for a period of 90 days, the information described below currently in your possession in a form that includes the complete record. This request applies only retrospectively. It does not in any way obligate you to capture and preserve new information that arises after the date of this request. This request applies to the following items, whether in electronic or other form, including information stored on backup media, if available:

b3 -
b7E

b3 -1
b7E -6

If you have questions regarding this request, please call me a

Sincerely,

David B. Fein
UNITED STATES ATTORNEY

Assistant United States Attorney

b6 -4
b7C -4

FD-1036 (Rev. 10-16-2009)

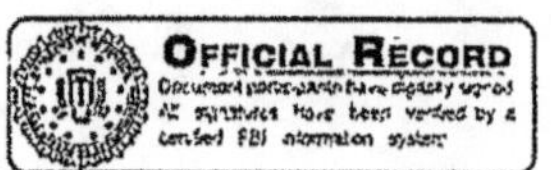

UNCLASSIFIED

FEDERAL BUREAU OF INVESTIGATION

Import Form

Form Type: OTHER **Date:** 12/17/2012

Title: (U) Preservation Letter to [redacted]

Approved By: [redacted]

Drafted By: [redacted]

b3 -1
b6 -1
b7C -1
b7E -6

Case ID #: 4-NH-2619946 (U) UNSUB(S)
Sandy Hook Elementary School
12 Dickinson St, Sandy Hook, CT-Victim
Firearms Act.
OO:NH

Synopsis: (U) A letter issued 12/14/2012 requesting preservation of [redacted]

b3 -1
b7E -

♦♦

UNCLASSIFIED

4-NH-2619946 Serial 58

FAX TRANSMISSION

United States Attorney
Connecticut
157 Church St., 23rd floor
New Haven, Connecticut 06510

To ATTN:	[redacted]		b3 -1 b7E -6
Fax			
From	[redacted] Assistant United States Attorney	Voice [redacted]	b6 -4 b7C -4
Fax	[redacted]		

Date December 14, 2012 **Pages** 3, including this page

Subject Preservation letter under 18 U.S.C. § 2703(f)

U.S. Department of Justice

United States Attorney
Connecticut

157 Church St., 23rd floor
New Haven, Connecticut 06510

PHONE: 203.821.3796
FAX: 203.773.5373

December 14, 2012

b3 -1
b7E -6

Re: Request for Preservation of Records

Dear

Pursuant to Title 18, United States Code, Section 2703(f), this letter is a formal request for the preservation of all stored communications, records, and other evidence in your possession regarding the following email account(s) pending further legal process:

I request that you not disclose the existence of this request to the subscriber or any other person, other than as necessary to comply with this request. If compliance with this request might result in a permanent or temporary termination of service or otherwise alert any user of as to your actions to preserve the information described below, please contact me as soon as possible and before taking action.

b3 -1
b7E -

I request that you preserve, for a period of 90 days, the information described below currently in your possession in a form that includes the complete record. This request applies only retrospectively. It does not in any way obligate you to capture and preserve new information that arises after the date of this request. This request applies to the following items, whether in electronic or other form, including information stored on backup media, if available:

b3 -
b7E

b3 -1
b7E -6

If you have questions regarding this request, please call me a

Sincerely,

David B. Fein
UNITED STATES ATTORNEY

b6 -4
b7C -4

Assistant United States Attorney

FD-1036 (Rev. 10-16-2009)

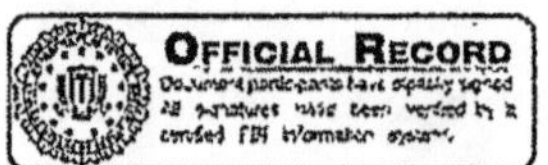

FEDERAL BUREAU OF INVESTIGATION

Import Form

Form Type: OTHER **Date:** 12/17/2012

Title: (U) Preservation Letter: [redacted]

Approved By: [redacted]

Drafted By: [redacted]

b3 -1
b6 -1
b7C -1
b7E -6

Case ID #: 4-NH-2619946 (U) UNSUB(S)
Sandy Hook Elementary School
12 Dickinson St, Sandy Hook, CT-Victim
Firearms Act.
OO:NH

Synopsis: (U) A 12/17/2012 request for the preservation of [redacted]

b3 -
b7E

♦♦

4-NH-2619946 Serial 59

U.S. Department of Justice

United States Attorney
Connecticut

157 Church St., 23rd floor
New Haven, Connecticut 06510

PHONE: 203.821.3796
FAX: 203.773.5373

December 17, 2012

b3 -1
b7E -6

Re: Request for Preservation of Records

Dear

Pursuant to Title 18, United States Code, Section 2703(f), this letter is a formal request for the preservation of all stored communications, records, and other evidence in your possession regarding

b3 -1
b7E -6

Specifically, please preserve, for a period of 90 days, the contents of any communication or file related to This request applies to records whether in electronic or other form, including information stored on backup media, if available.

Sincerely,

David B. Fein
UNITED STATES ATTORNEY

b6 -4
b7C -4

Assistant United States Attorney

FD-1036 (Rev. 10-16-2009)

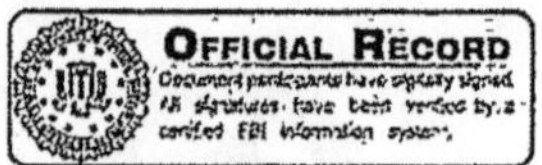

UNCLASSIFIED

FEDERAL BUREAU OF INVESTIGATION

Import Form

Form Type: OTHER **Date:** 12/17/2012

Title: (U) Preservation letter: [redacted]

Approved By: [redacted]

Drafted By: [redacted]

b3 -1
b6 -1
b7C -1
b7E -6

Case ID #: 4-NH-2619946 (U) UNSUB(S)
Sandy Hook Elementary School
12 Dickinson St, Sandy Hook, CT-Victim
Firearms Act.
OO:NH

Synopsis: (U) A 12/17/12 request for the preservation of [redacted]

b3 -
b7E

♦♦

UNCLASSIFIED

4-NH-2619946 Serial 60

U.S. Department of Justice

United States Attorney
Connecticut

157 Church St., 23rd floor
New Haven, Connecticut 06510

PHONE: 203.821.3796
FAX: 203.773.5373

December 17, 2012

Re: Request for Preservation of Records

b3 -1
b7E -6

Dear

Pursuant to Title 18, United States Code, Section 2703(f), this letter is a formal request for the preservation of

b3 -1
b7E -6

Specifically, please preserve, for a period of 90 days, the contents of any communication or file related to

This request applies to records whether in electronic or other form, including information stored on backup media, if available.

Sincerely,

David B. Fein
UNITED STATES ATTORNEY

b6 -4
b7C -4

Assistant United States Attorney

FD-302 (Rev. 5-8-10)

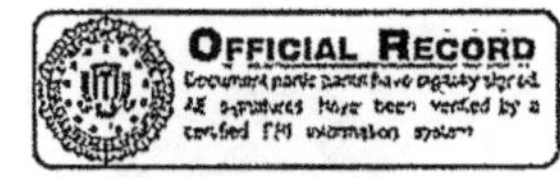

FEDERAL BUREAU OF INVESTIGATION

Date of entry 12/17/2012

SENSITIVE PATIENT MEDICAL INFORMATION

Maintain and use only if necessary for official duties and disseminate only to persons with a need to know; safeguard and protect from inadvertent disclosure.

was interviewed telephonically at After being advised of the identity of the interviewing Agent, SA and the nature of the interview provided the following information: b6 -1, b7C -1

contacted the FBI out of concern following her interview of a patient on Saturday, December 15th, 2012. b6 -5 b7C -

he ranted that he he was going to kill the and then kill himself.

b6 -5 b7C -

did not know if has access to weapons, ammunition or any other material which would assist him in carrying out his threat. believes it is her duty to bring this to the FBI's attention because it was her understanding that was planning on returning to Connecticut for Christmas. It was her opinion fascination with the Sandy Hook school shooting would escalate if he were to return to Connecticut stated that she was uncomfortable enough that if were to be released, she believed should be watched by law enforcement. b6 -5 b7C -

Investigation on 12/17/2012 at New Haven, Connecticut, United States (Phone)

File # 4-NH-2619946 Date drafted 12/17/2012 b6 b7

by

4-NH-2619946 Serial 61

b6 -5, 6
b7C -5, 6

[Administrative Note: Public source checks linked [redacted] to an address at [redacted] Also listed at that address is [redacted]

b6 -5
b7C -5

made claims to have posted items on line regarding the Newtown shooting.

b6 -5,
b7C -5,

Follow-up call to SA

b6 -1,
b7C -1

uncomfortable enough

→ should be watched

2:55 pm 12/17/12

kill & self

- from firearm in CT

b6 -5,
b7C -5

- not know @ guns access to carry out threat

FD-302 (Rev. 5-8-10)

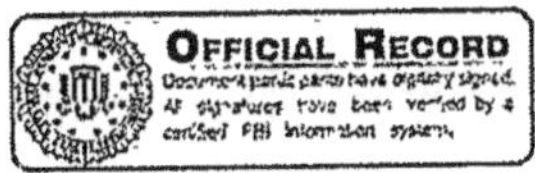

FEDERAL BUREAU OF INVESTIGATION

Date of entry 12/18/2012

[redacted] date of birth: [redacted] [redacted] cell# [redacted] was interviewed at [redacted] [redacted] After being advised of the identity of the interviewing Agent and the nature of the interview, [redacted] provided the following information: b6 -2 b7C -2

[redacted] b6 -2 b7C -2

[redacted] b6 -2 b7C -2

Investigation on 12/14/2012 at [redacted] United States (In Person)

File # 4-NH-2619946 Date drafted 12/15/2012 b6 -1, 2 b7C -1, 2

by [redacted]

4-NH-2619946 Serial 62

FD-302 (Rev. 5-8-10)

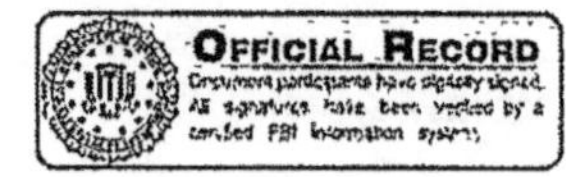

FEDERAL BUREAU OF INVESTIGATION

Date of entry 12/18/2012

Danbury Hospital, 24 Hospital Avenue, Danbury, Connecticut, 06810, telephone number was interviewed. After the undersigned agent identified himself and the nature of the interview, provided the following information: b6 b7C

On Monday, December 17, 2012, attended a memorial service at Danbury Hospital for one of the child victim's of the Sandy Hook Elementary School shootings. the service was being held in the hospital's auditorium for employees only. A short time after the conclusion of the service was still in the auditorium with was confronted by a white male, approximately 60 years-old, who told that his name was b6 -2, b7C -2,

was not invited to the closed memorial service. When asked why he was there, told him, among other things, that he had an "intelligence background" with "special clearance" and that he had been brought into the Sandy Hook Elementary School as a consultant after the shootings. b6 -2 b7C -2

was agitated b6 -2 b7C

also handed a business card to The business card had printed on it only the name, the telephone number, and the e-mail address, b6 -2 b7C -

is not sure how entered the hospital. Another employee of the hospital approached and and told that he was needed elsewhere. walked away. eventually left the auditorium and the hospital. b6 -2 b7C

Investigation on 12/17/2012 at Danbury, Connecticut, United States (Phone)

File # 4-NH-2619946 Date drafted 12/18/2012

by b6 b7C

This document contains neither recommendations nor conclusions of the FBI. It is the property of the FBI and is loaned to your agency; it and its contents are not to be distributed outside your agency.

4-NH-2619946 Serial 103

4-NH-2619946

Continuation of FD-302 of [redacted] , On 12/17/2012 , Page 2 of 2

b6 -6
b7C -6

(Administrative: [redacted]

b6 -2
b7C -2

[redacted] can be further described as:

b6 -2
b7C -2

tel cll

12/17/12

pcr Danbury Hosp.

60 yrs old

Subject white male.

b6 -2,
b7C -2,

uninvited

- showed up at memorial service
- I was at Sandy Hook school, special clearan
→ in the school
- I have an intelligence background

not sure how he entered the hospital

business card

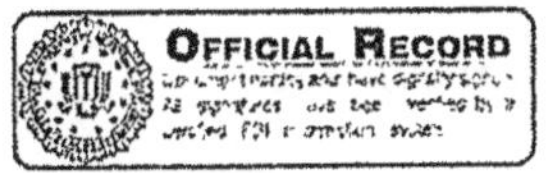

FEDERAL BUREAU OF INVESTIGATION

Date of entry 12/18/2012

At approximately 8:48 p.m. on 12/14/2012, Supervisory Special Agent (SSA) [redacted] of the Federal Bureau of Investigation (FBI) telephonically contacted [redacted] at [redacted] (Note: [redacted] [redacted] had provided [redacted] contact information to a Special Agent with [redacted] b6 -1, 2, 5 b7C -1, 2, 5

At approximately 9:10 p.m., [redacted] met SSA [redacted] b6 -1, 2, 5 b7C -1, 2, 5

Investigation on 12/14/2012 at [redacted] United States (In Person) b6 -1, 2 b7C -1, 2

File # 4-NH-2619946 Date drafted 12/18/2012

by [redacted]

4-NH-2619946 Serial 104

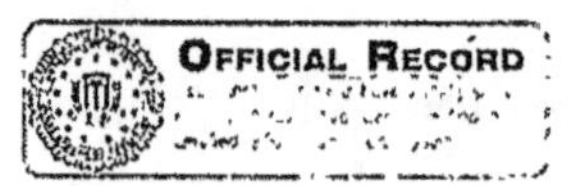

FEDERAL BUREAU OF INVESTIGATION

Date of entry 12/18/2012

date of birth (DOB): DOB: and date of birth: were interviewed jointly at their residence located at Newtown, Connecticut, telephone: After being advised of the identity of the interviewing Agents and the nature of the interview, the family provided the following information: b6 b7

On 12/16/2012, the family received four (4) telephone calls from telephone number (676)-843-7000. The first call occurred at approximately 9:30 a.m. (EST). stated she answered the telephone with "hello", heard two clicks, and then heard a male voice state, "This is Adama Lanza. I'm going to kill you." hung up the telephone. b6 b7

After the first call, the family received three (3) more telephone calls from the same number with the last one occurring at approximately 11:22 a.m. (EST). Of the three other calls, the caller left two (2) threatening messages that were recorded by the voicemail account. provided that she deleted the two threatening messages from the family's voicemail account. reported the threatening calls to the authorities. b b

described the two threatening messages on the family's voicemail account. stated that the first voicemail sounded like a computerized-voice which stated, "This is Adam Lanza. You're going to be dead by tomorrow." b6 b7

then provided that the voice on the second voicemail message sounded to be male, "Deep and raspy", and later categorized it as younger voice with no accent, and it sounded "freaky". furthered that the second voicemail contained a similar threat as the first voicemail but provided more details. According to the second voicemail repeated that the caller was Adama Lanza, that "I'm going to fucking kill you", and "I'm going to shoot you in the face with a shotgun". b6 b7

provided that he worked b b

Investigation on 12/16/2012 at Newtown, Connecticut, United States (In Person)

File # 4-NH-2619946 Date drafted 12/18/2012

by b b

4-NH-2619946 Serial 65

b6 -7
b7C -7

provided she was [redacted]

b6 -7
b7C -7

On the same date the [redacted] family received the threatening phone calls, five other families received similar threatening phone calls from the telephone number (676)-843-7000. After providing the [redacted] family with names of the other families who received the threatening calls, the [redacted] family provided they did not know any of the other families.

b6 -7
b7C -7

[redacted] provided that the [redacted] family's telephone number [redacted] is listed in the telephone book.

b6 -7
b7C -7

646-843-7000

12/16/12

b6
b7C

father

(4 call)

First — 9:30 am — — Click click — Hello — This is Adam (Freaky)
I'm going to kill you Lanza.
Hang-up —

last — 11:22 am

— Called back —

11:00 1 2 Voicemails
I'm going to kill you.

2 Voices — 1 raspy voice
(computer) — 1 computer generated

1. This is Adam Lanza
You're going to be dead Robot — Deep
by tomorrow. — I'm going to f'ing kill you

(Deep, Raspy) — Male — No accent — Younger

2. More detail. I'm going to
shoot you in the face.
— Freaky

FEDERAL BUREAU OF INVESTIGATION

Date of entry 12/18/2012

date of birth (DOB): and DOB: were interviewed at their residence of Newtown, Connecticut, telephone: Also present for the interview was friend DOB: After being advised of the identity of the interviewing Agents and the nature of the interview, and provided the following information: b6 -7 b7C -7

On 12/16/2012, at approximately 9:24 a.m. (EST), the family received a telephone call on their home number from telephone number (676)-873-7000. answered the telephone. After said "hello" twice, heard a click and then a male voice stated "I'm Adam Lanza". hung up the phone. described the male voice as "creepy and young". b6 -7 b7C -7

At approximately 9:25 a.m. (EST), the caller called the telephone number a second time but let the call go to the voicemail account. The caller left the following message on the voicemail account: b6 -7 b7C -7

"(Sound of a toilet flushing then a pause) This is Adam Lanza. I'm going to fucking kill you. You're dead. You're dead. Do you hear me? You're fucking dead." (Hang-up)

provided that she listened to the voicemail as described above soon after told her about the first call. then contacted the authorities. b6 -7 b7C -7

Prior to playing the voicemail for interviewing Agents, requested that and leave the room as she did not want either of them to hear the message. then played the voicemail for the interviewing agents twice. Special Agent was able to make a copy of the recording with an application on his blackberry. An electronic copy of the recording is attached to this communication. b6 -1, 7 b7C -1, 7

At approximately 11:23 a.m. (EST), the Caller Identification system (Caller ID) provided the family received a third call from the same number as listed above but no message was left. stated no b6 -7 b7C -7

Investigation on 12/16/2012 at Newtown, Connecticut, United States (In Person)

File # 4-NH-2619946 Date drafted 12/18/2012

by b6 -1 b7C -1

4-NH-2619946 Serial 66

b6
b7C

one was at the [redacted] residence at the time of the third call.

[redacted] further provided that the [redacted] Caller ID showed that the telephone number (646)-843-7000 belonged to "iCall Inc."

[redacted] worked since [redacted] spouse, [redacted] DOB: [redacted] is [redacted] Neither [redacted] nor the older daughter were at the residence during the interview or when the threatening telephone calls were placed to the home.

On the same date, five other families received similar threatening telephone calls from telephone number (676)-873-7000. After interviewing agents provided the names of the other families to [redacted] and [redacted] and [redacted] provided that neither of them knew the other families.

[redacted] stated that the family's telephone number is listed in the telephone book.

1st Home

- 9:24 a.m. -

- [redacted] - 9:35 a.m. 12/14/12 [redacted]

11:23 am. - Not home

1) [redacted] - Oldest Daughter
2) [redacted]
3) [redacted]

b6 -7
b7C -7

Hello (twice)

- [redacted] Male - I'm Adam Lanza - Hung-up
- Creepy, young

- 2nd Voice mail -

[redacted]

- Caller - Voicemail - (Toilet - fishing) This is Adam Lanza - I'm going to fucking kill you. You're dead. You're dead. Do you hear me? You're fucking dead.

listed.

- Hung up -

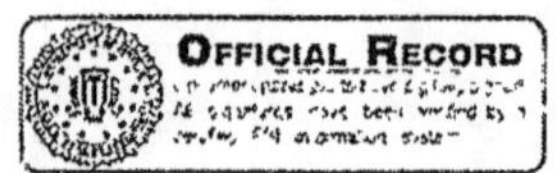

UNCLASSIFIED//~~FOUO~~

FEDERAL BUREAU OF INVESTIGATION

Electronic Communication

Title: (U) [redacted] **Date:** 12/18/2012 b7E -6,

To: [redacted]

From: NEW HAVEN
NH-9
Contact: [redacted] b6 -1 b7C -1

Approved By: A/SSA [redacted]

Drafted By: [redacted]

Case ID #: 4-NH-2619946 (U) UNSUB(S)
Sandy Hook Elementary School
12 Dickinson St, Sandy Hook, CT-Victim
Firearms Act.
OO:NH
[redacted] (U//~~FOUO~~) [redacted] b7A -1 b7E -4, 6,

Synopsis: (U) Request for [redacted] b6 - b7C -

Reference: 4-NH-2619946 Serial 1

Enclosure(s): Enclosed are the following items:
1. (U) Copy of CT State Search Warrant

Details:

New Haven Division is cooperating with the Connecticut State Police (CSP) in the investigation ofa mass shooting at Sandy Hook Elementary School, 12 Dickinson St, Sandy Hook, CT, on 12/14/2012. (See referenced serial for additional details regarding case background.)

UNCLASSIFIED//~~FOUO~~

4-NH-2619946 Serial 67

Title: (U) [redacted] b7E -6, 7

Re: 4-NH-2619946, 12/18/2012

During the investigation, CSP recovered a 500 GB Seagate Barracuda ST3500320AS hard drive, S/N 9QM34ZA8, from 36 Yogananda Street, Sandy Hook, CT, the home of suspect Adam Lanza. The drive has been opened and significantly damaged by force trauma as well as by being scratched with an implement.

New Haven is requesting assistance [redacted]

[redacted]

As this is a matter of national attention, it is of high priority. However, NH understands that the techniques involved will be very time-intensive. Therefore, no deadline is identified, but as rapid a response as is possible under the circumstances is requested. b7E -6, 7

[redacted]

The New Haven POC for this issue is SA [redacted] He can be reached at [redacted] (desk), or [redacted] (cell). b6 -1 b7C -1

♦♦

SEARCH AND SEIZURE WARRANT **STATE OF CONNECTICUT SUPERIOR COURT** **SEARCH AND SEIZURE WARRANT**

The foregoing Affidavit and Application for Search and Seizure Warrant having been presented to and been considered by the undersigned, a Judge of the Superior Court or a Judge Trial Referee, and the foregoing Affidavit having been subscribed and sworn to by the affiant(s) before me at the time it was presented, the undersigned (a) is satisfied therefrom that grounds exist for said application, and (b) finds that said affidavit established grounds and probable cause for the undersigned to issue this Search and Seizure Warrant, such probable cause being the following. From said affidavit, the undersigned finds that there is probable cause for the undersigned to believe that the property described in the foregoing affidavit and application is within or upon the person, if any, named or described in the foregoing affidavit and application, or the place or thing, if any, described in the foregoing affidavit and application, under the conditions and circumstances set forth in the foregoing affidavit and application, and that, therefore, a Search and Seizure warrant should issue for said property

NOW THEREFORE, by Authority of the State of Connecticut, I hereby command any Police Officer of a regularly organized police department, any State Police Officer, any inspector in the Division of Criminal Justice, or any conservation officer, special conservation officer or patrol officer acting pursuant to C.G.S. § 26-6 to whom these presents shall come within ten days after the date of this warrant to enter into or upon and search the place or thing described in the foregoing affidavit and application, or search the person described in the foregoing affidavit and application or both, to wit:

The residence of Nancy and Adam Lanza, 36 Yogananda Street in Sandy Hook, CT. The residence is a 2 story colonial style structure, with an attached two car garage. The house is pale yellow with dark green shutters and a dark green front door. The full address, 36 Yogananda Street is listed on the mailbox located in front of the house.

for the property described in the foregoing affidavit and application, to wit

Computers (including gaming devices and cellular telephones), zip disks, CD's, CDR's, DVD's, and other electronic storage media because; (1) The objects themselves may be instrumentalities, fruits, or evidence of a crime and (2) The objects may have been used to collect and store information about crimes in the form of electronic "data" (as defined by Connecticut General Statutes 53a-250(8)). Such data may include image files, video files, text files, or other electronically stored documents. Connecticut General Statutes define a "computer" as a programmable, electronic device capable of accepting and processing data, such as a gaming console, cellular telephone, and other similar devices.

[X] submit the property described in the foregoing affidavit and application to laboratory analysis and examination

Department of Public Safety Computer and Electronics Unit (278 Colony St in Meriden, CT) and/or other recognized and accredited forensic science laboratory for forensic examination and review.

and upon finding said property to seize the same, take and keep it in custody until the further order of the court, and with reasonable promptness make due return of this warrant accompanied by a written inventory of all property seized

[✓] The foregoing request that the judge or judge trial referee dispense with the requirement of C.G.S. § 54-33c that a copy of the warrant application and affidavit(s) in support of the warrant be given to the owner, occupant or person named therein and that the affidavit in support of such request also be included in such nondelivery is hereby:

[✓] GRANTED for a period of — NOT TO EXCEED 2 WEEKS BEYOND DATE WARRANT IS EXECUTED: Dec. 28, 2012

This order, or any extension thereof, dispensing with said requirement shall not limit disclosure of such application and affidavits to the attorney for a person arrested in connection with or subsequent to the execution of the search warrant unless, upon motion of the prosecuting authority within two weeks of such arraignment the court finds that the state's interest in continuing nondisclosure substantially outweighs the defendant's right to disclosure.

[ ] DENIED

[ ] Service of this Search Warrant upon the customer whose financial records are being sought is hereby waived, pursuant to C.G.S. § 36a-43 (a)

(NOTE: AFFIANT'S OATH MUST BE TAKEN PRIOR TO JUDGE / JUDGE TRIAL REFEREE SIGNING BELOW)

(This is page 7 of a 8 page Affidavit and Application.)

Signed at Newtown, Connecticut, on: Date Dec. 14 2012 At (Time) 7:25 [ ] a.m. [✓] p.m.

Signed (Judge/Judge Trial Referee) — Print name of Judicial Official: Hon. John F. Blawie

JD-CR-61

b6 b7

FD-302 (Rev. 5-8-10)

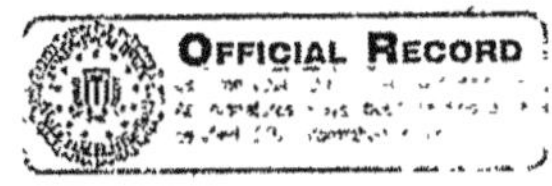

UNCLASSIFIED//~~FOUO~~

FEDERAL BUREAU OF INVESTIGATION

Date of entry 12/17/2012

[redacted] date of birth (DOB) [redacted] was interviewed at [redacted] [redacted] which is the office of his attorney, [redacted] telephone [redacted] employed by [redacted] [redacted] Immediately prior to the interview, [redacted] stated he was representing [redacted] [redacted] willing to answer questions and assist in the investigation. [redacted] [redacted] was going to be present during the interview. [redacted] [redacted] the interview began with [redacted] and the two listed FBI Special Agents. After being advised of the identity of the interviewing Special Agents, [redacted] provided the following information:

b6 -5, 6
b7C -5, 6

[redacted] stated that, on the evening of 12/11/2012, he went straight from work to his residence [redacted] [redacted]

b6 -6
b7C -6

[redacted]

b6 -6
b7C -6

[redacted]

b6 -6
b7C -6

UNCLASSIFIED//~~FOUO~~

Investigation on 12/16/2012 at [redacted] United States (In Person)

File # 4-NH-2619946 Date drafted 12/17/2012

b6 -1, 2
b7C -1, 2

by [redacted]

4-NH-2619946 Serial 68

b6
b7C

b6
b7C

b6
b7C

[redacted] stated ADAM LANZA had Asperger's Syndrome, which limited ADAM LANZA's ability to communicate well [redacted]

b6 -6,
b7C -6,

b6 -
b7C

b6
b7C

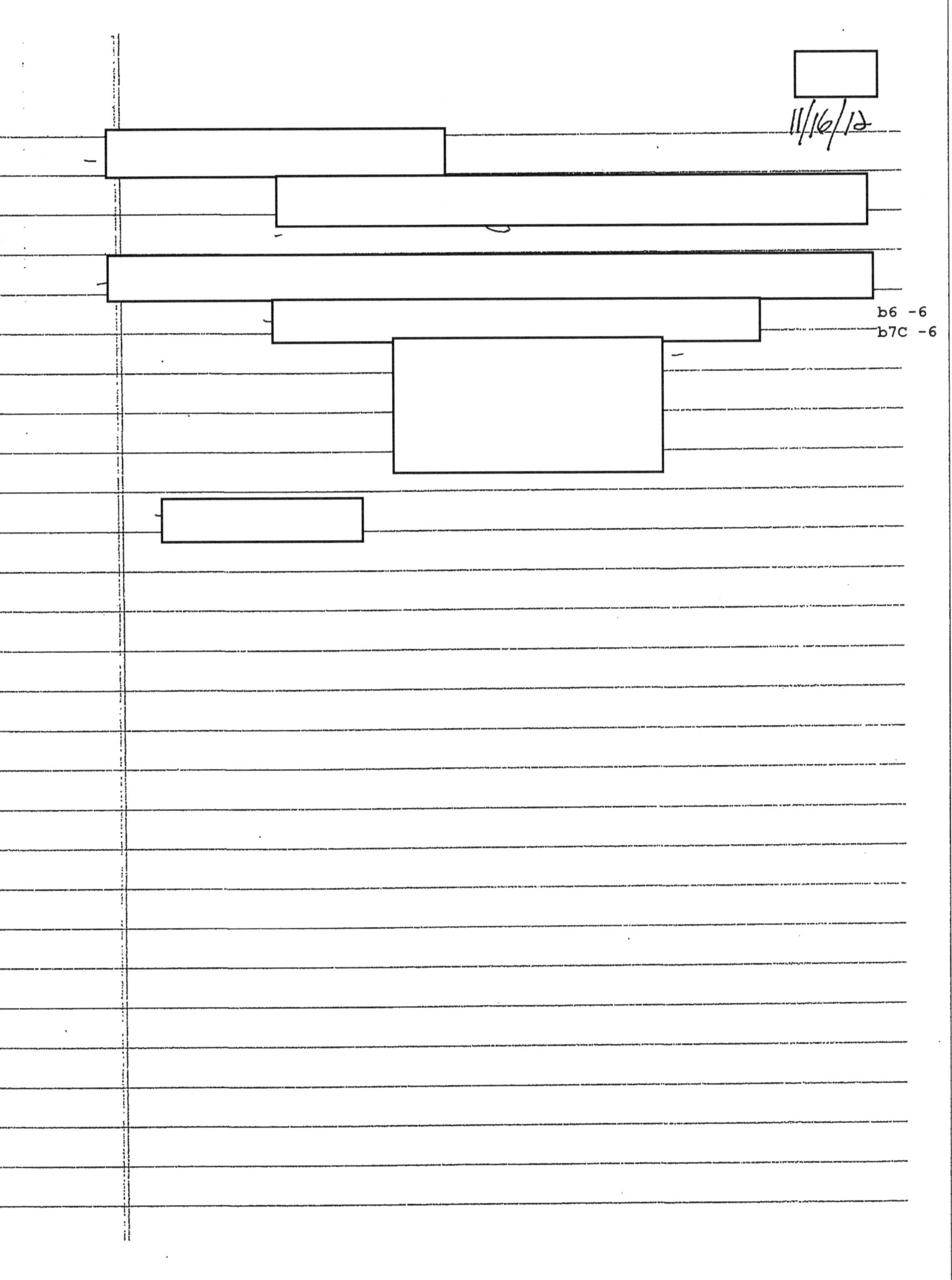

11/16/12

b6 -6
b7C -6

FD-1087 (Rev. 5-8-10)

UNCLASSIFIED

FEDERAL BUREAU OF INVESTIGATION

Evidence Log

Event Title: (U) Acquisition of [redacted] **Date:** 12/15/2012

To: [redacted] b3 -1 b6 -1, 2 b7C -1,

Approved By: SSA [redacted]

Drafted By: [redacted]

Case ID #: 4-NH-2619946 (U) UNSUB(S)
Sandy Hook Elementary School
12 Dickinson St, Sandy Hook, CT-Victim
Firearms Act.
OO:NH

FEDERAL GRAND JURY MATERIAL - DISSEMINATE PURSUANT TO RULE 6(E)
Do not disseminate except as authorized by federal rule of criminal procedure 6(e).

[redacted] b7E

Acquired By: [redacted] on 12/14/2012

Acquired From: (U) [redacted] b3 -1 b6 -1, 2 b7C -1,

Receipt Given?: No

Holding Office: NEW HAVEN

Details:

On 12/14/2012, a Federal Grand Jury subpoena was served on [redacted] b3 - b6 - b7C -

UNCLASSIFIED

4-NH-2619946
SERIAL 6

Title: (U) Acquisition of

Re: 4-NH-2619946, 12/15/2012

provided this information and subpoena return

b3 -1
b6 -1, 2
b7C -1, 2
b7E -6

Item Type	Description
	(U)
	Acquired On: 12/14/2012
	Located By:
	Other Locator:
	Location Area:
	Specific Location:

♦♦

FD-302 (Rev. 5-8-10)

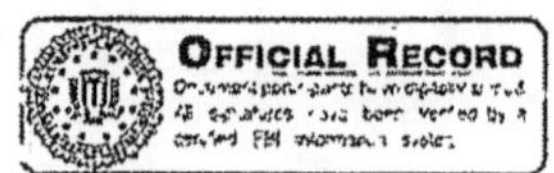

FEDERAL BUREAU OF INVESTIGATION

Date of entry 12/15/2012

On 12/14/2012, SA [redacted] and SA [redacted] conducted a search of [redacted] The search was conducted after consent was provided by way of a FD-26 Consent to Search form signed by [redacted] Also present during the search was [redacted] b6 -1, 2, b7C -1, 2,

During the search, the following items were found:

[redacted] b6 b7C

Each of the above items were photocopied and released to the FBI by [redacted] The original documents were placed back in [redacted] in their original locations upon being photocopied. b6 b7C

Enclosed with this document are the signed FD-26, photocopies of the aforementioned items, and a signed FD-597 Receipt.

Investigation on 12/14/2012 at [redacted], United States (In Person) b6 -1, b7C -1,

File # 4-NH-2619946 Date drafted 12/15/2012

by [redacted]

4-NH-2619946 Serial 7D

FD-26 (Rev. 7-20-94)

DEPARTMENT OF JUSTICE

FEDERAL BUREAU OF INVESTIGATION

CONSENT TO SEARCH

1. I have been asked by Special Agents of the Federal Bureau of Investigation to permit a complete search of:

(Describe the person(s), place(s), or thing(s) to be searched.)

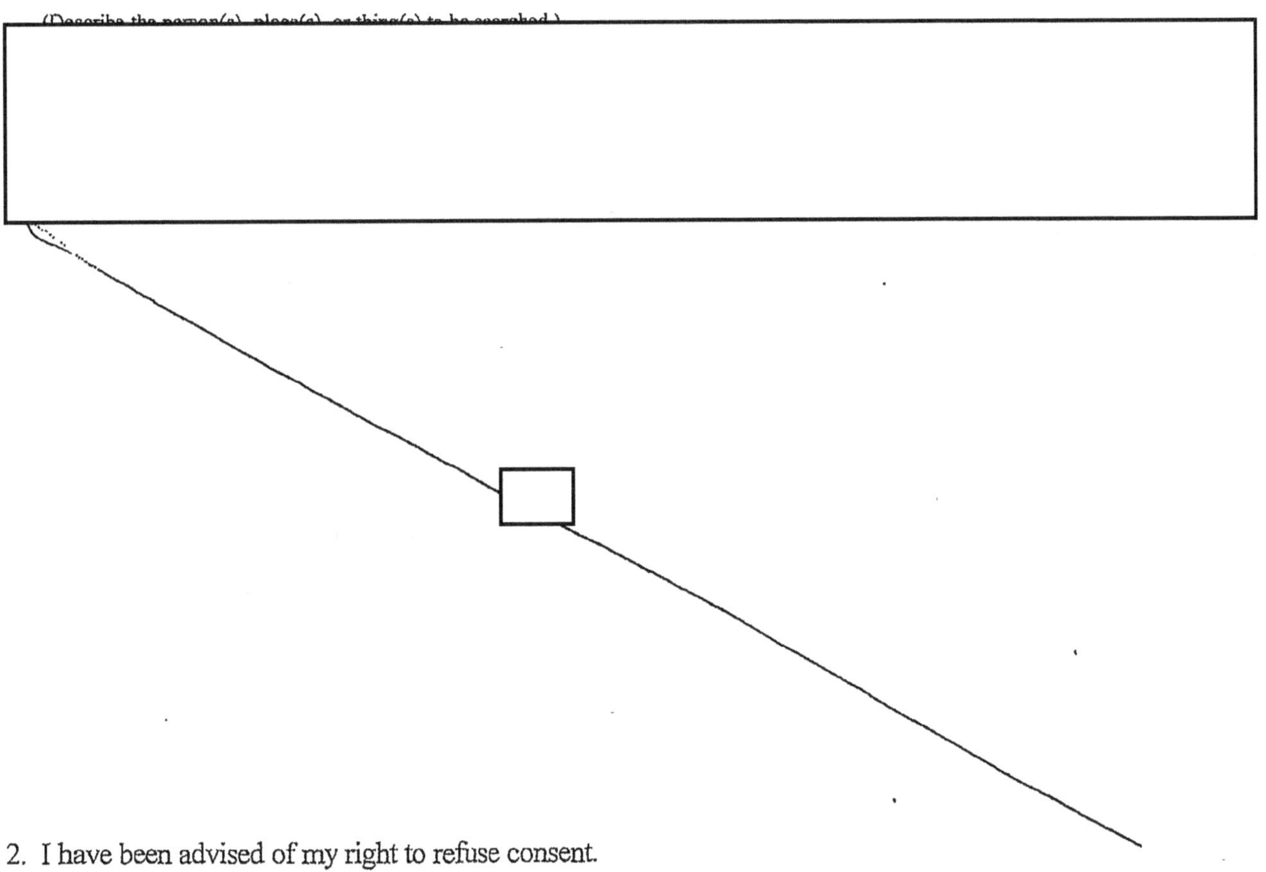

b6 -2
b7C -2

2. I have been advised of my right to refuse consent.

3. I give this permission voluntarily.

4. I authorize these agents to take any items which they determine may be related to their investigation.

14 DEC 12
Date

Witness

b6 -1, 5
b7C -1, 5

FD-597 (Rev 8-11-94)

UNITED STATES DEPARTMENT OF JUSTICE
FEDERAL BUREAU OF INVESTIGATION
Receipt for Property Received/Returned/Released/Seized

File # 4-NH-2619946

On (date) 12/14/12

item(s) listed below were:
- [x] Received From
- [ ] Returned To
- [ ] Released To
- [ ] Seized

(Name)

(Street Address)

(City)

b6 -
b7C

Description of Item(s): - Photocopies of

12/14/12

b6 -1,
b7C -1,

Received By:

Received From:

FEDERAL BUREAU OF INVESTIGATION
FOI/PA
DELETED PAGE INFORMATION SHEET
Civil Action# 16-cv-02136

Total Deleted Page(s) = 138
Page 4 ~ b3 - 1; b6 - 4; b7C - 4;
Page 5 ~ b3 - 1; b6 - 4; b7C - 4;
Page 7 ~ Duplicate;
Page 9 ~ b3 - 1; b6 - 4, 5; b7C - 4, 5;
Page 10 ~ b3 - 1; b6 - 4; b7C - 4;
Page 12 ~ Duplicate;
Page 14 ~ b3 - 1; b6 - 4; b7C - 4;
Page 15 ~ b3 - 1; b6 - 4; b7C - 4;
Page 17 ~ Duplicate;
Page 18 ~ b3 - 1; b6 - 4; b7C - 4;
Page 19 ~ b3 - 1; b6 - 4; b7C - 4;
Page 21 ~ Duplicate;
Page 23 ~ b3 - 1; b6 - 4; b7C - 4;
Page 24 ~ b3 - 1; b6 - 4; b7C - 4;
Page 26 ~ Duplicate;
Page 28 ~ b3 - 1; b6 - 4; b7C - 4;
Page 29 ~ b3 - 1; b6 - 4; b7C - 4;
Page 31 ~ Duplicate;
Page 33 ~ b3 - 1; b6 - 4; b7C - 4;
Page 34 ~ b3 - 1; b6 - 4; b7C - 4;
Page 36 ~ Duplicate;
Page 38 ~ b3 - 1; b6 - 4; b7C - 4;
Page 39 ~ b3 - 1; b6 - 4; b7C - 4;
Page 41 ~ Duplicate;
Page 44 ~ Duplicate;
Page 46 ~ b3 - 1; b6 - 4; b7C - 4;
Page 47 ~ b3 - 1; b6 - 4; b7C - 4;
Page 49 ~ Duplicate;
Page 51 ~ b3 - 1; b6 - 4; b7C - 4;
Page 52 ~ b3 - 1; b6 - 4; b7C - 4;
Page 54 ~ Duplicate;
Page 56 ~ b3 - 1; b6 - 4; b7C - 4;
Page 57 ~ b3 - 1; b6 - 4; b7C - 4;
Page 59 ~ Duplicate;
Page 61 ~ b3 - 1; b6 - 4; b7C - 4;
Page 62 ~ b3 - 1; b6 - 4; b7C - 4;
Page 64 ~ Duplicate;
Page 66 ~ b3 - 1; b6 - 4, 5; b7C - 4, 5;
Page 72 ~ b3 - 1; b6 - 1, 4, 5; b7C - 1, 4, 5;
Page 73 ~ b3 - 1;
Page 74 ~ b3 - 1;
Page 75 ~ b3 - 1;
Page 76 ~ b3 - 1;
Page 77 ~ b3 - 1;
Page 78 ~ b3 - 1;
Page 89 ~ b3 - 1; b6 - 4; b7C - 4;
Page 90 ~ b3 - 1; b6 - 4; b7C - 4;
Page 96 ~ b3 - 1; b6 - 1, 5; b7C - 1, 5;

Page 97 ~ b3 - 1; b6 - 1, 5; b7C - 1, 5;
Page 99 ~ b3 - 1; b6 - 4; b7C - 4;
Page 100 ~ b3 - 1; b6 - 4; b7C - 4;
Page 105 ~ b3 - 1; b6 - 4; b7C - 4;
Page 106 ~ b3 - 1; b6 - 4; b7C - 4;
Page 111 ~ b3 - 1; b6 - 4; b7C - 4;
Page 112 ~ b3 - 1; b6 - 4; b7C - 4;
Page 117 ~ b3 - 1; b6 - 4; b7C - 4;
Page 119 ~ b3 - 1; b6 - 4; b7C - 4;
Page 122 ~ b3 - 1; b6 - 4, 5; b7C - 4, 5;
Page 123 ~ b3 - 1; b6 - 4; b7C - 4;
Page 125 ~ Duplicate;
Page 127 ~ b3 - 1; b6 - 4, 5; b7C - 4, 5;
Page 128 ~ b3 - 1; b6 - 4; b7C - 4;
Page 130 ~ Duplicate;
Page 132 ~ b3 - 1; b6 - 4; b7C - 4;
Page 133 ~ b3 - 1; b6 - 4; b7C - 4;
Page 135 ~ Duplicate;
Page 137 ~ b3 - 1; b6 - 4, 5; b7C - 4, 5;
Page 138 ~ b3 - 1; b6 - 4; b7C - 4;
Page 140 ~ Duplicate;
Page 143 ~ Duplicate;
Page 147 ~ b6 - 2, 3; b7C - 2, 3;
Page 148 ~ b6 - 3, 6; b7C - 3, 6;
Page 149 ~ b6 - 6; b7C - 6;
Page 151 ~ b3 - 1; b6 - 5; b7C - 5;
Page 152 ~ b3 - 1; b6 - 4, 5; b7C - 4, 5;
Page 153 ~ b3 - 1; b6 - 5; b7C - 5;
Page 154 ~ b3 - 1;
Page 155 ~ b3 - 1;
Page 156 ~ b3 - 1; b6 - 5; b7C - 5;
Page 157 ~ b3 - 1;
Page 158 ~ b3 - 1;
Page 159 ~ b3 - 1; b6 - 5; b7C - 5;
Page 160 ~ b3 - 1;
Page 161 ~ b3 - 1; b6 - 5; b7C - 5;
Page 162 ~ b3 - 1; b6 - 5; b7C - 5;
Page 163 ~ b3 - 1; b6 - 5; b7C - 5;
Page 164 ~ b3 - 1; b6 - 5; b7C - 5;
Page 165 ~ b3 - 1; b6 - 5; b7C - 5;
Page 166 ~ b3 - 1; b6 - 5; b7C - 5;
Page 167 ~ b3 - 1; b6 - 5; b7C - 5;
Page 168 ~ b3 - 1; b6 - 5; b7C - 5;
Page 169 ~ b3 - 1; b6 - 5; b7C - 5;
Page 170 ~ b3 - 1;
Page 171 ~ b3 - 1; b6 - 5; b7C - 5;
Page 172 ~ b3 - 1; b6 - 5; b7C - 5;
Page 173 ~ b3 - 1; b6 - 5; b7C - 5;
Page 174 ~ b3 - 1; b6 - 5; b7C - 5;
Page 175 ~ b3 - 1; b6 - 5; b7C - 5;
Page 176 ~ b3 - 1; b6 - 5; b7C - 5;
Page 177 ~ b3 - 1; b6 - 5; b7C - 5;
Page 178 ~ b3 - 1; b6 - 5; b7C - 5;
Page 179 ~ b3 - 1;

Page 180 ~ b3 - 1;
Page 181 ~ b3 - 1; b6 - 5; b7C - 5;
Page 182 ~ b3 - 1;
Page 183 ~ b3 - 1; b6 - 5; b7C - 5;
Page 185 ~ b3 - 1; b6 - 1, 4; b7C - 1, 4;
Page 186 ~ b3 - 1; b6 - 1, 4; b7C - 1, 4;
Page 192 ~ b6 - 1; b7C - 1; b7E - 2;
Page 193 ~ b6 - 2; b7C - 2; b7E - 2;
Page 194 ~ b6 - 1; b7C - 1; b7E - 2;
Page 195 ~ b6 - 1; b7C - 1; b7E - 2;
Page 197 ~ b3 - 1; b6 - 4; b7C - 4;
Page 198 ~ b3 - 1; b6 - 4; b7C - 4;
Page 203 ~ b3 - 1; b6 - 4; b7C - 4;
Page 204 ~ b3 - 1; b6 - 4; b7C - 4;
Page 207 ~ Duplicate;
Page 210 ~ b3 - 1; b6 - 4; b7C - 4;
Page 211 ~ b3 - 1; b6 - 4; b7C - 4;
Page 216 ~ b3 - 1; b6 - 4; b7C - 4;
Page 217 ~ b3 - 1; b6 - 4; b7C - 4;
Page 223 ~ b3 - 1; b6 - 4, 5; b7C - 4, 5;
Page 224 ~ b3 - 1; b6 - 4; b7C - 4;
Page 226 ~ b3 - 1; b6 - 4, 5; b7C - 4, 5;
Page 227 ~ b3 - 1; b6 - 4; b7C - 4;
Page 231 ~ b3 - 1; b6 - 4; b7C - 4;
Page 232 ~ b3 - 1; b6 - 4; b7C - 4;
Page 237 ~ b3 - 1; b6 - 4; b7C - 4;
Page 238 ~ b3 - 1; b6 - 4; b7C - 4;
Page 243 ~ b3 - 1; b6 - 1, 2, 5; b7C - 1, 2, 5;
Page 244 ~ b3 - 1; b6 - 2; b7C - 2;
Page 245 ~ b3 - 1; b6 - 2; b7C - 2;
Page 246 ~ b3 - 1; b6 - 2; b7C - 2;
Page 247 ~ b3 - 1; b6 - 2; b7C - 2;
Page 248 ~ b3 - 1; b6 - 2; b7C - 2;
Page 249 ~ b3 - 1; b6 - 4, 5; b7C - 4, 5;
Page 251 ~ b3 - 1; b6 - 1, 5; b7C - 1, 5;
Page 252 ~ b3 - 1; b6 - 2; b7C - 2;

XXXXXXXXXXXXXXXXXXXXXXX
X Deleted Page(s) X
X No Duplication Fee X
X For this Page X
XXXXXXXXXXXXXXXXXXXXXXX

FD-1036 (Rev. 10-16-2009)

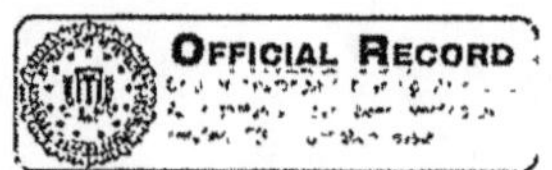

UNCLASSIFIED

FEDERAL BUREAU OF INVESTIGATION

Import Form

Form Type: OTHER **Date:** 12/17/2012

Title: (U) FGJ Subpoean to [redacted]

Approved By: [redacted]

Drafted By: [redacted]

b3 -1
b6 -1
b7C -1

Case ID #: 4-NH-2619946-GJ (U) Grand Jury Information

FEDERAL GRAND JURY MATERIAL - DISSEMINATE PURSUANT TO RULE 6(E)
Do not disseminate except as authorized by federal rule of criminal procedure 6(e).

Synopsis: (U) 12/14/2012 FGJ Subpoena to [redacted]

♦♦

UNCLASSIFIED

4-NH-2619946-GJ
SERIAL 1

AO 110 (Rev. 06/09) Subpoena to Testify Before a Grand Jury

UNITED STATES DISTRICT COURT

for the

District of Connecticut

SUBPOENA TO TESTIFY BEFORE A GRAND JURY

b3 -1

To:

[redacted] ED to appear in this United States district court at the time, date, and place shown below to testify before the court's grand jury. When you arrive, you must remain at the court until the judge or a court officer allows you to leave.

Place: United States Courthouse 141 Church Street New Haven, CT 06510	Date and Time:

You must also bring with you the following documents, electronically stored information, or objects *(blank if not applicable)*:

b3 -1

Date: December 14, 2012

CLERK OF COURT

Signature of Clerk or Deputy Clerk

The name, address, e-mail, and telephone number of the United States attorney, or assistant United States attorney, who requests this subpoena, are:

AUSA
157 Church St., 23rd floor
New Haven, CT 06510

Personal appearance is not required if documents are provided on or before the appearance date to: FBI S/A
600 State St.
New Haven CT 06510

b3 -1
b6 -1, 4
b7C -1, 4

FD-1036 (Rev. 10-16-2009)

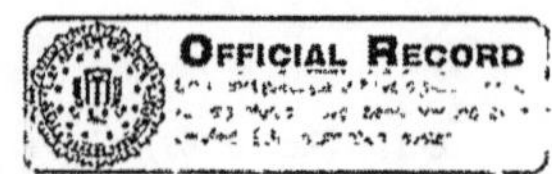

UNCLASSIFIED

FEDERAL BUREAU OF INVESTIGATION

Import Form

Form Type: FD-617 **Date:** 12/17/2012

Title: (U) FGJ Subpoena to [redacted]

Approved By: [redacted] b3 -1

b6 -1

Drafted By: [redacted] b7C -1

Case ID #: 4-NH-2619946-GJ (U) Grand Jury Information

FEDERAL GRAND JURY MATERIAL - DISSEMINATE PURSUANT TO RULE 6(E)
Do not disseminate except as authorized by federal rule of criminal procedure 6(e).

Synopsis: (U) 12/14/2012 FGJ Subpoena to [redacted]

[redacted] b3

♦♦

UNCLASSIFIED

4-NH-2619946-GJ
SERIAL 2

AO 110 (Rev. 06/09) Subpoena to Testify Before a Grand Jury

UNITED STATES DISTRICT COURT

for the

District of Connecticut

SUBPOENA TO TESTIFY BEFORE A GRAND JURY

To: [redacted]

b3 -1
b6 -5
b7C -5

YOU ARE COMMANDED to appear in this United States district court at the time, date, and place shown below to testify before the court's grand jury. When you arrive, you must remain at the court until the judge or a court officer allows you to leave.

Place: United States Courthouse, 141 Church Street, New Haven, CT 06510	Date and Time: [redacted]

You must also bring with you the following documents, electronically stored information, or objects *(blank if not applicable)*:

[redacted]

b3 -1

Date: December 14, 2012

CLERK OF COURT

Signature of Clerk or Deputy Clerk

The name, address, e-mail, and telephone number of the United States attorney, or assistant United States attorney, who requests this subpoena, are:

AUSA [redacted]
157 Church St., 23rd floor
New Haven, CT 06510

Personal appearance is not required if documents are provided on or before the appearance date to: FBI S/A [redacted]
600 State St.
New Haven CT 06510

b3 -1
b6 -1, 4
b7C -1, 4

FD-1036 (Rev. 10-16-2009)

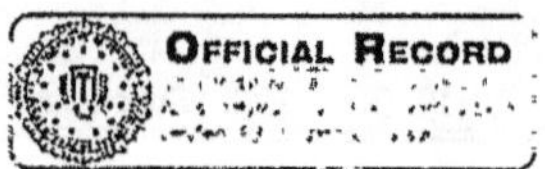

UNCLASSIFIED

FEDERAL BUREAU OF INVESTIGATION

Import Form

Form Type: FD-617 **Date:** 12/17/2012

Title: (U) 12/14/12 FGJ Subpoena to [redacted]

Approved By: [redacted] b3 -1

b6 -1

Drafted By: [redacted] b7C -

Case ID #: 4-NH-2619946-GJ (U) Grand Jury Information

FEDERAL GRAND JURY MATERIAL - DISSEMINATE PURSUANT TO RULE 6(E)
Do not disseminate except as authorized by federal rule of criminal procedure 6(e).

Synopsis: (U) 12/14/12 FGJ Subpoena to [redacted] b3 -

[redacted]

♦♦

UNCLASSIFIED

4-NH-2619946-GJ
SERIAL 3

AO 110 (Rev. 06/09) Subpoena to Testify Before a Grand Jury

UNITED STATES DISTRICT COURT

for the

District of Connecticut

SUBPOENA TO TESTIFY BEFORE A GRAND JURY

b3 -1

To:

~~YOU ARE COMMANDED~~ to appear in this United States district court at the time, date, and place shown below to testify before the court's grand jury. When you arrive, you must remain at the court until the judge or a court officer allows you to leave.

Place: United States Courthouse, 141 Church Street, New Haven, CT 06510	Date and Time:

You must also bring with you the following documents, electronically stored information, or objects *(blank if not applicable)*:

b3 -1

Date: December 14, 2012

CLERK OF COURT

Signature of Clerk or Deputy Clerk

The name, address, e-mail, and telephone number of the United States attorney, or assistant United States attorney, who requests this subpoena, are:

AUSA
157 Church St., 23rd floor
New Haven, CT 06510

Personal appearance is not required if documents are provided on or before the appearance date to: FBI S/A
600 State St.
New Haven CT 06510

b3 -1
b6 -1, 4
b7C -1, 4

AO 110 (Rev. 06/09) Subpoena to Testify Before a Grand Jury

UNITED STATES DISTRICT COURT

for the

District of Connecticut

SUBPOENA TO TESTIFY BEFORE A GRAND JURY

To:

b3 -1

YOU ARE COMMANDED to appear in this United States district court at the time, date, and place shown below to testify before the court's grand jury. When you arrive, you must remain at the court until the judge or a court officer allows you to leave.

Place: United States Courthouse 141 Church Street New Haven, CT 06510	Date and Time:

You must also bring with you the following documents, electronically stored information, or objects *(blank if not applicable)*:

b3

Date: December 14, 2012

CLERK OF COURT

Signature of Clerk or Deputy Clerk

The name, address, e-mail, and telephone number of the United States attorney, or assistant United States attorney, who requests this subpoena, are:

AUSA
157 Church St., 23rd floor
New Haven, CT 06510

Personal appearance is not required if documents are provided on or before the appearance date to: FBI S/A
600 State St.
New Haven CT 06510

b3 -1
b6 -1,
b7C -1,

FD-1036 (Rev. 10-16-2009)

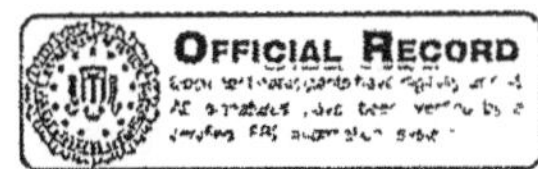

FEDERAL BUREAU OF INVESTIGATION

Import Form

Form Type: FD-617 **Date:** 12/17/2012

Title: (U) FGJ subpoean to [redacted]

b3 -1
b6 -1
b7C -1

Approved By: [redacted]

Drafted By: [redacted]

Case ID #: 4-NH-2619946-GJ (U) Grand Jury Information

FEDERAL GRAND JURY MATERIAL - DISSEMINATE PURSUANT TO RULE 6(E)
Do not disseminate except as authorized by federal rule of criminal procedure 6(e).

Synopsis: (U) A FGJ Subpoena issued to [redacted] on 12/14/12 for [redacted]

b3 -1
b6 -2
b7C -2

♦♦

4-NH-2619946-GJ
SERIAL 4

AO 110 (Rev. 06/09) Subpoena to Testify Before a Grand Jury

UNITED STATES DISTRICT COURT
for the
District of Connecticut

SUBPOENA TO TESTIFY BEFORE A GRAND JURY

To: b3 -1

YOU ARE COMMANDED to appear in this United States district court at the time, date, and place shown below to testify before the court's grand jury. When you arrive, you must remain at the court until the judge or a court officer allows you to leave.

Place:	Date and Time:
United States Courthouse 141 Church Street New Haven, CT 06510	

You must also bring with you the following documents, electronically stored information, or objects *(blank if not applicable)*:

b3 -
b6 -
b7C

Date: December 14, 2012

CLERK OF COURT

Signature of Clerk or Deputy Clerk

The name, address, e-mail, and telephone number of the United States attorney, or assistant United States attorney, who requests this subpoena, are:

AUSA
157 Church St., 23rd floor
New Haven, CT 06510

Personal appearance is not required if documents are provided on or before the appearance date to: FBI S/A
600 State St.
New Haven CT 06510

b3 -1
b6 -1, 4
b7C -1, 4

FD-1036 (Rev. 10-16-2009)

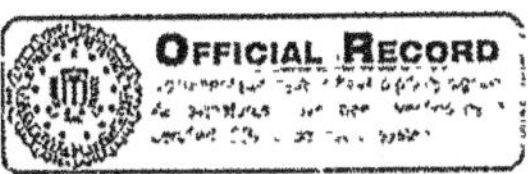

FEDERAL BUREAU OF INVESTIGATION

Import Form

Form Type: FD-617 **Date:** 12/17/2012

Title: (U) FGJ Subpoena to [redacted]

b3 -1
b6 -1
b7C -1

Approved By: [redacted]

Drafted By: [redacted]

Case ID #: 4-NH-2619946-GJ (U) Grand Jury Information

FEDERAL GRAND JURY MATERIAL - DISSEMINATE PURSUANT TO RULE 6(E)
Do not disseminate except as authorized by federal rule of criminal procedure 6(e).

Synopsis: (U) A FGJ subpoena issued to [redacted] on 4/14/12 for [redacted]

b3 -1
b6 -2
b7C -2

♦♦

4-NH-2619946-GJ
SERIAL 5

AO 110 (Rev. 06/09) Subpoena to Testify Before a Grand Jury

UNITED STATES DISTRICT COURT

for the

District of Connecticut

SUBPOENA TO TESTIFY BEFORE A GRAND JURY

To:

b3 -

YOU ARE COMMANDED to appear in this United States district court at the time, date, and place shown below to testify before the court's grand jury. When you arrive, you must remain at the court until the judge or a court officer allows you to leave.

Place: United States Courthouse 141 Church Street New Haven, CT 06510	Date and Time:

You must also bring with you the following documents, electronically stored information, or objects *(blank if not applicable)*:

b3 -
b6 -
b7C

Date: December 14, 2012

CLERK OF COURT

Signature of Clerk or Deputy Clerk

The name, address, e-mail, and telephone number of the United States attorney, or assistant United States attorney, who requests this subpoena, are:

AUSA
157 Church St., 23rd floor
New Haven, CT 06510

Personal appearance is not required if documents are provided on or before the appearance date to: FBI S/A
600 State St.
New Haven CT 06510

b3 -1
b6 -1,
b7C -1

FD-1036 (Rev. 10-16-2009)

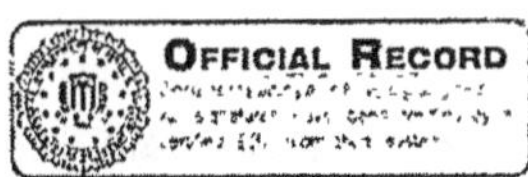

UNCLASSIFIED

FEDERAL BUREAU OF INVESTIGATION

Import Form

Form Type: FD-617 **Date:** 12/17/2012

Title: (U) FGJ subpoena issued to [redacted]

Approved By: [redacted]

Drafted By: [redacted]

b3 -1
b6 -1
b7C -1

Case ID #: 4-NH-2619946-GJ (U) Grand Jury Information

FEDERAL GRAND JURY MATERIAL - DISSEMINATE PURSUANT TO RULE 6(E)
Do not disseminate except as authorized by federal rule of criminal procedure 6(e).

Synopsis: (U) A 12/14/2012 FGJ Subpoena issued to [redacted]

b3 -1

♦♦

UNCLASSIFIED

4-NH-2619946-GJ
SERIAL 6

AO 110 (Rev. 06/09) Subpoena to Testify Before a Grand Jury

UNITED STATES DISTRICT COURT

for the

District of Connecticut

SUBPOENA TO TESTIFY BEFORE A GRAND JURY

To: b3 -

ED to appear in this United States district court at the time, date, and place shown below to testify before the court's grand jury. When you arrive, you must remain at the court until the judge or a court officer allows you to leave.

Place: United States Courthouse 141 Church Street New Haven, CT 06510	Date and Time:

You must also bring with you the following documents, electronically stored information, or objects *(blank if not applicable)*:

b3

Date: December 14, 2012

CLERK OF COURT

Signature of Clerk or Deputy Clerk

The name, address, e-mail, and telephone number of the United States attorney, or assistant United States attorney, who requests this subpoena, are:

AUSA
157 Church St., 23rd floor
New Haven, CT 06510

Personal appearance is not required if documents are provided on or before the appearance date to: FBI S/A
600 State St.
New Haven CT 06510

b3 -
b6 -
b7C

FD-1036 (Rev. 10-16-2009)

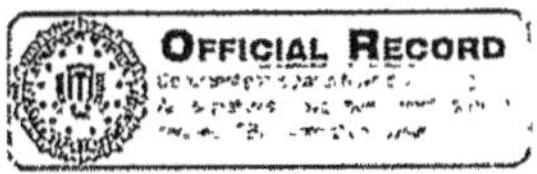

UNCLASSIFIED

FEDERAL BUREAU OF INVESTIGATION

Import Form

Form Type: FD-617. **Date:** 12/17/2012

Title: (U) FGJ Subpoena to [redacted]

b3 -1
b6 -1
b7C -1

Approved By: [redacted]

Drafted By: [redacted]

Case ID #: 4-NH-2619946-GJ (U) Grand Jury Information

FEDERAL GRAND JURY MATERIAL - DISSEMINATE PURSUANT TO RULE 6(E)
Do not disseminate except as authorized by federal rule of criminal procedure 6(e).

Synopsis: (U) A FGJ Subpoena dated 12/14/2012 issued to [redacted] b3 -1

[redacted]

♦♦

UNCLASSIFIED

4-NH-2619946-GJ
SERIAL 7

AO 110 (Rev. 06/09) Subpoena to Testify Before a Grand Jury

UNITED STATES DISTRICT COURT

for the

District of Connecticut

SUBPOENA TO TESTIFY BEFORE A GRAND JURY

To: b3 -

ANDED to appear in this United States district court at the time, date, and place shown below to testify before the court's grand jury. When you arrive, you must remain at the court until the judge or a court officer allows you to leave.

Place: United States Courthouse 141 Church Street New Haven, CT 06510	Date and Time:

You must also bring with you the following documents, electronically stored information, or objects *(blank if not applicable)*:

b3 -

Date: December 14, 2012

CLERK OF COURT

Signature of Clerk or Deputy Clerk

The name, address, e-mail, and telephone number of the United States attorney, or assistant United States attorney, who requests this subpoena, are:

AUSA
157 Church St., 23rd floor
New Haven, CT 06510

Personal appearance is not required if documents are provided on or before the appearance date to: FBI S/A
600 State St.
New Haven CT 06510

b3 -1
b6 -1,
b7C -1

FD-1036 (Rev. 10-16-2009)

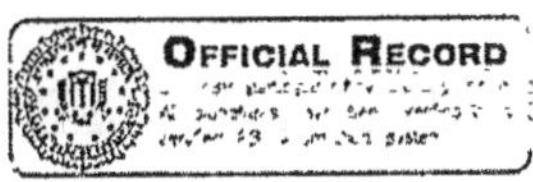

UNCLASSIFIED

FEDERAL BUREAU OF INVESTIGATION

Import Form

Form Type: FD-617 **Date:** 12/17/2012

Title: (U) FGJ Subpoean to [redacted]

b3 -1
b6 -1
b7C -1

Approved By: [redacted]

Drafted By: [redacted]

Case ID #: 4-NH-2619946-GJ (U) Grand Jury Information

FEDERAL GRAND JURY MATERIAL - DISSEMINATE PURSUANT TO RULE 6(E)
Do not disseminate except as authorized by federal rule of criminal procedure 6(e).

Synopsis: (U) FGJ Subpoena issued to [redacted] on 12/15/2012 for [redacted]

b3 -1

♦♦

UNCLASSIFIED

4-NH-2619946-GJ
SERIAL 8

AO 110 (Rev. 06/09) Subpoena to Testify Before a Grand Jury

UNITED STATES DISTRICT COURT

for the

District of Connecticut

SUBPOENA TO TESTIFY BEFORE A GRAND JURY

To:

YOU ARE COMMANDED to appear in this United States district court at the time, date, and place shown below to testify before the court's grand jury. When you arrive, you must remain at the court until the judge or a court officer allows you to leave. b3 -

Place: United States Courthouse 141 Church Street New Haven, CT 06510	Date and Time:

You must also bring with you the following documents, electronically stored information, or objects *(blank if not applicable)*:

b3

Date: 12/15/2012

CLERK OF COURT

UNITED STATES DISTRICT COURT DISTRICT OF CONNECTICUT FIAT JUSTITIA

Signature of Clerk or Deputy Clerk

The name, address, e-mail, and telephone number of the United States attorney, or assistant United States attorney, who requests this subpoena, are:

AUSA
1000 LaFayette Blvd., 10th Floor
Bridgeport, CT 06604

Personal appearance is not required if documents are provided on or before the appearance date to :
FBI S/A
600 State Street, New Haven, CT 06510

b6 -1,
b7C -1,

FD-1036 (Rev. 10-16-2009)

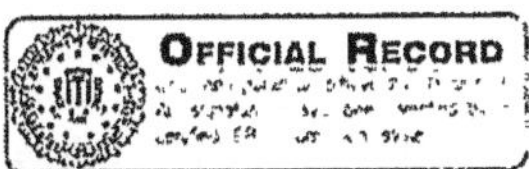

UNCLASSIFIED

FEDERAL BUREAU OF INVESTIGATION

Import Form

Form Type: FD-617 **Date:** 12/17/2012

Title: (U) FGJ Subpoena to [redacted]

b3 -1
b6 -1
b7C -1

Approved By: [redacted]

Drafted By: [redacted]

Case ID #: 4-NH-2619946-GJ (U) Grand Jury Information

FEDERAL GRAND JURY MATERIAL - DISSEMINATE PURSUANT TO RULE 6(E)
Do not disseminate except as authorized by federal rule of criminal procedure 6(e).

Synopsis: (U) A FGJ Subpoena issued on 12/16/12 to [redacted] b3 -1

◆◆

UNCLASSIFIED

4-NH-2619946-GJ
SERIAL 9

AO 110 (Rev. 06/09) Subpoena to Testify Before a Grand Jury

UNITED STATES DISTRICT COURT

for the

District of Connecticut

SUBPOENA TO TESTIFY BEFORE A GRAND JURY

To:

b3 -1

to appear in this United States district court at the time, date, and place shown below to testify before the court's grand jury. When you arrive, you must remain at the court until the judge or a court officer allows you to leave.

Place: United States Courthouse 141 Church Street New Haven, CT 06510	Date and Time:

You must also bring with you the following documents, electronically stored information, or objects *(blank if not applicable)*:

b3

Date: December 16, 2012

CLERK OF COURT

Signature of Clerk or Deputy Clerk

The name, address, e-mail, and telephone number of the United States attorney, or assistant United States attorney, who requests this subpoena, are:

AUSA
157 Church St., 23rd floor
New Haven, CT 06510

Personal appearance is not required if documents are provided on or before the appearance date to: FBI S/A
600 State St.
New Haven CT 06510

b3 -1
b6 -1, 4
b7C -1, 4

FD-1036 (Rev. 10-16-2009)

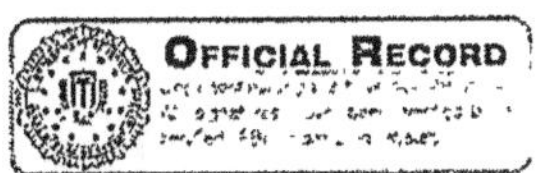

UNCLASSIFIED

FEDERAL BUREAU OF INVESTIGATION

Import Form

Form Type: FD-617 **Date:** 12/17/2012

Title: (U) FGJ Subpoena to [redacted]

b3 -1
b6 -1
b7C -1

Approved By: [redacted]

Drafted By: [redacted]

Case ID #: 4-NH-2619946-GJ (U) Grand Jury Information

FEDERAL GRAND JURY MATERIAL - DISSEMINATE PURSUANT TO RULE 6(E)
Do not disseminate except as authorized by federal rule of criminal procedure 6(e).

Synopsis: (U) A FGJ Subpoena issued to [redacted] on 12/14/2012 [redacted]

b3 -1

♦♦

UNCLASSIFIED

4-NH-2619946-GJ

SERIAL 10

AO 110 (Rev. 06/09) Subpoena to Testify Before a Grand Jury

UNITED STATES DISTRICT COURT

for the

District of Connecticut

SUBPOENA TO TESTIFY BEFORE A GRAND JURY

To:

b3 -1

D to appear in this United States district court at the time, date, and place shown below to testify before the court's grand jury. When you arrive, you must remain at the court until the judge or a court officer allows you to leave.

Place: United States Courthouse 141 Church Street New Haven, CT 06510	Date and Time:

You must also bring with you the following documents, electronically stored information, or objects *(blank if not applicable)*:

b3

Date: December 14, 2012

CLERK OF COURT

Signature of Clerk or Deputy Clerk

The name, address, e-mail, and telephone number of the United States attorney, or assistant United States attorney, who requests this subpoena, are:

AUS
157 Church St., 23rd floor
New Haven, CT 06510

Personal appearance is not required if documents are provided on or before the appearance date to: FBI S/A
600 State St.
New Haven CT 06510

b3 -1
b6 -1, 4
b7C -1,

FD-1036 (Rev. 10-16-2009)

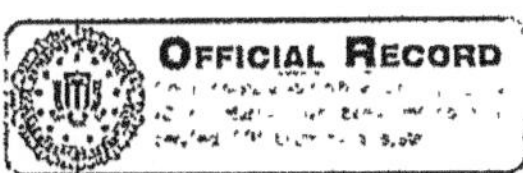

UNCLASSIFIED

FEDERAL BUREAU OF INVESTIGATION

Import Form

Form Type: FD-617 **Date:** 12/17/2012

Title: (U) FGJ Subpoena issued to [redacted]

Approved By: [redacted]

Drafted By: [redacted]

b3 -1
b6 -1
b7C -1

Case ID #: 4-NH-2619946-GJ (U) Grand Jury Information

FEDERAL GRAND JURY MATERIAL - DISSEMINATE PURSUANT TO RULE 6(E)
Do not disseminate except as authorized by federal rule of criminal procedure 6(e).

Synopsis: (U) A FGJ Subpoena issued on 12/14/12 to [redacted]

b3 -1

♦♦

UNCLASSIFIED

4-NH-2619946-GJ
SERIAL 11

AO 110 (Rev. 06/09) Subpoena to Testify Before a Grand Jury

UNITED STATES DISTRICT COURT

for the

District of Connecticut

SUBPOENA TO TESTIFY BEFORE A GRAND JURY

To: b3 -1

YOU ARE COMMANDED to appear in this United States district court at the time, date, and place shown below to testify before the court's grand jury. When you arrive, you must remain at the court until the judge or a court officer allows you to leave.

Place: United States Courthouse 141 Church Street New Haven, CT 06510	Date and Time:

You must also bring with you the following documents, electronically stored information, or objects *(blank if not applicable)*:

b3

Date: December 14, 2012

CLERK OF COURT

Signature of Clerk or Deputy Clerk

The name, address, e-mail, and telephone number of the United States attorney, or assistant United States attorney, who requests this subpoena, are:

AUSA
157 Church St., 23rd floor
New Haven, CT 06510

Personal appearance is not required if documents are provided on or before the appearance date to: FBI S/A
600 State St.
New Haven CT 06510

b3 -1
b6 -1,
b7C -1

FD-1036 (Rev. 10-16-2009)

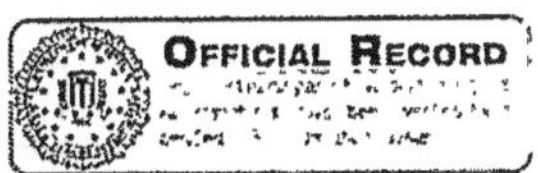

UNCLASSIFIED

FEDERAL BUREAU OF INVESTIGATION

Import Form

Form Type: FD-617

Date: 12/17/2012

Title: (U) [redacted]

Approved By: [redacted]

Drafted By: [redacted]

b3 -1
b6 -1
b7C -1

Case ID #: 4-NH-2619946-GJ (U) Grand Jury Information

FEDERAL GRAND JURY MATERIAL - DISSEMINATE PURSUANT TO RULE 6(E)
Do not disseminate except as authorized by federal rule of criminal procedure 6(e).

Synopsis: (U) A FGJ Subpoena issued to [redacted]

b3 -1
b6 -2
b7C -2

♦♦

UNCLASSIFIED

4-NH-2619946-GJ
SERIAL 12

AO 110 (Rev. 06/09) Subpoena to Testify Before a Grand Jury

UNITED STATES DISTRICT COURT

for the

District of Connecticut

SUBPOENA TO TESTIFY BEFORE A GRAND JURY

To:

b3

YOU ARE COMMANDED to appear in this United States district court at the time, date, and place shown below to testify before the court's grand jury. When you arrive, you must remain at the court until the judge or a court officer allows you to leave.

Place: United States Courthouse 141 Church Street New Haven, CT 06510	Date and Time:

You must also bring with you the following documents, electronically stored information, or objects *(blank if not applicable)*:

b3
b6
b7C

Date: December 14, 2012

CLERK OF COURT

Signature of Clerk or Deputy Clerk

The name, address, e-mail, and telephone number of the United States attorney, or assistant United States attorney, who requests this subpoena, are:

AUSA
157 Church St., 23rd floor
New Haven, CT 06510

Personal appearance is not required if documents are provided on or before the appearance date to: FBI S/A
600 State St.
New Haven CT 06510

b3 -1
b6 -1,
b7C -1

FD-302 (Rev. 5-8-10)

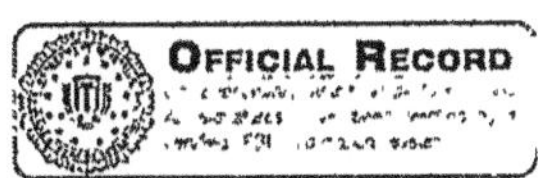

FEDERAL BUREAU OF INVESTIGATION

Date of entry 12/15/2012

FEDERAL GRAND JURY MATERIAL - DISSEMINATE PURSUANT TO RULE 6(E)
Do not disseminate except as authorized by federal rule of criminal procedure 6(e).

On 12/14/2012 at approximately 5:02 PM, a Federal Grand Jury subpoena was served on [redacted] The subpoena was served via e-mail. b3 -1 b6 -2, 5 b7C -2, 5

On 12/14/2012 at approximately 9:00 PM, [redacted] met with SA [redacted] and SA [redacted] to provide the Agents with [redacted] Also present during this meeting were [redacted] b3 -1 b6 -2, 5 b7C -2, 5

[redacted] will be submitted for storage to the New Haven Evidence Custodian. b3 -1

Investigation on 12/14/2012 at [redacted] United States (In Person, Email) b3 -1

File # 4-NH-2619946-GJ Date drafted 12/15/2012

by [redacted] b6 -1 b7C -1

4-NH-2619946-GJ
SERIAL 13

AO 110 (Rev. 06/09) Subpoena to Testify Before a Grand Jury

UNITED STATES DISTRICT COURT

for the

District of Connecticut

SUBPOENA TO TESTIFY BEFORE A GRAND JURY

To:

b3 -1
b6 -2, 5
b7C -2,

YOU ARE COMMANDED to appear in this United States district court at the time, date, and place shown below to testify before the court's grand jury. When you arrive, you must remain at the court until the judge or a court officer allows you to leave.

Place: United States Courthouse 141 Church Street New Haven, CT 06510	Date and Time:

You must also bring with you the following documents, electronically stored information, or objects *(blank if not applicable)*:

b3
b6
b7C

Date: December 14, 2012

CLERK OF COURT

Signature of Clerk or Deputy Clerk

The name, address, e-mail, and telephone number of the United States attorney, or assistant United States attorney, who requests this subpoena, are:

AUSA
157 Church St., 23rd floor
New Haven, CT 06510

Personal appearance is not required if documents are provided on or before the appearance date to: FBI S/A
600 State St.
New Haven CT 06510

b3 -
b6 -
b7C

PROOF OF SERVICE

This subpoena for *(name of individual or organization)* [redacted]
was received by me on *(date)* 12/14/2012 .

☒ I served the sub[redacted]s: served via email to [redacted]
on *(date)* 12/14/2012 ; or

☐ I returned the subpoena unexecuted because: ______________________

b3 -1
b6 -2, 5
b7C -2, 5

I declare under penalty of perjury that this inf[redacted]

Date: 12/15/2012

b6 -1
b7C -1

Special Agent [redacted]
Pri[redacted]

600 State St, New Haven, CT 06512
Server's address

Additional information regarding attempted service, etc:

From:
Sent: Friday, December 14, 2012 5:02 PM
To:
Subject: Re: (No Subject)
Attachments:

b3 -1
b6 -1, 6
b7C -1, 6

- please find attached subpoena for the email information we discussed.

Thank you,

From
To
Sent: Fri Dec 14 16:50:09 2012
Subject: RE: (No Subject)

b6 -1, 6
b7C -1, 6

I will have an IT contact for you in 10 minutes.

Sent with Good (www.good.com)

-----Original Message-----
From:
Sent: Friday, December 14, 2012 04:29 PM Eastern Standard Time
To:
Subject: Re: (No Subject)

b6 -1, 2, 6
b7C -1, 2, 6

for the subpoena, who is it being served on and what is the full corporate address? Thanks

(cell)

From
To
Sent: Fri Dec 14 16:22:29 2012
Subject: FW: (No Subject)

b6 -1, 2, 6
b7C -1, 2, 6

My contact info

b6 -6
b7C -6

Sent with Good (www.good.com)

-----Original Message-----
From:
Sent: Friday, December 14, 2012 04:18 PM Eastern Standard Time
To
Subject:

b6 -2, 6
b7C -2, 6

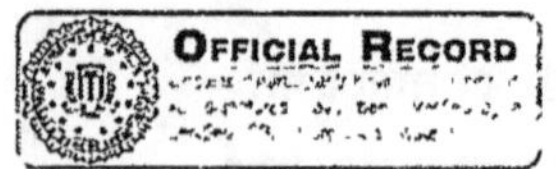

FEDERAL BUREAU OF INVESTIGATION

Date of entry 12/19/2012

FEDERAL GRAND JURY MATERIAL - DISSEMINATE PURSUANT TO RULE 6(E)
Do not disseminate except as authorized by federal rule of criminal procedure 6(e).

On 12/18/2012, writer served a Federal Grand Jury Subpoena on [redacted] The subpoena dated 12/18/2012 and issued by the United States District Court for the District of Connecticut, requested [redacted] b3 b6 b7C

On 12/18/2012, writer received the subpoena results [redacted] and noted results below. [redacted] as well as a copy of the subpoena will be filed in a 1-A envelope. b3 b6 b7C

[redacted] b3

Investigation on 12/18/2012 at Newtown, Connecticut, United States (Email)

File # 4-NH-2619946-GJ Date drafted 12/19/2012

by [redacted] b6 - b7C

4-NH-2619946-GJ
Serial 14

UNITED STATES DISTRICT COURT

for the

District of Connecticut

SUBPOENA TO TESTIFY BEFORE A GRAND JURY

To:

YOU ARE COMMANDED to appear in this United States district court at the time, date, and place shown below to testify before the court's grand jury. When you arrive, you must remain at the court until the judge or a court officer allows you to leave.

Place: United States District Court 915 Lafayette Boulevard Bridgeport, Connecticut	Date and Time:

b3 -1
b6 -1, 2, 5
b7C -1, 2, 5

You must also bring with you the following documents, electronically stored information, or objects *(blank if not applicable)*:

Personal appearance is not required if the subpoenaed materials are produced on or before the return date to FBI Special Agent If you have any questions about this subpoena, please contact Special Agent at

Date: 12/18/2012

CLERK OF COURT

Signature of Clerk or Deputy Clerk

The name, address, e-mail, and telephone number of the United States attorney, or assistant United States attorney, who requests this subpoena, are:

Assistant United States Attorney
United States Attorney's Office
1000 Lafayette Boulevard, 10th Floor
Bridgeport, Connecticut 06604

b6 -4
b7C -4

PROOF OF SERVICE

This subpoena for *(name of individual or organization)* [redacted]

was received by me on *(date)* 12/18/2012 .

☑ I served the subpoena by delivering a copy to the named person as follows: Served via email to [redacted] on *(date)* 12/18/2012 ; or

b3 -1
b6 -1,
b7C -1

☐ I returned the subpoena unexecuted because:

I declare under penalty of perjury that this information is true.

Date: 12/18/2012.

[redacted]
Server's signature

[redacted] FBI Special Agent
Printed name and title

600 State Street
New Haven, CT 06511
Server's address

Additional information regarding attempted service, etc:

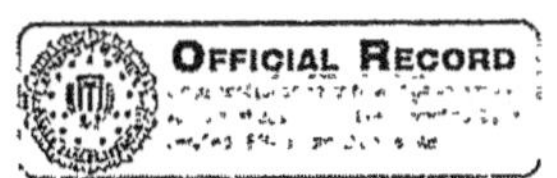

FEDERAL BUREAU OF INVESTIGATION

Date of entry 12/19/2012

FEDERAL GRAND JURY MATERIAL - DISSEMINATE PURSUANT TO RULE 6(E)
Do not disseminate except as authorized by federal rule of criminal procedure 6(e).

On 12/18/2012, writer served a Federal Grand Jury Subpoena on [redacted] Subpoena was sent via e-mail to [redacted] The subpoena dated 12/18/2012 and issued by the United States District Court for the District of Connecticut, requested [redacted]

b3 -1
b6 -2, 5
b7C -2, 5

Investigation on 12/18/2012 at Newtown, Connecticut, United States (Email)

File # 4-NH-2619946-GJ Date drafted 12/19/2012

by [redacted]

b6 -1
b7C -1

4-NH-2619946-GJ
SERIAL 15

FD-1036 (Rev. 10-16-2009)

UNCLASSIFIED

FEDERAL BUREAU OF INVESTIGATION

Import Form

Form Type: INSERT **Date:** 12/19/2012

Title: (U) Correction of Title for Serial 15

Approved By: A/SSA [redacted]

Drafted By: [redacted]

Case ID #: 4-NH-2619946-GJ (U) Grand Jury Information

b3 -1
b6 -1
b7C -1

Synopsis: (U) The title of Serial 15 should be Service of Subpoena to [redacted]

♦♦

UNCLASSIFIED

4-NH-2619946-GJ
SERIAL 16

4-NH-2619946-GJ

b3 -1
b6 -1
b7C -1

The title for Serial 15 should be "Service of Subpoena to

FD-302 (Rev. 5-8-10)

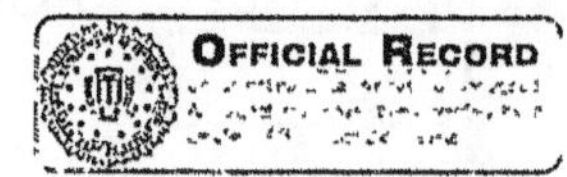

FEDERAL BUREAU OF INVESTIGATION

Date of entry 12/19/2012

FEDERAL GRAND JURY MATERIAL - DISSEMINATE PURSUANT TO RULE 6(E)
Do not disseminate except as authorized by federal rule of criminal procedure 6(e).

On 12/18/2012, writer served a Federal Grand Jury Subpoena on [redacted] [redacted] Subpoena was sent via e-mail to [redacted] and via overnight mail. The subpoena dated 12/18/2012 and issued by the United States District Court for the District of Connecticut, [redacted] [redacted]

b3

Investigation on 12/18/2012 at Newtown, Connecticut, United States (Email, Mail)

File # 4-NH-2619946-GJ Date drafted 12/19/2012

by [redacted]

b
b

This document contains neither recommendations nor conclusions of the FBI. It is the property of the FBI and is loaned to your agency; it and its contents are not to be distributed outside your agency.

4-NH-2619946-GJ
SERIAL 17

FD-302 (Rev. 5-8-10)

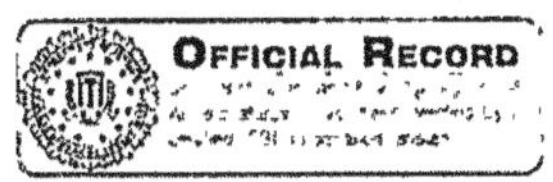

FEDERAL BUREAU OF INVESTIGATION

Date of entry 12/19/2012

FEDERAL GRAND JURY MATERIAL - DISSEMINATE PURSUANT TO RULE 6(E)
Do not disseminate except as authorized by federal rule of criminal procedure 6(e).

On 12/18/2012, writer served a subpoena to [redacted] [redacted] Subpoena results were received on 12/19/2012 from [redacted] A copy of the subpoena results will be filed in a 1-A. Results of Subpoena are as follows:

b3 -1
b6 -2, 5
b7C -2, 5

[redacted]

b3 -1
b6 -2
b7C -2

[redacted]

b3 -1
b6 -2
b7C -2

Investigation on 12/19/2012 at New Haven, Connecticut, United States (Email)

File # 4-NH-2619946-GJ Date drafted 12/19/2012

by [redacted]

b6 -1
b7C -1

4-NH-2619946-GJ
SERIAL 19

FD-302 (Rev. 5-8-10)

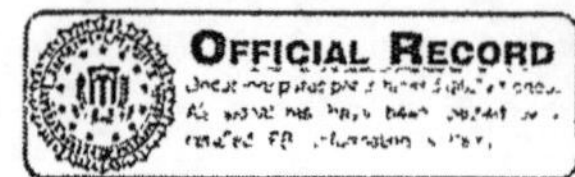

FEDERAL BUREAU OF INVESTIGATION

Date of entry 12/20/2012

On 12/19/2012, SA [redacted] received subpoena returns from [redacted]

b3 -1
b6 -1,
b7C -1

b

b

Investigation on 12/19/2012 at [redacted] United States (In Person)

b3 -1
b6 -1
b7C -1

File # 4-NH-2619946-GJ

Date drafted 12/20/2012

by [redacted]

4-NH-2619946-GJ

SERIAL 19

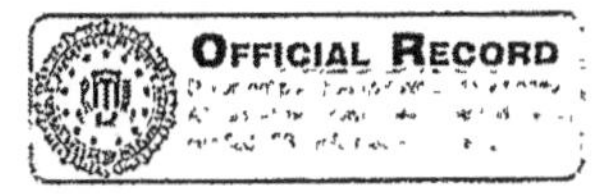

UNCLASSIFIED//~~FOUO~~

FEDERAL BUREAU OF INVESTIGATION

Date of entry 12/20/2012

FEDERAL GRAND JURY MATERIAL - DISSEMINATE PURSUANT TO RULE 6(E)
not disseminate except as authorized by federal rule of criminal procedure 6(e).

On December 20, 2012, Special Agent (SA) [redacted] faxed Federal Grand Jury subpoena number [redacted] to [redacted] The Federal Grand Jury subpoena required the production of the following: b3 -1 b6 -5 b7C -5

[redacted] b3 -1

Pursuant to the above referenced Federal Grand Jury Subpoena, on December, 20, 2012, SA [redacted] received [redacted]

[redacted] b3 -1 b6 -5 b7C -5

UNCLASSIFIED//~~FOUO~~

Investigation on 12/20/2012 at New Haven, Connecticut, United States (Email, Fax)

File # 4-NH-2619946-GJ Date drafted 12/20/2012

by [redacted] b6 -1 b7C -1

4-NH-2619946-GJ

SERIAL 20

b

b

The subpoena and subpoena return will be electronically filed as a 1A attachment to this document.

UNITED STATES DISTRICT COURT

for the

District of Connecticut

SUBPOENA TO TESTIFY BEFORE A GRAND JURY

To: b3 -1

D to appear in this United States district court at the time, date, and place shown below to testify before the court's grand jury. When you arrive, you must remain at the court until the judge or a court officer allows you to leave.

Place: United States Courthouse 141 Church Street New Haven, CT 06510	Date and Time:

You must also bring with you the following documents, electronically stored information, or objects *(blank if not applicable)*:

b3 -1

Date: December 20, 2012

CLERK OF COURT

Signature of Clerk or Deputy Clerk

The name, address, e-mail, and telephone number of the United States attorney, or assistant United States attorney, who requests this subpoena, are:

AUSA
157 Church St., 23rd floor
New Haven, CT 06510

Personal appearance is not required if documents are provided on or before the appearance date to: FBI S/A
600 State St.
New Haven CT 06510

b3 -1
b6 -1, 4
b7C -1, 4

PROOF OF SERVICE

This subpoena for *(name of individual or organization)* [redacted]
was received by me on *(date)* 12/20/2012 .

☑ I served the subpoena by delivering a copy to the named person as follows: I faxed the subpoena to [redacted] on *(date)* 12/20/2012 ; or b3 -1

☐ I returned the subpoena unexecuted because:

I declare under penalty of perjury that this information is true.

Date: 12/20/2012 [redacted]

b6 -1
b7C -

[redacted] Special Agent
Printed name and title

600 State Street New Haven, CT 06511
Server's address

Additional information regarding attempted service, etc:

FD-448
Revised
10-27-2004

FEDERAL BUREAU OF INVESTIGATION
FACSIMILE COVER SHEET

PRECEDENCE

○ Immediate ● Priority ○ Routine

CLASSIFICATION

○ Top Secret ○ Secret ○ Confidential ○ Sensitive ● Unclassified

TO

Name of Office:	Facsimile Number:	Date: **12/20/2012**
Attn:	Room:	Telephone Number:

FROM

Name of Office: **FBI New Haven**		Number of Pages: (including cover) **4**
Originator's Name: **SA**	Originator's Telephone Number:	Originator's Facsimile Number:

Approved:

b3 -1
b6 -1, 5
b7C -1, 5

DETAILS

Subject:

Special Handling Instructions:
Please note the subpoena requests that you refrain from disclosing the existence of the subpoena to any third party. If you have any questions or concerns, please feel free to e-mail:

Brief Description of Communication Faxed:

WARNING

Information attached to the cover sheet is U.S. Government Property. If you are not the intended recipient of this information disclosure, reproduction, distribution, or use of this information is prohibited (18.USC, § 641). Please notify the originator or local FBI Office immediately to arrange for proper disposition.

*************** -COMM. JOURNAL- ******************* DATE DEC-20-2012 ***** TIME 16:22 ********

MODE = MEMORY TRANSMISSION START=DEC-20 16:20 END=DEC-20 16:22

FILE NO.=192

STN NO.	COMM.	STATION NAME/EMAIL ADDRESS/TELEPHONE NO.	PAGES	DURATION
001	OK		004/004	00:01:11

-SQ 10

***** UF-8000 v2 ****************** -FBI NEW HAVEN - ***** - *********

FD-448
Revised
10-27-2004

FEDERAL BUREAU OF INVESTIGATION

FACSIMILE COVER SHEET

PRECEDENCE

○ Immediate ● Priority ○ Routine

CLASSIFICATION

○ Top Secret ○ Secret ○ Confidential ○ Sensitive ● Unclassified

TO

Name of Office:

Facsimile Number:

Date: 12/20/2012

b3 -1
b6 -1,
b7C -1

Attn:

Room:

Telephone Number:

FROM

Name of Office: **FBI New Haven**

Number of Pages: (including cover) 4

Originator's Name: **SA**

Originator's Telephone Number:

Originator's Facsimile Number:

Approved:

DETAILS

Subject:
FGJ Subpoen

Special Handling Instructions:
Please note the subpoena requests that you refrain from disclosing the existence of the subpoena to any third party. If you have any questions or concerns, please feel free to e-mail:

Brief Description of Communication Faxed:

WARNING

Information attached to the cover sheet is U.S. Government Property. If you are not the intended recipient of this information disclosure, reproduction, distribution, or use of this information is prohibited (18.USC, § 641). Please notify the originator or local FBI Office immediately to arrange for proper disposition.

From:
Sent: Thursday, December 20, 2012 4:20 PM
To:
Subject:
Attachments:

Attached is [redacted] that you requested.

b3 -1
b6 -1, 5
b7C -1, 5

Please find the records you requested attached herein. If you have any questions regarding these records, please refer to [redacted] case number listed in the subject line.

****This e-mail is in response to your request that these records be transmitted electronically. In receiving these documents electronically, you understand that this communication may not be secured and is subject to interception by third parties. You assume any liability for the release of this information via electronic mail. If you are not the intended recipient of this communication and you have received it in error, please notify the sender immediately and delete the original. Any other use of this email is prohibited.

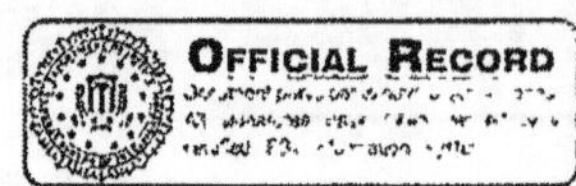

FEDERAL BUREAU OF INVESTIGATION

Import Form

Form Type: FD-617 **Date:** 12/21/2012

Title: (U) FGJ Subpoena to [redacted]

Approved By: SSA [redacted]

Drafted By: [redacted]

b3 -1
b6 -1
b7C -1

Case ID #: 4-NH-2619946-GJ (U) Grand Jury Information

FEDERAL GRAND JURY MATERIAL - DISSEMINATE PURSUANT TO RULE 6(E)
Do not disseminate except as authorized by federal rule of criminal procedure 6(e).

Synopsis: (U) FGJ Subpoena issued to [redacted] on 12/18/2012 [redacted]

b3 -1
b6 -2
b7C -

♦♦

4-NH-2619946-GJ
SERIAL 21

AO 110 (Rev. 06/09) Subpoena to Testify Before a Grand Jury

UNITED STATES DISTRICT COURT

for the

District of Connecticut

SUBPOENA TO TESTIFY BEFORE A GRAND JURY

To:

b3 -1

) to appear in this United States district court at the time, date, and place shown below to testify before the court's grand jury. When you arrive, you must remain at the court until the judge or a court officer allows you to leave.

Place: United States Courthouse 141 Church Street New Haven, CT 06510	Date and Time:

You must also bring with you the following documents, electronically stored information, or objects *(blank if not applicable)*:

b3 -1
b6 -2
b7C -2

Date: December 18, 2012

CLERK OF COURT

Signature of Clerk or Deputy Clerk

The name, address, e-mail, and telephone number of the United States attorney, or assistant United States attorney, who requests this subpoena, are:

AUSA
157 Church St., 23rd floor
New Haven, CT 06510

Personal appearance is not required if documents are provided on or before the appearance date to: FBI S/A
600 State St.
New Haven CT 06510

b3 -1
b6 -1, 4
b7C -1, 4

FD-448
Revised
10-27-2004

FEDERAL BUREAU OF INVESTIGATION
FACSIMILE COVER SHEET

PRECEDENCE

( ) Immediate (•) Priority ( ) Routine

CLASSIFICATION

( ) Top Secret ( ) Secret ( ) Confidential (•) Sensitive ( ) Unclassified

TO

Name of Office:	Facsimile Number:	Date:
		12/18/2012
Attn:	Room:	Telephone Number:

FROM

Name of Office:		Number of Pages: (including cover)
FBI New Haven		**4**
Originator's Name:	Originator's Telephone Number:	Originator's Facsimile Number:
SA		

Approved:
4-NH-2619946

b3 -1
b6 -1
b7C -1

DETAILS

Subject:

Special Handling Instructions:
SA may be reached a s well.

Brief Description of Communication Faxed:

WARNING

Information attached to the cover sheet is U.S. Government Property. If you are not the intended recipient of this information disclosure, reproduction, distribution, or use of this information is prohibited (18.USC, § 641). Please notify the originator or local FBI Office immediately to arrange for proper disposition.

MODE = MEMORY TRANSMISSION START=DEC-18 17:05 END=DEC-18 17:06

FILE NO.=162

STN NO.	COMM.	STATION NAME/EMAIL ADDRESS/TELEPHONE NO.	PAGES	DURATION
001	OK	[redacted]	004/004	00:01:33

-SQ 10 -

***** UF-8000 v2 ****************** -FBI NEW HAVEN - ***** - [redacted] *******

FD-448
Revised
10-27-2004

FEDERAL BUREAU OF INVESTIGATION
FACSIMILE COVER SHEET

b3 -1
b6 -1
b7C -1

PRECEDENCE

○ Immediate ◉ Priority ○ Routine

CLASSIFICATION

○ Top Secret ○ Secret ○ Confidential ◉ Sensitive ○ Unclassified

TO

Name of Office: [redacted]
Facsimile Number: [redacted]
Date: **12/18/2012**
Attn: [redacted]
Room:
Telephone Number:

FROM

Name of Office: **FBI New Haven**
Number of Pages: (including cover) **4**
Originator's Name: **SA** [redacted]
Originator's Telephone Number: [redacted]
Originator's Facsimile Number:
Approved: **4-NH-2619946**

DETAILS

Subject: [redacted]

Special Handling Instructions:
SA [redacted] **may be reached at** [redacted] **as well.**

Brief Description of Communication Faxed:

WARNING

Information attached to the cover sheet is U.S. Government Property. If you are not the intended recipient of this information disclosure, reproduction, distribution, or use of this information is prohibited (18.USC, § 641). Please notify the originator or local FBI Office immediately to arrange for proper disposition.

FD-1036 (Rev. 10-16-2009)

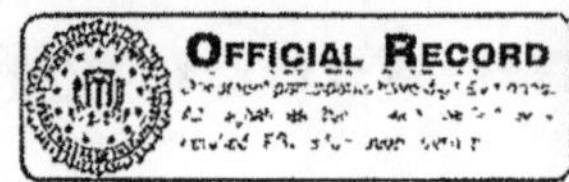

FEDERAL BUREAU OF INVESTIGATION

Import Form

Form Type: FD-617 **Date:** 12/20/2012

Title: (U) FGJ Subpoena to [redacted]

b3 -1
b6 -1
b7C -1

Approved By: SSA [redacted]

Drafted By: [redacted]

Case ID #: 4-NH-2619946-GJ (U) Grand Jury Information

FEDERAL GRAND JURY MATERIAL - DISSEMINATE PURSUANT TO RULE 6(E)
Do not disseminate except as authorized by federal rule of criminal procedure 6(e).

Synopsis: (U) FGJ Subpoena issued to [redacted] on [redacted]

b3 -1
b6 -2
b7C -

♦♦

4-NH-2619946-GJ
SERIAL 22

AO 110 (Rev. 06/09) Subpoena to Testify Before a Grand Jury

UNITED STATES DISTRICT COURT

for the

District of Connecticut

SUBPOENA TO TESTIFY BEFORE A GRAND JURY

To: b3 -1

YOU ARE COMMANDED to appear in this United States district court at the time, date, and place shown below to testify before the court's grand jury. When you arrive, you must remain at the court until the judge or a court officer allows you to leave.

Place: United States Courthouse 141 Church Street New Haven, CT 06510	Date and Time:

You must also bring with you the following documents, electronically stored information, or objects *(blank if not applicable)*:

b3 -1
b6 -2
b7C -2

Date: December 18, 2012

CLERK OF COURT

Signature of Clerk or Deputy Clerk

The name, address, e-mail, and telephone number of the United States attorney, or assistant United States attorney, who requests this subpoena, are:

AUSA
157 Church St., 23rd floor
New Haven, CT 06510

Personal appearance is not required if documents are provided on or before the appearance date to: FBI S/A
600 State St.
New Haven CT 06510

b3 -1
b6 -1, 4
b7C -1, 4

FD-448
Revised
10-27-2004

FEDERAL BUREAU OF INVESTIGATION
FACSIMILE COVER SHEET

PRECEDENCE

○ Immediate ◉ Priority ○ Routine

CLASSIFICATION

○ Top Secret ○ Secret ○ Confidential ◉ Sensitive ○ Unclassified

TO

Name of Office:	Facsimile Number:	Date: **12/18/2012**
Attn:	Room:	Telephone Number:

FROM

Name of Office: **FBI New Haven**		Number of Pages: (including cover) **4**
Originator's Name: **SA**	Originator's Telephone Number:	Originator's Facsimile Number:

Approved:
4-NH-2619946

b3 -1
b6 -1
b7C -1

DETAILS

Subject:

Special Handling Instructions:
SA may be reached at as well.

Brief Description of Communication Faxed:

WARNING

Information attached to the cover sheet is U.S. Government Property. If you are not the intended recipient of this information disclosure, reproduction, distribution, or use of this information is prohibited (18.USC, § 641). Please notify the originator or local FBI Office immediately to arrange for proper disposition.

*************** -COMM. JOURNAL- ******************* DATE DEC-18-2012 ***** TIME 17:09 ********

MODE = MEMORY TRANSMISSION START=DEC-18 17:07 END=DEC-18 17:09

FILE NO.=163

STN NO.	COMM.	STATION NAME/EMAIL ADDRESS/TELEPHONE NO.	PAGES	DURATION
001	OK		004/004	00:01:55

-SQ 10 -

***** UF-8000 v2 ******************* -FBI NEW HAVEN - ***** - *********

FD-448
Revised
10-27-2004

FEDERAL BUREAU OF INVESTIGATION

FACSIMILE COVER SHEET

PRECEDENCE

○ Immediate ◉ Priority ○ Routine

CLASSIFICATION

○ Top Secret ○ Secret ○ Confidential ◉ Sensitive ○ Unclassified

b3 -1
b6 -1
b7C -1

TO

Name of Office:

Facsimile Number:

Date: **12/18/2012**

Attn:

Room:

Telephone Number:

FROM

Name of Office: **FBI New Haven**

Number of Pages: (including cover) **4**

Originator's Name: **SA**

Originator's Telephone Number:

Originator's Facsimile Number:

Approved: **4-NH-2619946**

DETAILS

Subject:

Special Handling Instructions:
SA may be reached at as well.

Brief Description of Communication Faxed:

WARNING

Information attached to the cover sheet is U.S. Government Property. If you are not the intended recipient of this information disclosure, reproduction, distribution, or use of this information is prohibited (18.USC, § 641). Please notify the originator or local FBI Office immediately to arrange for proper disposition.

FD-1036 (Rev. 10-16-2009)

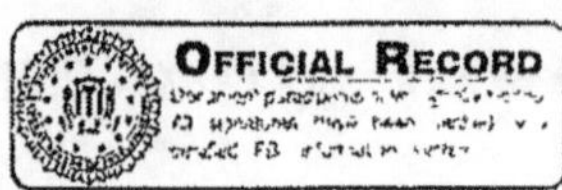

UNCLASSIFIED//~~FOUO~~

FEDERAL BUREAU OF INVESTIGATION

Import Form

Form Type: FD-617 **Date:** 12/21/2012

Title: (U) FGJ Subpoena to [redacted]

Approved By: SSA [redacted]

b3 -1
b6 -1
b7C -1

Drafted By: [redacted]

Case ID #: 4-NH-2619946-GJ (U) Grand Jury Information

FEDERAL GRAND JURY MATERIAL - DISSEMINATE PURSUANT TO RULE 6(E)

Do not disseminate except as authorized by federal rule of criminal procedure 6(e).

Synopsis: (U) FGJ Subpoena issued to [redacted] on 12/18/2012 [redacted] b3

[redacted]

♦♦

UNCLASSIFIED//~~FOUO~~

4-NH-2619946-GJ

SERIAL 23

AO 110 (Rev. 06/09) Subpoena to Testify Before a Grand Jury

UNITED STATES DISTRICT COURT

for the

District of Connecticut

SUBPOENA TO TESTIFY BEFORE A GRAND JURY

b3 -1

To:

DED to appear in this United States district court at the time, date, and place shown below to testify before the court's grand jury. When you arrive, you must remain at the court until the judge or a court officer allows you to leave.

Place: United States Courthouse 141 Church Street New Haven, CT 06510	Date and Time:

You must also bring with you the following documents, electronically stored information, or objects *(blank if not applicable)*:

b3 -1

Date: December 18, 2012

CLERK OF COURT

Signature of Clerk or Deputy Clerk

The name, address, e-mail, and telephone number of the United States attorney, or assistant United States attorney, who requests this subpoena, are:

AUS
157 Church St., 23rd floor
New Haven, CT 06510

Personal appearance is not required if documents are provided on or before the appearance date to: FBI S/A
600 State St.
New Haven CT 06510

b3 -1
b6 -1, 4
b7C -1, 4

FD-448
Revised
10-27-2004

FEDERAL BUREAU OF INVESTIGATION

FACSIMILE COVER SHEET

PRECEDENCE

( ) Immediate (•) Priority ( ) Routine

CLASSIFICATION

( ) Top Secret ( ) Secret ( ) Confidential (•) Sensitive ( ) Unclassified

TO

Name of Office: [redacted]	Facsimile Number: [redacted]	Date: **12/18/2012**
Attn: [redacted]	Room:	Telephone Number:

FROM

Name of Office: **FBI New Haven**		Number of Pages: (including cover) **4**
Originator's Name: **SA** [redacted]	Originator's Telephone Number: [redacted]	Originator's Facsimile Number: [redacted]
Approved: **4-NH-2619946**		

b3 -1
b6 -1
b7C -

DETAILS

Subject:
Federal Grand Jury Subpoena [redacted]

Special Handling Instructions:
SA [redacted] **may be reached at** [redacted] **as well.**

Brief Description of Communication Faxed:

WARNING

Information attached to the cover sheet is U.S. Government Property. If you are not the intended recipient of this information disclosure, reproduction, distribution, or use of this information is prohibited (18.USC, § 641). Please notify the originator or local FBI Office immediately to arrange for proper disposition.

************** -COMM. JOURNAL- ****************** DATE DEC-18-2012 ***** TIME 17:04 ********

MODE = MEMORY TRANSMISSION START=DEC-18 17:02 END=DEC-18 17:04

FILE NO.=161

STN NO.	COMM.	STATION NAME/EMAIL ADDRESS/TELEPHONE NO.	PAGES	DURATION
001	OK		004/004	00:01:17

-SQ 10 -

***** UF-8000 v2 ****************** -FBI NEW HAVEN - ***** - *********

FD-448
Revised
10-27-2004

FEDERAL BUREAU OF INVESTIGATION
FACSIMILE COVER SHEET

PRECEDENCE

○ Immediate ◉ Priority ○ Routine

CLASSIFICATION

○ Top Secret ○ Secret ○ Confidential ◉ Sensitive ○ Unclassified

b3 -1
b6 -1
b7C -1

TO

Name of Office:

Facsimile Number:

Date: **12/18/2012**

Attn:

Room:

Telephone Number:

FROM

Name of Office: **FBI New Haven**

Number of Pages: (including cover) **4**

Originator's Name: **SA**

Originator's Telephone Number:

Originator's Facsimile Number:

Approved: **4-NH-2619946**

DETAILS

Subject:
Federal Grand Jury Subpoe

Special Handling Instructions:
S[redacted] may be reached a[redacted] as well.

Brief Description of Communication Faxed:

WARNING

Information attached to the cover sheet is U.S. Government Property. If you are not the intended recipient of this information disclosure, reproduction, distribution, or use of this information is prohibited (18.USC, § 641). Please notify the originator or local FBI Office immediately to arrange for proper disposition.

FD-1057 (Rev. 5-8-10)

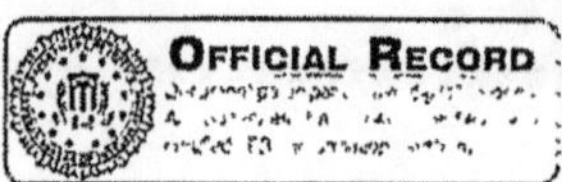

UNCLASSIFIED

FEDERAL BUREAU OF INVESTIGATION

Electronic Communication

Title: (U) [redacted] **Date:** 12/21/2012 b3

From: NEW HAVEN
NH-13
Contact: [redacted]

Approved By: A/SSRA [redacted] b6 -1 b7C -1

Drafted By: [redacted]

Case ID #: 4-NH-2619946-GJ (U) Grand Jury Information

FEDERAL GRAND JURY MATERIAL - DISSEMINATE PURSUANT TO RULE 6(E)
Do not disseminate except as authorized by federal rule of criminal procedure 6(e).

Synopsis: (U) FGJ subpoena requesting [redacted]

Enclosure(s): Enclosed are the following items:
1. (U) FGJ subpoena to [redacted]

b3 -1
b6 -2
b7C -

Details:

On 12/20/2012, a Federal Grand Jury subpoena was served to [redacted]

♦♦

UNCLASSIFIED

4-NH-2619946-GJ

SERIAL 24

AO 110 (Rev. 06/09) Subpoena to Testify Before a Grand Jury

UNITED STATES DISTRICT COURT

for the

District of Connecticut

SUBPOENA TO TESTIFY BEFORE A GRAND JURY

To:

b3 -1

ED to appear in this United States district court at the time, date, and place shown below to testify before the court's grand jury. When you arrive, you must remain at the court until the judge or a court officer allows you to leave.

Place: United States Courthouse 141 Church Street New Haven, CT 06510	Date and Time:

You must also bring with you the following documents, electronically stored information, or objects *(blank if not applicable)*:

b3 -1
b6 -2
b7C -2

Date: December 20, 2012

CLERK OF COURT

Signature of Clerk or Deputy Clerk

The name, address, e-mail, and telephone number of the United States attorney, or assistant United States attorney, who requests this subpoena, are:

AUSA
157 Church St., 23rd floor
New Haven, CT 06510

Personal appearance is not required if documents are provided on or before the appearance date to: FBI S/A
600 State St.
New Haven CT 06510

b3 -1
b6 -1, 4
b7C -1, 4

PROOF OF SERVICE

This subpoena for *(name of individual or organization)* [redacted]

was received by me on *(date)* 12/20/2012

☒ I served the subpoena by delivering a copy to the named person as follows: b3 -

[redacted] on *(date)* 12/20/12 ; or

☐ I returned the subpoena unexecuted because:

I declare under penalty of perjury that this information is true.

Date: 12/20/2012

[redacted] b6 -
b7C
[redacted] /IOA

600 State St.
New Haven CT 06511

Server's address

Additional information regarding attempted service, etc:

FD-1036 (Rev. 10-16-2009)

UNCLASSIFIED

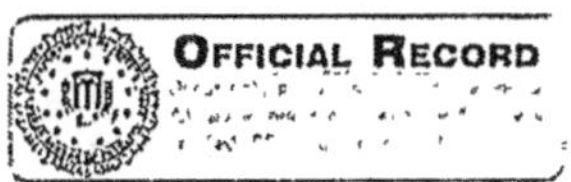

FEDERAL BUREAU OF INVESTIGATION

Import Form

Form Type: FD-617

Date: 12/27/2012

Title: (U) FGJ Subpoena issued to [redacted]

Approved By: A/SSA [redacted]

Drafted By: [redacted]

b3 -1
b6 -1, 2
b7C -1, 2

Case ID #: 4-NH-2619946-GJ (U) Grand Jury Information

FEDERAL GRAND JURY MATERIAL - DISSEMINATE PURSUANT TO RULE 6(E)
Do not disseminate except as authorized by federal rule of criminal procedure 6(e).

Synopsis: (U) FGJ Subpoena issued to [redacted]
[redacted]

b3 -1
b6 -2
b7C -2

♦♦

UNCLASSIFIED

4-NH-2619946-GJ
SERIAL 25

AO 110 (Rev. 06/09) Subpoena to Testify Before a Grand Jury

UNITED STATES DISTRICT COURT

for the

District of Connecticut

SUBPOENA TO TESTIFY BEFORE A GRAND JURY

To:

b3 -1
b6 -5
b7C -

YOU ARE COMMANDED to appear in this United States district court at the time, date, and place shown below to testify before the court's grand jury. When you arrive, you must remain at the court until the judge or a court officer allows you to leave.

Place: United States Courthouse, 141 Church Street, New Haven, CT 06510	Date and Time:

You must also bring with you the following documents, electronically stored information, or objects *(blank if not applicable)*:

b3
b6
b7C

Date: December 14, 2012

CLERK OF COURT

Signature of Clerk or Deputy Clerk

The name, address, e-mail, and telephone number of the United States attorney, or assistant United States attorney, who requests this subpoena, are:

AUSA
157 Church St., 23rd floor
New Haven, CT 06510

Personal appearance is not required if documents are provided on or before the appearance date to: FBI S/A
600 State St.
New Haven CT 06510

b3 -1
b6 -1,
b7C -1

D-1036 (Rev. 10-16-2009)

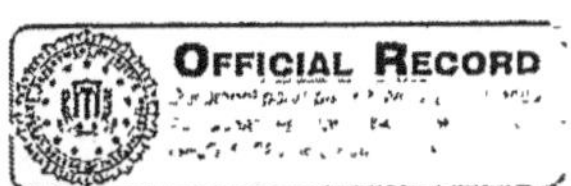

UNCLASSIFIED

FEDERAL BUREAU OF INVESTIGATION

Import Form

Form Type: FD-617 **Date:** 12/27/2012

Title: (U) FGJ Subpoena to [redacted]

Approved By: A/SSA [redacted]

Drafted By: [redacted]

b3 -1
b6 -1, 2
b7C -1, 2

Case ID #: 4-NH-2619946-GJ (U) Grand Jury Information

FEDERAL GRAND JURY MATERIAL - DISSEMINATE PURSUANT TO RULE 6(E)
Do not disseminate except as authorized by federal rule of criminal procedure 6(e).

Synopsis: (U) FGJ Subpoena issued to [redacted]

b3 -1
b6 -2
b7C -2

♦♦

UNCLASSIFIED

4-NH-2619946-GJ
SERIAL 26

UNITED STATES DISTRICT COURT

for the

District of Connecticut

SUBPOENA TO TESTIFY BEFORE A GRAND JURY

To:

b3 -1
b6 -2,
b7C -2

YOU ARE COMMANDED to appear in this United States district court at the time, date, and place shown below to testify before the court's grand jury. When you arrive, you must remain at the court until the judge or a court officer allows you to leave.

Place: United States Courthouse 141 Church Street New Haven, CT 06510	Date and Time:

You must also bring with you the following documents, electronically stored information, or objects *(blank if not applicable)*:

b3
b6
b7C

Date: December 14, 2012

CLERK OF COURT

Signature of Clerk or Deputy Clerk

The name, address, e-mail, and telephone number of the United States attorney, or assistant United States attorney, who requests this subpoena, are:

AUSA
157 Church St., 23rd floor
New Haven, CT 06510

Personal appearance is not required if documents are provided on or before the appearance date to: FBI S/
600 State St.
New Haven CT 06510

b3 -1
b6 -1,
b7C -1

D-1036 (Rev. 10-16-2009)

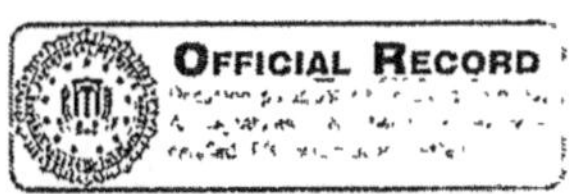

UNCLASSIFIED

FEDERAL BUREAU OF INVESTIGATION

Import Form

Form Type: FD-617 **Date:** 12/27/2012

Title: (U) FGJ Subpoena to [redacted]

Approved By: A/SSA [redacted]

Drafted By: [redacted]

b3 -1
b6 -1
b7C -1

Case ID #: 4-NH-2619946-GJ (U) Grand Jury Information

FEDERAL GRAND JURY MATERIAL - DISSEMINATE PURSUANT TO RULE 6(E)
Do not disseminate except as authorized by federal rule of criminal procedure 6(e).

Synopsis: (U) FGJ Subpoena issued to [redacted] on 12/18/2012 for [redacted]

b3 -1
b6 -2
b7C -2

♦♦

UNCLASSIFIED

4-NH-2619946-GJ
SERIAL 27

UNITED STATES DISTRICT COURT

for the

District of Connecticut

SUBPOENA TO TESTIFY BEFORE A GRAND JURY

To: b3 -1

to appear in this United States district court at the time, date, and place shown below to testify before the court's grand jury. When you arrive, you must remain at the court until the judge or a court officer allows you to leave.

Place: United States Courthouse 141 Church Street New Haven, CT 06510	Date and Time:

You must also bring with you the following documents, electronically stored information, or objects *(blank if not applicable)*:

b3
b6
b7C

Date: December 18, 2012

CLERK OF COURT

Signature of Clerk or Deputy Clerk

The name, address, e-mail, and telephone number of the United States attorney, or assistant United States attorney, who requests this subpoena, are:

AUSA
157 Church St., 23rd floor
New Haven, CT 06510

Personal appearance is not required if documents are provided on or before the appearance date to: FBI S/A
600 State St.
New Haven CT 06510

b3 -1
b6 -1,
b7C -1

)-1036 (Rev. 10-16-2009)

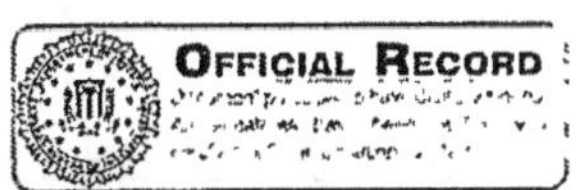

UNCLASSIFIED

FEDERAL BUREAU OF INVESTIGATION

Import Form

Form Type: FD-617 **Date:** 12/27/2012

Title: (U) FGJ Subpoena to [redacted]

Approved By: A/SSA [redacted]

b3 -1
b6 -1, 2
b7C -1, 2

Drafted By: [redacted]

Case ID #: 4-NH-2619946-GJ (U) Grand Jury Information

FEDERAL GRAND JURY MATERIAL - DISSEMINATE PURSUANT TO RULE 6(E)
Do not disseminate except as authorized by federal rule of criminal procedure 6(e).

Synopsis: (U) FGJ Subpoena issued to [redacted]

b3 -1
b6 -2
b7C -2

♦♦

UNCLASSIFIED

4-NH-2619946-GJ
SERIAL 28

UNITED STATES DISTRICT COURT

for the

District of Connecticut

SUBPOENA TO TESTIFY BEFORE A GRAND JURY

b3 -1
b6 -5
b7C -5

To:

appear in this United States district court at the time, date, and place shown below to testify before the court's grand jury. When you arrive, you must remain at the court until the judge or a court officer allows you to leave.

Place: United States Courthouse 141 Church Street New Haven, CT 06510	Date and Time:

You must also bring with you the following documents, electronically stored information, or objects *(blank if not applicable)*:

b3 -
b6 -
b7C

Date: December 18, 2012

CLERK OF COURT

Signature of Clerk or Deputy Clerk

The name, address, e-mail, and telephone number of the United States attorney, or assistant United States attorney, who requests this subpoena, are:

AUSA
157 Church St., 23rd floor
New Haven, CT 06510

Personal appearance is not required if documents are provided on or before the appearance date to: FBI S/A
600 State St.
New Haven CT 06510

b3 -1
b6 -1,
b7C -1,

FD-1036 (Rev. 10-16-2009)

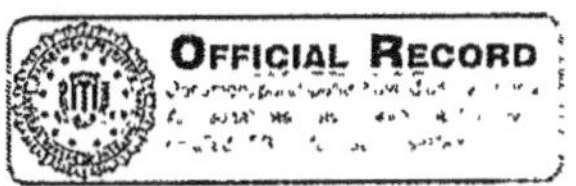

UNCLASSIFIED

FEDERAL BUREAU OF INVESTIGATION

Import Form

Form Type: FD-617 **Date:** 12/27/2012

Title: (U) FGJ Subpoena to

Approved By: A/SSA

Drafted By:

b3 -1
b6 -1, 2
b7C -1, 2

Case ID #: 4-NH-2619946-GJ (U) Grand Jury Information

FEDERAL GRAND JURY MATERIAL - DISSEMINATE PURSUANT TO RULE 6(E)
Do not disseminate except as authorized by federal rule of criminal procedure 6(e).

Synopsis: (U) FGJ Subpoena issued to on 12/19/2012 for

b3 -1
b6 -2
b7C -2

♦♦

UNCLASSIFIED

4-NH-2619946-GJ
SERIAL 29

AO 110 (Rev. 06/09) Subpoena to Testify Before a Grand Jury

UNITED STATES DISTRICT COURT

for the

District of Connecticut

SUBPOENA TO TESTIFY BEFORE A GRAND JURY

To

YOU ARE COMMANDED to appear in this United States district court at the time, date, and place shown below to testify before the court's grand jury. When you arrive, you must remain at the court until the judge or a court officer allows you to leave. b3 -

Place: United States District Court 915 Lafayette Boulevard Bridgeport, Connecticut	Date and Time:

You must also bring with you the following documents, electronically stored information, or objects *(blank if not applicable)*:

b3 -1
b6 -1
b7C -

Date: 12/19/2012

CLERK OF COURT

Signature of Clerk or Deputy Clerk

The name, address, e-mail, and telephone number of the United States attorney, or assistant United States attorney, who requests this subpoena, are:

Assistant United States Attorney
United States Attorney's Office b6 -4
1000 Lafayette Boulevard, 10th Floor b7C -4
Bridgeport, Connecticut 06604

FD-302 (Rev. 5-8-10)

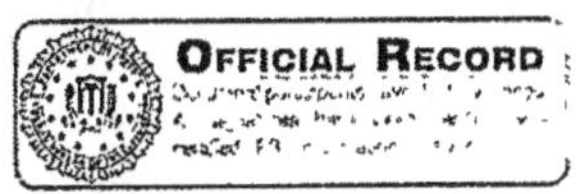

FEDERAL BUREAU OF INVESTIGATION

Date of entry 12/21/2012

FEDERAL GRAND JURY MATERIAL - DISSEMINATE PURSUANT TO RULE 6(E)
Do not disseminate except as authorized by federal rule of criminal procedure 6(e).

On 12/21/2012, Supervisory Special Agent [redacted] received [redacted] The records were produced via UPS pursuant to a Federal Grand Jury subpoena addressed to [redacted] b3 -1 b6 -5 b7C -5

Investigation on 12/21/2012 at New Haven, Connecticut, United States (, Other (UPS))

File # 4-NH-2619946-GJ Date drafted 12/21/2012

by [redacted] b6 -1 b7C -1

This document contains neither recommendations nor conclusions of the FBI. It is the property of the FBI and is loaned to your agency; it and its contents are not to be distributed outside your agency.

4-NH-2619946-GJ
SERIAL 30

AO 110 (Rev. 06/09) Subpoena to Testify Before a Grand Jury

UNITED STATES DISTRICT COURT

for the

District of Connecticut

SUBPOENA TO TESTIFY BEFORE A GRAND JURY

b3 -1
b6 -1, 5
b7C -1,

To:

YOU ARE COMMANDED to appear in this United States district court at the time, date, and place shown below to testify before the court's grand jury. When you arrive, you must remain at the court until the judge or a court officer allows you to leave.

Place: Grand Jury Room United States District Court & Federal Building 915 Lafayette Blvd Bridgeport, CT 06604	Date and Time:

You must also bring with you the following documents, electronically stored information, or objects *(blank if not applicable)*:

b3 -
b6 -
b7C

Date: 12/18/2012

CLERK OF COURT

Signature of Clerk or Deputy Clerk

UNITED STATES DISTRICT COURT DISTRICT OF CONNECTICUT FIAT JUSTITIA

The name, address, e-mail, and telephone number of the United States attorney, or assistant United States attorney, who requests this subpoena, are:

ASSISTANT UNITED STATES ATTORNEY
UNITED STATES ATTORNEY'S OFFICE
1000 LAFAYETTE BLVD., 10TH FLOOR
BRIDGEPORT, CT 06604

b6 -4
b7C -4

Control No:

CERTIFICATE OF AUTHENTICITY

I, ___, hereby certify that:

1. I am the custodian of records at ___ ("the Company"), located at ___

2. I have examined the records of the Company, and they contain the attached documents, each of which is the original or the duplicate of the original records, described more particularly as

   true and complete

b3 -1
b6 -1, 5
b7C -1, 5

3. The information in these records was recorded at or near the time of the occurrence of the matters set forth therein, by a person with knowledge of these matters or with information transmitted from such a person.

4. These records are made, and are kept, as a regular practice in the ordinary course of business.

I certify under penalty of perjury that the foregoing is true and correct.

Executed on 12/18/12, in ___
(date) (city) (state)

name:

address

telephone number:

FD-448
Revised
10-27-2004

FEDERAL BUREAU OF INVESTIGATION
FACSIMILE COVER SHEET

PRECEDENCE

(•) Immediate ( ) Priority ( ) Routine

CLASSIFICATION

( ) Top Secret ( ) Secret ( ) Confidential (•) Sensitive ( ) Unclassified

TO

Name of Office:

Facsimile Number:

Date: **12/18/2012**

b3 -1
b6 -1,
b7C -1

Attn:

Room:

Telephone Number:

FROM

Name of Office:
Federal Bureau of Investigation - Boston

Number of Pages: (including cover)
8

Originator's Name:
SA

Originator's Telephone Number:

Originator's Facsimile Number:

Approved:
Y

DETAILS

Subject:
Grand Jury Subpoena related to

Special Handling Instructions:
Please deliver to Also please confirm receipt of this subpoena to SA at or Thank you.

b3 -1
b6 -1, 5
b7C -1, 5

Brief Description of Communication Faxed:
Cover sheet: Grand Jury Subpoena

WARNING

Information attached to the cover sheet is U.S. Government Property. If you are not the intended recipient of this information disclosure, reproduction, distribution, or use of this information is prohibited (18.USC, § 641). Please notify the originator or local FBI Office immediately to arrange for proper disposition.

-1036 (Rev. 10-16-2009)

UNCLASSIFIED//~~FOUO~~

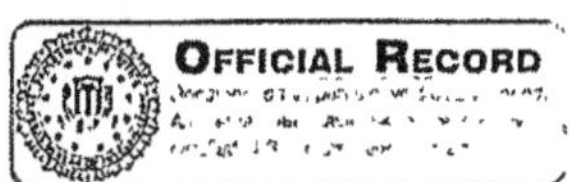

FEDERAL BUREAU OF INVESTIGATION

Import Form

Form Type: FD-617 **Date:** 12/21/2012

Title: (U) FGJ Subpoena to [redacted]

Approved By: SSA [redacted]

Drafted By: [redacted]

b3 -1
b6 -1
b7C -1

Case ID #: 4-NH-2619946-GJ (U) Grand Jury Information

FEDERAL GRAND JURY MATERIAL - DISSEMINATE PURSUANT TO RULE 6(E)
Do not disseminate except as authorized by federal rule of criminal procedure 6(e).

Synopsis: (U) FGJ Subpoena issued to [redacted] [redacted] on 12/19/2012 [redacted]

b3 -1
b6 -2
b7C -2

Enclosure(s): Enclosed are the following items:
1. (U//~~FOUO~~) [redacted]

b7E -2

♦♦

UNCLASSIFIED//~~FOUO~~

4-NH-2619946-GJ
SERIAL 31

AO 110 (Rev. 06/09) Subpoena to Testify Before a Grand Jury

UNITED STATES DISTRICT COURT

for the

District of Connecticut

SUBPOENA TO TESTIFY BEFORE A GRAND JURY

To:

b3 -

ar in this United States district court at the time, date, and place shown below to testify before the court's grand jury. When you arrive, you must remain at the court until the judge or a court officer allows you to leave.

Place: United States Courthouse 141 Church Street New Haven, CT 06510	Date and Time:

You must also bring with you the following documents, electronically stored information, or objects *(blank if not applicable)*:

SEE ATTACHMENT

Date: December 19, 2012

CLERK OF COURT

Signature of Clerk or Deputy Clerk

The name, address, e-mail, and telephone number of the United States attorney, or assistant United States attorney, who requests this subpoena, are:

AUS
157 Church St., 23rd floor
New Haven, CT 06510

Personal appearance is not required if documents are provided on or before the appearance date to: FBI S/A
600 State St.
New Haven CT 06510

b3 -1
b6 -1,
b7C -1,

ATTACHMENT

b3 -1
b6 -2
b7C -2

PROOF OF SERVICE

This subpoena for *(name of individual or organization)* [redacted]
was received by me on *(date)* 12/19/2012 .

☒ I served the subpoena by delivering a copy to the named person as follows: [redacted] b3

[redacted] on *(date)* 12/19/2012 ; or

☐ I returned the subpoena unexecuted because: _______________

I declare under penalty of perjury that this information is true.

Date: 12/19/2012

[redacted]
Server's signature

[redacted] SPECIAL AGENT
Printed name and title

b3 -
b6 -
b7C

FBI, 600 STATE STREET, NEW HAVEN, CONNECTICUT
Server's address

Additional information regarding attempted service, etc: Served via facsimile to [redacted]

FD-448
Revised
10-27-2004

FEDERAL BUREAU OF INVESTIGATION
FACSIMILE COVER SHEET

PRECEDENCE

(•) Immediate ( ) Priority ( ) Routine

CLASSIFICATION

( ) Top Secret ( ) Secret ( ) Confidential ( ) Sensitive (•) Unclassified

TO

ame of Office: [redacted]
Facsimile Number: [redacted]
Date: **12/19/2012**
ttn:
Room:
Telephone Number:

FROM

ame of Office: **BI, New Haven Division**
Number of Pages: (including cover) **5**
b3 -1
b6 -1
b7C -1
riginator's Name: A [redacted]
Originator's Telephone Number: [redacted]
Originator's Facsimile Number:
pproved:

DETAILS

ubject: [redacted]
riginator's Email: [redacted]

pecial Handling Instructions:

rief Description of Communication Faxed:

WARNING

nformation attached to the cover sheet is U.S. Government Property. If you are not the intended recipient of this information disclosure, eproduction, distribution, or use of this information is prohibited (18.USC, § 641). Please notify the originator or local FBI Office nmediately to arrange for proper disposition.

*************** -COMM. JOURNAL- ******************* DATE DEC-19-2012 ***** TIME 17:49 ********

MODE = MEMORY TRANSMISSION START=DEC-19 17:48 END=DEC-19 17:49

FILE NO.=183

STN NO.	COMM.	STATION NAME/EMAIL ADDRESS/TELEPHONE NO.	PAGES	DURATION
001	OK		005/005	00:00:51

-SQ 10 -

***** UF-8000 v2 ******************* -FBI NEW HAVEN - ***** - *********

b3 -1
b6 -1
b7C -1

FD-448
Revised
10-27-2004

FEDERAL BUREAU OF INVESTIGATION
FACSIMILE COVER SHEET

PRECEDENCE

(•) Immediate ( ) Priority ( ) Routine

CLASSIFICATION

( ) Top Secret ( ) Secret ( ) Confidential ( ) Sensitive (•) Unclassified

TO

Facsimile Number:
Date: **12/19/2012**
Attn:
Room:
Telephone Number:

FROM

Name of Office: **FBI, New Haven Division**
Number of Pages: (including cover) **5**
Originator's Name: **SA**
Originator's Telephone Number:
Originator's Facsimile Number:
Approved:

DETAILS

Subject:
Originator's Email:

Special Handling Instructions:

Brief Description of Communication Faxed:

WARNING

Information attached to the cover sheet is U.S. Government Property. If you are not the intended recipient of this information disclosure, reproduction, distribution, or use of this information is prohibited (18.USC, § 641). Please notify the originator or local FBI Office immediately to arrange for proper disposition.

D-1036 (Rev. 10-16-2009)

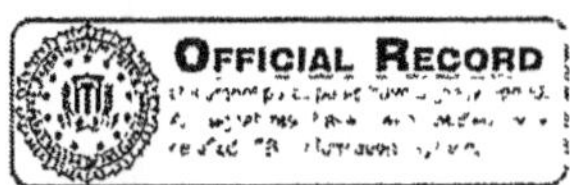

UNCLASSIFIED//~~FOUO~~

FEDERAL BUREAU OF INVESTIGATION

Import Form

Form Type: FD-617 **Date:** 12/21/2012

Title: (U) FGJ Subpoena to [redacted]

Approved By: SSA [redacted]

Drafted By: [redacted]

b3 -1
b6 -1
b7C -1

Case ID #: 4-NH-2619946-GJ (U) Grand Jury Information

FEDERAL GRAND JURY MATERIAL - DISSEMINATE PURSUANT TO RULE 6(E)
Do not disseminate except as authorized by federal rule of criminal procedure 6(e).

Synopsis: (U) FGJ Subpoena issued to [redacted] on 12/19/2012 for [redacted]

b3 -1
b6 -2
b7C -2

♦♦

UNCLASSIFIED//~~FOUO~~

4-NH-2619946-GJ
SERIAL 32

AO 110 (Rev. 06/09) Subpoena to Testify Before a Grand Jury

UNITED STATES DISTRICT COURT

for the

District of Connecticut

SUBPOENA TO TESTIFY BEFORE A GRAND JURY

To:

b3 -1

ED to appear in this United States district court at the time, date, and place shown below to testify before the court's grand jury. When you arrive, you must remain at the court until the judge or a court officer allows you to leave.

Place: United States Courthouse 141 Church Street New Haven, CT 06510	Date and Time:

You must also bring with you the following documents, electronically stored information, or objects *(blank if not applicable)*:

b3
b6
b7C

Date: December 19, 2012

CLERK OF COURT

Signature of Clerk or Deputy Clerk

The name, address, e-mail, and telephone number of the United States attorney, or assistant United States attorney, who requests this subpoena, are:

AUSA
157 Church St., 23rd floor
New Haven, CT 06510

Personal appearance is not required if documents are provided on or before the appearance date to: FBI S/A
600 State St.
New Haven CT 06510

b3 -1
b6 -1,
b7C -1,

FD-448
Revised
10-27-2004

FEDERAL BUREAU OF INVESTIGATION
FACSIMILE COVER SHEET

PRECEDENCE

( ) Immediate (•) Priority ( ) Routine

CLASSIFICATION

( ) Top Secret ( ) Secret ( ) Confidential (•) Sensitive ( ) Unclassified

TO

Name of Office: [redacted]	Facsimile Number: [redacted]	Date: **12/19/2012**
Attn: [redacted]	Room:	Telephone Number:

FROM

Name of Office: **FBI New Haven**		Number of Pages: (including cover) **4**
Originator's Name: **SA** [redacted]	Originator's Telephone Number: [redacted]	Originator's Facsimile Number: [redacted]
Approved: **4-NH-2619946**		

b3 -1
b6 -1
b7C -1

DETAILS

Subject:
Federal Grand Jury Subpoena [redacted]

Special Handling Instructions:
SA [redacted] **may be reached at** [redacted] **as well.**

Brief Description of Communication Faxed:

WARNING
Information attached to the cover sheet is U.S. Government Property. If you are not the intended recipient of this information disclosure, reproduction, distribution, or use of this information is prohibited (18.USC, § 641). Please notify the originator or local FBI Office immediately to arrange for proper disposition.

*************** -COMM. JOURNAL- ******************* DATE DEC-19-2012 ***** TIME 17:57 ********

MODE = MEMORY TRANSMISSION START=DEC-19 17:56 END=DEC-19 17:57

FILE NO.=186

STN NO.	COMM.	STATION NAME/EMAIL ADDRESS/TELEPHONE NO.	PAGES	DURATION
001	OK		004/004	00:00:41

-SQ 10

***** UF-8000 v2 ******************* -FBI NEW HAVEN - ***** - *********

FD-448
Revised
10-27-2004

FEDERAL BUREAU OF INVESTIGATION

FACSIMILE COVER SHEET

PRECEDENCE

○ Immediate ◉ Priority ○ Routine

CLASSIFICATION

○ Top Secret ○ Secret ○ Confidential ◉ Sensitive ○ Unclassified

b3 -1
b6 -1
b7C -1

TO

Name of Office:	Facsimile Number:	Date: **12/19/2012**
Attn:	Room:	Telephone Number:

FROM

Name of Office: **FBI New Haven**		Number of Pages: (including cover) **4**
Originator's Name: **SA**	Originator's Telephone Number:	Originator's Facsimile Number:

Approved:
4-NH-2619946

DETAILS

Subject:
Federal Grand Jury Subpoena

Special Handling Instructions:
SA may be reached at as well.

Brief Description of Communication Faxed:

WARNING

Information attached to the cover sheet is U.S. Government Property. If you are not the intended recipient of this information disclosure, reproduction, distribution, or use of this information is prohibited (18.USC, § 641). Please notify the originator or local FBI Office immediately to arrange for proper disposition.

FD-1036 (Rev. 10-16-2009)

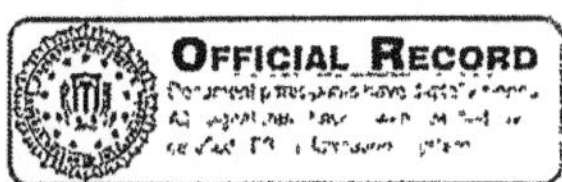

FEDERAL BUREAU OF INVESTIGATION

Import Form

Form Type: FD-617 **Date:** 12/21/2012

Title: (U) FGJ Subpoena [redacted]

Approved By: SSA [redacted]

Drafted By: [redacted]

b3 -1
b6 -1
b7C -1

Case ID #: 4-NH-2619946-GJ (U) Grand Jury Information

FEDERAL GRAND JURY MATERIAL - DISSEMINATE PURSUANT TO RULE 6(E)
Do not disseminate except as authorized by federal rule of criminal procedure 6(e).

Synopsis: (U) FGJ Subpoena issued to [redacted] on 12/19/2012 [redacted]

b3 -1
b6 -2
b7C -2

♦♦

4-NH-2619946-GJ
SERIAL 33

AO 110 (Rev. 06/09) Subpoena to Testify Before a Grand Jury

UNITED STATES DISTRICT COURT

for the

District of Connecticut

SUBPOENA TO TESTIFY BEFORE A GRAND JURY

To: b3 -1

YOU ARE COMMANDED to appear in this United States district court at the time, date, and place shown below to testify before the court's grand jury. When you arrive, you must remain at the court until the judge or a court officer allows you to leave.

Place: United States Courthouse 141 Church Street New Haven, CT 06510	Date and Time:

You must also bring with you the following documents, electronically stored information, or objects *(blank if not applicable)*:

b3 -1
b6 -2
b7C -

Date: December 19, 2012

CLERK OF COURT

Signature of Clerk or Deputy Clerk

The name, address, e-mail, and telephone number of the United States attorney, or assistant United States attorney, who requests this subpoena, are:

AUSA
157 Church St., 23rd floor
New Haven, CT 06510

Personal appearance is not required if documents are provided on or before the appearance date to: FBI S/A
600 State St.
New Haven, CT 06510

b3 -1
b6 -1,
b7C -1

FD-448
Revised
10-27-2004

FEDERAL BUREAU OF INVESTIGATION
FACSIMILE COVER SHEET

PRECEDENCE

( ) Immediate (•) Priority ( ) Routine

CLASSIFICATION

( ) Top Secret ( ) Secret ( ) Confidential (•) Sensitive ( ) Unclassified

TO

Name of Office: [redacted]	Facsimile Number: [redacted]	Date: **12/19/2012**
Attn: [redacted]	Room:	Telephone Number:

FROM

Name of Office: **FBI New Haven**		Number of Pages: (including cover) **4**
Originator's Name: **SA** [redacted]	Originator's Telephone Number: [redacted]	Originator's Facsimile Number: [redacted]

Approved:
4-NH-2619946

b3 -1
b6 -1
b7C -1

DETAILS

Subject: [redacted]

Special Handling Instructions:
S[redacted] may be reached a[redacted] as well.

Brief Description of Communication Faxed:

WARNING

Information attached to the cover sheet is U.S. Government Property. If you are not the intended recipient of this information disclosure, reproduction, distribution, or use of this information is prohibited (18.USC, § 641). Please notify the originator or local FBI Office immediately to arrange for proper disposition.

*************** -COMM. JOURNAL- ****************** DATE DEC-19-2012 ***** TIME 13:50 ********

MODE = MEMORY TRANSMISSION   START=DEC-19 13:49   END=DEC-19 13:50

FILE NO.=176

STN NO.	COMM.	STATION NAME/EMAIL ADDRESS/TELEPHONE NO.	PAGES	DURATION
001	OK		004/004	00:01:20

-SQ 10   -

***** UF-8000 v2 ****************** -FBI NEW HAVEN   - ***** -   ********

FD-448
Revised
10-27-2004

FEDERAL BUREAU OF INVESTIGATION

FACSIMILE COVER SHEET

PRECEDENCE

○ Immediate   ◉ Priority   ○ Routine

CLASSIFICATION

○ Top Secret   ○ Secret   ○ Confidential   ◉ Sensitive   ○ Unclassified

b3 -1
b6 -1
b7C -1

TO

Name of Office:

Date: **12/19/2012**

Name: Room: Telephone Number:

FROM

Name of Office: **FBI New Haven**

Number of Pages: (including cover) **4**

Originator's Name: **S**

Originator's Telephone Number: Originator's Facsimile Number:

Approved:
4-NH-2619946

DETAILS

Subject:

Special Handling Instructions:
S   may be reached at   as well.

Brief Description of Communication Faxed:

WARNING

Information attached to the cover sheet is U.S. Government Property. If you are not the intended recipient of this information disclosure, reproduction, distribution, or use of this information is prohibited (18.USC, § 641). Please notify the originator or local FBI Office immediately to arrange for proper disposition.

D-1036 (Rev. 10-16-2009)

UNCLASSIFIED//~~FOUO~~

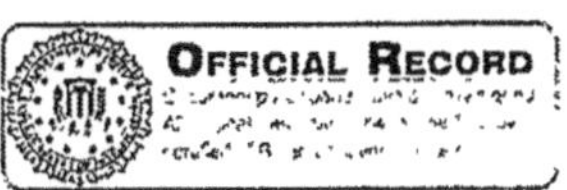

FEDERAL BUREAU OF INVESTIGATION

Import Form

Form Type: FD-617 **Date:** 12/21/2012

Title: (U) FGJ Subpoena [redacted]

Approved By: SSA [redacted]

b3 -1
b6 -1
b7C -1

Drafted By: [redacted]

Case ID #: 4-NH-2619946-GJ (U) Grand Jury Information

FEDERAL GRAND JURY MATERIAL - DISSEMINATE PURSUANT TO RULE 6(E)
Do not disseminate except as authorized by federal rule of criminal procedure 6(e).

Synopsis: (U) FGJ Subpoena issued to [redacted] on 12/18/2012 [redacted]

b3 -1
b6 -2
b7C -2

♦♦

UNCLASSIFIED//~~FOUO~~

4-NH-2619946-GJ
SERIAL 34

AO 110 (Rev. 06/09) Subpoena to Testify Before a Grand Jury

UNITED STATES DISTRICT COURT

for the

District of Connecticut

SUBPOENA TO TESTIFY BEFORE A GRAND JURY

To:

b3 -1

YOU ARE COMMANDED to appear in this United States district court at the time, date, and place shown below to testify before the court's grand jury. When you arrive, you must remain at the court until the judge or a court officer allows you to leave.

Place: United States Courthouse 141 Church Street New Haven, CT 06510	Date and Time:

You must also bring with you the following documents, electronically stored information, or objects *(blank if not applicable)*:

b3 -
b6 -
b7C

Date: December 18, 2012

CLERK OF COURT

Signature of Clerk or Deputy Clerk

The name, address, e-mail, and telephone number of the United States attorney, or assistant United States attorney, who requests this subpoena, are:

AUSA
157 Church St., 23rd floor
New Haven, CT 06510

Personal appearance is not required if documents are provided on or before the appearance date to: FBI S/A
600 State St.
New Haven CT 06510

b3 -1
b6 -1,
b7C -1,

FD-448
Revised
10-27-2004

FEDERAL BUREAU OF INVESTIGATION

FACSIMILE COVER SHEET

PRECEDENCE

( ) Immediate (•) Priority ( ) Routine

CLASSIFICATION

( ) Top Secret ( ) Secret ( ) Confidential (•) Sensitive ( ) Unclassified

TO

Name of Office:	Facsimile Number:	Date: **12/18/2012**
Attn:	Room:	Telephone Number:

FROM

Name of Office: **FBI New Haven**		Number of Pages: (including cover) **4**
Originator's Name: **SA**	Originator's Telephone Number:	Originator's Facsimile Number:
Approved: **4-NH-2619946**		

b3 -1
b6 -1
b7C -1

DETAILS

Subject:
Federal Grand Jury Subpoena

Special Handling Instructions:
SA may be reached at as well.

Brief Description of Communication Faxed:

WARNING

Information attached to the cover sheet is U.S. Government Property. If you are not the intended recipient of this information disclosure, reproduction, distribution, or use of this information is prohibited (18.USC, § 641). Please notify the originator or local FBI Office immediately to arrange for proper disposition.

*************** -COMM. JOURNAL- ******************* DATE DEC-18-2012 ***** TIME 21:29 ********

MODE = MEMORY TRANSMISSION START=DEC-18 21:28 END=DEC-18 21:29

FILE NO.=174

STN NO.	COMM.	STATION NAME/EMAIL ADDRESS/TELEPHONE NO.	PAGES	DURATION
001	OK		004/004	00:01:27

-SQ 10 -

***** UF-8000 v2 ****************** -FBI NEW HAVEN - ***** - ********

FD-448
Revised
10-27-2004

FEDERAL BUREAU OF INVESTIGATION
FACSIMILE COVER SHEET

b3 -1
b6 -1
b7C -1

PRECEDENCE

○ Immediate ◉ Priority ○ Routine

CLASSIFICATION

○ Top Secret ○ Secret ○ Confidential ◉ Sensitive ○ Unclassified

TO

Name of Office:

Facsimile Number:

Date: **12/18/2012**

Attn:

Room:

Telephone Number:

FROM

Name of Office: **FBI New Haven**

Number of Pages: (including cover) **4**

Originator's Name: **SA**

Originator's Telephone Number:

Originator's Facsimile Number:

Approved: **4-NH-2619946**

DETAILS

Subject:
Federal Grand Jury Subpoena

Special Handling Instructions:
SA may be reached at as well.

Brief Description of Communication Faxed:

WARNING
Information attached to the cover sheet is U.S. Government Property. If you are not the intended recipient of this information disclosure, reproduction, distribution, or use of this information is prohibited (18.USC, § 641). Please notify the originator or local FBI Office immediately to arrange for proper disposition.

FD-1036 (Rev. 10-16-2009)

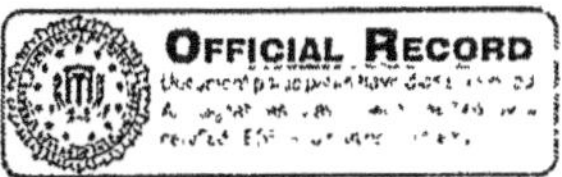

FEDERAL BUREAU OF INVESTIGATION

Import Form

Form Type: FD-617 **Date:** 12/21/2012

Title: (U) FGJ Subpoena to

Approved By: SSA

Drafted By:

b3 -1
b6 -1
b7C -1

Case ID #: 4-NH-2619946-GJ (U) Grand Jury Information

FEDERAL GRAND JURY MATERIAL - DISSEMINATE PURSUANT TO RULE 6(E)
Do not disseminate except as authorized by federal rule of criminal procedure 6(e).

Synopsis: (U) FGJ Subpoena issued to on 12/18/2012

b3 -1
b6 -2
b7C -2

♦♦

4-NH-2619946-GJ
SERIAL 35

AO 110 (Rev. 06/09) Subpoena to Testify Before a Grand Jury

UNITED STATES DISTRICT COURT

for the

District of Connecticut

SUBPOENA TO TESTIFY BEFORE A GRAND JURY

To:

b3 -1

ppear in this United States district court at the time, date, and place shown below to testify before the court's grand jury. When you arrive, you must remain at the court until the judge or a court officer allows you to leave.

Place: United States Courthouse 141 Church Street New Haven, CT 06510	Date and Time:

You must also bring with you the following documents, electronically stored information, or objects *(blank if not applicable)*:

b3 -
b6 -
b7C

Date: December 18, 2012

CLERK OF COURT

Signature of Clerk or Deputy Clerk

The name, address, e-mail, and telephone number of the United States attorney, or assistant United States attorney, who requests this subpoena, are:

AUS
157 Church St., 23rd floor
New Haven, CT 06510

Personal appearance is not required if documents are provided on or before the appearance date to: FBI S/A
600 State St.
New Haven CT 06510

b3 -1
b6 -1,
b7C -1,

FD-448
Revised
10-27-2004

FEDERAL BUREAU OF INVESTIGATION
FACSIMILE COVER SHEET

PRECEDENCE

Immediate ◉ Priority Routine

CLASSIFICATION

Top Secret Secret Confidential ◉ Sensitive Unclassified

TO

Name of Office:	Facsimile Number:	Date: **12/18/2012**
Attn:	Room:	Telephone Number:

FROM

Name of Office: **FBI New Haven**		Number of Pages: (including cover) **4**
Originator's Name: **SA**	Originator's Telephone Number:	Originator's Facsimile Number:
Approved: **4-NH-2619946**		

b3 -1
b6 -1
b7C -1

DETAILS

Subject:
Federal Grand Jury Subpoena

Special Handling Instructions:
S may be reached a as well.

Brief Description of Communication Faxed:

WARNING

Information attached to the cover sheet is U.S. Government Property. If you are not the intended recipient of this information disclosure, reproduction, distribution, or use of this information is prohibited (18.USC, § 641). Please notify the originator or local FBI Office immediately to arrange for proper disposition.

FD-448
Revised
10-27-2004

FEDERAL BUREAU OF INVESTIGATION
FACSIMILE COVER SHEET

PRECEDENCE

( ) Immediate (•) Priority ( ) Routine

CLASSIFICATION

( ) Top Secret ( ) Secret ( ) Confidential (•) Sensitive ( ) Unclassified

TO

Name of Office:	Facsimile Number:	Date:
		12/18/2012
Attn:	Room:	Telephone Number:

FROM

Name of Office:	Number of Pages: (including cover)
FBI New Haven	**4**

Originator's Name:	Originator's Telephone Number:	Originator's Facsimile Number:
SA		

Approved:
4-NH-2619946

b3 -1
b6 -1
b7C -

DETAILS

Subject:
Federal Grand Jury Subpoena

Special Handling Instructions:
SA may be reached at as well.

Brief Description of Communication Faxed:

BAD FAX #

WARNING
Information attached to the cover sheet is U.S. Government Property. If you are not the intended recipient of this information disclosure, reproduction, distribution, or use of this information is prohibited (18.USC, § 641). Please notify the originator or local FBI Office immediately to arrange for proper disposition.

*************** -COMM. JOURNAL- ******************* DATE DEC-18-2012 ***** TIME 20:16 ********

MODE = MEMORY TRANSMISSION START=DEC-18 20:15 END=DEC-18 20:16

FILE NO.=173

STN NO.	COMM.	STATION NAME/EMAIL ADDRESS/TELEPHONE NO.	PAGES	DURATION
001	OK		004/004	00:00:42

-SQ 10 -

***** UF-8000 v2 ******************* -FBI NEW HAVEN - ***** - ********

FD-448 Revised 10-27-2004

FEDERAL BUREAU OF INVESTIGATION

FACSIMILE COVER SHEET

PRECEDENCE

○ Immediate ◉ Priority ○ Routine

CLASSIFICATION

○ Top Secret ○ Secret ○ Confidential ◉ Sensitive ○ Unclassified

TO

Name of Office: Facsimile Number: Date: 12/18/2012

Attn: Room: Telephone Number:

b3 -1
b6 -1
b7C -1

FROM

Name of Office: **FBI New Haven** Number of Pages: (including cover) 4

Originator's Name: **SA** Originator's Telephone Number: Originator's Facsimile Number:

Approved:
4-NH-2619946

DETAILS

Subject:
Federal Grand Jury Subpoena

Special Handling Instructions:
SA may be reached at as well.

Brief Description of Communication Faxed:

WARNING

Information attached to the cover sheet is U.S. Government Property. If you are not the intended recipient of this information disclosure, reproduction, distribution, or use of this information is prohibited (18.USC, § 641). Please notify the originator or local FBI Office immediately to arrange for proper disposition.

FD-1036 (Rev. 10-16-2009)

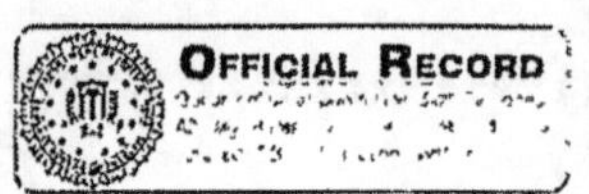

UNCLASSIFIED//~~FOUO~~

FEDERAL BUREAU OF INVESTIGATION

Import Form

Form Type: FD-617 **Date:** 12/21/2012

Title: (U) FGJ Subpoena to [redacted]

Approved By: SSA [redacted]

Drafted By: [redacted]

b3 -1
b6 -1
b7C -1

Case ID #: 4-NH-2619946-GJ (U) Grand Jury Information

FEDERAL GRAND JURY MATERIAL - DISSEMINATE PURSUANT TO RULE 6(E)
Do not disseminate except as authorized by federal rule of criminal procedure 6(e).

Synopsis: (U) FGJ Subpoena issued to [redacted] on 12/18/2012 [redacted]

[redacted]

b3 -1
b6 -2
b7C -2

♦♦

UNCLASSIFIED//~~FOUO~~

4-NH-2619946-GJ
SERIAL 36

AO 110 (Rev. 06/09) Subpoena to Testify Before a Grand Jury

UNITED STATES DISTRICT COURT

for the

District of Connecticut

SUBPOENA TO TESTIFY BEFORE A GRAND JURY

To:

b3 -1
b6 -5
b7C -5

YOU ARE COMMANDED to appear in this United States district court at the time, date, and place shown below to testify before the court's grand jury. When you arrive, you must remain at the court until the judge or a court officer allows you to leave.

Place: United States Courthouse 141 Church Street New Haven, CT 06510	Date and Time:

You must also bring with you the following documents, electronically stored information, or objects *(blank if not applicable)*:

b3 -1
b6 -2
b7C -2

Date: December 18, 2012

CLERK OF COURT

Signature of Clerk or Deputy Clerk

The name, address, e-mail, and telephone number of the United States attorney, or assistant United States attorney, who requests this subpoena, are:

AUSA
157 Church St., 23rd floor
New Haven, CT 06510

Personal appearance is not required if documents are provided on or before the appearance date to: FBI S/A
600 State St.
New Haven CT 06510

b3 -1
b6 -1, 4
b7C -1, 4

UNITED STATES DISTRICT COURT

for the

District of Connecticut

SUBPOENA TO TESTIFY BEFORE A GRAND JURY

To: b3 -1 b6 -5 b7C -5

ear in this United States district court at the time, date, and place shown below to testify before the court's grand jury. When you arrive, you must remain at the court until the judge or a court officer allows you to leave.

Place:	Date and Time:
United States Courthouse 141 Church Street New Haven, CT 06510	

You must also bring with you the following documents, electronically stored information, or objects *(blank if not applicable)*:

b3 -
b6 -
b7C

Date: December 18, 2012

CLERK OF COURT

Signature of Clerk or Deputy Clerk

The name, address, e-mail, and telephone number of the United States attorney, or assistant United States attorney, who requests this subpoena, are:

AUSA
157 Church St., 23rd floor
New Haven, CT 06510

Personal appearance is not required if documents are provided on or before the appearance date to: FBI S/A
600 State St.
New Haven CT 06510

b3 -1
b6 -1, 4
b7C -1,

Legal Request

b3 -1
b6 -1, 5
b7C -1, 5

Sent: Tuesday, December 18, 2012 18:18

To:

Attachments:

Please find a preservation request and Federal Grand Jury Subpoena attached to this email. Please call or email with any questions.

Should you need an amended subpoena, I'm happy to provide the appropriate legal process.

b3 -1
b6 -1, 2, 5
b7C -1, 2, 5

Regards,

Special Agent, FBI
(desk)
203-777-6311 (FBI New Haven switchboard)

b7E -5

FD-1036 (Rev. 10-16-2009)

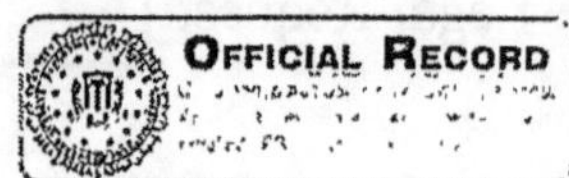

UNCLASSIFIED//~~FOUO~~

FEDERAL BUREAU OF INVESTIGATION

Import Form

Form Type: FD-617 **Date:** 12/21/2012

Title: (U) FGJ Subpoena to [redacted]

Approved By: SSA [redacted]

Drafted By: [redacted]

b3 -1
b6 -1
b7C -1

Case ID #: 4-NH-2619946-GJ (U) Grand Jury Information

FEDERAL GRAND JURY MATERIAL - DISSEMINATE PURSUANT TO RULE 6(E)
Do not disseminate except as authorized by federal rule of criminal procedure 6(e).

Synopsis: (U) FGJ Subpoena issued to [redacted] on 12/18/2012 [redacted]

[redacted]

b3 -
b6 -
b7C

♦♦

UNCLASSIFIED//~~FOUO~~

4-NH-2619946-GJ
SERIAL 37

AO 110 (Rev. 06/09) Subpoena to Testify Before a Grand Jury

UNITED STATES DISTRICT COURT

for the

District of Connecticut

SUBPOENA TO TESTIFY BEFORE A GRAND JURY

To: b3 -1

ED to appear in this United States district court at the time, date, and place shown below to testify before the court's grand jury. When you arrive, you must remain at the court until the judge or a court officer allows you to leave.

Place: United States Courthouse 141 Church Street New Haven, CT 06510	Date and Time:

You must also bring with you the following documents, electronically stored information, or objects *(blank if not applicable)*:

b3 -1
b6 -2
b7C -2

Date: December 18, 2012

CLERK OF COURT

Signature of Clerk or Deputy Clerk

The name, address, e-mail, and telephone number of the United States attorney, or assistant United States attorney, who requests this subpoena, are:

AUSA
157 Church St., 23rd floor
New Haven, CT 06510

Personal appearance is not required if documents are provided on or before the appearance date to: FBI S/A
600 State St.
New Haven CT 06510

b3 -1
b6 -1, 4
b7C -1, 4

FD-448
Revised
10-27-2004

FEDERAL BUREAU OF INVESTIGATION

FACSIMILE COVER SHEET

PRECEDENCE

( ) Immediate (•) Priority ( ) Routine

CLASSIFICATION

( ) Top Secret ( ) Secret ( ) Confidential (•) Sensitive ( ) Unclassified

TO

Name of Office:	Facsimile Number:	Date:
		12/18/2012
Attn:	Room:	Telephone Number:

FROM

Name of Office:		Number of Pages: (including cover)
FBI New Haven		**4**
Originator's Name:	Originator's Telephone Number:	Originator's Facsimile Number:
SA		
Approved:		
4-NH-2619946		

b3
b6
b7C

DETAILS

Subject:
Federal Grand Jury Subpoena

Special Handling Instructions:
SA may be reached at as well.

Brief Description of Communication Faxed:

WARNING

Information attached to the cover sheet is U.S. Government Property. If you are not the intended recipient of this information disclosure, reproduction, distribution, or use of this information is prohibited (18.USC, § 641). Please notify the originator or local FBI Office immediately to arrange for proper disposition.

*************** -COMM. JOURNAL- ******************* DATE DEC-18-2012 ***** TIME 17:02 ********

MODE = MEMORY TRANSMISSION START=DEC-18 17:01 END=DEC-18 17:02

FILE NO.=160

STN NO.	COMM.	STATION NAME/EMAIL ADDRESS/TELEPHONE NO.	PAGES	DURATION
001	OK		004/004	00:00:38

-SQ 10

***** UF-8000 v2 ****************** -FBI NEW HAVEN - ***** - ********

FD-448
Revised
10-27-2004

FEDERAL BUREAU OF INVESTIGATION
FACSIMILE COVER SHEET

PRECEDENCE

○ Immediate ◉ Priority ○ Routine

CLASSIFICATION

○ Top Secret ○ Secret ○ Confidential ◉ Sensitive ○ Unclassified

TO

Date:
12/18/2012

Attn: Room: Telephone Number:

b3 -1
b6 -1
b7C -1

FROM

Name of Office:
FBI New Haven

Number of Pages: (including cover)
4

Originator's Name: S
Originator's Telephone Number: Originator's Facsimile Number:

Approved:
4-NH-2619946

DETAILS

Subject:
Federal Grand Jury Subpoena

Special Handling Instructions:
SA may be reached at as well.

Brief Description of Communication Faxed:

WARNING
Information attached to the cover sheet is U.S. Government Property. If you are not the intended recipient of this information disclosure, reproduction, distribution, or use of this information is prohibited (18.USC, § 641). Please notify the originator or local FBI Office immediately to arrange for proper disposition.

FD-1036 (Rev. 10-16-2009)

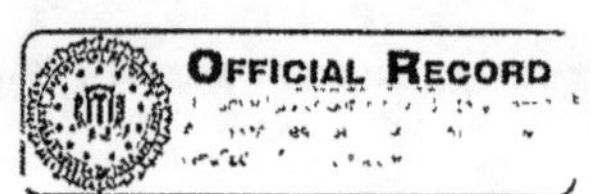

UNCLASSIFIED//~~FOUO~~

FEDERAL BUREAU OF INVESTIGATION

Import Form

Form Type: FD-617 **Date:** 01/03/2013

Title: (U) FGJ Subpoena to [redacted]

Approved By: SSA [redacted]

b3 -1
b6 -1
b7C -1

Drafted By: [redacted]

Case ID #: 4-NH-2619946-GJ (U) Grand Jury Information

FEDERAL GRAND JURY MATERIAL - DISSEMINATE PURSUANT TO RULE 6(E)
Do not disseminate except as authorized by federal rule of criminal procedure 6(e).

Synopsis: (U) FGJ Subpoena issued to [redacted] on 12/20/2012 [redacted]
[redacted]

b3 -1
b6 -2
b7C -

♦♦

UNCLASSIFIED//~~FOUO~~

4-NH-2619946-GJ
SERIAL 38

AO 110 (Rev. 06/09) Subpoena to Testify Before a Grand Jury

UNITED STATES DISTRICT COURT

for the

District of Connecticut

SUBPOENA TO TESTIFY BEFORE A GRAND JURY

To:

b3 -1

YOU ARE COMMANDED to appear in this United States district court at the time, date, and place shown below to testify before the court's grand jury. When you arrive, you must remain at the court until the judge or a court officer allows you to leave.

Place: United States Courthouse 141 Church Street New Haven, CT 06510	Date and Time:

You must also bring with you the following documents, electronically stored information, or objects *(blank if not applicable)*:

b3 -1
b6 -2
b7C -2

Date: December 20, 2012

CLERK OF COURT

Signature of Clerk or Deputy Clerk

The name, address, e-mail, and telephone number of the United States attorney, or assistant United States attorney, who requests this subpoena, are:

AUSA
157 Church St., 23rd floor
New Haven, CT 06510

Personal appearance is not required if documents are provided on or before the appearance date to: FBI S/A
600 State St.
New Haven CT 06510

b3 -1
b6 -1, 4
b7C -1, 4

FD-448
Revised
10-27-2004

FEDERAL BUREAU OF INVESTIGATION

FACSIMILE COVER SHEET

PRECEDENCE

○ Immediate ◉ Priority ○ Routine

CLASSIFICATION

○ Top Secret ○ Secret ○ Confidential ◉ Sensitive ○ Unclassified

TO

Name of Office:	Facsimile Number:	Date: **12/20/2012**
	Room:	Telephone Number:

FROM

Name of Office: **FBI New Haven**		Number of Pages: (including cover) **4**
Originator's Name: **SA**	Originator's Telephone Number:	Originator's Facsimile Number:

Approved:
4-NH-2619946

b3 -
b6 -
b7C

DETAILS

Subject:
Federal Grand Jury Subpoena

Special Handling Instructions:
SA may be reached at as well.

Brief Description of Communication Faxed:

WARNING

Information attached to the cover sheet is U.S. Government Property. If you are not the intended recipient of this information disclosure, reproduction, distribution, or use of this information is prohibited (18.USC, § 641). Please notify the originator or local FBI Office immediately to arrange for proper disposition.

*************** -COMM. JOURNAL- ******************* DATE DEC-20-2012 ***** TIME 14:14 ********

MODE = MEMORY TRANSMISSION   START=DEC-20 14:13   END=DEC-20 14:14

FILE NO.=190

STN NO.	COMM.	STATION NAME/EMAIL ADDRESS/TELEPHONE NO.	PAGES	DURATION
001	OK	[redacted]	004/004	00:00:34

-SQ 10 -

***** UF-8000 v2 ****************** -FBI NEW HAVEN - ***** - [redacted] ********

FD-448 Revised 10-27-2004

FEDERAL BUREAU OF INVESTIGATION

FACSIMILE COVER SHEET

PRECEDENCE

○ Immediate ◉ Priority ○ Routine

CLASSIFICATION

○ Top Secret ○ Secret ○ Confidential ◉ Sensitive ○ Unclassified

b3 -1
b6 -1
b7C -1

TO

Name of Office: [redacted]   [redacted]   Date: 12/20/2012

Attn: [redacted]   Room: Telephone Number:

FROM

Name of Office: FBI New Haven   Number of Pages: (including cover) 4

Originator's Name: SA [redacted]   Originator's Telephone Number: [redacted]   Originator's Facsimile Number:

Approved:
4-NH-2619946

DETAILS

Subject:
Federal Grand Jury Subpoena [redacted]

Special Handling Instructions:
SA [redacted] may be reached at [redacted] as well.

Brief Description of Communication Faxed:

WARNING

Information attached to the cover sheet is U.S. Government Property. If you are not the intended recipient of this information disclosure, reproduction, distribution, or use of this information is prohibited (18.USC, § 641). Please notify the originator or local FBI Office immediately to arrange for proper disposition.

FD-302 (Rev. 5-8-10)

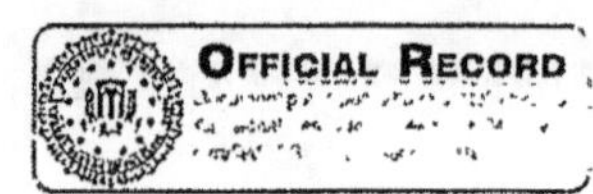

UNCLASSIFIED//~~FOUO~~

FEDERAL BUREAU OF INVESTIGATION

Date of entry 01/03/2013

FEDERAL GRAND JURY MATERIAL - DISSEMINATE PURSUANT TO RULE 6(E)
Do not disseminate except as authorized by federal rule of criminal procedure 6(e).

On December 18, 2012, [redacted] responded to a Federal Grand Jury Subpoena that was issued on 12/18/2012 [redacted]

[redacted]

b3 -
b6 -
b7C -

The [redacted] response is maintained in a 1A.

UNCLASSIFIED//~~FOUO~~

Investigation on 12/18/2012 at New Haven, Connecticut, United States (Email)

File # 4-NH-2619946-GJ Date drafted 01/03/2013

by [redacted]

b6 -
b7C

4-NH-2619946-GJ
SERIAL 39

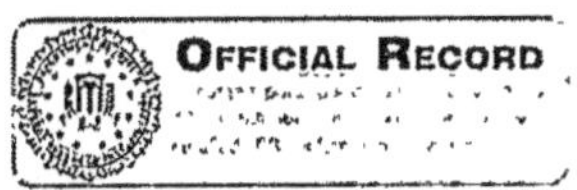

UNCLASSIFIED//~~FOUO~~

FEDERAL BUREAU OF INVESTIGATION

Date of entry 01/03/2013

FEDERAL GRAND JURY MATERIAL - DISSEMINATE PURSUANT TO RULE 6(E)
Do not disseminate except as authorized by federal rule of criminal procedure 6(e).

On December 20, 2012, [redacted] responded to a Federal Grand Jury Subpoena that was issued on 12/18/2012 [redacted]

[redacted]

b3 -1
b6 -2
b7C -2

The [redacted] response is maintained in a 1A.

UNCLASSIFIED//~~FOUO~~

Investigation on 12/20/2012 at New Haven, Connecticut, United States (Fax)

File # 4-NH-2619946-GJ Date drafted 01/03/2013

by [redacted]

b6 -1
b7C -1

4-NH-2619946-GJ SERIAL 10

FEDERAL BUREAU OF INVESTIGATION
FOI/PA
DELETED PAGE INFORMATION SHEET
Civil Action# 16-cv-02136

Total Deleted Page(s) = 102
Page 8 ~ b6 - 2; b7C - 2; b7E - 6;
Page 9 ~ b6 - 2; b7C - 2; b7E - 6;
Page 10 ~ b6 - 2; b7C - 2; b7E - 6;
Page 11 ~ b6 - 2; b7C - 2; b7E - 6;
Page 12 ~ b6 - 2; b7C - 2; b7E - 6;
Page 13 ~ b6 - 2; b7C - 2; b7E - 6;
Page 14 ~ b6 - 2; b7C - 2; b7E - 6;
Page 15 ~ b6 - 2; b7C - 2; b7E - 6;
Page 16 ~ b6 - 2; b7C - 2; b7E - 6;
Page 17 ~ b6 - 2; b7C - 2; b7E - 6;
Page 18 ~ b6 - 2; b7C - 2; b7E - 6;
Page 20 ~ b6 - 2; b7C - 2; b7E - 6;
Page 21 ~ b6 - 2; b7C - 2; b7E - 6;
Page 22 ~ b6 - 2; b7C - 2; b7E - 6;
Page 23 ~ b6 - 2; b7C - 2; b7E - 6;
Page 24 ~ b6 - 2; b7C - 2; b7E - 6;
Page 25 ~ b6 - 2; b7C - 2; b7E - 6;
Page 26 ~ b6 - 2; b7C - 2; b7E - 6;
Page 27 ~ b6 - 2; b7C - 2; b7E - 6;
Page 28 ~ b6 - 2; b7C - 2; b7E - 6;
Page 29 ~ b6 - 2; b7C - 2; b7E - 6;
Page 30 ~ b6 - 2; b7C - 2; b7E - 6;
Page 31 ~ b6 - 2; b7C - 2; b7E - 6;
Page 32 ~ b6 - 2; b7C - 2; b7E - 6;
Page 34 ~ b6 - 2; b7C - 2; b7E - 6;
Page 35 ~ b6 - 2; b7C - 2; b7E - 6;
Page 36 ~ b6 - 2; b7C - 2; b7E - 6;
Page 37 ~ b6 - 2; b7C - 2; b7E - 6;
Page 38 ~ b6 - 2; b7C - 2; b7E - 6;
Page 39 ~ b6 - 2; b7C - 2; b7E - 6;
Page 40 ~ b6 - 2; b7C - 2; b7E - 6;
Page 41 ~ b6 - 2; b7C - 2; b7E - 6;
Page 45 ~ b3 - 1; b6 - 4, 5; b7C - 4, 5;
Page 46 ~ b3 - 1; b6 - 4; b7C - 4;
Page 49 ~ b3 - 1; b6 - 1, 4, 5; b7C - 1, 4, 5;
Page 51 ~ b3 - 1; b6 - 4; b7C - 4;
Page 52 ~ b3 - 1; b6 - 4; b7C - 4;
Page 55 ~ b3 - 1; b6 - 1, 4; b7C - 1, 4;
Page 57 ~ b3 - 1; b6 - 4; b7C - 4;
Page 58 ~ b3 - 1; b6 - 4; b7C - 4;
Page 61 ~ b3 - 1; b6 - 1, 4; b7C - 1, 4;
Page 63 ~ b3 - 1; b6 - 4; b7C - 4;
Page 64 ~ b3 - 1; b6 - 4; b7C - 4;
Page 68 ~ b3 - 1; b6 - 1, 4; b7C - 1, 4;
Page 70 ~ b3 - 1; b6 - 4; b7C - 4;
Page 71 ~ b3 - 1; b6 - 4; b7C - 4;
Page 73 ~ Duplicate;
Page 75 ~ b3 - 1; b6 - 1, 4; b7C - 1, 4;

Page 79 ~ b6 - 2; b7C - 2;
Page 80 ~ b6 - 2; b7C - 2;
Page 81 ~ b6 - 2; b7C - 2;
Page 82 ~ b6 - 2; b7C - 2; b7E - 3;
Page 83 ~ b6 - 2; b7C - 2; b7E - 3;
Page 84 ~ b6 - 2; b7C - 2;
Page 85 ~ b6 - 2; b7C - 2;
Page 86 ~ b6 - 1, 2; b7C - 1, 2;
Page 87 ~ b6 - 2; b7C - 2;
Page 88 ~ b6 - 2; b7C - 2;
Page 89 ~ b6 - 2; b7C - 2;
Page 91 ~ b3 - 1; b6 - 4; b7C - 4;
Page 92 ~ b3 - 1; b6 - 4; b7C - 4;
Page 95 ~ b3 - 1; b6 - 1; b7C - 1;
Page 97 ~ b3 - 1; b6 - 4; b7C - 4;
Page 98 ~ b3 - 1; b6 - 4; b7C - 4;
Page 101 ~ b3 - 1; b6 - 1, 4; b7C - 1, 4;
Page 103 ~ b3 - 1; b6 - 4; b7C - 4;
Page 104 ~ b3 - 1; b6 - 4; b7C - 4;
Page 107 ~ b3 - 1; b6 - 1; b7C - 1;
Page 127 ~ b6 - 5, 6; b7C - 5, 6; b7D - 1;
Page 128 ~ b6 - 5, 6; b7C - 5, 6; b7D - 1;
Page 129 ~ b6 - 5, 6; b7C - 5, 6; b7D - 1;
Page 130 ~ b6 - 5, 6; b7C - 5, 6; b7D - 1;
Page 131 ~ b6 - 3, 5, 6; b7C - 3, 5, 6; b7D - 1;
Page 186 ~ b3 - 1; b6 - 4; b7C - 4;
Page 187 ~ b3 - 1; b6 - 4; b7C - 4;
Page 191 ~ b3 - 1; b6 - 4; b7C - 4;
Page 192 ~ b3 - 1; b6 - 4; b7C - 4;
Page 195 ~ b3 - 1; b6 - 1; b7C - 1;
Page 197 ~ b3 - 1; b6 - 4; b7C - 4;
Page 198 ~ b3 - 1; b6 - 4; b7C - 4;
Page 201 ~ b3 - 1; b6 - 1; b7C - 1;
Page 205 ~ b6 - 2, 4; b7C - 2, 4;
Page 250 ~ b6 - 2; b7C - 2;
Page 251 ~ b6 - 2; b7C - 2;
Page 252 ~ b6 - 2; b7C - 2;
Page 253 ~ b6 - 1, 2; b7C - 1, 2;
Page 254 ~ b6 - 2; b7C - 2;
Page 255 ~ b6 - 2; b7C - 2;
Page 256 ~ b6 - 2; b7C - 2;
Page 257 ~ b6 - 1, 2; b7C - 1, 2;
Page 258 ~ b6 - 2; b7C - 2;
Page 259 ~ b6 - 2; b7C - 2;
Page 260 ~ b6 - 1, 2; b7C - 1, 2;
Page 279 ~ b6 - 2; b7C - 2;
Page 280 ~ b6 - 2; b7C - 2;
Page 281 ~ b6 - 2; b7C - 2;
Page 282 ~ b6 - 2, 5; b7C - 2, 5;
Page 283 ~ b6 - 2, 5; b7C - 2, 5;
Page 284 ~ b6 - 2, 5; b7C - 2, 5;
Page 285 ~ b6 - 2, 5; b7C - 2, 5;
Page 286 ~ b6 - 2, 5; b7C - 2, 5;
Page 287 ~ b6 - 2, 5; b7C - 2, 5;

```
XXXXXXXXXXXXXXXXXXXXXXXX
X   Deleted Page(s)    X
X   No Duplication Fee X
X   For this Page      X
XXXXXXXXXXXXXXXXXXXXXXXX
```

FD-1057 (Rev. 5-8-10)

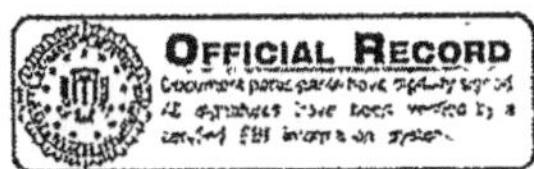

UNCLASSIFIED

FEDERAL BUREAU OF INVESTIGATION

Electronic Communication

Title: (U) Open case

Date: 12/14/2012

To: [redacted]

NH-4 (SSA)
NH-CDC (CDC)
[redacted]

b6 -1
b7C -1

From: NEW HAVEN
NH-4
Contact: [redacted]

Approved By: A/SSA [redacted]

Drafted By: [redacted]

b6 -1
b7C -1

Case ID #: 4-NH-2619946 (U) UNSUB(S)
Sandy Hook Elementary School
12 Dickinson St, Sandy Hook, CT-Victim
Firearms Act.
OO:NH

Synopsis: (U) [redacted]

b7E -1

Details:

For information of New Haven, on December 14, 2012 FBI New Haven was contacted by the Newtown Connecticut Police Department who requested immediate assistance with an active shooter who had entered an elementary school and opened fire, injuring and killing students and school faculty. Specific information concerning the incident is as follows:

UNCLASSIFIED

4-NH-2619946 Serial 1

Title: (U) Open case
Re: 4-NH-2619946, 12/14/2012

Adam P. Lanza, the shooter, has been identified by [redacted] [redacted] as autistic and had a personality disorder. At this time, Adam Lanza appears to be the sole shooter. [redacted] b6 - b7C

[redacted]

Nancy Lanza's status has not been confirmed; however, the female victim at 36 Yogananda Street resembles Nancy Lanza.

Chronological details of the shooting are as follows:

At 9:40AM, initial call-in to Newtown emergency services/911 was received from Sandy Hook Elementary School, Newtown CT, that shots had been fired within the school.

As of 3:10 PM, there were a total of 27 dead, 20 children and 6 adults (not including the gunman). The gunman was described as a 20-year-old white male wearing combat gear with ties to New Jersey. He died of a self-inflicted gunshot wound to the head. A Bushmaster long gun and one Glock pistol were recovered at the scene.

As of 1:05 PM, an unidentified gunman was discovered at scene with an apparent self-inflicted gunshot wound to the head. Witness reports confirm one shooter. A vehicle associated with the shooting had Connecticut license plates 872YEO; the vehicle was registered to Nancy Lanza, of 36 Yogananda Street, Sandy Hook, Connecticut. Tags 872YEO are associated with a black 2010 Honda Civic. Nancy Lanza and [redacted] [redacted] utilize telephone number 203-426-8167 and 203-364-9879, [redacted] son, Adam P. Lanza (DOB 4/22/1992). [redacted] [redacted] Adam P. Lanza had no criminal backgrounds. b6 - b7C

[redacted] [redacted] Nancy and [redacted] Lanza were divorced as of 2009. FBI New Haven provided an update indicating that ATF went into the 36 Yogananda Street address with a robot. The first floor was clear, but b6 - b7C the second floor bedroom of 36 Yogananda Street contained a deceased female, believed to be Nancy Lanza, with a gunshot wound to the head. The identity of the deceased female has not been confirmed.

As of 2:41 PM, FBI New Haven confirmed that Adam P. Lanza was the shooter. [redacted] b6 -2 b7C -2

[redacted] was being interviewed by Newtown Police Department. As of 2:58 PM, [redacted] involvement in this incident is unknown. b6 -2 b7C -2

[redacted] b6 -2 b7C -2

As of 3:10 PM, the following weapons registered to Nancy Lanza are unaccounted for: Enfield Albion NO 4 NKI HCZ2273A (or HC22273A), a Sig Sauer P22G UU676027, and an Izhmash SAIGA 12 H08402282. [redacted] b6 -2 b7C -2

[redacted] Adam was a functioning autistic with a personality disorder and was a recluse. [redacted] b6 -2 b7C -2

As of 3:34 PM, FBI New Haven indicated that the residence at 36 Yogananda Street was cleared by bomb technicians. The house was very clean, ammo and guns were found, as well as Adam's computer. The hard drive was severely damaged, and was removed and left near the tower. Additionally, Connecticut State Police received a telephone call from a woman [redacted] who claimed that her son was playing Call of Duty: Black Ops with an individual who told him to "watch the news tomorrow." This lead is currently being worked. b7D -1

Title: (U) Open case
Re: 4-NH-2619946, 12/14/2012

b6 -2
b7C -2

FBI New Haven is coordinating with FBI LA regarding b6 -2 b7C -2

b6 -2
b7C -

Therefore it is respectfully requested that this matter be opened and assigned to SA b6 -1 b7C -

♦♦

FD-1036 (Rev. 10-16-2009)

UNCLASSIFIED

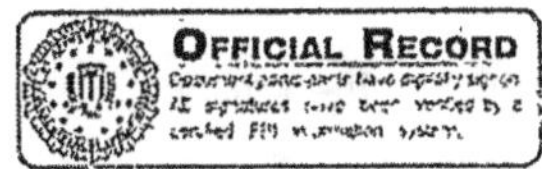

FEDERAL BUREAU OF INVESTIGATION

Import Form

Form Type: OTHER

Date: 12/15/2012

Title: (U) [redacted]

Approved By: [redacted]

Drafted By: [redacted]

b6 -1, 2
b7C -1, 2
b7E -6

Case ID #: 4-NH-2619946

(U) UNSUB(S)
Sandy Hook Elementary School
12 Dickinson St, Sandy Hook, CT-Victim
Firearms Act.
OO:NH

Synopsis: (U) [redacted]

b6 -2
b7C -2
b7E -6

♦♦

UNCLASSIFIED

Sandy Hook-5

4-NH-2619946 Serial 2

FD-1036 (Rev. 10-16-2009)

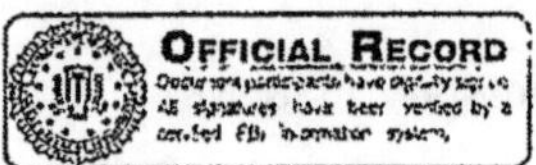

UNCLASSIFIED

FEDERAL BUREAU OF INVESTIGATION

Import Form

Form Type: OTHER **Date:** 12/15/2012

Title: (U) [redacted]

Approved By: [redacted]

Drafted By: [redacted]

b6 -1, 2
b7C -1, 2
b7E -6

Case ID #: 4-NH-2619946 (U) UNSUB(S)
Sandy Hook Elementary School
12 Dickinson St, Sandy Hook, CT-Victim
Firearms Act.
OO:NH

Synopsis: (U) [redacted]

b6 -
b7C
b7E

♦♦

UNCLASSIFIED

Sandy Hook-17

4-NH-2619946 Serial 3

FD-1036 (Rev. 10-16-2009)

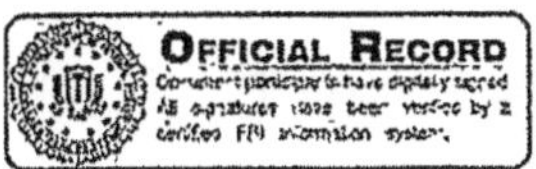

UNCLASSIFIED

FEDERAL BUREAU OF INVESTIGATION

Import Form

Form Type: OTHER **Date:** 12/15/2012

Title: (U) [redacted]

Approved By: [redacted]

b6 -1, 2
b7C -1, 2
b7E -6

Drafted By: [redacted]

Case ID #: 4-NH-2619946 (U) UNSUB(S)
Sandy Hook Elementary School
12 Dickinson St, Sandy Hook, CT-Victim
Firearms Act.
OO:NH

Synopsis: (U) [redacted]

b6 -2
b7C -2
b7E -6

♦♦

UNCLASSIFIED

4-NH-2619946 Serial 4

FD-302 (Rev. 5-8-10)

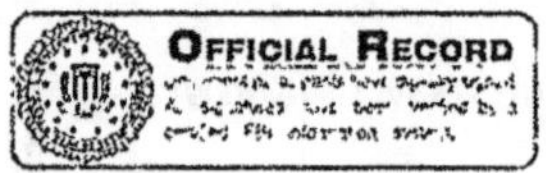

FEDERAL BUREAU OF INVESTIGATION

Date of entry 12/17/2012

[redacted] date of birth [redacted] social security account number [redacted] cellular telephone number [redacted] was interviewed [redacted] by Special Agent [redacted] and Task Force Officer [redacted] After being advised of the identity of the interviewing agents and the nature of the interview, [redacted] provided the following information:

b6 -1, 2, 4
b7C -1, 2,

[redacted]

b6 -2
b7C -

[redacted]

b6 -
b7C -

[redacted]

b6 -
b7C -

[redacted]

b6 -
b7C

Investigation on 12/14/2012 at [redacted] United States (In Person)

b6 -1,
b7C -1,

File # 4-NH-2619946 Date drafted 12/17/2012

by [redacted]

Sandy Hook-

4-NH-2619946 Serial 5

b6 -2
b7C -2

b6 -2
b7C -2

b6 -2
b7C -2

FD-302 (Rev. 5-8-10)

FEDERAL BUREAU OF INVESTIGATION

Date of entry 12/15/2012

On December 15, 2012, Special Agent (SA) [redacted] served [redacted] Federal Grand Jury subpoena number [redacted] issued by the United States District Court for the District of CT, via facsimile.

b3 -1
b6 -1, 5
b7C -1,

Investigation on 12/15/2012 at New Haven, Connecticut, United States (, Other (Subpoena Service))

File # 4-NH-2619946 Date drafted 12/15/2012

by [redacted]

b6 -1
b7C -

This document contains neither recommendations nor conclusions of the FBI. It is the property of the FBI and is loaned to your agency; it and its contents are not to be distributed outside your agency.

AO 110 (Rev. 06/09) Subpoena to Testify Before a Grand Jury

UNITED STATES DISTRICT COURT

for the

District of Connecticut

SUBPOENA TO TESTIFY BEFORE A GRAND JURY

To: [redacted]

b3 -1
b6 -5
b7C -5

YOU ARE COMMANDED to appear in this United States district court at the time, date, and place shown below to testify before the court's grand jury. When you arrive, you must remain at the court until the judge or a court officer allows you to leave.

Place: United States Courthouse 141 Church Street New Haven, CT 06510	Date and Time: [redacted]

You must also bring with you the following documents, electronically stored information, or objects *(blank if not applicable)*:

[redacted]

b3 -1

Date: December 15, 2012

CLERK OF COURT

Signature of Clerk or Deputy Clerk

The name, address, e-mail, and telephone number of the United States attorney, or assistant United States attorney, who requests this subpoena, are:

AUSA [redacted]

Personal appearance is not required if documents are provided on or before the appearance date to: FBI S/A [redacted]
600 State St.
New Haven CT 06510

b3 -1
b6 -1, 4
b7C -1, 4

PROOF OF SERVICE

This subpoena for *(name of individual or organization)* [redacted]
was received by me on *(date)* 12/15/12 .

☑ I served the subpoena by delivering a copy to the named person as follows: [redacted]
[redacted] on *(date)* 12/15/12 ; or

☐ I returned the subpoena unexecuted because:

I declare under penalty of perjury that this information is true.

Date: 12/15/12

[redacted]

b3

b6 -
b7C

[redacted] Special Agent
Printed name and title

2 Union Plaza, Ste. 301, New London, CT 06320
Server's address

Additional information regarding attempted service, etc:

FD-302 (Rev. 5-8-10)

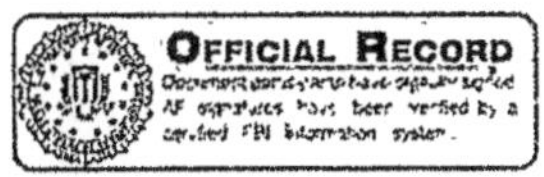

FEDERAL BUREAU OF INVESTIGATION

Date of entry 12/15/2012

On December 15, 2012, Special Agent (SA) [redacted] served [redacted] [redacted] [redacted] Federal Grand Jury subpoena number [redacted] issued by the United States District Court for the District of Connecticut, via facsimile.

b3 -1
b6 -1
b7C -1

Investigation on 12/15/2012 at New Haven, Connecticut, United States (, Other (Subpoean Service))

File # 4-NH-2619946 Date drafted 12/15/2012

by [redacted]

b6 -1
b7C -1

4-NH-2619946 Serial 7

AO 110 (Rev. 06/09) Subpoena to Testify Before a Grand Jury

UNITED STATES DISTRICT COURT

for the

District of Connecticut

SUBPOENA TO TESTIFY BEFORE A GRAND JURY

To:

b3 -1

to appear in this United States district court at the time, date, and place shown below to testify before the court's grand jury. When you arrive, you must remain at the court until the judge or a court officer allows you to leave.

Place: United States Courthouse 141 Church Street New Haven, CT 06510	Date and Time:

You must also bring with you the following documents, electronically stored information, or objects *(blank if not applicable)*:

b3

Date: December 15, 2012

CLERK OF COURT

Signature of Clerk or Deputy Clerk

The name, address, e-mail, and telephone number of the United States attorney, or assistant United States attorney, who requests this subpoena, are:

AUSA
157 Church St., 23rd floor
New Haven, CT 06510

Personal appearance is not required if documents are provided on or before the appearance date to: FBI S/A
600 State St.
New Haven CT 06510

b3 -1
b6 -1,
b7C -1,

PROOF OF SERVICE

This subpoena for *(name of individual or organization)* [redacted]
was received by me on *(date)* 12/15/12 .

☑ I served the subpoena [redacted] follows: [redacted] b3 -1
via fax [redacted]
on *(date)* 12/15/12 ; or

☐ I returned the subpoena unexecuted because:

I declare under penalty of perjury that this information is true.

Date: 12/15/12

[redacted] b6 -1 b7C -1

[redacted] Special Agent
Printed name and title

2 Union Plaza, Ste. 301, New London CT 06320
Server's address

Additional information regarding attempted service, etc:

FD-302 (Rev. 5-8-10)

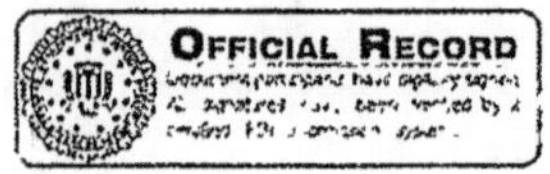

FEDERAL BUREAU OF INVESTIGATION

Date of entry 12/15/2012

On December 15, 2012, Special Agent (SA) [redacted] served [redacted] [redacted] [redacted] Federal Grand Jury subpoena number [redacted] issued by the United States District Court for the District of Connecticut, via facsimile.

b3
b6
b7C

Investigation on 12/15/2012 at New Haven, Connecticut, United States (, Other (Subpoena Service))

File # 4-NH-2619946 Date drafted 12/15/2012

by [redacted]

b6 -1
b7C -1

4-NH-2619946 Serial 8

AO 110 (Rev. 06/09) Subpoena to Testify Before a Grand Jury

UNITED STATES DISTRICT COURT

for the

District of Connecticut

SUBPOENA TO TESTIFY BEFORE A GRAND JURY

To:

b3 -1

YOU ARE COMMANDED to appear in this United States district court at the time, date, and place shown below to testify before the court's grand jury. When you arrive, you must remain at the court until the judge or a court officer allows you to leave.

Place: United States Courthouse 141 Church Street New Haven, CT 06510	Date and Time:

You must also bring with you the following documents, electronically stored information, or objects *(blank if not applicable)*:

b3 -1

Date: December 15, 2012

CLERK OF COURT

Signature of Clerk or Deputy Clerk

The name, address, e-mail, and telephone number of the United States attorney, or assistant United States attorney, who requests this subpoena, are:

AUSA
157 Church St., 23rd floor
New Haven, CT 06510

Personal appearance is not required if documents are provided on or before the appearance date to: FBI S/A
600 State St.
New Haven CT 06510

b3 -1
b6 -1, 4
b7C -1, 4

PROOF OF SERVICE

This subpoena for *(name of individual or organization)* [redacted]

was received by me on *(date)* 12/15/12 .

☑ I served the subpoena by delivering a copy to the named person as follows: [redacted] b3

[redacted] on *(date)* 12/15/12 ; or

☐ I returned the subpoena unexecuted because:

I declare under penalty of perjury that this information is true.

Date: 12/15/12

[redacted] b6 - b7C

[redacted] Special Agent

Printed name and title

2 Union Plaza, Ste 301 New London CT 06320

Server's address

Additional information regarding attempted service, etc:

FD-302 (Rev. 5-8-10)

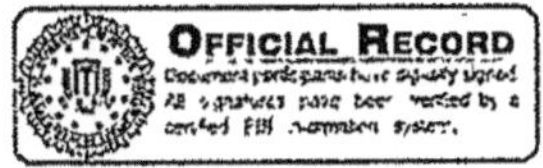

FEDERAL BUREAU OF INVESTIGATION

Date of entry 12/15/2012

On December 15, 2012, Special Agent (SA) [redacted] served [redacted] [redacted] [redacted] Federal Grand Jury subpoena number [redacted] issued by the United States District Court for the District of Connecticut, via facsimile. b3 -1 b6 -1 b7C -1

Investigation on 12/15/2012 at New Haven, Connecticut, United States (, Other (Subpoena Service))

File # 4-NH-2619946 Date drafted 12/15/2012

by [redacted] b6 -1 b7C -1

4-NH-2619946 Serial 9

AO 110 (Rev. 06/09) Subpoena to Testify Before a Grand Jury

UNITED STATES DISTRICT COURT

for the

District of Connecticut

SUBPOENA TO TESTIFY BEFORE A GRAND JURY

To:

b3 -1

to appear in this United States district court at the time, date, and place shown below to testify before the court's grand jury. When you arrive, you must remain at the court until the judge or a court officer allows you to leave.

Place: United States Courthouse 141 Church Street New Haven, CT 06510	Date and Time:

You must also bring with you the following documents, electronically stored information, or objects *(blank if not applicable)*:

b3 -

Date: December 15, 2012

CLERK OF COURT

Signature of Clerk or Deputy Clerk

The name, address, e-mail, and telephone number of the United States attorney, or assistant United States attorney, who requests this subpoena, are:

AUSA
157 Church St., 23rd floor
New Haven, CT 06510

Personal appearance is not required if documents are provided on or before the appearance date to: FBI S/A
600 State St.
New Haven CT 06510

b3
b6
b7

Sandy Hook-

PROOF OF SERVICE

This subpoena for *(name of individual or organization)* ____________________
was received by me on *(date)* ______________ .

☐ I served the subpoena by delivering a copy to the named person as follows: ______________
____
____ on *(date)* ____________ ; or

☐ I returned the subpoena unexecuted because: ______________________________
____ .

I declare under penalty of perjury that this information is true.

Date: ______________

____
Server's signature

____
Printed name and title

____
Server's address

Additional information regarding attempted service, etc:

PROOF OF SERVICE

This subpoena for *(name of individual or organization)* [redacted]
was received by me on *(date)* 12/15/12 .

☑ I served the subpoena by delivering a copy to the named person as follows: [redacted]
[redacted] via fax [redacted]
on *(date)* 12/15/12 ; or

☐ I returned the subpoena unexecuted because:

b3 -1

I declare under penalty of perjury that this information is true.

Date: 12/15/12

[redacted]

[redacted] Special Agent
Printed name and title

b6 -1
b7C -1

2 Union Plaza, Ste. 301, New London CT 06320
Server's address

Additional information regarding attempted service, etc:

FD-302 (Rev. 5-8-10)

OFFICIAL RECORD

FEDERAL BUREAU OF INVESTIGATION

Date of entry 12/15/2012

On December 15, 2012, Special Agent (SA) [redacted] served [redacted] [redacted] [redacted] Federal Grand Jury subpoena number [redacted] issued by the United States District Court for the District of Connecticut, via facsimile.

b3 -1
b6 -1
b7C -1

Investigation on 12/15/2012 at New Haven, Connecticut, United States (, Other (Subpoena Service))

File # 4-NH-2619946 Date drafted 12/15/2012

by [redacted]

b6 -1
b7C -1

4-NH-2619946 Serial 10.

UNITED STATES DISTRICT COURT

for the

District of Connecticut

SUBPOENA TO TESTIFY BEFORE A GRAND JURY

To:

b3 -1

YOU ARE COMMANDED to appear in this United States district court at the time, date, and place shown below to testify before the court's grand jury. When you arrive, you must remain at the court until the judge or a court officer allows you to leave.

Place: United States Courthouse 141 Church Street New Haven, CT 06510	Date and Time:

You must also bring with you the following documents, electronically stored information, or objects *(blank if not applicable)*:

b3 -1

Date: December 15, 2012

CLERK OF COURT

Signature of Clerk or Deputy Clerk

The name, address, e-mail, and telephone number of the United States attorney, or assistant United States attorney, who requests this subpoena, are:

AUSA
157 Church St., 23rd floor
New Haven, CT 06510

Personal appearance is not required if documents are provided on or before the appearance date to: FBI S/A
600 State St.
New Haven, CT 06510

b3 -1
b6 -1,
b7C -1,

PROOF OF SERVICE

This subpoena for *(name of individual or organization)* ______
was received by me on *(date)* 12/15/12 .

☑ I served the subpoena by delivering a copy to the named person as follows: ______ via fax ______
on *(date)* 12/15/12 ; or

☐ I returned the subpoena unexecuted because: ______

b3 -1

I declare under penalty of perjury that this information is true.

Date: 12/15/12

______
Server's signature

______ Special Agent
Printed name and title

b6 -1
b7C -1

2 Union Plaza Ste. 301, New London CT 06320
Server's address

Additional information regarding attempted service, etc:

FD-1057 (Rev. 5-8-10)

UNCLASSIFIED

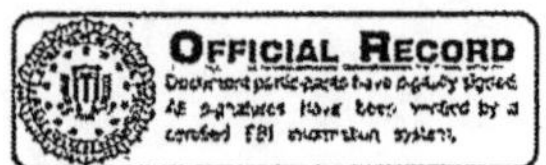

FEDERAL BUREAU OF INVESTIGATION

Electronic Communication

Title: (U) Case EC - [redacted] Fraudulent Facebook Page

Date: 12/15/2012

From: NEW HAVEN
NH-7
Contact: [redacted]

b6 -1, 2
b7C -1,

Approved By: SSA [redacted]

Drafted By: [redacted]

Case ID #: 4-NH-2619946

(U) UNSUB(S)
Sandy Hook Elementary School
12 Dickinson St, Sandy Hook, CT-Victim
Firearms Act.
OO:NH

Synopsis: (U) To document email, LinkedIn account, [redacted] [redacted] and criminal background regarding [redacted] [redacted]

b6 -2
b7C -
b7E -
b7E -1

Enclosure(s): Enclosed are the following items:
1. (U) 1. Email 2. LinkedIn account 3. [redacted] b7E
4. criminal background

Details:

On 12/15/2012, Special Agent (SA) [redacted] received an e-mail from SA [redacted] regarding follow-up on a possible fraudulent Facebook page created by [redacted] in the name of Adam Lanza regarding captioned investigation.

b6 -1,
b7C -1

SA [redacted] was requested to positively identify [redacted] namely, personal identifiers and current residence location; afterwhich, send a lead to the appropriate FBI Division to conduct an interview of [redacted]

b6 -1,
b7C -1

A search on LinkedIn revealed [redacted] is [redacted]

b6 -2
b7C -

UNCLASSIFIED

4-NH-2619946 Serial 11

Title: (U) Case EC - [redacted] Fraudulent Facebook Page
Re: 4-NH-2619946, 12/15/2012

b6 -2
b7C -2

[redacted] to the present.

b6 -2
b7C -2

[redacted]

b6 -2
b7C -2
b7E -3

[redacted]

b6 -2
b7C -2

SA [redacted] was advised by SA [redacted] to not send a lead for [redacted] to be interviewed until [redacted]

b3 -1
b6 -1, 2
b7C -1, 2

♦♦

From:
Sent: Saturday, December 15, 2012 10:41 AM
To:
Subject: FW: followup on Facebook account found by USMS
Attachments: Picture (Device Independent Bitmap) 1.jpg

b6 -1, 4
b7C -1, 4

From:
Sent: Saturday, December 15, 2012 10:34 AM
To
Subject: Fw: followup on Facebook account found by USMS

is interested in pursuing obstruction or any other potential charges against who created a bogus facebook page in the name of after the shooting took place. This action caused investigators to waste several hours and took law enforcement away from other important work.

b6 -1,
b7C -1,

Accordingly, we are requesting that an immediate lead be set for Seattle to interview and inquire about his intent in creating the facebook page and any potential links to

Everything we know about (not much) is included in the email below. If you can get someone to find more info on him and then cut the lead that would be great. Once we have the name of an agent in Seattle we will send a list of questions - we are working on more specific questions now.

Thanks,

From (USACT)
To
Sent: Sat Dec 15 10:18:26 2012
Subject: Fw: followup on Facebook account found by USMS

b6 1, 2,
b7C 1, 2,

From: (USACT)
Sent: Friday, December 14, 2012 11:36 PM
To: (USACT) (USACT) USACT) (USACT)
Cc (FBI)
Subject: followup on Facebook account found by USMS

The Facebook account found by the USMS appears to have been created by in the Seattle area, after the news broke. Here is a picture of from his LinkedIn account. No obvious leads to pursue.

FD-302 (Rev. 5-8-10)

OFFICIAL RECORD

FEDERAL BUREAU OF INVESTIGATION

Date of entry 12/17/2012

On December 17, 2012, Special Agent (SA) [redacted] served [redacted] [redacted] Federal Grand Jury subpoena number [redacted] issued by the United States District Court for the District of Connecticut, via FedEx.

b3 -1
b6 -1
b7C -1

Investigation on 12/17/2012 at New London, Connecticut, United States (, Other (Subpoena Service))

File # 4-NH-2619946 Date drafted 12/17/2012

by [redacted]

b6 -1
b7C -1

4-NH-2619946 Serial 12

AO 110 (Rev. 06/09) Subpoena to Testify Before a Grand Jury

UNITED STATES DISTRICT COURT

for the

District of Connecticut

SUBPOENA TO TESTIFY BEFORE A GRAND JURY

To:

b3 -

YOU ARE COMMANDED to appear in this United States district court at the time, date, and place shown below to testify before the court's grand jury. When you arrive, you must remain at the court until the judge or a court officer allows you to leave.

Place: United States Courthouse 141 Church Street New Haven, CT 06510	Date and Time:

You must also bring with you the following documents, electronically stored information, or objects *(blank if not applicable)*:

b3
b6
b7C

Date: December 15, 2012

CLERK OF COURT

Signature of Clerk or Deputy Clerk

The name, address, e-mail, and telephone number of the United States attorney, or assistant United States attorney, who requests this subpoena, are:

AUSA
157 Church St., 23rd floor
New Haven, CT 06510

Personal appearance is not required if documents are provided on or before the appearance date to: FBI S/A
600 State St.
New Haven CT 06510

b3 -1
b6 -1
b7C -

Sandy Hook-

PROOF OF SERVICE

This subpoena for *(name of individual or organization)* ______________________
was received by me on *(date)* 12/15/12 .

☑ I served the subpoena by deli... ______________________ person as follows: ______________
____
____ on *(date)* 12/17/12 ; or

☐ I returned the subpoena unexecuted because: ______________________
____

b3 -1

I declare under penalty of perjury that this information is true.

Date: 12/17/12

____

b6 -1
b7C -1

______________________ Special Agent
Printed name and title

2 Union Plaza, Ste. 301, New London CT 06320
Server's address

Additional information regarding attempted service, etc:

FD-302 (Rev. 5-8-10)

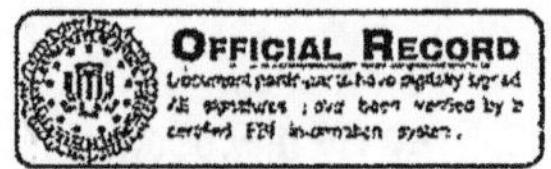

FEDERAL BUREAU OF INVESTIGATION

Date of entry 12/17/2012

On December 17, 2012, Special Agent (SA) [redacted] served [redacted] Federal Grand Jury subpoena number [redacted] issued by the United States District Court for the District of Connecticut, via facsimile.

b3 -1
b6 -1
b7C -

Investigation on 12/17/2012 at New London, Connecticut, United States (, Other (Subpoena Service))

File # 4-NH-2619946 Date drafted 12/17/2012

by [redacted]

b6 -
b7C -

AO 110 (Rev. 06/09) Subpoena to Testify Before a Grand Jury

UNITED STATES DISTRICT COURT

for the

District of Connecticut

SUBPOENA TO TESTIFY BEFORE A GRAND JURY

To:

b3 -1

YOU ARE COMMANDED to appear in this United States district court at the time, date, and place shown below to testify before the court's grand jury. When you arrive, you must remain at the court until the judge or a court officer allows you to leave.

Place: United States Courthouse 141 Church Street New Haven, CT 06510	Date and Time:

You must also bring with you the following documents, electronically stored information, or objects *(blank if not applicable)*:

b3 -1

Date: December 15, 2012

CLERK OF COURT

Signature of Clerk or Deputy Clerk

The name, address, e-mail, and telephone number of the United States attorney, or assistant United States attorney, who requests this subpoena, are:

AUSA
157 Church St., 23rd floor
New Haven, CT 06510

Personal appearance is not required if documents are provided on or before the appearance date to: FBI S/A
600 State St.
New Haven CT 06510

b3 -1
b6 -1, 4
b7C -1. 4

PROOF OF SERVICE

This subpoena for *(name of individual or organization)* ______
was received by me on *(date)* 12/15/12 .

☑ I served the subpoena by delivering a copy to the named person as follows: ______
______
______ on *(date)* 12/17/12 ; or

☐ I returned the subpoena unexecuted because: ______
______

b3

I declare under penalty of perjury that this information is true.

Date: 12/17/12 ______
Server's signature

b6 -1
b7C -

______ Special Agent
Printed name and title

2 Union Plaza, Ste. 301, New London CT 06320
Server's address

Additional information regarding attempted service, etc:

FD-302 (Rev. 5-8-10)

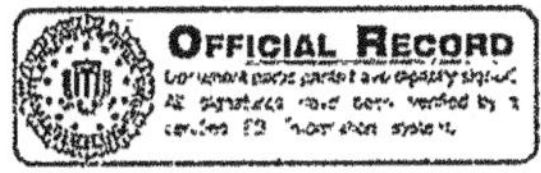

FEDERAL BUREAU OF INVESTIGATION

Date of entry 12/17/2012

On December 17, 2012, Special Agent (SA) [redacted] served [redacted] [redacted] Federal Grand Jury subpoena number [redacted] issued by the United States District Court for the District of Connecticut, via FedEx. b3 -1 b6 -1 b7C -1

Investigation on 12/17/2012 at New London, Connecticut, United States (, Other (Subpoena Service))

File # 4-NH-2619946 Date drafted 12/17/2012

by [redacted] b6 -1 b7C -1

4-NH-2619946 Serial 14

AO 110 (Rev. 06/09) Subpoena to Testify Before a Grand Jury

UNITED STATES DISTRICT COURT
for the
District of Connecticut

SUBPOENA TO TESTIFY BEFORE A GRAND JURY

To: b3

YOU ARE COMMANDED to appear in this United States district court at the time, date, and place shown below to testify before the court's grand jury. When you arrive, you must remain at the court until the judge or a court officer allows you to leave.

Place: United States Courthouse 141 Church Street New Haven, CT 06510	Date and Time:

You must also bring with you the following documents, electronically stored information, or objects *(blank if not applicable)*:

b3

Date: December 15, 2012

CLERK OF COURT

Signature of Clerk or Deputy Clerk

The name, address, e-mail, and telephone number of the United States attorney, or assistant United States attorney, who requests this subpoena, are:

AUSA
157 Church St., 23rd floor
New Haven, CT 06510

Personal appearance is not required if documents are provided on or before the appearance date to: FBI S/A
600 State St.
New Haven CT 06510

b3 -1
b6 -1
b7C -

Sandy Hoo

PROOF OF SERVICE

This subpoena for *(name of individual or organization)* [redacted]
was received by me on *(date)* 12/15/12.

☑ I served the subpoena by delivering a copy to the named person as follows: [redacted]
[redacted] via FedEx
on *(date)* 12/17/12 ; or

☐ I returned the subpoena unexecuted because:

b3 1

I declare under penalty of perjury that this information is true.

Date: 12/17/12

[redacted]
Server's signature

[redacted] Special Agent
Printed name and title

b6 -1
b7C -1

2 Union Plaza, Ste. 301, New London CT 06320
Server's address

Additional information regarding attempted service, etc:

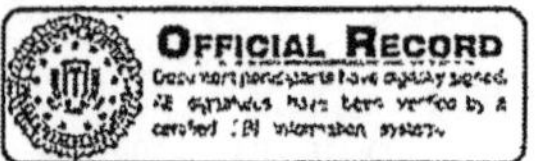

FEDERAL BUREAU OF INVESTIGATION

Date of entry 12/16/2012

[REDACTED] date of birth [REDACTED] and [REDACTED] date of birth, [REDACTED] of [REDACTED] Sandy Hook, Connecticut, 06482, home telephone number [REDACTED] and cellular telephone of [REDACTED] were interviewed at their residence. After being advised of the identity of the interviewing Agents and the nature of the interview, [REDACTED] provided the following information: b6 -6 b7C -

[REDACTED] moved to [REDACTED] years ago. The [REDACTED] used to have Nancy Lanza ("Nancy") and her sons, Adam Lanza ("Adam") and [REDACTED] over [REDACTED] every year. The [REDACTED] was in [REDACTED] When Adam Lanza was in ninth grade, Nancy told [REDACTED] that Adam had hacked into a government computer system. Adam had made it through the second level of security and when he tried to breach the third level the screen went black and the authorities showed up at the Lanza's door at 36 Yogananda Street. Nancy believed that the authorities that showed up at her door were either the FBI or the CIA. Nancy had to convince the authorities that her son was just very intelligent and was challenging himself to see if he could hack into a government system. The authorities told Nancy that if her son was that smart he could have a job with them someday. b6 -2, b7C -2,

Adam was always a troubled kid and was interested in Japanese techno music. [REDACTED] was [REDACTED] and [REDACTED] never met the father. [REDACTED] had thought that [REDACTED] was [REDACTED] for [REDACTED] drove [REDACTED] Nancy did not have a job and never worked at Sandy Hook Elementary School. Nancy got all her money from the divorce [REDACTED] Nancy had season tickets to the Boston Red Sox and attended many games. [REDACTED] b6 -2, b7C -2,

Nancy was a gun nut. [REDACTED] Nancy got into a verbal confrontation about Nancy's fascination for guns. [REDACTED] Nancy told [REDACTED] that she "loved the feeling and power of a gun in her hand". b6 -6 b7C -

[REDACTED] would have their neighbors over for drinks or b6 - b7C

Investigation on 12/15/2012 at Sandy Hook, Connecticut, United States (In Person)

File # 4-NH-2619946 Date drafted 12/16/2012

by [REDACTED] b6 - b7C

b6 -6
b7C -6

dinner parties, [redacted] would leave invitations in all of the neighbors mailboxes. For one particular party [redacted] Nancy never RSVP'd and when [redacted] asked Nancy why she never responded, Nancy told [redacted] that "because there was no return address on the envelope she had thought there was anthrax in it".

b6 -6
b7C -6

Nancy never let anyone come into her home. If one of the neighbors was picking up [redacted] Adam, Nancy would tell them to wait in the driveway. Nancy had her clothes custom made by [redacted] woman on [redacted] in Newtown, CT. Nancy was friendly with this woman. [redacted] had thought the woman's name was [redacted] or something similar (believed to be called [redacted] Newtown, CT, [redacted] Nancy was also friendly with the [redacted] who owned [redacted] located on [redacted] Newtown, CT, [redacted]

b6 -2, 5, 6
b7C -2, 5, 6

Around 9:00 AM on 12/14/2012 [redacted] heard about two to three shots fired. He had thought it was just a hunter as the hunters are often close to their home.

b6 -6
b7C -6

cell

home 12/15/12

Sandy Hook CT 06482 moved here

told by neighbor

Nancy Lanza told neighbors her son hacked into computer systems - he got into 2nd level letter computer FBI or CIA - when got in to 3rd level they shut him down and showed up at house - This was when he was in ninth grade

b6 -6
b7C -6

Lanzas used to come over [redacted]

[redacted]

Always a troubled kid

FBI/~~CIA~~ told Lanza if
he was smart he could
have a job if he was
that intelligent when he
grows up mother had to
convince FBI/CIA that
her son was just intelligent and just
trying to see if he could hack into system

Nancy was friendly
with [redacted]

[redacted]

Nancy was against ~~gun~~ -She
[illegible] the [illegible] power [illegible]

b6 -5, 6
b7C -5, 6

the taller

knows her

b6 -5, 6
b7C -5, 6

Didnt let anyone in house -
would tell people wait outside

b6 -2
b7C -2

Adam was into japanese techno music

She got all her money from the divorce - she had season tickets to red sox

b6 -2, 6
b7C -2, 6

Around 9 am [redacted] heard 2-3 shots - thought it was a hunter really close to his house

[redacted] said Lanza did not
walk e school - did not work at all

[redacted] when talking
about guns [redacted] + Nancy got
confrontational

b6 -
b7C -

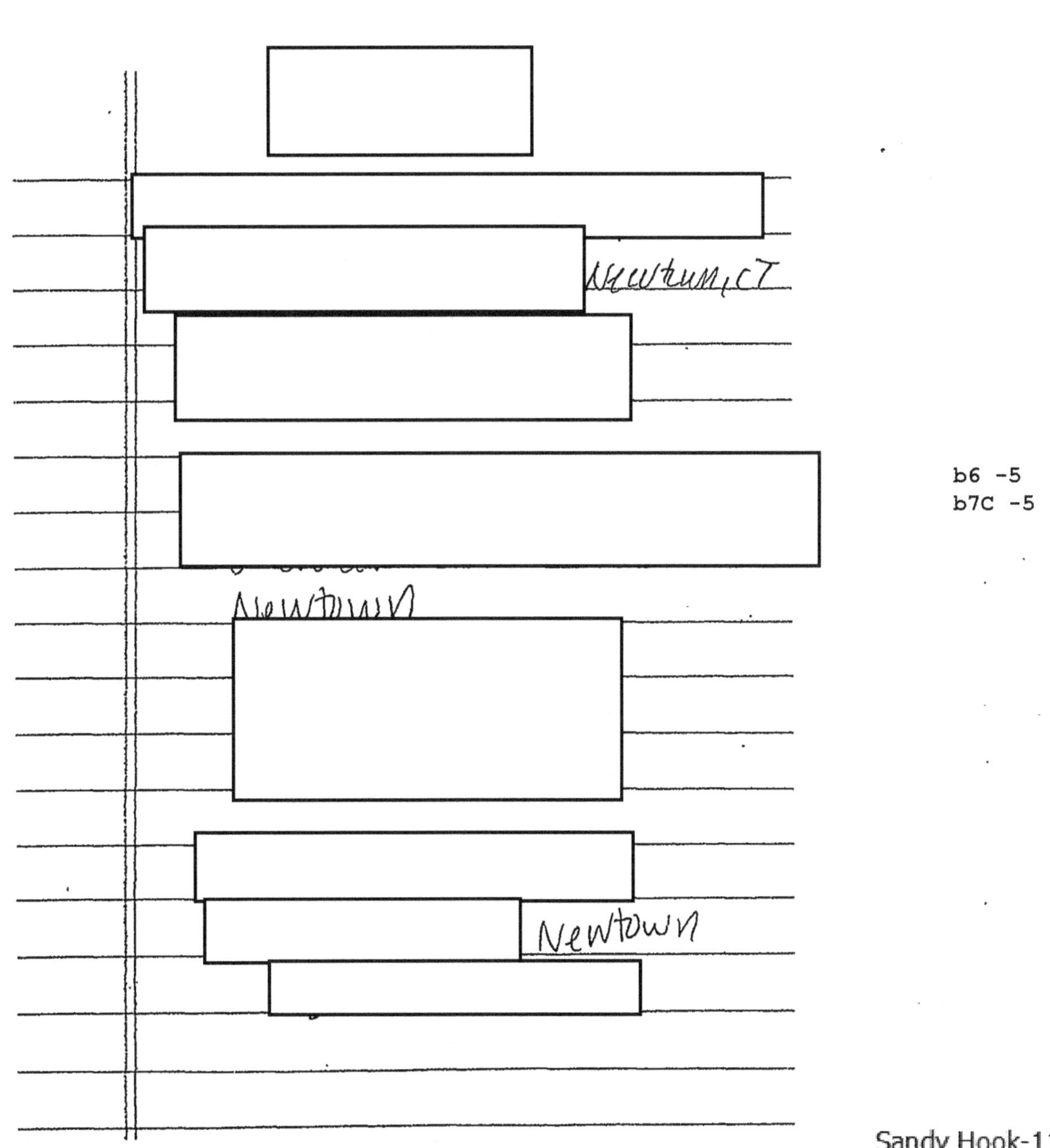

b6 -5
b7C -5

FD-302 (Rev. 5-8-10)

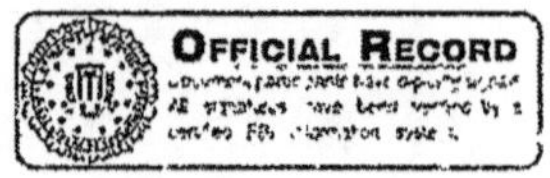

FEDERAL BUREAU OF INVESTIGATION

Date of entry 12/17/2012

Special Agent (SA) [redacted] and SA [redacted] conducted the following neighborhood canvas in Sandy Hook, Connecticut on 12/14/2012:

[redacted] No one was present at the address as of 5:14pm b6 -1, 5 b7C -1,

[redacted]: No one was present at the address as of 5:17pm

[redacted] [redacted] and [redacted] cellular telephone number [redacted] were interviewed by Special Agent [redacted] and Special Agent [redacted] After being advised as to the nature of the interview and the identities of the interviewing agents, [redacted] and [redacted] provided the following information: b6 -1, b7C -1,

Nothing unusual occurred in the neighborhood in the last 24 hours. They were not familiar with the LANZA family. The last time they saw a young kid around the LANZA house would have been four years ago. [redacted] advised that [redacted] b6 -6 b7C -

[redacted]: [redacted] cellular telephone number [redacted] home telephone number [redacted] was interviewed by Special Agent [redacted] and Special Agent [redacted] After being advised as to the nature of the interview and the identities of the interviewing agents, [redacted] provided the following information: b6 -1, b7C -1,

Nothing unusual occurred in the neighborhood in the last 24 hours. [redacted] [redacted] did not know the LANZA's. b6 -6 b7C -

[redacted]: [redacted] was interviewed by Special Agent [redacted] and Special Agent [redacted] After being advised as to the nature of the interview and the identities of the interviewing agents, [redacted] provided the following information: b6 -1, 6 b7C -1,

[redacted] did not see anything unusual in the last 24 hours. b6 -6 b7C -

[redacted]: [redacted] and [redacted] home telephone number b6 -6 b7C -

Investigation on 12/14/2012 at Sandy Hook, Connecticut, United States (In Person)

File # 4-NH-2619946 Date drafted 12/17/2012

by [redacted] b6 - b7C

[redacted] cellular telephone number [redacted] were interviewed by Special Agent [redacted] and Special Agent [redacted] After being advised as to the nature of the interview and the identities of the interviewing agents, [redacted] an[redacted] provided the following information:

b6 -1, 6
b7C -1, 6

Nothing unusual occurred in the neighborhood in the last 24 hours. They were not familiar with the LANZA family. [redacted]

b6 -6
b7C -5, 6

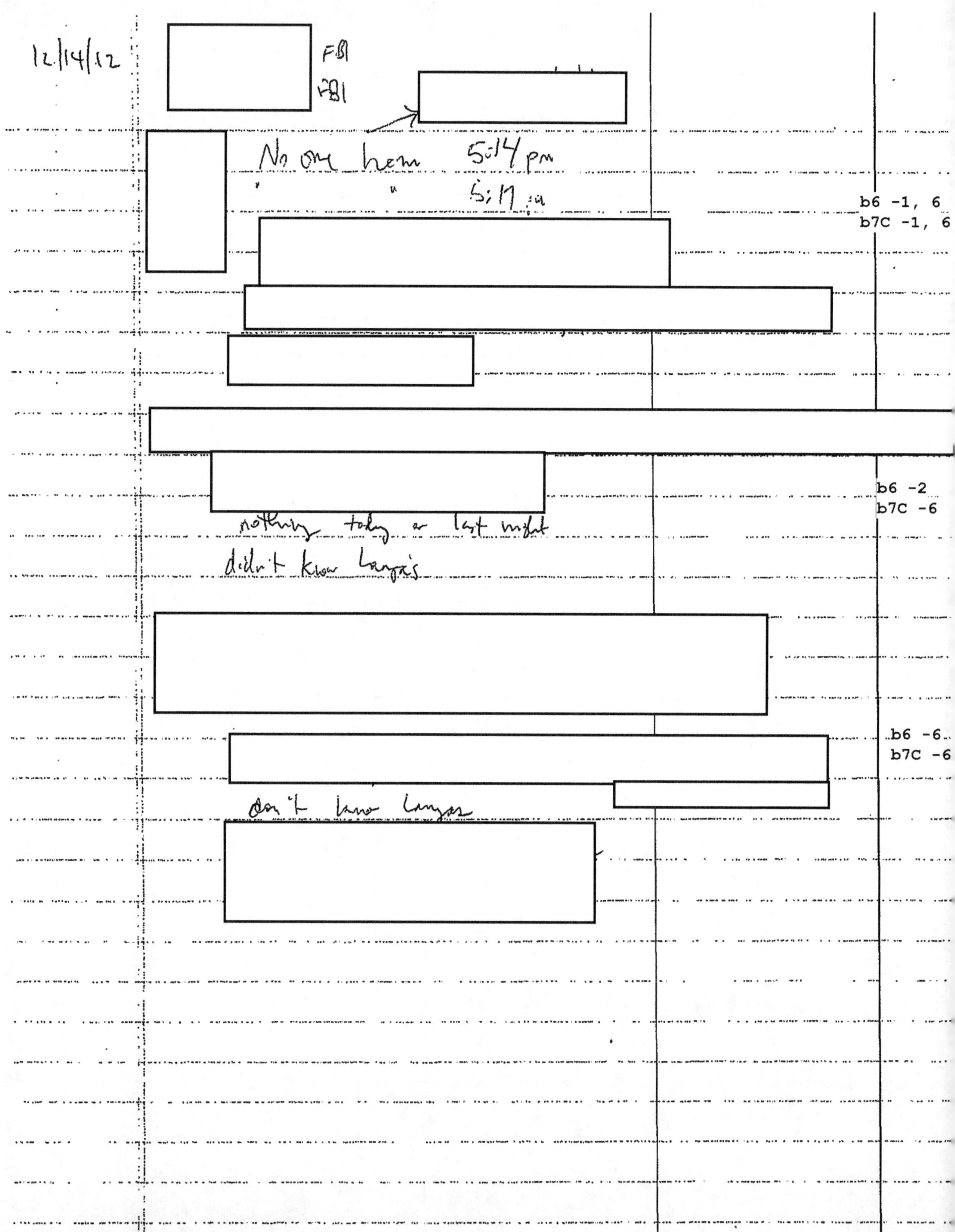

12/14/12

FBI

FBI

No one home 5:14 pm

" " 5:17 pm

b6 -1, 6
b7C -1, 6

b6 -2
b7C -6

nothing today or last night

didn't know Lanza's

b6 -6
b7C -6

don't know Lanzas

FD-302 (Rev. 5-8-10)

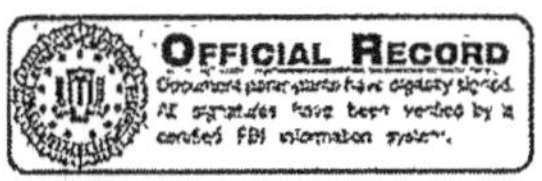

FEDERAL BUREAU OF INVESTIGATION

Date of entry 12/17/2012

[redacted] date of birth, [redacted] and [redacted] [redacted] date of birth, [redacted] of [redacted] Sandy Hook, Connecticut, 06482, home telephone number [redacted] cellular telephone of [redacted] and cellular telephone of [redacted] [redacted] were interviewed telephonically. After being advised of the identity of the interviewing Agent and the nature of the interview, the [redacted]'s provided the following information: b6 -6 b7C -6

There was a trail to the state forest adjacent to their neighborhood where [redacted] took her dogs twice a week. Generally [redacted] did not see anyone when she was on these walks. On Thursday, December 13, 2012, around 1:00 PM Diane was coming back from her walk while on the phone [redacted] [redacted] and she saw a man in an orange poncho sitting up on a hill. The man looked like he was contemplating [redacted] believed the man to be a hunter, however, she thought it was strange that a hunter would be out at 1:00 PM when they are usually hunting at dawn or dusk. [redacted] did not have any further description of the man and did not see any weapons near the man but mentioned that she thought Adam Lanza was not as thin as the photo that was going around of him. b6 -5, 6 b7C -5, 6

[redacted] take a longer hike usually once a week on Sunday. On Sunday December 9, 2012, [redacted] and [redacted] were hiking in the state forest and they took a trail that they had not previously taken. About 1.5 miles from their home they noticed a double tent with a tarp over it and some other items that appeared to be there for quite some time. The odd part about this trail was that it looked like it at just been cleared with a leaf blower as usually the trails are covered with leaves. This trail was in the same general vicinity of where [redacted] saw the man in the orange poncho, however, not the same exact area. On Sunday, December 16, 2012, [redacted] and [redacted] were taking their longer weekly hike and the tent was still in the same place and the trail still looked like it had recently been cleared. [redacted] and [redacted] did not see anyone near the tent or any weapons from their vantage point of the tent. b6 -6 b7C -6

Investigation on 12/16/2012 at Sandy Hook, Connecticut, United States (Phone, Email)

File # 4-NH-2619946 Date drafted 12/17/2012

by [redacted] b6 -1 b7C -1

4-NH-2619946 Serial 17

12/16/2012

trail to state forest
takes Dogs there 2X week
generally never sees anyone

- Thursday 12/13 coming back
talking to
a man in an orange poncho
sitting up on hill ≈ 1 pm
who would be hunting at 1??
usually dusk/dawn

- hard to tell description - doesn't
think Adam is as thin as
picture showing

b6 -5, 6
b7C -5, 6

different area than where saw man

- last Sunday 12/9 coming back on a trail that had been cleared (like someone had just cleaned it)

- saw double tents w/ tarp over it last Sunday - still there today 12/16 noone there

- man in orange poncho sitting there contemplating

- did not see a rifle, gun

From:
To:
Sent: Sun Dec 16 17:18:50 2012
Subject: Fwd: Campsite in woods

b6 -1, 6
b7C -1, 6

Special Agent

We live at in Sandy Hook, You and your partner visited our house Friday evening - we didn't have much of value to tell you I'm afraid. This afternoon my wife and I were taking our weekly hike in the state forest adjacent to the neighborhood and thought of something to pass on to you. Approx 1.5 miles from our house in a remote part of the woods is a large tent and other items that appear to have been there for quite some time. We first noticed it last weekend when we took an unmarked trail we had never hiked. It didn't occur to us to mention it to you all on Froday evening but we thought about it today. I am attaching a photo I took of the site.

b6 -
b7C

In addition, my wife remembers seeing a man in the woods, in the same general vicinity as the tent, with a gun on Thursday, 12/13/2012 at approx 1 pm. Likely a hunter, but she wanted to inform you about this.

It's likely this is nothing, but that is for you all to determine. If you would like to ask us anything about this site please contact us. my cell is home is my wife cell is

thank you,

---------- Forwarded message ----------
From:
Date: Sun, Dec 16, 2012 at 4:53 PM
Subject: Campsite in woods
To:

b6 -6
b7C -6

Sent from my iPhone

b6 -6
b7C -6

FD-302 (Rev. 5-8-10)

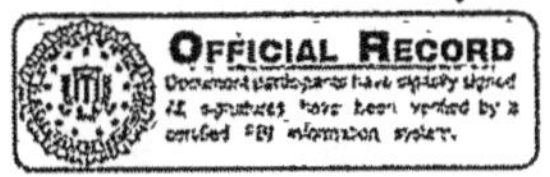

FEDERAL BUREAU OF INVESTIGATION

Date of entry 12/17/2012

[redacted] date of birth [redacted] was interviewed at her residence located at [redacted] Also present during the interview were [redacted] and [redacted] After being advised of the identity of the interviewing Agent and the nature of the interview, [redacted] and [redacted] provided the following information: b6 -6 b7C -6 b7D -1

(**Agent Note:** [redacted] requested the identities of [redacted] be protected. Henceforth, [redacted] will be referred to as the Reporting Party (RP) and [redacted] (B1) and [redacted] (B2). **End Note**) b6 -6 b7C -6 b7D -1

[redacted] b6 -5 b7C -5 b7D -1

[redacted] b6 -6 b7C -6 b7D -1

[redacted] b6 -6 b7C -6 b7D -1

Investigation on 12/14/2012 at [redacted] United States (In Person) b6 -1, 6 b7C -1, 6 b7D -1

File # 4-NH-2619946 Date drafted 12/17/2012

by [redacted]

4-NH-2619946 Serial 18

b6 -
b7C -
b7D -

[redacted]

b6 -3
b7C -
b7D -

The RP, B1, and B2 were cooperative during the interview and open to being re-contacted by writer for further questioning if necessary.

FD-302 (Rev. 5-8-10)

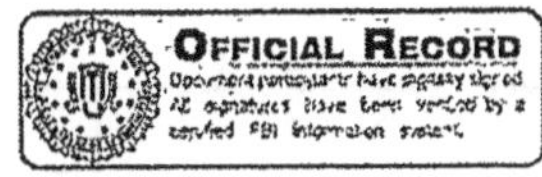

FEDERAL BUREAU OF INVESTIGATION

Date of entry 12/15/2012

On 12/14/2012, [redacted] contacted FBI New Haven regarding [redacted] [redacted] [redacted] cellular telephone number [redacted] e-mail address [redacted] was advised of the identity of the interviewing Agent. He provided the following information: b6 -2, 6 b7C -2, 6

[redacted] b6 -2 b7C -2

[redacted] b6 -2, 6 b7C -2, 6

[redacted] advised [redacted] would provide law enforcement with all necessary information regarding [redacted] b6 -2, 6 b7C -2, 6

Investigation on 12/14/2012 at New Haven, Connecticut, United States (Phone, Email)

File # 4-NH-2619946 Date drafted 12/15/2012

by [redacted] b6 -1 b7C -1

4-NH-2619946 Serial 19

From:
Sent: Friday, December 14, 2012 4:40 PM
To:
Subject: RE: (No Subject)
Attachments:

b3 -1
b6 -1, 6
b7C -1, 6

Cell

Sent with Good (www.good.com)

-----Original Message-----
From:
Sent: Friday, December 14, 2012 04:29 PM Eastern Standard Time
To:
Subject: Re: (No Subject)

b3 -1
b6 -1, 6
b7C -1, 6

for the subpoena, who is it being served on and what is the full corporate address? Thanks

(cell)

From
To:
Sent: Fri Dec 14 16:22:29 2012
Subject: FW: (No Subject)

b6 -1, 2, 6
b7C -1, 2, 6

Cell

My contact info

Sent with Good (www.good.com)

-----Original Message-----
From: [redacted]
Sent: Friday, December 14, 2012 04:18 PM Eastern Standard Time
To [redacted]
Subject:

b6 -2, 6
b7C -2, 6

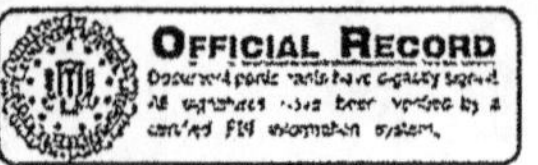

UNCLASSIFIED

FEDERAL BUREAU OF INVESTIGATION

Evidence Log

Event Title: (U) [redacted] interview **Date:** 12/17/2012

Approved By: SSA [redacted] b6 -1, 2 b7C -1, 2

Drafted By: [redacted]

Case ID #: 4-NH-2619946 (U) UNSUB(S)
Sandy Hook Elementary School
12 Dickinson St, Sandy Hook, CT-Victim
Firearms Act.
OO:NH

[redacted] b7E -1

Acquired By: [redacted] on 12/14/2012 b6 -1 b7C -1

Acquired From: (U) Self generated

Receipt Given?: No

Holding Office: [redacted]

Details: b6 -2 b7C - b7E -

[redacted] interview conducted on 12/14/2012, in [redacted]
[redacted]

Item Type	Description
[redacted]	(U) [redacted] interview conducted on 12/14/2012, [redacted] Acquired On: 12/17/2012 [redacted]

b6 -2 b7C - b7E -

UNCLASSIFIED

Title: (U) [redacted] interview
Re: 4-NH-2619946, 12/17/2012

b6 -2
b7C -2

♦♦

FD-1087 (Rev. 5-8-10)

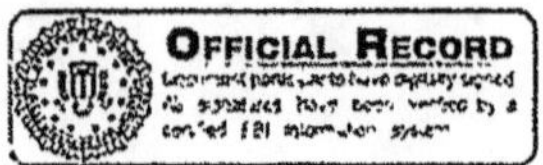

UNCLASSIFIED

FEDERAL BUREAU OF INVESTIGATION

Evidence Log

Event Title: (U) [redacted] interview **Date:** 12/17/2012

Approved By: SSA [redacted] b6 -1, 6 b7C -1,

Drafted By: [redacted]

Case ID #: 4-NH-2619946 (U) UNSUB(S)
Sandy Hook Elementary School
12 Dickinson St, Sandy Hook, CT-Victim
Firearms Act.
OO:NH

[redacted] b7E -

Acquired By: [redacted] on 12/14/2012 b6 -1 b7C -

Acquired From: (U) Self generated

Receipt Given?: No

Holding Office: [redacted]

Details: b6 b7C b7E

[redacted] interview conducted on 12/14/2012, in [redacted] [redacted]

Item Type	**Description**
[redacted]	(U) [redacted] interview conducted on 12/14/2012, in [redacted] Acquired On: 12/17/2012 [redacted]

b6 - b7C b7E

UNCLASSIFIED

This document contains neither recommendations nor conclusions of the FBI. It is the property of the FBI and is loaned to your agency; it and its contents are not to be distributed outside your agency.

Sandy Hook-

4-NH-2619946 Serial 21

Title: (U) [redacted] interview
Re: 4-NH-2619946, 12/17/2012

b6 -6
b7C -6

♦♦

FD-1087 (Rev. 5-8-10)

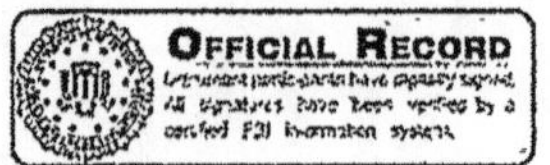

UNCLASSIFIED

FEDERAL BUREAU OF INVESTIGATION

Evidence Log

Event Title: (U) [redacted] **Date:** 12/17/2012

Approved By: SSA [redacted] b6 -1, 2 b7C -1, 2

Drafted By: [redacted]

Case ID #: 4-NH-2619946 (U) UNSUB(S)
Sandy Hook Elementary School
12 Dickinson St, Sandy Hook, CT-Victim
Firearms Act.
OO:NH

[redacted] b7E -1

Acquired By: [redacted] on 12/14/2012

b6 -1, 2
b7C -1, 2

Acquired From: (U [redacted]

Receipt Given?: No

Holding Office: NEW HAVEN

Details:

[redacted] b6 -
b7C

Item Type [redacted]

Description
(U) [redacted]
Acquired On: 12/14/2012
Located By: [redacted]
Location Area: [redacted]
Specific Location: [redacted]

b6 -1,
b7C -1,
b7E -6

UNCLASSIFIED

This document contains neither recommendations nor conclusions of the FBI. It is the property of the FBI and is loaned to your agency; it and its contents are not to be distributed outside your agency.

4-NH-2619946 Serial 22

Title: (U) [redacted]

Re: 4-NH-2619946, 12/17/2012

b6 -2
b7C -2

♦♦

FD-1087 (Rev. 5-8-10)

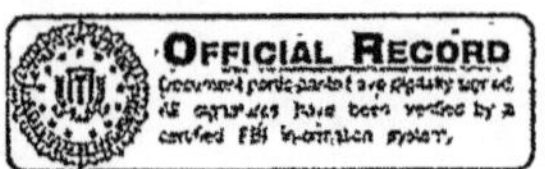

UNCLASSIFIED

FEDERAL BUREAU OF INVESTIGATION

Evidence Log

Event Title: (U) [redacted] **Date:** 12/17/2012

Approved By: SSA [redacted] b6 -1, 2 b7C -1, 2

Drafted By: [redacted]

Case ID #: 4-NH-2619946 (U) UNSUB(S)
Sandy Hook Elementary School
12 Dickinson St, Sandy Hook, CT-Victim
Firearms Act.
OO:NH

[redacted] b7E -

Acquired By: [redacted] on 12/14/2012 b6 -1, b7C -1

Acquired From: (U [redacted]

Receipt Given?: No

Holding Office: NEW HAVEN

Details:

[redacted] b6 - b7C

Item Type	Description
[redacted]	(U) [redacted] [redacted] Acquired On: 12/14/2012 Located By: [redacted] Location Area: [redacted] Specific Location: [redacted] [redacted]

b6 - b7C b7E

UNCLASSIFIED

This document contains neither recommendations nor conclusions of the FBI. It is the property of the FBI and is loaned to your agency; it and its contents are not to be distributed outside your agency.

4-NH-2619946 Serial 23

Title: (U[redacted]

Re: 4-NH-2619946, 12/17/2012

b6 -2
b7C -2

♦♦

FD-1087 (Rev. 5-8-10)

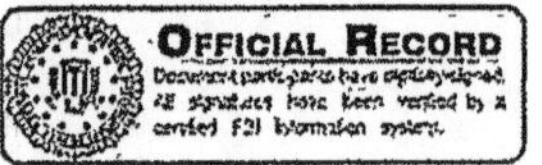

UNCLASSIFIED

FEDERAL BUREAU OF INVESTIGATION

Evidence Log

Event Title: (U) [redacted] **Date:** 12/17/2012

Approved By: SSA [redacted] b6 -1, 2 b7C -1,

Drafted By: [redacted]

Case ID #: 4-NH-2619946 (U) UNSUB(S)
Sandy Hook Elementary School
12 Dickinson St, Sandy Hook, CT-Victim
Firearms Act.
OO:NH

[redacted] b7E -1

Acquired By: [redacted] on 12/14/2012 b6 -1, 2 b7C -1,

Acquired From: (U [redacted]

Receipt Given?: No

Holding Office: NEW HAVEN

Details:

[redacted] b6 -2 b7C -

Item Type	Description
[redacted]	(U) [redacted]

Acquired On: 12/14/2012
Located By: [redacted] b6 -1, 2
Location Area: [redacted] b7C -1,
Specific Location: [redacted] b7E -6
[redacted]

UNCLASSIFIED

Title: (U)[redacted]

Re: 4-NH-2619946, 12/17/2012

b6 -2
b7C -2

♦♦

FD-1087 (Rev. 5-8-10)

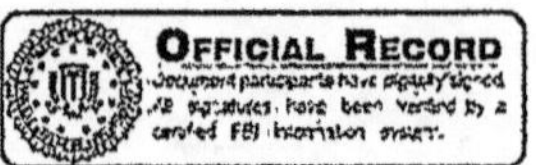

UNCLASSIFIED

FEDERAL BUREAU OF INVESTIGATION

Evidence Log

Event Title: (U) [redacted] **Date:** 12/17/2012

Approved By: SSA [redacted] b6 -1, 2 b7C -1, 2

Drafted By: [redacted]

Case ID #: 4-NH-2619946 (U) UNSUB(S)
Sandy Hook Elementary School
12 Dickinson St, Sandy Hook, CT-Victim
Firearms Act.
OO:NH

[redacted] b7E -

Acquired By: [redacted] on 12/14/2012 b6 -1, 2 b7C -1, 2

Acquired From: (U [redacted]

Receipt Given?: No

Holding Office: NEW HAVEN

Details:

[redacted] b6 b7C

Item Type	Description
[redacted]	(U) [redacted] [redacted] Acquired On: 12/14/2012 Located By: [redacted] Location Area: [redacted] Specific Location: [redacted] [redacted]

b6 -1, b7C -1, b7E -6

UNCLASSIFIED

Title: (U) [redacted]
Re: 4-NH-2619946, 12/17/2012

b6 -2
b7C -2

◆◆

FD-1087 (Rev. 5-8-10)

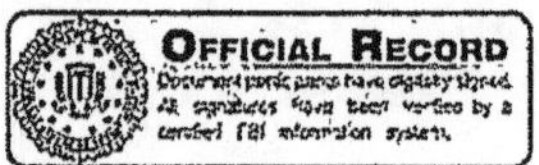

UNCLASSIFIED

FEDERAL BUREAU OF INVESTIGATION

Evidence Log

Event Title: (U) [redacted] **Date:** 12/17/2012

Approved By: SSA [redacted] b6 -1, 2 b7C -1, 2

Drafted By: [redacted]

Case ID #: 4-NH-2619946 (U) UNSUB(S)
Sandy Hook Elementary School
12 Dickinson St, Sandy Hook, CT-Victim
Firearms Act.
OO:NH

[redacted] b7E -1

Acquired By: [redacted] on 12/14/2012 b6 -1, 2

Acquired From: (U [redacted] b7C -1,

Receipt Given?: No

Holding Office: NEW HAVEN

Details:

[redacted] b6 - b7C

Item Type [redacted]

Description
(U) [redacted]
[redacted]
Acquired On: 12/14/2012
Located By: [redacted]
Location Area: [redacted]
Specific Location: [redacted]
[redacted]

b6 -1, b7C -1, b7E -6

UNCLASSIFIED

4-NH-2619946 Serial 21

Title: (U[redacted]

Re: 4-NH-2619946, 12/17/2012

b6 -2
b7C -2

♦♦

FD-1087 (Rev. 5-8-10)

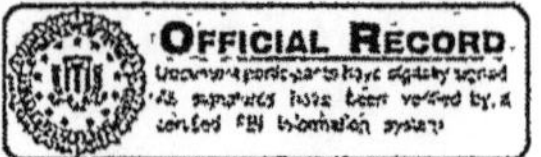

UNCLASSIFIED

FEDERAL BUREAU OF INVESTIGATION

Evidence Log

Event Title: (U) [redacted] **Date:** 12/17/2012

Approved By: SSA [redacted]

b6 -1, 2
b7C -1, 2

Drafted By: [redacted]

Case ID #: 4-NH-2619946 (U) UNSUB(S)
Sandy Hook Elementary School
12 Dickinson St, Sandy Hook, CT-Victim
Firearms Act.
OO:NH

[redacted] b7E -1

Acquired By: [redacted] on 12/14/2012

b6 -1, 2
b7C -1, 2

Acquired From: (U) [redacted]

Receipt Given?: No

Holding Office: NEW HAVEN

Details:

[redacted]

b6 -2
b7C -2

Item Type	Description
[redacted]	(U) [redacted]
	[redacted]
	Acquired On: 12/14/2012
	Located By: [redacted]
	Location Area: [redacted]
	Specific Location: [redacted]
	[redacted]

b6 -1, 2
b7C -1, 2
b7E -6

UNCLASSIFIED

This document contains neither recommendations nor conclusions of the FBI. It is the property of the FBI and is loaned to your agency; it and its contents are not to be distributed outside your agency.

Title: (U) [redacted]

Re: 4-NH-2619946, 12/17/2012

b6 -2
b7C -2

♦♦

FD-1087 (Rev. 5-8-10)

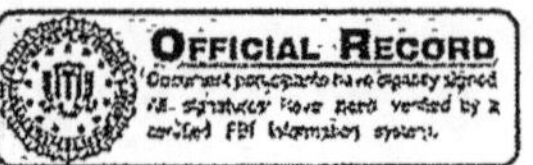

UNCLASSIFIED

FEDERAL BUREAU OF INVESTIGATION

Evidence Log

Event Title: (U) [redacted] **Date:** 12/17/2012

Approved By: SSA [redacted]

b6 -1, 2
b7C -1, 2

Drafted By: [redacted]

Case ID #: 4-NH-2619946 (U) UNSUB(S)
Sandy Hook Elementary School
12 Dickinson St, Sandy Hook, CT-Victim
Firearms Act.
OO:NH

[redacted] b7E -1

Acquired By: [redacted] on 12/14/2012

b6 -1, 2
b7C -1, 2

Acquired From: (U [redacted]

Receipt Given?: No

Holding Office: NEW HAVEN

Details:

[redacted] b6 -2
b7C -

Item Type	Description
[redacted]	(U) [redacted] [redacted] Acquired On: 12/14/2012 Located By: [redacted] Location Area: [redacted] Specific Location: [redacted] [redacted]

b6 -1, 2
b7C -1, 2
b7E -6

UNCLASSIFIED

4-NH-2619946 Serial 28

Title: (U) [redacted]
Re: 4-NH-2619946, 12/17/2012

b6 -2
b7C -2

♦♦

FD-1087 (Rev. 5-8-10)

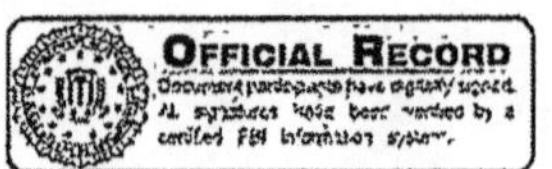

UNCLASSIFIED

FEDERAL BUREAU OF INVESTIGATION

Evidence Log

Event Title: (U) [redacted] **Date:** 12/17/2012

Approved By: SSA [redacted] b6 -1, 2 b7C -1, 2

Drafted By: [redacted]

Case ID #: 4-NH-2619946 (U) UNSUB(S)
Sandy Hook Elementary School
12 Dickinson St, Sandy Hook, CT-Victim
Firearms Act.
OO:NH

[redacted] b7E -1

Acquired By: [redacted] on 12/14/2012 b6 -1, 2 b7C -1, 2

Acquired From: (U) [redacted]

Receipt Given?: No

Holding Office: NEW HAVEN

Details:

[redacted] b6 -2 b7C -

Item Type	Description
[redacted]	(U) [redacted] [redacted] Acquired On: 12/14/2012 Located By: [redacted] Location Area: [redacted] Specific Location: [redacted] [redacted]

b6 -1, 2
b7C -1, 2
b7E -6

UNCLASSIFIED

4-NH-2619946 Serial 29

Title: (U)[redacted]

Re: 4-NH-2619946, 12/17/2012

b6 -2
b7C -2

♦♦

FD-1087 (Rev. 5-8-10)

UNCLASSIFIED

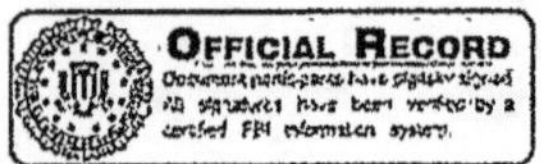

FEDERAL BUREAU OF INVESTIGATION

Evidence Log

Event Title: (U) Search Warrant Executed At [redacted] **Date:** 12/17/2012

Approved By: [redacted]

b6 -1, 2
b7C -1, 2

Drafted By: [redacted]

Case ID #: 4-NH-2619946 (U) UNSUB(S)
Sandy Hook Elementary School
12 Dickinson St, Sandy Hook, CT-Victim
Firearms Act.
OO:NH

[redacted] b7E -1

Acquired By: [redacted] on 12/15/2012

Acquired From: (U) [redacted]
United States

b6 -1, 2
b7C -1, 2

Receipt Given?: Yes

Holding Office: NEW HAVEN

Details:

Evidence seized from [redacted]
12/14 through 12/15/2012.

b6 -
b7C

Item Type **Description**

UNCLASSIFIED

This document contains neither recommendations nor conclusions of the FBI. It is the property of the FBI and is loaned to your agency; it and its contents are not to be distributed outside your agency.

Sandy Hook-1

4-NH-2619946 Serial 3C

Title: (U) Search Warrant Executed At [redacted] b6 -2 b7C -2
Re: 4-NH-2619946, 12/17/2012

[redacted] (U) [redacted]

Acquired On: 12/14/2012
Located By: [redacted] b6 -1, 2
Other Locator: [redacted] b7C -1, 2
Location Area: Room J b7E -6
Specific Location: [redacted]

[redacted] (U) [redacted]

Acquired On: 12/14/2012 b6 -1, 2
Located By: [redacted] b7C -1, 2
Other Locator: [redacted] b7E -6
Location Area: ROOM H
Specific Location: [redacted]

[redacted] (U) [redacted]

Acquired On: 12/14/2012 b6 -1, 2
Located By: [redacted] b7C -1, 2
Other Locator: [redacted] b7E -6
Location Area: ROOM H
Specific Location: [redacted]

[redacted] (U) [redacted]

Acquired On: 12/14/2012
Located By: [redacted] b6 -1, 2
Other Locator: [redacted] b7C -1, 2
Location Area: ROOM O b7E -6
Specific Location: [redacted]

Title: (U) Search Warrant Executed At [redacted] b6 -2 b7C -
Re: 4-NH-2619946, 12/17/2012

(U)
Acquired On: 12/14/2012
Located By:
Other Locator:
Location Area: ROOM O
Specific Location:

b6 -1, 2
b7C -1,
b7E -6

(U)
Acquired On: 12/15/2012
Located By:
Other Locator:
Location Area: ROOM Q
Specific Location:
1

b6 -1, 2
b7C -1,
b7E -6

(U)
Acquired On: 12/15/2012
Located By:
Other Locator:
Location Area: ROOM V
Specific Location:

b6 -1, 2
b7C -1,
b7E -6

(U)
Acquired On: 12/15/2012
Located By:
Other Locator:
Location Area: ROOM N
Specific Location:

b6 -1, 2
b7C -1,
b7E -6

Title: (U) Search Warrant Executed At [redacted] b6 -2 b7C -2

Re: 4-NH-2619946, 12/17/2012

[redacted] (U) [redacted]

Acquired On: 12/15/2012
Located By: [redacted]
Other Locator: [redacted]
Location Area: ROOM N
Specific Location: [redacted]

b6 -1, 2
b7C -1, 2
b7E -6

[redacted] (U) [redacted]

Acquired On: 12/15/2012
Located By: [redacted]
Other Locator: [redacted]
Location Area: ROOM O
Specific Location: [redacted]

b6 -1, 2
b7C -1, 2
b7E -6

[redacted] (U) [redacted]

b6 -1, 2
b7C -1, 2
b7E -6

Acquired On: 12/14/2012
Located By: [redacted]
Other Locator: [redacted]
Location Area: ROOM E
Specific Location: [redacted]

Title: (U) Search Warrant Executed At [redacted] b6 -2
Re: 4-NH-2619946, 12/17/2012 b7C -2

[redacted] (U) [redacted]
Acquired On: 12/15/2012
Located By: [redacted]
Other Locator: [redacted] b6 -1, 2
Location Area: ROOM O b7C -1,
Specific Location: [redacted] b7E -6
[redacted]

[redacted] (U) [redacted]
Acquired On: 12/14/2012
Located By: [redacted] b6 -1,
Other Locator: [redacted] b7C -1,
Location Area: ROOM E b7E -6
Specific Location: [redacted]

[redacted] (U) [redacted]
[redacted]
Acquired On: 12/14/2012 b6 -1,
Located By: [redacted] b7C -1
Other Locator: [redacted] b7E -6
Location Area: ROOM E
Specific Location: [redacted]

[redacted] (U) [redacted]
[redacted]
Acquired On: 12/14/2012
Located By: [redacted] b6 -1,
Other Locator: [redacted] b7C -1
Location Area: ROOM E b7E -6
Specific Location: [redacted]

Title: (U) Search Warrant Executed At [redacted] b6 -2 b7C -2
Re: 4-NH-2619946, 12/17/2012

[redacted] (U) [redacted]
Acquired On: 12/14/2012
Located By: [redacted]
Other Locator: [redacted]
Location Area: ROOM E
Specific Location: [redacted]

b6 -1, 2
b7C -1, 2
b7E -6

[redacted] (U) [redacted]
Acquired On: 12/14/2012
Located By: [redacted]
Other Locator: [redacted]
Location Area: ROOM E
Specific Location: [redacted]

b6 -1, 2
b7C -1, 2
b7E -6

[redacted] (U) [redacted]
Acquired On: 12/14/2012
Located By: [redacted]
Other Locator: [redacted]
Location Area: ROOM E
Specific Location: [redacted]

b6 -1, 2
b7C -1, 2
b7E -6

[redacted] (U) [redacted]
Acquired On: 12/15/2012
Located By: [redacted]
Other Locator: [redacted]
Location Area: ROOM E
Specific Location: [redacted]

b6 -1, 2
b7C -1, 2
b7E -6

[redacted] (U) [redacted]
Acquired On: 12/15/2012
Located By: [redacted]
Other Locator: [redacted]
Location Area: ROOM E
Specific Location: [redacted]

b6 -1, 2
b7C -1, 2
b7E -6

Title: (U) Search Warrant Executed At [redacted] b6 -2
Re: 4-NH-2619946, 12/17/2012 b7C -

[redacted] (U) [redacted]
Acquired On: 12/15/2012
Located By: [redacted] b6 -1, 2
Other Locator: [redacted] b7C -1,
Location Area: ROOM E b7E -6
Specific Location: [redacted]

[redacted] (U) [redacted]
Acquired On: 12/15/2012
Located By: [redacted] b6 -1, 2
Other Locator: [redacted] b7C -1,
Location Area: ROOM E b7E -6
Specific Location: [redacted]

[redacted] (U) [redacted]
[redacted]
Acquired On: 12/15/2012
Located By: [redacted] b6 -1, 2
Other Locator: [redacted] b7C -1,
Location Area: ROOM E b7E -6
Specific Location: [redacted]

[redacted] (U) [redacted]
[redacted]
Acquired On: 12/15/2012 b6 -1
Located By: [redacted] b7C -
Other Locator: [redacted] b7E -
Location Area: ROOM E
Specific Location: [redacted]

[redacted] (U) [redacted]
[redacted]
Acquired On: 12/15/2012
Located By: [redacted] b6 -1
Other Locator: [redacted] b7C -
Location Area: ROOM E b7E -
Specific Location: [redacted]

Title: (U) Search Warrant Executed At [redacted] b6 -2 b7C -2
Re: 4-NH-2619946, 12/17/2012

[redacted] (U) [redacted]

[redacted]

b6 -1, 2
b7C -1, 2
b7E -6

Acquired On: 12/15/2012
Located By: [redacted]
Other Locator: [redacted]
Location Area: ROOM E
Specific Location: [redacted]

♦♦

FD-1087 (Rev. 5-8-10)

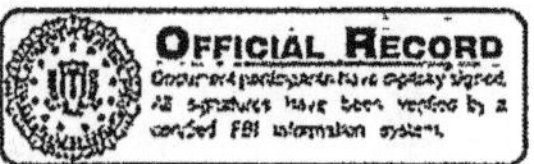

UNCLASSIFIED//~~FOUO~~

FEDERAL BUREAU OF INVESTIGATION

Evidence Log

Event Title: (U//FOUO) [redacted] Evidence from [redacted] [redacted] search

Date: 12/17/2012

Approved By: [redacted]

b6 -1, 2
b7C -1, 2
b7E -7

Drafted By: [redacted]

Case ID #: 4-NH-2619946

(U) UNSUB(S)
Sandy Hook Elementary School
12 Dickinson St, Sandy Hook, CT-Victim
Firearms Act.
OO:NH

[redacted]

b7E -1

Acquired By: [redacted] on 12/15/2012

Acquired From: (U//~~FOUO~~) [redacted]

b6 -1, 2
b7C -1, 2

Receipt Given?: Yes

Holding Office: NEW HAVEN

Details:

The purpose of this communication is to submit the following items of evidence to NH Evidence Control:

[redacted]

b7E

[redacted]

UNCLASSIFIED//~~FOUO~~

4-NH-2619946 Serial 3

Title: (U//~~FOUO~~) Evidence from consent search
Re: 4-NH-2619946, 12/17/2012

b6 -2
b7C -2
b7E -7

Item Type	Description
	(U//~~FOUO~~) Acquired On: 12/15/2012 Receipt Number: 28 Located By: Other Locator: Location Area: Room J and Room Q Specific Location:
	(U//~~FOUO~~) Acquired On: 12/15/2012 Receipt Number: 29 Located By: Other Locator: Location Area: Room J Specific Location:

b6 -1, 2
b7C -1, 2
b7E -6

b6 -1, 2
b7C -1, 2
b7E -6

♦♦

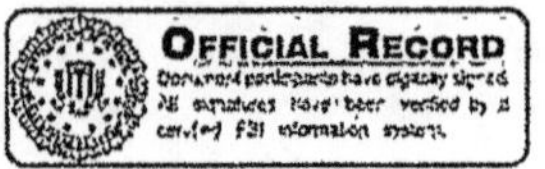

FEDERAL BUREAU OF INVESTIGATION

Date of entry 12/16/2012

[redacted] date of birth [redacted] of [redacted] [redacted] Sandy Hook, Connecticut, 06482, was interviewed at his residence. After being advised of the identity of the interviewing Agents and the nature of the interview, [redacted] provided the following information: b6 - b7C

[redacted] knew that the Lanza's were divorced. [redacted] [redacted] knew Adam Lanza. b6 -5, b7C -5,

[redacted] never really saw the Lanza's. [redacted] [redacted] did not see or hear anything unusual on 12/14/2012. b6 b7C

Investigation on 12/14/2012 at Sandy Hook, Connecticut, United States (In Person)

File # 4-NH-2619946 Date drafted 12/16/2012

by [redacted] b6 b7C

4-NH-2619946 Serial 3

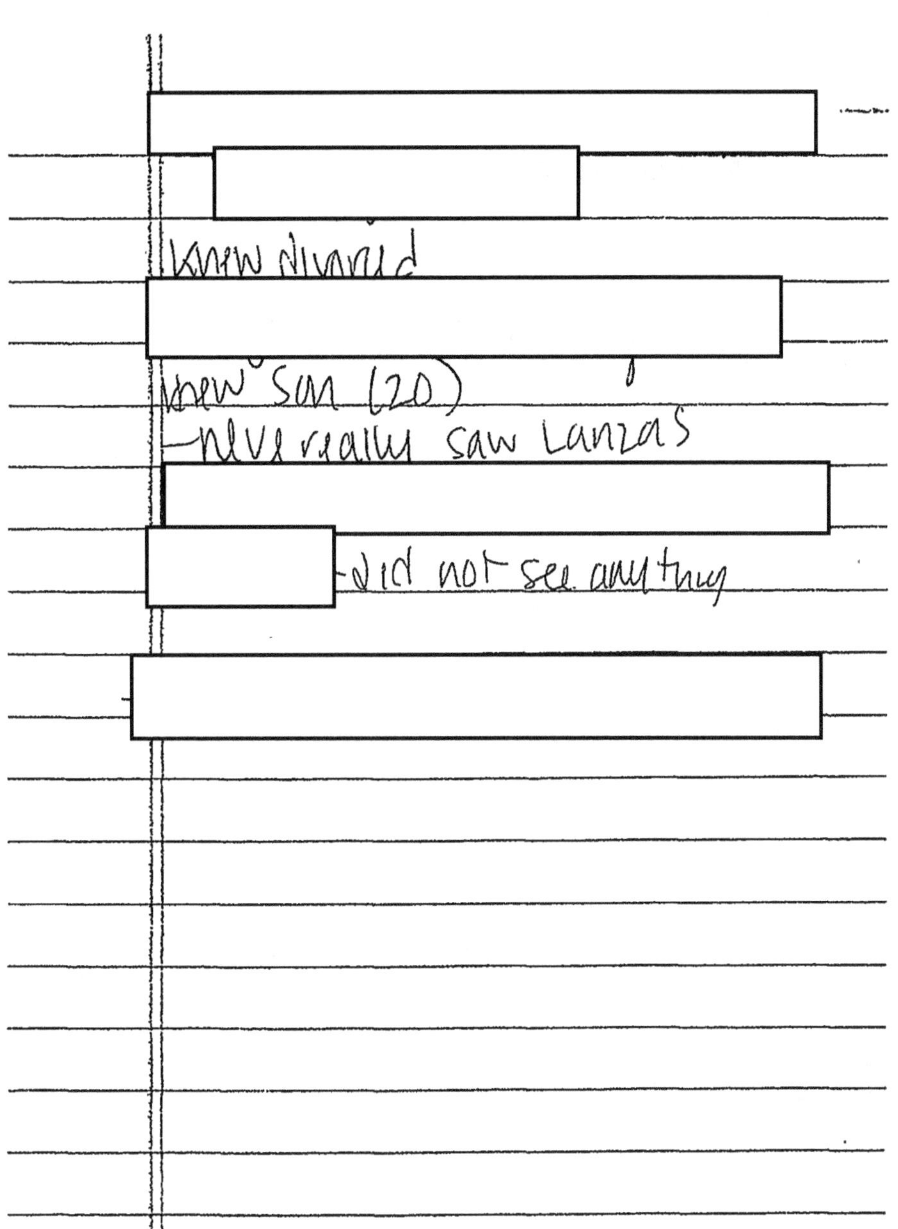

knew divorced
knew son (20)
-never really saw Lanzas
-did not see anything

b6 -5, 6
b7C -5, 6

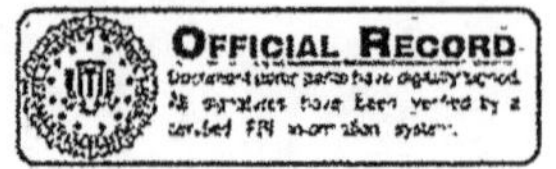

FEDERAL BUREAU OF INVESTIGATION

Date of entry 12/17/2012

[redacted] date of birth (DOB)[redacted] residence address [redacted] Texas, cellular telephone number [redacted] was interviewed telephonically. After being advised of the identity of the interviewing Agent and the nature of the interview, [redacted] provided the following information: b6 - b7C

[redacted] b6 - b7C

At the news of the shooting, he began doing his own research of the [redacted] who he thought from the news was the shooter. b6 - b7C

He looked up [redacted] Facebook account and noticed that [redacted] had changed his Facebook avatar on 12/08/12. The new photo was of a male wearing all black clothes and sunglasses. [redacted] found this suspicious because that was similar to what the shooter in CT was wearing. b6 -2, 6 b7C -2, 6

There were a number of posts on [redacted] Facebook page by [redacted] The comments said, "Looks like you're dressed like and assassin." [redacted] thought he was referencing a violent video game. [redacted] also made reference to [redacted] wearing a trench coat [redacted] thought this was similar to the "trench coat mafia" and the Columbine HS shooters. [redacted] final post said,"This can only turn out awesome." b6 -2, 5 b7C -2,

[redacted] "read between the lines" and believed [redacted] may have had advance knowledge of the shootings. [redacted] could not access [redacted] Facebook account, it had been locked out. b6 -5, 6 b7C -5, 6

[redacted] later found out that the shooter was not [redacted] but [redacted] ADAM LANZA, thus nullifying his thought that [redacted] had prior knowledge. b6 -2, 5 b7C -2,

Investigation on 12/14/2012 at Houston, Texas, United States (Phone)

File # 4-NH-2619946 Date drafted 12/17/2012

by [redacted] b6 -1 b7C -

FD-302 (Rev. 5-8-10)

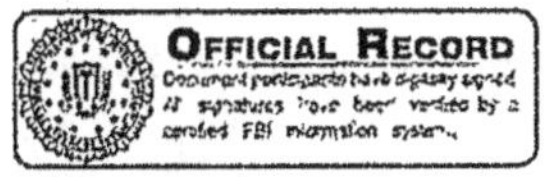

FEDERAL BUREAU OF INVESTIGATION

Date of entry 12/17/2012

[redacted] home telephone number [redacted] residence address [redacted] Sandy Hook, Connecticut, was interviewed at her residence by Special Agent (SA) [redacted] and SA [redacted] After being advised of the identities of the interviewing Agents and the nature of the interview, [redacted] provided the following information: b6 -1, 7 b7C -1, 7

[redacted] father, [redacted] received a threatening phone call. SA [redacted] examined the caller ID for the home telephone number, [redacted] which showed calls on 12/16/2012, at 12:14pm, 12:16pm, and 12:20pm, from telephone number 646-843-7000, ICALLED INC. [redacted] stated her father, [redacted] answered the first call and an unknown male said in substance, "I'm Adam Lanza, I'm going to kill you." [redacted] argued with the caller and ended the call. The unknown male called the second time and called [redacted] a "faggot." [redacted] hung up on the caller on the third call. b6 -7 b7C -7

SA [redacted] then called [redacted] stated the caller on the first call stated, "I'm Adam Lanza and you are going to be dead." After arguing with the caller, the caller stated, "No, I'm really going to kill you." [redacted] stated the caller did not have a noticeable accent. b6 -1, 7 b7C -1, 7

Investigation on 12/16/2012 at Sandy Hook, Connecticut, United States (In Person, Phone)

File # 4-NH-2619946 Date drafted 12/17/2012

by [redacted] b6 -1 b7C -1

4-NH-2619946 Serial 34

12/16/12

646-843-7000

I call inc

12:20 pm

12:24 , 16 , 12:20

b6 -7
b7C -7

answered

Adam Lanza , I'm going to kill you

→ argument , ended call

1st call yell   2nd call yell fizzy   3rd call hang up

home phone called

on phone

I'm AL and you are going to be dead

No accent (foreign)

– no I'm really going to kill you

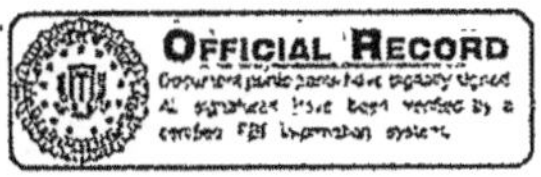

FEDERAL BUREAU OF INVESTIGATION

Date of entry 12/17/2012

[redacted] date of birth [redacted] residence address [redacted] Sandy Hook, Connecticut, was interviewed at his residence. Also present during the interview was [redacted] date of birth [redacted] After being advised of the identities of the interviewing Agents and the nature of the interview, [redacted] and [redacted] provided the following information: b6 -6 b7C -6

[redacted] and [redacted] have lived at [redacted] for the past [redacted] years. [redacted] b6 -5, 6 b7C -5, 6

[redacted] and [redacted] didn't know the LANZA family. They never had any interaction with the anyone in the LANZA family. [redacted] and [redacted] never saw any children at 36 Yogananda Street. The only activity they saw at 36 Yogananda Street was a lady arriving and departing in an automobile. b6 -6 b7C -6

On December 14, 2012, [redacted] was at home in the morning between 8:00am and 9:00am. She then left her residence and returned home around 9:30am. [redacted] left home early in the morning and returned home at noon on December 14, 2012. b6 -6 b7C -6

[redacted] b6 -5 b7C -5

[redacted] mentioned that he witnessed, four to five years ago, a kid dressed in all black walk up Yogananda Street to the bus stop and turned around and walked away. [redacted] didn't know who the kid was or where he came from. b6 -6 b7C -6

Investigation on 12/14/2012 at Sandy Hook, Connecticut, United States (In Person)

File # 4-NH-2619946 Date drafted 12/17/2012

by [redacted] b6 -1 b7C -1

4-NH-2619946 Serial 35

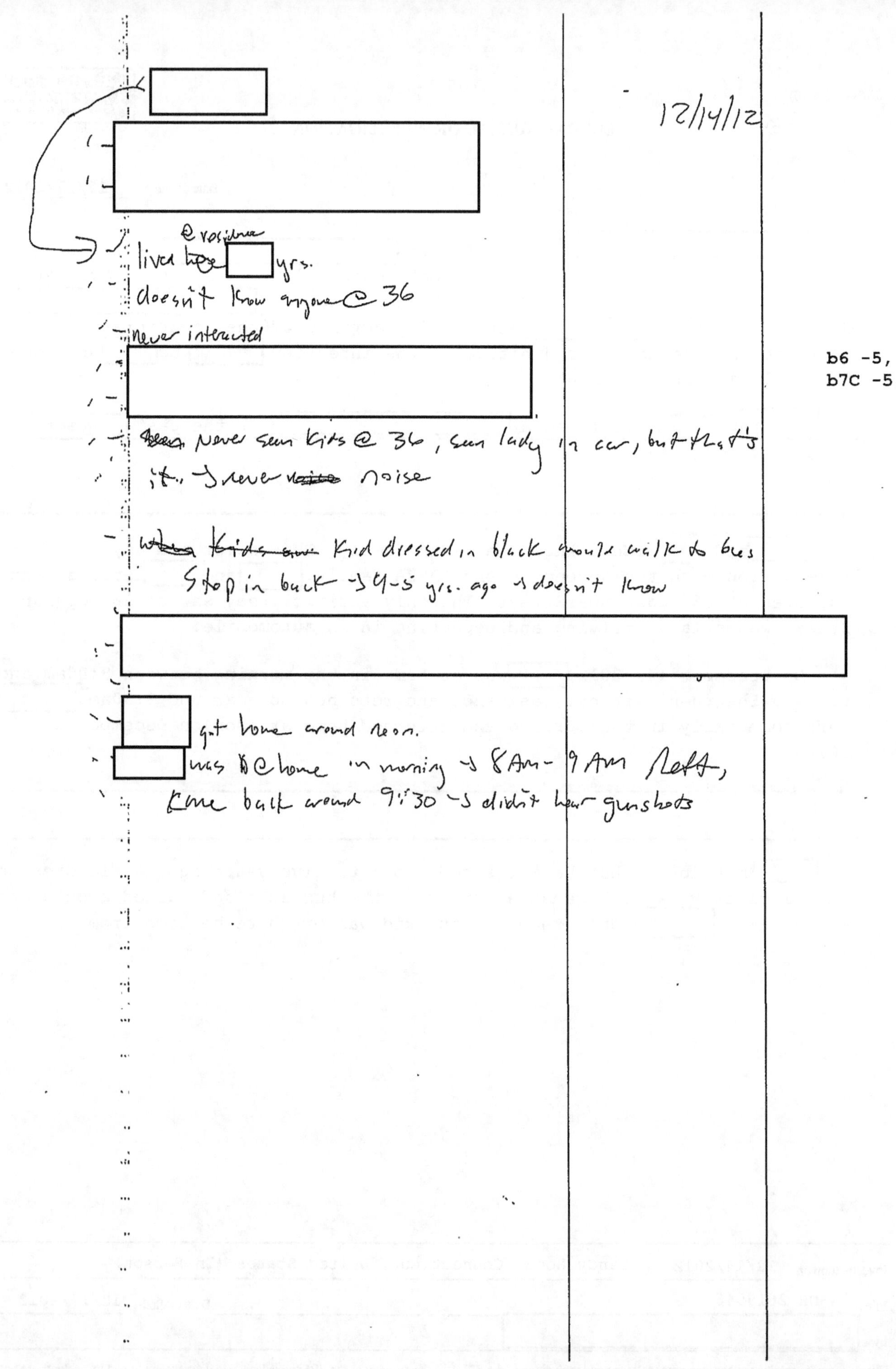

12/14/12

lived ~~here~~ @ residence [redacted] yrs.

doesn't know anyone @ 36

never interacted

~~Seen~~ Never seen kids @ 36, seen lady in car, but that's it. → never ~~noise~~ noise

~~When~~ ~~kids~~ ~~are~~ Kid dressed in black would walk to bus stop in back → 4-5 yrs. ago → doesn't know

[redacted] got home around noon.

[redacted] was ~~to~~ @ home in morning → 8AM-9AM left, came back around 9:30 → didn't hear gunshots

b6 -5, 6
b7C -5, 6

FD-302 (Rev. 5-8-10)

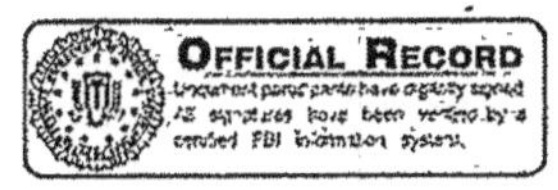

FEDERAL BUREAU OF INVESTIGATION

Date of entry 12/17/2012

Special Agent (SA) [redacted] and SA [redacted] attempted to interview [redacted] on 12/16/2012 at 5:10pm at his residence [redacted] Sandy Hook, Connecticut, telephone number [redacted] No one answered the door and no one answered the home telephone, which could be heard ringing in the house. There was no way to leave a voicemail. b6 -1, 5 b7C -1, 5

Investigation on 12/16/2012 at Sandy Hook, Connecticut, United States (In Person, Phone)

File # 4-NH-2619946 Date drafted 12/17/2012

by [redacted] b6 -1 b7C -1

4-NH-2619946 Serial 26

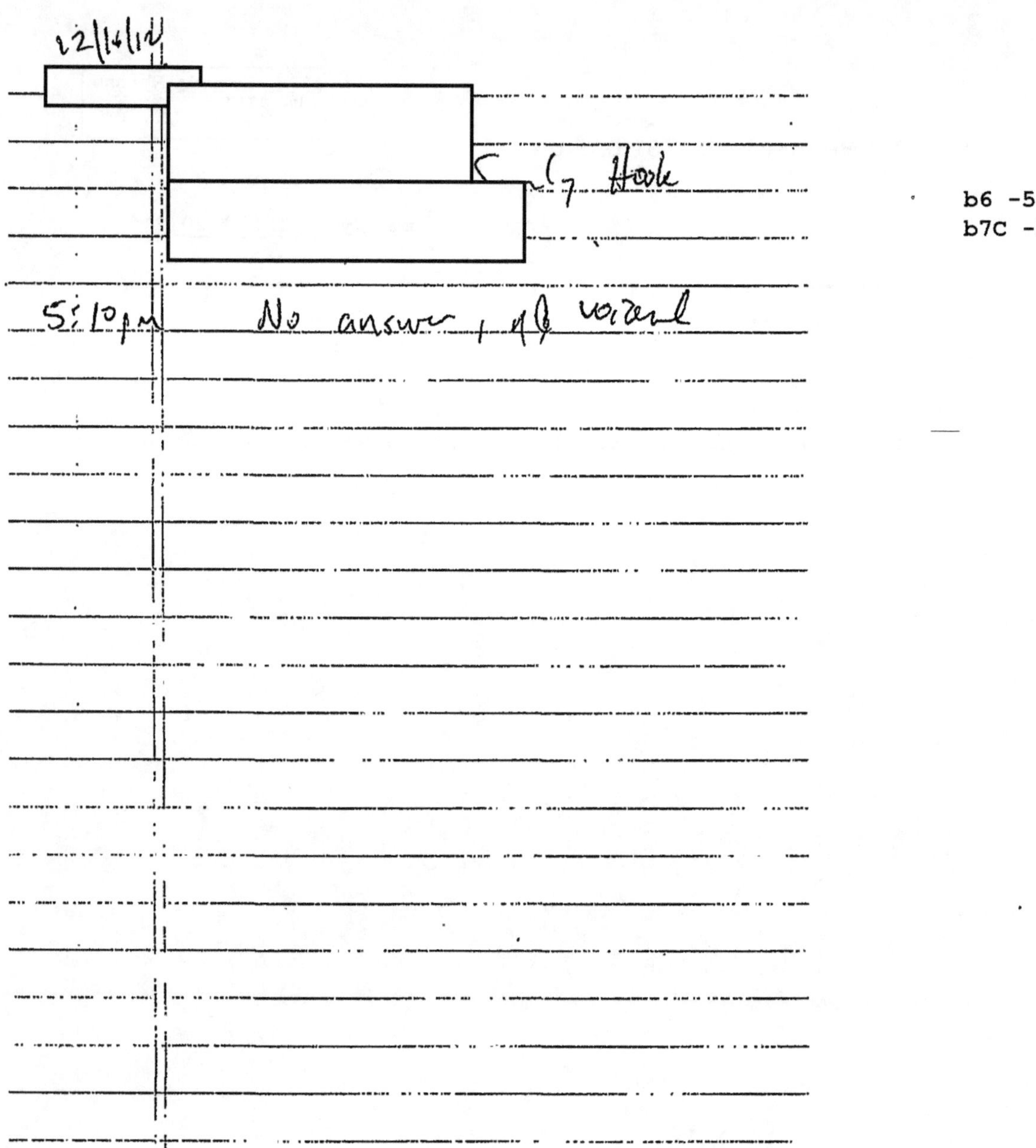

b6 -5
b7C -5

FD-302 (Rev. 5-8-10)

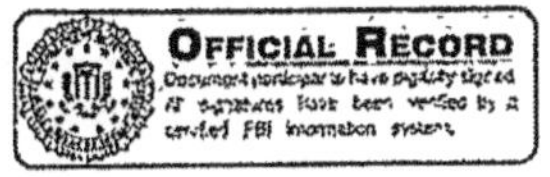

FEDERAL BUREAU OF INVESTIGATION

Date of entry 12/17/2012

[redacted] date of birth (DOB) [redacted] residence address [redacted] [redacted] was interviewed in the driveway of his residence. After being advised of the identities of the interviewing Agents and the nature of the interview, [redacted] provided the following information: b6 -6 b7C -6

[redacted] advised that he did not know the LANZA family. He never heard other neighbors speak about the LANZA family. [redacted] did not observe any suspicious activity in his neighborhood over the past few weeks. The neighborhood has always been very quiet. b6 -6 b7C -6

On the morning of December 14, 2012, [redacted] was at work [redacted] b6 -5, 6 b7C -5, 6

[redacted] advised [redacted] b6 -6, 7 b7C -6, 7

[redacted] advised that he would be willing to cooperate further as it was deemed necessary. b6 -6 b7C -6

Investigation on 12/14/2012 at Sandy Hook, Connecticut, United States (In Person)

File # 4-NH-2619946 Date drafted 12/17/2012

by [redacted] b6 -1 b7C -1

4-NH-2619946 Serial 37

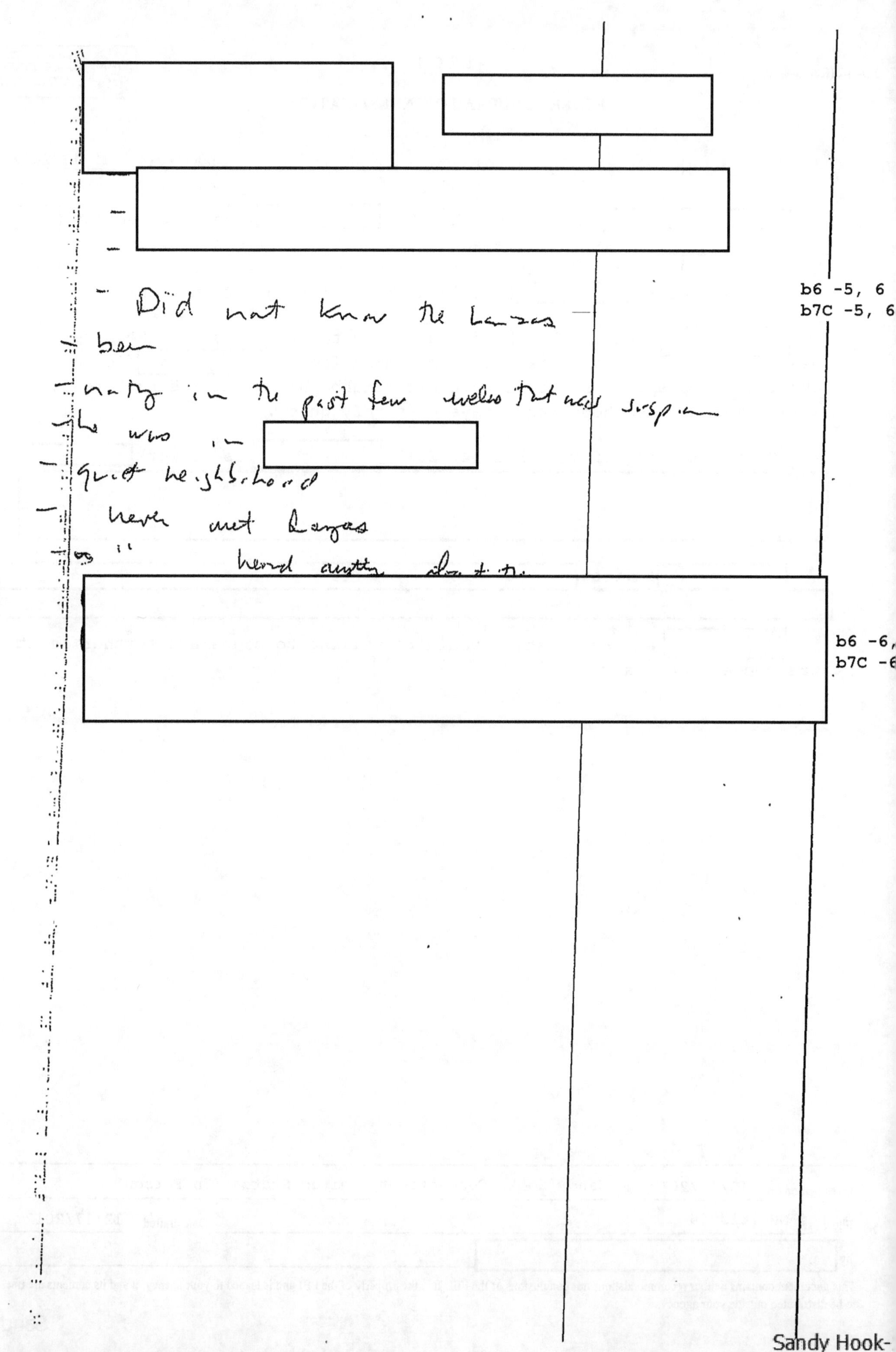

Did not know the Lanzas
been
nothing in the past few weeks that was suspicious
he was in
Quiet neighborhood
never met Lanzas
heard anything about it

b6 -5, 6
b7C -5, 6

b6 -6,
b7C -6

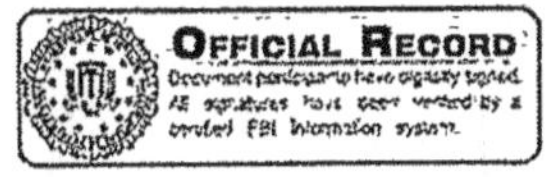

FEDERAL BUREAU OF INVESTIGATION

Date of entry 12/17/2012

[redacted] date of birth (DOB) [redacted] residence address [redacted] [redacted] Newtown, Connecticut, was interviewed at her residence. After being advised of the identities of the interviewing Agents and the nature of the interview [redacted] provided the following information: b6 -7 b7C -7

On December 16, 2012, an unidentified male left a voice message on [redacted] answering machine at approximately 9:00am. The voicemail stated, "this is ADAM LANZA, I'm going to kill you. hahaha." [redacted] accidentally erased the voicemail message. [redacted] did not receive any other threatening phone calls on December 16th. b6 -7 b7C -7

[redacted] advised [redacted] b6 -7 b7C -7

[redacted] b6 -7 b7C -7

[redacted] advised that she would be willing to cooperate further as it was deemed necessary. b6 -7 b7C -7

Investigation on 12/16/2012 at Newtown, Connecticut, United States (In Person)

File # 4-NH-2619946 Date drafted 12/17/2012

by [redacted] b6 -1 b7C -1

4-NH-2619946 Serial 38

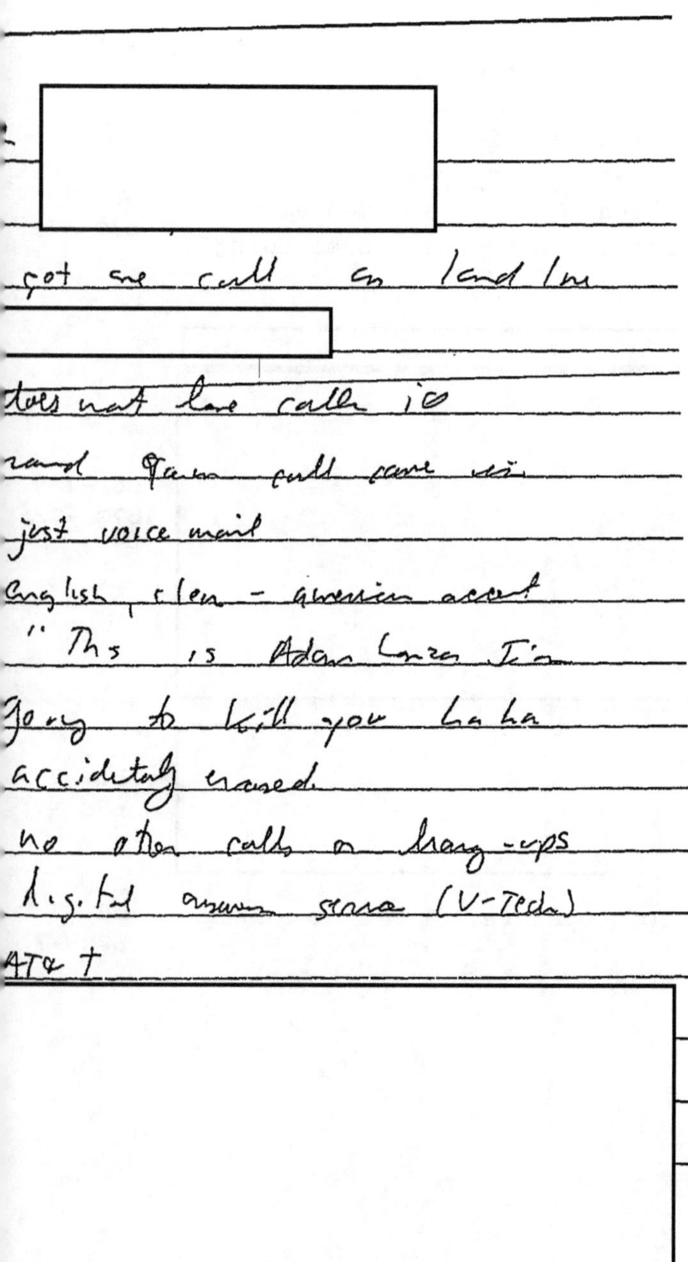

got one call on land line

does not have caller ID

around 9am call came in

just voice mail

English, clear - american accent

" This is Adam Lanza I'm

going to kill you haha

accidentally erased.

no other calls or hang-ups

digital answering system (V-Tech)

AT&T

b6 -7
b7C -7

b6 -7
b7C -7

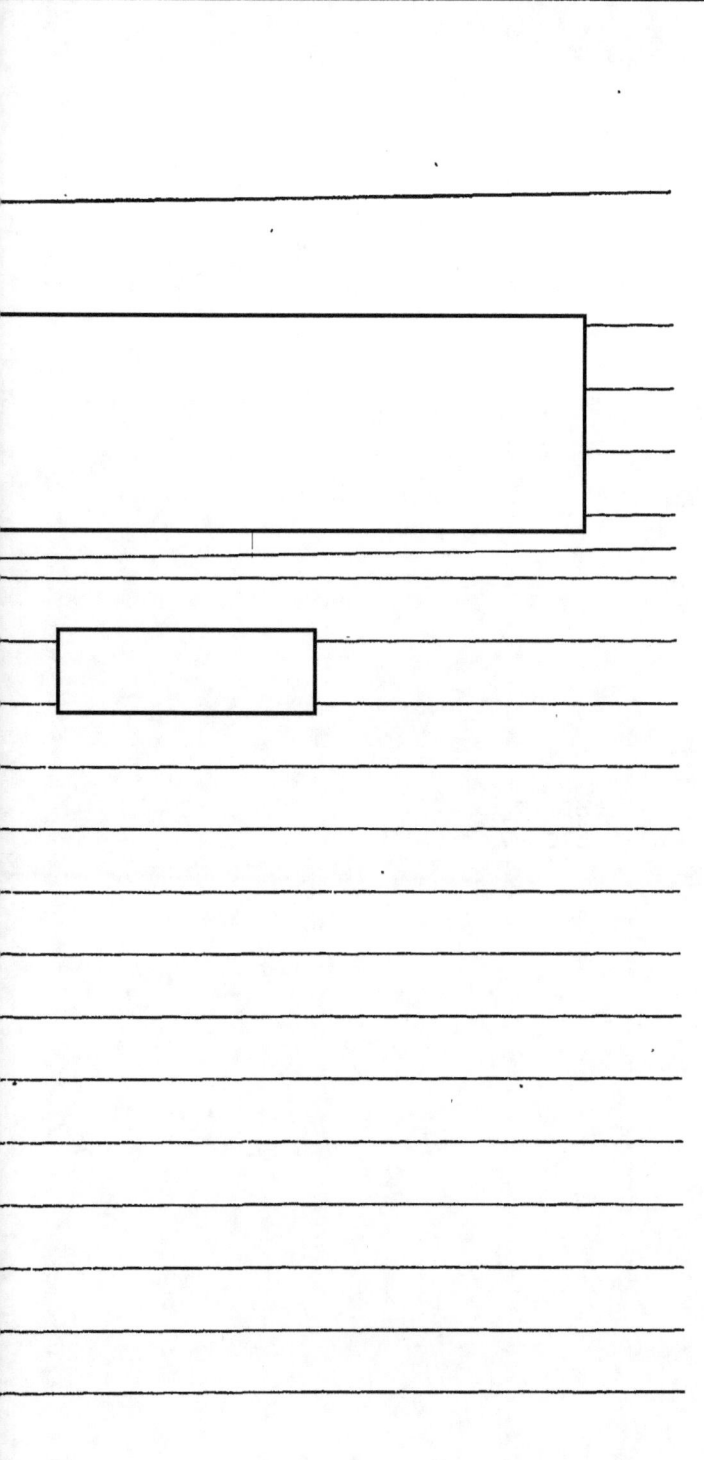

b6 -7
b7C -7

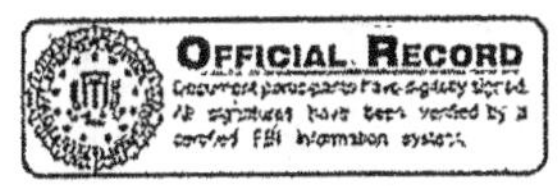

FEDERAL BUREAU OF INVESTIGATION

Date of entry 12/17/2012

[redacted] date of birth [redacted] residence address [redacted] [redacted] Newtown, Connecticut, home telephone number [redacted] was interviewed at his residence. Also present during the interview were [redacted] children, [redacted] date of birth [redacted] and [redacted] date of birth [redacted] After being advised of the identities of the interviewing Agents and the nature of the interview, the [redacted] family provided the following information: b6 -7 b7C -7

The [redacted] family received a threatening telephone call between 9:00am and 10:00am on December 16, 2012. [redacted] a friend of [redacted] answered the telephone. The caller identified himself as ADAM LANZA and said "I'm going to kill you." b6 -7 b7C -7

The [redacted] family received additional telephone calls on their residence land line. The unidentified male left two threatening voice messages. Administrative note: [redacted] consented to the Agents recording the voice messages left by the unidentified caller. SA [redacted] recorded the voice messages with his Federal Bureau of Investigation (FBI) issued Blackberry. The recording will be preserved and maintained in the case file. b6 -1, 7 b7C -1, 7

[redacted] answered the telephone twice and spoke to the unidentified caller. The caller threatened to kill [redacted] family. [redacted] asked the caller some questions and the caller was responsive. b6 -7 b7C -7

The [redacted] family received more than five threatening telephone calls on December 16, 2012. The caller spoke English. Each time, the caller identified himself as ADAM LANZA. b6 -7 b7C -7

[redacted] advised that he would be willing to cooperate further as it was deemed necessary. b6 -7 b7C -7

Investigation on 12/16/2012 at Newtown, Connecticut, United States (In Person)

File # 4-NH-2619946 Date drafted 12/17/2012

by [redacted] b6 -1 b7C -1

4-NH-2619946 Serial 39

b6 -7
b7C -

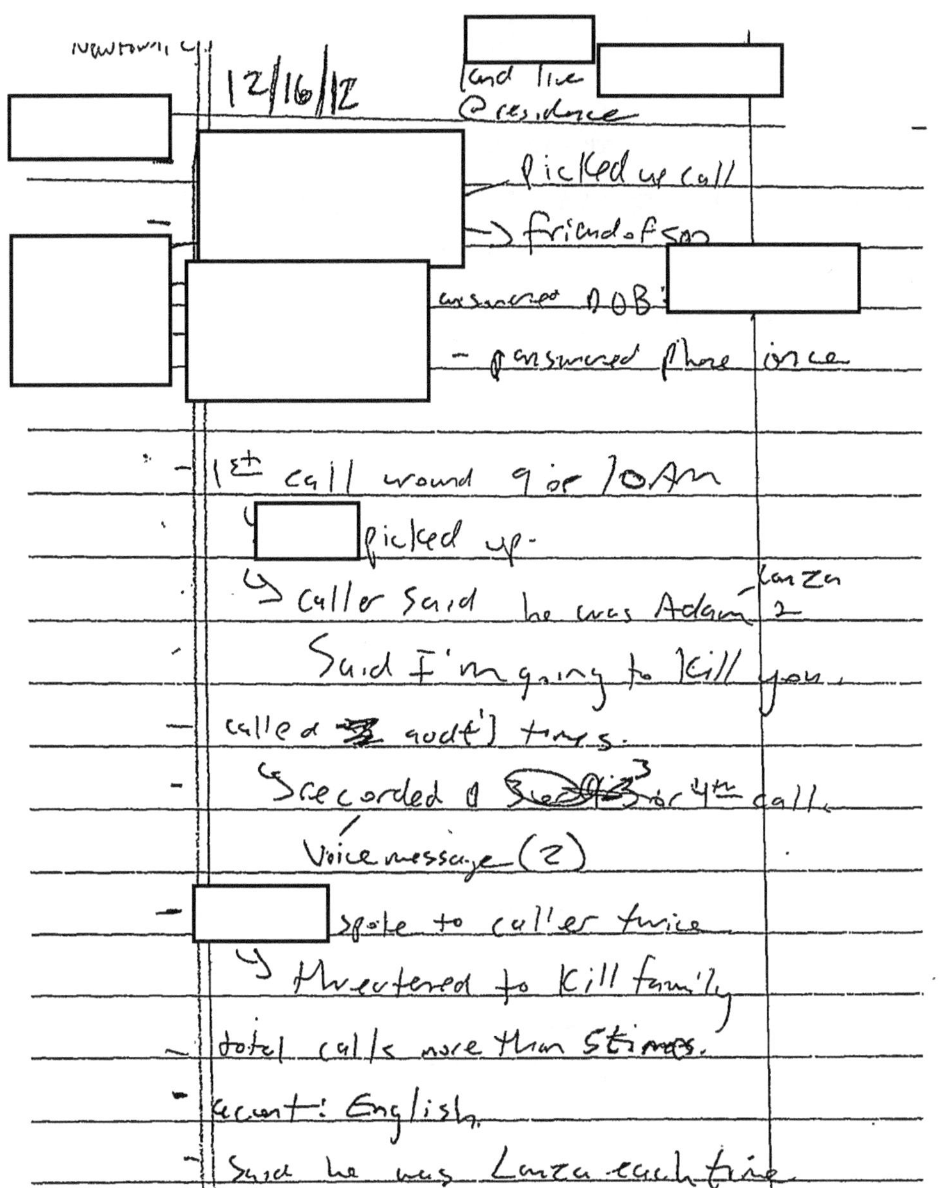
Newtown, CT
12/16/12
land line
@residence
picked up call
friend of son
answered DOB:
- answered phone once
- 1st call around 9 or 10AM
picked up.
caller said he was Adam Lanza 2
Said I'm going to kill you.
- called 3 add'l times.
- recorded 3 or 4th call
Voice message (2)
- spoke to caller twice
threatened to kill family
- total calls more than 5 times.
- accent: English.
- Said he was Lanza each time
- Consented to taking voice message -

b6 -7
b7C -7

FD-1057 (Rev. 5-8-10)

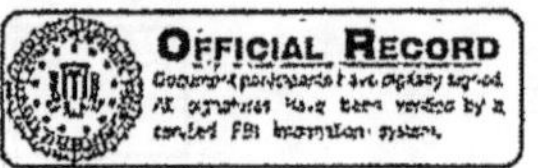

UNCLASSIFIED

FEDERAL BUREAU OF INVESTIGATION

Electronic Communication

Title: (U) Request to interview [redacted] **Date:** 12/18/2012

To: [redacted]

From: NEW HAVEN
NH-7
Contact: [redacted]

b6 -1,
b7C -1,

Approved By: [redacted]

Drafted By: [redacted]

Case ID #: 4-NH-2619946 (U) UNSUB(S)
Sandy Hook Elementary School
12 Dickinsòn St, Sandy Hook, CT-Victim
Firearms Act.
OO:NH

Synopsis: (U) Lead to interview [redacted] for the Newtown, CT school system.

b6 -6
b7C -

[redacted]

b7E -

Details:

At 9:40 AM on 14 December 2012, initial call-in to Newtown emergency services (911) was received from Sandy Hook Elementary School in Newtown, Connecticut, that shots had been fired within the school. The gunman, Adam P. Lanza, (DOB:04/22/1992) shot out the windows at the front of the elementary school in order to gain access. Two law enforcement officers arrived during the shooting, at which time the suspect ducked into a classroom and shot himself. The shooter attended the school as a child, but no other relationship between Adam P. Lanza and Sandy Hook Elementary School has been established. There were a total of 28 dead, 20 children and 8 adults (seven at the school, including the gunman, and his mother at their 36 Yogananda Street residence).

UNCLASSIFIED

4-NH-2619946 Serial 40

Title: (U) Request to interview [redacted] b6 -6 b7C -6

Re: 4-NH-2619946, 12/18/2012

In connection with the investigation into the attack on the Sandy Hook Elementary School on 12/14/2012, Connecticut State Police is requesting FBI assistance in interviewing [redacted] former [redacted] [redacted] for the Newtown, CT school system. [redacted] has been interviewed by numerous media outlets and claims extensive knowledge of the suspect, Adam Lanza. [redacted] b6 -6 b7C -6

[redacted] b6 -6 b7C -6 b7E -3

♦♦

FD-302 (Rev. 5-8-10)

FEDERAL BUREAU OF INVESTIGATION

Date of entry 12/18/2012

On December 17, 2012, [redacted] was contacted at his place of employment, [redacted] After being advised of the identity of the Agent, [redacted] was served with Federal Grand Jury subpoena number [redacted] issued by the United States District Court for the District of CT.

b3 -1
b6 -5
b7C -

Investigation on 12/18/2012 at New London, Connecticut, United States (, Other (Subpoena Service))

File # 4-NH-2619946 Date drafted 12/18/2012

by [redacted]

b6 -1
b7C -

This document contains neither recommendations nor conclusions of the FBI. It is the property of the FBI and is loaned to your agency; it and its contents are not to be distributed outside your agency.

AO 110 (Rev. 06/09) Subpoena to Testify Before a Grand Jury

UNITED STATES DISTRICT COURT

for the

District of Connecticut

SUBPOENA TO TESTIFY BEFORE A GRAND JURY

To: b3 -1

YOU ARE COMMANDED to appear in this United States district court at the time, date, and place shown below to testify before the court's grand jury. When you arrive, you must remain at the court until the judge or a court officer allows you to leave.

Place: United States Courthouse 141 Church Street New Haven, CT 06510	Date and Time:

You must also bring with you the following documents, electronically stored information, or objects *(blank if not applicable)*:

b3 -1

Date: ______________ CLERK OF COURT

December 15, 2012

Signature of Clerk or Deputy Clerk

The name, address, e-mail, and telephone number of the United States attorney, or assistant United States attorney, who requests this subpoena, are:

AUSA
1000 Lafayette Blvd, 10th Floor
Bridgeport, CT 06604

Personal appearance is not required if documents are provided on or before the appearance date to: FBI S/A
600 State St.
New Haven CT 06510

b6 -1, 4
b7C -1, 4

PROOF OF SERVICE

This subpoena for *(name of individual or organization)*

was received by me on *(date)* 12/15/12

✓ I served the subpoena by delivering a copy to the named person as follows:

on *(date)* 12/17/12 ; or

O I returned the subpoena unexecuted because:

I declare under penalty of perjury that this information is true.

Date: 12/17/12

Special Agent
Printed name and title

2 Union Plaza, Ste. 301, New London, CT 06320
Server's address

b3
b6
b7

b6
b7

Additional information regarding attempted service, etc:

FD-302 (Rev. 5-8-10)

FEDERAL BUREAU OF INVESTIGATION

Date of entry 12/18/2012

On December 17, 2012, Special Agent (SA) [redacted] served [redacted], [redacted] Federal Grand Jury subpoena number [redacted] issued by the United States District Court for the District of Connecticut, via FedEx.

b3 -1
b6 -1
b7C -1

Investigation on 12/18/2012 at New London, Connecticut, United States (, Other (Subpoena Service))

File # 4-NH-2619946 Date drafted 12/18/2012

by [redacted]

b6 -1
b7C -1

4-NH-2619946 Serial 42

UNITED STATES DISTRICT COURT

for the

District of Connecticut

SUBPOENA TO TESTIFY BEFORE A GRAND JURY

To:

b3 -

to appear in this United States district court at the time, date, and place shown below to testify before the court's grand jury. When you arrive, you must remain at the court until the judge or a court officer allows you to leave.

Place: United States Courthouse 141 Church Street New Haven, CT 06510	Date and Time:

You must also bring with you the following documents, electronically stored information, or objects *(blank if not applicable)*:

b3

Date: December 15, 2012

CLERK OF COURT

Signature of Clerk or Deputy Clerk

The name, address, e-mail, and telephone number of the United States attorney, or assistant United States attorney, who requests this subpoena, are:

AUSA
157 Church St., 23rd floor
New Haven, CT 06510

Personal appearance is not required if documents are provided on or before the appearance date to: FBI S/A
600 State St.
New Haven CT 06510

b3 -1
b6 -1, 4
b7C -1,

PROOF OF SERVICE

This subpoena for *(name of individual or organization)* ______
was received by me on *(date)* 12/15/12 .

☑ I served the subpoena by delivering a copy to the named person as follows: ______
______ via Fed Ex
on *(date)* 12/17/12 ; or

☐ I returned the subpoena unexecuted because: ______

b3

I declare under penalty of perjury that this information is true.

Date: 12/17/12

b6 -1
b7C -1

______ Special Agent
Printed name and title

2 Union Plaza, Ste. 301, New London CT 06320
Server's address

Additional information regarding attempted service, etc:

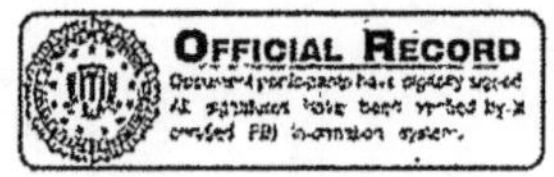

FEDERAL BUREAU OF INVESTIGATION

Date of entry 12/18/2012

On December 17, 2012, Special Agent (SA) [redacted] served [redacted] Federal Grand Jury subpoena number [redacted] issued by the United States District Court for the District of Connecticut, via FedEx.

b3 -
b6 -
b7C

Investigation on 12/18/2012 at New London, Connecticut, United States (, Other (Subpoena Service))

File # 4-NH-2619946 Date drafted 12/18/2012

by [redacted]

b6 -
b7C

AO 110 (Rev. 06/09) Subpoena to Testify Before a Grand Jury

UNITED STATES DISTRICT COURT

for the

District of Connecticut

SUBPOENA TO TESTIFY BEFORE A GRAND JURY

To:

b3 -1

YOU ARE COMMANDED to appear in this United States district court at the time, date, and place shown below to testify before the court's grand jury. When you arrive, you must remain at the court until the judge or a court officer allows you to leave.

Place: United States Courthouse 141 Church Street New Haven, CT 06510	Date and Time:

You must also bring with you the following documents, electronically stored information, or objects *(blank if not applicable)*:

b3 -1

Date: December 15, 2012

CLERK OF COURT

Signature of Clerk or Deputy Clerk

The name, address, e-mail, and telephone number of the United States attorney, or assistant United States attorney, who requests this subpoena, are:

AUSA
157 Church St., 23rd floor
New Haven, CT 06510

Personal appearance is not required if documents are provided on or before the appearance date to: FBI S/A
600 State St.
New Haven CT 06510

b3 -1
b6 -1, 4
b7C -1, 4

PROOF OF SERVICE

This subpoena for *(name of individual or organization)* [redacted]

was received by me on *(date)* 12/15/12.

☑ I served the subpoena by delivering a copy to the named person as follows: [redacted]

[redacted] via Fed Ex

on *(date)* 12/17/12 ; or

☐ I returned the subpoena unexecuted because:

I declare under penalty of perjury that this information is true.

Date: 12/17/12

[redacted]

[redacted] Special Agent

Printed name and title

2 Union Plaza, Ste. 301, New London, CT 06320

Server's address

Additional information regarding attempted service, etc:

FD-302 (Rev. 5-8-10)

FEDERAL BUREAU OF INVESTIGATION

Date of entry 12/18/2012

[redacted] (PROTECT IDENTIY), [redacted] [redacted] telephone number [redacted] contacted the Newtown Command Post anonymously with information. A search of data bases revealed the above information being connected to the telephone number on which the anonymous call was made. Writer then telephonically contacted [redacted] After being advised of the identity of the interviewing Agent and the nature of the interview, [redacted] provided the following information: b6 -6 b7C -6 b7D -1

[redacted] confirmed his identity and address and provided his date of birth as [redacted] b6 -6 b7C -6 b7D -1

[redacted]

[redacted] b6 -5, 6 b7C -5, 6 b7D -1

[redacted] b6 -5, 6 b7C -5, 6 b7D -1

Investigation on 12/16/2012 at Newtown, Connecticut, United States (Phone)

File # 4-NH-2619946 Date drafted 12/18/2012

by [redacted] b6 -1 b7C -1

4-NH-2619946 Serial 44

b6 -
b7C
b7D

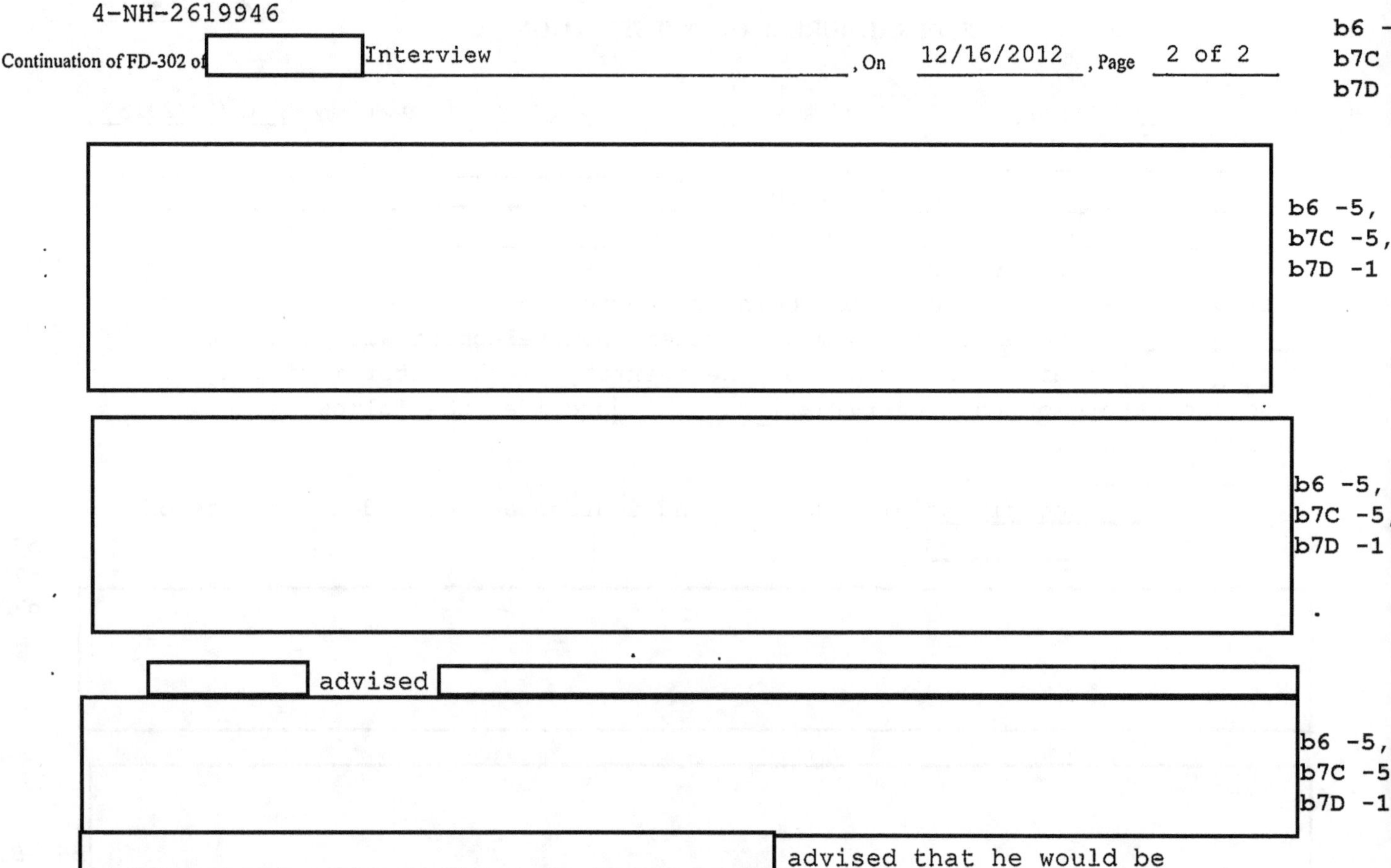

b6 -5,
b7C -5,
b7D -1

b6 -5,
b7C -5,
b7D -1

[redacted] advised [redacted]

b6 -5,
b7C -5
b7D -1

[redacted] advised that he would be willing to cooperate further as it was deemed necessary.

FD-1057 (Rev. 5-8-10)

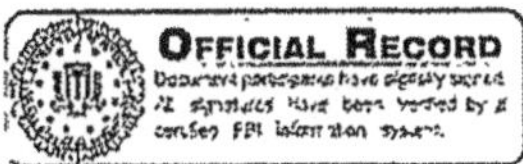

UNCLASSIFIED

FEDERAL BUREAU OF INVESTIGATION

Electronic Communication

Title: (U) [redacted] **Date:** 12/18/2012

From: NEW HAVEN
NH-3
Contact: [redacted] b6 -1, 2 b7C -1, 2

Approved By: [redacted]

Drafted By: [redacted]

Case ID #: 4-NH-2619946 (U) UNSUB(S)
Sandy Hook Elementary School
12 Dickinson St, Sandy Hook, CT-Victim
Firearms Act.
OO:NH

Synopsis: (U) To document Amtrak train ticket information related to [redacted] in the case file.

[redacted] b6 -2 b7C -2 b7E -1

Enclosure(s): Enclosed are the following items:
1. (U) Amtrak Tickets for [redacted]

Details:

On 12/17/2012, [redacted] Amtrak Police Department, Rail Security Team, NJTTF, telephone [redacted] advised that [redacted] b6 -2, 4 b7C -2, 4

♦♦

UNCLASSIFIED

Sandy Hook-202

4-NH-2619946 Serial 45

FD-302 (Rev. 5-8-10)

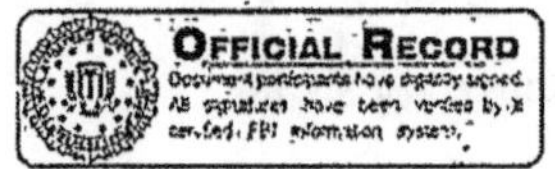

FEDERAL BUREAU OF INVESTIGATION

Date of entry 12/17/2012

The following are the results of a neighborhood canvass conducted in conjunction with captioned investigation. The canvass occurred on December 14, 2012. The addresses covered in this summary of the canvass were homes number [REDACTED] and [REDACTED] Newtown, Connecticut: b6 -5, b7C -5,

[REDACTED]: [REDACTED] date of birth [REDACTED] and [REDACTED] date of birth [REDACTED] would not know any of the residents at 36 Yogananda Street even if they saw pictures of them. The [REDACTED] have lived in their home since [REDACTED]. They did not see or hear anything unusual in their neighborhood for the past several days, including today. b6 -6 b7C -

[REDACTED] frequently walks the neighborhood and has noticed that the residents of 36 Yogananda Street always have many empty bottles of bottled water out on the street in their recycling when it is collected each week. She never saw anyone outside house number thirty-six on her walks. b6 - b7C -

The telephone number for the [REDACTED] home is [REDACTED] b6 - b7C

[REDACTED]: There was no response to Agents knocking on the door and ringing the doorbell of this address. It appeared that there was no one home. b6 - b7C -

Investigation on 12/14/2012 at Newtown, Connecticut, United States (In Person)

File # 4-NH-2619946 Date drafted 12/18/2012

by [REDACTED] b6 b7C

4-NH-2619946 Serial 46

FD-302 (Rev. 5-8-10)

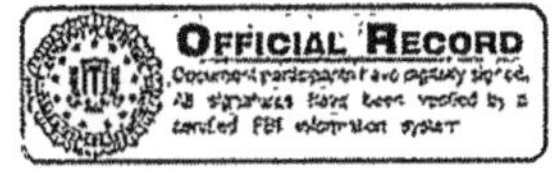

FEDERAL BUREAU OF INVESTIGATION

Date of entry 12/17/2012

male, date of birth was interviewed at his residence, located at Sandy Hook, Connecticut, by the undersigned agents. Also interviewed was female, date of birth Their home telephone number is and cellular telephone number is After being advised of the identities of the interviewing Agents and the nature of the interview, and provided the following information: b6 -6 b7C -6

and have lived in this house for approximately years. b6 -6 b7C -6

Neither nor knew NANCY LANZA (NANCY) very well. NANCY never made an effort to introduce herself to and and had heard that the couple living at 36 Yogananda Street were getting a divorce. They did not know NANCY's former husband well, either. b6 -6 b7C -6

and weren't even sure of NANCY's last name until they heard it mentioned on news reports earlier today. They thought that NANCY had one son, but learned through the news reports that she had another son living in another State. and were unaware of the violence that had been inflicted upon NANCY until they heard about it on the news. b6 -6 b7C -6

At approximately 10:00 a.m. today, while was at work, the Newtown Police Department told she had to evacuate her residence immediately. did as she was instructed by the police, and only returned to her home in the early evening. date of birth residing at was with when this happened, but has since returned to his residence. Neither nor thought that would know any more about the LANZA family than they did. b6 -5, 6 b7C -5, 6

Investigation on 12/14/2012 at Sandy Hook, Connecticut, United States (In Person)

File # 4-NH-2619946 Date drafted 12/17/2012

by b6 -1 b7C -1

4-NH-2619946 Serial 47

FD-302 (Rev. 5-8-10)

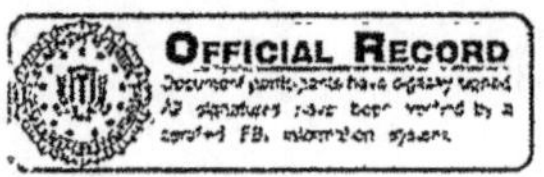

FEDERAL BUREAU OF INVESTIGATION

Date of entry 12/17/2012

[redacted] date of birth (DOB) [redacted] residence address [redacted] telephone number [redacted] was interviewed telephonically. After being advised of the identity of the interviewing Agent and the nature of the interview, [redacted] provided the following information: b6 -6 b7C -6

[redacted] advised that [redacted] stated on his Facebook page that ADAM LANZA and [redacted] were his heroes. [redacted] thought that [redacted] was friends with the LANZA brothers on Facebook. [redacted] also observed a Facebook conversation between [redacted] and another individual on Facebook. In the conversation [redacted] told the individual that he was moving to Canada and that if everything would have worked out, they would have made a lot of money. [redacted] was not certain if those statements were related to the LANZA brothers. [redacted] eventually removed those comments from his Facebook wall. [redacted] also had a picture of [redacted] on his Facebook page. [redacted] thought that [redacted] lived in Connecticut at one time, but she was not certain. [redacted] has never met [redacted] in person, but she believed that he currently resided in Indiana. b6 -5, b7C -5,

[redacted] advised that she would be willing to cooperate further as it was deemed necessary. b6 -6 b7C -6

Investigation on 12/15/2012 at Bridgeport, Connecticut, United States (In Person)

File # 4-NH-2619946 Date drafted 12/17/2012

by [redacted] b6 b7C

4-NH-2619946 Serial 48

12/15/12
Telephone

FB - Concerns

states that Lanza's are heroes

Also thought that Lanza's were friends w/

FB conversation b/t & friend → "More to Canada, if everything worked out, they would have ~~gotten paid~~ made a lot of $. → Lanzas?

removed those comments from FB wall

Thought that lived in CT @ some time

never met in person, but believes live in Indiana

b6 -5, 6
b7C -5, 6

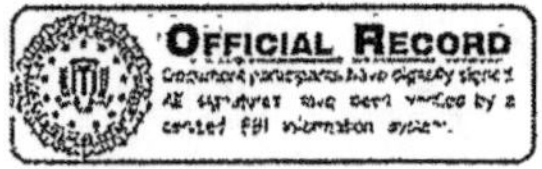

FEDERAL BUREAU OF INVESTIGATION

Date of entry 12/18/2012

[redacted] date of birth (DOB) [redacted] SSN: [redacted] Cell: [redacted] was interviewed at [redacted] After being advised of the identity of the interviewing Agent and the nature of the interview, [redacted] provided the following information: b6 b7C

[redacted] b6 -5, b7C -5

[redacted] went to the Worcester rifle range to shoot Adam's two rifles. [redacted]

[redacted] Adam's schooling which began at Sandy Hook Elementary School for grades K-4th. Adam then moved onto Newtown Middle School for grades 5th-7th. Around 7th grade Adam moved to St. Mary's Catholic School. Once completing middle school Adam moved onto Newtown High School where he completed 9th grade and then Nancy [redacted] thought it was best to remove Adam from school and home school him through graduation. Around Adam's 6th grade he was diagnosed with Asperger's and a great deal of school and societal stresses started to present and was the reason why he moved to St. Mary's Catholic School. [redacted] Adam was bullied, but not excessively, for his social awkwardness and his physical gate, both results of his disease. Adam continued in school until his 9th grade year when stresses over papers, classes, pressure from grades and b6 - b7C

Investigation on 12/14/2012 at [redacted] United States (In Person) b6 -1, b7C -1

File # 4-NH-2619946 Date drafted 12/18/2012

by [redacted]

b6 -6
b7C -6

dealing with his disease he finally was removed from school. Adam never completely accepted that he had a disease and therefore never took any of his medication he was prescribed. [redacted] Adam was in complete denial of his disease from diagnosis and therefore was not on disability because of this denial.

b6 -6
b7C -6

[redacted] Adam was a member of the tech club, but never was able to maintain any of the relationship he established there. [redacted] Adam [redacted] never had got in trouble in school or with the police [redacted] nor [redacted] demonstrate any violent tendencies as far as [redacted] knew when it came to harming animals, or getting into fights. [redacted]

b6 -5, 6
b7C -5, 6

November 2012 Nancy [redacted] to chip in for buying Adam a computer or parts for a computer for Adam to build himself. [redacted] summarizes the reason why Nancy wanted to do this as Adam has become a shut in and he hasn't gone anywhere in 3 months, his battery in his car is dead because it's been sitting there so long. [redacted] could tell that Nancy was worried about Adam.

b6 -6
b7C -6

Adam's hobbies would vary over the course of time since he would find one interest and then not care about it every few months. Some of Adam's hobbies included building computers, online gaming, and writing, poetry, hiking, and shooting. Some of the walks [redacted] Adam would take would be around Sandy Hook Elementary School [redacted] Adam [redacted] loved this school and liked to visit. [redacted] took Adam to the range once or twice [redacted] only knew of Adam having two rifles, one black single barrel shotgun and one black large caliber rifle. [redacted] never knew that Adam owned any pistols or any other rifles, but does remember Nancy taking Adam to pistol safety courses so he could fire a pistol at the local range. [redacted] did not know how or why Adam became involved in firearms as a hobby.

b6 -6
b7C -6

[redacted] never knew Adam to have any interest in social media such as Facebook, Myspace, forums, or anything of the same. [redacted] gave the one email address he knew of Adam's as blarvink@gmail.com. [redacted] also stated that this blarvink user name was what Adam used on all of his online gaming community account. [redacted] believed Adam played mostly fantasy role playing games, but couldn't remember any of their names.

b6 -6
b7C -6

Adam had a cell phone but would never use it. [redacted] would attempt to call him on it, but it would only go to voice mail so he would mainly just email Adam when he would try to reach him. The number [redacted] had for Adam in

b6 -6
b7C -6

b6
b7C

his cell phone was 203-364-9879.

Nancy would take care of all of Adam's needs. She would shop for him, cook him food, do his laundry, and other household choirs. However, she never cleaned his room, nor was allowed in his room. Adam's room was his personal space that no one else was allowed into. [redacted] also mentioned that Adam would sometimes sleep on the floor, or sleep without pillows and some other strange behaviors [redacted] and Nancy just accepted as part of the disease [redacted] said Adam never appreciated what Nancy did for him.

b6
b7C

FD-302 (Rev. 5-8-10)

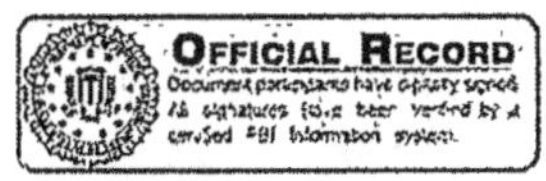

FEDERAL BUREAU OF INVESTIGATION

Date of entry 12/18/2012

[redacted] date of birth (DOB) [redacted] residing at [redacted] Cell [redacted] was interviewed at [redacted] on 12/14/2012. After being advised of the identity of the interviewing Agent and the nature of the interview, [redacted] provided the following information: b6 -6 b7C -6

On 12/14/2012 [redacted] left his residence for work, [redacted] at approximately 8:50am. [redacted] purchased coffee at a Dunkin Donuts at [redacted] with his Bank of America Credit Card and arrived at his office at approximately 9:45am. b6 -6 b7C -6

[redacted] b6 -5, 6 b7C -5, 6

Investigation on 12/14/2012 at [redacted] United States (In Person)

File # 4-NH-2619946 Date drafted 12/18/2012 b6 -1, 6 b7C -1, 6

by [redacted]

4-NH-2619946 Serial 50

b6
b7C

b6
b7C

b6 -5,
b7C -5

ADAM was diagnosed with Ashberger's Syndrome, a form of autism, in approximately the 8th grade. He left high school in either the 9th or 10th grade, and essentially became a "recluse", shutting himself in his bedroom, playing video games all day. He attended a few courses at Western Connecticut State University, but never attended full time.

b6
b7C

b6
b7C

stated that ADAM has no friends, no associates, no girlfriend, but is very "computer savvy", and spends most of his time on his computer. At some point ADAM worked briefly at a computer repair shop in Newtown, but never held any other job, including summer work while still in school.

ADAM became very interested in firearms, and at one point considered joining the military. ADAM enjoyed target shooting,

b6
b7C

ADAM and NANCY owned at least four guns; a black AR-15 semi-automatic

b6 -6
b7C -6

.223 rifle, a Lee Enfield .308 rifle, a "semi-automatic" shotgun and a .45cal pistol [redacted] believed all the weapons had been legally purchased by NANCY, and were registered in her name, but that ADAM actually owned the AR-15, and that all the weapons were kept in a gun safe in ADAM's bedroom closet.

b6 -6
b7C -6

[redacted] advised that ADAM had taken an NRA safety certification course that allowed him to fire the .45cal pistol at the Danbury range, and that to his knowledge ADAM was able to purchase all his ammunition legally.

b6 -6
b7C -6

[redacted] advised that ADAM and NANCY had a "close relationship", and as he had no outside friends, she became the only person ADAM would talk to. Although ADAM spent the majority of his time playing video games, they were non-violent games. His favorite was Super Mario Brothers. Although he often became frustrated at not being able to "express himself", ADAM never became violent. He never used drugs or alcohol, and actually "hated the thought of it". [redacted] could provide no explanation or motive for ADAM's actions.

b6 -6
b7C -6

[redacted]

b6 -6
b7C -6

FEDERAL BUREAU OF INVESTIGATION

Date of entry 12/17/2012

[redacted] date of birth (DOB) [redacted] residence address [redacted] Sandy Hook, Connecticut, was interviewed at his residence. Also present at the interview was [redacted] [redacted] DOB [redacted] After being advised of the identities of the interviewing Agents and the nature of the interview, [redacted] and [redacted] provided the following information: b6 -6 b7C -

[redacted] and [redacted] advised they did not know the residents who lived at 36 Yogananda Street, Sandy Hook, Connecticut. [redacted] and [redacted] moved to their current residence in [redacted] Since that time, they have not had any interactions with the family residing at 36 Yogananda Street. b6 - b7C -

[redacted] and [redacted] were not home on the morning of December 14, 2012. They did not notice any suspicious activity in their neighborhood within the past few weeks. b6 - b7C

[redacted] b6 -5 b7C -

[redacted] and [redacted] advised that they would be willing to cooperate further as it was deemed necessary. b6 - b7C

Investigation on 12/14/2012 at Sandy Hook, Connecticut, United States (In Person)

File # 4-NH-2619946 Date drafted 12/17/2012

by [redacted] b6 b7C

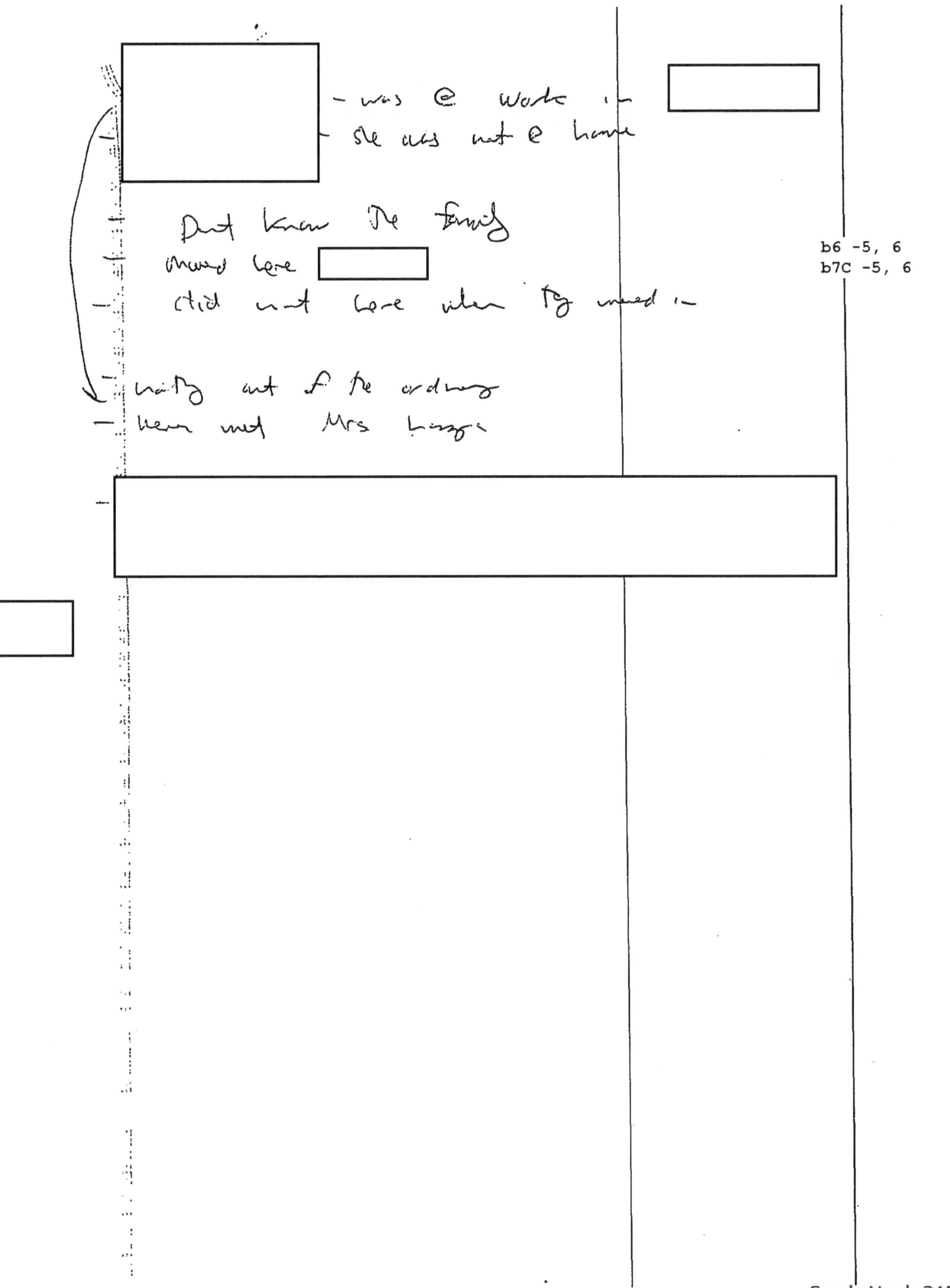

- was @ work in
- she was not @ home

Dont know the family
moved here
did not here when they moved in

- mainly out of the ordinary
- never met Mrs Lanza

b6 -5, 6
b7C -5, 6

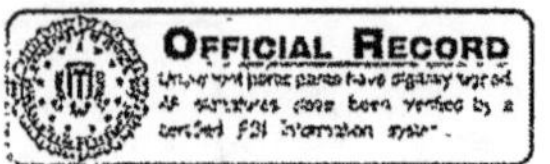

FEDERAL BUREAU OF INVESTIGATION

Electronic Communication

Title: (U) [redacted] Information **Date:** 12/17/2012

From: NEW HAVEN
NH-3
Contact: [redacted]

b6 -1, 2
b7C -1,

Approved By: [redacted]

Drafted By: [redacted]

Case ID #: 4-NH-2619946 (U) UNSUB(S)
Sandy Hook Elementary School
12 Dickinson St, Sandy Hook, CT-Victim
Firearms Act.
OO:NH

Synopsis: (U) To document [redacted] information in case file.

b6 -2
b7C -2
b7E -1

Details:

On 12/14/2012, [redacted] telephone number [redacted] advised [redacted]

b6 -
b7C

♦♦

4-NH-2619946 Serial 52

UNCLASSIFIED

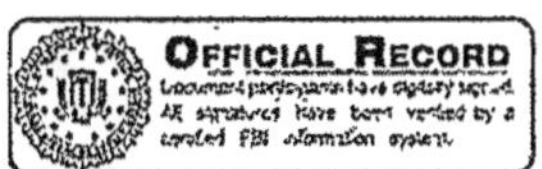

FEDERAL BUREAU OF INVESTIGATION

Electronic Communication

Title: (U) [redacted] Information **Date:** 12/17/2012

From: NEW HAVEN
NH-3
Contact: [redacted]

b6 -1, 2
b7C -1, 2

Approved By: [redacted]

Drafted By: [redacted]

Case ID #: 4-NH-2619946 (U) UNSUB(S)
Sandy Hook Elementary School
12 Dickinson St, Sandy Hook, CT-Victim
Firearms Act.
OO:NH

Synopsis: (U) To document [redacted] information in the case file.

b6 -2
b7C -2

[redacted]

b7E -1

Details:

On 12/14/2012, writer met with [redacted] provided the below listed [redacted] information [redacted]

b6 -2, 6
b7C -2, 6

[redacted]

b6 -2
b7C -2

UNCLASSIFIED

4-NH-2619946 Serial 53

Title: (U) [redacted] Information b6 -2 b7C -2
Re: 4-NH-2619946, 12/17/2012

[redacted] b6 -2 b7C -2

[redacted] advised that [redacted] records associated with [redacted] could be released with a subpoena requesting this information. b6 -2, b7C -2,

♦♦

FD-1057 (Rev. 5-8-10)

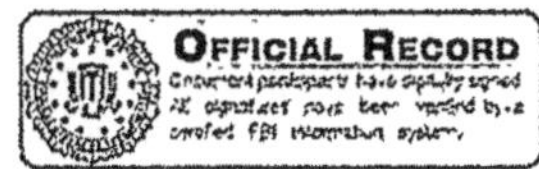

UNCLASSIFIED

FEDERAL BUREAU OF INVESTIGATION

Electronic Communication

Title: (U) Agency Checks **Date:** 12/17/2012

From: NEW HAVEN
NH-3
Contact: [redacted]

Approved By: [redacted] b6 -1 b7C -1

Drafted By: [redacted]

Case ID #: 4-NH-2619946 (U) UNSUB(S)
Sandy Hook Elementary School
12 Dickinson St, Sandy Hook, CT-Victim
Firearms Act.
OO:NH

Synopsis: (U) To document agency checks in case file.

[redacted] b7E -1

Details:

(U) NJTTF reports [redacted]

[redacted] b7E -3

UNCLASSIFIED

4-NH-2619946 Serial 54

Title: (U) Agency Checks
Re: 4-NH-2619946, 12/17/2012

b7E -3

Title: (U) Agency Checks
Re: 4-NH-2619946, 12/17/2012

b7E -3

♦♦

FD-1036 (Rev. 10-16-2009)

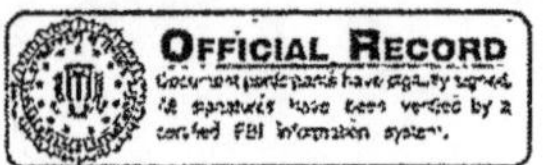

UNCLASSIFIED

FEDERAL BUREAU OF INVESTIGATION

Import Form

Form Type: OTHER **Date:** 12/17/2012

Title: (U) 12/15/12 Preservation letter to [redacted] b3 -1 b7E -6

Approved By: [redacted]

Drafted By: [redacted] b6 -1 b7C -1

Case ID #: 4-NH-2619946 (U) UNSUB(S)
Sandy Hook Elementary School
12 Dickinson St, Sandy Hook, CT-Victim
Firearms Act.
OO:NH

Synopsis: (U) 12/15/12 Preservation letter to [redacted]

[redacted] b3 -1 b6 -2 b7C -2 b7E -6

♦♦

UNCLASSIFIED

FAX TRANSMISSION

United States Attorney
Connecticut
157 Church St., 23rd floor
New Haven, Connecticut 06510

To ATTN:	[redacted]		b3 -1 b7E -6
Fax	[redacted]		
From	[redacted] Assistant United States Attorney	Voice [redacted]	b6 -4 b7C -4
Fax	[redacted]		
Date	December 15, 2012	Pages 3, including this page	
Subject	Preservation letter under 18 U.S.C. § 2703(f)		

U.S. Department of Justice

United States Attorney
Connecticut

157 Church St., 23rd floor
New Haven, Connecticut 06510

PHONE: 203.821.3796
FAX: 203.773.5373

December 15, 2012

b3 -
b7E

Re: Request for Preservation of Records

Dear

Pursuant to Title 18, United States Code, Section 2703(f), this letter is a formal request for the preservation of all stored communications, records, and other evidence in your possession regarding the following screen names pending further legal process:

b3 -1
b6 -2
b7C -2
b7E -6

I request that you not disclose the existence of this request to the subscriber or any other person, other than as necessary to comply with this request. If compliance with this request might result in a permanent or temporary termination of service to or otherwise alert any user of as to your actions to preserve the information described below, please contact me as soon as possible and before taking action.

b3 -1
b7E -

I request that you preserve, for a period of 90 days, the information described below currently in your possession in a form that includes the complete record. This request applies only retrospectively. It does not in any way obligate you to capture and preserve new information that arises after the date of this request. This request applies to the following items, whether in electronic or other form, including information stored on backup media, if available:

b3 -
b7E

b3 -1
b7E -6

If you have questions regarding this request, please call me at [redacted]

Sincerely,

David B. Fein
UNITED STATES ATTORNEY

[redacted]

b6 -4
b7C -4

Assistant United States Attorney

FD-1036 (Rev. 10-16-2009)

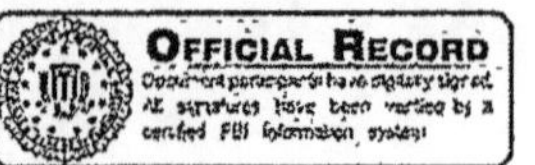

UNCLASSIFIED

FEDERAL BUREAU OF INVESTIGATION

Import Form

Form Type: OTHER **Date:** 12/17/2012

Title: (U) 12/15/12 Preservation letter to [redacted] b3 -1 b7E -6

Approved By: [redacted]

Drafted By: [redacted] b6 -1 b7C -1

Case ID #: 4-NH-2619946 (U) UNSUB(S)
Sandy Hook Elementary School
12 Dickinson St, Sandy Hook, CT-Victim
Firearms Act.
OO:NH

Synopsis: (U) 12/15/12 Preservation letter to [redacted]

[redacted] b3 -1 b6 -2 b7C -2 b7E -6

♦♦

UNCLASSIFIED

4-NH-2619946 Serial 56

U.S. Department of Justice

United States Attorney
District of Connecticut

1000 Lafayette Boulevard, 10th Floor
Bridgeport, Connecticut 06604

(203) 696-3000
Fax (203) 579-5550

December 15, 2012

VIA FACSIMILE

b3 -1
b7E -6

Re: Preservation Letter

Dear Sir or Madam:

You are hereby requested to preserve, under the provisions of Title 18, United States Code, Section 2703(f)(1), all communications, records, and other evidence in your possession including records stored on backup media, associated with

b3 -1
b6 -2
b7C -2
b7E -6

You are requested not to disclose the existence of this request or its contents to the subscribers or to any other person; other than as necessary to comply with this request. If compliance with this request might result in a permanent or temporary termination of service or otherwise might alert any user of as to your actions to preserve the information described below, please contact me as soon as possible before taking action.

b3 -1
b7E -6

I request that you preserve, for a period of 90 days, the information described below currently in your possession in a form that includes the complete record. This request applies only retrospectively. It does not in any way obligate you to capture and preserve new information that arises after the date of this request. This request applies to the following items, whether in electronic or other form, including information stored on backup media if available:

b3 -
b7E

If you have questions regarding this request, please call me at [redacted] Thank you for your assistance in this matter.

Very truly yours,

DAVID B. FEIN
UNITED STATES ATTORNEY

b6 -4
b7C -4

ASSISTANT UNITED STATES ATTORNEY

FD-1036 (Rev. 10-16-2009)

UNCLASSIFIED

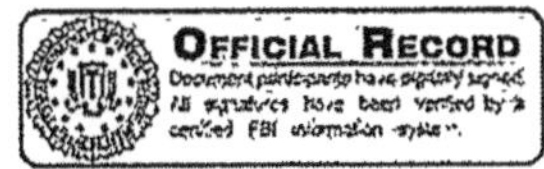

FEDERAL BUREAU OF INVESTIGATION

Import Form

Form Type: OTHER **Date:** 12/17/2012

Title: (U) 12/14/12 Preservation letter to [redacted]

Approved By: [redacted]

Drafted By: [redacted]

b3 -1
b6 -1
b7C -1
b7E -6

Case ID #: 4-NH-2619946 (U) UNSUB(S)
Sandy Hook Elementary School
12 Dickinson St, Sandy Hook, CT-Victim
Firearms Act.
OO:NH

Synopsis: (U) A 12/14/12 preservation letter to [redacted] prior to legal process: [redacted]

b3 -1
b7E -6

♦♦

UNCLASSIFIED

4-NH-2619946 Serial 57

FAX TRANSMISSION

United States Attorney
Connecticut
157 Church St., 23rd floor
New Haven, Connecticut 06510

To	[redacted]		
Fax	[redacted]		
From	[redacted] Assistant United States Attorney	**Voice**	[redacted]
Fax	[redacted]		
Date	December 14, 2012	**Pages**	3, including this page
Subject	Preservation letter under 18 U.S.C. § 2703(f)		

b3 -1
b7E -6

b6 -4
b7C -4

U.S. Department of Justice

United States Attorney
Connecticut

157 Church St., 23rd floor
New Haven, Connecticut 06510

PHONE: 203.821.3796
FAX: 203.773.5373

December 14, 2012

b3 -1
b7E -6

Re: Request for Preservation of Records

Dea

Pursuant to Title 18, United States Code, Section 2703(f), this letter is a formal request for the preservation of all stored communications, records, and other evidence in your possession regarding the following

I request that you not disclose the existence of this request to the subscriber or any other person, other than as necessary to comply with this request. If compliance with this request might result in a permanent or temporary termination of service to or otherwise alert any user of as to your actions to preserve the information described below, please contact me as soon as possible and before taking action. b3 -1 b7E -6

I request that you preserve, for a period of 90 days, the information described below currently in your possession in a form that includes the complete record. This request applies only retrospectively. It does not in any way obligate you to capture and preserve new information that arises after the date of this request. This request applies to the following items, whether in electronic or other form, including information stored on backup media, if available:

b3 -1
b7E -6

b3 -
b7E

If you have questions regarding this request, please call me a

Sincerely,

b6 -4
b7C -4

David B. Fein
UNITED STATES ATTORNEY

Assistant United States Attorney

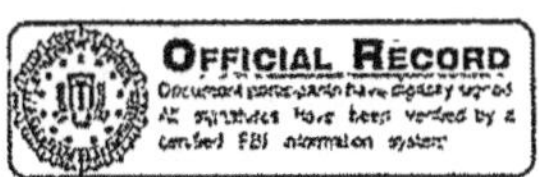

UNCLASSIFIED

FEDERAL BUREAU OF INVESTIGATION

Import Form

Form Type: OTHER

Date: 12/17/2012

Title: (U) Preservation Letter to [redacted]

Approved By: [redacted]

Drafted By: [redacted]

b3 -1
b6 -1
b7C -1
b7E -6

Case ID #: 4-NH-2619946

(U) UNSUB(S)
Sandy Hook Elementary School
12 Dickinson St, Sandy Hook, CT-Victim
Firearms Act.
OO:NH

Synopsis: (U) A letter issued 12/14/2012 requesting preservation of [redacted]

b3 -1
b7E -6

♦♦

UNCLASSIFIED

4-NH-2619946 Serial 58

FAX TRANSMISSION

United States Attorney
Connecticut
157 Church St., 23rd floor
New Haven, Connecticut 06510

To ATTN:			b3 -1 b7E -6
Fax			
From	Assistant United States Attorney	Voice	b6 -4 b7C -4
Fax			
Date	December 14, 2012	**Pages**	3, including this page
Subject	Preservation letter under 18 U.S.C. § 2703(f)		

U.S. Department of Justice

United States Attorney
Connecticut

157 Church St., 23rd floor
New Haven, Connecticut 06510

PHONE: 203.821.3796
FAX: 203.773.5373

December 14, 2012

b3 -1
b7E -6

Re: Request for Preservation of Records

Dea

Pursuant to Title 18, United States Code, Section 2703(f), this letter is a formal request for the preservation of all stored communications, records, and other evidence in your possession regarding the following email account(s) pending further legal process:

I request that you not disclose the existence of this request to the subscriber or any other person, other than as necessary to comply with this request. If compliance with this request might result in a permanent or temporary termination of service or otherwise alert any user of as to your actions to preserve the information described below, please contact me as soon as possible and before taking action.

b3 -1
b7E -6

I request that you preserve, for a period of 90 days, the information described below currently in your possession in a form that includes the complete record. This request applies only retrospectively. It does not in any way obligate you to capture and preserve new information that arises after the date of this request. This request applies to the following items, whether in electronic or other form, including information stored on backup media, if available:

b3 -1
b7E -6

b3 -
b7E

If you have questions regarding this request, please call me a

Sincerely,

David B. Fein
UNITED STATES ATTORNEY

Assistant United States Attorney

b6 -4
b7C -4

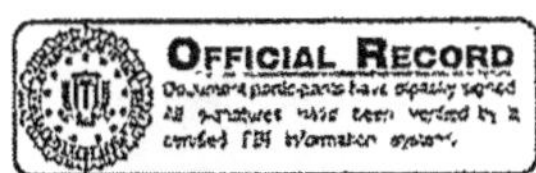

UNCLASSIFIED

FEDERAL BUREAU OF INVESTIGATION

Import Form

Form Type: OTHER **Date:** 12/17/2012

Title: (U) Preservation Letter: [redacted]

Approved By: [redacted]

Drafted By: [redacted]

b3 -1
b6 -1
b7C -1
b7E -6

Case ID #: 4-NH-2619946 (U) UNSUB(S)
Sandy Hook Elementary School
12 Dickinson St, Sandy Hook, CT-Victim
Firearms Act.
OO:NH

Synopsis: (U) A 12/17/2012 request for the preservation of [redacted]

b3 -1
b7E -6

♦♦

UNCLASSIFIED

4-NH-2619946 Serial 59

U.S. Department of Justice

United States Attorney
Connecticut

157 Church St., 23rd floor
New Haven, Connecticut 06510

PHONE: 203.821.3796
FAX: 203.773.5373

December 17, 2012

b3 -1
b7E -6

Re: Request for Preservation of Records

Dear

Pursuant to Title 18, United States Code, Section 2703(f), this letter is a formal request for the preservation of all stored communications, records, and other evidence in your possession regarding

b3 -1
b7E -6

Specifically, please preserve, for a period of 90 days, the contents of any communication or file related to

This request applies to records whether in electronic or other form, including information stored on backup media, if available.

Sincerely,

David B. Fein
UNITED STATES ATTORNEY

b6 -4
b7C -4

Assistant United States Attorney

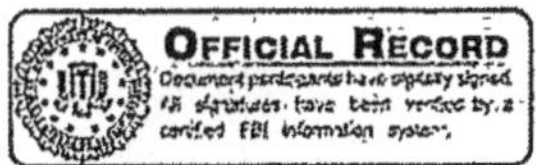

UNCLASSIFIED

FEDERAL BUREAU OF INVESTIGATION

Import Form

Form Type: OTHER **Date:** 12/17/2012

Title: (U) Preservation letter: [redacted]

Approved By: [redacted]

Drafted By: [redacted]

b3 -1
b6 -1
b7C -1
b7E -6

Case ID #: 4-NH-2619946 (U) UNSUB(S)
Sandy Hook Elementary School
12 Dickinson St, Sandy Hook, CT-Victim
Firearms Act.
OO:NH

Synopsis: (U) A 12/17/12 request for the preservation of [redacted]

b3 -1
b7E -6

♦♦

UNCLASSIFIED

4-NH-2619946 Serial 60

U.S. Department of Justice

United States Attorney
Connecticut

157 Church St., 23rd floor
New Haven, Connecticut 06510

PHONE: 203.821.3796
FAX: 203.773.5373

December 17, 2012

Re: Request for Preservation of Records

b3 -1
b7E -6

Dear

Pursuant to Title 18, United States Code, Section 2703(f), this letter is a formal request for the preservation of

b3 -
b7E

Specifically, please preserve, for a period of 90 days, the contents of any communication or file related to This request applies to records whether in electronic or other form, including information stored on backup media, if available.

Sincerely,

David B. Fein
UNITED STATES ATTORNEY

b6 -4
b7C -4

Assistant United States Attorney

FD-302 (Rev. 5-8-10)

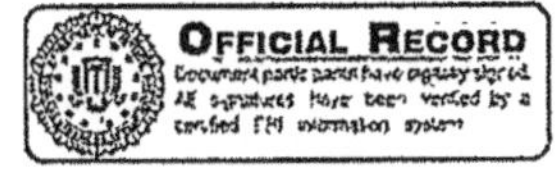

FEDERAL BUREAU OF INVESTIGATION

Date of entry 12/17/2012

SENSITIVE PATIENT MEDICAL INFORMATION

Maintain and use only if necessary for official duties and disseminate only to persons with a need to know; safeguard and protect from inadvertent disclosure.

[redacted] was interviewed telephonically at [redacted] After being advised of the identity of the interviewing Agent, SA [redacted] and the nature of the interview [redacted] provided the following information: b6 -1, 6 b7C -1, 6

[redacted] contacted the FBI out of concern following her interview of a patient [redacted] on Saturday, December 15th, 2012. [redacted] b6 -5, 6 b7C -5, 6

[redacted] he ranted that he he was going to kill the [redacted] and then kill himself.

[redacted] b6 -5, 6 b7C -5, 6

[redacted]

[redacted] did not know if [redacted] has access to weapons, ammunition or any other material which would assist him in carrying out his threat. [redacted] believes it is her duty to bring this to the FBI's attention because it was her understanding that [redacted] was planning on returning to Connecticut for Christmas. It was her opinion [redacted] fascination with the Sandy Hook school shooting would escalate if he were to return to Connecticut [redacted] stated that she was uncomfortable enough that if [redacted] were to be released, she believed [redacted] should be watched by law enforcement. b6 -5, 6 b7C -5, 6

Investigation on 12/17/2012 at New Haven, Connecticut, United States (Phone)

File # 4-NH-2619946 Date drafted 12/17/2012

by [redacted] b6 -1 b7C -1

4-NH-2619946 Serial 61

b6 -5, b7C -5

[Administrative Note: Public source checks linked [redacted] to an address at [redacted] Also listed at that address is [redacted]

b6 -5 b7C -5

made claims to have posted items on line regarding the Newtown shooting.

b6 -5, 6
b7C -5, 6

Follow-up call to SA

b6 -1, 5
b7C -1, 5

uncomfortable enough

→ should be watched

2:55 pm 12/17/12

kill & self

- from town in CT

b6 -5, 6
b7C -5, 6

- not know @ guns access to carry out threat

FD-302 (Rev. 5-8-10)

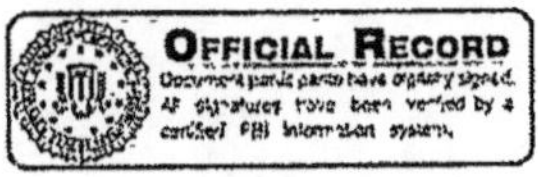

FEDERAL BUREAU OF INVESTIGATION

Date of entry 12/18/2012

[redacted] date of birth: [redacted] [redacted] cell# [redacted] was interviewed at [redacted] [redacted] After being advised of the identity of the interviewing Agent and the nature of the interview, [redacted] provided the following information: b6 -2 b7C -2

[redacted] b6 -2 b7C -2

[redacted] b6 -2 b7C -2

Investigation on 12/14/2012 at [redacted] United States (In Person)

File # 4-NH-2619946 Date drafted 12/15/2012 b6 -1, b7C -1,

by [redacted]

4-NH-2619946 Serial 62

FD-302 (Rev. 5-8-10)

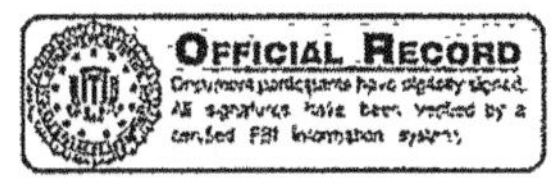

FEDERAL BUREAU OF INVESTIGATION

Date of entry 12/18/2012

[REDACTED] Danbury Hospital, 24 Hospital Avenue, Danbury, Connecticut, 06810, telephone number [REDACTED] [REDACTED] was interviewed. After the undersigned agent identified himself and the nature of the interview, [REDACTED] provided the following information: b6 -6 b7C -6

On Monday, December 17, 2012, [REDACTED] attended a memorial service at Danbury Hospital for one of the child victim's of the Sandy Hook Elementary School shootings. [REDACTED] the service was being held in the hospital's auditorium for employees only. A short time after the conclusion of the service [REDACTED] was still in the auditorium with [REDACTED] [REDACTED] was confronted by a white male, approximately 60 years-old, who told that his name was [REDACTED] b6 -2, 6, 7 b7C -2, 6, 7

[REDACTED] was not invited to the closed memorial service. When [REDACTED] asked [REDACTED] why he was there, [REDACTED] told him, among other things, that he had an "intelligence background" with "special clearance" and that he had been brought into the Sandy Hook Elementary School as a consultant after the shootings. b6 -2, 6 b7C -2, 6

[REDACTED] was agitated [REDACTED] b6 -2, 6 b7C -2, 6

[REDACTED] also handed a business card to [REDACTED] The business card had printed on it only the name, [REDACTED] the telephone number, [REDACTED] [REDACTED] and the e-mail address, [REDACTED] b6 -2, 6 b7C -2, 6

[REDACTED] is not sure how [REDACTED] entered the hospital. Another employee of the hospital approached [REDACTED] and [REDACTED] and told [REDACTED] that he was needed elsewhere. [REDACTED] walked away. [REDACTED] eventually left the auditorium and the hospital. b6 -2, 6 b7C -2, 6

Investigation on 12/17/2012 at Danbury, Connecticut, United States (Phone)

File # 4-NH-2619946 Date drafted 12/18/2012

by [REDACTED] b6 -1 b7C -1

4-NH-2619946 Serial 63

b6
b7C

(Administrative: [redacted]

b6
b7C

[redacted] can be further described as:

b6 -
b7C -

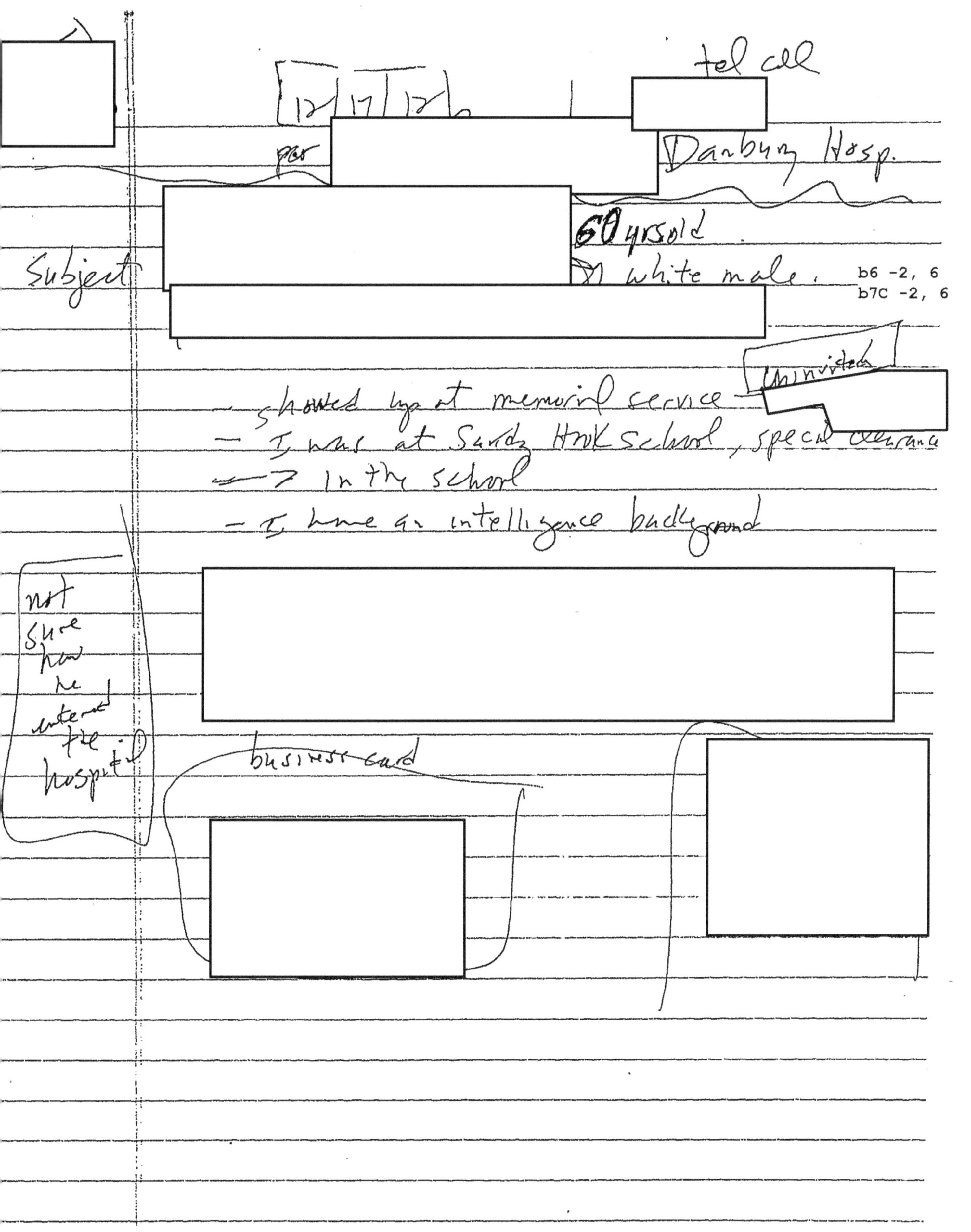

tel call
12/17/12
per
Danbury Hosp.
60 yrs old
white male.
Subject
b6 -2, 6
b7C -2, 6
uninvited
- showed up at memorial service
- I was at Sandy Hook School, special clearance
-> in the school
- I have an intelligence background
not sure how he entered the hospital
business card

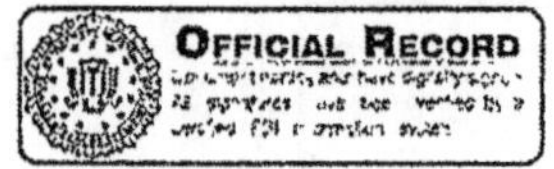

FEDERAL BUREAU OF INVESTIGATION

Date of entry 12/18/2012

At approximately 8:48 p.m. on 12/14/2012, Supervisory Special Agent (SSA) [redacted] of the Federal Bureau of Investigation (FBI) telephonically contacted [redacted] at [redacted] (Note: [redacted] [redacted] had provided [redacted] contact information to a Special Agent with [redacted] b6 -1, 2 b7C -1,

At approximately 9:10 p.m., [redacted] met SSA [redacted] b6 -1, b7C -1,

Investigation on 12/14/2012 at [redacted] United States (In Person) b6 -1, 2 b7C -1, 2

File # 4-NH-2619946 Date drafted 12/18/2012

by [redacted]

FD-302 (Rev. 5-8-10)

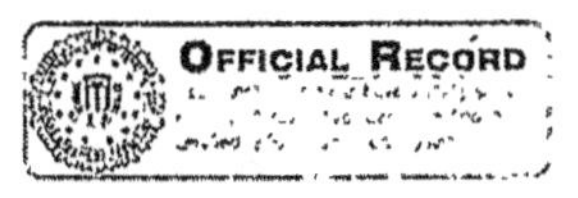

FEDERAL BUREAU OF INVESTIGATION

Date of entry 12/18/2012

[REDACTED] date of birth (DOB): [REDACTED] DOB: [REDACTED] and [REDACTED] date of birth: [REDACTED] were interviewed jointly at their residence located at [REDACTED] [REDACTED] Newtown, Connecticut, telephone: [REDACTED] After being advised of the identity of the interviewing Agents and the nature of the interview, the [REDACTED] family provided the following information: b6 -7 b7C -7

On 12/16/2012, the [REDACTED] family received four (4) telephone calls from telephone number (676)-843-7000. The first call occurred at approximately 9:30 a.m. (EST). [REDACTED] stated she answered the telephone with "hello", heard two clicks, and then heard a male voice state, "This is Adama Lanza. I'm going to kill you." [REDACTED] hung up the telephone. b6 -7 b7C -7

After the first call, the [REDACTED] family received three (3) more telephone calls from the same number with the last one occurring at approximately 11:22 a.m. (EST). Of the three other calls, the caller left two (2) threatening messages that were recorded by the [REDACTED] voicemail account. [REDACTED] provided that she deleted the two threatening messages from the family's voicemail account. [REDACTED] reported the threatening calls to the authorities. b6 -7 b7C -7

[REDACTED] described the two threatening messages on the family's voicemail account. [REDACTED] stated that the first voicemail sounded like a computerized-voice which stated, "This is Adam Lanza. You're going to be dead by tomorrow." b6 -7 b7C -7

[REDACTED] then provided that the voice on the second voicemail message sounded to be male, "Deep and raspy", and later categorized it as younger voice with no accent, and it sounded "freaky". [REDACTED] furthered that the second voicemail contained a similar threat as the first voicemail but provided more details. According to [REDACTED] [REDACTED] the second voicemail repeated that the caller was Adama Lanza, that "I'm going to fucking kill you", and "I'm going to shoot you in the face with a shotgun". b6 -7 b7C -7

[REDACTED] provided that he worked [REDACTED] [REDACTED] b6 -7 b7C -7

Investigation on 12/16/2012 at Newtown, Connecticut, United States (In Person)

File # 4-NH-2619946 Date drafted 12/18/2012

by [REDACTED] b6 -1 b7C -1

4-NH-2619946 Serial 65

b6 b7C

provided she was [redacted]

b6 b7C

On the same date the [redacted] family received the threatening phone calls, five other families received similar threatening phone calls from the telephone number (676)-843-7000. After providing the [redacted] family with names of the other families who received the threatening calls, the [redacted] family provided they did not know any of the other families.

b6 b7C

[redacted] provided that the [redacted] family's telephone number [redacted] is listed in the telephone book.

b6 b7C

646-843-7000

12/16/12

b6 -7
b7C -7

fathe

(4 call)
First — 9:30 am — Click click — (Freaky) Hello — This is Adam I'm going to kill you Lanza.
last — 11:22 am Hang-up —
— Called back —
I'm going to kill you.

11:00 1 2 Voicemails
2 Voices — 1 raspy voice
— 1 computer generated

(computer)
1. This is Adam Lanza
You're going to be dead Robot — Deep
by tomorrow. — I'm going to f'ing kill you

(Deep, Raspy) — Male — No accent — Younger
2. More detail. I'm going to shoot you in the face.
— Freaky

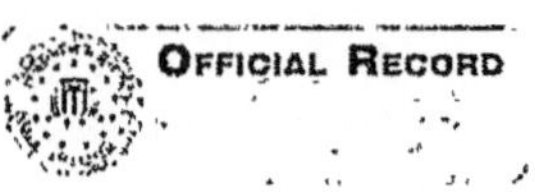

FEDERAL BUREAU OF INVESTIGATION

Date of entry 12/18/2012

[redacted] date of birth (DOB): [redacted] and [redacted] DOB: [redacted] were interviewed at their residence of [redacted] Newtown, Connecticut, telephone: [redacted] Also present for the interview was [redacted] friend [redacted] DOB: [redacted] After being advised of the identity of the interviewing Agents and the nature of the interview, [redacted] and [redacted] provided the following information: b6 b7C

On 12/16/2012, at approximately 9:24 a.m. (EST), the [redacted] family received a telephone call on their home number [redacted] from telephone number (676)-873-7000. [redacted] answered the telephone. After [redacted] said "hello" twice, [redacted] heard a click and then a male voice stated "I'm Adam Lanza". [redacted] hung up the phone [redacted] described the male voice as "creepy and young". b6 b7C

At approximately 9:25 a.m. (EST), the caller called the [redacted] telephone number a second time but [redacted] let the call go to the [redacted] voicemail account. The caller left the following message on the [redacted] voicemail account: b6 b7C

"(Sound of a toilet flushing then a pause) This is Adam Lanza. I'm going to fucking kill you. You're dead. You're dead. Do you hear me? You're fucking dead." (Hang-up)

[redacted] provided that she listened to the voicemail as described above soon after [redacted] told her about the first call. [redacted] then contacted the authorities. b6 b7C

Prior to playing the voicemail for interviewing Agents, [redacted] requested that [redacted] and [redacted] leave the room as she did not want either of them to hear the message [redacted] then played the voicemail for the interviewing agents twice. Special Agent [redacted] was able to make a copy of the recording with an application on his blackberry. An electronic copy of the recording is attached to this communication. b6 -1, b7C -1

At approximately 11:23 a.m. (EST), the [redacted] Caller Identification system (Caller ID) provided the [redacted] family received a third call from the same number as listed above but no message was left. [redacted] stated no b6 b7C

Investigation on 12/16/2012 at Newtown, Connecticut, United States (In Person)

File # 4-NH-2619946 Date drafted 12/18/2012

by [redacted] b6 b7C

4-NH-2619946 Serial 66

b6 -7
b7C -7

one was at the [redacted] residence at the time of the third call.

b6 -7
b7C -7

[redacted] further provided that the [redacted] Caller ID showed that the telephone number (646)-843-7000 belonged to "iCall Inc."

b6 -7
b7C -7

[redacted] worked since [redacted] [redacted] [redacted] spouse, [redacted] DOB: [redacted] is [redacted] [redacted] [redacted] Neither [redacted] nor the older daughter were at the residence during the interview or when the threatening telephone calls were placed to the home.

b6 -7
b7C -7

On the same date, five other families received similar threatening telephone calls from telephone number (676)-873-7000. After interviewing agents provided the names of the other families to [redacted] and [redacted] and [redacted] provided that neither of them knew the other families.

b6 -7
b7C -7

b6 -7
b7C -7

[redacted] stated that the family's telephone number is listed in the telephone book.

b6 -7
b7C -7

1st Home

- 9:24 a.m. -

- 9:35 a.m. 12/16/12

11:23 am. - Not home

1) - Oldest Daughter

2.

3.

b6 -
b7C -

Hello (twice)

Male - I'm Adam Lanza - Hung-up

- Creepy, young

- 2nd Voice mail -

- Caller - Voicemail - [Toilet - Flushing] "This is Adam Lanza - I'm going to fucking kill you. You're dead. You're dead. Do you hear me? You're fucking dead."

listed. - Hung up -

FD-1057 (Rev. 5-8-10)

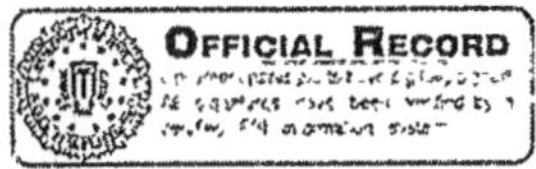

FEDERAL BUREAU OF INVESTIGATION

Electronic Communication

Title: (U) [redacted] **Date:** 12/18/2012 b7E -6, 7

To: [redacted]

From: NEW HAVEN
NH-9
Contact: [redacted] b6 -1 b7C -1

Approved By: A/SSA [redacted]
[redacted]

Drafted By: [redacted]

Case ID #: 4-NH-2619946 (U) UNSUB(S)
Sandy Hook Elementary School
12 Dickinson St, Sandy Hook, CT-Victim
Firearms Act.
OO:NH
[redacted] (U//~~FOUO~~) [redacted] b7A -1 b7E -4, 6, 7

Synopsis: (U) Request for [redacted]
[redacted]
[redacted] b6 -1 b7C -1

Reference: 4-NH-2619946 Serial 1

Enclosure(s): Enclosed are the following items:
1. (U) Copy of CT State Search Warrant

Details:

New Haven Division is cooperating with the Connecticut State Police (CSP) in the investigation ofa mass shooting at Sandy Hook Elementary School, 12 Dickinson St, Sandy Hook, CT, on 12/14/2012. (See referenced serial for additional details regarding case background.)

Title: (U) [redacted] b7E -6, 7
Re: 4-NH-2619946, 12/18/2012

During the investigation, CSP recovered a 500 GB Seagate Barracuda ST3500320AS hard drive, S/N 9QM34ZA8, from 36 Yogananda Street, Sandy Hook, CT, the home of suspect Adam Lanza. The drive has been opened and significantly damaged by force trauma as well as by being scratched with an implement.

New Haven is requesting assistance [redacted]

As this is a matter of national attention, it is of high priority. However, NH understands that the techniques involved will be very time-intensive. Therefore, no deadline is identified, but as rapid a response as is possible under the circumstances is requested. b7E -6,

[redacted]

The New Haven POC for this issue is SA [redacted] He can be reached at [redacted] (desk), or [redacted] (cell). b6 - b7C

♦♦

7

12-18-12;14:40 ;NEWTOWN-EOC 12035035388 ;2032704365 # 2/ 2

SEARCH AND SEIZURE WARRANT | **STATE OF CONNECTICUT SUPERIOR COURT** | **SEARCH AND SEIZURE WARRANT**

The foregoing Affidavit and Application for Search and Seizure Warrant having been presented to and been considered by the undersigned, a Judge of the Superior Court or a Judge Trial Referee, and the foregoing Affidavit having been subscribed and sworn to by the affiant(s) before me at the time it was presented, the undersigned (a) is satisfied therefrom that grounds exist for said application, and (b) finds that said affidavit established grounds and probable cause for the undersigned to issue this Search and Seizure Warrant, such probable cause being the following. From said affidavit, the undersigned finds that there is probable cause for the undersigned to believe that the property described in the foregoing affidavit and application is within or upon the person, if any, named or described in the foregoing affidavit and application, or the place or thing, if any, described in the foregoing affidavit and application, under the conditions and circumstances set forth in the foregoing affidavit and application, and that, therefore, a Search and Seizure warrant should issue for said property

NOW THEREFORE, by Authority of the State of Connecticut, I hereby command any Police Officer of a regularly organized police department, any State Police Officer, any inspector in the Division of Criminal Justice, or any conservation officer, special conservation officer or patrol officer acting pursuant to C.G.S. § 26-6 to whom these presents shall come within ten days after the date of this warrant to enter into or upon and search the place or thing described in the foregoing affidavit and application, or search the person described in the foregoing affidavit and application or both, to wit:

The residence of Nancy and Adam Lanza, 36 Yogananda Street in Sandy Hook, CT. The residence is a 2 story colonial style structure, with an attached two car garage. The house is pale yellow with dark green shutters and a dark green front door. The full address, 36 Yogananda Street is listed on the mailbox located in front of the house.

for the property described in the foregoing affidavit and application, to wit

Computers (including gaming devices and cellular telephones), zip disks, CD's, CDR's, DVD's, and other electronic storage media because; (1) The objects themselves may be instrumentalities, fruits, or evidence of a crime and (2) The objects may have been used to collect and store information about crimes in the form of electronic "data" (as defined by Connecticut General Statutes 53a-250(8)). Such data may include image files, video files, text files, or other electronically stored documents. Connecticut General Statutes define a "computer" as a programmable, electronic device capable of accepting and processing data, such as a gaming console, cellular telephone, and other similar devices.

[X] submit the property described in the foregoing affidavit and application to laboratory analysis and examination

Department of Public Safety Computer and Electronics Unit (278 Colony St in Meriden, CT) and/or other recognized and accredited forensic science laboratory for forensic examination and review.

and upon finding said property to seize the same, take and keep it in custody until the further order of the court, and with reasonable promptness make due return of this warrant accompanied by a written inventory of all property seized

[✓] The foregoing request that the judge or judge trial referee dispense with the requirement of C.G.S. § 54-33c that a copy of the warrant application and affidavit(s) in support of the warrant be given to the owner, occupant or person named therein and that the affidavit in support of such request also be included in such nondelivery is hereby:

[✓] GRANTED for a period of — NOT TO EXCEED 2 WEEKS BEYOND DATE WARRANT IS EXECUTED: Dec. 28, 2012

This order, or any extension thereof, dispensing with said requirement shall not limit disclosure of such application and affidavits to the attorney for a person arrested in connection with or subsequent to the execution of the search warrant unless, upon motion of the prosecuting authority within two weeks of such arraignment the court finds that the state's interest in continuing nondisclosure substantially outweighs the defendant's right to disclosure.

[ ] DENIED

[ ] Service of this Search Warrant upon the customer whose financial records are being sought is hereby waived, pursuant to C.G.S. § 36a-43 (a)

(NOTE: AFFIANT'S OATH MUST BE TAKEN PRIOR TO JUDGE / JUDGE TRIAL REFEREE SIGNING BELOW)

(This is page 7 of a 8 page Affidavit and Application.)

Signed at Newtown, Connecticut, on:	Date: Dec. 14, 2012	At (Time): 7:25	[ ] a.m. [✓] p.m.
Signed (Judge/Judge Trial Referee)	Print name of Judicial Official: Hon. John F. Blawie		

JD-CR-61

b6 -3
b7C -3

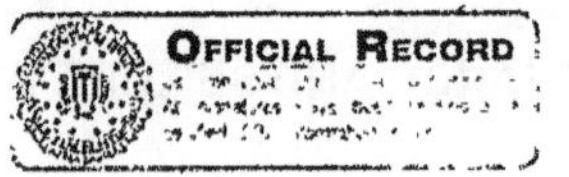

UNCLASSIFIED//~~FOUO~~

FEDERAL BUREAU OF INVESTIGATION

Date of entry 12/17/2012

[redacted] date of birth (DOB) [redacted] was interviewed at [redacted] [redacted] which is the office of his attorney, [redacted] telephone [redacted] employed by [redacted] [redacted] Immediately prior to the interview, [redacted] stated he was representing [redacted] [redacted] willing to answer questions and assist in the investigation. [redacted] [redacted] was going to be present during the interview. [redacted] [redacted] the interview began with [redacted] and the two listed FBI Special Agents. After being advised of the identity of the interviewing Special Agents, [redacted] provided the following information: b6 -5, b7C -5,

[redacted] stated that, on the evening of 12/11/2012, he went straight from work to his residence [redacted] [redacted] b6 b7C

[redacted] b6 b7C

[redacted] b6 b7C

UNCLASSIFIED//~~FOUO~~

Investigation on 12/16/2012 at [redacted] United States (In Person)

File # 4-NH-2619946 Date drafted 12/17/2012 b6 -1, b7C -1,

by [redacted]

b6 -6
b7C -6

b6 -6
b7C -6

b6 -6
b7C -6

stated ADAM LANZA had Asperger's Syndrome, which limited ADAM LANZA's ability to communicate well

b6 -6, 7
b7C -6, 7

b6 -6
b7C -6

b6 -6
b7C -6

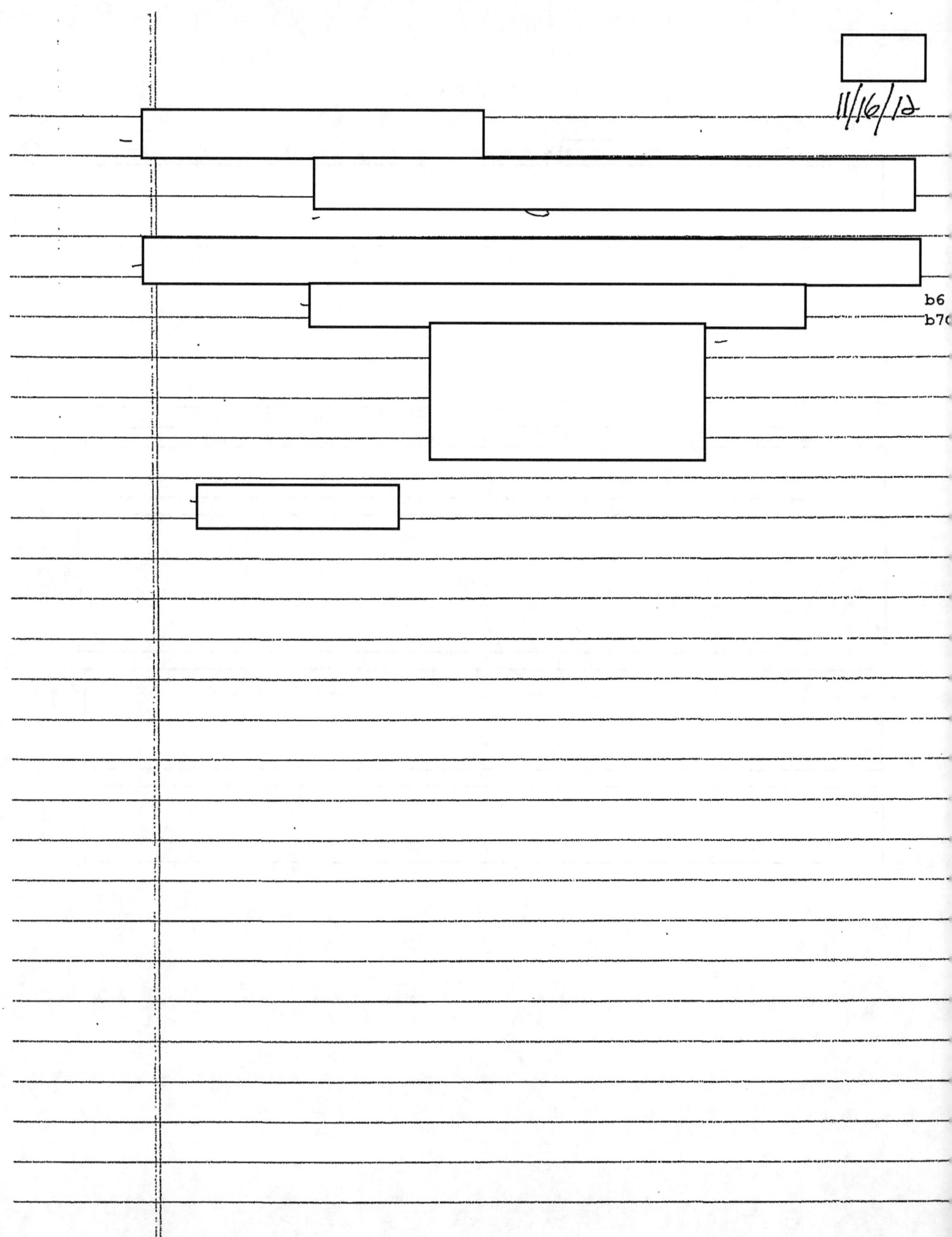
11/16/12
b6
b7C

FD-1087 (Rev. 5-8-10)

UNCLASSIFIED

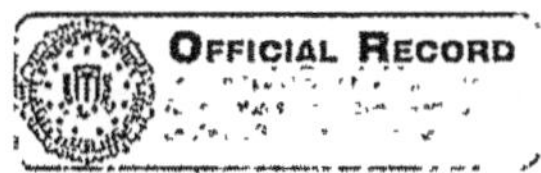

FEDERAL BUREAU OF INVESTIGATION

Evidence Log

Event Title: (U) Acquisition of [redacted]

Date: 12/15/2012

To: [redacted]

b3 -1
b6 -1, 2
b7C -1, 2

Approved By: SSA [redacted]

Drafted By: [redacted]

Case ID #: 4-NH-2619946

(U) UNSUB(S)
Sandy Hook Elementary School
12 Dickinson St, Sandy Hook, CT-Victim
Firearms Act.
OO:NH

FEDERAL GRAND JURY MATERIAL - DISSEMINATE PURSUANT TO RULE 6(E)
Do not disseminate except as authorized by federal rule of criminal procedure 6(e).

[redacted] b7E -1

Acquired By: [redacted] on 12/14/2012

Acquired From: (U) [redacted]

b3 -1
b6 -1, 2
b7C -1, 2

Receipt Given?: No

Holding Office: NEW HAVEN

Details:

On 12/14/2012, a Federal Grand Jury subpoena was served on [redacted]

b3 -1
b6 -2
b7C -2

UNCLASSIFIED

This document contains neither recommendations nor conclusions of the FBI. It is the property of the FBI and is loaned to your agency; it and its contents are not to be distributed outside your agency.

4-NH-2619946
SERIAL 69

Title: (U) Acquisition of

Re: 4-NH-2619946, 12/15/2012

provided this information and subpoena return

b3 -1
b6 -1, 2
b7C -1,
b7E -6

Item Type	Description
	(U)
	Acquired On: 12/14/2012 Located By: Other Locator: Location Area: Specific Location:

♦♦

FD-302 (Rev. 5-8-10)

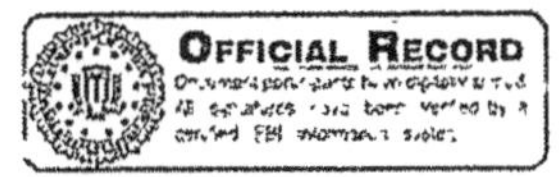

FEDERAL BUREAU OF INVESTIGATION

Date of entry 12/15/2012

On 12/14/2012, SA [redacted] and SA [redacted] conducted a search of [redacted] The search was conducted after consent was provided by way of a FD-26 Consent to Search form signed by [redacted] Also present during the search was [redacted] b6 -1, 2, 5 b7C -1, 2, 5

During the search, the following items were found:

[redacted] b6 -2 b7C -2

Each of the above items were photocopied and released to the FBI by [redacted] The original documents were placed back in [redacted] in their original locations upon being photocopied. b6 -2 b7C -2

Enclosed with this document are the signed FD-26, photocopies of the aforementioned items, and a signed FD-597 Receipt.

Investigation on 12/14/2012 at [redacted], United States (In Person) b6 -1, 2 b7C -1, 2

File # 4-NH-2619946 Date drafted 12/15/2012

by [redacted]

4-NH-2619946 Serial 70

FD-26 (Rev. 7-20-94)

DEPARTMENT OF JUSTICE

FEDERAL BUREAU OF INVESTIGATION

CONSENT TO SEARCH

1. I have been asked by Special Agents of the Federal Bureau of Investigation to permit a complete search of:

(Describe the person(s), place(s), or thing(s) to be searched.)

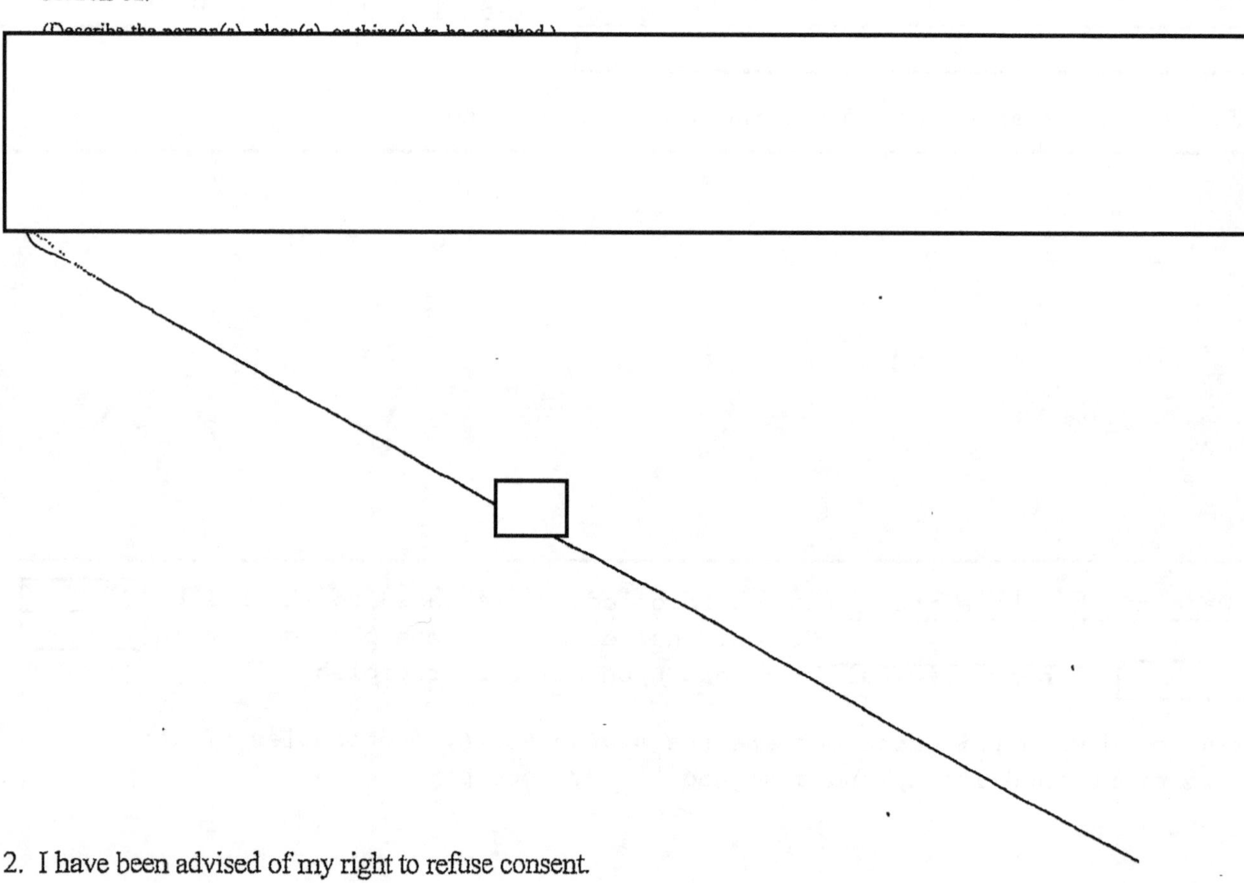

b6 -
b7C

2. I have been advised of my right to refuse consent.

3. I give this permission voluntarily.

4. I authorize these agents to take any items which they determine may be related to their investigation.

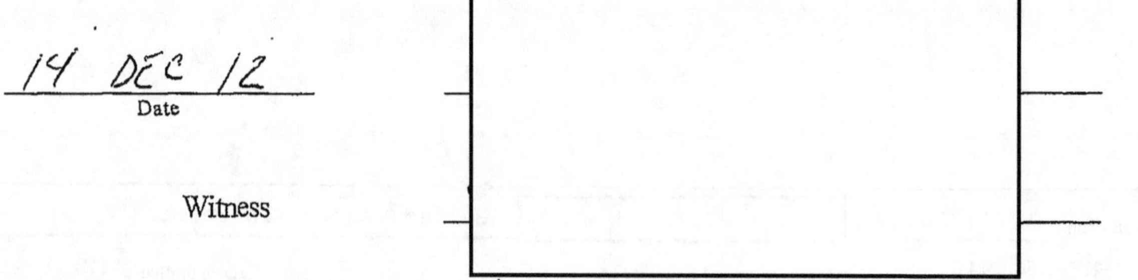

14 DEC 12
Date

Witness

b6 -1,
b7C -1,

FD-597 (Rev 8-11-94)

UNITED STATES DEPARTMENT OF JUSTICE
FEDERAL BUREAU OF INVESTIGATION
Receipt for Property Received/Returned/Released/Seized

File # 4-NH-2619946

On (date) 12/14/12

item(s) listed below were:
☒ Received From
☐ Returned To
☐ Released To
☐ Seized

(Name)

(Street Address)

(City)

b6 -2
b7C -2

Description of Item(s): - Photocopies of

12/14/12

b6 -1, 5
b7C -1, 5

Received By:

Received From:

FEDERAL BUREAU OF INVESTIGATION
FOI/PA
DELETED PAGE INFORMATION SHEET
Civil Action# 16-cv-02136

Total Deleted Page(s) = 138
Page 4 ~ b3 - 1; b6 - 4; b7C - 4;
Page 5 ~ b3 - 1; b6 - 4; b7C - 4;
Page 7 ~ Duplicate;
Page 9 ~ b3 - 1; b6 - 4, 5; b7C - 4, 5;
Page 10 ~ b3 - 1; b6 - 4; b7C - 4;
Page 12 ~ Duplicate;
Page 14 ~ b3 - 1; b6 - 4; b7C - 4;
Page 15 ~ b3 - 1; b6 - 4; b7C - 4;
Page 17 ~ Duplicate;
Page 18 ~ b3 - 1; b6 - 4; b7C - 4;
Page 19 ~ b3 - 1; b6 - 4; b7C - 4;
Page 21 ~ Duplicate;
Page 23 ~ b3 - 1; b6 - 4; b7C - 4;
Page 24 ~ b3 - 1; b6 - 4; b7C - 4;
Page 26 ~ Duplicate;
Page 28 ~ b3 - 1; b6 - 4; b7C - 4;
Page 29 ~ b3 - 1; b6 - 4; b7C - 4;
Page 31 ~ Duplicate;
Page 33 ~ b3 - 1; b6 - 4; b7C - 4;
Page 34 ~ b3 - 1; b6 - 4; b7C - 4;
Page 36 ~ Duplicate;
Page 38 ~ b3 - 1; b6 - 4; b7C - 4;
Page 39 ~ b3 - 1; b6 - 4; b7C - 4;
Page 41 ~ Duplicate;
Page 44 ~ Duplicate;
Page 46 ~ b3 - 1; b6 - 4; b7C - 4;
Page 47 ~ b3 - 1; b6 - 4; b7C - 4;
Page 49 ~ Duplicate;
Page 51 ~ b3 - 1; b6 - 4; b7C - 4;
Page 52 ~ b3 - 1; b6 - 4; b7C - 4;
Page 54 ~ Duplicate;
Page 56 ~ b3 - 1; b6 - 4; b7C - 4;
Page 57 ~ b3 - 1; b6 - 4; b7C - 4;
Page 59 ~ Duplicate;
Page 61 ~ b3 - 1; b6 - 4; b7C - 4;
Page 62 ~ b3 - 1; b6 - 4; b7C - 4;
Page 64 ~ Duplicate;
Page 66 ~ b3 - 1; b6 - 4, 5; b7C - 4, 5;
Page 72 ~ b3 - 1; b6 - 1, 4, 5; b7C - 1, 4, 5;
Page 73 ~ b3 - 1;
Page 74 ~ b3 - 1;
Page 75 ~ b3 - 1;
Page 76 ~ b3 - 1;
Page 77 ~ b3 - 1;
Page 78 ~ b3 - 1;
Page 89 ~ b3 - 1; b6 - 4; b7C - 4;
Page 90 ~ b3 - 1; b6 - 4; b7C - 4;
Page 96 ~ b3 - 1; b6 - 1, 5; b7C - 1, 5;

Page 97 ~ b3 - 1; b6 - 1, 5; b7C - 1, 5;
Page 99 ~ b3 - 1; b6 - 4; b7C - 4;
Page 100 ~ b3 - 1; b6 - 4; b7C - 4;
Page 105 ~ b3 - 1; b6 - 4; b7C - 4;
Page 106 ~ b3 - 1; b6 - 4; b7C - 4;
Page 111 ~ b3 - 1; b6 - 4; b7C - 4;
Page 112 ~ b3 - 1; b6 - 4; b7C - 4;
Page 117 ~ b3 - 1; b6 - 4; b7C - 4;
Page 119 ~ b3 - 1; b6 - 4; b7C - 4;
Page 122 ~ b3 - 1; b6 - 4, 5; b7C - 4, 5;
Page 123 ~ b3 - 1; b6 - 4; b7C - 4;
Page 125 ~ Duplicate;
Page 127 ~ b3 - 1; b6 - 4, 5; b7C - 4, 5;
Page 128 ~ b3 - 1; b6 - 4; b7C - 4;
Page 130 ~ Duplicate;
Page 132 ~ b3 - 1; b6 - 4; b7C - 4;
Page 133 ~ b3 - 1; b6 - 4; b7C - 4;
Page 135 ~ Duplicate;
Page 137 ~ b3 - 1; b6 - 4, 5; b7C - 4, 5;
Page 138 ~ b3 - 1; b6 - 4; b7C - 4;
Page 140 ~ Duplicate;
Page 143 ~ Duplicate;
Page 147 ~ b6 - 2, 3; b7C - 2, 3;
Page 148 ~ b6 - 3, 6; b7C - 3, 6;
Page 149 ~ b6 - 6; b7C - 6;
Page 151 ~ b3 - 1; b6 - 5; b7C - 5;
Page 152 ~ b3 - 1; b6 - 4, 5; b7C - 4, 5;
Page 153 ~ b3 - 1; b6 - 5; b7C - 5;
Page 154 ~ b3 - 1;
Page 155 ~ b3 - 1;
Page 156 ~ b3 - 1; b6 - 5; b7C - 5;
Page 157 ~ b3 - 1;
Page 158 ~ b3 - 1;
Page 159 ~ b3 - 1; b6 - 5; b7C - 5;
Page 160 ~ b3 - 1;
Page 161 ~ b3 - 1; b6 - 5; b7C - 5;
Page 162 ~ b3 - 1; b6 - 5; b7C - 5;
Page 163 ~ b3 - 1; b6 - 5; b7C - 5;
Page 164 ~ b3 - 1; b6 - 5; b7C - 5;
Page 165 ~ b3 - 1; b6 - 5; b7C - 5;
Page 166 ~ b3 - 1; b6 - 5; b7C - 5;
Page 167 ~ b3 - 1; b6 - 5; b7C - 5;
Page 168 ~ b3 - 1; b6 - 5; b7C - 5;
Page 169 ~ b3 - 1; b6 - 5; b7C - 5;
Page 170 ~ b3 - 1;
Page 171 ~ b3 - 1; b6 - 5; b7C - 5;
Page 172 ~ b3 - 1; b6 - 5; b7C - 5;
Page 173 ~ b3 - 1; b6 - 5; b7C - 5;
Page 174 ~ b3 - 1; b6 - 5; b7C - 5;
Page 175 ~ b3 - 1; b6 - 5; b7C - 5;
Page 176 ~ b3 - 1; b6 - 5; b7C - 5;
Page 177 ~ b3 - 1; b6 - 5; b7C - 5;
Page 178 ~ b3 - 1; b6 - 5; b7C - 5;
Page 179 ~ b3 - 1;

Page 180 ~ b3 - 1;
Page 181 ~ b3 - 1; b6 - 5; b7C - 5;
Page 182 ~ b3 - 1;
Page 183 ~ b3 - 1; b6 - 5; b7C - 5;
Page 185 ~ b3 - 1; b6 - 1, 4; b7C - 1, 4;
Page 186 ~ b3 - 1; b6 - 1, 4; b7C - 1, 4;
Page 192 ~ b6 - 1; b7C - 1; b7E - 2;
Page 193 ~ b6 - 2; b7C - 2; b7E - 2;
Page 194 ~ b6 - 1; b7C - 1; b7E - 2;
Page 195 ~ b6 - 1; b7C - 1; b7E - 2;
Page 197 ~ b3 - 1; b6 - 4; b7C - 4;
Page 198 ~ b3 - 1; b6 - 4; b7C - 4;
Page 203 ~ b3 - 1; b6 - 4; b7C - 4;
Page 204 ~ b3 - 1; b6 - 4; b7C - 4;
Page 207 ~ Duplicate;
Page 210 ~ b3 - 1; b6 - 4; b7C - 4;
Page 211 ~ b3 - 1; b6 - 4; b7C - 4;
Page 216 ~ b3 - 1; b6 - 4; b7C - 4;
Page 217 ~ b3 - 1; b6 - 4; b7C - 4;
Page 223 ~ b3 - 1; b6 - 4, 5; b7C - 4, 5;
Page 224 ~ b3 - 1; b6 - 4; b7C - 4;
Page 226 ~ b3 - 1; b6 - 4, 5; b7C - 4, 5;
Page 227 ~ b3 - 1; b6 - 4; b7C - 4;
Page 231 ~ b3 - 1; b6 - 4; b7C - 4;
Page 232 ~ b3 - 1; b6 - 4; b7C - 4;
Page 237 ~ b3 - 1; b6 - 4; b7C - 4;
Page 238 ~ b3 - 1; b6 - 4; b7C - 4;
Page 243 ~ b3 - 1; b6 - 1, 2, 5; b7C - 1, 2, 5;
Page 244 ~ b3 - 1; b6 - 2; b7C - 2;
Page 245 ~ b3 - 1; b6 - 2; b7C - 2;
Page 246 ~ b3 - 1; b6 - 2; b7C - 2;
Page 247 ~ b3 - 1; b6 - 2; b7C - 2;
Page 248 ~ b3 - 1; b6 - 2; b7C - 2;
Page 249 ~ b3 - 1; b6 - 4, 5; b7C - 4, 5;
Page 251 ~ b3 - 1; b6 - 1, 5; b7C - 1, 5;
Page 252 ~ b3 - 1; b6 - 2; b7C - 2;

XXXXXXXXXXXXXXXXXXXXXXXX
X Deleted Page(s) X
X No Duplication Fee X
X For this Page X
XXXXXXXXXXXXXXXXXXXXXXXX

FD-1036 (Rev. 10-16-2009)

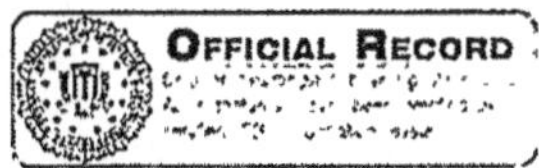

UNCLASSIFIED

FEDERAL BUREAU OF INVESTIGATION

Import Form

Form Type: OTHER **Date:** 12/17/2012

Title: (U) FGJ Subpoean to [redacted]

Approved By: [redacted]

Drafted By: [redacted]

b3 -1
b6 -1
b7C -1

Case ID #: 4-NH-2619946-GJ (U) Grand Jury Information

FEDERAL GRAND JURY MATERIAL - DISSEMINATE PURSUANT TO RULE 6(E)
Do not disseminate except as authorized by federal rule of criminal procedure 6(e).

Synopsis: (U) 12/14/2012 FGJ Subpoena to [redacted] b3 -1

♦♦

UNCLASSIFIED

Sandy Hook-286

4-NH-2619946-GJ
SERIAL 1

UNITED STATES DISTRICT COURT

for the

District of Connecticut

SUBPOENA TO TESTIFY BEFORE A GRAND JURY

To:

b3 -1

ED to appear in this United States district court at the time, date, and place shown below to testify before the court's grand jury. When you arrive, you must remain at the court until the judge or a court officer allows you to leave.

Place: United States Courthouse 141 Church Street New Haven, CT 06510	Date and Time:

You must also bring with you the following documents, electronically stored information, or objects *(blank if not applicable)*:

b3

Date: December 14, 2012

CLERK OF COURT

Signature of Clerk or Deputy Clerk

The name, address, e-mail, and telephone number of the United States attorney, or assistant United States attorney, who requests this subpoena, are:

AUSA
157 Church St., 23rd floor
New Haven, CT 06510

Personal appearance is not required if documents are provided on or before the appearance date to: FBI S/A
600 State St.
New Haven CT 06510

b3 -1
b6 -1, 4
b7C -1,

FD-1036 (Rev. 10-16-2009)

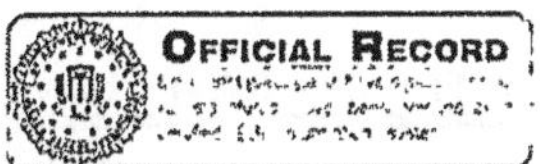

UNCLASSIFIED

FEDERAL BUREAU OF INVESTIGATION

Import Form

Form Type: FD-617 **Date:** 12/17/2012

Title: (U) FGJ Subpoena to [redacted]

Approved By: [redacted] b3 -1 b6 -1 b7C -1

Drafted By: [redacted]

Case ID #: 4-NH-2619946-GJ (U) Grand Jury Information

FEDERAL GRAND JURY MATERIAL - DISSEMINATE PURSUANT TO RULE 6(E)
Do not disseminate except as authorized by federal rule of criminal procedure 6(e).

Synopsis: (U) 12/14/2012 FGJ Subpoena to [redacted]

[redacted] b3 -1

♦♦

UNCLASSIFIED

4-NH-2619946-GJ
SERIAL 2

AO 110 (Rev. 06/09) Subpoena to Testify Before a Grand Jury

UNITED STATES DISTRICT COURT

for the

District of Connecticut

SUBPOENA TO TESTIFY BEFORE A GRAND JURY

To: b3 -1 b6 -5 b7C -5

YOU ARE COMMANDED to appear in this United States district court at the time, date, and place shown below to testify before the court's grand jury. When you arrive, you must remain at the court until the judge or a court officer allows you to leave.

Place: United States Courthouse 141 Church Street New Haven, CT 06510	Date and Time:

You must also bring with you the following documents, electronically stored information, or objects *(blank if not applicable)*:

b3

Date: December 14, 2012

CLERK OF COURT

Signature of Clerk or Deputy Clerk

The name, address, e-mail, and telephone number of the United States attorney, or assistant United States attorney, who requests this subpoena, are:

AUSA
157 Church St., 23rd floor
New Haven, CT 06510

Personal appearance is not required if documents are provided on or before the appearance date to: FBI S/A
600 State St.
New Haven CT 06510

b3 -1 b6 -1 b7C -

FD-1036 (Rev. 10-16-2009)

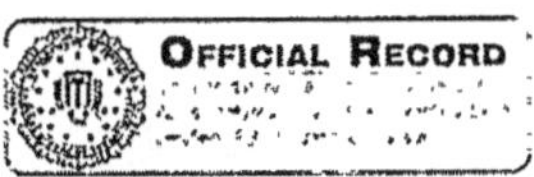

UNCLASSIFIED

FEDERAL BUREAU OF INVESTIGATION

Import Form

Form Type: FD-617 **Date:** 12/17/2012

Title: (U) 12/14/12 FGJ Subpoena to [redacted]

Approved By: [redacted]

Drafted By: [redacted]

b3 -1
b6 -1
b7C -1

Case ID #: 4-NH-2619946-GJ (U) Grand Jury Information

FEDERAL GRAND JURY MATERIAL - DISSEMINATE PURSUANT TO RULE 6(E)
Do not disseminate except as authorized by federal rule of criminal procedure 6(e).

Synopsis: (U) 12/14/12 FGJ Subpoena to [redacted]

b3 -1

♦♦

UNCLASSIFIED

4-NH-2619946-GJ
SERIAL 3

UNITED STATES DISTRICT COURT

for the

District of Connecticut

SUBPOENA TO TESTIFY BEFORE A GRAND JURY

To: b3 -1

YOU ARE COMMANDED to appear in this United States district court at the time, date, and place shown below to testify before the court's grand jury. When you arrive, you must remain at the court until the judge or a court officer allows you to leave.

Place: United States Courthouse, 141 Church Street, New Haven, CT 06510	Date and Time:

You must also bring with you the following documents, electronically stored information, or objects *(blank if not applicable)*:

b3 -

Date: December 14, 2012

CLERK OF COURT

Signature of Clerk or Deputy Clerk

The name, address, e-mail, and telephone number of the United States attorney, or assistant United States attorney, who requests this subpoena, are:

AUS
157 Church St., 23rd floor
New Haven, CT 06510

Personal appearance is not required if documents are provided on or before the appearance date to: FBI S/A
600 State St.
New Haven CT 06510

b3 -1
b6 -1, 4
b7C -1,

AO 110 (Rev. 06/09) Subpoena to Testify Before a Grand Jury

UNITED STATES DISTRICT COURT

for the

District of Connecticut

SUBPOENA TO TESTIFY BEFORE A GRAND JURY

To: b3 -1

YOU ARE COMMANDED to appear in this United States district court at the time, date, and place shown below to testify before the court's grand jury. When you arrive, you must remain at the court until the judge or a court officer allows you to leave.

Place: United States Courthouse 141 Church Street New Haven, CT 06510	Date and Time:

You must also bring with you the following documents, electronically stored information, or objects *(blank if not applicable)*:

b3 -1

Date: December 14, 2012

CLERK OF COURT

Signature of Clerk or Deputy Clerk

The name, address, e-mail, and telephone number of the United States attorney, or assistant United States attorney, who requests this subpoena, are:

AUS
157 Church St., 23rd floor
New Haven, CT 06510

Personal appearance is not required if documents are provided on or before the appearance date to: FBI S/A
600 State St.
New Haven CT 06510

b3 -1
b6 -1, 4
b7C -1, 4

FD-1036 (Rev. 10-16-2009)

UNCLASSIFIED

FEDERAL BUREAU OF INVESTIGATION

Import Form

Form Type: FD-617 **Date:** 12/17/2012

Title: (U) FGJ subpoean to [redacted]

b3 -1
b6 -1
b7C -1

Approved By: [redacted]

Drafted By: [redacted]

Case ID #: 4-NH-2619946-GJ (U) Grand Jury Information

FEDERAL GRAND JURY MATERIAL - DISSEMINATE PURSUANT TO RULE 6(E)
Do not disseminate except as authorized by federal rule of criminal procedure 6(e).

Synopsis: (U) A FGJ Subpoena issued to [redacted] on 12/14/12 for [redacted]

b3 -1
b6 -2
b7C -2

♦♦

UNCLASSIFIED

Sandy Hook-3

4-NH-2619946-GJ
SERIAL 4

AO 110 (Rev. 06/09) Subpoena to Testify Before a Grand Jury

UNITED STATES DISTRICT COURT

for the

District of Connecticut

SUBPOENA TO TESTIFY BEFORE A GRAND JURY

To: b3 -1

D to appear in this United States district court at the time, date, and place shown below to testify before the court's grand jury. When you arrive, you must remain at the court until the judge or a court officer allows you to leave.

Place: United States Courthouse 141 Church Street New Haven, CT 06510	Date and Time:

You must also bring with you the following documents, electronically stored information, or objects *(blank if not applicable)*:

b3 -1
b6 -2
b7C -2

Date: December 14, 2012

CLERK OF COURT

Signature of Clerk or Deputy Clerk

The name, address, e-mail, and telephone number of the United States attorney, or assistant United States attorney, who requests this subpoena, are:

AUSA
157 Church St., 23rd floor
New Haven, CT 06510

Personal appearance is not required if documents are provided on or before the appearance date to: FBI S/A
600 State St.
New Haven CT 06510

b3 -1
b6 -1, 4
b7C -1, 4

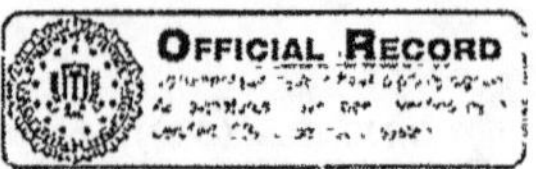

UNCLASSIFIED

FEDERAL BUREAU OF INVESTIGATION

Import Form

Form Type: FD-617 **Date:** 12/17/2012

Title: (U) FGJ Subpoena to [redacted]

b3 -1
b6 -1
b7C -1

Approved By: [redacted]

Drafted By: [redacted]

Case ID #: 4-NH-2619946-GJ (U) Grand Jury Information

FEDERAL GRAND JURY MATERIAL - DISSEMINATE PURSUANT TO RULE 6(E)
Do not disseminate except as authorized by federal rule of criminal procedure 6(e).

Synopsis: (U) A FGJ subpoena issued to [redacted] on 4/14/12 for [redacted]

b3 -
b6 -
b7C

♦♦

UNCLASSIFIED

UNITED STATES DISTRICT COURT

for the

District of Connecticut

SUBPOENA TO TESTIFY BEFORE A GRAND JURY

To: b3 -1

YOU ARE COMMANDED to appear in this United States district court at the time, date, and place shown below to testify before the court's grand jury. When you arrive, you must remain at the court until the judge or a court officer allows you to leave.

Place: United States Courthouse 141 Church Street New Haven, CT 06510	Date and Time:

You must also bring with you the following documents, electronically stored information, or objects *(blank if not applicable)*:

b3 -1
b6 -2
b7C -2

Date: December 14, 2012

CLERK OF COURT

Signature of Clerk or Deputy Clerk

The name, address, e-mail, and telephone number of the United States attorney, or assistant United States attorney, who requests this subpoena, are:

AUSA
157 Church St., 23rd floor
New Haven, CT 06510

Personal appearance is not required if documents are provided on or before the appearance date to: FBI S/A
600 State St.
New Haven CT 06510

b3 -1
b6 -1, 4
b7C -1, 4

FD-1036 (Rev. 10-16-2009)

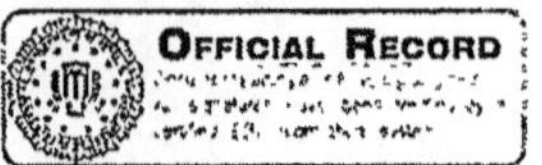

UNCLASSIFIED

FEDERAL BUREAU OF INVESTIGATION

Import Form

Form Type: FD-617 **Date:** 12/17/2012

Title: (U) FGJ subpoena issued to [redacted]

Approved By: [redacted]

Drafted By: [redacted]

b3 -1
b6 -1
b7C -1

Case ID #: 4-NH-2619946-GJ (U) Grand Jury Information

FEDERAL GRAND JURY MATERIAL - DISSEMINATE PURSUANT TO RULE 6(E)
Do not disseminate except as authorized by federal rule of criminal procedure 6(e).

Synopsis: (U) A 12/14/2012 FGJ Subpoena issued to [redacted]

b3 -1

♦♦

UNCLASSIFIED

Sandy Hook-31

4-NH-2619946-GJ
SERIAL 6

UNITED STATES DISTRICT COURT

for the

District of Connecticut

SUBPOENA TO TESTIFY BEFORE A GRAND JURY

To: b3 -1

ED to appear in this United States district court at the time, date, and place shown below to testify before the court's grand jury. When you arrive, you must remain at the court until the judge or a court officer allows you to leave.

Place: United States Courthouse 141 Church Street New Haven, CT 06510	Date and Time:

You must also bring with you the following documents, electronically stored information, or objects *(blank if not applicable)*:

b3 -1

Date: December 14, 2012

CLERK OF COURT

Signature of Clerk or Deputy Clerk

The name, address, e-mail, and telephone number of the United States attorney, or assistant United States attorney, who requests this subpoena, are:

AUSA
157 Church St., 23rd floor
New Haven, CT 06510

Personal appearance is not required if documents are provided on or before the appearance date to: FBI S/A
600 State St.
New Haven CT 06510

b3 -1
b6 -1, 4
b7C -1, 4

FD-1036 (Rev. 10-16-2009)

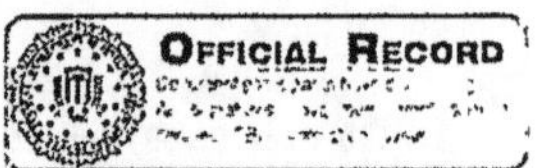

UNCLASSIFIED

FEDERAL BUREAU OF INVESTIGATION

Import Form

Form Type: FD-617. **Date:** 12/17/2012

Title: (U) FGJ Subpoena to [redacted]

Approved By: [redacted]

Drafted By: [redacted]

b3 -1
b6 -1
b7C -1

Case ID #: 4-NH-2619946-GJ (U) Grand Jury Information

FEDERAL GRAND JURY MATERIAL - DISSEMINATE PURSUANT TO RULE 6(E)
Do not disseminate except as authorized by federal rule of criminal procedure 6(e).

Synopsis: (U) A FGJ Subpoena dated 12/14/2012 issued to [redacted]

b3 -

♦♦

UNCLASSIFIED

Sandy Hook-32

4-NH-2619946-GJ
SERIAL 7

AO 110 (Rev. 06/09) Subpoena to Testify Before a Grand Jury

UNITED STATES DISTRICT COURT

for the

District of Connecticut

SUBPOENA TO TESTIFY BEFORE A GRAND JURY

To: b3 -1

ANDED to appear in this United States district court at the time, date, and place shown below to testify before the court's grand jury. When you arrive, you must remain at the court until the judge or a court officer allows you to leave.

Place: United States Courthouse 141 Church Street New Haven, CT 06510	Date and Time:

You must also bring with you the following documents, electronically stored information, or objects *(blank if not applicable)*:

b3 -1

Date: December 14, 2012

CLERK OF COURT

Signature of Clerk or Deputy Clerk

The name, address, e-mail, and telephone number of the United States attorney, or assistant United States attorney, who requests this subpoena, are:

AUSA
157 Church St., 23rd floor
New Haven, CT 06510

Personal appearance is not required if documents are provided on or before the appearance date to: FBI S/A
600 State St.
New Haven CT 06510

b3 -1
b6 -1, 4
b7C -1, 4

FD-1036 (Rev. 10-16-2009)

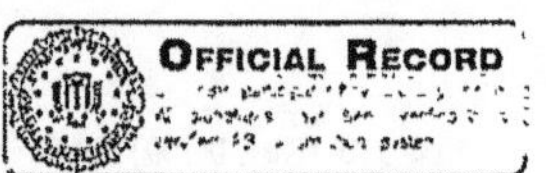

UNCLASSIFIED

FEDERAL BUREAU OF INVESTIGATION

Import Form

Form Type: FD-617 **Date:** 12/17/2012

Title: (U) FGJ Subpoean to [redacted]

b3 -1
b6 -1
b7C -1

Approved By: [redacted]

Drafted By: [redacted]

Case ID #: 4-NH-2619946-GJ (U) Grand Jury Information

FEDERAL GRAND JURY MATERIAL - DISSEMINATE PURSUANT TO RULE 6(E)
Do not disseminate except as authorized by federal rule of criminal procedure 6(e).

Synopsis: (U) FGJ Subpoena issued to [redacted] on 12/15/2012 for [redacted]

b3 -

♦♦

UNCLASSIFIED

Sandy Hook-3

4-NH-2619946-GJ
SERIAL 8

AO 110 (Rev. 06/09) Subpoena to Testify Before a Grand Jury

UNITED STATES DISTRICT COURT

for the

District of Connecticut

SUBPOENA TO TESTIFY BEFORE A GRAND JURY

To: [redacted]

YOU ARE COMMANDED to appear in this United States district court at the time, date, and place shown below to testify before the court's grand jury. When you arrive, you must remain at the court until the judge or a court officer allows you to leave. b3 -1

Place: United States Courthouse 141 Church Street New Haven, CT 06510	Date and Time: [redacted]

You must also bring with you the following documents, electronically stored information, or objects *(blank if not applicable)*:

[redacted] b3 -1

Date: 12/15/2012

CLERK OF COURT

Signature of Clerk or Deputy Clerk

The name, address, e-mail, and telephone number of the United States attorney, or assistant United States attorney, who requests this subpoena, are:

AUSA [redacted]
1000 LaFayette Blvd., 10th Floor
Bridgeport, CT 06604
[redacted]

Personal appearance is not required if documents are provided on or before the appearance date to :
FBI S/A [redacted]
600 State Street, New Haven, CT 06510
[redacted]

b6 -1, 4
b7C -1, 4

FD-1036 (Rev. 10-16-2009)

UNCLASSIFIED

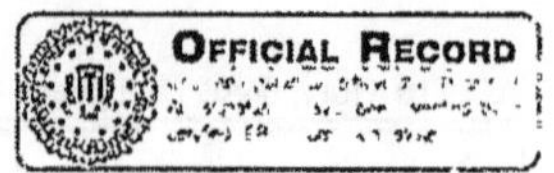

FEDERAL BUREAU OF INVESTIGATION

Import Form

Form Type: FD-617 **Date:** 12/17/2012

Title: (U) FGJ Subpoena to [redacted]

Approved By: [redacted]

Drafted By: [redacted]

b3 -1
b6 -1
b7C -1

Case ID #: 4-NH-2619946-GJ (U) Grand Jury Information

FEDERAL GRAND JURY MATERIAL - DISSEMINATE PURSUANT TO RULE 6(E)
Do not disseminate except as authorized by federal rule of criminal procedure 6(e).

Synopsis: (U) A FGJ Subpoena issued on 12/16/12 to [redacted]

b3

♦♦

UNCLASSIFIED

4-NH-2619946-GJ
SERIAL 9

UNITED STATES DISTRICT COURT
for the
District of Connecticut

SUBPOENA TO TESTIFY BEFORE A GRAND JURY

To: b3 -1

to appear in this United States district court at the time, date, and place shown below to testify before the court's grand jury. When you arrive, you must remain at the court until the judge or a court officer allows you to leave.

Place: United States Courthouse 141 Church Street New Haven, CT 06510	Date and Time:

You must also bring with you the following documents, electronically stored information, or objects *(blank if not applicable)*:

b3 -1

Date: December 16, 2012

CLERK OF COURT

Signature of Clerk or Deputy Clerk

The name, address, e-mail, and telephone number of the United States attorney, or assistant United States attorney, who requests this subpoena, are:

AUSA
157 Church St., 23rd floor
New Haven, CT 06510

Personal appearance is not required if documents are provided on or before the appearance date to: FBI S/A
600 State St.
New Haven CT 06510

b3 -1
b6 -1, 4
b7C -1, 4

FD-1036 (Rev. 10-16-2009)

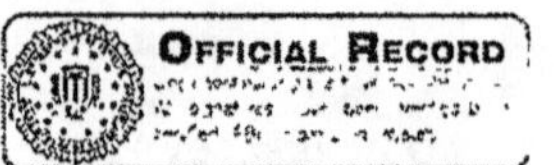

UNCLASSIFIED

FEDERAL BUREAU OF INVESTIGATION

Import Form

Form Type: FD-617 **Date:** 12/17/2012

Title: (U) FGJ Subpoena to [redacted]

Approved By: [redacted]

Drafted By: [redacted]

b3 -1
b6 -1
b7C -1

Case ID #: 4-NH-2619946-GJ (U) Grand Jury Information

FEDERAL GRAND JURY MATERIAL - DISSEMINATE PURSUANT TO RULE 6(E)
Do not disseminate except as authorized by federal rule of criminal procedure 6(e).

Synopsis: (U) A FGJ Subpoena issued to [redacted] on 12/14/2012 [redacted] b3

♦♦

UNCLASSIFIED

Sandy Hook-

4-NH-2619946-GJ

SERIAL 10

AO 110 (Rev. 06/09) Subpoena to Testify Before a Grand Jury

UNITED STATES DISTRICT COURT

for the

District of Connecticut

SUBPOENA TO TESTIFY BEFORE A GRAND JURY

To:

b3 -1

D to appear in this United States district court at the time, date, and place shown below to testify before the court's grand jury. When you arrive, you must remain at the court until the judge or a court officer allows you to leave.

Place: United States Courthouse 141 Church Street New Haven, CT 06510	Date and Time:

You must also bring with you the following documents, electronically stored information, or objects *(blank if not applicable)*:

b3 -1

Date: December 14, 2012

CLERK OF COURT

Signature of Clerk or Deputy Clerk

The name, address, e-mail, and telephone number of the United States attorney, or assistant United States attorney, who requests this subpoena, are:

AUS
157 Church St., 23rd floor
New Haven, CT 06510

Personal appearance is not required if documents are provided on or before the appearance date to: FBI S/A
600 State St.
New Haven CT 06510

b3 -1
b6 -1, 4
b7C -1, 4

FD-1036 (Rev. 10-16-2009)

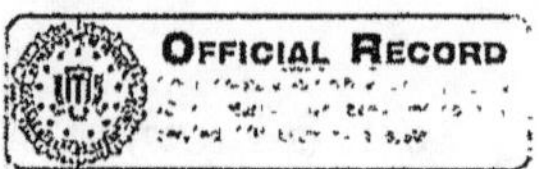

UNCLASSIFIED

FEDERAL BUREAU OF INVESTIGATION

Import Form

Form Type: FD-617 **Date:** 12/17/2012

Title: (U) FGJ Subpoena issued to [redacted]

Approved By: [redacted] b3 -1 b6 -1 b7C -1

Drafted By: [redacted]

Case ID #: 4-NH-2619946-GJ (U) Grand Jury Information

FEDERAL GRAND JURY MATERIAL - DISSEMINATE PURSUANT TO RULE 6(E)
Do not disseminate except as authorized by federal rule of criminal procedure 6(e).

Synopsis: (U) A FGJ Subpoena issued on 12/14/12 to [redacted] b3

♦♦

UNCLASSIFIED

Sandy Hook-33

4-NH-2619946-GJ
SERIAL 11

UNITED STATES DISTRICT COURT

for the

District of Connecticut

SUBPOENA TO TESTIFY BEFORE A GRAND JURY

To: b3 -1

YOU ARE COMMANDED to appear in this United States district court at the time, date, and place shown below to testify before the court's grand jury. When you arrive, you must remain at the court until the judge or a court officer allows you to leave.

Place: United States Courthouse 141 Church Street New Haven, CT 06510	Date and Time:

You must also bring with you the following documents, electronically stored information, or objects *(blank if not applicable)*:

b3 -1

Date: December 14, 2012

CLERK OF COURT

Signature of Clerk or Deputy Clerk

The name, address, e-mail, and telephone number of the United States attorney, or assistant United States attorney, who requests this subpoena, are:

AUSA
157 Church St., 23rd floor
New Haven, CT 06510

Personal appearance is not required if documents are provided on or before the appearance date to: FBI S/A
600 State St.
New Haven CT 06510

b3 -1
b6 -1, 4
b7C -1, 4

FD-1036 (Rev. 10-16-2009)

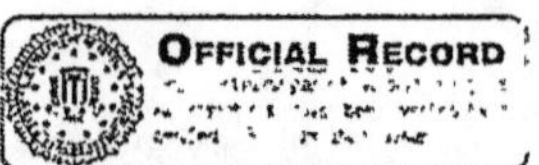

UNCLASSIFIED

FEDERAL BUREAU OF INVESTIGATION

Import Form

Form Type: FD-617 **Date:** 12/17/2012

Title: (U) [redacted]

Approved By: [redacted]

Drafted By: [redacted]

b3 -1
b6 -1
b7C -1

Case ID #: 4-NH-2619946-GJ (U) Grand Jury Information

FEDERAL GRAND JURY MATERIAL - DISSEMINATE PURSUANT TO RULE 6(E)
Do not disseminate except as authorized by federal rule of criminal procedure 6(e).

Synopsis: (U) A FGJ Subpoena issued to [redacted]

b3 -
b6 -
b7C -

♦♦

UNCLASSIFIED

Sandy Hook-3

4-NH-2619946-GJ
SERIAL 12

AO 110 (Rev. 06/09) Subpoena to Testify Before a Grand Jury

UNITED STATES DISTRICT COURT

for the

District of Connecticut

SUBPOENA TO TESTIFY BEFORE A GRAND JURY

To:

b3 -1

YOU ARE COMMANDED to appear in this United States district court at the time, date, and place shown below to testify before the court's grand jury. When you arrive, you must remain at the court until the judge or a court officer allows you to leave.

Place: United States Courthouse 141 Church Street New Haven, CT 06510	Date and Time:

You must also bring with you the following documents, electronically stored information, or objects *(blank if not applicable)*:

b3 -1
b6 -2
b7C -2

Date: December 14, 2012

CLERK OF COURT

Signature of Clerk or Deputy Clerk

The name, address, e-mail, and telephone number of the United States attorney, or assistant United States attorney, who requests this subpoena, are:

AUSA
157 Church St., 23rd floor
New Haven, CT 06510

Personal appearance is not required if documents are provided on or before the appearance date to: FBI S/A
600 State St.
New Haven CT 06510

b3 -1
b6 -1, 4
b7C -1, 4

FD-302 (Rev. 5-8-10)

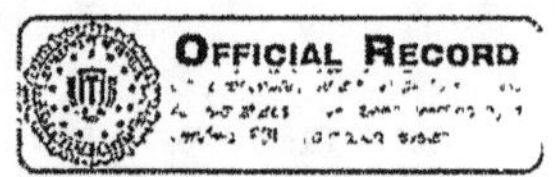

FEDERAL BUREAU OF INVESTIGATION

Date of entry 12/15/2012

FEDERAL GRAND JURY MATERIAL - DISSEMINATE PURSUANT TO RULE 6(E)
Do not disseminate except as authorized by federal rule of criminal procedure 6(e).

On 12/14/2012 at approximately 5:02 PM, a Federal Grand Jury subpoena was served on [redacted] The subpoena was served via e-mail. b3 -1 b6 -2 b7C -

On 12/14/2012 at approximately 9:00 PM, [redacted] met with SA [redacted] and SA [redacted] to provide the Agents with [redacted] Also present during this meeting were [redacted] b3 -1 b6 -2 b7C -

[redacted] will be submitted for storage to the New Haven Evidence Custodian. b3

Investigation on 12/14/2012 at [redacted] United States (In Person, Email) b3 -

File # 4-NH-2619946-GJ Date drafted 12/15/2012 b6 -

by [redacted] b7C

4-NH-2619946-GJ

SERIAL 13

UNITED STATES DISTRICT COURT

for the

District of Connecticut

SUBPOENA TO TESTIFY BEFORE A GRAND JURY

To:

b3 -1
b6 -2, 5
b7C -2, 5

YOU ARE COMMANDED to appear in this United States district court at the time, date, and place shown below to testify before the court's grand jury. When you arrive, you must remain at the court until the judge or a court officer allows you to leave.

Place: United States Courthouse 141 Church Street New Haven, CT 06510	Date and Time:

You must also bring with you the following documents, electronically stored information, or objects *(blank if not applicable)*:

b3 -1
b6 -2
b7C -2

Date: December 14, 2012

CLERK OF COURT

Signature of Clerk or Deputy Clerk

The name, address, e-mail, and telephone number of the United States attorney, or assistant United States attorney, who requests this subpoena, are:

AUSA
157 Church St., 23rd floor
New Haven, CT 06510

Personal appearance is not required if documents are provided on or before the appearance date to: FBI S/A
600 State St.
New Haven CT 06510

b3 -1
b6 -1, 4
b7C -1, 4

PROOF OF SERVICE

This subpoena for *(name of individual or organization)* [redacted]
was received by me on *(date)* 12/14/2012 .

☒ I served the sub[redacted]s: served via email to [redacted]
on *(date)* 12/14/2012 ; or

☐ I returned the subpoena unexecuted because: ______________

b3 -1
b6 -2,
b7C -2

I declare under penalty of perjury that this inf[redacted]

Date: 12/15/2012 [redacted]

b6
b7C

Special Agent [redacted]
Pri[redacted]

600 State St, New Haven, CT 06512
Server's address

Additional information regarding attempted service, etc:

From:
Sent: Friday, December 14, 2012 5:02 PM
To:
Subject: Re: (No Subject)
Attachments:

b3 -1
b6 -1, 6
b7C -1, 6

- please find attached subpoena for the email information we discussed.

Thank you,

From
To
Sent: Fri Dec 14 16:50:09 2012
Subject: RE: (No Subject)

b6 -1, 6
b7C -1, 6

I will have an IT contact for you in 10 minutes.

Sent with Good (www.good.com)

-----Original Message-----
From:
Sent: Friday, December 14, 2012 04:29 PM Eastern Standard Time
To:
Subject: Re: (No Subject)

b6 -1, 2, 6
b7C -1, 2, 6

for the subpoena, who is it being served on and what is the full corporate address? Thanks

(cell)

From
To
Sent: Fri Dec 14 16:22:29 2012
Subject: FW: (No Subject)

b6 -1, 2, 6
b7C -1, 2, 6

My contact info

b6 -6
b7C -6

Sent with Good (www.good.com)

-----Original Message-----
From:
Sent: Friday, December 14, 2012 04:18 PM Eastern Standard Time
To
Subject:

b6 -2, 6
b7C -2, 6

FD-302 (Rev. 5-8-10)

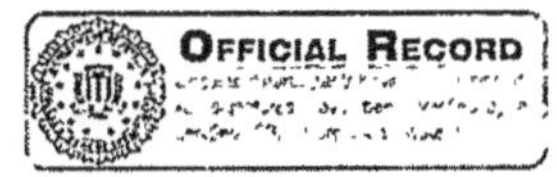

FEDERAL BUREAU OF INVESTIGATION

Date of entry 12/19/2012

FEDERAL GRAND JURY MATERIAL - DISSEMINATE PURSUANT TO RULE 6(E)
Do not disseminate except as authorized by federal rule of criminal procedure 6(e).

On 12/18/2012, writer served a Federal Grand Jury Subpoena on [redacted] The subpoena dated 12/18/2012 and issued by the United States District Court for the District of Connecticut, requested [redacted] b3 -1 b6 -2 b7C -2

On 12/18/2012, writer received the subpoena results [redacted] and noted results below. [redacted] as well as a copy of the subpoena will be filed in a 1-A envelope. b3 -1 b6 -5 b7C -5

[redacted] b3 -1

Investigation on 12/18/2012 at Newtown, Connecticut, United States (Email)

File # 4-NH-2619946-GJ Date drafted 12/19/2012

by [redacted] b6 -1 b7C -1

4-NH-2619946-GJ

SERIAL 14

UNITED STATES DISTRICT COURT

for the

District of Connecticut

SUBPOENA TO TESTIFY BEFORE A GRAND JURY

To:

YOU ARE COMMANDED to appear in this United States district court at the time, date, and place shown below to testify before the court's grand jury. When you arrive, you must remain at the court until the judge or a court officer allows you to leave.

Place: United States District Court 915 Lafayette Boulevard Bridgeport, Connecticut	Date and Time:

b3 -1
b6 -1, 2
b7C -1,

You must also bring with you the following documents, electronically stored information, or objects *(blank if not applicable)*:

Personal appearance is not required if the subpoenaed materials are produced on or before the return date to FBI Special Agent If you have any questions about this subpoena, please contact Special Agent at

Date: 12/18/2012

CLERK OF COURT

Signature of Clerk or Deputy Clerk

The name, address, e-mail, and telephone number of the United States attorney, or assistant United States attorney, who requests this subpoena, are:

Assistant United States Attorney
United States Attorney's Office
1000 Lafayette Boulevard, 10th Floor
Bridgeport, Connecticut 06604

b6
b7C

PROOF OF SERVICE

This subpoena for *(name of individual or organization)* [redacted]
was received by me on *(date)* 12/18/2012.

☑ I served the subpoena by delivering a copy to the named person as follows: Served via email to [redacted] on *(date)* 12/18/2012 ; or

☐ I returned the subpoena unexecuted because:

I declare under penalty of perjury that this information is true.

Date: 12/18/2012

[redacted]
Server's signature

[redacted] FBI Special Agent
Printed name and title

600 State Street
New Haven, CT 06511
Server's address

Additional information regarding attempted service, etc:

b3 -1
b6 -1, 5
b7C -1, 5

FD-302 (Rev. 5-8-10)

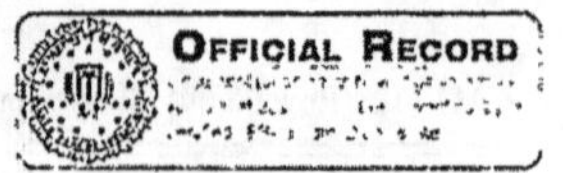

FEDERAL BUREAU OF INVESTIGATION

Date of entry 12/19/2012

FEDERAL GRAND JURY MATERIAL - DISSEMINATE PURSUANT TO RULE 6(E)
Do not disseminate except as authorized by federal rule of criminal procedure 6(e).

On 12/18/2012, writer served a Federal Grand Jury Subpoena on [redacted] Subpoena was sent via e-mail to [redacted] The subpoena dated 12/18/2012 and issued by the United States District Court for the District of Connecticut, requested [redacted]

b3 -1
b6 -2,
b7C -2,

Investigation on 12/18/2012 at Newtown, Connecticut, United States (Email)

File # 4-NH-2619946-GJ Date drafted 12/19/2012

by [redacted]

b6 -1
b7C -

This document contains neither recommendations nor conclusions of the FBI. It is the property of the FBI and is loaned to your agency; it and its contents are not to be distributed outside your agency.

Sandy Hook-

4-NH-2619946-GJ
SERIAL 15

FD-1036 (Rev. 10-16-2009)

UNCLASSIFIED

FEDERAL BUREAU OF INVESTIGATION

Import Form

Form Type: INSERT **Date:** 12/19/2012

Title: (U) Correction of Title for Serial 15

Approved By: A/SSA [redacted]

Drafted By: [redacted]

Case ID #: 4-NH-2619946-GJ (U) Grand Jury Information

b3 -1
b6 -1
b7C -1

Synopsis: (U) The title of Serial 15 should be Service of Subpoena to [redacted]

♦♦

UNCLASSIFIED

4-NH-2619946-GJ
SERIAL 16

4-NH-2619946-GJ

b3
b6
b7

The title for Serial 15 should be "Service of Subpoena to

FD-302 (Rev. 5-8-10)

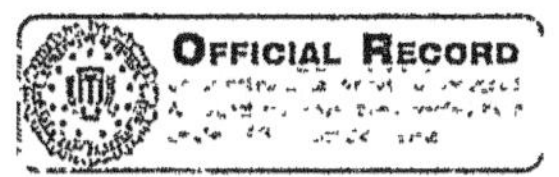

FEDERAL BUREAU OF INVESTIGATION

Date of entry 12/19/2012

FEDERAL GRAND JURY MATERIAL - DISSEMINATE PURSUANT TO RULE 6(E)
Do not disseminate except as authorized by federal rule of criminal procedure 6(e).

On 12/18/2012, writer served a Federal Grand Jury Subpoena on [redacted] Subpoena was sent via e-mail to [redacted] and via overnight mail. The subpoena dated 12/18/2012 and issued by the United States District Court for the District of Connecticut, [redacted]

b3 -1

Investigation on 12/18/2012 at Newtown, Connecticut, United States (Email, Mail)

File # 4-NH-2619946-GJ Date drafted 12/19/2012

by [redacted]

b6 -1
b7C -1

4-NH-2619946-GJ
SERIAL 17

FD-302 (Rev. 5-8-10)

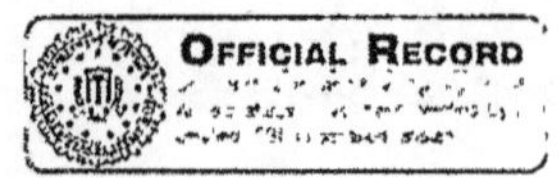

FEDERAL BUREAU OF INVESTIGATION

Date of entry 12/19/2012

FEDERAL GRAND JURY MATERIAL - DISSEMINATE PURSUANT TO RULE 6(E)
Do not disseminate except as authorized by federal rule of criminal procedure 6(e).

On 12/18/2012, writer served a subpoena to [redacted] [redacted] Subpoena results were received on 12/19/2012 from [redacted] A copy of the subpoena results will be filed in a 1-A. Results of Subpoena are as follows:

b3 -1
b6 -2,
b7C -2,

[redacted]

b3 -
b6 -
b7C

[redacted]

b3 -
b6 -
b7C

Investigation on 12/19/2012 at New Haven, Connecticut, United States (Email)

b6 -1
b7C -1

File # 4-NH-2619946-GJ

Date drafted 12/19/2012

by [redacted]

Sandy Hook-

4-NH-2619946-GJ

SERIAL 1[illegible]

FEDERAL BUREAU OF INVESTIGATION

Date of entry 12/20/2012

On 12/19/2012, SA [redacted] received subpoena returns from [redacted]

[redacted]

b3 -1
b6 -1, 5
b7C -1, 5

[redacted]

b3 -1

[redacted]

b3 -1

[redacted]

b3 -1

b3 -1
b6 -1
b7C -1

Investigation on 12/19/2012 at [redacted] United States (In Person)

File # 4-NH-2619946-GJ Date drafted 12/20/2012

by [redacted]

4-NH-2619946-GJ
SERIAL 19

FD-302 (Rev. 5-8-10)

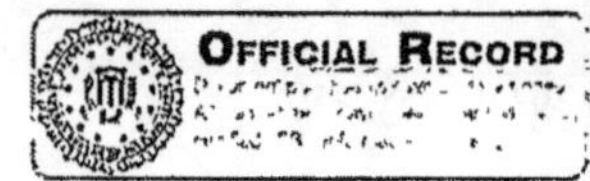

UNCLASSIFIED//~~FOUO~~

FEDERAL BUREAU OF INVESTIGATION

Date of entry 12/20/2012

FEDERAL GRAND JURY MATERIAL - DISSEMINATE PURSUANT TO RULE 6(E)
Do not disseminate except as authorized by federal rule of criminal procedure 6(e).

On December 20, 2012, Special Agent (SA) [redacted] faxed Federal Grand Jury subpoena number [redacted] to [redacted] [redacted] [redacted] The Federal Grand Jury subpoena required the production of the following: b3 b6 b7C

[redacted] b3

Pursuant to the above referenced Federal Grand Jury Subpoena, on December, 20, 2012, SA [redacted] received [redacted]

[redacted] b3 b6 b7

UNCLASSIFIED//~~FOUO~~

Investigation on 12/20/2012 at New Haven, Connecticut, United States (Email, Fax) b6 - b7C

File # 4-NH-2619946-GJ Date drafted 12/20/2012

by [redacted]

4-NH-2619946-GJ
SERIAL 20

b3 -1

b3 -1

The subpoena and subpoena return will be electronically filed as a 1A attachment to this document.

UNITED STATES DISTRICT COURT

for the

District of Connecticut

SUBPOENA TO TESTIFY BEFORE A GRAND JURY

To: b3 -1

D to appear in this United States district court at the time, date, and place shown below to testify before the court's grand jury. When you arrive, you must remain at the court until the judge or a court officer allows you to leave.

Place: United States Courthouse 141 Church Street New Haven, CT 06510	Date and Time:

You must also bring with you the following documents, electronically stored information, or objects *(blank if not applicable)*:

b3

Date: December 20, 2012

CLERK OF COURT

Signature of Clerk or Deputy Clerk

The name, address, e-mail, and telephone number of the United States attorney, or assistant United States attorney, who requests this subpoena, are:

AUSA
157 Church St., 23rd floor
New Haven, CT 06510

Personal appearance is not required if documents are provided on or before the appearance date to: FBI S/A
600 State St.
New Haven CT 06510

b3 -1
b6 -1,
b7C -1,

PROOF OF SERVICE

This subpoena for *(name of individual or organization)* [redacted]
was received by me on *(date)* 12/20/2012 .

☑ I served the subpoena by delivering a copy to the named person as follows: I faxed the subpoena to [redacted] on *(date)* 12/20/2012 ; or b3 -1

☐ I returned the subpoena unexecuted because: ____________

I declare under penalty of perjury that this information is true.

Date: 12/20/2012 [redacted] b6 -1 b7C -1

[redacted] Special Agent
Printed name and title

660 State Street New Haven, CT 06511
Server's address

Additional information regarding attempted service, etc:

FD-448
Revised
10-27-2004

FEDERAL BUREAU OF INVESTIGATION
FACSIMILE COVER SHEET

PRECEDENCE

( ) Immediate (•) Priority ( ) Routine

CLASSIFICATION

( ) Top Secret ( ) Secret ( ) Confidential ( ) Sensitive (•) Unclassified

TO

Name of Office:	Facsimile Number:	Date:
[redacted]	[redacted]	**12/20/2012**

Attn:	Room:	Telephone Number:
[redacted]		

FROM

Name of Office:		Number of Pages: (including cover)
FBI New Haven		**4**

Originator's Name:	Originator's Telephone Number:	Originator's Facsimile Number:
SA [redacted]	[redacted]	[redacted]

Approved:

b3 -1
b6 -1, 5
b7C -1, 5

DETAILS

Subject:
[redacted]

Special Handling Instructions:
Please note the subpoena requests that you refrain from disclosing the existence of the subpoena to any third party. If you have any questions or concerns, please feel free to e-mail:
[redacted]

Brief Description of Communication Faxed:

WARNING

Information attached to the cover sheet is U.S. Government Property. If you are not the intended recipient of this information disclosure, reproduction, distribution, or use of this information is prohibited (18.USC, § 641). Please notify the originator or local FBI Office immediately to arrange for proper disposition.

Sandy Hook-3

*************** -COMM. JOURNAL- ******************* DATE DEC-20-2012 ***** TIME 16:22 ********

MODE = MEMORY TRANSMISSION START=DEC-20 16:20 END=DEC-20 16:22

FILE NO.=192

STN NO.	COMM.	STATION NAME/EMAIL ADDRESS/TELEPHONE NO.	PAGES	DURATION
001	OK	[redacted]	004/004	00:01:11

-SQ 10

***** UF-8000 v2 ****************** -FBI NEW HAVEN - ***** - [redacted] *********

FD-448
Revised
10-27-2004

FEDERAL BUREAU OF INVESTIGATION
FACSIMILE COVER SHEET

PRECEDENCE

( ) Immediate (•) Priority ( ) Routine

CLASSIFICATION

( ) Top Secret ( ) Secret ( ) Confidential ( ) Sensitive (•) Unclassified

TO

Name of Office: [redacted]	Facsimile Number: [redacted]	Date: 12/20/2012
Attn: [redacted]	Room:	Telephone Number:

FROM

Name of Office: FBI New Haven	Number of Pages: (including cover) 4	
Originator's Name: SA [redacted]	Originator's Telephone Number: [redacted]	Originator's Facsimile Number:
Approved:		

b3 -1
b6 -1, 5
b7C -1, 5

DETAILS

Subject:
FGJ Subpoen[redacted]

Special Handling Instructions:
Please note the subpoena requests that you refrain from disclosing the existence of the subpoena to any third party. If you have any questions or concerns, please feel free to e-mail: [redacted]

Brief Description of Communication Faxed:

WARNING
Information attached to the cover sheet is U.S. Government Property. If you are not the intended recipient of this information disclosure, reproduction, distribution, or use of this information is prohibited (18.USC, § 641). Please notify the originator or local FBI Office immediately to arrange for proper disposition.

FD-302 (Rev. 5-8-10)

FEDERAL BUREAU OF INVESTIGATION

Date of entry 12/17/2012

[redacted] and [redacted] Street, Sandy Hook, Connecticut were interviewed at their residence. After being advised of the identity of the interviewing Agents and the nature of the interview, [redacted] and [redacted] provided the following information: b6 -6 b7C -6

They lived at [redacted] for the past [redacted] years. [redacted] The LANZAS were married until a few years ago. [redacted] heard NANCY LANZA make a derogatory remark about her ex-husband after the divorce but she and NANCY LANZA were not friends. They had coffee once in all the years they lived there. [redacted] believed that the ex-husband would get the boys on the weekends. b6 -6 b7C -6

They knew that the younger LANZA boy had a hard time in public school so the LANZAS put him in catholic school at St. Rose's for a short time but that did not work out either. NANCY LANZA asked [redacted] about St. Rose's [redacted] recalled that NANCY mentioned her younger boy was very involved with Japanese Manga which are some type of comics and that he did not relate well with other kids. NANCY LANZA pulled him out of St. Rose's because he was flunking religion. [redacted] did not know if the younger LANZA finished high school. He may have finished online. b6 -6 b7C -6

[redacted] She said that there were always cars going up and down the driveway at strange hours of the night. [redacted] b6 -6 b7C -6

Investigation on 12/14/2012 at Newtown, Connecticut, United States (In Person)

File # 4-NH-2619946 Date drafted 12/17/2012

by [redacted] b6 -1 b7C -1

4-NH-2619946 Serial 71

12/13/12

b6 -6
b7C -6

Always cars [illegible] down the driveway – strange hours of the night

the past

lived here years –

she [illegible] always [illegible]

about ex husband after divorce. wouldn't [illegible] boys [illegible].

Had coffee w/ Nancy once –

Younger boy went to ST. Rose He had hard time in public school so tried catholic school but that didn't last long either.

Nancy had asked about ST. Rose

said younger one didn't get along.

Younger kid very into w/ Japanese Manga (comics)

didn't relate well w/ other kids. He was fidgety in religious class so she pulled him out.

Nancy didn't work when kids were in school.

May have finished HS online – not sure of that.

10:35 AM approx heard dogs barking

10:40 were evacuated by PD

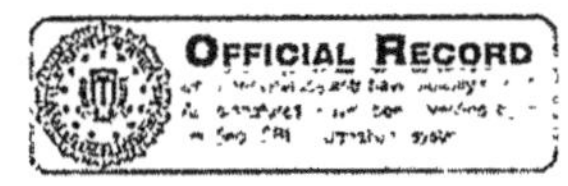

FEDERAL BUREAU OF INVESTIGATION

Date of entry 12/19/2012

[redacted] date of birth [redacted] was interviewed at his residence located, at [redacted] On 12/15/2012 at approximately 8:00PM, writer contacted [redacted] at the captioned residence. After being advised of the identity of the interviewing Agent and the nature of the interview, [redacted] provided the following information: b6 -1, 6 b7C -1, 6 b7D -1

[redacted] lives at the listed residence with his wife [redacted] and their family. For employment, [redacted] travels [redacted] b6 -6 b7C -6 b7D -1

[redacted]

[redacted] called [redacted] and they both provided verbal consent for writer to take [redacted] for further investigation. Writer provided a handwritten authorization, which [redacted] signed, explaining what items were to be taken and later to be returned. [redacted] [redacted] (See attached documents) b6 -6 b7C -6 b7D -1 b7E -6

Investigation on 12/15/2012 at [redacted] United States (In Person)

File # 4-NH-2619946 Date drafted 12/19/2012

by [redacted]

b6 -1, 6 b7C -1, 6 b7D -1

4-NH-3619946 Serial 72

(AT 8:20pm 12/15/12), I SA [redacted]

received verbal consent from [redacted]

to temporary take in my possession their property, [redacted] for further investigation.

[redacted]

[redacted] All items will be returned as it is taken on this day,

b6 -1, b7C -1 b7D -1 b7E -6

FD-941 (2-26-01)

CONSENT TO SEARCH COMPUTER(S)

I, ______________________________, have been asked by Special Agents of the Federal Bureau of Investigation (FBI) to permit a complete search by the FBI or its designees of any and all computers, any electronic and/or optical data storage and/or retrieval system or medium, and any related computer peripherals, described below:

____
CPU Make, Model & Serial Number (if available)

____
Storage or Retrieval Media, Computer Peripherals

____

____

and located at ______________________________, which I own, possess, control, and/or have access to, for any evidence of a crime or other violation of the law. The required passwords, logins, and/or specific directions for computer entry are as follows: ______________________________.

I have been advised of my right to refuse to consent to this search, and I give permission for this search, freely and voluntarily, and not as the result of threats or promises of any kind.

I authorize those Agents to take any evidence discovered during this search, together with the medium in/on which it is stored, and any associated data, hardware, software and computer peripherals.

______________ Date	______________________ Signature
______________ Date	______________________ Signature of Witness
	______________________ Printed Full Name of Witness
	______________________ Location

See handwritten verbal/written consent for [redacted] (see attached)

b7D -1
b7E -6

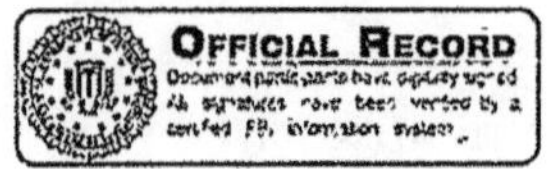

FEDERAL BUREAU OF INVESTIGATION

Date of entry 12/19/2012

On 12/17/12, writer and Task Force Officer (TFO) [redacted] contacted [redacted] at her residence located at [redacted] b6 -4, b7C -4, b7D -1

Writer and TFO [redacted] returned and provided RP with her property, [redacted] In the presence of writer and TFO [redacted] RP signed the FD-597 receipt for property returned and FD-941 page 2 consent to search computer forms. (See attached signed forms) b6 -4, b7C -4, b7D -1, b7E -6

RP further clarified on 12/14/12, she called the Connecticut State Police with the information she had from her cell phone [redacted] at approximately 12:45PM. At approximately 1:37PM, the RP received a call from the Connecticut State Police. At approximately 3:25PM, the RP sent an e-mail to Connecticut State Police Detective [redacted] of the information she reported. RP provided writer and TFO [redacted] with her e-mail address of [redacted] b6 -3, 4, b7C -3, 4, b7D -1

b6 -1, 4, b7C -1, 4, b7D -1

Investigation on 12/17/2012 at [redacted] United States (In Person)

File # 4-NH-2619946 Date drafted 12/19/2012

by [redacted]

FD-597 (Rev 8-11-94)

UNITED STATES DEPARTMENT OF JUSTICE
FEDERAL BUREAU OF INVESTIGATION
Receipt for Property Received/Returned/Released/Seized

File # 4-NH-2619946

On (date) 12/17/12

item(s) listed below were:
☐ Received From
☒ Returned To
☐ Released To
☐ Seized

(Name)

(Street Address)

(City)

b6 -6
b7C -6
b7D -1
b7E -6

Description of Item(s):

Received By

Received From

(Signature)

b6 -1, 6
b7C -1,
b7D -1

This is to certify that on 12/17/12 at 4:19pm

Special Agents of the Federal Bureau of Investigation, U.S. Department of Justice, conducted a complete search of any and all computers, any electronic and/or optical data storage and/or retrieval system, and any related computer peripherals.

I certify that nothing was removed from my custody by those Agents.

(Signed

b6 -4, 6
b7C -4,
b7D -1

Witnessed:

Special Agent
Federal Bureau of Investigation
U.S. Department of Justice

U.S. Department of Justice

FD-1057 (Rev. 5-8-10)

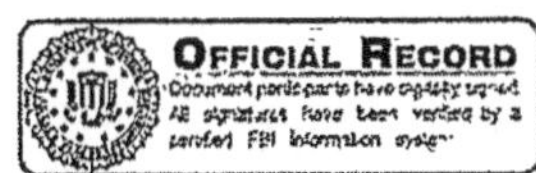

UNCLASSIFIED

FEDERAL BUREAU OF INVESTIGATION

Electronic Communication

Title: (U) [redacted] examined by North Texas Regional Computer Forensic Laboratory

Date: 12/19/2012

b7D -1
b7E -6

To: [redacted]

From: DALLAS
CT3
Contact: [redacted]

b6 -1
b7C -1

Approved By: SSA [redacted]

Drafted By: [redacted]

Case ID #: 4-NH-2619946 (U) UNSUB(S)
Sandy Hook Elementary School
12 Dickinson St, Sandy Hook, CT-Victim
Firearms Act.
OO:NH

Synopsis: (U) To document report of examination of [redacted] [redacted] by North Texas Regional Computer Forensic Laboratory (NTRCFL).

b7D -1
b7E -6

[redacted]

b7E -1

Enclosure(s): Enclosed are the following items:
1. (U) NTRCFL report of examination
2. (U) NTRCFL property/evidence receipt

Details:

On 12/15/12, writer provided Senior Forensic Examiner [redacted] of the NTRCFL, [redacted] for further examination. (See attached NTRCFL Property/Evidence Receipt)

b6 -1
b7C -1
b7D -1
b7E -6

UNCLASSIFIED

4-NH-2619946 Serial 74

Title: (U) [redacted] examined by North Texas Regional Computer Forensic Laboratory
Re: 4-NH-2619946, 12/19/2012

b7D -
b7E -

On 12/17/12, the NTRCFL completed their examination of [redacted] and returned the listed items to writer. (See attached NTRCFL Report of Examination)

♦♦

301 North Market St suite 500
5th floor
Dallas, Texas 75202

REPORT OF EXAMINATION

To: SA [redacted]
Federal Bureau of Investigation
Dallas Division
[redacted]

Date: December 16, 2012

Case ID No.: 4-NH-2619946

Lab No.: R2[redacted]

b6 -1
b7C -1
b7D -1

Reference: Communication dated December 15, 2012

Ref. No.: N/A

Title: UNSUB; FIREARMS ACT

Date specimen(s) received: December 15, 2012

Specimens: [redacted]

b7D -1
b7E -6

Request:

SA[redacted] requested tha[redacted] be examined and information found on the device be provided to him.

b6 -1
b7C -1
b7D -1
b7E -8

Summary of Examination:

The evidence item was processe[redacted] [redacted] This device has[redacted] [redacted]

b7D -1
b7E -8

Details of Examination:

The following processes were performed on submitted[redacted]

- The evidence items were photographed and initialed
- The date is correct[redacted] [redacted]

b7E -8

- The device has
- The This identification is unique to
-
-
- The only information

b7D
b7E

The following items were generated during the examination process:

Disposition of Evidence:

and were returned to the Evidence Control Technician. The notes of the examination were placed in the case file and will be retained with the case file by the North Texas Regional Computer Forensics Laboratory along with a copy of the item. A copy of this report will be given to the Case Agent along with three (3) copies of and the original evidence items.

b7D
b7E

b7D

Examiner: [redacted] b6 -1 b7C -1

NTRCFL
Dallas Division
Computer Analysis Response Team

4-NH-2619946

Property / Evidence Receipt

301 North Market Street, suite 500 Dallas, Texas 75202
Office number: 972-559-5800 Fax number 972-559-5881

NTRCFL # R2-_____ - __________

On (date) 12 / 13 / 12

(time) _____:_____am / pm

The item(s) listed below were:

X Received from

____ Returned to

____ Checked out

____ Returned to ECF

Name: [redacted] b6 - b7C

Agency: FBI

Address: __________

Description of Item(s):

[redacted] b7D -1 b7E -6

Received by: [redacted] Received from: [redacted] b6 -1 b7C -1

Witnessed by: __________

Property / Evidence Receipt

301 North Market Street, suite 500 Dallas, Texas 75202
Office number: 972-559-5800 Fax number 972-559-5881

NTRCFL # R2-[redacted]

Page 1 of 1 b7D -1

On (date) 12 / 17 / 2012

(time) _____:_____ am / pm

The item(s) listed below were:

___ Received from
X Returned to
___ Checked out
___ Returned to ECF

b6 -1
b7C -1

Name: [redacted]

Agency: FBI- Dallas

Address: ____________________

Description of Item(s):

Report of Examination [redacted]

[redacted]

b7D -1
b7E -6

Received by [redacted] Received from [redacted]

b6 -1
b7C -1

Witnessed by:

FD-1057 (Rev. 5-8-10)

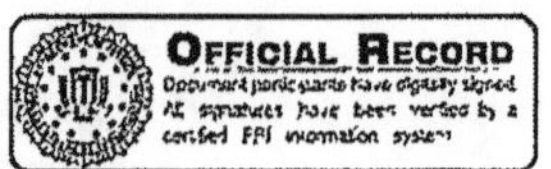

UNCLASSIFIED

FEDERAL BUREAU OF INVESTIGATION

Electronic Communication

Title: (U) Interview of [redacted] **Date:** 12/17/2012

From: NEW HAVEN
NH-MRA
Contact: [redacted]

b6 -1, 7
b7C -1, 7

Approved By: [redacted]

Drafted By: [redacted]

Case ID #: 4-NH-2619946 (U) UNSUB(S)
Sandy Hook Elementary School
12 Dickinson St, Sandy Hook, CT-Victim
Firearms Act.
OO:NH

Synopsis: (U) Interview of Mr. & Mrs. [redacted] who received threatening message on there answering machine.

b6 -7
b7C -7
b7E -1

[redacted]

Enclosure(s): Enclosed are the following items:
1. (U) Interview Notes

Details:

On December 16, 2012, [redacted] born [redacted] and his wife [redacted] born [redacted] were interviewed at there home located at [redacted] Newtown, Connecticut. Present during the interview was this writer and SA [redacted] After being advised of the nature of the interview and the identity of the interviewing Agents, [redacted] provided the following information:

b6 -1,
b7C -1,

The [redacted] currently reside at the above address and [redacted] [redacted] During the morning of December 16, 2012, [redacted] left his residence around 8:00 a.m. to eat breakfast. [redacted] had left earlier than him to go

b6 -7
b7C -

UNCLASSIFIED

4-NH-2619946 Serial 76

Title: (U) Interview of [redacted] b6 -7 b7C -7
Re: 4-NH-2619946, 12/17/2012

Christmas shopping [redacted] Upon his return, he discovered a missed telephone call on his home phone number [redacted] [redacted] advised that he then checked the voice mail messages on their home telephone answering machine. The message was as follows "This is Adam Lanza. I'm gonna kill you. Your dead." The caller identification read the incoming call was from telephone number 1-646-843-7100. The [redacted] did not recognize the voice or the incoming number. (Investigative Note: This writer made a copy of the voice recording and advised [redacted] to maintain the recording.) b6 -5, 7 b7C -5, 7

[redacted] advised that [redacted] [redacted] advised that she is still employed [redacted] [redacted] advised that his number is listed in the phone book and he provides both his cell and home phone number [redacted] for emergency issues. b6 -7 b7C -7

[redacted] was amenable to re-contact and could be reached at his home number (listed above) or his cellular telephone number, [redacted] b6 -7 b7C -7

♦♦

"This is Adam Lanza..
I'm gonna kill you
Your dead" Sunday 9:12 AM
from 1646 843-7[illegible]00

- do not recognize voice.

NEWTON CT.

b6 -7
b7C -7

live alone. no private # no other calls or friends received calls.

provide both

cell + home

cell #

b6 -7
b7C -7

FD-1057 (Rev. 5-8-10)

UNCLASSIFIED

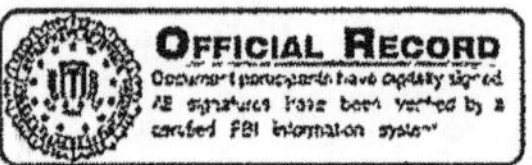

FEDERAL BUREAU OF INVESTIGATION

Electronic Communication

Title: (U) Interview request at Bank of San Antonio

Date: 12/19/2012

To: [redacted]

From: NEW HAVEN
NH-8
Contact: [redacted]

b6 -1
b7C -1

Approved By: [redacted]

Drafted By: [redacted]

Case ID #: 4-NH-2619946 (U) UNSUB(S)
Sandy Hook Elementary School
12 Dickinson St, Sandy Hook, CT-Victim
Firearms Act.
OO:NH

Synopsis: (U) Interviews to be conducted, immediately, at Bank of San Antonio.

[redacted] b7E -1

Details:

A call was placed to the Bank of San Antonio, (210)271-3065, this morning, December 19, 2012, at 9:53am from the same number that made the Newtown bomb threats. The bank personnel should be asked if they received a bomb threat this morning and/or if they received any suspicious calls to the above captioned #. Bank information is as follows:

Bank of San Antonio

911 North Frio Street

UNCLASSIFIED

4-NH-2619946 Serial 79

Title: (U) Interview request at Bank of San Antonio
Re: 4-NH-2619946, 12/19/2012

San Antonio, TX

♦♦

FD-1057 (Rev. 5-8-10)

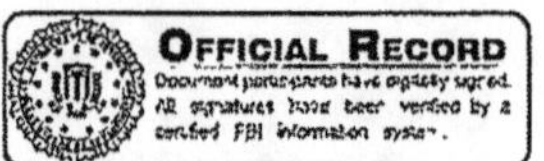

UNCLASSIFIED//~~FOUO~~

FEDERAL BUREAU OF INVESTIGATION

Electronic Communication

Title: (U//~~FOUO~~) Request Charlotte Division to locate and interview [redacted]

Date: 12/19/2012

From: NEW HAVEN
NH-10
Contact: [redacted]

b6 -1, 2
b7C -1, 2

Approved By: SSA [redacted]

Drafted By: [redacted]

Case ID #: 4-NH-2619946

(U) UNSUB(S)
Sandy Hook Elementary School
12 Dickinson St, Sandy Hook, CT-Victim
Firearms Act.
OO:NH

LAW ENFORCEMENT SENSITIVE

This information is the property of the FBI and may be distributed to state, tribal, or local government law enforcement officials with a need-to-know. Further distribution without FBI authorization is prohibited. Precautions should be taken to ensure this information is stored and/or destroyed in a manner that precludes unauthorized access.

Synopsis: (U//~~FOUO~~) New Haven respectfully requests Charlotte Division locate and interview [redacted] residence address [redacted]

[redacted]

b6 -
b7C

Enclosure(s): Enclosed are the following items:

b7E -1,

1. (U) [redacted]
2. (U) [redacted]
3. (U//~~FOUO~~) [redacted]

Details:

For information of Charlotte, on December 14, 2012 FBI New Haven was

UNCLASSIFIED//~~FOUO~~

4-NH-2619946 Serial 78

Sandy Hook-

b6 -2
b7C -2

contacted by the Newtown Connecticut Police Department who requested immediate assistance with an active shooter who had entered the Sandy Hook Elementary School and opened fire, resulting in the death of 20 students and 6 school faculty. Specific information concerning the incident is as follows:

The shooter was identified as Adam P. Lanza, DOB: 04/22/1992, residence address 36 Yoganda Street, Newtown, Connecticut. Lanza died at the scene with an apparent self-inflicted gunshot wound to the head. New Haven subsequently opened a case to support the investigation of the following violations: aiding and abetting and conspiracy for 922(g)(2)(a) -unlawful for individual to possess firearm that has moved in interstate commerce in school zone, 922(g)(3)(a) - discharging in school zone; 922(j) stolen guns.

New Haven's investigation revealed Lanza utilized the e-mail account blarvink@gmail.com.

b6 -2
b7C -2

Title: (U//~~FOUO~~) Request Charlotte Division to locate and interview

b6 -2
b7C -2

Re: 4-NH-2619946, 12/19/2012

OTHER Sealed Pursuant to Court Order

b6 -2,
b7C -2,

b6 -2
b7C -2
OTHER Sealed Pursuant to Court Order

Title: (U//~~FOUO~~) Request Charlotte Division to locate and interview [redacted]

b6 -2
b7C -2

Re: 4-NH-2619946, 12/19/2012

New Haven respectfully requests Charlotte locate and interview [redacted] [redacted] residence address [redacted] [redacted] and ascertain the following information:

[redacted]

b6 -2
b7C -2
b7E -6

♦♦

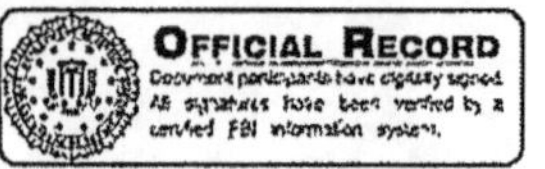

FEDERAL BUREAU OF INVESTIGATION

Date of entry 12/19/2012

(U)On December 19, 2012 at approximately 2:15PM, Supervisory Special Agent (SSA) [redacted] FBI, conducted a telephonic interview of [redacted] via conference call. [redacted] conference call I.D. [redacted] Also present on the conference call were [redacted] and [redacted] The purpose of the interview was to obtain clarification [redacted] regarding a CZ-83 pistol and a kidney/gastrointestinal health condition pertaining to [redacted] Adam Lanza. During the interview [redacted] provided the following information: b6 -1, b7C -1 b7E -5

CZ 83

(U) [redacted] was unaware of what a CZ 83 was but assumed it was a type of weapon. He explained that in addition [redacted] he would [redacted] [redacted] was uncertain as to whether or not Nancy had even purchased the CZ 83 for Adam. (For purposes of clarity first names will be used through the rest of this report). b6 - b7C -

(U)Around Christmas, 2010, [redacted] was planning on accompanying Adam to the [redacted] wanted to [redacted] and wished to participate in [redacted] When [redacted] learned that Adam was developing an interest in weapons, [redacted] purchased various boxes of [redacted] rents various types of [redacted] therefore [redacted] purchased a variety [redacted] just in case Adam wanted to try [redacted] never did accompany Adam to [redacted] and [redacted] believed that the boxes [redacted] b6 - b7C

Adam's Physical Health

(U)Regarding e-mail traffic between [redacted] and Nancy concerning Adam's kidney and gall bladder tests, [redacted] said that he was not present during the tests and therefore he did not know the names of any of the doctors who b6 -6 b7C -

Investigation on 12/19/2012 at New Haven, Connecticut, United States (Phone)

File # 4-NH-2619946 Date drafted 12/19/2012

by [redacted] b6 - b7C

b6 -6
b7C -6

performed the tests. He received all of his information regarding Adam's health second hand from Nancy and was not made aware of any results of the tests so he concluded that there were no problems. Although Adam occasionally had difficulty sleeping, Adam was not experiencing any physical pain. [redacted] believed that the tests were performed as a result of Adam, who possessed a naturally thin build, losing so much weight; Adam weighed about 85 pounds.

b6 -6
b7C -6

(U) [redacted] said that [redacted]

b6 -6
b7C -6

The Relationship Between [redacted] and Adam

(U) [redacted]

b6 -6
b7C -6

(U) The interview concluded at approximately 2:38 PM.

12/19/12 2:15 PM

conf. I.D.

CZ 83 - no idea, assumed it's gun

2010

Christmas -

varying interest bought

b6 -6
b7C -6
b7E -5

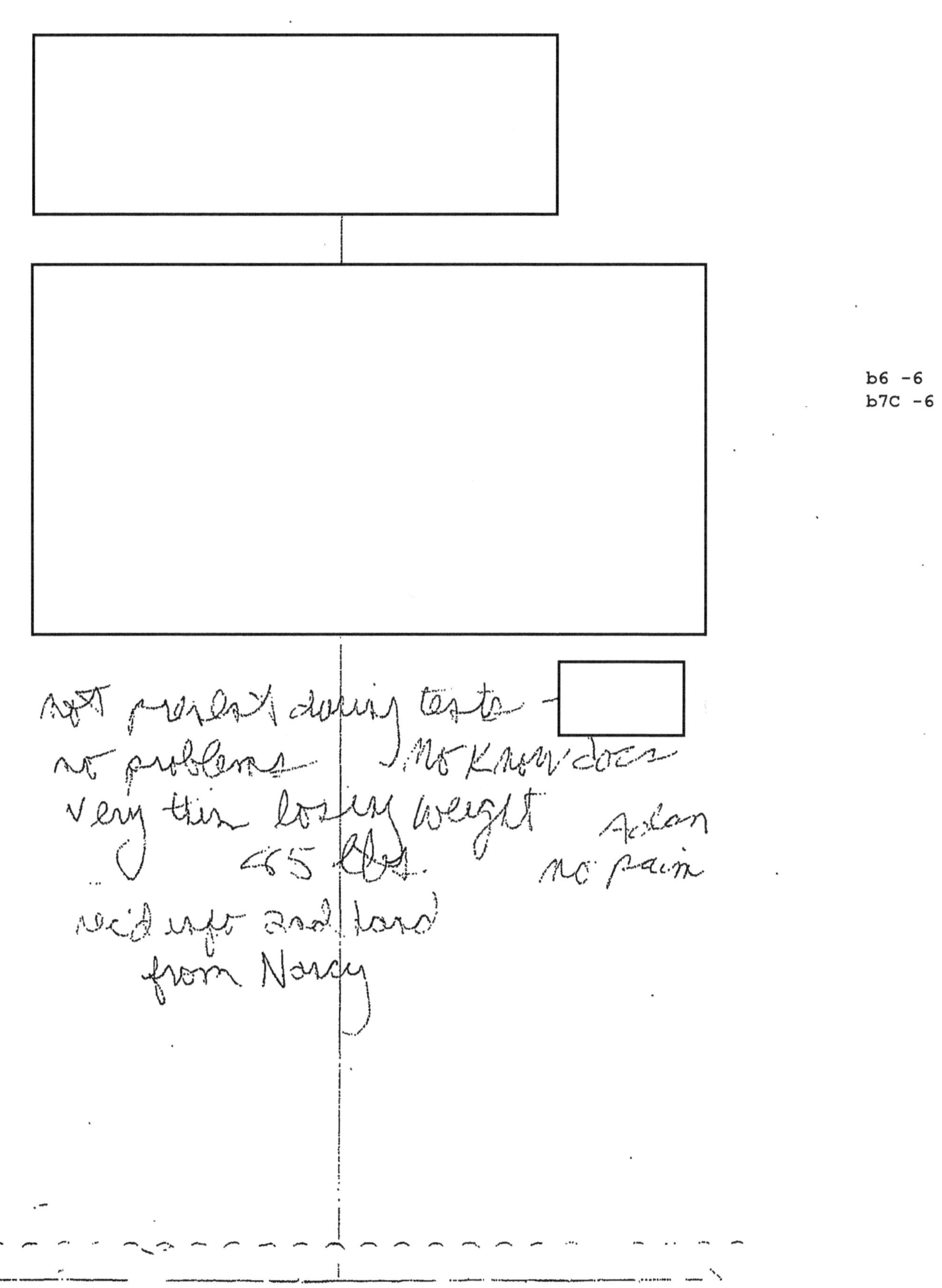

not present during tests —
no problems
no known docs
very thin losing weight
Adam
no pain
rec'd info 2nd hand
from Nancy

b6 -6
b7C -6

b6 -6
b7C -6

vito ends 2:38

FD-302 (Rev. 5-8-10)

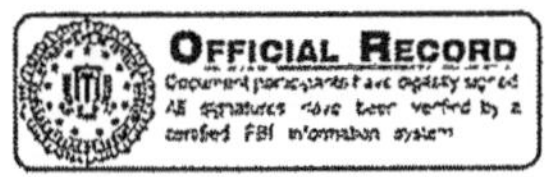

FEDERAL BUREAU OF INVESTIGATION

Date of entry 12/19/2012

[redacted] was interviewed at his place of employment (the above referenced address). After being apprised of the identity of the interviewing Agent and the nature of the interview, [redacted] provided the following information: b6 -6 b7C -6

[redacted] b6 -2, 6 b7C -2, 6

Investigation on 12/18/2012 at [redacted] United States (In Person) b6 -1, 2 b7C -1, 2

File # 4-NH-2619946 Date drafted 12/19/2012

by [redacted]

4-NH-2619946 Serial 80

FD-1087 (Rev. 5-8-10)

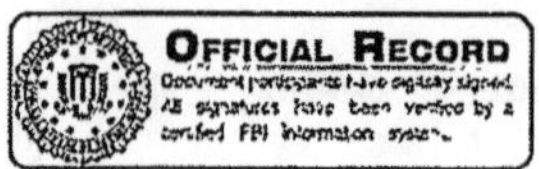

UNCLASSIFIED

FEDERAL BUREAU OF INVESTIGATION

Evidence Log

Event Title: (U) evidence log 121912 **Date:** 12/19/2012

Approved By: A/SSA [redacted]

Drafted By: [redacted]

b6 -1
b7C -1

Case ID #: 4-NH-2619946 (U) UNSUB(S)
Sandy Hook Elementary School
12 Dickinson St, Sandy Hook, CT-Victim
Firearms Act.
OO:NH

[redacted]

b7E -1

Acquired By: [redacted]

Acquired From: (U) Trooper [redacted]
Connecicut State Police
Troop A
Southbury

b6 -1, 3
b7C -1, 3

Receipt Given?: No

Holding Office: NEW HAVEN

Details:

To enter evidence obtained from Connecticut State Police Troop A regarding the above-captioned case from search at 36 Yogananda Street, Sandy Hook Ct

Item Type **Description**

UNCLASSIFIED

This document contains neither recommendations nor conclusions of the FBI. It is the property of the FBI and is loaned to your agency; it and its contents are not to be distributed outside your agency.

4-NH-2619946 Serial 8

Title: (U) evidence log 121912
Re: 4-NH-2619946, 12/19/2012

1B CART (U) CSP #3 Sony Playstation 2 seized Southwest second floor room.
Acquired On: 12/19/2012
Located By: [redacted]
Location Area: Southwest Second Floor
Specific Location: Bedroom
Device Type: Other
Number of Devices Collected: 1

b6 -1
b7C -1
b7E -6

1B CART (U) Dell Laptop Imperiron 6000
Acquired On: 12/19/2012
Located By: [redacted]
Location Area: Desk North Wall of Den
Specific Location: Den
Device Type: Other
Number of Devices Collected: 1

b6 -1
b7C -1
b7E -6

1B CART (U) 2010 Honda paper work, 6 CDRs, Handwritten notes on local gun shops, Garmin GPS,
Acquired On: 12/19/2012
Located By: [redacted]
Location Area: Northeast Bedroom
Specific Location: Closet
Device Type: Other
Number of Devices Collected: 1

b6 -1
b7C -1
b7E -6

1B CART (U) One At&T telephone with digital answering sytem
Acquired On: 12/19/2012
Located By: [redacted]
Location Area: 1st Floor
Specific Location: Office
Device Type: Other
Number of Devices Collected: 1

b6 -1
b7C -1
b7E -6

1B CART (U) One X Box 360
Acquired On: 12/19/2012
Located By: [redacted]
Location Area: Basement
Specific Location: Basement
Device Type: Other
Number of Devices Collected: 1

b6 -1
b7C -1
b7E -6

Title: (U) evidence log 121912
Re: 4-NH-2619946, 12/19/2012

1B CART	(U) One X Box Acquired On: 12/19/2012 Located By: [redacted] Location Area: 2nd Flr Southwest Bedroom Specific Location: TV Cart Device Type: Other Number of Devices Collected: 1	b6 -1 b7C -1
1B CART	(U) One shoe box containing video games parts and memory cards Acquired On: 12/19/2012 Located By: [redacted] Location Area: 2nd flr Southwest Bedroom Specific Location: Under TV on shelf Device Type: Other Number of Devices Collected: 1	b6 -1 b7C -1
1B CART	(U) One USB device Acquired On: 12/19/2012 Located By: [redacted] Location Area: 2nd flr Hall bathroom Specific Location: underbathroom sink Device Type: Other Number of Devices Collected: 1	b6 -1 b7C -1
1B CART	(U) One western digital harddrive Acquired On: 12/19/2012 Located By: [redacted] Location Area: basement Specific Location: floor Device Type: Other Number of Devices Collected: 1	b6 -1 b7C -1
1B CART	(U) One LG Verizon cell phone Acquired On: 12/19/2012 Located By: [redacted] Location Area: 2nd floor hall bathroom Specific Location: Under sink Device Type: Other Number of Devices Collected: 1	b6 -1 b7C -1

Title: (U) evidence log 121912
Re: 4-NH-2619946, 12/19/2012

1B CART	(U) One hard drive platter Acquired On: 12/19/2012 Located By: [redacted] Location Area: 2nd floor Southeast bedroom Specific Location: closet shelf Device Type: Other Number of Devices Collected: 1	b6 -1 b7C -1
1B CART	(U) One black Apple I Phone Acquired On: 12/19/2012 Located By: [redacted] Location Area: North living room Specific Location: 1st floor Device Type: Other Number of Devices Collected: 1	b6 -1 b7C -1
1B CART	(U) One Transcend external hard drive Acquired On: 12/19/2012 Located By: [redacted] Location Area: Southeast Bedroom Specific Location: Closet Device Type: Other Number of Devices Collected: 1	b6 -1 b7C -1
1B CART	(U) One brother fax machine Acquired On: 12/19/2012 Located By: [redacted] Location Area: 1st floor Office Specific Location: Office Device Type: Other Number of Devices Collected: 1	b6 -1 b7C -1
1B CART	(U) One black computer tower Acquired On: 12/19/2012 Located By: [redacted] Location Area: 2nd floor southwest bedroom Specific Location: bedroom Device Type: Other Number of Devices Collected: 1	b6 -1 b7C -1

Title: (U) evidence log 121912
Re: 4-NH-2619946, 12/19/2012

♦♦

FD-302 (Rev. 5-8-10)

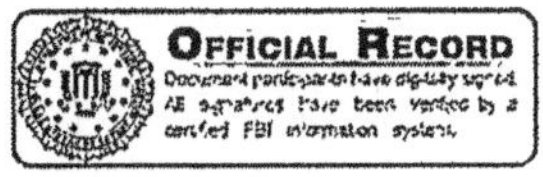

FEDERAL BUREAU OF INVESTIGATION

Date of entry 12/20/2012

On 12/19/2012, Amtrak Police INV/TFO [redacted] advised [redacted]

b6 -2, 4
b7C -2, 4
b7E -7

Investigation on 12/19/2012 at New Haven, Connecticut, United States (Email)

File # 4-NH-2619946 Date drafted 12/20/2012

by [redacted]

b6 -1
b7C -1

4-NH-2619946 Serial 82

FEDERAL BUREAU OF INVESTIGATION

Date of entry 12/17/2012

From December 14, 2012 through December 15, 2012, the Federal Bureau of Investigation (FBI) New Haven Field Office (NHFO) Evidence Response Team (ERT) executed a consent search at [redacted] [redacted] provided consent to search and a signed FD-26, Consent to Search form. b6 -2 b7C -2

The search began on December 14, 2012 at approximately 9:25pm and ended on December 15, 2012 at approximately 3:39am.

On Saturday, December 15, 2012, at approximately 4:27am, evidence items [redacted] were secured at an FBI facility in locked, sealed storage until Monday, December 17, 2012, when they were transported to the FBI NHFO at 600 State Street, New Haven, Connecticut and turned over to Evidence Control at approximately 11:40am. [redacted] was photographed but not seized and [redacted] [redacted] were maintained by SA [redacted] and documented separately. b6 -1 b7C -1 b7E -6

Further details regarding the search are stored in a 1A attachment in the substantive case file, 4-NH-2619946, to include the photo logs, printouts of thumbnails of the photos, sketches, a handwritten FD-597, the ERT Final Casebook, notes, three (3) DVDs containing the original photos, three (3) DVDs containing copies of the photos, and the room letter labels. A copy of the FD-26, Consent to Search form, is also included in the 1A attachments.

Investigation on 12/14/2012 at [redacted] United States (In Person)

File # 4-NH-2619946 Date drafted 12/17/2012 b6 -1, 2 b7C -1,

by [redacted]

FD-597 (Rev 8-11-94)

UNITED STATES DEPARTMENT OF JUSTICE
FEDERAL BUREAU OF INVESTIGATION
Receipt for Property Received/Returned/Released/Seized

File # 4-NH-2619946

On (date) 12/15/2012

item(s) listed below were:
☐ Received From
☐ Returned To
☐ Released To
☒ Seized

(Name) [redacted]
(Street Address) [redacted]
(City) [redacted]

b6 -2
b7C -2

Description of Item(s): Document with name and address of [redacted]

[redacted]

b6 -2
b7C -2

[redacted] 12/15/2012

b6 -1
b7C -1

Received By: [redacted] (Signature)

Received From: NOT PRESENT (Signature)

DEPARTMENT OF JUSTICE

FEDERAL BUREAU OF INVESTIGATION

CONSENT TO SEARCH

1. I have been asked by Special Agents of the Federal Bureau of Investigation to permit a complete search of:

b6 -2
b7C -2

2. I have been advised of my right to refuse consent.
3. I give this permission voluntarily.
4. I authorize these agents to take any items which they determine may be related to their investigation.

12/14/2012

WITNESS

b6 -1, 2
b7C -1, 2

FBI

EVIDENCE RESPONSE TEAM

CASEBOOK

DATE OF ARRIVAL
12/14/2012

TIME OF ARRIVAL
8:55 PM

CASE IDENTIFIER
4-NH-2619946

TEAM LEADER

b6 -1
b7C -1

LOCATION

b6
b7C

b6 -2
b7C -2

DEC 14, 2012 08:55 PM
4-NH-2619946

ADMINISTRATIVE WORKSHEET

General Information

Location	
Date/Time of Arrival	Dec 14, 2012 08:55 PM
Case ID	4-NH-2619946
Latitude & Longitude	Lat. Long.
Condition of Scene on Arrival	Secured FBI
Lighting	Indoor Lighting
Weather	Indoors
General Description	
Person in Charge on Arrival	SA
Control of Scene Obtained From	FBI
Date/Time of Control Acquisition	Dec 14, 2012 09:25 PM

b6 -1, 2
b7C -1, 2

Persons On Scene

b6 -1, 2, 3, 4
b7C -1, 2, 3, 4

Name	Status	Comment
	Law Enforcement	Entry and scene security
	Law Enforcement	IRS. Entry team and scene security
	Law Enforcement	. Entry and scene security
	Law Enforcement	Entry and scene security
	Law Enforcement	CSP Emergency Services Unit. Bomb tech
	Law Enforcement	Entry and scene security
	Law Enforcement	FBI entry team and scene security
	Law Enforcement	CSP. Entry and scene security

Team Roster

Name	Responsibility	Agency
	Team Lead	FBI
	Custodian/Searcher/Finder	FBI
	Photo Log	FBI
	Photographer	FBI
	Searcher/Finder	FBI
	Searcher/Finder	FBI
	Searcher/Finder	FBI

b6 -1
b7C -1

b6 -2
b7C -

ADMINISTRATIVE WORKSHEET

		Searcher/Finder	FBI
		Searcher/Finder	FBI
		Searcher/Finder	FBI
		Searcher/Finder	FBI
		Sketcher	FBI
		Coordinator	FBI
		Computer	FBI

b6 -1
b7C -1

Notes

Preliminary Survey/Evidence Evaluation (Notes/Observations)	
Special Situations, Conditions, and/or Specialists Used (Notes/Observations)	
Crime Scene Conference (Notes/Observations)	
Final Survey (Notes/Observations)	
Narrative (Notes/Observations)	

b6 -1, 2, 3
b7C -1, 2, 3

b6 -2
DEC 14, 2012 08:55 PM b7C -2
4-NH-2619946

ADMINISTRATIVE WORKSHEET

Search Completion

Release of Scene Authorized By	SA
Release of Scene To	Not applicable
Date/Time of Scene Release	Dec 15, 2012 03:39 AM

b6 -1
b7C -1

Administrative Log

Date/Time	Log Entry
Dec 14, 2012 09:25 PM	**Preliminary Survey begins**
Dec 14, 2012 10:00 PM	**Called SABT regarding SABT advised save to begin search, but team should remain out of until removed.**
Dec 14, 2012 10:18 PM	**Begin photos**
Dec 14, 2012 10:35 PM	**CSP ESUTFC arrived.**
Dec 14, 2012 10:49 PM	**Search begins**
Dec 14, 2012 11:35 PM	**CSP ESUTFC removed and cleared the scene.**
Dec 15, 2012 01:12 AM	**SA and TFO left scene.**
Dec 15, 2012 03:20 AM	**Final Survey begins**
Dec 15, 2012 03:39 AM	**ERT departs, scene secured and released.**

b6 -1, 2, 3
b7C -1, 2, 3

b6
b7C

DEC 14, 2012 08:55 PM
4-NH-2619946

EVIDENCE RECOVERY LOG

Evidence Recovery Log

Item #	Description	Recovered By	Observed By	Date Found
				12/14/2012

Where Found	Packaging/Marking	Grid	Room/Area	Comments
			J	

b6 -1, 2
b7C -1,
b7E -6

Item #	Description	Recovered By	Observed By	Date Found
				12/14/2012

Where Found	Packaging/Marking	Grid	Room/Area	Comments
			H	

b6 -1, 2
b7C -1, 2
b7E -6

Item #	Description	Recovered By	Observed By	Date Found
				12/14/2012

Where Found	Packaging/Marking	Grid	Room/Area	Comments
			H	

b6 -1, 2
b7C -1,
b7E -6

b6 -2
b7C -2

DEC 14, 2012 08:55 PM
4-NH-2619946

EVIDENCE RECOVERY LOG

b6 -2
b7C -2

Item #	Description	Recovered By	Observed By		Date Found
					12/14/2012
	Where Found	Packaging/Marking	Grid	Room/Area	Comments
				O	

b6 -1, 2
b7C -1, 2
b7E -6

Item #	Description	Recovered By	Observed By		Date Found
					12/14/2012
	Where Found	Packaging/Marking	Grid	Room/Area	Comments
				Q	

b6 -1, 2
b7C -1, 2
b7E -6

Item #	Description	Recovered By	Observed By		Date Found
					12/15/2012
	Where Found	Packaging/Marking	Grid	Room/Area	Comments
				Q	

b6 -1, 2
b7C -1, 2
b7E -6

Item #	Description	Recovered By	Observed By		Date Found
					12/15/2012
	Where Found	Packaging/Marking	Grid	Room/Area	Comments
				V	

b6 -1, 2
b7C -1, 2
b7E -6

b6
b7C

EVIDENCE RECOVERY LOG

b6
b7C

Item #	Description	Recovered By	Observed By		Date Found
					12/15/2012
	Where Found	Packaging/Marking	Grid	Room/Area	Comments
				N	

b6 -1, 2
b7C -1, 2
b7E -6

Item #	Description	Recovered By	Observed By		Date Found
					12/15/2012
	Where Found	Packaging/Marking	Grid	Room/Area	Comments
				N	

b6 -1, 2
b7C -1, 2
b7E -6

Item #	Description	Recovered By	Observed By		Date Found
					12/15/2012
	Where Found	Packaging/Marking	Grid	Room/Area	Comments
				O	

b6 -1, 2
b7C -1, 2
b7E -6

Item #	Description	Recovered By	Observed By	Date Found
				12/14/2012

b6 -1, 2
b7C -1, 2
b7E -6

b6 -2
b7C -2

DEC 14, 2012 08:55 PM
4-NH-2619946

EVIDENCE RECOVERY LOG

Where Found	Packaging/Marking	Grid	Room/Area	Comments
			E	

b6 -2
b7C -2

Item #	Description	Recovered By	Observed By	Date Found
				12/15/2012

Where Found	Packaging/Marking	Grid	Room/Area	Comments
			O	

b6 -1, 2
b7C -1, 2
b7E -6

b6
b7C

DEC 14, 2012 08:55 PM
4-NH-2619946

EVIDENCE RECOVERY LOG

Item #	Description	Recovered By	Observed By		Date Found
					12/14/2012
	Where Found	Packaging/Marking	Grid	Room/Area	Comments
				E	

b6 -1,
b7C -1,
b7E -6

Item #	Description	Recovered By	Observed By		Date Found
					12/14/2012
	Where Found	Packaging/Marking	Grid	Room/Area	Comments
				E	

b6 -1, 2
b7C -1,
b7E -6

Item #	Description	Recovered By	Observed By		Date Found
					12/14/2012
	Where Found	Packaging/Marking	Grid	Room/Area	Comments
				E	

b6 -1, 2
b7C -1,
b7E -6

Item #	Description	Recovered By	Observed By		Date Found
					12/14/2012
	Where Found	Packaging/Marking	Grid	Room/Area	Comments

b6 -1
b7C -
b7E -

b6 -2
b7C -2

DEC 14, 2012 08:55 PM
4-NH-2619946

EVIDENCE RECOVERY LOG

				E	

b6 -2
b7C -2

Item #	Description	Recovered By	Observed By		Date Found
					12/14/2012
	Where Found	Packaging/Marking	Grid	Room/Area	Comments
				E	

b6 -1, 2
b7C -1, 2
b7E -6

Item #	Description	Recovered By	Observed By		Date Found
					12/14/2012
	Where Found	Packaging/Marking	Grid	Room/Area	Comments
				E	

b6 -1, 2
b7C -1, 2
b7E -6

Item #	Description	Recovered By	Observed By		Date Found
					12/15/2012
	Where Found	Packaging/Marking	Grid	Room/Area	Comments
				E	

b6 -1, 2
b7C -1, 2
b7E -6

Item #	Description	Recovered By	Observed By	Date Found
				12/15/2012

b6 -1, 2
b7C -1, 2
b7E -6

b6 -
b7C

DEC 14, 2012 08:55 PM
4-NH-2619946

EVIDENCE RECOVERY LOG

Item #	Description	Recovered By	Observed By	Date Found

	Where Found	Packaging/Marking	Grid	Room/Area	Comments
				E	

b6 -2
b7C -

Item #	Description	Recovered By	Observed By	Date Found
				12/15/2012

	Where Found	Packaging/Marking	Grid	Room/Area	Comments
				E	

b6 -1, 2
b7C -1, 2
b7E -6

Item #	Description	Recovered By	Observed By	Date Found
				12/15/2012

	Where Found	Packaging/Marking	Grid	Room/Area	Comments
				E	

b6 -1, 2
b7C -1, 2
b7E -6

Item #	Description	Recovered By	Observed By	Date Found
				12/15/2012

	Where Found	Packaging/Marking	Grid	Room/Area	Comments
				E	

b6 -1, 2
b7C -1, 2
b7E -6

Item #	Description	Recovered By	Observed By	Date Found
				12/15/2012

b6 -1, 2
b7C -1, 2
b7E -6

b6 -2
b7C -2

DEC 14, 2012 08:55 PM
4-NH-2619946

EVIDENCE RECOVERY LOG

b6 -2
b7C -2

Where Found	Packaging/Marking	Grid	Room/Area	Comments
			E	

Item #	Description	Recovered By	Observed By	Date Found
				12/15/2012

Where Found	Packaging/Marking	Grid	Room/Area	Comments
			E	

b6 -1, 2
b7C -1, 2
b7E -6

Item #	Description	Recovered By	Observed By	Date Found
				12/15/2012

b6 -1, 2
b7C -1, 2
b7E -6

b6
b7C

DEC 14, 2012 08:55 PM
4-NH-2619946

EVIDENCE RECOVERY LOG

Where Found	Packaging/Marking	Grid	Room/Area	Comments
			E	

b6
b7

Item #	Description	Recovered By	Observed By	Date Found
				12/15/2012

b6 -1, 2
b7C -1, 2
b7E -6, 7

Where Found	Packaging/Marking	Grid	Room/Area	Comments
			Q	

Item #	Description	Recovered By	Observed By	Date Found
				12/15/2012

b6 -1, 2
b7C -1,
b7E -6,

Where Found	Packaging/Marking	Grid	Room/Area	Comments
			J	

PHOTOGRAPHIC LOG

GENERAL INFORMATION

DATE 12/14/2012
CASE ID 4-NH-2619946
LOCATION [redacted]
PREPARER/ASSISTANT SA [redacted]
REMARKS Card 1

b6 -1, 2
b7C -1, 2

PHOTO#	DESCRIPTION OF PHOTOGRAPHIC SUBJECT / MISCELLANEOUS COMMENTS

b7E -6

PHOTOGRAPHIC LOG

GENERAL INFORMATION

DATE 12/14/2012
CASE ID 4-NH-2619946
LOCATION [redacted]
PREPARER/ASSISTANT SA [redacted]
REMARKS card 1

b6 -1,
b7C -1,

PHOTO#	DESCRIPTION OF PHOTOGRAPHIC SUBJECT / MISCELLANEOUS COMMENTS

b7E -

PHOTOGRAPHIC LOG

GENERAL INFORMATION

DATE 12/14/2012
CASE ID 4-NH-2619946
LOCATION
PREPARER/ASSISTANT SA
REMARKS card 1

b6 -1, 2
b7C -1, 2

PHOTO#	DESCRIPTION OF PHOTOGRAPHIC SUBJECT / MISCELLANEOUS COMMENTS

b7E -6

PHOTOGRAPHIC LOG

GENERAL INFORMATION

DATE 12/14/2012
CASE ID 4-NH-2619946
LOCATION
PREPARER/ASSISTANT SA
REMARKS card 1

b6 -1,
b7C -1

PHOTO#	DESCRIPTION OF PHOTOGRAPHIC SUBJECT / MISCELLANEOUS COMMENTS

b7E

PHOTOGRAPHIC LOG

GENERAL INFORMATION

DATE 12/14/2012
CASE ID 4-NH-2619946
LOCATION
PREPARER/ASSISTANT SA
REMARKS card 1

b6 -1, 2
b7C -1, 2

PHOTO#	DESCRIPTION OF PHOTOGRAPHIC SUBJECT / MISCELLANEOUS COMMENTS

b6 -2
b7C -2
b7E -6

PHOTOGRAPHIC LOG

GENERAL INFORMATION

DATE 12/14/2012
CASE ID 4-NH-2619946
LOCATION
PREPARER/ASSISTANT SA
REMARKS card 1 / card 2

b6 -1,
b7C -1,

PHOTO#	DESCRIPTION OF PHOTOGRAPHIC SUBJECT / MISCELLANEOUS COMMENTS

b6 -1,
b7C -1,
b7E -6

PHOTOGRAPHIC LOG

GENERAL INFORMATION

DATE 12/14/2012
CASE ID 4-NH-2619946
LOCATION [redacted]
PREPARER/ASSISTANT SA [redacted]
REMARKS card 2

b6 -1, 2
b7C -1, 2

PHOTO#	DESCRIPTION OF PHOTOGRAPHIC SUBJECT / MISCELLANEOUS COMMENTS

b7E -6

PHOTOGRAPHIC LOG

GENERAL INFORMATION

DATE 12/14/2012
CASE ID 4-NH-2619946
LOCATION
PREPARER/ASSISTANT SA
REMARKS card 2

b6 -1,
b7C -1

PHOTO#	DESCRIPTION OF PHOTOGRAPHIC SUBJECT / MISCELLANEOUS COMMENTS

b7E

PHOTOGRAPHIC LOG

GENERAL INFORMATION

DATE 12/14/2012
CASE ID 4-NH-2619946
LOCATION
PREPARER/ASSISTANT SA
REMARKS card 2

b6 -1, 2
b7C -1, 2

PHOTO#	DESCRIPTION OF PHOTOGRAPHIC SUBJECT / MISCELLANEOUS COMMENTS

b6 -2
b7C -2
b7E -6

PHOTOGRAPHIC LOG

GENERAL INFORMATION

DATE 12/14/2012
CASE ID 4-NH-2619946
LOCATION
PREPARER/ASSISTANT SA
REMARKS card 2

b6 -1,
b7C -1,

PHOTO#	DESCRIPTION OF PHOTOGRAPHIC SUBJECT / MISCELLANEOUS COMMENTS

b7E

PHOTOGRAPHIC LOG

GENERAL INFORMATION

DATE 12/14/2012
CASE ID 4-NH-2619946
LOCATION [redacted]
PREPARER/ASSISTANT SA [redacted]
REMARKS card 2

b6 -1, 2
b7C -1, 2

PHOTO#	DESCRIPTION OF PHOTOGRAPHIC SUBJECT / MISCELLANEOUS COMMENTS

b7E -6

PHOTOGRAPHIC LOG

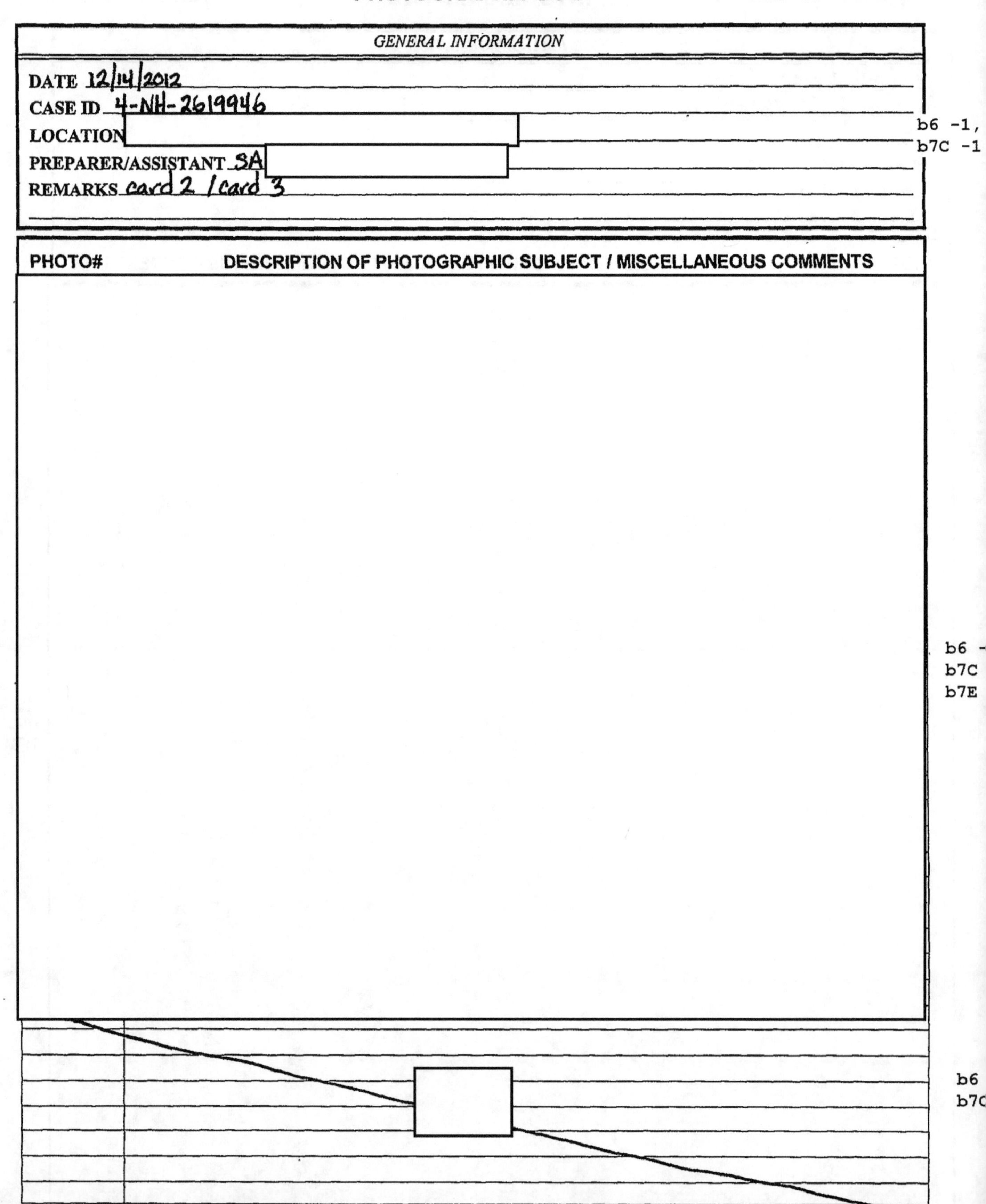

GENERAL INFORMATION

DATE 12/14/2012
CASE ID 4-NH-2619946
LOCATION
PREPARER/ASSISTANT SA
REMARKS card 2 / card 3

b6 -1, b7C -1

PHOTO#	DESCRIPTION OF PHOTOGRAPHIC SUBJECT / MISCELLANEOUS COMMENTS

b6 - b7C b7E

b6 b7C

FD-302 (Rev. 5-8-10)

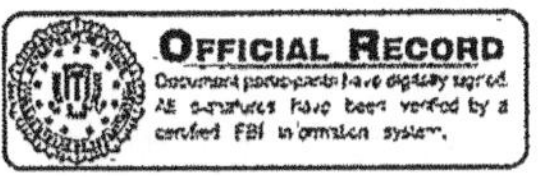

FEDERAL BUREAU OF INVESTIGATION

Date of entry 12/20/2012

On 12/14/2012 [redacted] search was conducted [redacted] The search team consisted of FBI Special Agent's (SA's) [redacted] and [redacted] The following events took place and the approximate times listed:

b6 -1, 2, 3
b7C -1, 2, 3

Time	Event
4:18pm	Search team conducted the [redacted] search [redacted]
4:34pm	Search completed. No items seized or taken. [redacted]
7:00pm	FBI SA's [redacted] and [redacted]
7:30pm	SA [redacted] re-entered [redacted] at the direction of FBI SA [redacted] SA

b6 -1, 2, 3
b7C -1, 2, 3
b7E -6

Investigation on 12/14/2012 at [redacted] United States (In Person)

b6 -1, 2
b7C -1, 2

File # 4-NH-2619946 Date drafted 12/20/2012

by [redacted]

4-NH-2619946 Serial 84

b6 -2
b7C -2

[redacted] b6 -1, 2 b7C -1, b7E -6

7:36pm	SA [redacted] b6 -1, b7C -1,
8:30pm	SA [redacted] b6 -1, 2, b7C -1, 2
8:45pm	[redacted] b6 -2, 5 b7C -2,
9:00pm	SA [redacted] advised [redacted] the FBI was securing the operation and departing the scene as per FBI Supervisory Special Agent [redacted] b6 -1, 3 b7C -1,
9:15pm	SA [redacted] SA [redacted] and SA [redacted] b6 -1, 2 b7C -1, b7E -6
9:30pm	Operation terminated.

FD-302 (Rev. 5-8-10)

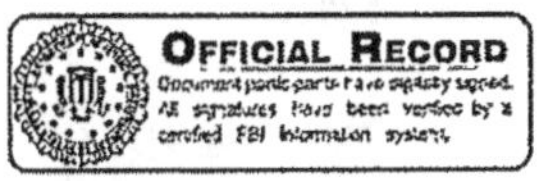

FEDERAL BUREAU OF INVESTIGATION

Date of entry 12/20/2012

On December 18, 2012, at approximately 5:15 PM, [redacted] Date of Birth (DOB): [redacted] SSAN: [redacted] [redacted] (mobile) was advised of the identities of the interviewing agents and the purpose of the interview. Present during the interview were SA [redacted] /FBI, SA [redacted] /FBI and TFO [redacted] /FBI. Family members present during the interview were [redacted] [redacted], DOB: [redacted] SSAN: [redacted] and [redacted] dob: [redacted] SSAN: [redacted]. [redacted] was told the purpose of the interview was to ascertain any information he may have pertaining to ADAM LANZA [redacted] [redacted] participation in the High School Tech Club at the Newtown High School in Newtown, CT. [redacted] was interviewed at his residence and voluntarily provided the following information: b6 -1, 5, 6 b7C -1, 5, 6

[redacted] was born in [redacted] and attended High School in the Newtown, CT. After High School, [redacted] became employed at [redacted] [redacted] [redacted] has held multiple positions [redacted] b6 -6 b7C -6

[redacted] resided at [redacted] Newtown. [redacted] b6 -5, 6 b7C -5, 6

[redacted] remained with the Board of Education [redacted]. [redacted] b6 -6 b7C -6

Investigation on 12/18/2012 at [redacted] United States (In Person)

File # 4-NH-2619946 Date drafted 12/18/2012 b6 -1, 6 b7C -1, 6

by [redacted]

This document contains neither recommendations nor conclusions of the FBI. It is the property of the FBI and is loaned to your agency; it and its contents are not to be distributed outside your agency.

4-NH-2619946 Serial 85

b6 -
b7C -

[redacted]

b6 -
b7C

[redacted]

b6
b7C

[redacted] employed as [redacted]
[redacted]

[redacted] first became familiar with the Lanza Family through after school activities at Newtown High School. [redacted] The club was an after school activity that allowed students to explore technology and its applications. [redacted] first met ADAM LANZA while he was a student at the Middle School in Newtown. ADAM would often come to Tech Club functions [redacted]

b6 -
b7C

[redacted] described ADAM LANZA as one not willing to talk much. ADAM didn't have much contact with other students and it was very hard to communicate with him. ADAM did not have good social skills and would often become withdrawn in a social environment. [redacted] determined early on that ADAM LANZA had some issues. [redacted] knew Mrs. LANZA from his dealing with the Tech Club. Mrs. Lanza would often attend functions of the Tech Club.

b6
b7C

[redacted] stated that when ADAM LANZA reached high school, he became a member of the Tech Club. [redacted] remembers that ADAM dealt poorly with other students but did not show any signs of violence. [redacted] remembers that he had to watch ADAM when he was working with tools because he could hurt himself. ADAM's mother cautioned [redacted] that ADAM does not feel pain like other children and that care was needed when he was working around tools in Tech Club.

b6
b7C

b6 -6
b7C -6

[redacted]

b6 -6
b7C -6

[redacted] had discussions with Mrs. LANZA about ADAM LANZA's issues. Mrs. LANZA told [redacted] that ADAM had several disorders to include Autism and Asperger Syndrome. There was one other disorder that [redacted] and Mrs. LANZA discussed but [redacted] cannot remember that name. [redacted] remembers ADAM being on some type of medication but he cannot remember their names.

b6 -6
b7C -6

[redacted] would have contact with Mrs. LANZA when ADAM would have episodes at school. These episodes would last about 15 minutes or so and often would require a call to Mrs. LANZA who would respond from work. ADAM would become withdrawn but did not show any signs of violence during these episodes. ADAM was more likely to be victimized then to act in violence against another person. ADAM LANZA would have a Teacher's Aid with him during the school day. ADAM was "inclusive" in the classroom and would be removed to a special classroom for specialized training.

b6 -6
b7C -6

[redacted] remembers that Mrs. LANZA was a teacher or volunteer and would come from work to respond to ADAM's episodes. [redacted] does not recall ADAM any episodes during after school activities in the Tech Club. [redacted] may have sent ADAM home during an "overnight" Tech Club activity at school. [redacted]

[redacted]

b6 -5, 6
b7C -5, 6

[redacted] learned that [redacted] of Newtown had spoken to the media sometime after the shooting incident at Sandy Hook Elementary School. [redacted] spoke to [redacted] and referred them to [redacted]

b6 -5, 6
b7C -5,

[redacted] initial decision to speak to the media was based on his belief that he could raise awareness about being observant to warning signs in children's behavior. [redacted] admits he does not have much experience in dealing with the media. Once involved with the media, his message was lost and the media just wanted to concentrate on ADAM. [redacted] has agreed to speak [redacted]

b6 -6
b7C -6

[redacted] has not seen or had any contact with ADAM LANZA for his family since 2008. [redacted]

b6 -6
b7C -6

 b6 -6 b7C -

[redacted] has not had any electronic communication, to include social media sites or email, with any members of the LANZA family [redacted] b6 - b7C

[redacted] b6 - b7C

[redacted] and [redacted] expressed their frustration with the media. Since [redacted] has made comments on different media outlets; the couple has been inundated with inquiries for comments. Both admit this is overwhelming and has affected their family. b6 -5, 6 b7C -5,

[redacted] and [redacted] were provided the number of the FBI's Victim/Witness Coordinator Specialist for the [redacted]. [redacted] were advised to call the VCS for assistance. b6 -5, 6 b7C -5,

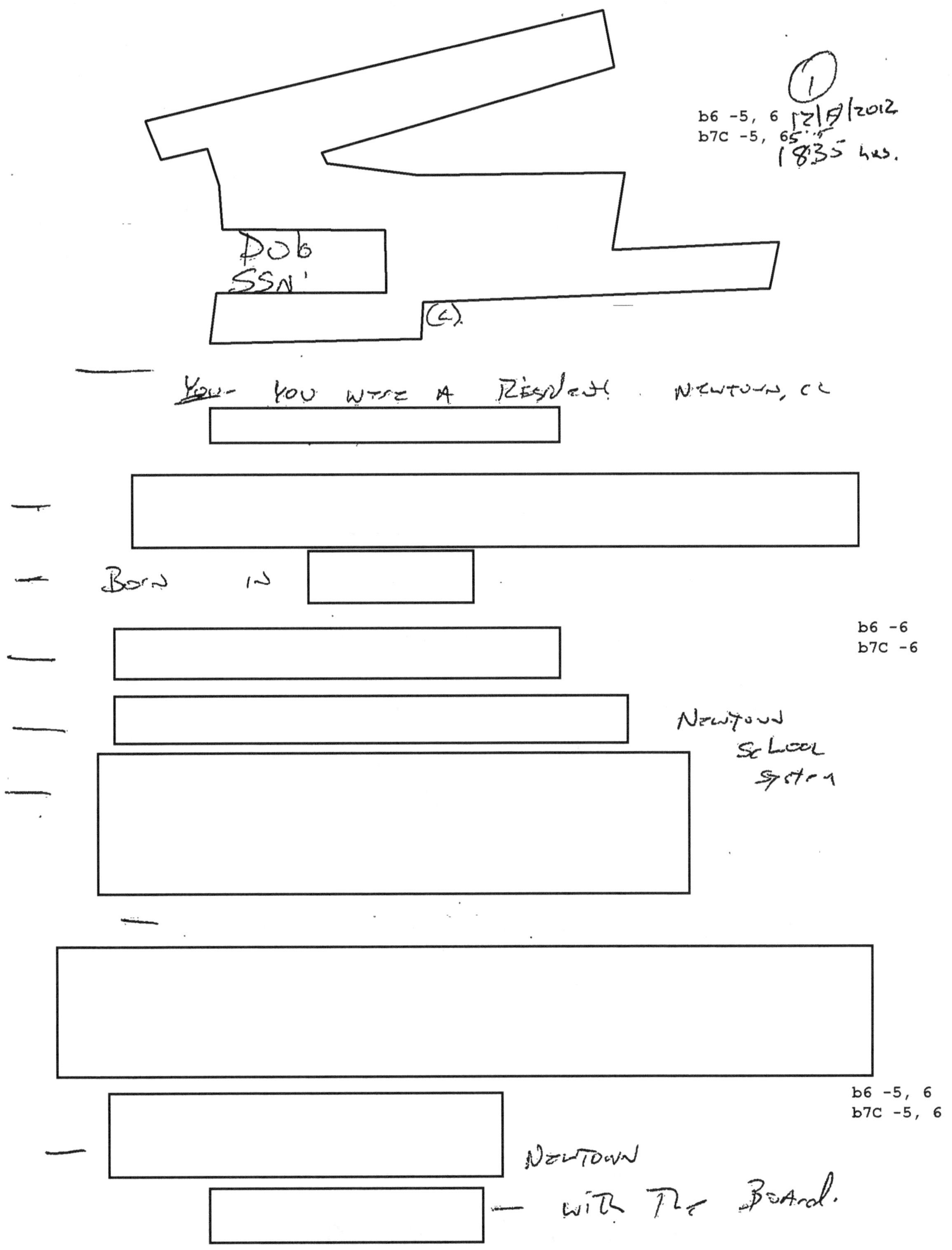

①
b6 -5, 6 12/15/2012
b7C -5, 6
1835 hrs.
DOB
SSN
(c).
You - You were a Resident Newtown, CT
Born in
b6 -6
b7C -6
Newtown
School
System
b6 -5, 6
b7C -5, 6
Newtown
with The Board.

3

—

—

—

b6 -5, b7C -5

—

—

b6 -5
b7C -5

— Met Adam Thought Tech Club
— middle School.

— Newtown, CT middle School,

— ~~His Tea.~~ Interacted with Him ~~Tech Club~~

—

b6 -5
b7C -5

— One That Didn't want to Talk To

— No contact

— No verbal comm

- Determining Early on That He Had Some issues

—

~~Me~~ Knew Mrs. Lanza for her Dealing in The Tech club
[redacted]

— The Tech club was @ The High School in Newtown

— [redacted]

b6 -5
b7C -5

— [redacted]

b6 -5
b7C -5

— Seeing Adam Daily

— [redacted]

→ [redacted]

b6 -6
b7C -6

—

(5)

—

—

b6
b7

Alan Lanza
→ Withdrawn

— Had Discussion with his mother

— Several Disorders
— Autistic Assburgers

— Does other can't remember

— Mother told him he was able to Feel sensation of pain Assoc with activities of the tech club

—

b6 -5
b7C -

—

— Dealt poorly with other kids
— no signs of violence

— [redacted box]

b6 -5
b7C -5

— No violence signs
— Likely to be victimize

—

— Contact with mother mostly During Activities of the ~~at~~ Tech Club
— supportive of the child's events

— Episode = Total withdrawal.
— ~~Mother~~ would Respond in 15 mins
— Adam would Respond to her

Can't Recall his meds that Adam was on.

7

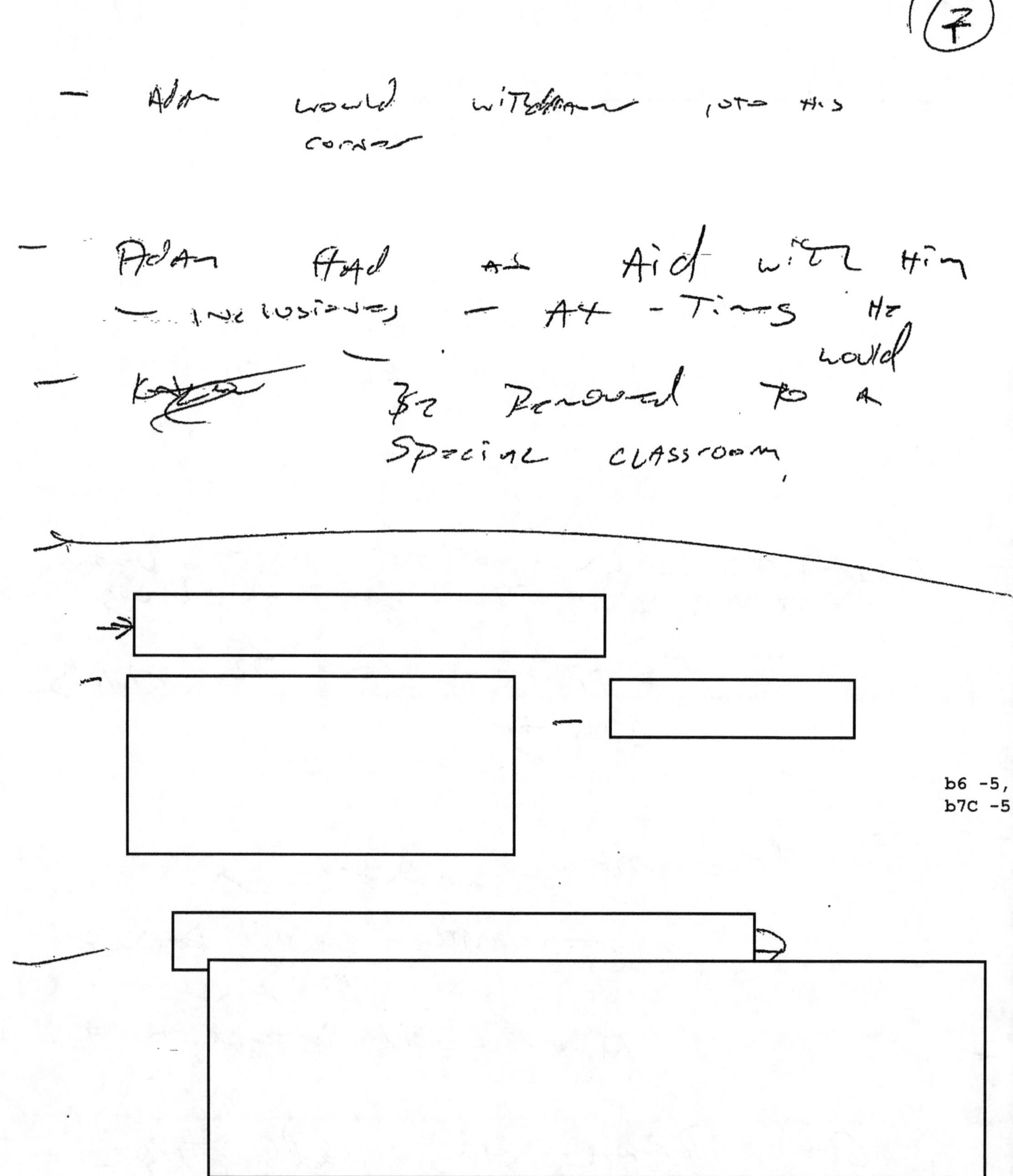

- Adam would withdraw into his corner

- Adam had an Aid with him
  - inclusion – At times he would be removed to a special classroom.

b6 -5,
b7C -5,

(8)

Talking to media

— His intentions was to get this out to the public for signs to look for in child's behavior

— Don't have much have experience dealing with media.

—

—

b6 -5, 6
b7C -5, 6

—

—

—

b6 -6
b7C -6

Last saw had contact with Adam was 200[illegible]

~ No FB or Email contact

—

b6 -5
b7C -5

—

(9)

- Remember Mrs LANZA was a teacher / or volunteer and come from work to attend to an episode

- He would come out of it.

- Don't remember ~~[illegible]~~, heard any episode in Tech. CLUB

MAY HAVE SENT HIM HOME ON ONCE BECAUSE OVERNIGHT @ THE SCHOOL

-

b6
b7C

- Victim witness Name provided

- Provided Name of VC witness

FD-1057 (Rev. 5-8-10)

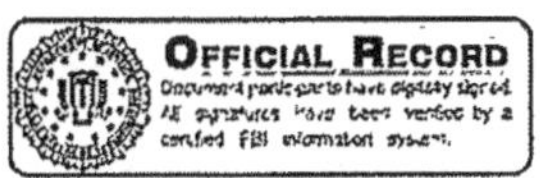

UNCLASSIFIED

FEDERAL BUREAU OF INVESTIGATION

Electronic Communication

Title: (U) [redacted] located and interviewed

Date: 12/21/2012

To: [redacted]

From: CHARLOTTE
CE07
Contact: [redacted]

b6 -1, 2
b7C -1, 2

Approved By: A/SSA [redacted]

Drafted By: [redacted]

Case ID #: 4-NH-2619946 (U) UNSUB(S)
Sandy Hook Elementary School
12 Dickinson St, Sandy Hook, CT-Victim
Firearms Act.
OO:NH

Synopsis: (U) [redacted] was located and interviewed at the request of New Haven Division. Lead Covered.

[redacted]

b6 -2
b7C -2
b7E -1

Details:

[redacted] contacted the writer on the evening of 12/19/2012 requesting investigative assistance with tracking down [redacted] [redacted] is believed to have been living at [redacted] [redacted] with [redacted] [redacted] and [redacted] may be [redacted]

[redacted]

b6 -1, 2, 5
b7C -1, 2, 5

[redacted] requested the writer locate and interview [redacted] in accordance with referenced lead.

The writer contacted [redacted] at

b6 -2
b7C -2

UNCLASSIFIED

4-NH-2619946 Serial 86

Title: (U) [redacted] located and interviewed
Re: 4-NH-2619946, 12/21/2012

b6 -2
b7C -2

approximately 8:00pm on 12/19/2012 to request assistance with locating and interviewing [redacted] Two [redacted] deputies assisted the writer with this task and conducted a cursory search of [redacted] living quarters and had casual conversations with [redacted] Results of the writer's interview with [redacted] can be found in the corresponding FD-302 in this case file. Results of the [redacted] search, interviews, and other observations from the writer not included in the FD-302 follow:

b6 -1, 2
b7C -1, 2

[redacted]

b6 -2
b7C -2

[redacted]

b6 -2
b7C -2

[redacted]

b6
b7C

Title: (U) [redacted] located and interviewed
Re: 4-NH-2619946, 12/21/2012

b6 -2
b7C -2

[redacted]

b6 -2
b7C -2

[redacted]

b6 -2
b7C -2

[redacted] stated that [redacted]

b6 -2
b7C -2

Title: (U) [redacted] located and interviewed
Re: 4-NH-2619946, 12/21/2012

b6 -2
b7C -2

[redacted]

b6 -2
b7C -2

[redacted]

b6 -
b7C
b7E

As there is no apparent connection to LANZA [redacted] Charlotte Division considers this lead covered. Charlotte Division will assist New Haven Division if further information or action from [redacted] or [redacted] is required.

b6 -2, 6
b7C -2,

♦♦

FD-1057 (Rev. 5-8-10)

UNCLASSIFIED

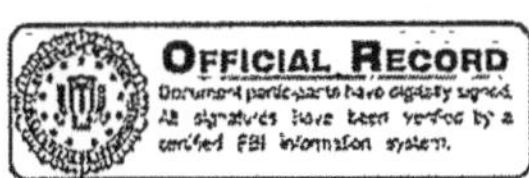

FEDERAL BUREAU OF INVESTIGATION

Electronic Communication

Title: (U) To Document a [redacted] [redacted] **Date:** 12/21/2012

To: [redacted]

From: SAN DIEGO b6 -1
SD-CT1 b7C -1
Contact: [redacted] b7E -3

Approved By: SSA [redacted]

Drafted By: [redacted]

Case ID #: 4-NH-2619946 (U) UNSUB(S)
Sandy Hook Elementary School
12 Dickinson St, Sandy Hook, CT-Victim
Firearms Act.
OO:NH

Synopsis: (U) Writer executed a [redacted] [redacted] [redacted] b6 -2 b7C -2 b7E -1, 3

Administrative Notes: (U) Below investigative support provided to the New Haven FBI Office in furtherance of their captioned matter.

Enclosure(s): Enclosed are the following items:
1. (U) [redacted] b6 -2
2. (U) [redacted] b7C -2
3. (U) [redacted]

Details:

On December 20, 2012, writer contacted [redacted] [redacted] with regards to the address: b7E -3

UNCLASSIFIED

Sandy Hook-1324

4-NH-2619946 Serial 87

Title: (U) To Document [redacted] b7E

Re: 4-NH-2619946, 12/21/2012

[redacted] b6 - b7C b7E

♦♦

FD-302 (Rev. 5-8-10)

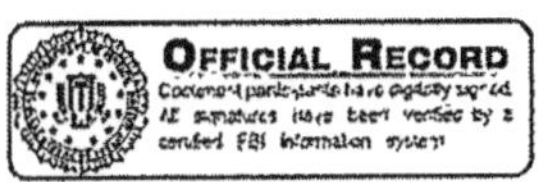

UNCLASSIFIED//~~FOUO~~

FEDERAL BUREAU OF INVESTIGATION

Date of entry 12/21/2012

b6 -1, 2
b7C -1, 2
b7E -10

On December 20, 2012, a physical surveillance was conducted in the area of [redacted] The surveillance was conducted by SA [redacted] and SA [redacted] The following observations were made during the surveillance:

EVENT_TIMELINE

19:30 [redacted]

[redacted]

b6 -2
b7C -2
b7E -10

UNCLASSIFIED//~~FOUO~~

Investigation on 12/20/2012 at [redacted] United States (In Person)

File # 4-NH-2619946 Date drafted 12/21/2012

by [redacted]

b7C -1, 2
b7E -10

4-NH-2619946 Serial 88

b6 -2
b7C -2
b7E -10

4-NH-2619946

[redacted]

19:50 Surveillance terminated.

FD-1036 (Rev. 10-16-2009)

UNCLASSIFIED

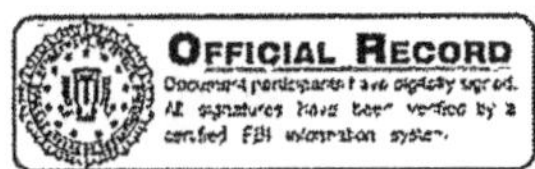

FEDERAL BUREAU OF INVESTIGATION

Import Form

Form Type: OTHER

Date: 12/22/2012

Title: (U) Operational Plan

Approved By: A/SSA [redacted]
ASAC [redacted]

b6 -1
b7C -1

Drafted By: [redacted]

Case ID #: 4-NH-2619946

(U) UNSUB(S)
Sandy Hook Elementary School
12 Dickinson St, Sandy Hook, CT-Victim
Firearms Act.
OO:NH

Synopsis: (U) Columbia division operational plan for [redacted]
[redacted]

b7E -11

♦♦

UNCLASSIFIED

Sandy Hook-1331

4-NH-2619946 Serial 89

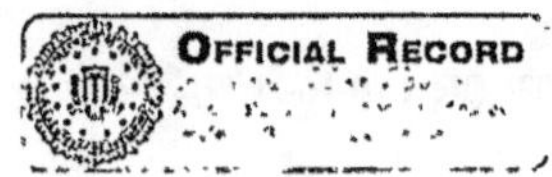

UNCLASSIFIED

FEDERAL BUREAU OF INVESTIGATION

Import Form

Form Type: OTHER **Date:** 12/21/2012

Title: (U)

Approved By: SSA

Drafted By:

b6 -1
b7C -1
OTHER Sealed Pursuant to Court Order

Case ID #: 4-NH-2619946

(U) UNSUB(S)
Sandy Hook Elementary School
12 Dickinson St, Sandy Hook, CT-Victim
Firearms Act.
OO:NH

INFORMATION UNDER COURT ORDER

Disclosure of this information is restricted by court order. Consult with the assigned Assistant United States Attorney before disseminating within or outside the FBI.

Synopsis: (U)

b6 -2
b7C -2
OTHER Sealed Pursuant to Court Order

♦♦

UNCLASSIFIED

4-NH-2619946
SERIAL 90

FD-1036 (Rev. 10-16-2009)

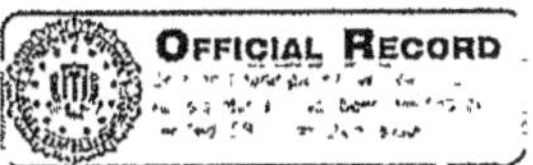

UNCLASSIFIED

FEDERAL BUREAU OF INVESTIGATION

Import Form

Form Type: OTHER

Date: 12/21/2012

Title: (U) [redacted]

[redacted]

b6 -1
b7C -1
OTHER Sealed Pursuant to Court Order

Approved By: SSA [redacted]

Drafted By: [redacted]

Case ID #: 4-NH-2619946

(U) UNSUB(S)
Sandy Hook Elementary School
12 Dickinson St, Sandy Hook, CT-Victim
Firearms Act.
OO:NH

INFORMATION UNDER COURT ORDER

Disclosure of this information is restricted by court order. Consult with the assigned Assistant United States Attorney before disseminating within or outside the FBI.

Synopsis: (U) [redacted]

[redacted]

b6 -2
b7C -2
OTHER Sealed Pursuant to Court Order

♦♦

UNCLASSIFIED

4-NH-2619946
SERIAL 91

FD-1036 (Rev. 10-16-2009)

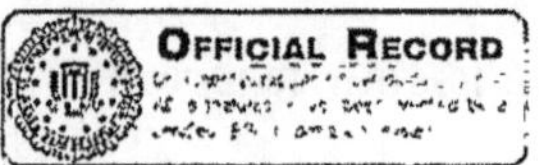

UNCLASSIFIED

FEDERAL BUREAU OF INVESTIGATION

Import Form

Form Type: OTHER

Date: 12/21/2012

Title: (U) [redacted]

Approved By: SSA [redacted]

Drafted By: [redacted]

b6 -1
b7C -1
OTHER Sealed Pursuant to Court Order

Case ID #: 4-NH-2619946

(U) UNSUB(S)
Sandy Hook Elementary School
12 Dickinson St, Sandy Hook, CT-Victim
Firearms Act.
OO:NH

INFORMATION UNDER COURT ORDER

Disclosure of this information is restricted by court order. Consult with the assigned Assistant United States Attorney before disseminating within or outside the FBI.

Synopsis: (U) [redacted]

b6 -1
b7C -1
OTHER Sealed Pursuant to Court Order

♦♦

UNCLASSIFIED

FD-1036 (Rev. 10-16-2009)

UNCLASSIFIED

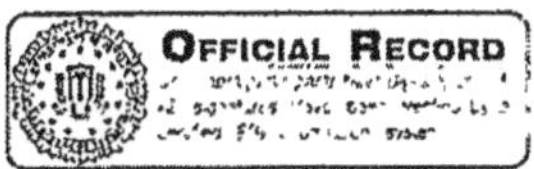

FEDERAL BUREAU OF INVESTIGATION

Import Form

Form Type: OTHER **Date:** 12/21/2012

Title: (U) [redacted]

Approved By: SSA [redacted]

Drafted By: [redacted]

b6 -1
b7C -1
OTHER Sealed Pursuant to Court Order

Case ID #: 4-NH-2619946 (U) UNSUB(S)
Sandy Hook Elementary School
12 Dickinson St, Sandy Hook, CT-Victim
Firearms Act.
OO:NH

INFORMATION UNDER COURT ORDER

Disclosure of this information is restricted by court order. Consult with the assigned Assistant United States Attorney before disseminating within or outside the FBI.

Synopsis: (U) [redacted]

b6 -2
b7C -2
OTHER Sealed Pursuant to Court Order

♦♦

UNCLASSIFIED

4-NH-2619946
SERIAL 93

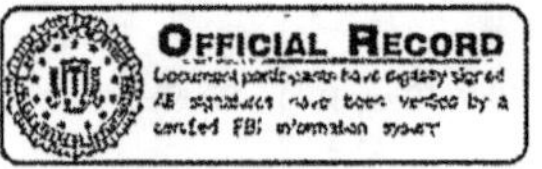

FEDERAL BUREAU OF INVESTIGATION

Date of entry 12/26/2012

[redacted] white male, date of birth (DOB) [redacted] Social Security Account Number (SSAN) [redacted] [redacted] was interviewed at [redacted] [redacted] Also present was [redacted] of the [redacted] and [redacted] [redacted] After being advised of the identity of the interviewing Agent and the nature of the interview, [redacted] provided the following information: b6 -3, b7C -3

[redacted] indicated he had information regarding the shooting that occurred at SANDY HOOK ELEMENTARY SCHOOL. [redacted] b6 -5 b7C -5

[redacted] [redacted] allegedly overheard the conversation and informed [redacted] that [redacted] LANZA, was also very interested in assault weapons. As the discussion progressed, [redacted] stated that [redacted] LANZA, possessed an assault weapon and that she was scared of him. LANZA allegedly told [redacted] that he planned to kill his mother and children at SANDY HOOK in Newton, Connecticut. b6 -5, b7C -5

[redacted] in December of 2008, [redacted] While there [redacted] could not get over the information he had regarding LANZA. [redacted] called SANDY HOOK [redacted] and spoke to [redacted] [redacted] (phonetic), [redacted] explained to [redacted] what he had been told by [redacted] stated she had previous run-ins with LANZA, and requested that [redacted] contact the NEWTON POLICE DEPARTMENT (NPD). b6 -5, b7C -5

[redacted] called the NPD and told them he had information about LANZA threatening to kill his mother and shoot children at SANDY HOOK. [redacted] was told by NPD that LANZA'S mother owned the guns and that there was nothing b6 - b7C

Investigation on 12/20/2012 at [redacted] United States (In Person) b6 -1, b7C -1

File # 4-NH-2619946 Date drafted 12/26/2012

by [redacted]

b6 -2
b7C -2

NPD could do about it. [redacted] alleges that NPD threatened to contact the [redacted]

b6 -6
b7C -6

[redacted] called [redacted] with the information he received from NPD, and [redacted] insisted [redacted] call the State Police. [redacted] refused as he was scared of the threats from NPD, and told [redacted] to leave him alone. [redacted] insisted she come to [redacted] to speak with [redacted] and convince him to return to Connecticut with her to speak with the authorities. [redacted] told [redacted] not to come looking for him in [redacted] and he wanted to stay out of it.

b6 -5, 6
b7C -5, 6

A short while later, [redacted] was in [redacted] While there, [redacted] learned a woman had been traveling around in the area looking for him, and asking for him by name. While [redacted] was at [redacted] he found the woman that was looking for him. [redacted] stated that it was [redacted]

b6 -5, 6
b7C -5, 6

[redacted] spoke with [redacted] and she pleaded with him to go to Connecticut and tell the authorities what he knew about LANZA. [redacted] refused and told [redacted] she needed to leave town. [redacted] was staying at the SUPER 8 in [redacted] was escorted out of [redacted] and back to [redacted] was told to fly back to Connecticut from [redacted] which she apparently did.

b6 -5, 6
b7C -5, 6

[redacted] indicated this time frame was sometime between December 6, 2008 and December 24, 2008. [redacted] remembered these dates, as he [redacted]

b6 -6
b7C -6

[redacted] talked to [redacted] again [redacted] called her [redacted] was upset with [redacted] for informing [redacted] about LANZA. Apparently [redacted] had contacted [redacted] as well. [redacted] had told LANZA of the incident and LANZA had threatened to make it seem like [redacted] would be involved if a shooting ever took place.

b6 -5, 6
b7C -5, 6

[redacted] has not talked to [redacted] since the phone call [redacted] Per [redacted] LANZA hated his mother and SANDY HOOK, because his mother had worked there. LANZA apparently felt that his mother loved the students more than him.

b6 -5, 6
b7C -5, 6

b6 -6
b7C -

[redacted] stated that he made all of his phone calls to [redacted] and the NPD from [redacted] land line, [redacted] said his story could be verified from the phone records from [redacted] house, and possibly the flight records of [redacted] from traveling from Connecticut to [redacted] believed that [redacted] was in [redacted] sometime around December 18 through December 24, 2008.

b6 -5,
b7C -5

[redacted] stated he had read about the shooting and watched the events on television. He was coming forward with this information because he felt bad about not doing more to try and prevent the incident from occurring.

b6 -
b7C -

[redacted] provided a printout [redacted] which is attached to this document.

b6 -3,
b7C -3

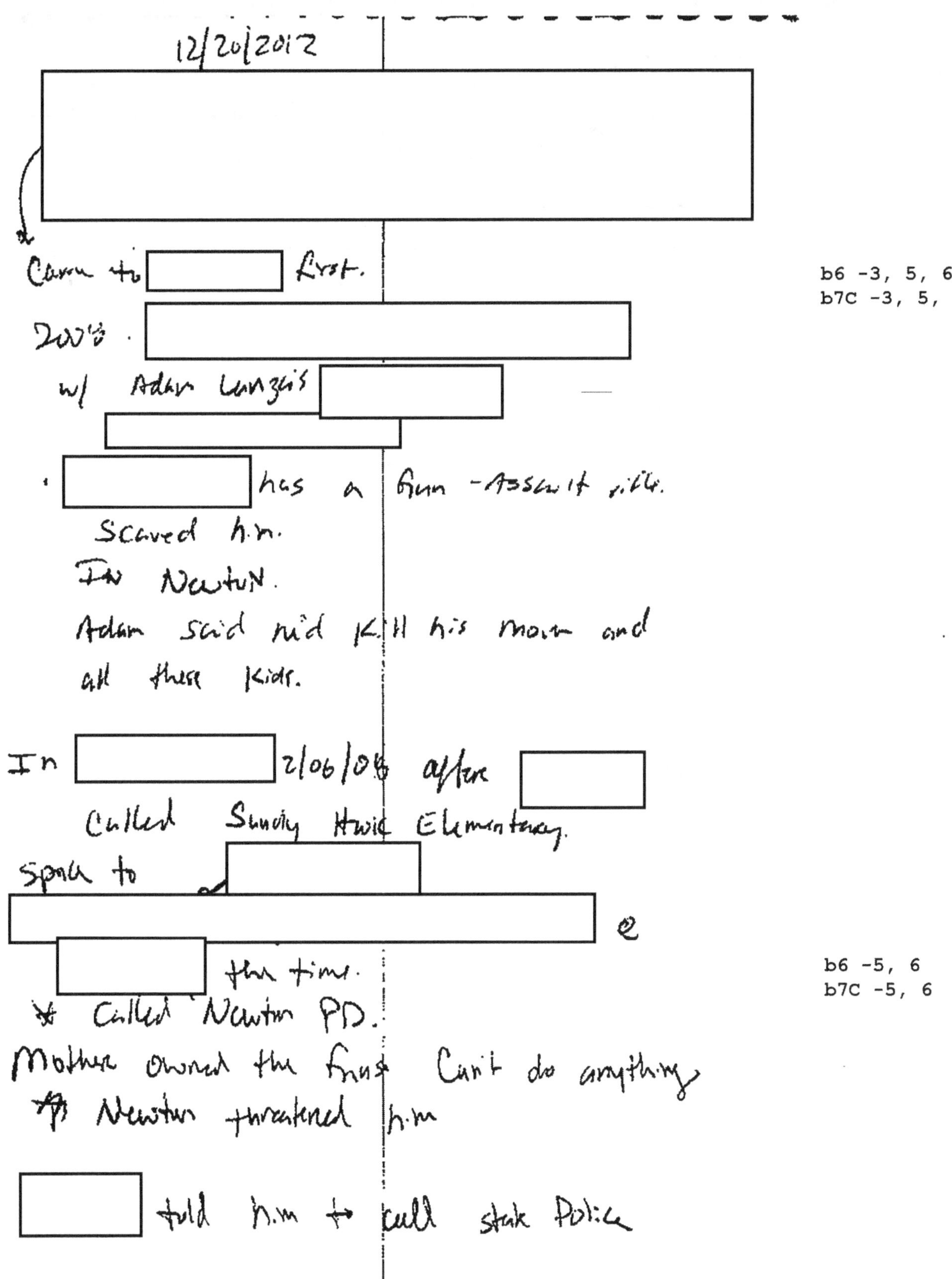

12/20/2012

Came to first.

2008.

w/ Adam Lanza's

has a Gun - Assault rifle.

Scared him.

In Newton.

Adam said he'd Kill his mom and all these Kids.

In 2/06/08 after

Called Sandy Hook Elementary.

Spoke to

@

the time.

* Called Newton PD.

Mother owned the guns Can't do anything

Newton threatened him

told him to call state Police

b6 -3, 5, 6
b7C -3, 5, 6

b6 -5, 6
b7C -5, 6

Said she was coming to get him. Buffer 12/24/08

In came looking for him. -

She was in

Begged him to go to Connecticut.

Super 8 in is where she was staying.

Flew with back to CT.

Talked to after the incident. He called her from

- she wasn't happy he told

b6 -5,
b7C -5,

Adam Threatened to make [redacted] seem like he was involved.

[redacted] afraid his name might be in Adam's computer.

[redacted]

• Never spoke to Adam

[redacted]

[redacted]

b6 -6
b7C -6

✱ - Sister here in [redacted]

12/14 - 12/24 - 2008 is when he thinks she was here

[redacted]

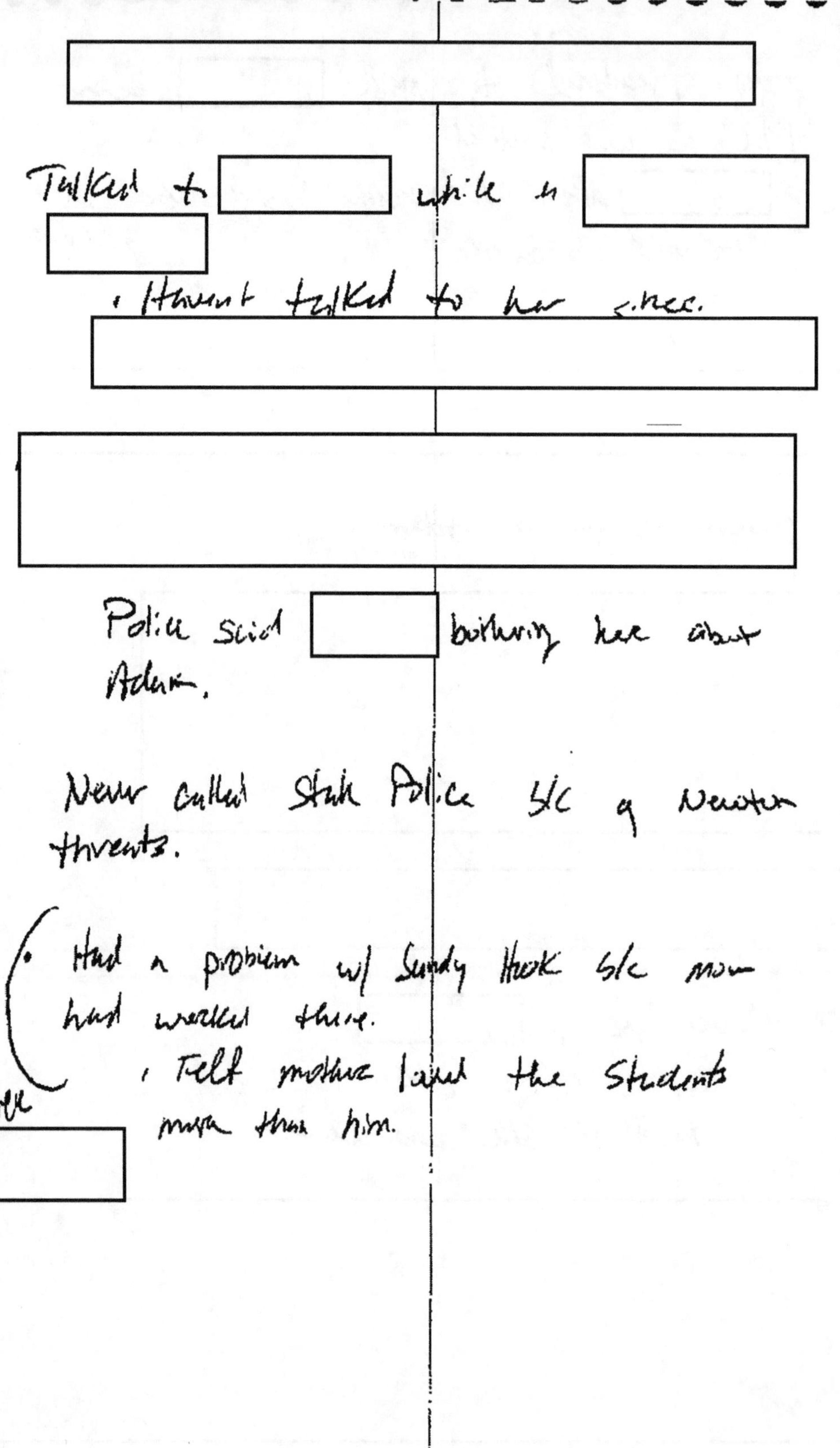

Talked to [redacted] while in [redacted] [redacted]

- Haven't talked to her since.

[redacted]

[redacted]

Police said [redacted] bothering her about Adam.

Never called State Police b/c of Newtown threats.

- Had a problem w/ Sandy Hook b/c mom had worked there.
  - Felt mother loved the students more than him.

DCF [redacted]

b6 -5, 6
b7C -5, 6

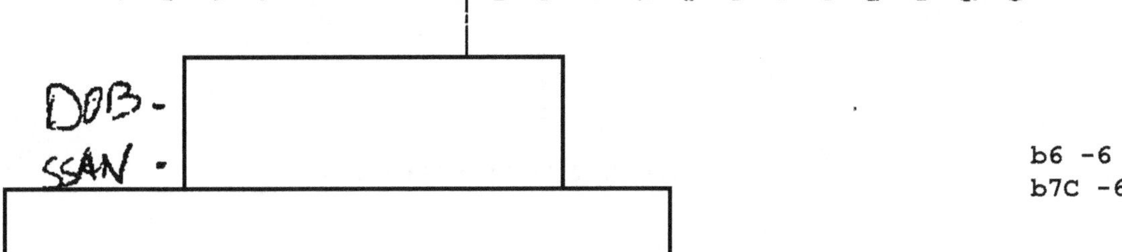

b6 -6
b7C -6

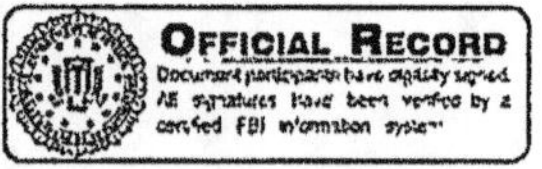

FEDERAL BUREAU OF INVESTIGATION

Date of entry 12/21/2012

[redacted] date of birth: [redacted] white male, hair: blonde, eyes: blue, height: 5'7", [redacted] drivers license number: [redacted] expiration date [redacted] residence address: [redacted] [redacted] was located and interviewed in the presence of [redacted] date of birth: [redacted] social security number: [redacted] and [redacted] date of birth: [redacted] social security number: [redacted] [redacted] and [redacted] were also present at all times during this interview. After being advised of the identity of the interviewing agent and the purpose of the interview, [redacted] voluntarily provided the following information: b6 -2, b7C -2,

[redacted] was aware of the shooting at Sandy Hook Elementary School in Newtown, Connecticut but stated he had no advance knowledge that such an event was going to occur. [redacted] said it was a constant topic of conversation at work, where he served as [redacted] b6 -2 b7C -

[redacted] has never knowingly had contact with ADAM LANZA.

[redacted] has had a Facebook account in the past but has not used it in some time. [redacted] Most of [redacted] online social activity involves tweeting through his twitter handle, [redacted] also does a lot of online gaming on various consoles to include his personal computer, XBOX360, and Play Station 3. [redacted] uses various gamer tags, also known as nicknames or nicks, to include but not limited to [redacted] and [redacted] (note: the gamer tag [redacted] was phonetically spelled as [redacted] could not recall how it was spelled) [redacted] does maintain active XBOX Live and Play Station Network online gaming accounts. [redacted] logged onto his XBOX Live account and only had 15 friends listed. [redacted] stated b6 - b7C

Investigation on 12/19/2012 at [redacted] United States (In Person) b6 -1, b7C -1

File # 4-NH-2619946 Date drafted 12/21/2012

by [redacted]

b6 -2
b7C -2

that he had dropped all friends from his Play Station Network account. When [redacted] does play online video games, he normally plays with his online friends.

b6 -2
b7C -2

[redacted] has a large collection of video games and admitted he had a spending problem because of his love for video games. The games that [redacted] mostly plays are first person shooter, action, puzzle, and fighting games. [redacted] does not participate in chat/audio sessions while playing online but has heard conversations that other users have with one another. [redacted] had never participated in or heard others talk about mass shootings, massacres, murder, or anything along those lines while he played video games online. [redacted] stated that if he had knowledge of such conversations that he would have immediately reported them to the police. [redacted] also stated that intentionally harming children was "sick" and that "that bastard took the easy way out by killing himself and if I would have killed the shooter myself if I had the chance because of what he did to those kids" in reference to the shooting in Newtown, CT.

b6 -2
b7C -2

[redacted] doesn't use e-mail often. [redacted] has purchased video games online through the digital software distribution service known as Steam. [redacted] does maintain a dropbox account linked to his [redacted] address and uses it for storing free video games that he has downloaded from the Internet.

b6 -2
b7C -2

[redacted]

b6 -2
b7C -2

[redacted]

b6 -2
b7C -2

b6 -2
b7C -

b6 -
b7C

[redacted] did not recall any instances of strange conversations, e-mails, or other communications regarding events related to the Connecticut shooting or other massacres and mass killings.

b6 -
b7C

Interviewed w/ [redacted] present

12/19/12

DL

M 5'7 Blue eyes Blonde Hair

b6 -2, 5
b7C -2, 5

DOB:

No knowledge of Shooting / Lanza

No facebook

Twitter - Gaming only

Gmail - Not used after

Online Gaming

PC XBOX 360 PS3

FPS, Action, Puzzles, fighting

b6 -2
b7C -2

No talking / chatting

Dropbox

- stored video games

Usually play w/ friends

~~Know of~~ Doesn't listen to convos but would report it

b6 -2, 5
b7C -2, 5

15 friends on XBOX360
0 friends on PS3

FD-1057 (Rev. 5-8-10)

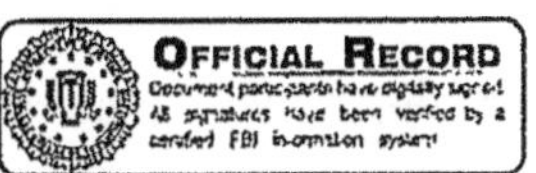

UNCLASSIFIED

FEDERAL BUREAU OF INVESTIGATION

Electronic Communication

Title: (U) Lead Coverage **Date:** 12/26/2012

From: MEMPHIS
ME-COLUMBIA RA
Contact: [redacted]

Approved By: SSA [redacted]

Drafted By: [redacted]

b6 -1
b7C -1

Case ID #: 4-NH-2619946 (U) UNSUB(S)
Sandy Hook Elementary School
12 Dickinson St, Sandy Hook, CT-Victim
Firearms Act.
OO:NH

Synopsis: (U) Lead Coverage

[redacted] b7E -1

Details:

On December 18, 2012, [redacted] was interviewed in reference Serial #40, Lead Coverage.

b6 -6
b7C -6

FD-302 prepared and uploaded to captioned matter.

♦♦

UNCLASSIFIED

4-NH-2619946 Serial 96

FD-1087 (Rev. 5-8-10)

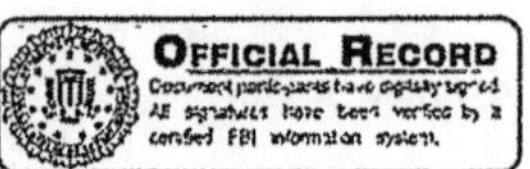

UNCLASSIFIED

FEDERAL BUREAU OF INVESTIGATION

Evidence Log

Event Title: (U) 4-NH-2619946 **Date:** 12/26/2012

Approved By: [redacted]

Drafted By: [redacted]

b6 -1
b7C -1

Case ID #: 4-NH-2619946

(U) UNSUB(S)
Sandy Hook Elementary School
12 Dickinson St, Sandy Hook, CT-Victim
Firearms Act.
OO:NH

[redacted] b7E -1

Acquired By: [redacted] on 12/16/2012

b6 -1
b7C -1

Acquired From: (U) Volunteered
Newtown, Connecticut

Receipt Given?: No

Holding Office: NEW HAVEN

Details: *No Details Provided*

Item Type	Description
1D	(U) Volunteered; 12/16/12; 1 orig.computer disk containing threatening phone call left for resident of Newtown, CT Acquired On: 12/16/2012 ELSUR Evidence Type: Other Intercept Type: Volunteered/Subpoenaed Medium Media Type: Computer Disk Original Type: Original

♦♦

UNCLASSIFIED

4-NH-2619946 Serial 97

FD-1087 (Rev. 5-8-10)

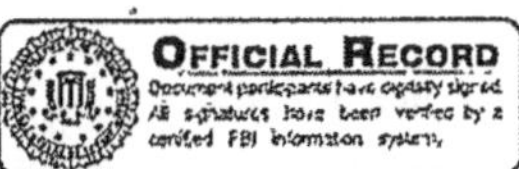

UNCLASSIFIED

FEDERAL BUREAU OF INVESTIGATION

Evidence Log

Event Title: (U) [redacted] **Date:** 12/26/2012

Approved By: [redacted]

Drafted By: [redacted]

b6 -1
b7C -1
OTHER Sealed Pursuant to Court Order

Case ID #: 4-NH-2619946

(U) UNSUB(S)
Sandy Hook Elementary School
12 Dickinson St, Sandy Hook, CT-Victim
Firearms Act.
OO:NH

b7E -1

b6 -1, 2
b7C -1, 2
OTHER Sealed Pursuant to Court Order

UNCLASSIFIED

4-NH-2619946 Serial 98

FD-1087 (Rev. 5-8-10)

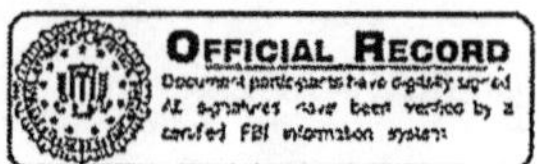

UNCLASSIFIED

FEDERAL BUREAU OF INVESTIGATION

Evidence Log

Event Title: (U) CART **Date:** 12/21/2012

Approved By: A/SSA [redacted]

Drafted By: [redacted]

b6 -1
b7C -1

Case ID #: 4-NH-2619946 (U) UNSUB(S)
Sandy Hook Elementary School
12 Dickinson St, Sandy Hook, CT-Victim
Firearms Act.
OO:NH

[redacted]

b7E -1

Acquired By: [redacted] on 12/19/2012

b6 -1
b7C -1

Acquired From: (U) CART Exam

Receipt Given?: No

Holding Office: NEW HAVEN

Details:

[redacted]

Item Type	Description
1B CART	(U) [redacted] [redacted] Acquired On: 12/19/2012 Located By: [redacted] Location Area: CART Specific Location: CART Device Type: [redacted] Number of Devices Collected: [redacted]

b6 -1, 2
b7C -1, 2

UNCLASSIFIED

4-NH-2619946 Serial 99

Title: (U) CART
Re: 4-NH-2619946, 12/21/2012

♦♦

FD-1087 (Rev. 5-8-10)

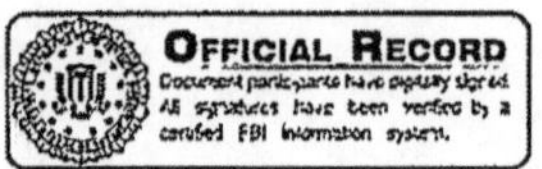

UNCLASSIFIED

FEDERAL BUREAU OF INVESTIGATION

Evidence Log

Event Title: (U) CART **Date:** 12/21/2012

Approved By: A/SSA [redacted]

Drafted By: [redacted]

b6 -1
b7C -1

Case ID #: 4-NH-2619946 (U) UNSUB(S)
Sandy Hook Elementary School
12 Dickinson St, Sandy Hook, CT-Victim
Firearms Act.
OO:NH

[redacted] b7E -1

Acquired By: [redacted] b6 -1 b7C -1

Acquired From: (U) CART Exam.

Receipt Given?: No

Holding Office: NEW HAVEN

Details:

[redacted]

Item Type	Description
1B CART	(U) [redacted]

b6 -1, 2
b7C -1,

Acquired On: 12/21/2012
Located By: [redacted]
Location Area: CART
Specific Location: CART
Device Type: [redacted]
Number of Devices Collected: [redacted]

UNCLASSIFIED

4-NH-2619946 Serial 100

Title: (U) CART
Re: 4-NH-2619946, 12/21/2012

♦♦

FEDERAL BUREAU OF INVESTIGATION
FOI/PA
DELETED PAGE INFORMATION SHEET
Civil Action# 16-cv-02136

Total Deleted Page(s) = 27
Page 3 ~ Referral/Consult;
Page 6 ~ Duplicate;
Page 7 ~ Duplicate;
Page 8 ~ Duplicate;
Page 9 ~ Duplicate;
Page 10 ~ Duplicate;
Page 11 ~ Duplicate;
Page 13 ~ Duplicate;
Page 15 ~ Duplicate;
Page 16 ~ Duplicate;
Page 17 ~ Duplicate;
Page 18 ~ Duplicate;
Page 20 ~ Duplicate;
Page 22 ~ Duplicate;
Page 24 ~ Duplicate;
Page 26 ~ Duplicate;
Page 28 ~ Duplicate;
Page 30 ~ Duplicate;
Page 31 ~ Duplicate;
Page 32 ~ Duplicate;
Page 34 ~ Duplicate;
Page 35 ~ Referral/Consult;
Page 36 ~ Referral/Consult;
Page 37 ~ Referral/Consult;
Page 38 ~ Referral/Consult;
Page 39 ~ Referral/Consult;
Page 43 ~ Duplicate;

XXXXXXXXXXXXXXXXXXXXXXXX
X Deleted Page(s) X
X No Duplication Fee X
X For this Page X
XXXXXXXXXXXXXXXXXXXXXXXX

FD-340a (Rev. 1-27-03)

(Title) 1A's

(File No.) 4-NH-2619946

Item	Date	To be returned Yes	No		Disposition

FD-340 (Rev. 4-11-03)

File Number 4-NH-2619946 - 1A 10

Field Office Acquiring Evidence New Haven, CT

Serial # of Originating Document ________

Date Received 12/15/2012

From ________
(Name of Contributor/Interviewee)

____
(Address)

____
(City and State)

By SA [redacted] b6 -1 b7C -1

To Be Returned ☐ Yes ☑ No

Receipt Given ☐ Yes ☑ No

Grand Jury Material - Disseminate Only Pursuant to Rule 6 (e) Federal Rules of Criminal Procedure

☐ Yes ☑ No

Federal Taxpayer Information (FTI)

☐ Yes ☑ No

Title:

Sandy Hook Elementary

Reference: ________
(Communication Enclosing Material)

Description: ☑ Original notes re interview of

1) [redacted] b6 -6 b7C -6

FD-340 (Rev. 3-8-01)

Universal Case File Number ~~[illegible]~~ 4-NH-2619946-1A11

Field Office Acquiring Evidence NH

Serial # of Originating Document 16

Date Received 12/14/2012

From ______________________________

(Name of Contributor)

____

(Address of Contributor)

____

(City and State)

By SA [redacted] b6 -1 b7C -1

To Be Returned ☐ Yes ☑ No

Receipt Given ☐ Yes ☑ No

Grand Jury Material - Disseminate Only Pursuant to Rule 6 (e)
Federal Rules of Criminal Procedure

☐ Yes ☑ No

Federal Taxpayer Information (FTI)

☐ Yes ☑ No

Title: Sandy Hook Elementary

Reference: ______________________________

(Communication Enclosing Material)

Description: ☐ Original notes re interview of

Neighborhood Canvass 12-14-2012

FD-340 (Rev. 4-11-03)

File Number 4-NH-2619946 - 1A12

Field Office Acquiring Evidence New Haven

Serial # of Originating Document

Date Received 12/14/2012

From

(Name of Contributor/Interviewee)

(Address)

(City and State)

By SA [redacted]

b6
b7C

To Be Returned ☐ Yes ☑ No

Receipt Given ☐ Yes ☑ No

Grand Jury Material - Disseminate Only Pursuant to Rule 6 (e) Federal Rules of Criminal Procedure

☐ Yes ☑ No

Federal Taxpayer Information (FTI)

☐ Yes ☐ No

Title:

Sandy Hook Elementary

Reference:

(Communication Enclosing Material)

Description: ☑ Original notes re interview of

1) Interview w/ [redacted]

2) Campsite photo

3) email from [redacted]

b6 -6
b7C -6

FD-340 (Rev. 4-11-03)

File Number 4-NH-2619946 -1A16

Field Office Acquiring Evidence New Haven

Serial # of Originating Document ______

Date Received 12/14/2012

From ______
(Name of Contributor/Interviewee)

______
(Address)

______
(City and State)

By SA [redacted]

b6 -1
b7C -1

To Be Returned ☐ Yes ☑ No

Receipt Given ☐ Yes ☑ No

Grand Jury Material - Disseminate Only Pursuant to Rule 6 (e)
Federal Rules of Criminal Procedure

☐ Yes ☑ No

Federal Taxpayer Information (FTI)

☐ Yes ☑ No

Title:

Sandy Hook Elementary

Reference: ______
(Communication Enclosing Material)

Description: ☑ Original notes re interview of

1) Interview of [redacted]

b6 -6
b7C -6

FD-340 (Rev. 3-8-01)

Universal Case File Number 4-NH-2619946 - 1A17

Field Office Acquiring Evidence NH

Serial # of Originating Document 34

Date Received 12/16/2012

From ____________________
(Name of Contributor)

____
(Address of Contributor)

____
(City and State)

By SA [redacted] b6 -1 b7C -1

To Be Returned ☐ Yes ☑ No

Receipt Given ☐ Yes ☑ No

Grand Jury Material - Disseminate Only Pursuant to Rule 6 (e)
Federal Rules of Criminal Procedure

☐ Yes ☑ No

Federal Taxpayer Information (FTI)

☐ Yes ☑ No

Title:

Sandy Hook Elementary

Reference: ____________________
(Communication Enclosing Material)

Description: ☑ Original notes re interview of

[redacted] & [redacted] b6 -7 b7C -7

FD-340c (4-11-03)

File Number 4-NH-2619946-1A18

Field Office Acquiring Evidence New Haven

Serial # of Originating Document 35

Date Received 12/14/12

From [redacted] b6 -6 b7C -6

(Name of Contributor/Interviewee)

(Address)

Sandy Hook, Connecticut

By SA [redacted] b6 -1 b7C -1

To Be Returned ☐ Yes ☑ No

Receipt Given ☐ Yes ☑ No

Grand Jury Material - Disseminate Only Pursuant to Rule 6 (e) Federal Rules of Criminal Procedure

☐ Yes ☑ No

Federal Taxpayer Information (FTI)

☐ Yes ☑ No

Title:

Reference:

(Communication Enclosing Material)

Description: ☑ Original notes re interview of [redacted] b6 -6 b7C -6

FD-340 (Rev. 3-8-01)

Universal Case File Number 4-NH-2619946-1A19

Field Office Acquiring Evidence NH

Serial # of Originating Document 36

Date Received 12/18/2012

From

(Name of Contributor)

(Address of Contributor)

(City and State)

By SA [redacted]

b6 -1
b7C -1

To Be Returned ☐ Yes ☑ No

Receipt Given ☐ Yes ☑ No

Grand Jury Material - Disseminate Only Pursuant to Rule 6 (e) Federal Rules of Criminal Procedure

☐ Yes ☑ No

Federal Taxpayer Information (FTI)

☐ Yes ☑ No

Title: Sandy Hook Elementary

Reference:

(Communication Enclosing Material)

Description: ☐ Original notes re interview of

Attempted [redacted] interview

b6 -5
b7C -5

FD-340c (4-11-03)

File Number 4- NH- 2619946-1A20

Field Office Acquiring Evidence NHo

Serial # of Originating Document 37

Date Received 12/14/2012

From [redacted] b6 -6 b7C -6

(Name of Contributor/Interviewee)

[redacted]

(Address)

Newtown, Connecticut

(City and State)

By SA [redacted] b6 -1 b7C -1

To Be Returned ☐ Yes ☒ No

Receipt Given ☐ Yes ☒ No

Grand Jury Material - Disseminate Only Pursuant to Rule 6 (e) Federal Rules of Criminal Procedure

☐ Yes ☒ No

Federal Taxpayer Information (FTI)

☐ Yes ☒ No

Title: (U) UNSUB(s)
Sandy Hook Elementary School
12 Dickenson St, Sandy Hook, CT
Firearms Act

Reference: FD-302 of [redacted]

(Communication Enclosing Material)

b6 -6 b7C -6

Description: ☒ Original notes re interview of [redacted]

FD-340c (4-11-03)

File Number 4-NH-2619946-A 21

Field Office Acquiring Evidence NHO

Serial # of Originating Document 38

Date Received 12/16/2012

From [redacted]
(Name of Contributor/Interviewee)

[redacted]
(Address)

b6 -7
b7C -7

Newtown, Connecticut
(City and State)

By SA [redacted]

b6 -1
b7C -1

To Be Returned ☐ Yes ☑ No

Receipt Given ☐ Yes ☑ No

Grand Jury Material - Disseminate Only Pursuant to Rule 6 (e)
Federal Rules of Criminal Procedure
☐ Yes ☑ No

Federal Taxpayer Information (FTI)
☐ Yes ☑ No

Title: (U) UNSUB(s)
Sandy Hook Elementary School
12 Dickinson St, Sandy Hook, CT
Firearms act

Reference: FD-302 of [redacted]
(Communication Enclosing Material)

b6 -7
b7C -7

Description: ☒ Original notes re interview of [redacted]

FD-340 (Rev. 3-8-01)

Universal Case File Number 4-NH-2619946-1A22

Field Office Acquiring Evidence New Haven

Serial # of Originating Document

Date Received 12/16/12

From [redacted] b6 -7 b7C -7

(Name of Contributor)

(Address of Contributor)

Newtown, Connecticut

(City and State)

By SA [redacted] b6 -1 b7C -1

To Be Returned ☐ Yes ☑ No

Receipt Given ☐ Yes ☑ No

Grand Jury Material - Disseminate Only Pursuant to Rule 6 (e) Federal Rules of Criminal Procedure

☐ Yes ☑ No

Federal Taxpayer Information (FTI)

☐ Yes ☑ No

Title:

Reference:

(Communication Enclosing Material)

Description: ☑ Original notes re interview of b6 -7 b7C -7

[redacted]

FD-340c (4-11-03)

File Number 4 - NH - 2619946 1A28

Field Office Acquiring Evidence NH

Serial # of Originating Document

Date Received 14 DEC 12

From FBI

(Name of Contributor/Interviewee)

(Address)

(City and State)

By SA [redacted] b6 -1 b7C -1

To Be Returned ☐ Yes ☑ No

Receipt Given ☐ Yes ☑ No

Grand Jury Material - Disseminate Only Pursuant to Rule 6 (e)
Federal Rules of Criminal Procedure

☐ Yes ☑ No

Federal Taxpayer Information (FTI)

☐ Yes ☑ No

Title: SANDY HOOK ELEMENTARY SCHOOL
12 DICKINSON ST, SANDY HOOK, CT - VICTIM
FIREARMS ACT
OO:NH

Reference:

(Communication Enclosing Material)

Description: ☐ Original notes re interview of

14 DEC 12 - NEIGHBORHOOD CANVASS
RESULTS FOR HOUSE #S [redacted] AND b6 -5, 6 b7C -5, 6
[redacted] NEWTOWN, CT

* ASSOCIATED WITH SERIAL #46

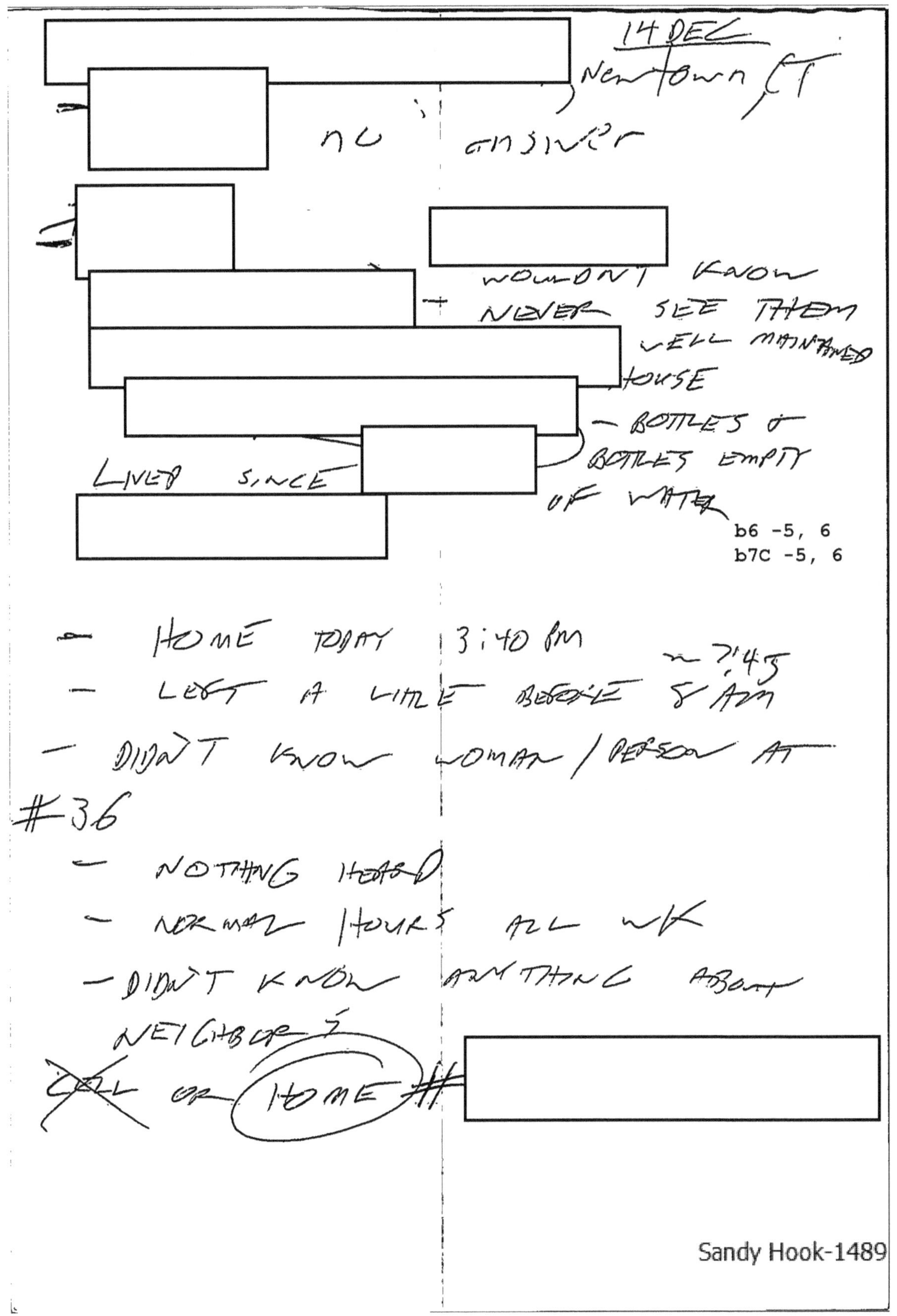

14 DEC

Newtown, CT

no answer

wouldn't know

never see them

well maintained

house

- bottles of bottles empty of water

Lived since

b6 -5, 6
b7C -5, 6

- Home today 3:40 pm
- Left a little before 8 am ~7:45
- Didn't know woman / person at #36
- Nothing heard
- Normal hours all wk
- Didn't know anything about neighbors

~~Cell~~ or Home #

FD-340c (4-11-03)

File Number 4-NH-261 99461-A 29

Field Office Acquiring Evidence NHO

Serial # of Originating Document 48

Date Received 12/15/2012

From [redacted]
(Name of Contributor/Interviewee)

[redacted]
(Address)

[redacted]
(City and State)

b6 -6
b7C -6

By SA [redacted]

b6 -1
b7C -1

To Be Returned ☐ Yes ☒ No

Receipt Given ☐ Yes ☒ No

Grand Jury Material - Disseminate Only Pursuant to Rule 6 (e)
Federal Rules of Criminal Procedure

☐ Yes ☒ No

Federal Taxpayer Information (FTI)

☐ Yes ☒ No

Title: (U) Unsub(s)
Sandy Hook Elementary School
12 Dickinson St., Sandy Hook, CT -
Firearms Act

Reference: FD-302 of [redacted]
(Communication Enclosing Material)

b6 -6
b7C -6

Description: ☒ Original notes re interview of [redacted]

FD-1057 (Rev. 5-8-10)

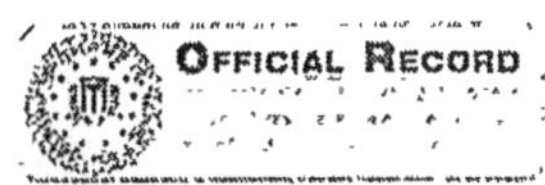

FEDERAL BUREAU OF INVESTIGATION

Electronic Communication

Title: (U) Subfile Opening Document **Date:** 03/22/2013

From: NEW HAVEN
NH-BRA2
Contact: [ ]

Approved By: SSRA [ ]

b6 -1
b7C -1

Drafted By: [ ]

Case ID #: 356A-NH-2619946-CLASSIFIED (U) ADAM PETER LANZA
Sandy Hook Elementary School
12 Dickinson St, Sandy Hook,
CT-Victim
Firearms Act.
OO:NH

Synopsis: (U) To open classified subfile.

~~Reason: 1.4(b), (c), (d)~~
~~Derived From: FBI~~
~~NSISC-20090615~~
~~Declassify On: 20380322~~

DECLASSIFIED BY: NSICG C28W34B64
ON 01-20-2017

Details:

Request to open classified subfile for retention of serials related to the use of classified techniques.

♦♦

~~SECRET//NOFORN~~

4-NH-2619946-CLASSIFIED
SERIAL 1

FD-1036 (Rev. 10-16-2009)

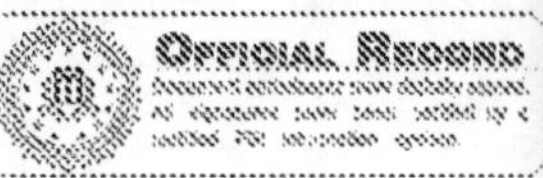

UNCLASSIFIED

FEDERAL BUREAU OF INVESTIGATION

Import Form

Form Type: OTHER **Date:** 11/27/2013

Title: (U) Sandy Hook Elementary School Shooting Final Report

Approved By: A/LEGAT [redacted]

b6 -1
b7C -1
b7E -4, 7

Drafted By: [redacted]

Case ID #: [redacted] (U) TRAINING PROVIDED [redacted]

Synopsis: (U) Sandy Hook Elementary School Shooting Final Report

ALL INFORMATION CONTAINED
HEREIN IS UNCLASSIFIED
DATE 03-03-2017 BY J37J85T94 NSICG

♦♦

UNCLASSIFIED

Report of the State's Attorney for the Judicial District of Danbury on the Shootings at Sandy Hook Elementary School and 36 Yogananda Street, Newtown, Connecticut on December 14, 2012

OFFICE OF THE STATE'S ATTORNEY
JUDICIAL DISTRICT OF DANBURY
Stephen J. Sedensky III, State's Attorney

November 25, 2013

TABLE OF CONTENTS

APPENDIX[1]

Search Warrants

[1] Because of its volume, the Appendix to this report is published as a separate document. Some of the search warrants and reports contained in the Appendix have been redacted to meet court orders, exceptions to the Freedom of Information Act, protect the identity of witnesses, protect records of child abuse or personal identification information.

EXECUTIVE SUMMARY

The purpose of this report is to identify the person or persons criminally responsible for the twenty-seven homicides that occurred in Newtown, Connecticut, on the morning of December 14, 2012, to determine what crimes were committed, and to indicate if there will be any state prosecutions as a result of the incident.

The State's Attorney for the Judicial District of Danbury is charged, pursuant to Article IV, Section 27 of the Constitution of the State of Connecticut and Connecticut General Statutes (C.G.S.) Sec. 51-276 *et seq.*, with the investigation and prosecution of all criminal offenses occurring within the Judicial District of Danbury. The Connecticut State Police have the responsibility to prevent and detect violations of the law and this State's Attorney has worked with and relied upon the Connecticut State Police since the incident occurred.

Since December 14, 2012, the Connecticut State Police and the State's Attorney's Office have worked with the federal authorities sharing responsibilities for various aspects of this investigation. Numerous other municipal, state and federal agencies assisted in the investigation. The investigation materials reflect thousands of law enforcement and prosecutor hours. Apart from physical evidence, the materials consist of more than seven-hundred individual files that include reports, statements, interviews, videos, laboratory tests and results, photographs, diagrams, search warrants and returns, as well as evaluations of those items.

In the course of the investigation, both state and federal law enforcement personnel received a large number of contacts purporting to provide information on the shootings and the shooter. Although many times these "leads" would go nowhere, each one was evaluated and often required substantial law enforcement time to pursue. An abundance of caution was used during the investigation to ensure that all leads were looked into, despite the fact that more than 40 such "leads" proved, after investigation, to be unsubstantiated. Information that was substantiated and relevant was made part of the investigation.

It is not the intent of this report to convey every piece of information contained in the voluminous investigation materials developed by the Connecticut State Police and other law enforcement agencies, but to provide information relevant to the purposes of this report. While no report is statutorily required of the State's Attorney once an investigation is complete, it has been the practice of State's Attorneys to issue reports on criminal investigations where there is no arrest and prosecution if the State's Attorney determines that some type of public statement is necessary. Given the gravity of the crimes committed on December 14, 2012, a report is in order.

On the morning of December 14, 2012, the shooter, age 20, heavily armed, went to Sandy Hook Elementary School (SHES) in Newtown, where he shot his way into the locked school building with a Bushmaster Model XM15-E2S rifle. He then shot and killed the principal and school psychologist as they were in the north hallway of the school responding to the noise of the shooter coming into the school. The shooter also shot and injured two other staff members who were also in the hallway.

The shooter then went into the main office, apparently did not see the staff who were hiding there, and returned to the hallway.

After leaving the main office, the shooter then went down the same hallway in which he had just killed two people and entered first grade classrooms 8 and 10, the order in which is unknown. While in those rooms he killed the two adults in each room, fifteen children in classroom 8 and five in classroom 10. All of the killings were done with the Bushmaster rifle.

He then took his own life with a single shot from a Glock 20, 10 mm pistol in classroom 10.

Prior to going to the school, the shooter used a .22 caliber Savage Mark II rifle to shoot and kill his mother in her bed at the home where they lived at 36 Yogananda Street in Newtown.

The response to these crimes began unfolding at 9:35:39 a.m. when the first 911 call was received by the Newtown Police Department. With the receipt of that call, the dispatching and the arrival of the police, the law enforcement response to the shootings began. It was fewer than four minutes from the time the first 911 call was received until the first police officer arrived at the school. It was fewer than five minutes from the first 911 call, and one minute after the arrival of the first officer, that the shooter killed himself. It was fewer than six minutes from the time the first police officer arrived on SHES property to the time the first police officer entered the school building. In fewer than 11 minutes twenty first-grade pupils and six adults had lost their lives.

The following weapons were recovered in the course of this investigation: (1) a Bushmaster Model XM15-E2S semi-automatic rifle, found in the same classroom as the shooter's body. All of the 5.56 mm shell casings from the school that were tested were found to have been fired from this rifle. (2) a Glock 20, 10 mm semi-automatic pistol found near the shooter's body and determined to have been the source of the self-inflicted gunshot wound by which he took his own life. (3) a Sig Sauer P226, 9 mm semi-automatic pistol found on the shooter's person. There is no evidence this weapon had been fired. (4) a Izhmash Saiga-12, 12 gauge semi-automatic shotgun found in the shooter's car in the parking lot outside the school, and which was secured in the vehicle's trunk by police responding to the scene. There is no evidence this weapon had been fired. (5) a Savage Mark II rifle found at 36 Yogananda Street on the floor of the master bedroom near the bed where the body of the shooter's mother was found. This rifle also was found to have fired the four bullets recovered during the autopsy of the shooter's mother.

All of the firearms were legally purchased by the shooter's mother. Additionally, ammunition of the types found had been purchased by the mother in the past, and there is no evidence that the ammunition was purchased by anyone else, including the shooter.

At the date of this writing, there is no evidence to suggest that anyone other than the shooter was aware of or involved in the planning and execution of the crimes that were committed on December 14, 2012, at Sandy Hook Elementary School and 36 Yogananda Street. From the time an unknown male was encountered by the Newtown police outside of the school during the initial response, until well after the staff and children had been evacuated, the thought that there may have been more than one shooter was a condition all responding law enforcement worked under as they cleared the school. Individuals located in the wooded areas surrounding the school as the searches and evacuations were taking place were initially treated as suspect and handled accordingly (including being handcuffed) until their identity could be determined. The circumstances surrounding all of these individuals were fully investigated and revealed no additional shooters. DNA testing of evidence recovered from both the school and 36 Yogananda Street also revealed no potential accessories or co-conspirators.

It is the conclusion of this State's Attorney that the shooter acted alone and was solely criminally responsible for his actions of that day. Moreover, none of the evidence developed to date demonstrates probable cause to believe that any other person conspired with the shooter to commit these crimes or aided and abetted him in doing so.

Unless additional – and at this time unanticipated – evidence is developed, there will be no state criminal prosecution as result of these crimes. With the issuance of this report, the investigation is closed. Should additional reliable information related to the existence of accessories or co-conspirators come to the attention of the investigators, the investigation will be reopened.[2]

In the course of his rampage the shooter committed a number of crimes in violation of our Connecticut Penal Code. The most significant are those where lives were taken and people were physically injured. In Sandy Hook Elementary School, the crime of Murder under Special Circumstances, in violation of C.G.S. Sec. 53a-54b, was committed twenty-six times and Attempted Murder under Special Circumstances in violation of C.G.S. Secs. 53a-49 and 53a-54b was committed twice as it relates to the two individuals who were shot by the shooter and survived. The crime of Murder in violation of C.G.S. Sec. 53a-54 was committed by the shooter in killing his mother.

The obvious question that remains is: "Why did the shooter murder twenty-seven people, including twenty children?" Unfortunately, that question may never be answered conclusively, despite the collection of extensive background information on the shooter through a multitude of interviews and other sources. The evidence clearly shows that the shooter planned his actions, including the taking of his own life, but there is no clear indication why he did so, or why he targeted Sandy Hook Elementary School.

It is known that the shooter had significant mental health issues that affected his ability to live a normal life and to interact with others, even those to whom he should have been close. As an adult he did not recognize or help himself deal with those issues. What contribution this made to the shootings, if any, is unknown as those mental health professionals who saw him did not see anything that would have predicted his future behavior. He had a familiarity with and access to firearms and ammunition and an obsession with mass murders, in particular the April 1999 shootings at Columbine High School in Colorado. Investigators however, have not discovered any evidence that the shooter voiced or gave any indication to others that he intended to commit such a crime himself.

---

[2] It should be noted that potentially important evidence, i.e., a computer hard drive recovered from the shooter's home, as of this date remains unreadable. Additional insight could be gained should efforts to recover data from the hard drive ever prove successful, which at this time appears highly improbable. It is because of this improbability, coupled with the current determination of no accessories or co-conspirators that the case is being closed.

This State's Attorney expresses his sincere sympathy and condolences to the victims of the incident of December 14, 2012, and to their families. He also expresses his appreciation for their continued patience and understanding during the course of the investigation and preparation of this report. He acknowledges and thanks law enforcement, which responded to Sandy Hook Elementary School in minutes and entered the building believing someone could be there ready to take *their* lives as well. He also acknowledges and thanks the staff of the Sandy Hook Elementary School who acted heroically. The combination saved many children's lives.

This report would not have been possible if not for the assistance and cooperation of numerous agencies at the state, local and federal levels of government. The State's Attorney expresses his sincere gratitude and appreciation to all of these agencies and to all of the men and women who contributed so much to this investigation. The assistance of federal authorities has been invaluable. Particularly worthy of special note are the men and women of the Connecticut State Police, and in particular, the Western District Major Crime Squad. The thoroughness and sensitivity with which they conducted their investigation is unmatched in my experience.

INTRODUCTION

On the morning of December 14, 2012, Adam Lanza, the shooter,[3] age 20, went to Sandy Hook Elementary School (also SHES) in Newtown, Connecticut, where he shot his way into the building and killed twenty children and six adults and wounded two other adults, all with a Bushmaster Model XM15-E2S rifle. The shooter then took his own life with a single shot from a Glock 20, 10 mm handgun. From the time the doors of the school were locked at 9:30 a.m. until the time it is believed the shooter killed himself at 9:40:03, fewer than 11 minutes had elapsed.

Prior to going to the school, the shooter used a .22 caliber Savage Mark II rifle to shoot and kill his mother in her bed. This occurred at the home where they lived at 36 Yogananda Street, also in Newtown.

With these unprecedented horrific crimes came a responsibility for an investigation to determine what crimes were committed and, more importantly, if the shooter acted alone. Any person who aided and abetted the shooter or who conspired with him had to be held accountable.

Beginning on December 14, 2012, the Connecticut State Police and the State's Attorney's Office worked in cooperation with the federal authorities sharing responsibilities for various aspects of the case. The federal involvement has been invaluable. Though some evidence is still being examined, there is no indication in the investigation by either state or federal authorities to date that the shooter acted with anyone on December 14, 2012, or had co-conspirators or accessories who could be prosecuted.

In addition to physical evidence,[4] the investigation materials contain over seven-hundred individual files that include reports, statements, interviews, videos, laboratory tests and results, photographs, diagrams, search warrants and search warrant returns as well as evaluations of those items. Investigators interviewed individuals who were present at SHES on December 14, 2012, and witnessed the incident, among them students, staff members, parents of students and neighbors. Special attention and consideration was given to the interviewing of child witnesses, given their traumatic experience. Also interviewed were police officers and other first responders who were present at SHES during the course of the incident itself and in the course of the subsequent search, evacuation of the school and processing of the scenes.

Investigators attempted to obtain as much information about the shooter's life as possible in an effort to determine the reasons or motives for his actions on December 14, 2012. Interviews were conducted with members of the shooter's family, those who knew the shooter or his family throughout his life, as well as teachers and school personnel who had been involved with him and his family over his time in Newtown.

Efforts were made within the limits of privacy laws to gather information on medical consultations and/or treatments the shooter was involved with over the course of his years in Newtown. In doing so, investigators found no evidence to suggest the shooter had taken any

[3] Throughout the remainder of this report Adam Lanza will be referred to as "the shooter."

[4] Over 270 evidence designations were used, many grouping related items as one number.

medication that would affect his behavior or by any means to explain his actions on December 14, 2012.

An investigation of this magnitude requires careful planning and review. The interviews took substantial time, first to identify which individuals should be interviewed and then to conduct the actual interviews. Physical evidence had to be examined and forensically reviewed. This included ballistics, fingerprint and DNA analysis. Additionally, all of the information collected had to be reviewed and summarized in written statements that have since become a part of the investigation, reflecting thousands of dedicated law enforcement and prosecutor hours.

I had been working closely with the Connecticut State Police, who conducted the state investigation, and federal law enforcement officers since December 2012. Once the investigation was delivered for my review, I took the time to read, digest, evaluate and summarize the material, mindful of the privacy interests involved and the approaching December 14, 2012, anniversary.

The federal authorities have stated that under federal law many of their reports and materials cannot become part of the public record due to rules regarding the dissemination of information obtained pursuant to grand jury subpoenas, sealed search warrants, and federal Freedom of Information law. Therefore, information obtained by federal authorities will not, for the most part, be incorporated into the Connecticut State Police criminal investigation file.

While the reports and materials will not be part of the state investigation record, such materials have been examined and considered by state law enforcement authorities. Based upon a review of all of the documentation, both state and federal, we are left confident at this time that the evidence developed to date does not reveal co-conspirators or accessories. Accordingly, as a result of the investigation to date, there will be no state criminal prosecution of anyone.

PURPOSE AND SCOPE OF REPORT

The State's Attorney's Office for the Judicial District of Danbury is charged, pursuant to Article IV, Sec. 27 of the Connecticut State Constitution[5] and Connecticut General Statutes (C.G.S.) Sec. 51-276[6] *et seq.*, with the investigation and prosecution of all criminal offenses occurring within the Judicial District of Danbury. The Connecticut State Police have the responsibility to prevent and detect violations of the law and this State's Attorney has worked with and relied upon the Connecticut State Police since the incident occurred. The investigation has been

---

[5] Connecticut Constitution Article 4, Sec. 27. There shall be established within the executive department a division of criminal justice *which shall be in charge of the investigation and prosecution of all criminal matters.* Said division shall include the chief state's attorney, who shall be its administrative head, and the state's attorneys for each judicial district, which districts shall be established by law. The prosecutorial power of the state shall be vested in a chief state's attorney and the state's attorney for each judicial district.

[6] Sec. 51-276. Division established. There is hereby established the Division of Criminal Justice within the Executive Department, which shall be in charge of the investigation and prosecution of all criminal matters in the Superior Court. The Division of Criminal Justice shall be an agency within the Executive Department with all management rights except appointment of all state's attorneys.

tirelessly conducted by the Connecticut State Police (also CSP) with the assistance of multiple local, state and federal agencies, both in and out of Connecticut.

While no report is statutorily required of the State's Attorney once the investigation is complete, it has been the practice of state's attorneys to issue reports on criminal investigations where there is no arrest and prosecution if the state's attorney determines that some type of public statement is necessary.[7] Given the gravity of the crimes committed on December 14, 2012, a report is in order.

The purpose of this report is to identify the person or persons criminally responsible for the twenty-seven homicides that occurred in Newtown, Connecticut,[8] on the morning of December 14, 2012, to determine what crimes were committed, and to indicate if there will be any state prosecutions as a result of the incident.

Many witnesses to this case have expressed great concern that their identities will be disclosed publicly and make them susceptible to threats or intimidation as a result of their cooperation or connection with the investigation.[9] This cooperation has been essential and greatly appreciated. As a result of the witnesses' concerns, this report will not identify lay witnesses, except where necessary.

Consistent with Public Act 13-311,[10] exceptions to the state Freedom of Information Act[11] and C.G.S. Sec. 17a-101k(a) [12] this report will not list the names of the twenty children killed in

---

[7] See for example: Statement of David I. Cohen, State's Attorney for the Judicial District of Stamford/Norwalk, in reference to the February 16, 2009, attack on Charla Nash by the Chimpanzee Named Travis, Issued December 7, 2009; Statement of the State's Attorney for the Judicial District of Stamford-Norwalk Concerning the Fatal Fire on December 25, 2011, at 2267 Shippan Avenue, Stamford, Issued June 8, 2012; and Report of the State's Attorney for the Judicial District of Ansonia-Milford on the Murder of Shangyl Rasim on January 17, 2010, Issued May 24, 2010.

[8] Newtown, Connecticut is within the Judicial District of Danbury.

[9] In fact, some witnesses have had that occur to them.

[10] An Act Limiting the Disclosure of Certain Records of Law Enforcement Agencies and Establishing a Task Force Concerning Victim Privacy Under the Freedom of Information Act.

[11] See C.G.S. Sec. 1-210.

[12] Sec. 17a-101k. Registry of findings of abuse or neglect of children maintained by Commissioner of Children and Families. Notice of finding of abuse or neglect of child. Appeal of finding. Hearing procedure. Appeal after hearing. Confidentiality. Regulations. (a) The Commissioner of Children and Families shall maintain a registry of the commissioner's findings of abuse or neglect of children pursuant to section 17a-101g that conforms to the requirements of this section. The regulations adopted pursuant to subsection (i) of this section shall provide for the use of the registry on a twenty-four-hour daily basis to prevent or discover abuse of children and the establishment of a hearing process for any appeal by a person of the commissioner's determination that such person is responsible for the abuse or neglect of a child pursuant to subsection (b) of section 17a-101g. The information contained in the registry and any other information relative to child abuse, wherever located, shall be confidential, subject to such statutes and regulations governing their use and access as shall conform to the requirements of federal law or regulations. Any violation of this section or the regulations adopted by the commissioner under this section shall be punishable by a fine of not more than one thousand dollars or imprisonment for not more than one year.

Sandy Hook Elementary School, nor will it recite 911 calls made from within the school on that morning or describe information provided by witnesses who were in the classrooms or heard what was occurring in the classrooms.

It is not the intent of this report to convey every piece of information contained in the voluminous investigation materials developed by the Connecticut State Police and other law enforcement agencies, but to provide information relevant to the purposes of this report.

To conclude that *all* such information, including the basic facts of the incident itself is confidential would prohibit even the disclosure of the children being killed. Such an interpretation would be unworkable and is not taken here. It is concluded though that the C.G.S. Sec. 17a-101k(a) is applicable in the present case and will be applied in the manner described.

SANDY HOOK ELEMENTARY SCHOOL - INCIDENT AND RESPONSE

Incident

On the morning of December 14, 2012, the shooter parked his 2010 Honda Civic next to a "No Parking" zone outside of Sandy Hook Elementary School in Newtown, Connecticut.[13] Shortly after 9:30 a.m. he approached the front entrance to the school.[14] He was armed with a Bushmaster Model XM15-E2S rifle (also Bushmaster rifle), a Glock 20, 10 mm pistol and a Sig Sauer P226, 9 mm pistol and a large supply of ammunition.

The doors to the school were locked, as they customarily were at this time, the school day having already begun. The shooter proceeded to shoot his way into the school building through the plate glass window to the right of the front lobby doors.

The main office staff reported hearing noises and glass breaking at approximately 9:35 a.m. and saw the shooter, a white male with a hat and sunglasses, come into the school building with a rifle type gun. The shooter walked normally, did not say anything and appeared to be breathing normally. He was seen shooting the rifle down the hallway.

Just down the hallway from the main office, in the direction that the shooter was to be seen firing, a 9:30 a.m. Planning and Placement Team (PPT) meeting was being held in room 9, a conference room. It was attended by Principal Dawn Hochsprung and School Psychologist Mary Sherlach, together with a parent and other school staff. Shortly after the meeting started, the attendees heard loud banging. The principal and school psychologist then left the room followed shortly after by a staff member. After leaving the room, Mrs. Hochsprung yelled "Stay put!"

As the staff member left the room, the staff member heard gunshots and saw Mrs. Hochsprung and Mrs. Sherlach fall down in front of the staff member. The staff member felt a gunshot hit the staff member's leg. Once down, the staff member was struck again by additional gunfire, but laid still in the hallway. Not seeing anyone in the hallway, the staff member crawled back into room 9 and held the door shut. A call to 911 was made and in the ensuing moments the telephone in room 9 was also used to turn on the school wide intercom system. This appears to have been done inadvertently, but provided notice to other portions of the building.[15]

---

[13] On December 13, 2012, the student enrollment was 489. Official attendance had not yet been recorded as of 9:30 a.m. on December 14, 2012. The staff for the school is 91, but on December 14, 2012, there were nine staff members absent. The staffing was at 82 for the day.

[14] A more complete description of the school building and the front entrance starts on page A119 of the Appendix. For the purposes of this report, the front of SHES faces north.

[15] Intercom system could be accessed from nine phones located in seven rooms. These telephones and rooms were three phones in the main office, the principal's office, the nurse's office (room 57), room 9 conference room, room 29, room 32 and room 60. The "All Call" which opens the intercom to the entire school was accessed by pressing "#0" from the telephones mentioned. The All Call-except quiet rooms was accessed by pressing "#1."

At the same time the shooter was firing in the hallway, another staff member was at the far east end of the hallway near classroom 1. The staff member was struck by a bullet in the foot and retreated into a classroom.

Both Dawn Hochsprung, age 47, and Mary Sherlach, age 56, died as a result of being shot. Both wounded staff members shot in the hallway were later evacuated to the hospital and survived.

After shooting and killing the two adults and wounding the two others, the shooter entered the main office. The office staff had taken shelter in the office. They heard sounds of the office door opening, footsteps walking inside the office and then back toward the office door. Staff members heard the door open a second time and then heard more gunfire from outside the office. They called 911.

Where the shooter specifically went next is unclear. The evidence and witness statements establish the shooter went down the hallway in an easterly direction ultimately entering first grade classrooms 8 and 10. The order is not definitively known. While in classrooms 8 and 10, the shooter shot and killed four adults and twenty children with the Bushmaster rifle. Twelve children survived, one from classroom 8 and eleven from classroom 10.

The shooter finally killed himself in classroom 10 with one gunshot to his head from a Glock 20, 10 mm pistol. This is believed to have occurred at 9:40:03.[16]

Classroom 8's substitute teacher was Lauren Rousseau, age 30, who was assisted by Rachel D'Avino, age 29, a behavioral therapist. Fifteen children were found by police. Fourteen who were deceased and one who was transported to Danbury Hospital and later pronounced dead. The two adults were found deceased close to the children. In all, seventeen people were killed in classroom 8. A sixteenth child survived and exited classroom 8 after the police arrived.

Classroom 10's teacher was Victoria Soto, age 27. Working with her was Anne Marie Murphy, age 52, a behavioral therapist. Five children were found, with Mrs. Murphy partially covering one child. Four of the five children were deceased. One of the five children was transported to the hospital and pronounced dead. Miss Soto was found deceased in the room near the north wall with a set of keys nearby. Nine children had run out of the room and survived. A police officer found two uninjured children in the class restroom.

In all, eighteen children and six adult school staff members were found deceased within the school. Two more children were pronounced dead at Danbury Hospital. Two other adult school staff members were injured and were treated at nearby hospitals and survived.

The two classrooms on either side of 8 and 10 were numbered 6 and 12. Classroom 6 was on the eastern side of classroom 8 and classroom 12 was on the western side of classroom 10. Staff and students hid in the class restrooms, locking the restroom doors from the inside.

---

[16] See the time line in the Appendix starting at page A84.

Throughout the rest of the school, staff and students hid themselves wherever they happened to be at the time they became aware of gunfire. The staff used various ways to keep the children calm, from reading to having them color or draw pictures. Those hiding in rooms closest to the shooter kept silent. Some people were able to escape out of the building prior to the police arrival and went to Sandy Hook center, nearby residences, or received rides from parents going to the school or from passersby.

One staff member heard a loud crashing noise and ran toward the front lobby. As the staff member got closer, bullet holes could be seen and gun powder smelled. Realizing what was going on, the staff member immediately called 911, turned and went back down the hall from where the staff member had come. During the incident, while staying on the line with the 911 operator, this staff member sent other staff to their rooms or had them stay in their rooms and this staff member went about locking doors. The staff member remained in the hallway on the telephone with the 911 operator until the police arrived.

Response

Upon the receipt of the first 911 call, law enforcement was immediately dispatched to the school. It was fewer than four minutes from the time the first 911 call was received until the first police officer arrived at SHES. It was fewer than five minutes from the time the first 911 call was received until the shooter killed himself. It was fewer than six minutes from the time the first police officer arrived on SHES property to the time the first police officer entered the school building.

Below is an abbreviated time line from the first 911 call received to the time the police entered the school building.[17]

9:35:39 - First 911 call to Newtown Police Department is received.

9:36:06 - Newtown Police Department dispatcher broadcasts that there is a shooting at Sandy Hook Elementary School.

9:37:38 - Connecticut State Police are dispatched to SHES for active shooter.

9:38:50 - CSP are informed that SHES is in lockdown.

9:39:00 - First Newtown police officer arrives behind SHES on Crestwood Rd.

9:39:13 - Two more Newtown officers arrive at SHES and park on the driveway near the ball field. Gunshots are heard in the background.

[17] See page A84 of the Appendix for full time line put together by the Connecticut State Police Western District Major Crime Squad. This time line was compiled from 911 calls, witness statements, police car cameras, police radio and police dispatch transmissions.

9:39:34 - Newtown officer encounters unknown male running along the east side of SHES with something in his hand.

9:40:03 - Last gunshot is heard. This is believed to be the final suicide shot from the shooter in classroom 10.

9:41:07 - Information is relayed as to the location of the last known gunshots heard within SHES, the front of the building.

9:41:24 - Newtown officer has unknown male prone on ground, starting information relay regarding possibly more than one shooter.

9:42:39 - Newtown officer calls out the license plate of the shooter's car.

9:44:47 - Newtown officers enter SHES.

9:46:23 - CSP arrive at SHES.

9:46:48 - CSP enter SHES.

As the gravity of the situation became known, local, state and federal agencies responded to the scene to assist.

From the time the unknown male was encountered by the Newtown police outside of SHES until after the staff and children were evacuated, all responding law enforcement operated under the belief that there may have been more than one shooter and acted accordingly.[18]

For example, K-9 units were brought in to search the area and officers were posted to act as lookouts to ensure the safety of those evacuating the school building. Some people were located in the areas surrounding the school as the searches and evacuations were taking place. Some of those individuals were treated initially as suspects and handled accordingly, including being handcuffed, until their identities and reason for being there could be determined.

Some of these detentions included:

1. The initial unknown male who turned out to be a parent with a cell telephone in his hand;
2. Two reporters located in the woods around SHES, who were held at gun point by Department of Energy and Environmental Protection (DEEP) police officers until their identities could be determined; and
3. A man from New York who was working in a nearby town and went to SHES after an application on his cell telephone alerted him to the situation at the school. He drove to the firehouse and went up to the school on foot. He was taken from the scene

[18] In fact, the possibility that there was more than one shooter remained a consideration beyond December 14, 2012. It was only after potential leads were investigated that investigators became confident that the shooter was not aided in any way by others and that no one knew of the shooter's plan prior to December 14, 2012.

of the school in handcuffs and later to Newtown Police Department. It was later determined that he did not have a connection to the shooting and had gone to SHES to see what was going on.

As noted above, on December 14, 2012, there was a concern that there may have been more than one shooter. This was based upon a number of factors:

1. The initial police encounter with the unknown male outside SHES;[19]
2. Reports by school personnel during the shooting on a 911 call of seeing someone running outside the school while the shooting was ongoing;
3. The location of two black zip up sweat jackets on the ground outside of the shooter's car;
4. The discovery of an Izhmash Saiga-12, 12 gauge shotgun and ammunition in the passenger compartment of the shooter's car. A police officer moved this shotgun and ammunition to the car's trunk for safety purposes;
5. Shell casings that were located outside of the school; and
6. The apparent sound of gunfire coming from outside of the school;

The subsequent investigation revealed there were no additional shooters based upon:

1. Searches of the area and examinations of local business security surveillance videos;
2. Persons detained revealed they were not connected to the shootings. In the case of the initial unknown male, he was identified as the parent of a student and had a cell telephone, rather than a weapon, in his hand;
3. Witness interviews which indicated that no witness saw anyone other than the shooter, with a firearm;
4. Witness interviews in which it was determined that a number of SHES staff had escaped from the school through a window and had been running outside the school building during the shootings;
5. The shotgun located in the shooter's car had been purchased by the shooter's mother previously;
6. The two sweat jackets were both C-Sport brand black zip up hooded sweat jackets with no size listed and were located immediately outside the shooter's car;[20] Both are believed to have been brought there by the shooter;[21]
7. The live shotgun shells (other than the one found on the shooter and the ones found in the shooter's car) that were located inside and outside of the school were in locations where first responders had been. Additionally, there were first responders who

[19] The man was later determined to be the parent of one of the school's children and the item in his hand was a cell telephone.

[20] See the Appendix at page A174.

[21] A parent who arrived at SHES as the shooting was taking place saw the shooter's car parked in front of the school with the passenger side door open and the two sweat jackets on the ground near the car. To the parent, the jackets looked like two black blankets on the ground.

reported missing live shotgun rounds. Moreover, the shells were found in locations where there had not been reported sightings of any non-law enforcement individuals;

8. There were no expended shotgun shells found in the actual crime scene nor were any expended 12 gauge shotgun pellets or slugs recovered;
9. The only expended casings located outside of the school building were 5.56 mm casings located just outside the school's front entrance, consistent with the shooter's entry into the school; and
10. The officer who heard what he believed to be outside gunfire was in a position to have heard the shooter's gunfire coming from window openings in the classroom in which the shooter was firing.

Stopping the active shooter was the first priority. Once that occurred, the location and treatment of the victims, the search for additional shooters, and the safe evacuation of the school were of primary importance.[22] The collection of evidence and the preservation and documentation of the crime scene, while important, came second.

Two command centers were set up, one at the firehouse on Riverside Road and the other at Newtown's Emergency Operations Center, located on the Newtown Fairfield Hills Campus. In the week immediately after the shootings, services to victims' families and victims, as well as support to the investigators in the school were handled out of the firehouse. All other aspects of the investigation not related to the school itself were run out of the Emergency Operations Center.

Investigation responsibilities were handled as follows:[23]

Connecticut State Police (CSP)

CSP-Western District Major Crime (WDMC) squad was the lead CSP unit for the entire investigation and acted as the coordinating law enforcement agency for other agencies and units of the CSP.[24] The van unit processed the interior of SHES.

CSP-Central District Major Crime (CDMC) squad van unit processed the exterior of SHES, including the shooter's car, and established the temporary morgue[25] with the

---

[22] One of the difficulties encountered was the inability of state police radios to operate within SHES.

[23] This report does not include a listing of all of the law-enforcement and non-law enforcement service providers and their actions. In the days and weeks that followed the tragedy, local, state and federal agencies provided help to the Town of Newtown and its families through counseling, funeral protection, traffic control, handling bomb threats as well as many other services. Additionally, the CSP set up an invaluable law enforcement liaison program with the families of the deceased victims in which a state or local police officer was specifically assigned to the family of a deceased victim to provide communication and protection in the days and weeks that followed December 14th.

[24] WDMC Squad and Van, as the lead CSP unit, over the course of the week that followed was there for seven days processing the interior scene, the shooter and victims' personal effects, including assisting with the packing and removal of furniture from the immediate scene.

[25] The Department of Public Health provided and set up the portable tent used for the temporary morgue.

OCME to identify and document the decedents prior to their being moved to the OCME in Farmington.[26] CDMC also attended the autopsies at the OCME and did a secondary search of 36 Yogananda Street, as well as photographing doors and locks in SHES.

Eastern District Major Crime (EDMC) squad processed the scene at 36 Yogananda Street and were the investigators for the shooting of Nancy Lanza, the shooter's mother.

CSP-Emergency Services Unit (ESU), Tactical Teams, were assigned to both SHES and 36 Yogananda Street to handle the clearing of the scenes and rendering them safe.[27]

CSP – Troop A, Southbury and CSP from other troops and units, in addition to being first responders, worked to secure the scene and worked with WDMC and the OCME.

Computer Crimes and Electronic Evidence Unit handled the seizure and examination of additional electronic evidence from 36 Yogananda Street together with EDMC, CDMC and WDMC.

CSP - Collision, Analysis and Reconstruction Squad (CARS) was assigned to produce the sketch maps for both the interior and exterior of the school.

CSP - On December 14, 2012, virtually every aspect of the CSP was engaged in the response to SHES and 36 Yogananda Street. For example, included in the first responders were troopers and detectives, not only from Troop A in Southbury, but other troops and units as well, including the Statewide Narcotics Task Force.

Department of Energy and Environmental Protection (DEEP) provided first responders at SHES.

Forensic Science Laboratory, Division of Scientific Services, Department of Emergency Services and Public Protection (DESPP) examined items seized and collected from SHES and 36 Yogananda Street.

Office of the Chief Medical Examiner (OCME) was responsible for investigating the cause and manner of the deaths involved in this case and worked with the CSP in setting up the temporary morgue at SHES that was used to identify and document the deceased prior to their being moved to Farmington.

Bureau of Alcohol, Tobacco, Firearms and Explosives (ATF) in addition to responding to both scenes, worked on the firearms aspect of the investigation.

---

[26] WDMC and CDMC personnel were also assigned and paired with the FBI to conduct interviews and neighborhood canvasses as well as assist with the identification of victims, investigate a report of another shooter at a hospital, as well as prepare search warrants and attend autopsies.

[27] There were numerous law enforcement agencies that worked on the clearing of SHES and the protection of those who were doing the clearing.

Federal Bureau of Investigation (FBI) – in addition to responding to the scenes, handled interviewing of witnesses and investigation both at a local level and on a national level. The Tactical Team assisted with the clearing of the school. The Behavioral Analysis Unit (BAU), as part of the search warrant execution for 36 Yogananda Street, was provided with materials for review. They provided their expertise in the preparation of witness interviews. The Victim Assistance Unit worked with victims' families, victims and witnesses.

United States Attorney's Office was stationed at the Emergency Operations Center overseeing the investigation into the possible commission of federal crimes and the issuance of federal legal process, as well as coordinating the various federal agencies involved in assisting with the state investigation.

United States Marshals Service, Technical Operations Group provided technical and investigation assistance.

United States Postal Service looked for mail that may have been relevant to the investigation.

Municipal Police Departments from around the state assisted throughout the Town of Newtown, including being first responders at SHES, handling calls in town and the tremendous inflow of media and visitors to the Town in the weeks after December 14, 2012.

Newtown Police Department in addition to being first responders, worked to secure the scene and assisted WDMC.

Office of the State's Attorney, Judicial District of Danbury (SAO) – oversaw the state investigation, working with the Connecticut State Police. Together with the assistance of the Office of the Chief State's Attorney, the SAO was stationed at the Emergency Operations Center starting December 14, 2012, and oversaw the legal issues and state aspect of the investigation including search warrant review, child witness issues, working with the federal authorities, etc.

SANDY HOOK ELEMENTARY SCHOOL – SCENE INVESTIGATION

On the afternoon of December 14, 2012, the WDMC and CDMC van units began documenting the crime scene and collecting evidence. The units could not begin this process until the scene was declared safe. The scene processing took seven days.

The scene was thoroughly processed, with the WDMC van unit handling the interior of SHES and the CDMC van unit covering the exterior. This processing included extensive written documentation as well as taking videos and thousands of photographs and measurements. In addition to the recovery of evidence, bullet trajectories were analyzed and documented.

My description of the scene processing starts with the front entrance and moves into the school building itself. This does not necessarily reflect the actual order in which the crime scene was processed. Many descriptions come directly from the investigation reports but are not in quotation marks to ease reading.

The conditions of windows and doors were documented, but some may have been disturbed by police and emergency personnel during the emergency response and protective sweep of the building. Similarly, other items of evidence, such as shell casings, may not have been found in their original positions because, as mentioned previously, the first priority was to locate and neutralize any active shooter, followed by the location and treatment of the victims, the search for additional shooters and the safe evacuation of the school. Only then could evidence collection begin.

Interior

Sandy Hook Elementary School was[28] a one story brick public school building of approximately 66,000 square feet, built in 1954. The building was on Dickinson Drive off of Riverside Road in the Sandy Hook section of Newtown. The front of the building sat in a magnetic northeast direction, but will be considered north for the purposes of this report. See the diagram at page 19.

SHES was rectangular in shape with four hallways in the main building and portable classrooms attached to the rear (south) side which were accessed from the south side of the main building. Classrooms on the exterior walls had even numbers and interior classrooms had odd numbers.

- **Main entrance**

The main entrance to the school was located next to the large glass window that the shooter shot out to enter the school. A patio area was just before the entrance doors. The entrance to the lobby consisted of two sets of locked full glass doors that opened outwardly using a pull handle. They were separated by a small vestibule. The doors were secured with an electronic locking mechanism. The doors could be opened from the inside with a horizontal push bar across the middle of the door.

The broken area of the window that the shooter shot out measured approximately 35.33 inches wide and 42.5 inches high.[29]

The exterior of the main entrance door way had a call box, buzzer system with a video camera. The call box was installed in 2005. The video camera did not record, but the video could be viewed live on three monitoring systems on the secretaries' desks in the main office, with no recording capabilities. The electronic unlocking of the front doors was done by using a "key button" on any of the three monitoring systems.

Glass shards were located just before and to the side of the outside entrance doors on the patio and plantings in the area and also on the floor in the lobby.[30] Eight expended brass colored 5.56

---

[28] SHES was demolished in October and November 2013.

[29] See the Appendix starting at page A168.

[30] See the Appendix at page A169 and A171.

mm bullet casings stamped with "S&B 60 5.56x45"[31] were located in the area outside the broken window and front entrance doors. These were seized.

The front entrance led into the school's lobby. The lobby measured approximately 28 feet north to south and 36 feet east to west. The southeast corner of the lobby allowed open access to the north hallway of the school. Sixteen brass colored expended 5.56 mm bullet casings were located on the floor within the lobby area and were seized. Furniture in the lobby area had holes consistent with having been struck by a bullet. There were eleven damaged areas consistent with bullet strikes in the lobby.

- **North Hallway**

The hallway on the north side of the building, where the shootings occurred, ran east to west and contained the lobby and main office, inside of which was the nurse's office. The hallway also contained rooms numbered 1-10, 11A-5 and 12. The bulk of the scene processing occurred in this area. See the diagram on page 19.

The ceiling as in the lobby was 8 feet high. And the width of the hall was 8.5 feet. The even numbered rooms were on the north side of the hallway with classroom 12 being the western most classroom and classroom 2 being the eastern most. The odd numbered rooms were on the south side of the hallway with the main office being the western most room and classroom 1 being the eastern most. East of the main office was a closet labeled "11A-5 storage" and the east of the closet was a conference room identified as Room 9.

The doors in the hallway all locked from the outside with a key. The interior door handles had no locking mechanism. All of the doors opened outwardly toward the hallway. All doors were solid wood with a circular window in the upper half of the door.[32]

All classrooms in the north hallway had a restroom and a closet. The restrooms were uniformly designed, approximately 4 feet 7 inches by 3 feet 6 inches with a solid wood door. The door of each restroom opened inward and away from the toilet. Each restroom door had a knob push button lock on the inside handle and a key lock on the outside handle.[33] The conference room did not have a restroom.

Classrooms in the north hallway 12 and 10, 8 and 6, 6 and 4, and 3 and 5 respectively had an interior door that was shared by the two classrooms.

---

[31] The ammunition used by the shooter in the Bushmaster rifle has been described as .223 caliber, 5.56 mm NATO and 5.56 X 45. All of these descriptions are for similar bullets (cartridges) that can be fired from the Bushmaster rifle. The ammunition that the shooter used in this case for the Bushmaster bore the stamp "S&B 60 5.56 X 45" on the base of the cartridges and will be referred to as a 5.56 mm round. The distinction between a .223 cal. and a 5.56 mm is not relevant to this report.

[32] See the Appendix at page A178 for an example of classroom door locks.

[33] See the Appendix at page A177 for an example of restroom door locks.

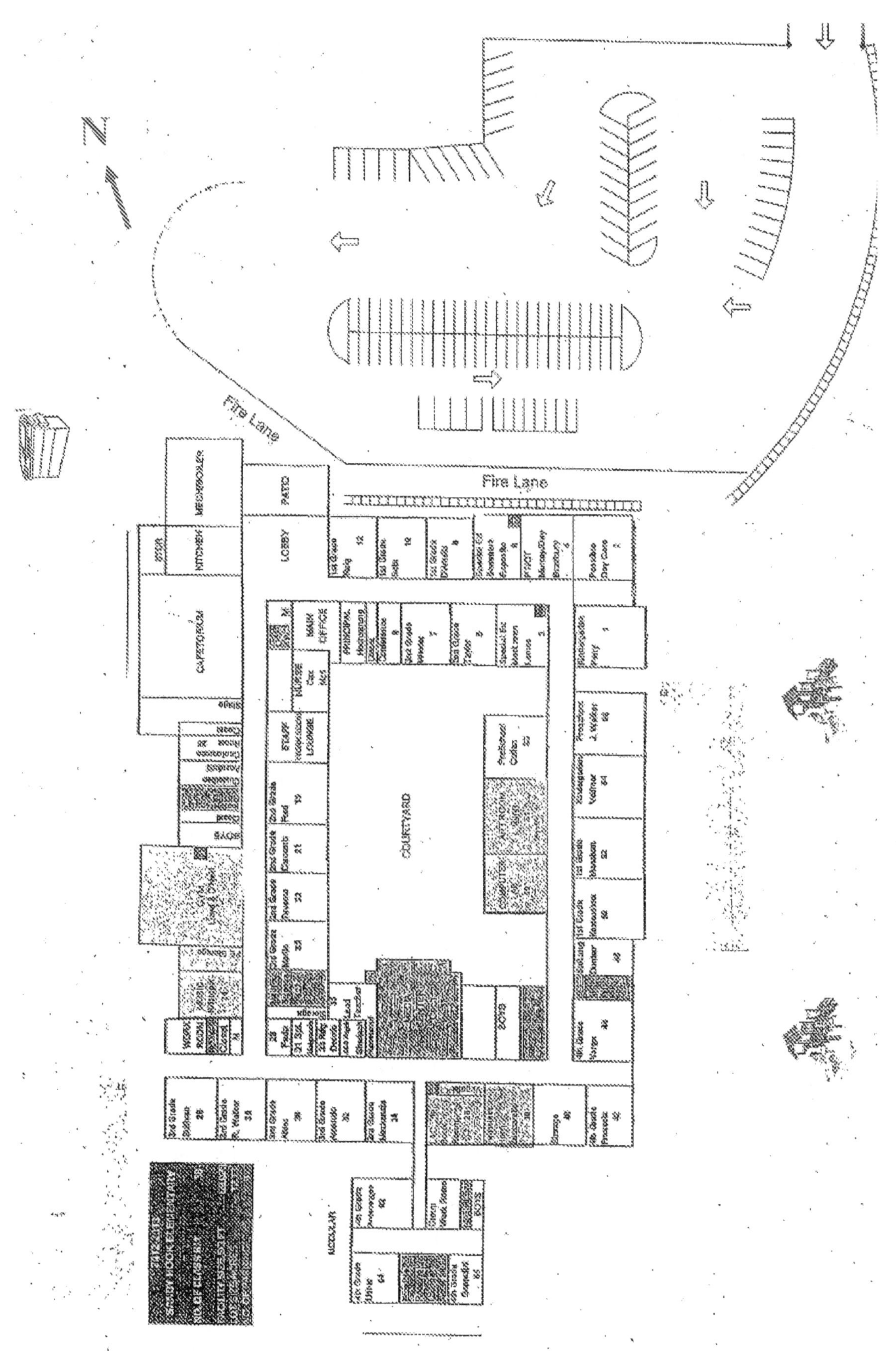

N
Fire Lane
Fire Lane
PATIO
LOBBY
KITCHEN
CAFETORIUM
MAIN OFFICE
STAFF LOUNGE
COURTYARD

The bodies of Mrs. Hochsprung and Mrs. Sherlach were located in the western-most area of the north hallway, near the lobby. One brass colored expended 5.56 mm casing was located and seized from the floor in the area of Mrs. Hochsprung and Mrs. Sherlach.[34] In addition to the 5.56 mm ballistics, one 10 mm shell casing was found in the north hallway and was later identified as having been fired from the Glock 20, 10 mm pistol found near the shooter.

- **Conference Room (Room 9)**

Conference room 9 was on the south side of the north hallway on the opposite side of the hallway and approximately 16 feet east of the door for classroom 12. The room had a telephone mounted in the center of the west wall.

- **Classroom 12**

Classroom 12 was located on the north side of the north hallway and was the first classroom east of the front lobby. The classroom door was located 23 feet east of the lobby. The window to the door was covered on the hallway side with dark colored paper that was there from a previous lockdown drill.

- **Classroom 10**

Classroom 10 was located on the north side of the north hallway and was the second classroom east of the front lobby. The hallway door was approximately 27 feet east of classroom 12. The window was not completely covered, but did have a decoration over part of the inside of the window.

The room measured 27 feet east to west and 30 feet north to south with carpeted floors and painted cinder block walls. There were large windows across the north wall, which provided a view into the front (north) parking lot. Fluorescent ceiling lights turned on automatically when the room was entered. As mentioned previously, there was a restroom in the room and a closet. This closet door had no lock. The door that provided access to classroom 12 was on the center of the west wall. This had a key lock on both sides and the door was unlocked. There was a telephone mounted on the south side of the east wall north of the closet. An Emergency Response Packet Plan was hanging on the south wall. The packet was above a map depicting the emergency evacuation route for this classroom.

The classroom door that opened into the north hallway could only be locked with a key from the outside (hallway side). The door was unlocked with no signs of forced entry.

In the window area for classroom 10 there were no less than nine holes consistent with being bullet holes. Investigators conducted a trajectory analysis of the shots that went through the window area of classroom 10. No determination could be made as to whether the shots through the window area were intended for the outside of the building. In other words, it could not be determined whether the shooter, while in classroom 10, had intentionally fired at something or

---

[34] See the Appendix starting at page A130 for a description of the ballistics evidence from the north hallway.

someone outside of the building. There was no indication that any shots through the window area of classroom 10 came from outside of the school. All of the evidence indicates that shots went out of the window area of classroom 10 and into the parking area north of the school.

Classroom 10 evidence is further described below.

- **Classroom 8**

Classroom 8 was located on the north side of the north hallway and was the third classroom east of the front lobby, with its entrance door approximately 27 feet east of classroom 10. As with the others, its classroom door opened out into the hallway and could only be locked from the hallway side with a key. The window was not covered. The classroom door to the hallway was unlocked with no signs of forced entry.

The room dimensions and construction were similar to those of classrooms 10 and 12. There was also a restroom in this classroom. The closet door in classroom 8 had no locking device. There were also large glass windows across the north wall providing a view into the front (north) parking lot of the school. There was a wall telephone in the room on the south side of the east wall, north of the closet. An "Emergency Response Plan" packet was hanging on the south wall adjacent to the east side of the entrance door. This packet was above a map depicting the emergency evacuation route for the classroom.

The door that connected into classroom 6 was on the north side of the east wall, had key locks on both sides of the door. The door was unlocked.

Ballistic evidence located in classroom 8 is described in the Appendix at page A134, which includes a total of twenty-four rounds of 5.56 mm ammunition found, of which ten rounds were in one PMAG 30 magazine, thirteen rounds were in another such magazine and one live round was on the floor. There was a third empty PMAG 30 magazine seized. There were a total of eighty expended 5.56 mm casings seized from classroom 8.

- **Classrooms 6 and 4**

Located on the floor of classroom 6 was one live round "Federal Tactical" 12 gauge shotgun slug shell (Exhibit 49). This shotgun shell was made of clear-like plastic and was different in color from the shotgun shell that was seized on the shooter's person. On the floor of classroom 4 was a blue colored 12 gauge slug shotgun shell with the word "Federal Premium Tactical Rifled slug" stamped on the side and "12 GA Made in USA stamped on the head of the shell (Exhibit 99). This shotgun shell was made of a blue colored plastic and also was different in color from the shotgun gun shell that was seized from the shooter's person.

As mentioned previously, the loose shotgun shells not found on the shooter were in locations where first responders had been and had reported missing shotgun shells. Additionally, there were no witness reports of any persons being seen with firearms other than first responders in those locations, there were no expended shotgun shell casings or projectiles recovered at the scene and the live shotgun shell on the shooter's person and those recovered from his car did not match any of those recovered from the three locations. No shotgun was recovered from the school. It is believed that these live shells were dropped by first responders.

- **Shooter**

Responding police officers found the shooter in classroom 10 northwest of the hallway entrance dead from a self-inflicted gunshot wound to the head. He was wearing a pale green pocket vest over a black polo style short sleeve shirt over a black t-shirt. He had yellow colored earplugs in each ear. He was wearing black cargo pocket pants, black socks, black sneakers, a black canvas belt and black fingerless gloves on each hand. He had an empty camouflage drop holster that was affixed to his right thigh.

After all of the victims were removed from the school, the shooter's body was removed once all firearms and ballistic evidence were recovered from his person. The body was moved to the OCME on December 15, 2012.

- **Weapons on Shooter and Ammunition in Classroom 10**

The weapons on the shooter together with a description of items seized related to the shooting are contained in the Appendix starting at page A136. On the shooter's person was a loaded semi-automatic Sig Sauer P226, 9 mm pistol and additional ammunition. Located near the shooter was a partially loaded Glock 20, 10 mm semi-automatic pistol that appeared to be jammed.

A Bushmaster Model XM15-E2S rifle was located some distance away from the shooter. The rifle's shoulder strap was attached in the front but disconnected at the butt of the rifle. The disconnected rear portion was the result of a failed nut attachment. It is unknown if the nut failed while the rifle was being used or as the result of being dropped or thrown to the floor.

The Bushmaster rifle was found with the safety in the "fire" position. There was one live 5.56 mm round in the chamber and one PMAG 30 magazine in the magazine well. The magazine contained fourteen live 5.56 mm rounds of ammunition. The rifle did not appear to have malfunctioned when observed by the WDMC van unit, but a CSP-ESU report described the weapon as appearing to have jammed. When tested later, the rifle functioned properly.

Two empty PMAG 30 magazines that were duct-taped together in a tactical configuration and one live 5.56 mm round were found near the rifle.

Officers found two-hundred-fifty-three live rounds on the shooter's body: one-hundred-sixteen 9 mm rounds, seventy-five rounds of 10 mm, sixty-one rounds of 5.56 mm and one 12 gauge shotgun shell. Officers also seized forty-six 5.56 mm live rounds. This consisted of fifteen from the rifle, one from the floor and thirty from the magazine under the body of the shooter, as well as thirteen 10 mm live rounds (nine from the Glock and four from the floor). There were forty-nine expended 5.56 mm casings seized and one 10 mm casing from classroom 10. Total live rounds seized were three-hundred-twelve and total expended casings seized from classroom 10 were fifty.

Exterior

CDMC processed the exterior of SHES.

- **Shooter's Car**

The shooter's car was found parked in front of the school, west of the front entrance, next to a "No Parking" zone. It was a black 2010 Honda Civic with Connecticut registration 872YEO. The car was registered to his mother, Nancy Lanza, but had been purchased for him.

Recovered from the car was an Izhmash Saiga-12, 12 gauge shotgun with two magazines containing a total of twenty rounds of ammunition.[35] The shotgun and ammunition were originally seen in the passenger compartment of the car and were moved by police to the car's trunk for safekeeping during the initial response and evacuation.

- **Parking Lot**

There were a number of cars parked in the north parking lot of SHES. Three of these cars were struck by gunfire. None of the cars struck belonged to law enforcement. A total of five strikes to those three cars were identified as having come from classroom 10. It could not be determined whether these shots were intended to go outside of the classroom.

Also found in the north parking lot, was a shotgun shell that was dropped by a first responder.

SANDY HOOK ELEMENTARY SCHOOL – AUTOPSY INFORMATION

Deceased victims were removed from the school building to a large military-style tent located in the north parking lot, near the front of the school. The Office of the Chief Medical Examiner sought to make positive identification of the victims through photos, school records and personal and clothing descriptions.

On Saturday, December 15, 2012, all of the victims were transported to the OCME in Farmington for autopsies; autopsies were performed the same day. The cause of death for all of the victims was determined to have been gunshot wounds; the manner of death was determined to have been homicide.[36]

Evidence collected during the autopsies was turned over to CDMC and forwarded to the Division of Scientific Services for examination. The Evidence Examination section of this report contains a summary of the results.

---

[35] A search warrant was obtained for the car. The search warrant return originally reported the amount of ammunition as seventy rounds. This was corrected to twenty rounds and the search warrant return was amended.

[36] Our law defines homicide as the killing of one human being by another human being.

36 YOGANANDA STREET, NEWTOWN, CT – INCIDENT AND RESPONSE

Incident

Sometime on the morning of December 14, 2012, before 9:30 a.m., the shooter shot and killed his mother, Nancy Lanza, in her bed at 36 Yogananda Street, Newtown. The weapon used was a .22 caliber Savage Mark II rifle. Someone in the area reported hearing "two or three" gunshots in the neighborhood between 8:00 a.m. and 9:00 a.m. That person thought them to be from hunters, though the person indicated the shots did "sound unusually close."

Between 9:30 a.m. and 10:00 a.m. there was a delivery made to the house. The delivery driver saw no one, did not see any vehicles in the driveway and the garage door was closed. A delivery slip was left and the driver continued on.

The mother was found by police dead in her bed when they entered the house. The rifle was found on the floor next to the bed.

Response

Once it was determined that the shooter's car was registered to his mother at 36 Yogananda Street, Newtown, Connecticut, the Newtown police went to the house and evacuated the surrounding homes. The CSP-ESU came to the scene to clear the residence of potential hazards, such as booby traps or trip wires.

36 YOGANANDA STREET, NEWTOWN, CT – SCENE INVESTIGATION

After the body of the shooter's mother was found and the scene declared safe, the process of obtaining search warrants for the house began, with the first warrant being reviewed and signed by a judge of the Superior Court at 5:29 p.m. on December 14, 2012, at the Emergency Operations Center.[37]

Additional search warrants were approved and issued as the search disclosed additional evidence. The investigation of the shooter's mother's killing and the scene processing was done by EDMC and the search for evidence at 36 Yogananda Street related to the shootings at SHES was investigated by both CDMC and WDMC. A list of the items seized from the home is contained in the search warrant returns in the Appendix, with some descriptions in the "Digital Image Report," starting at page A188 in the Appendix.[38]

---

[37] The Judicial Branch and the Honorable John F. Blawie are to be commended for their response to the SHES shootings. Judge Blawie was available at the Emergency Operations Center to review search warrants.

[38] A description of the home is also in the Appendix starting at page A181.

The weapon used to kill Nancy Lanza, the .22 cal. Savage Mark II rifle, was found near her bed and seized. In the chamber of the rifle was a spent .22 cal. shell casing and three live rounds were in the magazine. Three other spent .22 cal. shell casings were found in the room and seized.

The shooter's second floor bedroom windows were taped over with black trash bags. The second floor computer room also had its windows covered. There, investigators found a computer hard drive that appeared to have been intentionally damaged. To date, because of the extensive damage, forensic experts have not yet been able to recover any information from that hard drive.

In a typical criminal case, the investigation would remain open when potentially important evidence was still being examined. Given the improbability of any information being recovered from the damaged hard drive, this outstanding piece of evidence is not preventing the closure of this case now. Should any relevant information related to the existence of any accessory or co-conspirator be obtained from the hard drive, the case will be reopened.

Investigators found a large number of firearms and related items in the home. All firearms involved in these incidents were legally purchased by the shooter's mother over the years. The home also contained many edged weapons, knives, swords, spears, etc. A prescription bottle in the shooter's name for acetaminophen with codeine was found in the mother's bathroom, which was part of the master bedroom.

During the search of 36 Yogananda Street, a global positioning system (GPS) device was located in the shooter's room with various routes in the memory from April 25, 2012, through December 13, 2012. Investigation revealed that the GPS was purchased for the shooter.

The routes taken indicate a number of trips from 36 Yogananda Street to the area of a local theater where a commercial version of the game "Dance Dance Revolution" is located. Over that time period, trips were made that took the driver in the vicinity of some schools in Newtown, including SHES. On December 13, 2012, a trip was recorded from 2:09 p.m. to 2:32 p.m. starting and ending on Yogananda Street and driving in Sandy Hook, which is in the area of SHES, though the route does not indicate the shooter drove up to the school.

Numerous video games were located in the basement computer/gaming area. The list of video games includes, but is not limited to:

-"Left for Dead"
-"Metal Gear Solid"
-"Dead Rising"
-"Half Life"
-"Battlefield"
-"Call of Duty"
-"Grand Theft Auto"
-"Shin Megami Tensei"
-"Dynasty Warriors"
-"Vice City"
-"Team Fortress"
-"Doom"

Other items found and noted for this report are:

- A Christmas check from the mother to the shooter to purchase a CZ 83 firearm;[39]
- A New York Times article from February 18, 2008, regarding the school shooting at Northern Illinois University;
- Three photographs of what appear to be a dead human, covered in blood and wrapped in plastic;
- The book *Amish Grace: How Forgiveness Transcended Tragedy*, Jossey-Bass, 2007, by Donald B. Kraybill, Steven Nolt and David Weaver-Zercher;[40] and
- Photocopied newspaper articles from 1891 pertaining to the shooting of school children

While the vast majority of persons interviewed had no explanation for the shooter's actions, a review of electronic evidence or digital media that appeared to belong to the shooter, revealed that the shooter had a preoccupation with mass shootings, in particular the Columbine shootings[41] and a strong interest in firearms. For example, there was a spreadsheet with mass murders over the years listing information about each shooting.

The review of the electronic evidence also found many things that are on a typical hard drive or memory card that would probably have no relevance to the investigation either because of creation date or subject matter. That being said, the following selected topics or items were found within the digital evidence seized:

- Bookmarks pertaining to firearms, military, politics, mass murder, video games, music, books, Army Ranger, computers and programs, ammunition, candy, economic books
- Web page design folders
- Two videos showing suicide by gunshot
- Commercial movies depicting mass shootings
- The computer game titled "School Shooting" where the player controls a character who enters a school and shoots at students
- Screen shots (172) of the online game "Combat Arms"
- "Dance Dance Revolution" (DDR) game screen shots
- Videos of shooter playing DDR
- Images of the shooter holding a handgun to his head
- Images of the shooter holding a rifle to his head
- Five-second video (dramatization) depicting children being shot
- Images of shooter with a rifle, shotgun and numerous magazines in his pockets
- Documents on weapons and magazine capacity

---

[39] The return for the December 16, 2012, search warrant indicates that Exhibit #612 was a check for a "C183." A closer inspection of the check makes it clear that "CZ83" is written. A CZ 83 is a type of pistol. The check reads "Christmas Day" in the check's date section.

[40] In October 2006 a gunman entered a one-room Amish school in Pennsylvania, killed five children and leaving others wounded.

[41] The Columbine High School shootings occurred in April 1999 at Columbine High School in Colorado. Two shooters, in a planned attack, killed a number of students and a teacher and injured others.

- A document written showing the prerequisites for a mass murder spreadsheet
- A spreadsheet listing mass murders by name and information about the incident
- Materials regarding the topic of pedophilia and advocating for rights for pedophiles (not child pornography)[42]
- Large amount of materials relating to Columbine shootings and documents on mass murders
- Large amount of materials on firearms
- Comedy videos
- Music
- Images of hamsters
- Images of Lego creations

36 YOGANANDA STREET, NEWTOWN, CT – AUTOPSY INFORMATION

The OCME performed an autopsy on the body of Nancy Lanza, age 52, on December 16, 2012, at the OCME. The cause of death was determined to be multiple gunshots to the head. The manner of death was homicide.

SHOOTER - AUTOPSY INFORMATION

The autopsy of the shooter was conducted on December 16, 2012, at the OCME. The shooter, age 20, was 72 inches tall and weighed 112 pounds. No drugs were found in the shooter's system. The cause of death was determined to be a gunshot wound to the head. The manner of death was suicide.

INVESTIGATION TO DETERMINE ACCESSORIES AND/OR CO-CONSPIRATORS

The investigation sought to determine if the shooter was aided by or had conspired with anyone to commit these crimes. As detailed above, none of the persons found in the vicinity of SHES on December 14, 2012, played any role in the shootings. Most were attempting to escape the area; others were responding to the school after learning of the shootings. None had any association with the shooter.

Investigators then sought to determine if anyone had conspired with or aided the shooter before the shootings. To that end, investigators examined social contacts, writings, e-mails, internet blogs, telephone records and his general internet presence. One of the internet blogs on which the shooter posted focused on mass shootings and in particular the Columbine shootings. The shooter also exchanged e-mails with others who were interested in the topic of mass shootings. None of these communications, however, related to SHES or in any way suggested that the shooter intended to commit a mass shooting. Thus, the evidence as developed to date, does not demonstrate that any of those with whom he communicated conspired with the shooter or criminally aided and abetted him in committing the murders on December 14, 2012.

[42] No child pornography was seen on any of the digital media.

EVENTS AND BACKGROUND INFORMATION LEADING UP TO DECEMBER 14, 2012

Recent Background Information

As of December 14, 2012, the shooter and his mother lived at 36 Yogananda Street. This had been the family home for years, although only the shooter and his mother had resided in the house for an extended time.

Both the shooter's and his mother's bedrooms were on the second floor; the mother occupied the master bedroom.

In November 2012, the mother sought to buy the shooter another computer or parts for a computer for the shooter to build one himself. She was concerned about him and said that he hadn't gone anywhere in three months and would only communicate with her by e-mail, though they were living in the same house. The mother never expressed fear of the shooter, for her own safety or that of anyone else.

The mother said that she had plans to sell her home in Newtown and move to either Washington state or North Carolina. She reportedly had told the shooter of this plan and he apparently stated that he wanted to move to Washington. The intention was for the shooter to go to a special school in Washington or get a computer job in North Carolina. In order to effectuate the move, the mother planned to purchase a recreational vehicle (RV) to facilitate the showing and sale of the house and the eventual move to another state. The RV would provide the shooter with a place to sleep as he would not sleep in a hotel. In fact, during Hurricane Sandy in October 2012, with no power in the house, the shooter refused to leave the home and go to a hotel.

The mother wanted to buy the shooter a CZ 83 pistol for Christmas and had prepared a check for that purchase to give the shooter.

On December 10, 2012, the mother indicated to a friend that the shooter had bumped his head badly, there was some bleeding, but he was okay. This appeared to have occurred at 5:30 a.m. She then prepared for her trip to New Hampshire and cooked for the shooter before she left, leaving him his favorites.

During the week of December 10, 2012, the shooter's mother was out of town in New Hampshire. She arrived home Thursday evening December 13, 2012, at approximately 10:00 p.m.

As mentioned above, the GPS found in the home, revealed that on Thursday, December 13, 2012, the device was used. It recorded a trip from and back to 36 Yogananda Street with a route in the Sandy Hook area of Newtown between 2:09 p.m. and 2:32 p.m. The GPS did not report that the driver drove up to SHES. Presumably this was the shooter driving the black Honda Civic as this would have been the only car available to the shooter and it was reportedly his, having been purchased for him.

General Background Information

Investigators conducted many interviews with persons who knew the shooter and members of his family. As explained above, they did so principally to determine if anyone had conspired with the shooter or aided his crimes. But they also sought to ascertain what might have motivated him to murder children and their teachers and his mother.

The first question was whether the shooter had a reason specifically to target SHES or any student, teacher, or employee. No evidence suggests that he did. In fact, as best as can be determined, the shooter had no prior contact with anyone in the school that day. And, apart from having attended the school as a child, he appears to have had no continuing involvement with SHES.

More generally, those who knew the shooter describe him in contradictory ways. He was undoubtedly afflicted with mental health problems; yet despite a fascination with mass shootings and firearms, he displayed no aggressive or threatening tendencies. In some contexts he was viewed as having above-average intelligence; in others below-average. Some recalled that the shooter had been bullied; but others – including many teachers – saw nothing of the sort. With some people he could talk with them and be humorous; but many others saw the shooter as unemotional, distant, and remote.

What follows are some observations that investigators developed in attempting to determine the shooter's motive.

Parents

The shooter's mother and father Peter Lanza had been married to each other. They moved from New Hampshire to the Sandy Hook section of Newtown in 1998. In addition to the shooter, they had another son Ryan Lanza, who was four years older than the shooter.[43] In 2001 the shooter's parents separated. The children continued to reside with the mother. The parents subsequently divorced. The father remarried in 2011; the mother never remarried.

After college, the brother moved out of state. He reached out to the shooter a few times but the shooter did not respond. As of December 14, 2012, the older brother had not had contact with the shooter since 2010. The brother believed that the shooter and his mother had a close relationship. After his older brother left for college, the shooter reportedly became interested in firearms and at one point considered joining the military.

Both the shooter's mother and father indicated that the shooter was bullied growing up. The father indicated that it was not excessive and concerned his social awkwardness and physical gait. As expanded upon in the Education and Mental Health section below, other witnesses did not recall the shooter being overtly bullied. Nonetheless, the shooter appears to have had few friends growing up.

---

[43] Both the shooter's father and brother cooperated fully with the investigation.

The shooter's father saw him regularly until he turned 18. They would go hiking, play video games and other activities. They went shooting twice. The shooter had a cell phone but never used it. Calls all went to voice mail. His father would just e-mail him when he wanted to reach him.

The shooter's relationship with his father deteriorated in the last quarter of 2010 and the father last saw the shooter in that year. After that the father would reach out to the shooter by mail or through e-mails regularly, asking him to join him at various places for different activities. The shooter stopped responding at some point prior to December 2012.

One witness who knew the shooter in 2011 and 2012 said that he rarely mentioned his father or his brother; though he would mention briefly something he did with his father or brother in the past.

While it appears that the shooter's mother did volunteer at SHES, it was when the shooter was a student. There is no indication that she volunteered there in recent years.

The mother took care of all of the shooter's needs. The mother indicated that she did not work because of her son's condition. She worried about what would happen to the shooter if anything happened to her.

One witness indicated that the shooter did not have an emotional connection to his mother. Recently when his mother asked him if he would feel bad if anything happened to her, he replied, "No." Others, however, have indicated that they thought the shooter was close to his mother and she was the only person to whom the shooter would talk.

A person who knew the shooter in 2011 and 2012 said the shooter described his relationship with his mother as strained because the shooter said her behavior was not rational.

The shooter was particular about the food that he ate and its arrangement on a plate in relation to other foods on the plate. Certain types of dishware could not be used for particular foods. The mother would shop for him and cook to the shooter's specifications, though sometimes he would cook for himself. Reportedly the shooter did not drink alcohol, take drugs, prescription or otherwise, and hated the thought of doing any of those things.

The mother did the shooter's laundry on a daily basis as the shooter often changed clothing during the day. She was not allowed in the shooter's room, however, even to clean. No one was allowed in his room.

The shooter disliked birthdays, Christmas and holidays. He would not allow his mother to put up a Christmas tree. The mother explained it by saying that shooter had no emotions or feelings. The mother also got rid of a cat because the shooter did not want it in the house.

People Outside the Family

When the shooter had his hair cut, he did not like to be touched and did not like the sound of clippers, so they were not used much. He would sit with his hands in his lap and always look down, giving one word answers if the cutter tried to engage him in conversation.

Those who worked on the property at 36 Yogananda Street never entered the home. They spoke with the mother outside in the yard or at the bottom of driveway. They were instructed never to ring the doorbell and to make prior arrangements before using power equipment as her son had issues with loud noises. The shooter was observed at times coming and going from the residence.

There were a number of people who knew the mother over the years, some fairly well, who had never met the shooter – although were aware of his existence – and had never been inside her residence.

Shooter's Interests

Over the years his hobbies included building computers,[44] writing poetry and hiking. The shooter worked briefly at a computer repair shop. When he was younger he played the saxophone. The shooter had a cell phone but never used it.

Shooting was a pastime in which the family engaged. Over the years the shooter enjoyed target shooting and would go to a range with his brother and mother. The mother had grown up with firearms and had a pistol permit. The shooter did not. Both the mother and the shooter took National Rifle Association (NRA) safety courses. The mother thought it was good to learn responsibility for guns. Both would shoot pistols and rifles at a local range and the shooter was described as quiet and polite.

He played video games often, both solo at home and online. They could be described as both violent and non-violent. One person described the shooter as spending the majority of his time playing non-violent video games all day, with his favorite at one point being "Super Mario Brothers."

Another said he used the computer to play games online and communicate. Sometimes the shooter would not respond to e-mails and be unavailable for a couple of weeks. The shooter explained that he was "moping around." The shooter frequently formatted the hard drive of his computer as a way of "staying off the grid" and minimizing his internet trace.

Initially the shooter did not drive but he eventually got a driver's license and the Honda was purchased for him. The shooter was issued a driver's license in July 2010.

The shooter liked to play a game called "Dance Dance Revolution" (DDR), which is a music video game in which the player stands on a platform, watches a video screen and moves his feet

---

[44] By all accounts the shooter was extremely computer savvy.

as directed by the video. A home version of this was seen and photographed in the shooter's home.[45] Several videos of him playing DDR were found on digital media taken from the home.

The GPS found in the home and reportedly belonging to the shooter indicated that he regularly went to the area of a theater that had a commercial version of the DDR game in the lobby. In 2011 and up until a month before December 14, 2012, the shooter went to the theater and played the game. He went most every Friday through Sunday and played the game for four to ten hours.

The shooter was specific about the clothes he wore. He typically wore the same clothing when at the theater: a grey hoodie and slacks. After a snowstorm in 2011 the shooter was not seen at the theater until about February 2012. At that time he seemed more anti-social and no longer played DDR with others.

An acquaintance of the shooter from 2011 to June 2012 said that the shooter and the acquaintance played DDR quite a bit. They would play the game and occasionally see a movie. They did not play first person shooter games at the theater.[46] The shooter had stamina for DDR and never appeared winded unless really exhausted.

The acquaintance said the shooter seemed to enjoy nature and mentioned the possibility of going hiking more than once. The shooter was capable of laughing, smiling and making jokes, though always in a dry fashion. The shooter never mentioned being bullied while growing up. Topics of conversation included world and current events, and included chimpanzee society and how they interacted.

In the course of their conversations, the shooter indicated that he had an interest in mass murders and serial killing. They never spent a lot of time discussing them, but it would be a topic of conversation.[47] There were no conversations about weapons or shooting at a gun range.

Shooter – Education and Mental Health

The following background information is compiled from a variety of sources and may at times appear to be inconsistent. This is a function of the differing perspectives of those interviewed. The information also varied based upon the time period during which the witness knew or associated with the shooter or his family.

The shooter went through the Newtown public school system, though part of seventh grade and part of eighth grade were done at St. Rose of Lima School in Newtown.

---

[45] See the Appendix at page A197.

[46] Online first person shooter games that the shooter did play as determined by a search of the digital media in the home, "Combat Arms" and "World of Warcraft" were played on the computer using a keyboard to control the player.

[47] The shooter also wrote about all of these topics. Other topics of discussion included human nature, perception, judgment, morality, lack of control, prejudice, empathy, suicide, mental illness, existential crisis, urban exploration of abandoned areas, hiking and cookies.

While the shooter did attend SHES from 1998 to 2003, the first through fifth grade, he was never assigned to the classrooms where the shootings occurred. The shooter went for walks with his family around and near SHES after he had gotten out of the school. The shooter indicated that he loved the school and liked to go there.

According to some, the shooter was more social when he first moved to Connecticut and was younger. He would attend play groups and parties. The early school years have him portrayed as a nice kid, though sort of withdrawn. He loved music and played saxophone.

As he got older his condition seemed to worsen, he became more of a loner. As the shooter got into the higher grades of middle school, he did not like noise and confusion and began to have issues when he had to walk to different classes. As a result, in high school, the shooter was home schooled for a period of time. Though not in a mainstream setting, he could sit through a quiet lecture. The mother drove the shooter where he needed to go. He did not want to go to events with crowds.

He attended Newtown High School (NHS) with a combination of home schooling, tutoring and classes at NHS and Western Connecticut State University (WCSU). At NHS he was considered a special education student. Having enough credits, the shooter graduated from NHS in 2009. He continued to take classes at WCSU after high school graduation.

Various witnesses made the following observations about the shooter through his school years:

1. In the 2002-2003 school year, when the shooter was in the fifth grade, he was quiet, reluctant, very bright and had good ideas regarding creative writing. He wouldn't necessarily engage in conversation, but wouldn't ignore one. There was no recollection of him being bullied or teased.
2. The fifth grade was also the year that, related to a class project, the shooter produced the "Big Book of Granny" in which the main character has a gun in her cane and shoots people. The story includes violence against children. There is no indication this was ever handed in to the school.[48]
3. In the fifth grade the shooter indicated that he did not like sports, did not think highly of himself and believed that everyone else in the world deserved more than he did.
4. In intermediate school from 2002-2004 he was a quiet shy boy who participated in class and listened. He did not show enthusiasm, extreme happiness or extreme sadness. He was neutral.
5. In the fifth and sixth grades from 2003 to 2004 the shooter participated in concerts at school. He was not remembered by the teacher as having been bullied and the shooter had at least one friend.
6. A sixth grade teacher described the shooter as an average student with A's and B's; homework was never an issue. The shooter never made trouble or distracted others. He had friends and was friendly to others. He was a normal child with no oddities and there were no reports of bullying or teasing.

[48] See the Appendix starting at page A220.

7. In 2004 while at the intermediate school he was described as respectful and cooperated with others.
8. One person who remembered him from the middle school never saw the shooter bullied.
9. In seventh grade, a teacher described the shooter as intelligent but not normal, with anti-social issues. He was quiet, barely spoke and did not want to participate in anything. His writing assignments obsessed about battles, destruction and war, far more than others his age. The level of violence in the writing was disturbing. At the same time, when asked to write a poem, he was able to write a beautiful one and presented it in public.
10. In the ninth and tenth grades the shooter was reclusive, shutting himself in the bedroom and playing video games all day. In the upper classes the shooter compiled a journal instead of attending physical education.
11. In high school the shooter did not have good social skills. He did not show any signs of violence.
12. In high school the shooter would have "episodes"[49] and his mother would be called to the school. The episodes would last about fifteen minutes each. There were no signs of violence during any of these episodes and the shooter was more likely to be victimized than to act in violence against another.
13. In high school the shooter was not willing to talk much, hard to communicate with and had poor social skills. He often became withdrawn in a social environment. The shooter would have both inclusive class time and leave the class for specialized sessions.
14. At NHS the shooter was in the "Tech Club" in 2007–2008. He was remembered in a variety of ways including as a quiet person who was smart. He wore the same clothing repeatedly and might not speak to you, even if you were talking to him. He was not remembered to have been bullied or to have spoken about violence. The advisor looked out for him and tried to have him included wherever possible. He was also remembered for pulling his sleeves over his hand to touch something. He was not known to be a violent kid at all and never spoke of violence.
15. The shooter had a LAN party[50] at his home in 2008 with Tech Club members; no firearms were seen at the shooter's home.
16. In terms of video games, the shooter liked to play "Phantasy Star Online" (a role playing game), "Paper Mario," "Luigi's Mansion" and "Pikmin." He also liked Japanese animated films and television.

Over the years from the late 1990s and into the 2000s, the shooter had evaluations of various types, some of which were available to the investigators. In the late 1990s he was described as having speech and language needs. At that time he was also being followed medically for seizure activities. In preschool his conduct included repetitive behaviors, temper tantrums, smelling things that were not there, excessive hand washing and eating idiosyncrasies.

In 2005, the shooter was diagnosed with Asperger's Disorder and was described as presenting with significant social impairments and extreme anxiety. It was also noted that he lacked empathy and had very rigid thought processes. He had a literal interpretation of written and

---

[49] What these episodes were was unclear.

[50] This is a party where attendees eat pizza and play video games.

verbal material. In the school setting, the shooter had extreme anxiety and discomfort with changes, noise, and physical contact with others.

In 2006 the shooter had an overall IQ in the average range. He had no learning disability. Depending on the psychological test taken he could be average, below average or above average. Testing that required the touching of objects could not be done. It was reported that his school issues related to his identified emotional and/or Pervasive Developmental Disorder (PDD) spectrum behaviors. His high level of anxiety, Asperger's characteristics, Obsessive Compulsive Disorder (OCD) concerns and sensory issues all impacted his performance to a significant degree, limiting his participation in a general education curriculum. Tutoring, desensitization and medication were recommended. It was suggested that he would benefit by continuing to be eased into more regular classroom time and increasing exposure to routine events at school.

The shooter refused to take suggested medication and did not engage in suggested behavior therapies.

Over the years his mother consistently described the shooter as having Asperger's syndrome. She had a number of books in the home on the topic. She also described the shooter as being unable to make eye contact, sensitive to light and couldn't stand to be touched. Over time he had multiple daily rituals, an inability to touch door knobs,[51] repeated hand washing and obsessive clothes changing, to the point that his mother was frequently doing laundry.

In 2006, the shooter's mother noted that there were marked changes to the shooter's behavior around the seventh grade. Prior to that, he would ride his bike and do adventurous things such as climbing trees or climbing a mountain. He had stopped playing the saxophone. He had been in a school band but dropped out. He had withdrawn from playing soccer or baseball which he said he did not enjoy.

It is important to note that it is unknown, what contribution, if any, the shooter's mental health issues made to his attack on SHES. Those mental health professionals who saw him did not see anything that would have predicted his future behavior.

EVIDENCE EXAMINATION

Electronics

Examinations of the following seized items were done by the WDMC squad and the Computer Crimes and Electronic Evidence Laboratory of the Department of Emergency Services and Public Protection (DESPP).

Sony PlayStation 2: An older games history was found. Games located included "Dynasty Tactics," "Kingdom Hearts," "Kingdom Hearts 2," "Onimusha," "Dynasty Warriors," and "The Two Towers." The PlayStation 2 games could not be played with others over the internet.

[51] This included not opening doors for himself because he did not like touching the door handle or other metal objects, often going through a box of tissues a day to avoid the contact.

Xbox: A game history for the console and an indication of an Xbox Live user account were found. Games found in the gaming history included "Call of Duty 2: Big Red One," "Call of Duty: Finest Hour," "Dead or Alive 3," "Halo," "Halo 2," "Lego Star Wars," "MechAssault," "Mercenaries," "MGS2 Substance," "Panzer Dragoon ORTA," "PSO," "Shenmue II," "Spiderman," "Splinter Cell 2," "Splinter Cell-CT," "Star Wars Battlefront," "Star Wars Republic Commando," "Tenchu: Return from Darkness," "The Return of the King," and "Worms Forts Under Seige."

It was noted on both of the above items that the gaming history found may not be the complete history of those actually played. No evidence regarding the existence of any accessories or co-co-conspirators was found.

Xbox 360: Found to be damaged and inoperable.

Firearms and Related Evidence

Of the firearms seized in this case, five are directly involved, four from SHES and one from 36 Yogananda Street.

- **History**

All of the firearms below and involved in these cases were legally purchased by the shooter's mother. Additionally, ammunition of the type used in these cases had been purchased by the shooter's mother in the past. There is no reason to believe the ammunition used here was purchased by anyone else. The evidence does not show any ammunition purchases by the shooter.

The shooter did not have a permit to carry a pistol, nor had he ever had one. His mother had a valid pistol permit.

A pistol is defined as "… any firearm having a barrel less than twelve inches."[52] Both the Glock 20, 10 mm and the Sig Sauer P226, 9 mm qualify as pistols. They are firearms and their barrel lengths were less than 12 inches.

- **Firearms, Recovered Bullets and Fragments**

Recovered from Shooter's Honda Civic Outside of SHES

Izhmash Saiga-12, 12 gauge, semiautomatic shotgun: The Izhmash Saiga-12 was found in the shooter's Honda Civic that was parked outside SHES. It was tested and found to be operable without malfunction. There was no physical evidence indicating this weapon had been fired at SHES, i.e., the bullets, bullet fragments and expended shell casings recovered at the scene and from the OCME could not have been fired from this weapon.

---

[52] C.G.S. Sec. 53a-3(18).

Recovered from Classroom 10, SHES

Bushmaster Model XM15-E2S semiautomatic rifle: The Bushmaster rifle was found in classroom 10. The Bushmaster was tested and found to be operable without malfunction. All of the 5.56 mm shell casings from SHES that were tested were found to have been fired from this rifle. All of the bullets and fragments, recovered from SHES and the OCME that were tested, with the exception of those mentioned immediately below, are consistent with having been fired from the Bushmaster rifle.[53] They could not have been fired from the Saiga-12, the Glock 20 or the Sig Sauer P226.

Glock 20, 10 mm, semiautomatic pistol: The Glock 20 was found in classroom 10 near the shooter's body. The Glock 20 was tested and found to be operable without malfunction. It was found to have fired both of the 10 mm shell casings recovered at SHES. It was consistent with having fired the bullet that was recovered from the ceiling of classroom 8 in a location along the trajectory of the suicide shot of the shooter in classroom 10. It could have fired the three bullet fragments recovered from classroom 10. The three fragments together weigh less than one bullet and are presumed to have been parts of the same one bullet. Though all lacked sufficient striate for a positive identification, all had polygonal rifling consistent with the Glock 20. They could not have been fired from the Saiga-12, the Bushmaster or the Sig Sauer P226.

Sig Sauer P226, 9 mm, semiautomatic pistol: The Sig Sauer P226 was found in classroom 10 on the shooter's person. The Sig Sauer P226 was tested and found to be operable without malfunction. There was no physical evidence found indicating that this weapon had been fired at SHES, i.e. casings, bullets and bullet fragments recovered at the scene and from the OCME could not have been fired from this weapon.

The total weight of the guns and ammunition from the shooter at SHES was 30.47 lbs.[54]

Recovered from 36 Yogananda Street, Newtown, CT

Savage Mark II, .22 cal. Long Rifle, bolt action: The Savage Mark II rifle was found on the floor of the master bedroom near the bed where the body of the shooter's mother was found. The rifle was found to be operable without malfunction. The rifle was found to have fired the .22 cal. casing recovered from the rifle's chamber and the three .22 cal. casings found in the master bedroom. The rifle also was found to have fired the four bullets recovered during the autopsy of the shooter's mother.

---

[53] "No positive identification could be made to any of the bullet evidence submissions noted … … in 5.56 mm caliber. The physical condition of the bullet jacket surfaces were severely damaged and corroded. They all lacked individual striated marks of sufficient agreement for the identification process. The test fires also exhibited a lack of individual striated marks on the bullet surface for comparison purposes. This condition can be caused by fouling in the barrel of the rifle and the ammunition itself. The Bushmaster rifle cannot be eliminated as having fired the 5.56 caliber bullet evidence examined," quoting from the 6/19/13 Forensic Science Laboratory report.

[54] See the Appendix at page A141.

Other Testing

In the course of the investigation swabbings to test for DNA were taken from various pieces of evidence in the case, both at Sandy Hook Elementary School and 36 Yogananda Street. The purpose was to determine if anyone else had actively been involved in the planning or carrying out of the shootings. These swabbings were tested and compared to known samples in the case and no potential accessories or co-conspirators were revealed by the testing.[55]

MISCELLANEOUS INVESTIGATIVE LEADS

In the course of the investigation, law enforcement personnel received a large number of contacts purporting to provide information on the shootings and the shooter. This applied to both state and federal law enforcement. Information that was substantiated and relevant was made part of the investigation. Other information, after investigation was not substantiated.

Typically someone would call the CSP and leave a message that they had information relevant to the shootings at Sandy Hook Elementary School. In an abundance of caution, a detective was assigned to follow up on every "lead," regardless of its presumed validity.

Some of the more than forty unsubstantiated leads and information are described below because of their nature or mention in investigation documents.

1. In the December 14, 2012, 7:25 p.m. search warrant for 36 Yogananda Street, paragraphs 8 and 9 read as follows:

    8. That investigators determined that on 12/12/12, an individual logged onto a website called 4Chan.com and anonymously posted "I'm going to kill myself on Friday and it will make the news. be watching at 9:00 am." That another anonymous individual asked "Where at?" The first individual responded "I live in Connecticut, that's as much as I'll say."
    9. That additionally on 12/14/12, a concerned individual in Texas contacted the Hartford Police Department and reported that her son was playing a video game named 'Call of Duty' approximately 20 hours ago. She continued that a gamer with the screen name [RaWr]i<3EmoGirls (hereinafter "User") stated; "next week or very soon there maybe a shooting at my school and other schools so if i die remember me plz if I don't get on for 3-5 not including weeks that means i died and im being 100 percent serious." The User then stated: "something might go bad tomorrow this could possibly be my last moments alive.-." Finally, User stated, "as far as I know theres a list of ppl that are gunna get shot-. I hope I aint on it."

[55] Two of the items examined from outside the building of SHES, one from the shotgun in the shooter's car and a second from 36 Yogananda Street yielded DNA profiles consistent with the DNA profiles of two victims killed in SHES, one in each. It is strongly believed that this resulted from an accidental transference as a result of the unique circumstances of this case. There is no reason to believe that either victim would ever have come in contact with these items. The DESPP is conducting a separate protocol inquiry in an attempt to determine the reason that the DNA appears on the items.

Both of these leads were immediately investigated by federal law enforcement and found to have no validity and no relation to Newtown.[56]

2. A December 14, 2012, search of the Stamford residence of Peter Lanza, the father of the shooter, was conducted with the FBI. Some illegal fireworks were seized and secured. After consultation with David I. Cohen, the State's Attorney for the Judicial District of Stamford/Norwalk, and based on all of the circumstances involved, this state's attorney has decided to exercise his discretion and not prosecute Mr. Lanza for possession of the fireworks, which are in no way related to the events of December 14, 2012.
3. Dick's Sporting Goods – Police received a lead that the shooter had tried to buy ammunition at a Dick's Sporting Goods store. Store security surveillance videos were recovered and reviewed. None of the individuals depicted in the videos appear to be the shooter or connected to shooter.
4. A person called the police indicating that the shooter had tried to rent a room from her and indicated he was having problems with his mother. This proved to be unsubstantiated after an investigation.
5. Some callers indicated that they chatted with the shooter online in postings. These postings were determined to be false.
6. Numerous citizens in Newtown received calls on their telephones with messages left saying "I am [the shooter's name] and I am going to kill you." It was determined that these calls were made from out of state and the investigation is ongoing. Preliminary investigation results establish that the callers were not associated with the shooter.
7. CSP investigated a lead that the shooter went to Newtown High School before going to SHES. In the course of this investigation one parent refused to let her high school child be interviewed by police and related that a friend of the child had told the child they saw the shooter in the parking lot before the shooting. A review of Newtown High School video did not substantiate this claim.
8. There were reports of the shooter being at SHES on December 12, 2012, that were investigated and found not to be substantiated.
9. A report that a man claimed that while in Oklahoma a woman told him about the planned shooting before the shooting occurred. Federal law enforcement investigated this and found that it could not be true.

[56] These search warrants were applied for with information that was available at the time. Some of the information was later determined to be inaccurate.

DETERMINATIONS OF CRIMES COMMITTED

In the course of his rampage the shooter committed a number of state crimes. The most significant are those where lives were taken and people were specifically injured.

At Sandy Hook Elementary School, the crime of Murder under Special Circumstances[57] in violation of C.G.S. Sec. 53a-54b was committed twenty-six times. Attempted Murder under Special Circumstances[58] in violation of C.G.S. Secs. 53a-49 and 53a-54b was committed twice as it relates to the two individuals who were shot and survived. These crimes reflect the killings of the children and adults, as well as those physically injured.[59] The crime of Murder in violation of C.G.S. Sec. 53a-54a was committed by the shooter in killing his mother at 36 Yogananda Street.[60]

Also listed are other major crimes committed by the shooter on December 14, 2012.[61]

The major felonies[62] committed by the shooter in this case are:

- Murder with Special Circumstances
- Attempted Murder with Special Circumstances
- Assault in the First Degree[63]

---

[57] Sec. 53a-54b. Murder with special circumstances. A person is guilty of murder with special circumstances who is convicted of any of the following: (1)... ... (7) murder of two or more persons at the same time or in the course of a single transaction; or (8) murder of a person under sixteen years of age.

[58] Sec. 53a-49. Criminal attempt: Sufficiency of conduct; renunciation as defense. (a) A person is guilty of an attempt to commit a crime if, acting with the kind of mental state required for commission of the crime, he: ... ... (2) intentionally does or omits to do anything which, under the circumstances as he believes them to be, is an act or omission constituting a substantial step in a course of conduct planned to culminate in his commission of the crime.

[59] Though state law as to who is a "victim" in a criminal case is very broad, only those victims mentioned above will be discussed. Connecticut defines a "victim of crime" as an individual who suffers direct or threatened physical, emotional or financial harm as a result of a crime and includes immediate family members of a minor, incompetent individual or homicide victim and a person designated by a homicide victim in accordance with section 1-56r. See C.G.S. Sec. 1-1k.

[60] Sec. 53a-54a. Murder. (a) A person is guilty of murder when, with intent to cause the death of another person, he causes the death of such person or of a third person or causes a suicide by force, duress or deception; except that in any prosecution under this subsection, it shall be an affirmative defense that the defendant committed the proscribed act or acts under the influence of extreme emotional disturbance for which there was a reasonable explanation or excuse, the reasonableness of which is to be determined from the viewpoint of a person in the defendant's situation under the circumstances as the defendant believed them to be, provided nothing contained in this subsection shall constitute a defense to a prosecution for, or preclude a conviction of, manslaughter in the first degree or any other crime.

[61] The investigation has not discovered any evidence that Nancy Lanza was in any way aware of her son's plans.

[62] In any given situation, the facts giving rise to the commission of one crime will suffice to meet the elements of additional crimes. Here the focus will be on the major crimes committed and not go into every possible felony justified by the evidence.

- Burglary in the First Degree[64]
- Risk of Injury to a Minor[65]
- Possession of a Weapon on School Grounds[66]
- Carrying a Pistol Without a Permit,[67]

The crimes listed above all require some type of mental state whether it is a specific intent, knowledge or a general intent to do the prohibited act.

The intent to kill for the crime of murder can be seen in the circumstantial evidence such as the type of weapon used, the manner in which it was used, the type of wounds inflicted and the events leading to and immediately following the deaths, as well as with the shooter intending the natural consequences of his voluntary acts.[68]

Here the intent is clear from the evidence that the shooter intentionally armed himself heavily, drove to SHES, parked in a manner out of direct sight of the front door, shot his way into the building and immediately killed those who confronted him as well as those in classrooms 8 and 10. The evidence found at his home on the digital media further support his intentions to kill, both at the school and with his mother. Further the manner in which he killed his mother reflects the shooter's intent to kill her.

---

[63] Sec. 53a-59. Assault in the first degree: Class B felony: Nonsuspendable sentences. (a) A person is guilty of assault in the first degree when: (1) With intent to cause serious physical injury to another person, he causes such injury to such person or to a third person by means of a deadly weapon or a dangerous instrument;... ... or (5) with intent to cause physical injury to another person, he causes such injury to such person or to a third person by means of the discharge of a firearm.

[64] Sec. 53a-101. Burglary in the first degree: Class B felony. (a) A person is guilty of burglary in the first degree when (1) such person enters or remains unlawfully in a building with intent to commit a crime therein and is armed with explosives or a deadly weapon or dangerous instrument, or (2) such person enters or remains unlawfully in a building with intent to commit a crime therein and, in the course of committing the offense, intentionally, knowingly or recklessly inflicts or attempts to inflict bodily injury on anyone, or .....

[65] Sec. 53-21. Injury or risk of injury to, or impairing morals of, children. Sale of children. (a) Any person who (1) wilfully or unlawfully causes or permits any child under the age of sixteen years to be placed in such a situation that the life or limb of such child is endangered, the health of such child is likely to be injured or the morals of such child are likely to be impaired, or does any act likely to impair the health or morals of any such child, or ... ..., shall be guilty of a class C felony for a violation of subdivision (1) ....

[66] Sec. 53a-217b. Possession of a weapon on school grounds: Class D felony. (a) A person is guilty of possession of a weapon on school grounds when, knowing that such person is not licensed or privileged to do so, such person possesses a firearm or deadly weapon, as defined in section 53a-3, (1) in or on the real property comprising a public or private elementary or secondary school, or ....

[67] Sec. 29-35. Carrying of pistol or revolver without permit prohibited. Exceptions. (a) No person shall carry any pistol or revolver upon his or her person, except when such person is within the dwelling house or place of business of such person, without a permit to carry the same issued as provided in section 29-28.

[68] State v. Otto, 305 Conn. 51, 66-67 (2012).

Murder with Special Circumstances is met both in the killing of the children and in the killing of more than one person at the same time.

In this case the shooter's mental status is no defense to his conduct as the evidence shows he knew his conduct to be against the law. He had the ability to control his behavior to obtain the results he wanted, including his own death. This evidence includes his possession of materials related to mass murders, his removal of the GPS from his car, his utilization of ear plugs, the damaging of the hard drive and waiting for his mother's return from New Hampshire.[69]

The existence of an extreme emotional disturbance for which there is a reasonable explanation or excuse is also not present in this case.[70] It is clear that the shooter planned his crimes in advance and was under no extreme emotional disturbance for which there was a reasonable explanation or excuse.

---

[69] Sec. 53a-13. Lack of capacity due to mental disease or defect as affirmative defense. (a) In any prosecution for an offense, it shall be an affirmative defense that the defendant, at the time he committed the proscribed act or acts, lacked substantial capacity, as a result of mental disease or defect, either to appreciate the wrongfulness of his conduct or to control his conduct within the requirements of the law.

[70] Sec. 53a-54a. Murder. (a) A person is guilty of murder when, … …with intent to cause the death of another person, he causes the death of such person or of a third person or causes a suicide by force, duress or deception; except that in any prosecution under this subsection, it shall be an affirmative defense that the defendant committed the proscribed act or acts under the influence of extreme emotional disturbance for which there was a reasonable explanation or excuse, the reasonableness of which is to be determined from the viewpoint of a person in the defendant's situation under the circumstances as the defendant believed them to be, provided nothing contained in this subsection shall constitute a defense to a prosecution for, or preclude a conviction of, manslaughter in the first degree or any other crime.

CONCLUSION

With the issuance of this report, the investigation is closed.[71] If additional reliable information, related to the existence of others' involvement in the case, comes to the attention of the investigators, it is subject to being reopened. I do not anticipate that occurring. As of now, there will be no state prosecution of anyone as an accessory or co-conspirator.

Many people have asked why the shooter did what he did on December 14, 2012. Or, in the vernacular of the criminal justice system, "Did he have a motive to do what he did?" This investigation, with the substantial information available, does not establish a conclusive motive.

What we do know is that the shooter had significant mental health issues that, while not affecting the criminality of the shooter's mental state for the crimes or his criminal responsibility for them, did affect his ability to live a normal life and to interact with others, even those to whom he should have been close. Whether this contributed in any way is unknown. The shooter did not recognize or help himself deal with those issues. He had a familiarity with and access to firearms and ammunition and an obsession with mass murders, in particular the Columbine shootings.

There is no clear indication why Sandy Hook Elementary School was selected, other than perhaps its close proximity to the shooter's home.

What is clear is that on the morning of December 14, 2012, the shooter intentionally committed horrendous crimes, murdering 20 children and 6 adults in a matter of moments, with the ability and intention of killing even more. He committed these heinous acts after killing his own mother. The evidence indicates the shooter planned his actions, including the taking of his own life.

It is equally clear that law enforcement arrived at Sandy Hook Elementary School within minutes of the first shots being fired. They went into the school to save those inside with the knowledge that someone might be waiting to take *their* lives. It is also clear that the staff of Sandy Hook Elementary School acted heroically in trying to protect the children. The combination saved many children's lives.

November 25, 2013

Stephen J. Sedensky III
State's Attorney
Judicial District of Danbury

[71] There remain some outstanding reports, returns and an evidence examination evaluation to be filed.

ACKNOWLEDGEMENTS

Over the course of the last eleven months many agencies, governmental and private, have come together to assist the victims' families, victims, first responders, others affected by the crimes, the Connecticut State Police and the State's Attorney's Office for the Judicial District of Danbury.

I wish to thank the below agencies, listed alphabetically, for their investigative work, cooperation and assistance in this investigation. Though I have tried to list all of the agencies that provided assistance to the investigation, I suspect some will be inadvertently left out. For this I apologize.

- Connecticut State Police and in particular Western District Major Crime Squad[72]*
- Connecticut Intelligence Center (CTIC)
- Bureau of Alcohol, Tobacco, Firearms and Explosives
- Department of Emergency Services and Public Protection Forensic Science Laboratory
- Faculty of Finding Words-Connecticut, A ChildFirst State[73]
- Family & Children's Aid of Danbury[74]
- Federal Bureau of Investigation,[75] including Victim Services and Behavior Analysis units
- Gundersen Health System's National Child Protection Training Center
- Hoboken, New Jersey, Police Department
- Homeland Security
- Municipal police departments in Connecticut
- Newtown Police Department
- Office of the Chief Medical Examiner
- Office of the Chief State's Attorney[76]*
- State of Connecticut Judicial Branch
- United States Attorney's Office for the District of Connecticut*
- United States Drug Enforcement Agency
- United States Marshals Service

I would also like to thank the members of the Danbury State's Attorney's Office, in particular, Supervisory Assistant State's Attorney Warren Murray and Inspectors Donald Brown and John Mahoney for their assistance and support.

---

[72] The Western District Major Crime Squad under the leadership of Lt. David Delvecchia investigated this case with a thoroughness and sensitivity that is unmatched in my experience.

[73] Connecticut is a ChildFirst state whose one week program Finding Words Connecticut, Interviewing Children and Preparing for Court is funded by the Governor's Task Force on Justice for Abused Children.

[74] Family & Children's Aid of Danbury hosts the Multidisciplinary Investigation Team.

[75] This includes FBI agents across the country who sought out evidence and interviewed witnesses in many states.

[76] Chief State's Attorney Kevin T. Kane's counsel and assistance has been an invaluable asset to me and this case, together with the assistance of those in his office who worked on the case.

* I am grateful for the suggestions, editing and reviews of the drafts of this report provided by these organizations. Any errors that remain are mine.

FEDERAL BUREAU OF INVESTIGATION
FOI/PA
DELETED PAGE INFORMATION SHEET
Civil Action# 16-cv-02136

Total Deleted Page(s) = 346
Page 7 ~ b6 - 1, 2; b7C - 1, 2; OTHER - Sealed Pursuant to Court Order;
Page 23 ~ b6 - 5; b7C - 5; OTHER - Sealed Pursuant to Court Order;
Page 24 ~ Duplicate;
Page 25 ~ b6 - 5; b7C - 5; OTHER - Sealed Pursuant to Court Order;
Page 26 ~ b6 - 5; b7C - 5; OTHER - Sealed Pursuant to Court Order;
Page 27 ~ b6 - 5; b7C - 5; OTHER - Sealed Pursuant to Court Order;
Page 28 ~ b6 - 5; b7C - 5; OTHER - Sealed Pursuant to Court Order;
Page 29 ~ b6 - 5; b7C - 5; OTHER - Sealed Pursuant to Court Order;
Page 30 ~ b6 - 5; b7C - 5; OTHER - Sealed Pursuant to Court Order;
Page 31 ~ b6 - 5; b7C - 5; OTHER - Sealed Pursuant to Court Order;
Page 32 ~ b6 - 5; b7C - 5; OTHER - Sealed Pursuant to Court Order;
Page 33 ~ OTHER - Sealed Pursuant to Court Order;
Page 34 ~ OTHER - Sealed Pursuant to Court Order;
Page 35 ~ OTHER - Sealed Pursuant to Court Order;
Page 36 ~ b6 - 5; b7C - 5; OTHER - Sealed Pursuant to Court Order;
Page 37 ~ b6 - 5; b7C - 5; OTHER - Sealed Pursuant to Court Order;
Page 38 ~ b6 - 5; b7C - 5; OTHER - Sealed Pursuant to Court Order;
Page 39 ~ OTHER - Sealed Pursuant to Court Order;
Page 40 ~ b6 - 5; b7C - 5; OTHER - Sealed Pursuant to Court Order;
Page 41 ~ b6 - 5; b7C - 5; OTHER - Sealed Pursuant to Court Order;
Page 42 ~ b6 - 5; b7C - 5; OTHER - Sealed Pursuant to Court Order;
Page 43 ~ b6 - 5; b7C - 5; OTHER - Sealed Pursuant to Court Order;
Page 44 ~ b6 - 5; b7C - 5; OTHER - Sealed Pursuant to Court Order;
Page 45 ~ b6 - 5; b7C - 5; OTHER - Sealed Pursuant to Court Order;
Page 46 ~ b6 - 5; b7C - 5; OTHER - Sealed Pursuant to Court Order;
Page 47 ~ b6 - 5; b7C - 5; OTHER - Sealed Pursuant to Court Order;
Page 48 ~ b6 - 5; b7C - 5; OTHER - Sealed Pursuant to Court Order;
Page 49 ~ b6 - 5; b7C - 5; OTHER - Sealed Pursuant to Court Order;
Page 50 ~ b6 - 5; b7C - 5; OTHER - Sealed Pursuant to Court Order;
Page 51 ~ OTHER - Sealed Pursuant to Court Order;
Page 52 ~ b6 - 5; b7C - 5; OTHER - Sealed Pursuant to Court Order;
Page 53 ~ b6 - 5; b7C - 5; OTHER - Sealed Pursuant to Court Order;
Page 54 ~ b6 - 5; b7C - 5; OTHER - Sealed Pursuant to Court Order;
Page 55 ~ OTHER - Sealed Pursuant to Court Order;
Page 56 ~ OTHER - Sealed Pursuant to Court Order;
Page 57 ~ OTHER - Sealed Pursuant to Court Order;
Page 58 ~ OTHER - Sealed Pursuant to Court Order;
Page 59 ~ b6 - 5; b7C - 5; OTHER - Sealed Pursuant to Court Order;
Page 60 ~ b6 - 5; b7C - 5; OTHER - Sealed Pursuant to Court Order;
Page 61 ~ b6 - 5; b7C - 5; OTHER - Sealed Pursuant to Court Order;
Page 62 ~ b6 - 5; b7C - 5; OTHER - Sealed Pursuant to Court Order;
Page 63 ~ OTHER - Sealed Pursuant to Court Order;
Page 64 ~ b6 - 5; b7C - 5; OTHER - Sealed Pursuant to Court Order;
Page 65 ~ b6 - 5; b7C - 5; OTHER - Sealed Pursuant to Court Order;
Page 66 ~ b6 - 5; b7C - 5; OTHER - Sealed Pursuant to Court Order;
Page 67 ~ b6 - 5; b7C - 5; OTHER - Sealed Pursuant to Court Order;
Page 68 ~ OTHER - Sealed Pursuant to Court Order;
Page 69 ~ b6 - 5; b7C - 5; OTHER - Sealed Pursuant to Court Order;

Page 70 ~ OTHER - Sealed Pursuant to Court Order;
Page 71 ~ b6 - 5; b7C - 5; OTHER - Sealed Pursuant to Court Order;
Page 72 ~ b6 - 5; b7C - 5; OTHER - Sealed Pursuant to Court Order;
Page 73 ~ b6 - 5; b7C - 5; OTHER - Sealed Pursuant to Court Order;
Page 74 ~ b6 - 5; b7C - 5; OTHER - Sealed Pursuant to Court Order;
Page 75 ~ b6 - 5; b7C - 5; OTHER - Sealed Pursuant to Court Order;
Page 76 ~ b6 - 5; b7C - 5; OTHER - Sealed Pursuant to Court Order;
Page 77 ~ b6 - 5; b7C - 5; OTHER - Sealed Pursuant to Court Order;
Page 78 ~ OTHER - Sealed Pursuant to Court Order;
Page 79 ~ OTHER - Sealed Pursuant to Court Order;
Page 80 ~ OTHER - Sealed Pursuant to Court Order;
Page 81 ~ b6 - 5; b7C - 5; OTHER - Sealed Pursuant to Court Order;
Page 82 ~ b6 - 5; b7C - 5; OTHER - Sealed Pursuant to Court Order;
Page 83 ~ b6 - 5; b7C - 5; OTHER - Sealed Pursuant to Court Order;
Page 84 ~ b6 - 5; b7C - 5; OTHER - Sealed Pursuant to Court Order;
Page 85 ~ OTHER - Sealed Pursuant to Court Order;
Page 86 ~ OTHER - Sealed Pursuant to Court Order;
Page 87 ~ b6 - 5; b7C - 5; OTHER - Sealed Pursuant to Court Order;
Page 88 ~ b6 - 5; b7C - 5; OTHER - Sealed Pursuant to Court Order;
Page 89 ~ OTHER - Sealed Pursuant to Court Order;
Page 90 ~ OTHER - Sealed Pursuant to Court Order;
Page 91 ~ b6 - 5; b7C - 5; OTHER - Sealed Pursuant to Court Order;
Page 92 ~ b6 - 5; b7C - 5; OTHER - Sealed Pursuant to Court Order;
Page 93 ~ OTHER - Sealed Pursuant to Court Order;
Page 94 ~ b6 - 5; b7C - 5; OTHER - Sealed Pursuant to Court Order;
Page 95 ~ b6 - 5; b7C - 5; OTHER - Sealed Pursuant to Court Order;
Page 96 ~ OTHER - Sealed Pursuant to Court Order;
Page 97 ~ b6 - 5; b7C - 5; OTHER - Sealed Pursuant to Court Order;
Page 98 ~ OTHER - Sealed Pursuant to Court Order;
Page 99 ~ OTHER - Sealed Pursuant to Court Order;
Page 100 ~ OTHER - Sealed Pursuant to Court Order;
Page 101 ~ OTHER - Sealed Pursuant to Court Order;
Page 102 ~ OTHER - Sealed Pursuant to Court Order;
Page 103 ~ OTHER - Sealed Pursuant to Court Order;
Page 104 ~ OTHER - Sealed Pursuant to Court Order;
Page 105 ~ OTHER - Sealed Pursuant to Court Order;
Page 106 ~ b6 - 5; b7C - 5; OTHER - Sealed Pursuant to Court Order;
Page 107 ~ b6 - 5; b7C - 5; OTHER - Sealed Pursuant to Court Order;
Page 108 ~ OTHER - Sealed Pursuant to Court Order;
Page 109 ~ OTHER - Sealed Pursuant to Court Order;
Page 110 ~ OTHER - Sealed Pursuant to Court Order;
Page 111 ~ OTHER - Sealed Pursuant to Court Order;
Page 112 ~ OTHER - Sealed Pursuant to Court Order;
Page 113 ~ b6 - 5; b7C - 5; OTHER - Sealed Pursuant to Court Order;
Page 114 ~ b6 - 5; b7C - 5; OTHER - Sealed Pursuant to Court Order;
Page 115 ~ b6 - 5; b7C - 5; OTHER - Sealed Pursuant to Court Order;
Page 116 ~ b6 - 5; b7C - 5; OTHER - Sealed Pursuant to Court Order;
Page 117 ~ b6 - 5; b7C - 5; OTHER - Sealed Pursuant to Court Order;
Page 118 ~ b6 - 5; b7C - 5; OTHER - Sealed Pursuant to Court Order;
Page 119 ~ b6 - 5; b7C - 5; OTHER - Sealed Pursuant to Court Order;
Page 120 ~ OTHER - Sealed Pursuant to Court Order;
Page 121 ~ OTHER - Sealed Pursuant to Court Order;
Page 122 ~ b6 - 5; b7C - 5; OTHER - Sealed Pursuant to Court Order;
Page 123 ~ b6 - 5; b7C - 5; OTHER - Sealed Pursuant to Court Order;

Page 124 ~ b6 - 5; b7C - 5; OTHER - Sealed Pursuant to Court Order;
Page 125 ~ b6 - 5; b7C - 5; OTHER - Sealed Pursuant to Court Order;
Page 126 ~ b6 - 5; b7C - 5; OTHER - Sealed Pursuant to Court Order;
Page 127 ~ OTHER - Sealed Pursuant to Court Order;
Page 128 ~ b6 - 5; b7C - 5; OTHER - Sealed Pursuant to Court Order;
Page 129 ~ OTHER - Sealed Pursuant to Court Order;
Page 132 ~ b6 - 2; b7C - 2; OTHER - Sealed Pursuant to Court Order;
Page 133 ~ Duplicate;
Page 134 ~ b6 - 2; b7C - 2; OTHER - Sealed Pursuant to Court Order;
Page 135 ~ b6 - 2; b7C - 2; OTHER - Sealed Pursuant to Court Order;
Page 136 ~ b6 - 2, 5; b7C - 2, 5; OTHER - Sealed Pursuant to Court Order;
Page 137 ~ b6 - 5; b7C - 5; OTHER - Sealed Pursuant to Court Order;
Page 138 ~ OTHER - Sealed Pursuant to Court Order;
Page 139 ~ b6 - 2; b7C - 2; OTHER - Sealed Pursuant to Court Order;
Page 140 ~ b6 - 2; b7C - 2; OTHER - Sealed Pursuant to Court Order;
Page 141 ~ b6 - 2, 5; b7C - 2, 5; OTHER - Sealed Pursuant to Court Order;
Page 142 ~ b6 - 2; b7C - 2; OTHER - Sealed Pursuant to Court Order;
Page 143 ~ b6 - 2; b7C - 2; OTHER - Sealed Pursuant to Court Order;
Page 144 ~ b6 - 2; b7C - 2; OTHER - Sealed Pursuant to Court Order;
Page 145 ~ OTHER - Sealed Pursuant to Court Order;
Page 146 ~ b6 - 2; b7C - 2; OTHER - Sealed Pursuant to Court Order;
Page 147 ~ b6 - 2; b7C - 2; OTHER - Sealed Pursuant to Court Order;
Page 148 ~ b6 - 2; b7C - 2; OTHER - Sealed Pursuant to Court Order;
Page 149 ~ b6 - 2, 5; b7C - 2, 5; OTHER - Sealed Pursuant to Court Order;
Page 150 ~ b6 - 2; b7C - 2; OTHER - Sealed Pursuant to Court Order;
Page 151 ~ b6 - 2; b7C - 2; OTHER - Sealed Pursuant to Court Order;
Page 152 ~ b6 - 2, 5; b7C - 2, 5; OTHER - Sealed Pursuant to Court Order;
Page 153 ~ b6 - 5; b7C - 5; OTHER - Sealed Pursuant to Court Order;
Page 154 ~ b6 - 5; b7C - 5; OTHER - Sealed Pursuant to Court Order;
Page 155 ~ b6 - 5; b7C - 5; OTHER - Sealed Pursuant to Court Order;
Page 156 ~ b6 - 5; b7C - 5; OTHER - Sealed Pursuant to Court Order;
Page 157 ~ b6 - 5; b7C - 5; OTHER - Sealed Pursuant to Court Order;
Page 158 ~ b6 - 5; b7C - 5; OTHER - Sealed Pursuant to Court Order;
Page 159 ~ b6 - 5; b7C - 5; OTHER - Sealed Pursuant to Court Order;
Page 160 ~ b6 - 5; b7C - 5; OTHER - Sealed Pursuant to Court Order;
Page 161 ~ b6 - 5; b7C - 5; OTHER - Sealed Pursuant to Court Order;
Page 162 ~ b6 - 5; b7C - 5; OTHER - Sealed Pursuant to Court Order;
Page 163 ~ b6 - 5; b7C - 5; OTHER - Sealed Puruant to Court Order;
Page 164 ~ OTHER - Sealed Pursuant to Court Order;
Page 165 ~ OTHER - Sealed Pursuant to Court Order;
Page 166 ~ OTHER - Sealed Pursuant to Court Order;
Page 167 ~ OTHER - Sealed Pursuant to Court Order;
Page 168 ~ OTHER - Sealed Pursuant to Court Order;
Page 169 ~ OTHER - Sealed Pursuant to Court Order;
Page 170 ~ OTHER - Sealed Pursuant to Court Order;
Page 171 ~ OTHER - Sealed Pursuant to Court Order;
Page 172 ~ OTHER - Sealed Pursuant to Court Order;
Page 173 ~ OTHER - Sealed Pursuant to Court Order;
Page 174 ~ OTHER - Sealed Pursuant to Court Order;
Page 175 ~ OTHER - Sealed Pursuant to Court Order;
Page 176 ~ OTHER - Sealed Pursuant to Court Order;
Page 177 ~ OTHER - Sealed Pursuant to Court Order;
Page 178 ~ OTHER - Sealed Pursuant to Court Order;
Page 179 ~ OTHER - Sealed Pursuant to Court Order;

Page 180 ~ OTHER - Sealed Pursuant to Court Order;
Page 181 ~ OTHER - Sealed Pursuant to Court Order;
Page 182 ~ OTHER - Sealed Pursuant to Court Order;
Page 183 ~ OTHER - Sealed Pursuant to Court Order;
Page 184 ~ OTHER - Sealed Pursuant to Court Order;
Page 185 ~ OTHER - Sealed Pursuant to Court Order;
Page 186 ~ OTHER - Sealed Pursuant to Court Order;
Page 187 ~ OTHER - Sealed Pursuant to Court Order;
Page 188 ~ OTHER - Sealed Pursuant to Court Order;
Page 189 ~ OTHER - Sealed Pursuant to Court Order;
Page 190 ~ OTHER - Sealed Pursuant to Court Order;
Page 191 ~ OTHER - Sealed Pursuant to Court Order;
Page 192 ~ OTHER - Sealed Pursuant to Court Order;
Page 193 ~ OTHER - Sealed Pursuant to Court Order;
Page 194 ~ OTHER - Sealed Pursuant to Court Order;
Page 195 ~ OTHER - Sealed Pursuant to Court Order;
Page 196 ~ OTHER - Sealed Pursuant to Court Order;
Page 197 ~ OTHER - Sealed Pursuant to Court Order;
Page 198 ~ OTHER - Sealed Pursuant to Court Order;
Page 199 ~ OTHER - Sealed Pursuant to Court Order;
Page 200 ~ OTHER - Sealed Pursuant to Court Order;
Page 201 ~ OTHER - Sealed Pursuant to Court Order;
Page 202 ~ OTHER - Sealed Pursuant to Court Order;
Page 203 ~ OTHER - Sealed Pursuant to Court Order;
Page 204 ~ OTHER - Sealed Pursuant to Court Order;
Page 205 ~ OTHER - Sealed Pursuant to Court Order;
Page 206 ~ OTHER - Sealed Pursuant to Court Order;
Page 207 ~ OTHER - Sealed Pursuant to Court Order;
Page 208 ~ OTHER - Sealed Pursuant to Court Order;
Page 209 ~ OTHER - Sealed Pursuant to Court Order;
Page 210 ~ OTHER - Sealed Pursuant to Court Order;
Page 211 ~ OTHER - Sealed Pursuant to Court Order;
Page 212 ~ OTHER - Sealed Pursuant to Court Order;
Page 213 ~ OTHER - Sealed Pursuant to Court Order;
Page 214 ~ OTHER - Sealed Pursuant to Court Order;
Page 215 ~ OTHER - Sealed Pursuant to Court Order;
Page 216 ~ OTHER - Sealed Pursuant to Court Order;
Page 217 ~ OTHER - Sealed Pursuant to Court Order;
Page 218 ~ OTHER - Sealed Pursuant to Court Order;
Page 219 ~ OTHER - Sealed Pursuant to Court Order;
Page 220 ~ OTHER - Sealed Pursuant to Court Order;
Page 221 ~ OTHER - Sealed Pursuant to Court Order;
Page 222 ~ OTHER - Sealed Pursuant to Court Order;
Page 223 ~ OTHER - Sealed Pursuant to Court Order;
Page 224 ~ OTHER - Sealed Pursuant to Court Order;
Page 225 ~ OTHER - Sealed Pursuant to Court Order;
Page 226 ~ OTHER - Sealed Pursuant to Court Order;
Page 227 ~ OTHER - Sealed Pursuant to Court Order;
Page 228 ~ OTHER - Sealed Pursuant to Court Order;
Page 229 ~ OTHER - Sealed Pursuant to Court Order;
Page 236 ~ b6 - 1, 2; b7C - 1, 2; b7E - 6;
Page 237 ~ b6 - 1, 2; b7C - 1, 2; b7E - 6;
Page 238 ~ b6 - 1, 2; b7C - 1, 2; b7E - 6;
Page 239 ~ b6 - 1, 2; b7C - 1, 2; b7E - 6;

Page 240 ~ b6 - 1, 2; b7C - 1, 2; b7E - 6;
Page 241 ~ b6 - 1, 2; b7C - 1, 2; b7E - 6;
Page 242 ~ b6 - 2; b7C - 2; b7E - 6;
Page 250 ~ b6 - 2, 5; b7C - 2, 5;
Page 251 ~ b6 - 2, 5; b7C - 2, 5;
Page 252 ~ b6 - 2, 5; b7C - 2, 5;
Page 260 ~ b6 - 2, 5; b7C - 2, 5;
Page 261 ~ b6 - 2, 5; b7C - 2, 5;
Page 262 ~ b6 - 2, 5; b7C - 2, 5;
Page 263 ~ b6 - 2, 5; b7C - 2, 5;
Page 264 ~ b6 - 2, 5; b7C - 2, 5;
Page 265 ~ b6 - 2, 5; b7C - 2, 5;
Page 266 ~ b6 - 2, 5; b7C - 2, 5;
Page 267 ~ b6 - 2, 5; b7C - 2, 5;
Page 268 ~ b6 - 1, 2; b7C - 1, 2;
Page 269 ~ b6 - 1, 2; b7C - 1, 2;
Page 270 ~ b6 - 1, 2; b7C - 1, 2; OTHER - Sealed Pursuant to Court Order;
Page 276 ~ b6 - 2; b7C - 2;
Page 277 ~ b6 - 2; b7C - 2;
Page 278 ~ b6 - 2, 5; b7C - 2, 5;
Page 280 ~ b6 - 2; b7C - 2; b7E - 9; OTHER - Sealed Pursuant to Court Order;
Page 281 ~ b6 - 5; b7C - 5; b7E - 9; OTHER - Sealed Pursuant to Court Order;
Page 282 ~ b6 - 2, 5; b7C - 2, 5; b7E - 9; OTHER - Sealed Pursuant to Court Order;
Page 283 ~ b3 - 1; b6 - 1; b7C - 1; b7E - 9; OTHER - Sealed Pursuant to Court Order;
Page 284 ~ b3 - 1; b6 - 1; b7C - 1;
Page 286 ~ OTHER - Sealed Pursuant to Court Order;
Page 287 ~ b6 - 2; b7C - 2; OTHER - Sealed Pursuant to Court Order;
Page 288 ~ OTHER - Sealed Pursuant to Court Order;
Page 289 ~ b6 - 2; b7C - 2; OTHER - Sealed Pursuant to Court Order;
Page 290 ~ b6 - 1, 5; b7C - 1, 5; OTHER - Sealed Pursuant to Court Order;
Page 291 ~ b6 - 1, 5; b7C - 1, 5; OTHER - Sealed Pursuant to Court Order;
Page 293 ~ b6 - 1, 5; b7C - 1, 5; OTHER - Sealed Pursuant to Court Order;
Page 295 ~ OTHER - Sealed Pursuant to Court Order;
Page 296 ~ OTHER - Sealed Pursuant to Court Order;
Page 297 ~ b6 - 1; b7C - 1; b7E - 5; OTHER - Sealed Pursuant to Court Order;
Page 298 ~ b6 - 1; b7C - 1; b7E - 5; OTHER - Sealed Pursuant to Court Order;
Page 299 ~ b6 - 1; b7C - 1; b7E - 5; OTHER - Sealed Pursuant to Court Order;
Page 300 ~ b6 - 5; b7C - 5; OTHER - Sealed Pursuant to Court Order;
Page 301 ~ b6 - 5; b7C - 5; OTHER - Sealed Pursuant to Court Order;
Page 302 ~ b6 - 5; b7C - 5; OTHER - Sealed Pursuant to Court Order;
Page 303 ~ b6 - 5; b7C - 5; OTHER - Sealed Pursuant to Court Order;
Page 304 ~ b6 - 5; b7C - 5; OTHER - Sealed Pursuant to Court Order;
Page 305 ~ b6 - 5; b7C - 5; OTHER - Sealed Pursuant to Court Order;
Page 306 ~ b6 - 5; b7C - 5; OTHER - Sealed Pursuant to Court Order;
Page 307 ~ b6 - 5; b7C - 5; OTHER - Sealed Pursuant to Court Order;
Page 308 ~ b6 - 5; b7C - 5; OTHER - Sealed Pursuant to Court Order;
Page 309 ~ b6 - 5; b7C - 5; OTHER - Sealed Pursuant to Court Order;

Page 310 ~ b6 - 5; b7C - 5; OTHER - Sealed Pursuant to Court Order;
Page 311 ~ b6 - 5; b7C - 5; OTHER - Sealed Pursuant to Court Order;
Page 312 ~ b6 - 5; b7C - 5; OTHER - Sealed Pursuant to Court Order;
Page 313 ~ b6 - 5; b7C - 5; OTHER - Sealed Pursuant to Court Order;
Page 314 ~ b6 - 5; b7C - 5; OTHER - Sealed Pursuant to Court Order;
Page 315 ~ b6 - 5; b7C - 5; OTHER - Sealed Pursuant to Court Order;
Page 316 ~ b6 - 5; b7C - 5; OTHER - Sealed Pursuant to Court Order;
Page 317 ~ b6 - 5; b7C - 5; OTHER - Sealed Pursuant to Court Order;
Page 318 ~ b6 - 5; b7C - 5; OTHER - Sealed Pursuant to Court Order;
Page 319 ~ b6 - 5; b7C - 5; OTHER - Sealed Pursuant to Court Order;
Page 320 ~ b6 - 5; b7C - 5; OTHER - Sealed Pursuant to Court Order;
Page 321 ~ OTHER - Sealed Pursuant to Court Order;
Page 322 ~ OTHER - Sealed Pursuant to Court Order;
Page 323 ~ OTHER - Sealed Pursuant to Court Order;
Page 324 ~ b6 - 5; b7C - 5; OTHER - Sealed Pursuant to Court Order;
Page 325 ~ b6 - 5; b7C - 5; OTHER - Sealed Pursuant to Court Order;
Page 326 ~ b6 - 5; b7C - 5; OTHER - Sealed Pursuant to Court Order;
Page 327 ~ b6 - 5; b7C - 5; OTHER - Sealed Pursuant to Court Order;
Page 328 ~ b6 - 5; b7C - 5; OTHER - Sealed Pursuant to Court Order;
Page 329 ~ b6 - 5; b7C - 5; OTHER - Sealed Pursuant to Court Order;
Page 330 ~ b6 - 5; b7C - 5; OTHER - Sealed Pursuant to Court Order;
Page 331 ~ b6 - 5; b7C - 5; OTHER - Sealed Pursuant to Court Order;
Page 332 ~ b6 - 5; b7C - 5; OTHER - Sealed Pursuant to Court Order;
Page 333 ~ b6 - 5; b7C - 5; OTHER - Sealed Pursuant to Court Order;
Page 334 ~ b6 - 5; b7C - 5; OTHER - Sealed Pursuant to Court Order;
Page 335 ~ b6 - 5; b7C - 5; OTHER - Sealed Pursuant to Court Order;
Page 336 ~ b6 - 5; b7C - 5; OTHER - Sealed Pursuant to Court Order;
Page 337 ~ b6 - 5; b7C - 5; OTHER - Sealed Pursuant to Court Order;
Page 338 ~ b6 - 5; b7C - 5; OTHER - Sealed Pursuant to Court Order;
Page 339 ~ b6 - 5; b7C - 5; OTHER - Sealed Pursuant to Court Order;
Page 340 ~ b6 - 5; b7C - 5; OTHER - Sealed Pursuant to Court Order;
Page 341 ~ b6 - 5; b7C - 5; OTHER - Sealed Pursuant to Court Order;
Page 342 ~ b6 - 5; b7C - 5; OTHER - Sealed Pursuant to Court Order;
Page 343 ~ b6 - 5; b7C - 5; OTHER - Sealed Pursuant to Court Order;
Page 344 ~ b6 - 5; b7C - 5; OTHER - Sealed Pursuant to Court Order;
Page 345 ~ b6 - 5; b7C - 5; OTHER - Sealed Pursuant to Court Order;
Page 346 ~ b6 - 5; b7C - 5; OTHER - Sealed Pursuant to Court Order;
Page 347 ~ b6 - 5; b7C - 5; OTHER - Sealed Pursuant to Court Order;
Page 348 ~ b6 - 5; b7C - 5; OTHER - Sealed Pursuant to Court Order;
Page 349 ~ b6 - 5; b7C - 5; OTHER - Sealed Pursuant to Court Order;
Page 350 ~ b6 - 5; b7C - 5; OTHER - Sealed Pursuant to Court Order;
Page 351 ~ b6 - 5; b7C - 5; OTHER - Sealed Pursuant to Court Order;
Page 352 ~ b6 - 1, 5; b7C - 1, 5; b7E - 5; OTHER - Sealed Pursuant to Court Order;
Page 353 ~ b6 - 1, 5; b7C - 1, 5; b7E - 5; OTHER - Sealed Pursuant to Court Order;
Page 354 ~ b6 - 1, 5; b7C - 1, 5; b7E - 5; OTHER - Sealed Pursuant to Court Order;
Page 355 ~ b6 - 1, 5; b7C - 1, 5; b7E - 5; OTHER - Sealed Pursuant to Court Order;
Page 356 ~ b6 - 1, 5; b7C - 1, 5; b7E - 5; OTHER - Sealed Pursuant to Court Order;
Page 357 ~ b6 - 1, 5; b7C - 1, 5; b7E - 5; OTHER - Sealed Pursuant to Court Order;

Page 358 ~ b6 - 1, 5; b7C - 1, 5; b7E - 5; OTHER - Sealed Pursuant to Court Order;
Page 359 ~ b6 - 1, 5; b7C - 1, 5; b7E - 5; OTHER - Sealed Pursuant to Court Order;
Page 360 ~ b6 - 1, 5; b7C - 1, 5; b7E - 5; OTHER - Sealed Pursuant to Court Order;
Page 361 ~ b6 - 1, 5; b7C - 1, 5; b7E - 5; OTHER - Sealed Pursuant to Court Order;
Page 362 ~ b6 - 1, 5; b7C - 1, 5; b7E - 5; OTHER - Sealed Pursuant to Court Order;
Page 363 ~ b6 - 1, 5; b7C - 1, 5; b7E - 5; OTHER - Sealed Pursuant to Court Order;
Page 364 ~ b6 - 1, 5; b7C - 1, 5; b7E - 5; OTHER - Sealed Pursuant to Court Order;
Page 365 ~ b6 - 1, 5; b7C - 1, 5; b7E - 5; OTHER - Sealed Pursuant to Court Order;
Page 366 ~ b6 - 1, 5; b7C - 1, 5; b7E - 5; OTHER - Sealed Pursuant to Court Order;
Page 367 ~ b6 - 1, 5; b7C - 1, 5; b7E - 5; OTHER - Sealed Pursuant to Court Order;
Page 368 ~ b6 - 1, 5; b7C - 1, 5; b7E - 5; OTHER - Sealed Pursuant to Court Order;
Page 369 ~ b6 - 1, 5; b7C - 1, 5; b7E - 5; OTHER - Sealed Pursuant to Court Order;
Page 370 ~ b6 - 1, 5; b7C - 1, 5; b7E - 5; OTHER - Sealed Pursuant to Court Order;
Page 371 ~ b6 - 1, 5; b7C - 1, 5; b7E - 5; OTHER - Sealed Pursuant to Court Order;
Page 372 ~ b6 - 1, 5; b7C - 1, 5; b7E - 5; OTHER - Sealed Pursuant to Court Order;
Page 373 ~ b6 - 1, 5; b7C - 1, 5; b7E - 5; OTHER - Sealed Pursuant to Court Order;
Page 374 ~ b6 - 1, 5; b7C - 1, 5; b7E - 5; OTHER - Sealed Pursuant to Court Order;
Page 375 ~ b6 - 1; b7C - 1; b7E - 5; OTHER - Sealed Pursuant to Court Order;
Page 376 ~ b6 - 5; b7C - 5; OTHER - Sealed Pursuant to Court Order;
Page 377 ~ b6 - 5; b7C - 5; OTHER - Sealed Pursuant to Court Order;
Page 378 ~ OTHER - Sealed Pursuant to Court Order;
Page 379 ~ b6 - 1; b7C - 1; OTHER - Sealed Pursuant to Court Order;
Page 380 ~ OTHER - Sealed Pursuant to Court Order;
Page 381 ~ OTHER - Sealed Pursuant to Court Order;
Page 382 ~ OTHER - Sealed Pursuant to Court Order;
Page 383 ~ OTHER - Sealed Pursuant to Court Order;
Page 384 ~ OTHER - Sealed Pursuant to Court Order;
Page 385 ~ OTHER - Sealed Pursuant to Court Order;
Page 386 ~ OTHER - Sealed Pursuant to Court Order;
Page 387 ~ OTHER - Sealed Pursuant to Court Order;
Page 388 ~ OTHER - Sealed Pursuant to Court Order;
Page 389 ~ b6 - 5; b7C - 5; OTHER - Sealed Pursuant to Court Order;
Page 390 ~ b6 - 5; b7C - 5; OTHER - Sealed Pursuant to Court Order;
Page 391 ~ OTHER - Sealed Pursuant to Court Order;
Page 392 ~ OTHER - Sealed Pursuant to Court Order;
Page 394 ~ b6 - 5, 6; b7C - 5, 6;

Page 395 ~ b6 - 1, 2, 5, 6; b7C - 1, 2, 5, 6;
Page 397 ~ b6 - 1, 2; b7C - 1, 2; OTHER - Sealed Pursuant to Court Order;
Page 398 ~ b6 - 1, 2; b7C - 1, 2; OTHER - Sealed Pursuant to Court Order;
Page 399 ~ b6 - 1, 2; b7C - 1, 2; OTHER - Sealed Pursuant to Court Order;
Page 417 ~ b6 - 2, 5, 7; b7C - 2, 5, 7;

```
XXXXXXXXXXXXXXXXXXXXXXXX
X   Deleted Page(s)    X
X   No Duplication Fee X
X   For this Page      X
XXXXXXXXXXXXXXXXXXXXXXXX
```

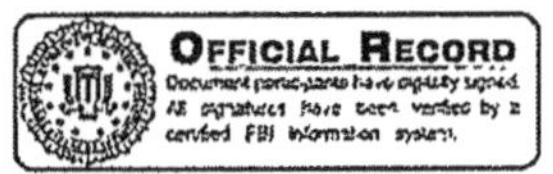

FEDERAL BUREAU OF INVESTIGATION

Date of entry 12/20/2012

On December 20, 2012, Special Agents (SAs) [redacted] and [redacted] [redacted] attempted to call telephone number [redacted] on two occasions. b6 -1, 2 b7C -1, 2

At approximately 12:45pm, SA [redacted] called telephone number [redacted] and received an automated notification that the call could not be completed as dialed. b6 -1, 2 b7C -1, 2 b7E -2

At approximately 12:50pm, SA [redacted] attempted to call telephone number [redacted] [redacted] and received an automated notification stating that, at the request of the subscriber, the phone did not accept incoming calls. b6 -1, 2 b7C -1, 2 b7E -2

Investigation on 12/20/2012 at New Haven, Connecticut, United States (Phone)

File # 4-NH-2619946 Date drafted 12/20/2012

by [redacted] b6 -1 b7C -1

4-NH-2619946 Serial 101

12/20/2012 FBI, 600 STATE STREET

12:45 PM START (CALL #1) NEW HAVEN, CT

VERSION:

"CALL CANNOT BE COMPLETED AS DIALED"

b6 -1, 2
b7C -1, 2
b7E -2

(CALL #2)

12:50PM -

MSG: ~~This phone doesn~~

This phone does not accept incoming calls at the request of the subscriber.

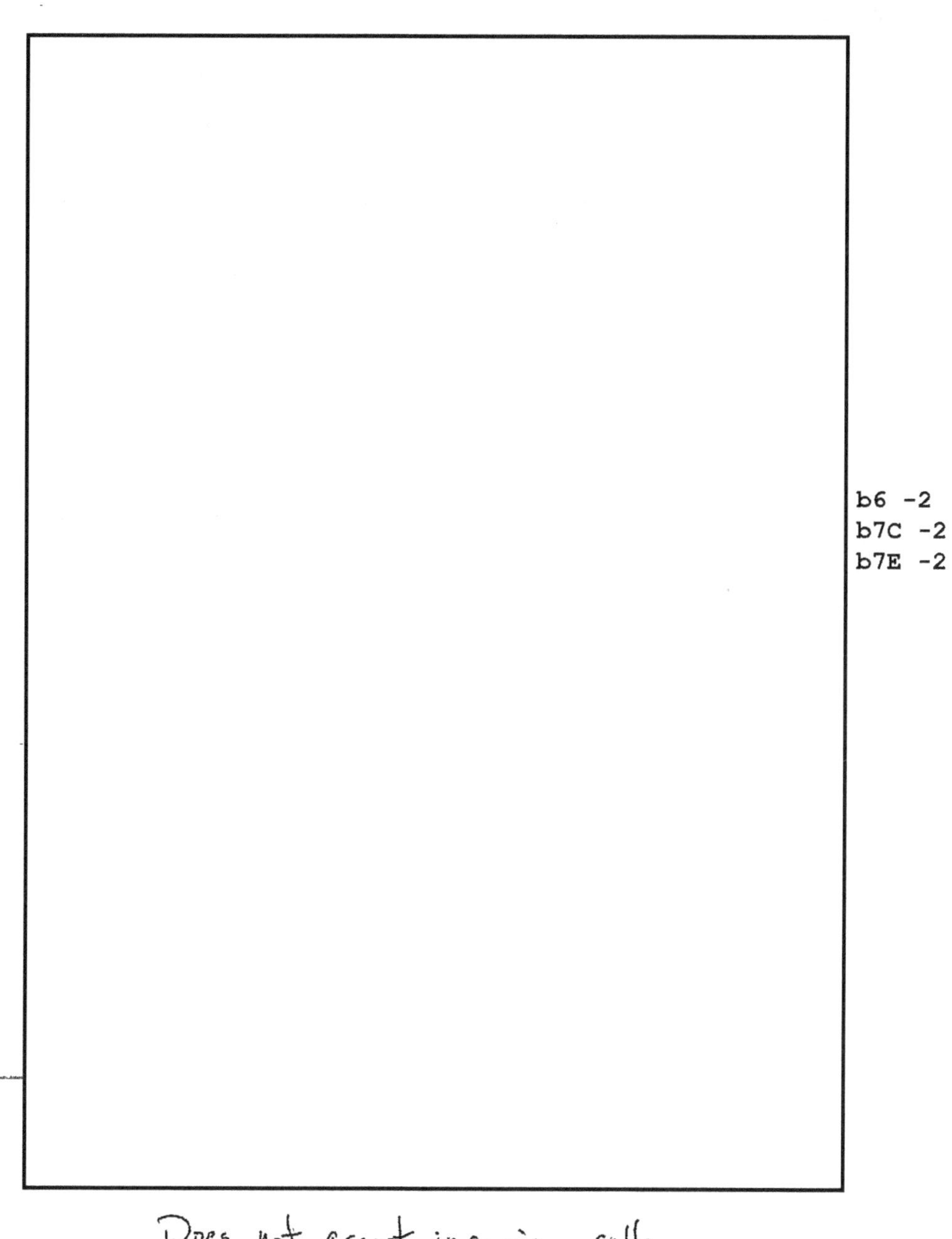

b6 -2
b7C -2
b7E -2

Does not accept incoming calls

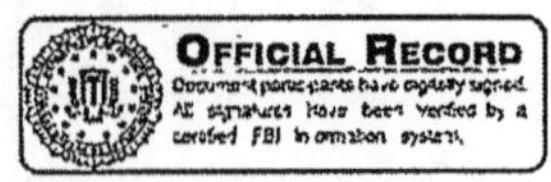

UNCLASSIFIED//~~FOUO~~

FEDERAL BUREAU OF INVESTIGATION

Date of entry 12/27/2012

b6 -1, 2
b7C -1, 2
OTHER Sealed Pursuant to Court Order

b6 -1, 2
b7C -1, 2
OTHER Sealed Pursuant to Court Order

UNCLASSIFIED//~~FOUO~~

Investigation on 12/23/2012 at [redacted] United States (In Person)

File # 4-NH-2619946 Date drafted 12/27/2012

by [redacted]

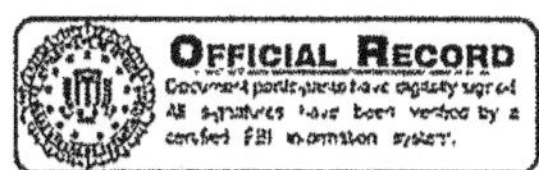

FEDERAL BUREAU OF INVESTIGATION

Date of entry 12/26/2012

[REDACTED] date of birth (DOB) [REDACTED] was interviewed at her residence located at [REDACTED] Also present during the interview was [REDACTED] After being advised of the identity of the interviewing Agents and the nature of the interview, [REDACTED] provided the following information: b6 -6 b7C -6

She advised that [REDACTED] friends of NANCY LANZA [REDACTED] [REDACTED] She stated that they maintained telephonic contact at [REDACTED] times a year and would try to see each other a couple times of year. b6 -6 b7C -6

[REDACTED] NANCY had spoke about her son ADAM LANZA. She had told [REDACTED] that although he had been diagnosed with Asperger's and personality disorder something had changed with him 3 months ago. NANCY had stated that ADAM had not left his bedroom in three months and would communicate with her by e-mail. NANCY had stated that he had become despondent and wanted to move to Seattle, Washington where it was dark and gloomy. NANCY advised [REDACTED] that they were going to put their Newtown house on the market in Spring of 2013 and move to Seattle to make ADAM happy. [REDACTED] stated that NANCY had boyfriend's but spent her life caring for ADAM and would not give up on him. NANCY had told the [REDACTED] that she had asked ADAM if he would miss her if something happened to her, and ADAM answered no, not really. NANCY seemed upset and concerned but thought his lack of emotion was part of his Aspergers. b6 -6 b7C -6

[REDACTED] stated that she knew that NANCY had one gun she would keep by her bed for protection. [REDACTED] stated that NANCY had gone to London last year and gone hawk hunting. [REDACTED] had never met ADAM and this summer when she visited NANCY she was not allowed in the house because it would upset and disrupt ADAM. [REDACTED] stated that she believed that NANCY did not work, maybe volunteered at the elementary b6 -5, 6 b7C -5, 6

Investigation on 12/15/2012 at [REDACTED] United States (In Person)

File # 4-NH-2619946 Date drafted 12/15/2012 b6 -1, 6 b7C -1, 6

by [REDACTED]

b6 -
b7C

school but was not a teacher. [redacted] stated that NANCY never told her if she had been assaulted by ADAM or was scared of him. [redacted] stated that NANCY never said if he was suicidal or had homicidal thoughts. [redacted] stated that ADAM was anti-social but had gone out with some friends in the past and would do DDR (Dance Dance Revolution) at a house or possible arcade or entertainment center in the Newtown area.

b6 -
b7C -

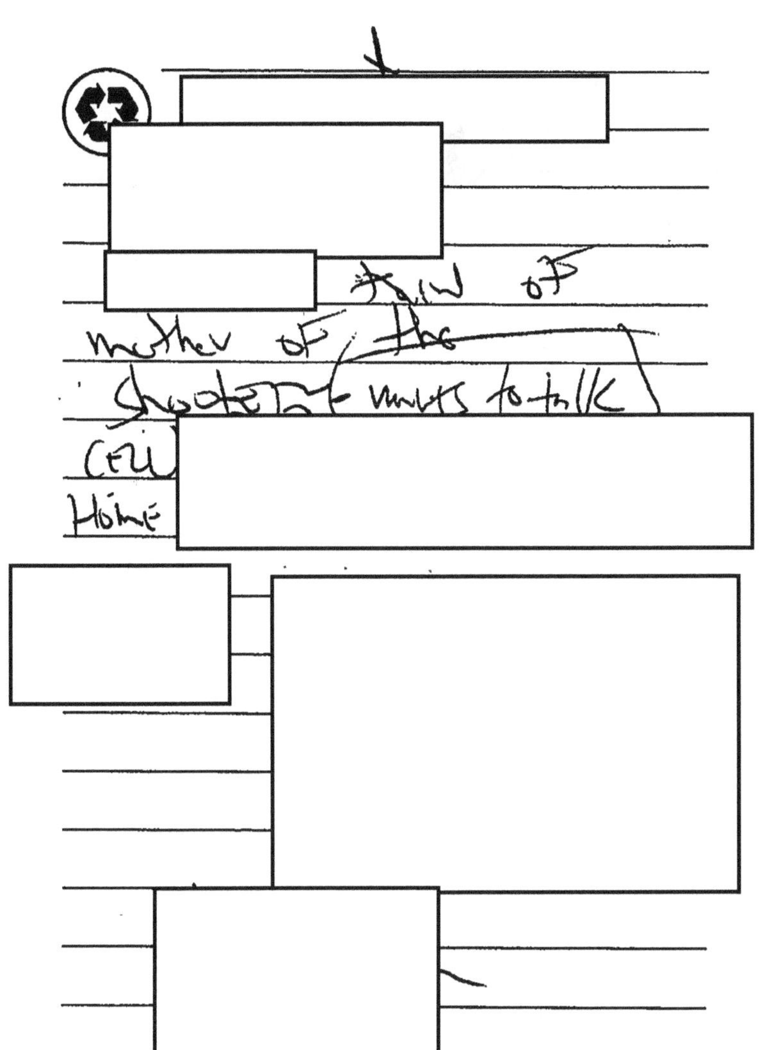

in law of
mother of the
shooter wants to talk
Cell
Home

b6 -6
b7C -6

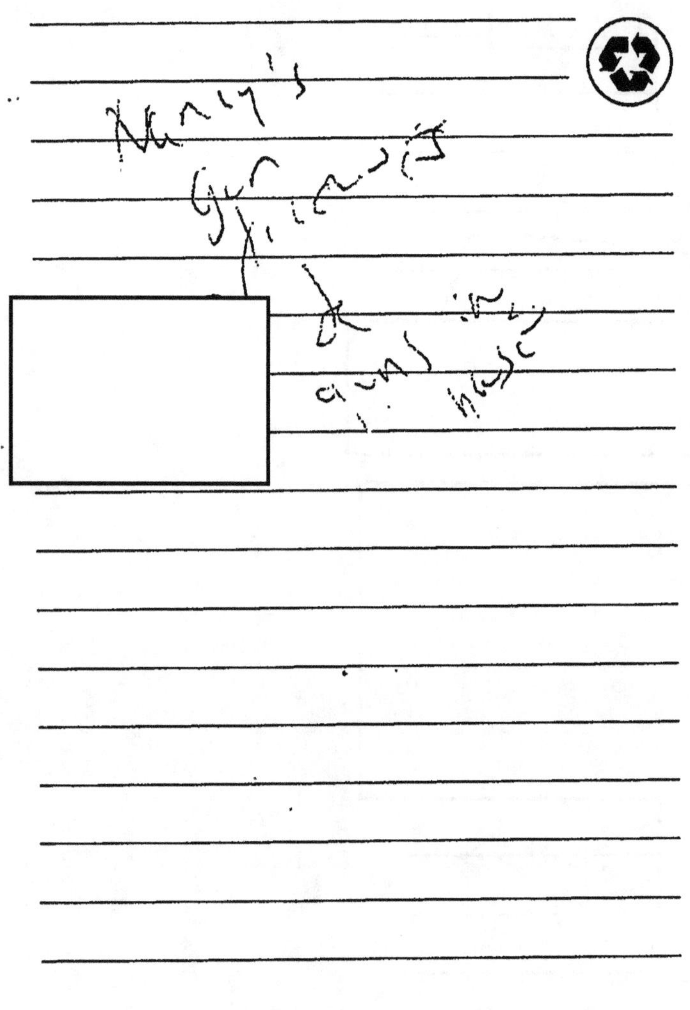

b6 -5
b7C -5

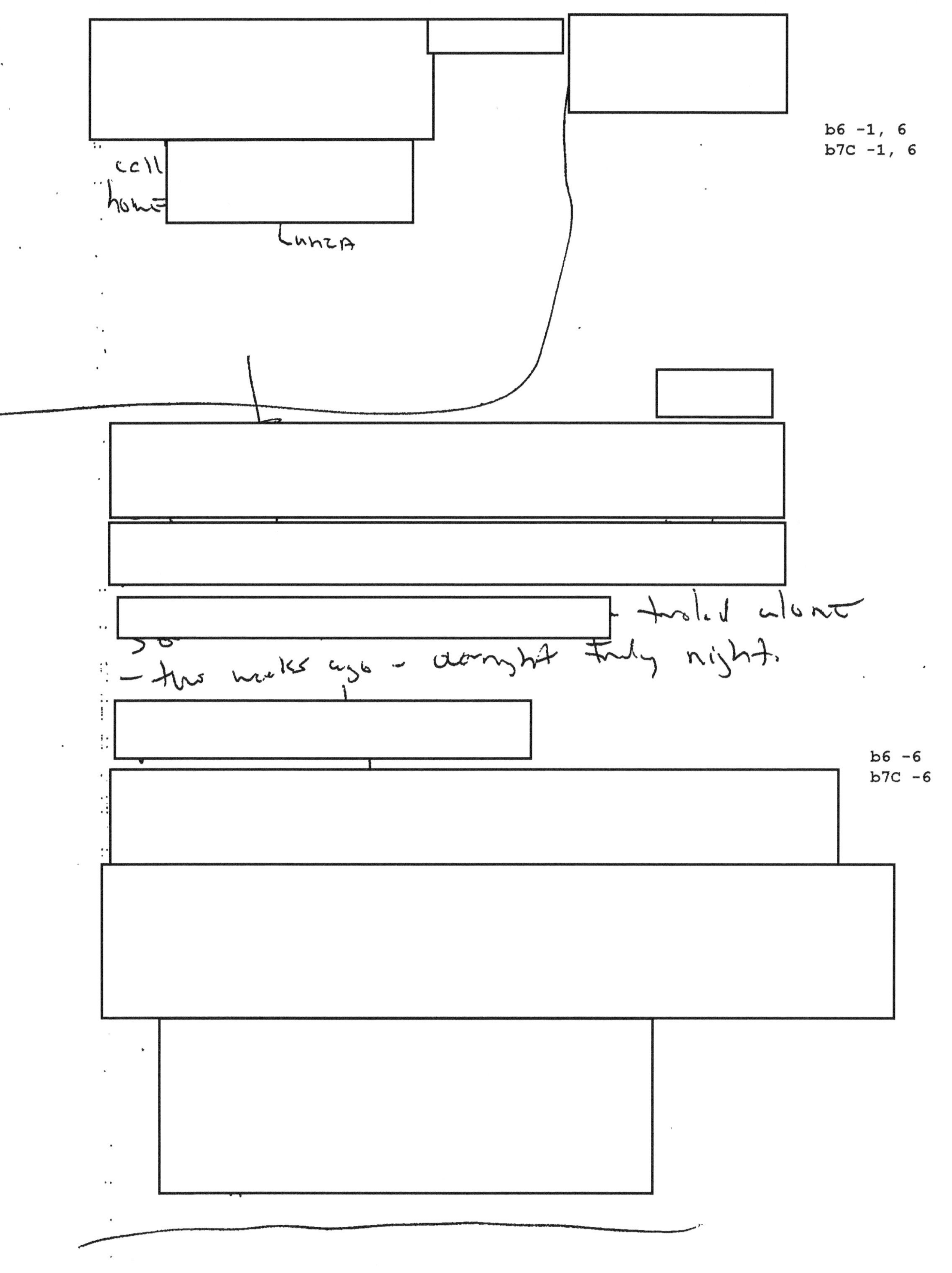

b6 -1, 6
b7C -1, 6

b6 -6
b7C -6

[redacted] time, she said [redacted] Adam always had anti-social behavior. (she knew that and was thinking of movement — he was despondent and hadn't left his bedroom in 3 months — She was a good parent (hypersensitivity) to sensory stimuli — (personality disorder) — (Asperger's Disease)

she wanted to move to Seattle cause he doesn't like the sun — [redacted] [redacted] (liked it gloomy — wouldn't eat in restaurants) —

have never met Adam [redacted] —
She was going to put house on market in Spring 2013

she said having a tough time — he hated Christmas —

communicate with her by e-mail — was in fear while in the house.

Nancy had a gun for protection (next to her bed) — [redacted]

violent videogames —

did hawk hunting in England — last year — She showed pictures in hunting gear

never went into house in Newtown — Adam wouldn't want anyone in

b6 -5
b7C -5

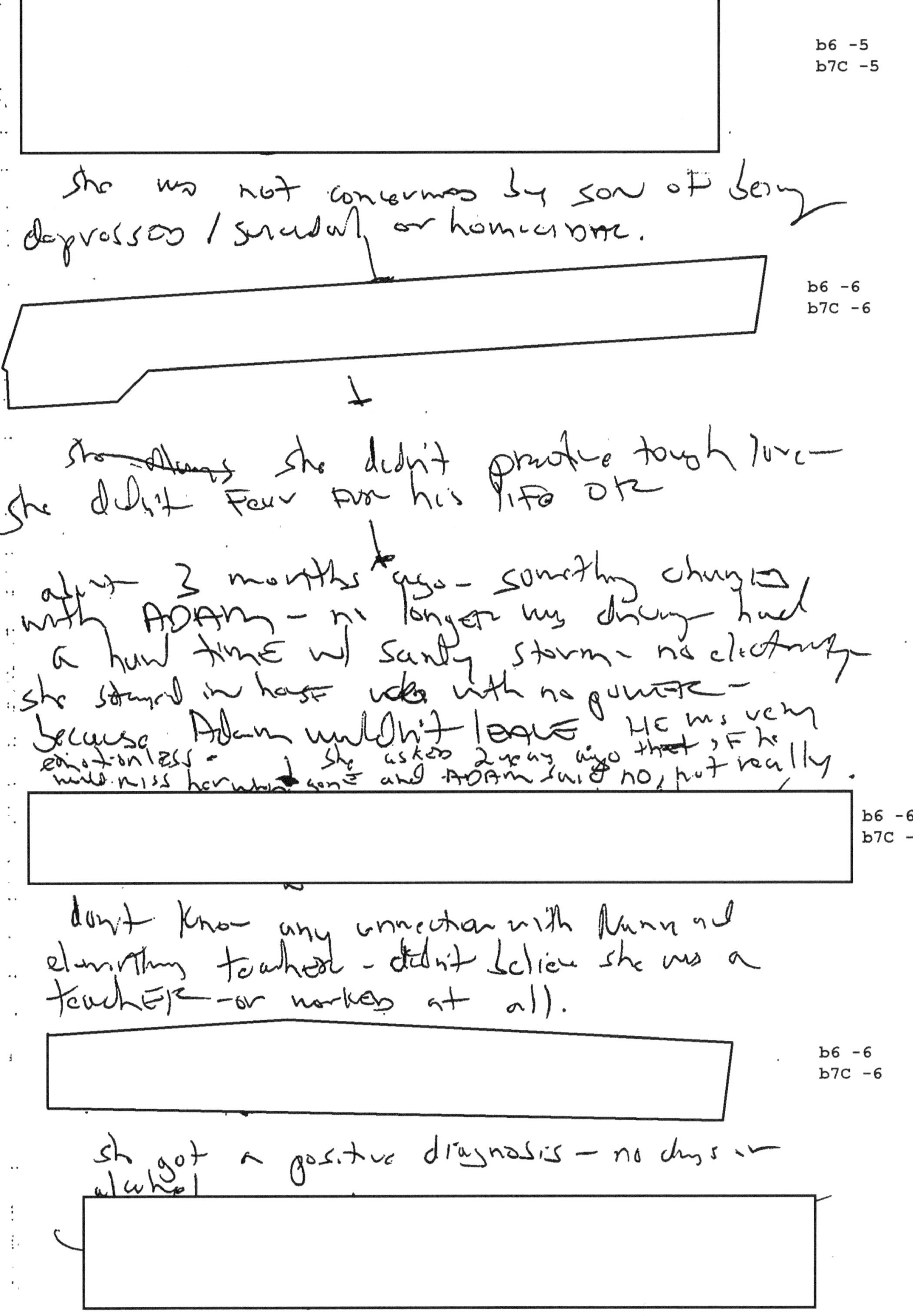

b6 -5
b7C -5

She was not concerned by son of being depressed / suicidal or homicidal.

b6 -6
b7C -6

She didn't practice tough love — she didn't fear for his life OK

about 3 months ago — something changed with ADAM — no longer was driving — had a hard time w/ Sandy storm — no electricity — she stayed in house with no power — because Adam wouldn't leave. HE was very emotionless — she asked 2 years ago that if he would miss her when gone and ADAM said no, not really.

b6 -6
b7C -6

don't know any connection with Nancy and elementary teacher — didn't believe she was a teacher — or worked at all.

b6 -6
b7C -6

She got a positive diagnosis — no drugs or alcohol

She didn't have any friends - none
type relationships - very intelligent - not
into sports.

Nov. 30 - 2 pictures on her
cell phone (of [redacted] Nancy) -
203-426-8167 - home
203-733-0943 = cell

11 pm - in kitchen

b6 -6
b7C -6

She would never give up on Adam -
had some boyfriends - but wouldn't get
serious.

Adam had issues w/ many classes & teachers
Didn't like kids in the hallway

FD-1087 (Rev. 5-8-10)

UNCLASSIFIED

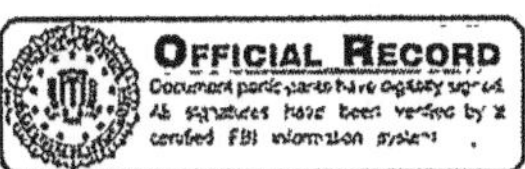

FEDERAL BUREAU OF INVESTIGATION

Evidence Log

Event Title: (U) Evidence received from the SD RCFL

Date: 12/27/2012

Approved By: [redacted]

Drafted By: [redacted]

b6 -1
b7C -1

Case ID #: 4-NH-2619946

(U) UNSUB(S)
Sandy Hook Elementary School
12 Dickinson St, Sandy Hook, CT-Victim
Firearms Act.
OO:NH

[redacted]

b7E -1

Acquired By: [redacted] on 12/27/2012

b6 -1
b7C -1

Acquired From: (U) SD RCFL

Receipt Given?: No

Holding Office: SAN DIEGO

Details: *No Details Provided*

[redacted]

b6 -1
b7C -1
OTHER Sealed Pursuant to Court Order

♦♦

UNCLASSIFIED

4-NH-2619946 Serial 104

FD-1057 (Rev. 5-8-10)

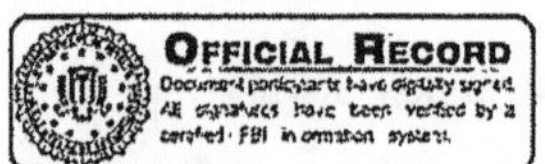

FEDERAL BUREAU OF INVESTIGATION

Electronic Communication

Title: (U) Request to transfer evidence from San Diego to New Haven

Date: 12/27/2012

To: [redacted]

From: NEW HAVEN
NH-10
Contact: [redacted]

b6 -1
b7C -1

Approved By: A/SSA [redacted]

Drafted By: [redacted]

Case ID #: 4-NH-2619946 (U) UNSUB(S)
Sandy Hook Elementary School
12 Dickinson St, Sandy Hook, CT-Victim
Firearms Act.
OO:NH

Synopsis: (U) Request to transfer CART evidence from San Diego to New Haven

[redacted]

b7E -1

Details:

[redacted]

b6 -2
b7C -2
OTHER Sealed Pursuant to Court Order

♦♦

4-NH-2619946 Serial 105

FD-71 (Rev. 5-8-10)

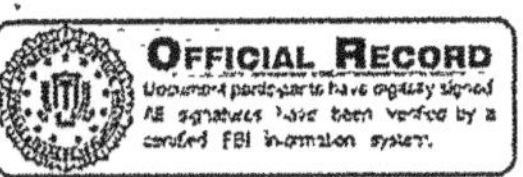

UNCLASSIFIED

FEDERAL BUREAU OF INVESTIGATION

Complaint Form

Title: (U) Complaint and Interview regarding [redacted]

Date: 12/20/2012

Approved By: A/SSRA [redacted]

b6 -1, 2, 4
b7C -1, 2, 4

Drafted By: [redacted]

Case ID #: 4-NH-2619946

(U) UNSUB(S)
Sandy Hook Elementary School
12 Dickinson St, Sandy Hook, CT-Victim
Firearms Act.
OO:NH

Complaint Synopsis: (U) To document results of the interview of [redacted] [redacted] predicated on a complaint by [redacted] who notified Little Rock Division that [redacted] posted Facebook/Internet comments in support of the December 14, 2012 massacre at Sandy Hook Elementary School in Newtown, Connecticut

b6 -2, 6
b7C -2, 6

[redacted]

b7E -1

Received On: 12/18/2012

Receipt Method: Telephone

Incident Type: Criminal Activity

Complaint Details:

On December 18, 2012, SSRA [redacted] Gulfport Resident Agency, telephonically notified SA [redacted] that the Little Rock Division received a complaint from [redacted] reporting that [redacted] posted a comment(s) on the Internet (Face Book) expressing support for the December 14, 2012 massacre at Sandy Hook Elementary School in Newtown, Connecticut. In the comment, [redacted] reportedly opined, "the death count was not high enough."

b6 -1, 2, 6
b7C -1, 2, 6

[redacted] white male, date of birth [redacted] social security account number [redacted] address [redacted]

b6 -2
b7C -2

UNCLASSIFIED

4-NH-2619946 Serial 106

b6 -2
b7C -2

[redacted] cellular telephone number [redacted] [redacted] was interviewed by Task Force Officer (TFO) [redacted] and TFO [redacted] [redacted] Pascagoula Resident Agency. The interview was conducted at the [redacted] [redacted] The identities of the interviewing agents and the nature of the interview were made known to [redacted]

b6 -2, 3,
b7C -2, 3

In summary, [redacted] identified himself as an Internet "TROLLER." [redacted] defined the term "TROLLER" as a person who, for entertainment value, enjoys finding Internet thread comments regarding sensitive issues and posts highly inflammatory and controversial opinions with the premeditated intent of agitating persons participating in the dialogue. Following initial denials [redacted] acknowledged posting a comment on his Face Book page regarding the Sandy Hook massacre and rendering his opinion that the death count was not high enough. Later during the interview, [redacted] recanted his admission and stated he did not have specific memory of posting the comment. [redacted] did admit having specific recollection of being involved in an Internet conversation thread regarding the massacre and mentally formulating the most heinous comment he could provide [redacted] opined the comment under inquiry is the most heinous comment he could think of and would be consistent with his thought process when "TROLLING."

b6 -2
b7C -2

[redacted]

b6 -2
b7C -

[redacted] described himself as an immature person who often uses poor

b6 -2
b7C -

b6 -2
b7C -2

judgment, [redacted] described the comment under inquiry as an act of extremely poor judgment [redacted] stated he sincerely objects to any form of violence, with the exception of violence required to defend ones family from physical harm. [redacted] adamantly denied ever committing a violent act. [redacted] also denied any past or present ideation of committing a violent act against a specific person or any ideation of committing a violent act based on opposition of a societal view. [redacted] denounced the December 14, 2012 massacre at Sandy Hook Elementary School in Newtown, Connecticut.

b6 -2
b7C -2

[redacted] acknowledged that he is the owner of a non-operational "Tech 9" handgun which he keeps to use as a ruse in the event an intruder ever enters his home and threatens the safety of his family [redacted] stated the non-operational "Tech 9" is the only weapon he owns.

b6 -2
b7C -2

[redacted]

b6 -2, 5
b7C -2, 5

Following their interview of [redacted] TFO [redacted] and TFO [redacted] interviewed [redacted] at her residence, [redacted] [redacted] voluntarily agreed to the interview and was made aware of the nature of the interview.

b6 -2, 3, 6
b7C -2, 3, 6

In summary [redacted] corroborated the information provided by [redacted] stated [redacted] [redacted] described [redacted] as non-violent. [redacted] validated that [redacted] is a "TROLLER" on the Internet. [redacted] stated [redacted] enjoys attempting to present himself as calloused even in his personal relationships. However, [redacted] routinely apologizes for inappropriate opinions and comments.

b6 -2, 6
b7C -2, 6

Title: (U) Complaint and Interview regarding [redacted] b6 -2 b7C -2
Re: 4-NH-2619946, 12/20/2012

A review of records on file with the National Crime Information Center (NCIC) revealed [redacted] has no identifiable criminal history. b6 -2 b7C -2

[redacted] b6 -2 b7C -2

◆◆

FD-302 (Rev. 5-8-10)

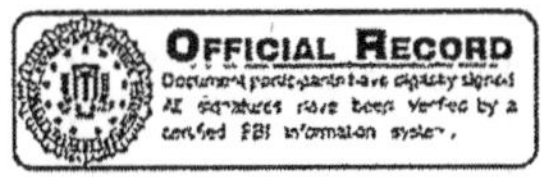

UNCLASSIFIED//~~FOUO~~

FEDERAL BUREAU OF INVESTIGATION

Date of entry 12/28/2012

b6 -1, 5
b7C -1, 5
OTHER Sealed Pursuant to Court Order

UNCLASSIFIED//~~F~~

Investigation on 12/14/2012 at New Haven, Connecticut, United States (

File # 4-NH-2619946 Date drafted 12/15/2012

by

4-NH-2619946 Serial 107

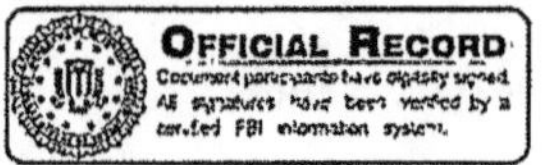

UNCLASSIFIED//~~FOUO~~

FEDERAL BUREAU OF INVESTIGATION

Date of entry 12/28/2012

UNCLASSIFIED//~~FOUO~~

b6 -2
b7C -2
OTHER Sealed Pursuant to Court Order

Investigation on 12/18/2012 at New Haven, Connecticut, United States ( )

File # 4-NH-2619946

Date drafted 12/19/2012

by

b6 -1
b7C -1

This document contains neither recommendations nor conclusions of the FBI. It is the property of the FBI and is loaned to your agency; it and its contents are not to be distributed outside your agency.

4-NH-2619946 Serial 108

FD-1057 (Rev. 5-8-10)

UNCLASSIFIED

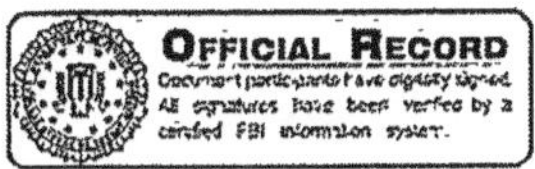

FEDERAL BUREAU OF INVESTIGATION

Electronic Communication

Title: (U) Internet Activity Report number [redacted] **Date:** 12/30/2012 b6 -2 b7C -2 b7E -7

From: COUNTERTERRORISM [redacted]
Contact: [redacted]

Approved By: A/UC [redacted] b6 -1 b7C -1

Drafted By: [redacted]

Case ID #: 4-NH-2619946 (U) UNSUB(S)
Sandy Hook Elementary School
12 Dickinson St, Sandy Hook, CT-Victim
Firearms Act.
OO:NH

Synopsis: (U) Internet Activity Report number [redacted] The information contained herein was received on the FBI's Internet web site as possibly being related to terrorist or other criminal activity. The submitted text has been incorporated into this communication. b6 -2 b7C -2

[redacted] b7E -1, 3, 7

Administrative Notes: [redacted]

[redacted]

Details:

On 12/27/2012, an Anonymous Individual (AI) reported that [redacted] [redacted] Date of Birth [redacted] told Adam Lanza to shoot up the school. b6 -2 b7C -2

[redacted] b6 -2 b7C -2 b7E -3

UNCLASSIFIED

Sandy Hook-1768

4-NH-2619946 Serial 109

Title: (U) Internet Activity Report number
Re: 4-NH-2619946, 12/30/2012

b6 -
b7C
b7E

♦♦

b6 -2
b7C -2

Title: (U) Internet Activity Report number [redacted]
Re: 4-NH-2619946, 12/30/2012

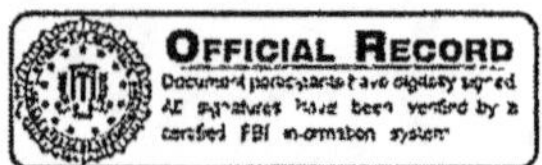

UNCLASSIFIED//~~FOUO~~

FEDERAL BUREAU OF INVESTIGATION

Electronic Communication

Title: (U//~~FOUO~~) NH [redacted] based on consent. **Date:** 12/17/2012 b6 -2 b7C -2 b7E -7

From: NEW HAVEN
NH-10
Contact: [redacted]

Approved By: [redacted] b6 -1 b7C -1

Drafted By: [redacted]

Case ID #: 4-NH-2619946 (U) UNSUB(S)
Sandy Hook Elementary School
12 Dickinson St, Sandy Hook, CT-Victim
Firearms Act.
OO:NH

[redacted] b7E -4

LAW ENFORCEMENT SENSITIVE

This information is the property of the FBI and may be distributed to state, tribal, or local government law enforcement officials with a need-to-know. Further distribution without FBI authorization is prohibited. Precautions should be taken to ensure this information is stored and/or destroyed in a manner that precludes unauthorized access.

Synopsis: (U//~~FOUO~~) New Haven [redacted] SA [redacted] pursuant to a consensual search [redacted] b6 -1 b7C - b7E -

[redacted] b7E -

Administrative Notes: (U//~~FOUO~~) [redacted] is filed in a 1A. On the date the search was executed, SA [redacted] b6 -1 b7C -

UNCLASSIFIED//~~FOUO~~

4-NH-2619946 Serial 11D

Title: (U//~~FOUO~~) NH [redacted] [redacted] based on consent.

Re: 4-NH-2619946, 12/17/2012

b6 -2
b7C -2
b7E -7

Enclosure(s): Enclosed are the following items:

1. (U//~~FOUO~~) [redacted]

b6 -2
b7C -2
b7E -7

Details:

[redacted]

b6 -1, 2, 5
b7C -1, 2,
b7E -6, 7

Title: (U//~~FOUO)~~ NH [redacted] [redacted] based on consent.
Re: 4-NH-2619946, 12/17/2012

b6 -2
b7C -
b7E -

[redacted]

b7E -

[redacted] original notes associated with the processing are maintained in a 1A. b7E -

♦♦

FD-302 (Rev. 5-8-10)

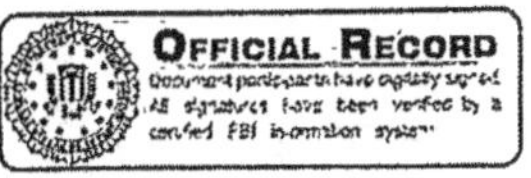

FEDERAL BUREAU OF INVESTIGATION

Date of entry 12/21/2012

CHIEF DONALD BRIGGS, KINGSTON POLICE DEPARTMENT (KPD), was interviewed at KPD, 16 Main Street, Kingston, New Hampshire(NH). After being advised of the identity of the interviewing Agents and the nature of the interview, CHIEF BRIGGS provided the following information:

[redacted] NANCY LANZA (nee CHAMPION), a victim of the December 14, 2012 mass shooting incident in Newtown, Connecticut (CT). [redacted] ADAM LANZA, NANCY LANZA's son [redacted] b6 -5 b7C -5

[redacted] b6 -5 b7C -5

[redacted] CHIEF BRIGGS could not recall if NANCY LANZA's son, ADAM LANZA, ever attended BAKIE SCHOOL. [redacted] b6 -5 b7C -5

[redacted] b6 -5 b7C -5

When NANCY LANZA (nee CHAMPION) married [redacted] built a home on the family homestead property and resided at what became [redacted] for several years until they moved to CT about 12 years ago. [redacted] b6 -5 b7C -5

Investigation on 12/14/2012 at Kingston, New Hampshire, United States (In Person)

File # 4-NH-2619946 Date drafted 12/27/2012

by [redacted] b6 -1 b7C -1

4-NH-2619946 Serial 111

b6 -
b7C

CHIEF BRIGGS provided no further information

b6 -
b7C

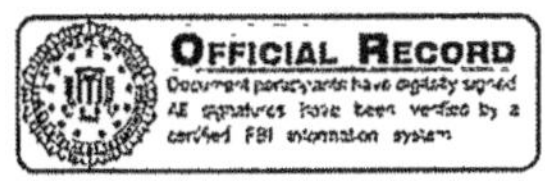

UNCLASSIFIED//~~FOUO~~

FEDERAL BUREAU OF INVESTIGATION

Date of entry 12/26/2012

On 12/23/2012, Special Agents of the Federal Bureau of Investigation (FBI) interviewed [redacted] SSAN [redacted] DOB [redacted] mobile telephone number [redacted] at her residence [redacted]

b6 -2
b7C -2
OTHER Sealed Pursuant to Court Order

[redacted] At that time, SA [redacted] and SA [redacted] advised [redacted] that they were working on the case involving a mass murder of school children and teachers in Newtown, Connecticut. [redacted] acknowledged that she was aware of the case and she listened carefully and sat relatively quietly, not asking any questions. [redacted]

b6 -1, 2
b7C -1, 2
OTHER Sealed Pursuant to Court Order

most fixated and disturbed internet associate she had ever encountered.

[redacted] agreed to speak to agents concerning this issue. [redacted] At approximately 9:13AM, SA [redacted] SA [redacted] and SA [redacted] met with [redacted] to [redacted] After being advised of the identities of the interviewing agents and the nature of the interview, [redacted] provided the following information:

b6 -1, 2
b7C -1, 2
OTHER Sealed Pursuant to Court Order

UNCLASSIFIED//~~FOUO~~

Investigation on 12/23/2012 at [redacted] United States (In Person)

File # 4-NH-2619946 Date drafted 12/25/2012

by [redacted]

b6 -
b7C

[redacted] first became aware of LANZA approximately two to two and a half years ago when she observed one of his postings on the web site columbinesupermassacrerpg.com. [redacted] LANZA's postings convinced [redacted] that he was very knowledgeable of Columbine and other murder events. [redacted] was aware that LANZA was working on a list, or spreadsheet, meticulously documenting the details of hundreds of spree killings and mass murders. After her first contact with LANZA, [redacted] communicated with him regularly, perhaps once a month on average, until early December 2012. [redacted] never communicated in any way other than emails and web postings. She never called LANZA by telephone or voice over internet. Similarly, she never engaged in instant messaging or other real time communication with LANZA.

b6 -
b7C

Throughout her online relationship with LANZA, [redacted] never had any idea who he was and did not know his first or last name. LANZA was a secretive guy. [redacted] was not sure where LANZA lived, but guessed it was in the New York area because he had referenced some murders that happened there. LANZA spoke very little about his family and personal life [redacted] also recalled LANZA posting that he liked the Harry Potter stories when he was a kid. LANZA liked the Harry Potter idea that at the age of eleven, the kids were taken away from their families.

b6 -
b7C

Although [redacted] did not know LANZA's true identity, over the years she became more familiar with his personality and thinking [redacted] found LANZA to have a distinct personality. She described LANZA as "the wierdest person online." He was singularly focused and obsessed with mass murders and spree killings. LANZA devoted almost all of his internet activity to researching and discussing mass murders and spree killings. From those communications, [redacted] came to know LANZA as extremely intelligent and serious. [redacted] also came to know LANZA as depressed and cynical regarding his view of life and people. LANZA had a very negative world view.

b6 -
b7C

LANZA's postings and messages made it clear that he was disturbed and depressed. [redacted] described it as a "functional depression." As far as [redacted] knew, LANZA had no effective coping mechanism to deal with his depression, but he was able to function. He seemed to "wallow" in it and ride out the low periods by hiding in his room and sleeping for 12 hours or more at a time. LANZA seemed to have no friends or people he could turn to for support or assistance and did not appear to have any enjoyment of life. LANZA portrayed himself as someone who lived an isolated life in which he was always in discomfort. LANZA believed he had issues with his sensory

b6 -
b7C

 b6 -2 b7C -2

inputs. He found food unappealing in terms of its taste and texture. He also complained that he could not find clothing that fit him comfortably. LANZA also wrote that light itself bothered him, writing that he hated natural light because it hurts his eyes. For that reason, he avoided daylight and stayed as much as he could in his house. LANZA did not consider death to be a negative. He saw it as an escape from his joyless existence. LANZA showed some interest in music, but only if it related in some way to spree killing or mass murder. Although LANZA occasionally wrote about committing suicide, [redacted] believed he was somehow managing his depression. b6 -2 b7C -2

LANZA made some reference to sexuality in his postings and writings. LANZA wrote that he believed he might be asexual. He wrote that he was sexually attracted to maybe only one or two people in his entire life and it was really not a factor for him. LANZA wrote at least one lengthy email to [redacted] expressing his views on pedophelia. LANZA possessed a hatred of pedophiles. He viewed pedophiles as a "threat" that would "influence a child." While he acknowledged it "could be unhealthy", LANZA described adult/child sexual relationships as possibly beneficial to both parties. LANZA felt "pity" for children. LANZA did not express any sexual interest of his own in children. b6 -2 b7C -2

In his writings, LANZA expressed a lot about his view of the world. For the most part, LANZA was angry and resentful about society's structure. LANZA thought of those who were successful in society as selfish, cruel and controlling. He believed that those in positions of authority were inappropriately controlling children and young adults. He believed that teachers and parents, too, were improperly controlling, smothering, and intentionally molding their students and children. LANZA thought of teachers as an extension of parents' control over children. Regarding children, [redacted] stated that LANZA "felt sorry for them." LANZA also felt that that people were "needlessly cruel" to animals. For that reason, he said he was a vegan. b6 -2 b7C -2

LANZA believed that spree killings and mass murders were merely a symptom caused by a broken society. LANZA talked about school killings and those who committed them with respect and understanding. To discuss these issues, LANZA used various forums. He used the e-mail addresses genericregistryemail@gmail.com and cryinghampster@yahoo.com. LANZA used the screen name "smiggles" on shockedbeyondbelief.com, which was preceded by columbinesupermassacrerpg.com. LANZA communicated regularly until the summer of 2012, when LANZA's postings stopped. LANZA later wrote that he had "committed virtual suicide." He wrote that he had destroyed the hard drive of his computer and lost all of his virtual identities. It took LANZA some time to get himself back online after the virtual suicide.

b6
b7C

At one time, LANZA was posting on Tumblr.com. LANZA was posting under the names "gayfortimk" (a reference to murderer TIM KRETSCHMER) and "queerforkimveer" (a reference to spree killer KIMVEER GILL). In those postings, [redacted] read about some nightmares that LANZA said he had. In one, LANZA wrote that in one of his nightmares, he was at a school and someone in his class shoved LANZA. In the dream, LANZA's teacher punished LANZA, not the person who shoved him. LANZA stormed out of the classroom, screaming at the teacher. In a second dream, LANZA was in a school when he saw some kids bullying another kid. The bullies were dumping out the backpack of the victim kid. The victim then took a gun out and started shooting the bullies. In the dream, LANZA was trying to help the shooter by telling him to watch out for people behind him who would try to stop him. In a third dream, LANZA said he was in mall when a mall shooting started. LANZA was in a shoe store and found himself with the shooter. LANZA was talking to the shooter and trying to convince the shooter to commit suicide before the police were able to arrest him.

b6
b7C

LANZA also posted some audio of himself calling into an internet radio show hosted by JOHN ZIRZAN. LANZA identified himself as GREG and called in about a story on the show about a chimpanzee or monkey was had been raised like a child. One day, the monkey was acting odd, so someone took him on a car ride, which usually calmed the monkey down. On this day, the monkey did not calm down and attacked a person, tearing the person's face off. LANZA was arguing that people were interpreting the monkey's reaction wrong on the radio show. In fact, the monkey was probably under great pressure and did not have any ability to express it. Having no way to relieve the pressure through expression, the monkey acted out in the only way it could and injured the person.

[redacted] is sure that the Tumblr dream postings and the audio posting were done by LANZA. She recognized the way he spoke and also messaged LANZA on Tumblr. At some time, LANZA confirmed to [redacted] that he had made the dream postings and the audio posting. LANZA deleted the Tumblr postings in or about November 2012.

b6
b7C

From all [redacted] knew about LANZA, he was a very unhappy and disturbed person, who was focused completely on spree killings and mass murders. Though LANZA was clearly obsessed with these ideas, [redacted] never saw anything in LANZA's writings that could be seen as direct indications that he would act out himself and commit a mass murder. LANZA demonstrated a "lack of enthusiasm." LANZA "casually mentioned suicide" but never openly expressed a desire to commit suicide. LANZA never smoked, consumed alcohol, or used drugs. LANZA never threatened to harm anyone and never wrote that he had guns or weapons in his home. His postings revealed he had extensive knowledge of the guns and ammunition that had been used in historical mass

b6
b7C

b6 -2
b7C -2

murders and spree killings, but never an indication that he possessed or used firearms himself.

Looking back at what she knew about LANZA, [redacted] is not shocked that he committed mass murder in Newtown. [redacted] does not know why LANZA would have chosen that time of place to commit the murders. He never suggested in any way that he was about to kill anyone. When asked why [redacted] thought that LANZA would have taken the lives of so many young and innocent children, [redacted] said she would guess that LANZA would have thought he was "saving them" or "protecting them." LANZA believed he was "taking them away from harmful influences," or those individuals who would control the children. Because he believed that death was an "escape from the pressures" of life, he could have thought he was helping the children that he killed. LANZA thought the children were "brain washed." LANZA would have thought differently about the teachers and adults who were killed. He would have considered them as controlling forces that "don't genuinely care" who needed to be killed. Even if LANZA saw a teacher trying to protect a child, he would have seen that act as an effort by the teacher to protect her "property" and not as an act of genuine love or devotion. Having learned that LANZA was responsible for the Newtown murders, [redacted] described LANZA as "more fucked up than I thought."

b6 -2
b7C -2

[redacted]

b6 -2
b7C -2

[redacted]

b6 -2, 5
b7C -2, 5

b6 -2
b7C -2

b6 -1,
b7C -1

b6 -
b7C

was cooperative

b6 -2
b7C -2
OTHER Sealed Pursuant to Court Order

12/23/2012
9:13a

b6 -1, 2
b7C -1, 2

Never knew GR was Adam - never knew
muttered children

Columbine Super Massacre RPG met
spree shootings - want to learn
Read "Columbine" 2-3 yrs ago

AL making spreadsheet - 2-3 yrs.
impression lived in NY
talk for week - drop off.
more frequent earlier this year

AL impression - very depressed cynical view of life/people
not out of control.
"functional depression"
didn't talk @ self - single mind
no knowledge of diagnosis
lost interest - moving on.

Troubling AL most? vegan 12 yrs people needlessly cruel

Children - feelings - dealt w/ pedophilia
felt sorry for them.

Mentioned own childhood in postings - Harry Potter be taken away

b6
b7C

No speaking, skype no IM
Never told real name
wierdest person online intelligent focused obsessed w/ spree killin

One primary - James Huberty

b6 -2, 5
b7C -2, 5

b7E

AL view: Society broken - people strike back.

AL Not focused on school shooting
Tim Krishner) AL mentioned
Peca Erik Avayan)

stumbled AL "gayfortimk" "queerfor kimveer" GN

AL experiences - dream/nightmares. • Tumblr • website read and deleted.

(1) controlling influence
impression bullied in school HS.
teacher punish him

(2) watch bully friend
boy had gun & spree shoot
helping friend (no gun)
Adam watching

(3) Mall shooting dream - shoestore w/ shooter - talk shooter into killing self
avoid jail

b7E -9

Sandy Hook-

Called to John Zerzan radio
≈ 1 year ago *call in talk @ case chimpanzee
chimp act odd - take for car ride
chimp attack friend was "Greg"
people interpret wrong - monkey give into pressure

b7E -9

b6 -2
b7C -2

on board AL post fact not opinion
spree kill - a type of mass murder 1 pers 1 location
mass murder - death 4+

talked to GR email no one known.
Not that interested in Columbine

b6 -5
b7C -5

Not interested in personal sharing on posts,
First name / state.

(AL) talk @ parents - smothering trying to mold.
mention had ~~mom~~ - in dream

AL Living conditions - hated natural light online alot
hurt eyes

(AL) Celebrate - never mentioned
post historic facts on 4/20 etc.

b6 -2, 5
b7C -2, 5

don't check email religiously
casually mentioned suicide lack of enthusiasm
consistent behavior over time.
~~ne~~ depressed / surpressed managed
unsure how relieved stress - focus on spree killings.
AL never used alc / drugs / smoke

AL lying on floor. ✓

Never mentioned: friends / dating.
thought "Asexual"
No religion - assume athiest - controlling influence
Comm - unsure shock beyond belief
Smiggles cryinghampster@yahoo. in Summer
GR email destroyed HD. in summer.
How destroy - commit virtual suicide - summer's 12

no idea if lying - being honest - impression

why not over summer - no idea no sense
deleted tumblr account Nov timeframe

b6 -2
b7C -2

Can use mom/dad computer.
Harry Potter books - movie - spree shootings
TV - ...
unsure gamer.

10:23 shows cooperation -

b6 -2
b7C -2

Plan to kill - "God no"
AL - sleep 12hrs - food unappealing
AL abuse - no indication
AL pedo - hatred of pedo - view as threat. - influence child
could be unhealthy - possible/beneficial to both parties
felt "pity" for children.
Killing kids was saving them "taking away from harmful influences."
"protecting them"
every thing AL wrote.. death escape from pressures.
spree killer should take own life

(AL) Children "brain washed"
Teacher "don't genuinely care" "protecting property"

Gun discussion - Columbine board
"paranoid" didn't
knowledge of guns re: spree killing

Re feeling AL "More F'd up than I thought"
encouraging discussion of beliefs - "serve as audience for ideas"
doesn't feel guilty

b6 -2,
b7C -2,

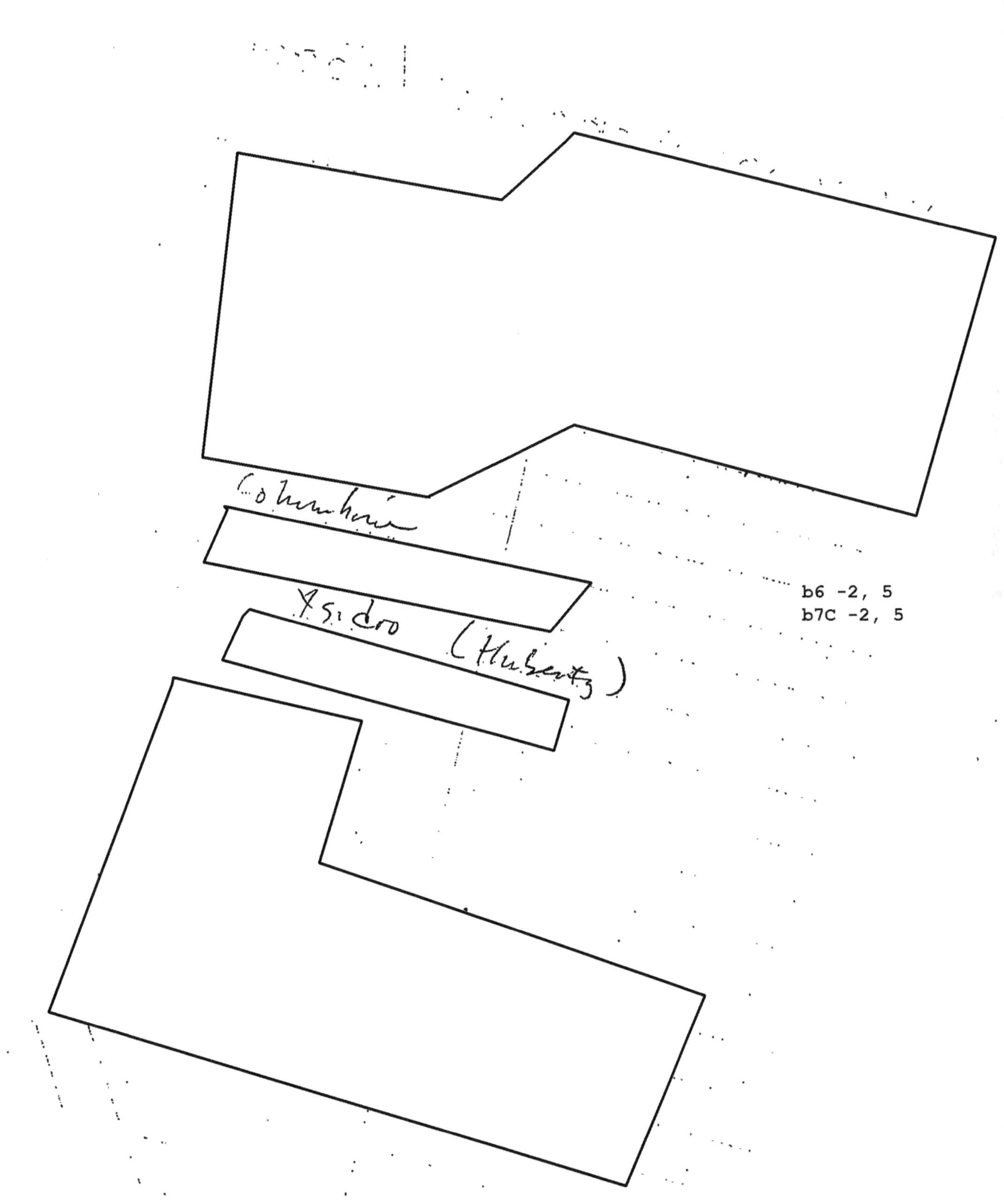

Columbia
Ysidro (Hubertz)
b6 -2, 5
b7C -2, 5

Message Columbine Spree Massacre RPG

[illegible] - She recalls [redacted]

At Least 2-7½ yrs ago. He kept [illegible]

— He was working on the list
on and off.
A month then regularly.

→ Mental - very depressed. Cynical.
negative world view.
Very serious. Single minded. b6 -2 b7C -2

[redacted] lost interest —
Adam was Vegan. People mistreating animals
animals suffering.
Pedophilia / [illegible]

He was really into Harry Potter

[redacted] b6 -2 b7C -2

Smart + focused Obsessed
Obsessed in Spree Killings.
James Holmes - no recall

Not to explain it.
Spree Killings are a Symptom

→ Focused on aversion of [illegible] culture
Tom Cruise —
[illegible] Eric Avinger —

Mentioned Them.
He had dreams, sometimes about [illegible]
Conformity.
He was in [illegible]

Blog site: Tumbler. Adam used gay for Tim K.

Showed in school. teacher [illegible] ...
[illegible] [illegible] person
storms out screams at [illegible]
(2) In hall. watching people [illegible]
a friend. [illegible] [illegible]
upside down
Kid later had a gun
Adam [illegible] watch a [illegible]
(1) [illegible]. [illegible] [illegible] mall. A
in a shoe store w/ shooter
Trying to talk the guy out
[illegible] himself so he [illegible] +
get [illegible]

Tim Kretschmer — [illegible] spree

Queer for Kinveer. (Kinveer bill)

writing style. Audio post, too

— He called a radio show a year ago.
John Zirzma radio show
He called in about. Monkey [illegible]
like a [illegible] [illegible] one day the
Chimp acted odd, [illegible]
car rider called [illegible] [illegible].
called friend to calm down.
— I D'd as Greg. He said people
interpret monkey as evil.
no monkey as pet
Adam [illegible] monkey [illegible] into
pressure + couldn't [illegible]

Call in on computer

Columbine super
Columbine guide. com
postings. [illegible]

b6 -2
b7C -2

- Shocked beyond belief.

- Adam not that interested in Columbine

- parents - generally try to mold the

~~He hated natural light. Hurts his eyes.~~

→ maybe. Share info

→ [redacted] April 20, Columbine
August — Hillcrest
Public Hawkins

Adam - talked about suicide
depressed - most men [illegible]
Adam appropriate [illegible]
no drugs

- He watched in it
no friends. dating
Hid in his room.
thought he was asexual.

—

Tumbler
Generic reg
(cryinghamster@yahoo.ca)
— over this summer
He destroyed his hard drive
Committed "virtual suicide" —
destroyed his identity.

b6 -2
b7C -2

no sense of
deleted Tumblr in Nov or earlier
from sleep for 12 hours.
found food unappealing. didn't like
taste, texture.
sensory issues
clothes not comfortable.
All music related to speech
pedophilia - never said he is it
said it could be helpful.
—>
Likes the philosophy - sorrowing posts.
death not negative
-> Death is an escape
A - Posted lots on guns. never said he
owned them
- memorized details

b6 -2
b7C -2

FD-1057 (Rev. 5-8-10)

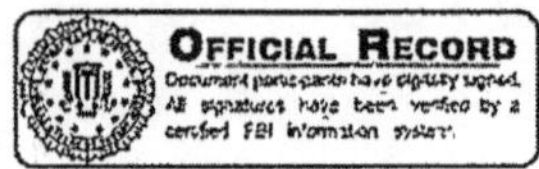

FEDERAL BUREAU OF INVESTIGATION

Electronic Communication

Title: (U) Online investigation - Summary as of 12/16/2012 6pm **Date:** 12/28/2012

From: NEW HAVEN
NH-10
Contact: [redacted]

Approved By: SSA [redacted]

Drafted By: [redacted]

b6 -1
b7C -1

Case ID #: 4-NH-2619946 (U) UNSUB(S)
Sandy Hook Elementary School
12 Dickinson St, Sandy Hook, CT-Victim
Firearms Act.
OO:NH

Synopsis: (U//~~FOUO~~) An investigative summary as to online investigation was provided to management on 12/16/2012. That summary is being recaptured in this communication for the file.

[redacted] b7E -1

Details:

An investigative summary of the initial online investigations undertaken following the Sandy Hook School shooting was prepared by SA [redacted] on 12/16/2012 at approximately 6pm. That summary is recaptured in this communication for the file.

b6 -1
b7C -1

Investigative Summary: Social Media/Cyber Matters as of 12/16/12 6:00pm

1 - Adam Lanza

[redacted] b7E -9

4-NH-2619946 Serial 113

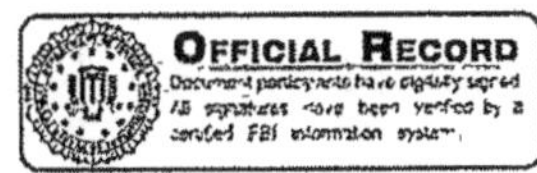

UNCLASSIFIED//~~FOUO~~

FEDERAL BUREAU OF INVESTIGATION

Date of entry 12/28/2012

b6 -1, 2
b7C -1, 2
OTHER Sealed Pursuant to Court Order

UNCLASSIFIED//FOUO

Investigation on 12/15/2012 at ~~New Haven, Connect~~icut, United States

File # 4-NH-2619946 Date drafted 12/21/2012

by

b6 -1
b7C -1

FD-302 (Rev. 5-8-10)

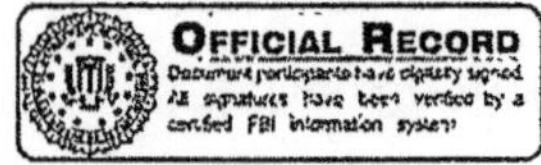

UNCLASSIFIED//FOUO

FEDERAL BUREAU OF INVESTIGATION

Date of entry 12/28/2012

b6 -1, 5
b7C -1, 5
OTHER Sealed Pursuant to Court Order

UNCLASSIFIED//FOUO

Investigation on 12/16/2012 at New Haven, Connecticut, United States

File # 4-NH-2619946 Date drafted 12/21/2012

by

b6 -1
b7C -1

This document contains neither recommendations nor conclusions of the FBI. It is the property of the FBI and is loaned to your agency; it and its contents are not to be distributed outside your agency.

UNCLASSIFIED//~~FOUO~~

-1, 6
: -1, 6
ER Sealed Pursuant to Court Order

FEDERAL BUREAU OF INVESTIGATION

Date of entry 12/27/2012

[redacted] date of birth (DOB) [redacted] was interviewed at [redacted] After being advised of the identity of the interviewing Agents, and the nature of the interview, [redacted] provided the following information:

[redacted] b6 -2, 6 b7C -2, 6

[redacted] b6 -2, 6 b7C -2, 6

[redacted] b6 -2, 6 b7C -2, 6

[redacted] b6 -2, 6 b7C -2, 6

[redacted] b6 -2, 5, 6 b7C -2, 5,

[redacted] b6 -1, 2 b7C -1, 2

UNCLASSIFIED//~~FOUO~~

Investigation on 12/23/2012 at [redacted] United States (In Person)

File # 4-NH-2619946 Date drafted 12/27/2012

by [redacted] b6 -1, 2 b7C -1, 2

This document contains neither recommendations nor conclusions of the FBI. It is the OTHER Sealed Pursuant to Court Order not to be distributed outside your agency.

4-NH-2619946 Serial 116

FD-1087 (Rev. 5-8-10)

UNCLASSIFIED//~~FOUO~~

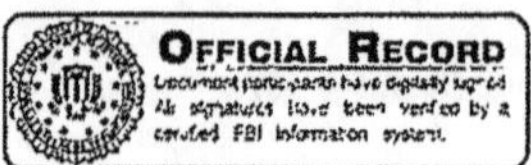

FEDERAL BUREAU OF INVESTIGATION

Evidence Log

Event Title: (U//~~FOUO~~)

Date: 01/02/2013

Approved By: SSA

b6 -1, 2
b7C -1, 2
OTHER Sealed Pursuant to Court Order

Drafted By:

Case ID #: 4-NH-2619946

(U) UNSUB(S)
Sandy Hook Elementary School
12 Dickinson St, Sandy Hook, CT-Victim
Firearms Act.
OO:NH

b7E -1

UNCLASSIFIED//~~FOUO~~

b6 -1, 2
b7C -1, 2
OTHER Sealed Pursuant to Court Order

4-NH-2619946 Serial 115

FD-1057 (Rev. 5-8-10)

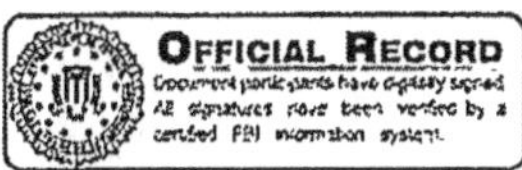

FEDERAL BUREAU OF INVESTIGATION

Electronic Communication

Title: (U) EMERGENCY VICTIM FUNDS AND BUDGET MATTERS, CRIMINAL CYBER RESPONSE SERVICES BRANCH; **Date:** 01/02/2013

To: [redacted]

From: DIRECTOR S OFFICE b6 -1
Contact: [redacted] b7C -1

Approved By: Kathryn McKay Turman

Drafted By: [redacted]

Case ID #: [redacted] b7E -4
4-NH-2619946 (U) UNSUB(S)
Sandy Hook Elementary School
12 Dickinson St, Sandy Hook, CT-Victim
Firearms Act.
OO:NH

Synopsis: (U) To document expenditures of the Terrorism Emergency Victim Assistance Funds following the shooting at Sandy Hook Elementary School in Newtown, CT.

Details:

On December 14, 2012 Adam Lanza killed twenty-seven people, including his mother, Nancy Lanza, and 26 students and staff at Sandy Hook Elementary School. The Office for Victim Assistance activated the Victim Assistance Rapid Deployment Team to respond to the shooting following a request for assistance from the Newtown Police Department and the Connecticut State Police. The Office for Victims of Crime authorized the use of Terrorism Emergency Victim Assistance funds to assist the victims of this mass fatality event. TEVAF assistance was requested and approved by OVA Program Director Turman [redacted] b6 -7 b7C -7

Title: (U) EMERGENCY VICTIM FUNDS AND BUDGET MATTERS, CRIMINAL CYBER RESPONSE SERVICES BRANCH;
Re: [redacted] 01/02/2013 b7E -4

Case Information: (NH-2619946) On December 14, 2012 Adam Lanza shot and killed his mother in their Newtown, CT home. He then traveled to Sandy Hook Elementary School and killed 20 students and six staff members before taking his own life. Four additional victims were injured during the shooting.

[redacted] b6 - b7C -

♦♦

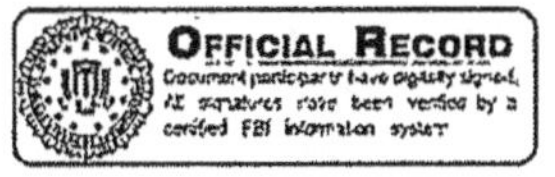

FEDERAL BUREAU OF INVESTIGATION

Date of entry 12/27/2012

[redacted] date of birth (DOB): [redacted] was interviewed at the residence of [redacted] After being advised of the identity of the interviewing Agents and the nature of the interview, [redacted] provided the following information: b6 -6 b7C -6

[redacted] NANCY JEAN LANZA (nee CHAMPION; DOB: September 6, 1960), a victim of the December 14, 2012 mass murders committed in Newtown, Connecticut (CT) by gunman, ADAM LANZA, son of NANCY LANZA [redacted] b6 -6 b7C -6

[redacted] b6 -5, 6 b7C -5, 6

[redacted] b6 -6 b7C -6

[redacted] provided the following background information regarding [redacted] NANCY LANZA. b6 -6 b7C -6

[redacted] advised that NANCY LANZA lives at 36 Yogananda Street, Sandy Hook, Connecticut (CT) with her adult son, ADAM LANZA. [redacted] stated that NANCY LANZA is not employed but does a lot of volunteer work at women's shelters and schools, including at SANDY HOOK ELEMENTARY SCHOOL where the shootings b6 -6 b7C -6

Investigation on 12/14/2012 at [redacted] United States (In Person) b6 -1, 6 b7C -1, 6

File # 4-NH-2619946 Date drafted 12/27/2012

by [redacted]

b6 -6
b7C -6

occurred earlier today. NANCY LANZA would donate clothing to the shelters and refurbish children's bicycles for donation. [redacted] does not know the nature of the volunteer work that NANCY LANZA performed at SANDY HOOK ELEMENTARY SCHOOL and does not think that NANCY LANZA has volunteered there in a long time.

b6 -6
b7C -6

NANCY LANZA attended primary grades in the public schools of Kingston, NH. NANCY LANZA married [redacted] in 1981. [redacted] built a house [redacted] and resided there for many years. [redacted] NANCY LANZA worked at JOHN HANCOCK and MORGAN STANLEY in Boston, MA.

b6 -
b7C

NANCY LANZA [redacted] had two children while residing in NH: [redacted] and ADAM LANZA, DOB: April 22, 1992, 20 years old.

b6 -5
b7C -

In approximately 1998, NANCY and [redacted] sold their home in East Kingston, NH and relocated to CT [redacted] when [redacted] and ADAM were approximately [redacted] and 6 years old, respectively. Just a couple of years later, NANCY and [redacted] separated. [redacted] NANCY LANZA had multiple sclerosis (MS) [redacted] Post-separation, NANCY LANZA remained in the marital home, 36 Yogananda St, Sandy Hook, CT. [redacted] ADAM LANZA lived with NANCY LANZA, who retained custody [redacted]

b6 -5,
b7C -5

[redacted]

b6 -5
b7C -5

[redacted] advised that ADAM is "not comfortable interacting with people" and was diagnosed with Asperger's Syndrome, a form of autism [redacted] is not sure if ADAM LANZA attended DJ BAKIE SCHOOL in East Kingston, NH before the family relocated to CT. ADAM LANZA was in Special Education classes when he

b6 -5,
b7C -5

b6 -6
b7C -6

attended school in Sandy Hook, CT. When ADAM LANZA reached puberty, NANCY LANZA took ADAM out of school "because she was nervous about him". ADAM took some classes at the public high school and was a member of the high school Tech Club. ADAM took some college courses (possibly at University of Connecticut?) and NANCY had to drop him off there because ADAM didn't drive. ADAM was always very mature and he did not like school because he thought all of the other kids were immature. NANCY LANZA was extremely private about her son, ADAM, and did not like to talk with family about ADAM's "issues". But NANCY LANZA knew since the time that ADAM was little that he had "issues". After NANCY [redacted] moved to CT, [redacted] ADAM experienced problems in both elementary and junior high school. NANCY LANZA only recently divulged ADAM's Asperger's diagnosis [redacted] a couple of years ago. NANCY LANZA later became very upset [redacted] when she learned [redacted] had shared the information [redacted] but NANCY LANZA felt that if [redacted] knew of his diagnosis they would think of him as weird. NANCY LANZA told [redacted] that ADAM was initially diagnosed with autism but later with Asperger's. [redacted] believes that NANCY LANZA was finally able to talk about ADAM over the last couple of years because she had less concern about him now. [redacted] stated that NANCY LANZA had ADAM in mental health counseling but that NANCY never discussed having ADAM on any type of medication.

b6 -5, 6
b7C -5, 6

ADAM LANZA is a vegan after previously being a vegetarian. ADAM is extremely smart. A couple of summers ago, ADAM had a job building computers for some guy. ADAM spent a lot of time on his computer but [redacted] does not think he was a "gamer". ADAM had no real friends. ADAM did not communicate [redacted] via e-mail or Facebook. [redacted] doubts that ADAM had a Facebook profile because he was not a social person. NANCY LANZA uses e-mail and her e-mail address is **njlanza1918@aol.com**; the significance of the "1918" in her e-mail address is related to the Red Sox's 1918 World Championship, as NANCY was an avid Red Sox fan.

b6 -5, 6
b7C -5, 6

[redacted] NANCY LANZA travelled often, [redacted] When NANCY travelled, she left ADAM home alone and he would be okay on his own.

b6 -5, 6
b7C -5, 6

However, NANCY LANZA had expressed concern about her son, ADAM, to [redacted] in the last couple of years, and as recently as two weeks ago [redacted] NANCY LANZA told [redacted] that she was very worried about what would happen to ADAM if anything ever happened to her. NANCY LANZA told [redacted] that ADAM was

b6 -6
b7C -6

b6 -
b7C

"doing better" but had gotten "weirded out" by Hurricame Sandy which hit the Northeast coast in late October 2012, and that she had to stay in her house with ADAM for several days without electricity because ADAM refused to leave and go to a hotel, and she would not leave him alone. [redacted] stated that she asked NANCY LANZ if she had made any arrangements for ADAM's care in the event that something happened to her, and NANCY LANZA told her that [redacted] would take care of ADAM. [redacted]

b6 -5, b7C -5

[redacted]

NANCY talked about a plan to move out of her big house in Sandy Hook, CT and relocate with ADAM to a house that had a mother-in-law suite for ADAM. NANCY told [redacted] that ADAM was doing better and was looking into going to college, perhaps to study history because he was very interested in history. NANCY LANZA said that she was looking at the Seattle, Washington area because ADAM would like the consistent weather there, or North Carolina [redacted] does not know if NANCY talked with ADAM about the idea of relocating. NANCY expressed her concern to [redacted] that ADAM can never live on his own and that's why she was considering buying a house with an in-law suite. To [redacted] knowledge, ADAM had a good relationship with his mother, NANCY. NANCY was extremely protective of ADAM. NANCY never expressed any concerns about ADAM being violent in any way. NANCY was not afraid of ADAM, but was afraid **for** him.

b6 -
b7C

[redacted] When NANCY and [redacted] separated and were later divorcing, ADAM LANZA's psychologist warned NANCY LANZA not to move ADAM out of the family home because he would not be able to handle it.

b6 -5
b7C -

NANCY LANZA told [redacted] that ADAM had begun driving lately. ADAM had previously not wanted to get a driver's license. NANCY also told [redacted] that ADAM has been taking private classes in Mandarin Chinese with a professor, as well as saxophone lessons, over the last couple of years.

b6 -
b7C -

When [redacted] saw NANCY LANZA [redacted] NANCY was getting ready to travel to London, England for Christmas. NANCY spoke of needing to buy new clothes and get her hair done. [redacted] stated that NANCY's Christmas travel plans could not have been the issue that made ADAM go on a shooting rampage today because NANCY travels all of the time and always leaves ADAM home. NANCY has a lot of friends and is a very social person. NANCY LANZA spends a lot of time at a restaurant next to a loal BIG Y store. [redacted]

b6 -5
b7C -

b6 -6
b7C -6

advised that about 4 or 5 years ago, NANCY turned down a marriage proposal from a man she was dating [redacted] because she would have had to move [redacted] and she would not leave ADAM. When she was dating this man, NANCY travelled [redacted] and left ADAM home alone, and ADAM was okay on his own. ADAM is able to cook his own food and care for himself when NANCY is away travelling.

b6 -5, 6
b7C -5,

[redacted]

b6 -5, 6
b7C -5,

[redacted] has never known ADAM to have a girlfriend or any friends at all.

b6 -5, 6
b7C -5,

[redacted] thinks that the concerns [redacted] NANCY LANZA, shared with her about ADAM LANZA over the last two years were probably "just the tip of the iceberg".

b6 -5, 6
b7C -5,

[redacted] advised that NANCY LANZA often took [redacted] ADAM, target shooting at a local range in CT. NANCY thought it was good for them to learn the responsibility of guns. NANCY LANZA owned several guns and had licenses for them. [redacted] could not explain why NANCY LANZA owned guns and stated that she did not think it was for reasons of self-defense. [redacted]

b6 -5, 6
b7C -5,

[redacted] advised that he knew NANCY LANZA to own a .45 caliber Governor handgun and a Ruger mini 14, .23 caliber gun. [redacted] NANCY LANZA had sold a gun recently. [redacted]

b6 -5, 6
b7C -5,

At the conclusion of the interview, SA [redacted] was notified by SSRA [redacted] that, per FBI-New Haven Command Post, NANCY LANZA had been officially identified as a deceased victim of today's mass shootings, and was shot in her home. SA [redacted]

b6 -1, 6
b7C -1,

b6 - b7C

FOLLOW-UP INTERVEIW OF [redacted] ON DECEMBER 15, 2012:

[redacted] advised that ADAM LANZA attended the SANDY HOOK ELEMENTARY SCHOOL where yesterday's shootings occurred. [redacted] recalled that it was ADAM's first school and that he had some kind of a problem in fourth grade. When ADAM was in middle school grades and had to change classrooms, he couldn't handle it. NANCY LANZA removed him from the public school and enrolled him in a small Catholic school for one year. ADAM did not do well there either and NANCY LANZA home-schooled him after that. b6 - b7C

[redacted] advised that NANCY LANZA told her that ADAM had no emotions or feelings; and that ADAM didn't care about birthdays or holidays and thought they were stupid. [redacted] recalled that NANCY LANZA had to get rid of a cat because ADAM was freaked out by it and couldn't handle it. b6 - b7C

[redacted]

[redacted] NANCY LANZA told her that her son, ADAM LANZA, had not left his bedroom in three months, and that despite the fact that NANCY and ADAM lived in the same house, NANCY has only been able to communicate with ADAM by e-mail. NANCY LANZA told [redacted] that ADAM had been freaked out by Hurricane Sandy in late October 2012. [redacted] told [redacted] that she had asked NANCY if she was afraid of ADAM and that NANCY had said no. [redacted] told [redacted] that she had urged NANCY LANZA to take some action regarding ADAM. [redacted] told [redacted] that NANCY talked about a plan to relocate with ADAM because ADAM wanted to go back to school. [redacted] advised that NANCY was looking into moving to Washington State or North Carolina. [redacted] told [redacted] that NANCY LANZA had discussed these moving plans with ADAM. b6 -5 b7C -

FOLLOW-UP INTERVIEW OF [redacted] ON DECEMBER 22, 2012:

[redacted]

b6 -5 b7C -

b6 -6
b7C -6

b6 -5, 6
b7C -5, 6

[redacted] advised that [redacted] bought NANCY a lot of guns and [redacted] wonders if any he bought for her were ones that ADAM LANZA used in his shooting rampage. [redacted]

b6 -5, 6
b7C -5, 6

[redacted] stated that she heard on the news that yesterday's victims at SANDY HOOK ELEMENTARY SCHOOL included the school's behavioral therapist, special education teacher, and psychologist. [redacted] wonders if ADAM knew those people and targeted them [redacted] also wondered if the classroom that ADAM shot children in was one of his former classrooms and if he went into the school with a plan.

b6 -6
b7C -6

[redacted] stated that she heard a news report about NANCY LANZA having recently filed legal documents seeking a conservatorship for ADAM. [redacted] inquired as to whether this has been corroborated by law enforcement. [redacted]

b6 -5, 6
b7C -5, 6

[redacted] provided no further information.

b6 -6
b7C -6

(Rev. 07-21-2011)

FEDERAL BUREAU OF INVESTIGATION

Serial Moved to Another Case

Action Performed By: [redacted] **Action Date:** 02/06/2013 b6 -1 b7C -1

Original Form Type: OTHER (Import)

From Case ID #: 4-NH-2619946

To Case ID #: [redacted] b7E

Justification: Move to another case (Incorrect Filing): Serial was inadvertently uploaded to the wrong case file

♦♦

FD-1087 (Rev. 5-8-10)

UNCLASSIFIED

FEDERAL BUREAU OF INVESTIGATION

Evidence Log

b7E -6

Event Title: (U) [redacted] **Date:** 01/03/2013

Approved By: SSA [redacted]

b6 -1
b7C -1

Drafted By: [redacted]

Case ID #: 4-NH-2619946 (U) UNSUB(S)
Sandy Hook Elementary School
12 Dickinson St, Sandy Hook, CT-Victim
Firearms Act.
OO:NH

[redacted] b7E -1

Acquired By: [redacted] on 01/03/2013

b6 -1
b7C -1

Acquired From: (U) Forensic exam

Receipt Given?: No

Holding Office: NEW HAVEN

Details:

[redacted]

b6 -1
b7C -1
b7E -6

UNCLASSIFIED

This document contains neither recommendations nor conclusions of the FBI. It is the property of the FBI and is loaned to your agency; it and its contents are not to be distributed outside your agency.

4-NH-2619946 Serial 121

Title: (U) [redacted]
Re: 4-NH-2619946, 01/03/2013

b7E -6

♦♦

FD-1087 (Rev. 5-8-10)

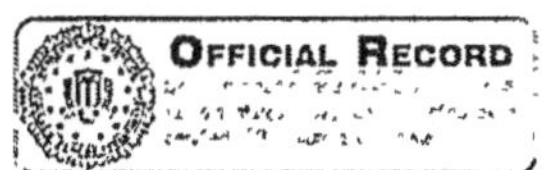

UNCLASSIFIED

FEDERAL BUREAU OF INVESTIGATION

Evidence Log

Event Title: (U) Acquisition of [redacted]

Date: 01/03/2013

To: [redacted]

b3 -1
b6 -1
b7C -1

Approved By: [redacted]

Drafted By: [redacted]

Case ID #: 4-NH-2619946 (U) UNSUB(S)
Sandy Hook Elementary School
12 Dickinson St, Sandy Hook, CT-Victim
Firearms Act.
OO:NH

FEDERAL GRAND JURY MATERIAL - DISSEMINATE PURSUANT TO RULE 6(E)
Do not disseminate except as authorized by federal rule of criminal procedure 6(e).

[redacted]

b7E -1

Acquired By: [redacted] on 12/21/2012

Acquired From: (U [redacted]

b3 -1
b6 -1, 5
b7C -1, 5

Receipt Given?: Yes

Holding Office: NEW HAVEN

Details:

On 12/14/2012, a Federal Grand Jury subpoena was served on [redacted] [redacted] On

b3 -1
b6 -2
b7C -2

UNCLASSIFIED

4-NH-2619946 SERIAL 122

Title: (U) Acquisition of [redacted] b3

Re: 4-NH-2619946, 01/03/2013

12/21/2012, [redacted]

b3 -1
b6 -1,
b7C -1

♦♦

FD-302 (Rev. 5-8-10)

FEDERAL BUREAU OF INVESTIGATION

Date of entry 12/19/2012

[redacted] date of birth: [redacted] Social Security Account Number: [redacted] was interviewed at [redacted] [redacted] After being advised of the identity of the interviewing Agent and the nature of the interview, [redacted] provided the following information: b6 -2 b7C -2

[redacted] b6 -2, 5 b7C -2, 5

[redacted]

[redacted] was acting out of emotion [redacted] He was reacting to the shooting at the school (Sandy Hook Elementary School). [redacted] spoke about the shooting in an immature fashion. He should not have reacted like he did. [redacted] b6 -2, 5, 7 b7C -2, 5, 7

[redacted] b6 -2, 5 b7C -2, 5

[redacted] b6 -2, 5 b7C -2, 5

[redacted] does not own or have access to firearms. He only has an "EMT" b6 -2 b7C -2

Investigation on 12/18/2012 at [redacted] United States (In Person) b6 -1, 2 b7C -1, 2

File # 4-NH-2619946 Date drafted 12/19/2012

by [redacted]

4-NH-2619946 Serial 123

b6 -2
b7C -

knife. He has never been hunting or to a gun range but he looks forward to doing both.

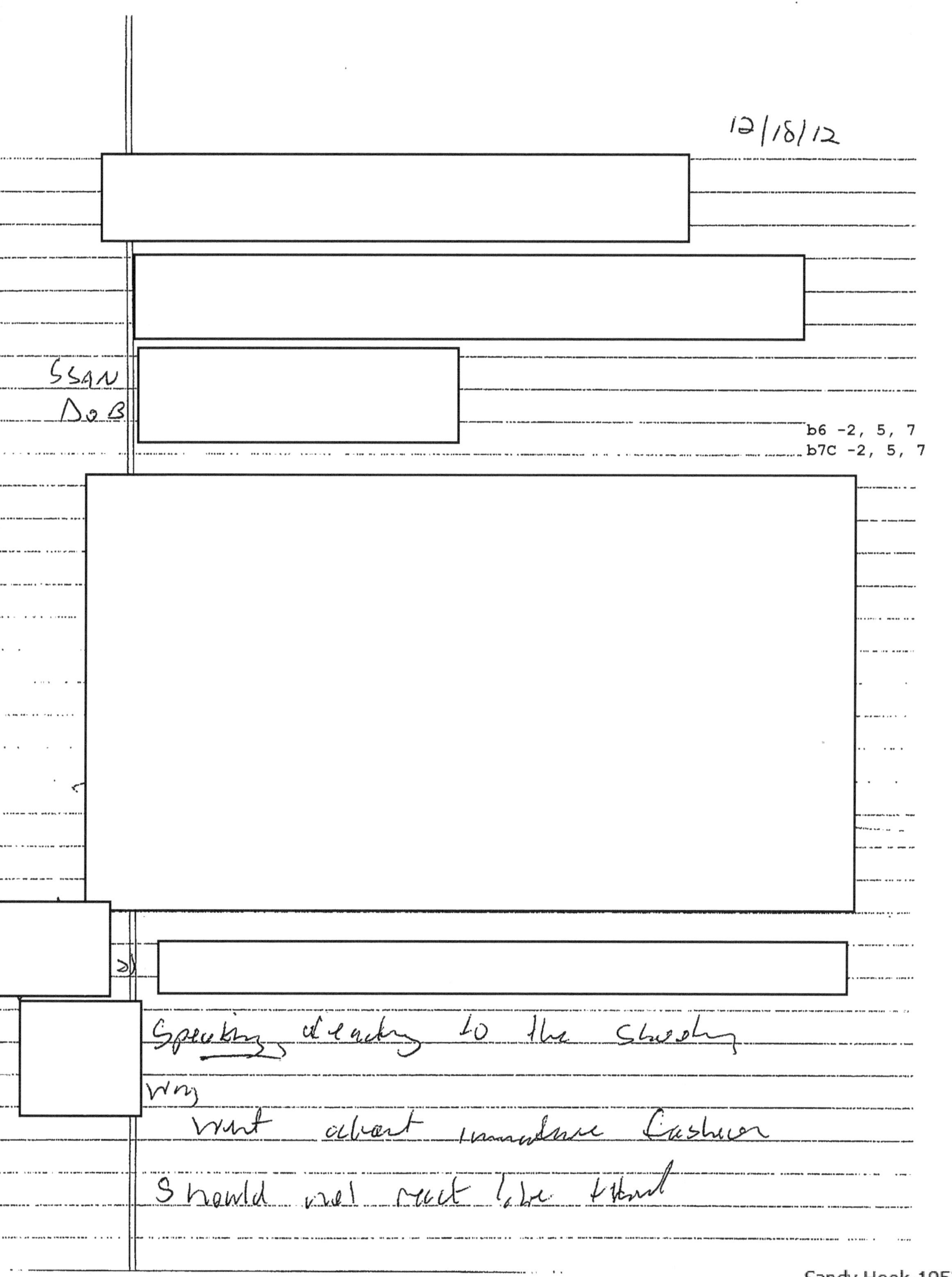

12/18/12

SSAN

DoB

b6 -2, 5, 7
b7C -2, 5, 7

2)

Speaking clearly to the shooting

way

went about immediate cashier

Should not react like that

b6 -2, 5
b7C -2, 5

"EMT knife"

FD-302 (Rev. 5-8-10)

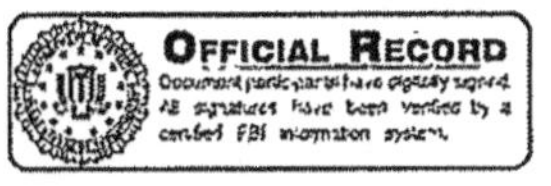

FEDERAL BUREAU OF INVESTIGATION

Date of entry 12/28/2012

On December 18, 2012, [redacted] (date of birth: [redacted] [redacted] cellular telephone number [redacted] was interviewed via prior arrangement at [redacted] Also present during the interview was [redacted] and [redacted] After being advised of the identities of the interviewing agents and the nature and purpose of the interview, [redacted] provided the following information: b6 -5, 6 b7C -5, 6

[redacted] NANCY [redacted] had two sons [redacted] and ADAM LANZA (ADAM). b6 -5, 6 b7C -5, 6

[redacted] b6 -5, 6 b7C -5, 6

[redacted] stated NANCY was very smart in school and NANCY finished high school early. After graduating high school, NANCY attended the UNIVERSITY OF NEW HAMPSHIRE for approximately three years. At the time NANCY's main focus of study was English, Spanish, and also possibly Social Services. [redacted] stated NANCY was very bright and only needed a few credits to graduate. [redacted] stated NANCY did not graduate from college as a result of NANCY's relationship and eventual marriage [redacted] b6 -5, 6 b7C -5, 6

[redacted] b6 -5, 6 b7C -5, 6

Investigation on 12/18/2012 at [redacted] United States (In Person) b6 -1, 6 b7C -1, 6

File # 4-NH-2619946 Date drafted 12/19/2012

by [redacted]

This document contains neither recommendations nor conclusions of the FBI. It is the property of the FBI and is loaned to your agency; it and its contents are not to be distributed outside your agency.

4-NH-2619946 Serial 124

b6 -6
b7C -6

[redacted]

b6 -5
b7C -5

After the wedding, NANCY [redacted] lived in Haverhill, Massachusetts for a couple of years. [redacted] NANCY opened a laundry, the FRONT STREET LAUNDRY, in Exeter, New Hampshire. NANCY was a hard worker and also worked as a hostess at the 1686 HOUSE restaurant to bring in additional money. [redacted] NANCY moved from Haverhill, Massachusetts, back to [redacted] in Kingston, New Hampshire during 1986. [redacted]

b6 -5,
b7C -5

[redacted] NANCY eventually sold the laundry and started working at JOHN HANCOCK in Boston, Massachusetts. During this timeframe, [redacted] ADAM were born. [redacted] believed [redacted] ADAM attended daycare while NANCY worked in Boston. [redacted] stated ADAM may have attended the D.J. BAKIE ELEMENTARY SCHOOL, but NANCY [redacted] moved to Connecticut during 1995 or 1996. [redacted] NANCY moved to Connecticut [redacted] believed [redacted] NANCY specifically chose to move to Newtown, Connecticut because of the school system there. [redacted].

b6 -5,
b7C -5

[redacted]

b6 -5,
b7C -5

[redacted] NANCY was private, but NANCY remained in contact and was very generous for various holidays and birthdays of family members.

b6 -
b7C

b6 -6
b7C -6

[redacted]

b6 -6
b7C -6

[redacted] believed NANCY's relationship with [redacted] ADAM was good. [redacted] recalled a phone conversation about three years ago with NANCY. [redacted] asked NANCY about the kids and NANCY replied, "Everything is fine." During telephone conversations with NANCY, [redacted] never spoke to ADAM on the telephone. When [redacted] would ask to speak to ADAM, NANCY would indicate ADAM was busy or not home or just not available. [redacted] recalled even as a young child ADAM did not like to talk on the telephone. [redacted] believed when ADAM first moved to Connecticut he was more of a social kid and would attend various play groups and parties [redacted] stated as ADAM became older he was more of a loner and an odd kid. [redacted] particularly noticed during the last couple of years ADAM had become more of a loner.

b6 -5, 6
b7C -5, 6

[redacted] NANCY never confirmed any type of medical condition or diagnosis of ADAM [redacted]

b6 -6
b7C -6

[redacted]

b6 -5, 6
b7C -5, 6

[redacted] stated ADAM loved music and ADAM could also play the saxophone.

b6 -5, 6
b7C -5, 6

[redacted] stated ADAM's demeanor as a teenager was "good but rigid". [redacted] stated ADAM took the board games very seriously and no one could joke around or ignore the rules of the board game when ADAM was playing.

b6 -6
b7C -6

b6 -
b7C -

[redacted] stated ADAM liked to use the computer, [redacted]

b6 -5,
b7C -5

[redacted] recalled ADAM was very concerned about the environment and ADAM would walk around the island [redacted] picking up trash [redacted] ADAM liked to spend time outdoors and was a "big hiker" who liked to climb. [redacted] when ADAM was 9 years old when he climbed up the Liberty Trail of Mt. Washington [redacted] stated the climb was no problem for ADAM, which was a very impressive feat for a 9 year old. [redacted] recalled another instance with ADAM was 13 or 14 years old when ADAM [redacted] climbed up and down Mt. Washington on the same day. [redacted] stated ADAM had indicated he wanted to climb every mountain in New Hampshire.

b6 -5,
b7C -5

[redacted] was not aware of any sports ADAM participated in at school. [redacted] believed ADAM had been in the Computer Club or the Tech Club at the public high school in Newtown, Connecticut. [redacted] believed ADAM attended the SANDY HOOK ELEMENTARY SCHOOL in Newtown, Connecticut [redacted] stated NANCY transferred ADAM to ST. ANNE'S SCHOOL at some point during Middle School. [redacted] stated ADAM did not like noise or confusion and ADAM began to have issues in school once he was required to walk to different classes during the school day. [redacted] stated ST. ANNE'S was a smaller school and academically ADAM did well at ST. ANNE'S. In high school [redacted] stated ADAM was home-schooled through the school. [redacted] stated NANCY would take ADAM to the school for advanced courses, but ADAM was not in the mainstream school setting. [redacted] stated ADAM had issues moving through the school between classes, but ADAM could sit through a quiet lecture without a problem. NANCY would take ADAM back and forth to school a couple of times a day to accommodate ADAM's schedule.

b6 -
b7C

[redacted]

[redacted] explained that over the last couple of years NANCY had indicated ADAM did not want to go to events with crowds of people. [redacted] NANCY told people that ADAM does not like crowds.

b6 -
b7C

[redacted]

b6
b7C

b6 -6
b7C -6

[redacted] b6 -6 b7C -6

[redacted] b6 -5, 6 b7C -5, 6

[redacted] did not have any e-mail contact with ADAM. [redacted] b6 -5, 6 b7C -5, 6

NANCY never spoke to [redacted] about any medication ADAM may have been taking. [redacted] b6 -5, 6 b7C -5, 6

[redacted] believed NANCY was more interested in collecting jewelry than collecting guns. [redacted] stated NANCY lived alone after the divorce and NANCY primarily had a gun for protection. [redacted] stated as NANCY began dating again after the divorce, NANCY could engage in conversations with guys to talk about guns or target shooting to develop rapport during a date, but NANCY was not a gun enthusiast. [redacted] never heard NANCY mention a Glock handgun or a Sig Sauer handgun. b6 -5, 6 b7C -5, 6

[redacted] vaguely remembered NANCY approaching [redacted] years ago asking for a recommendation for a gun to purchase for protection. [redacted] recommended a Smith & Wesson .38 Snubby to NANCY as a good gun for protection. b6 -5, 6 b7C -5, 6

Also during the discussion concerning guns, [redacted] vaguely remembered NANCY mentioning something about an AR-15 rifle approximately ten years ago [redacted] could not recall any other details about this conversation with NANCY. b6 -6 b7C -6

[redacted] b6 -5, 6 b7C -5, 6

b6 - b7C

[redacted] believed the last time they knew of ADAM shooting a gun was approximately six to eight years ago [redacted] ADAM may have shot a .22 rifle.

b6 -5, b7C -5

[redacted] stated during the last couple of years ADAM had been going back to school and was taking courses in the Chinese language. [redacted] believed ADAM was driving himself to the Chinese classes. [redacted] stated NANCY had encouraged ADAM to get his driver's license and ADAM eventually obtained a driver's license even though ADAM really did want to have one. [redacted] ADAM was more of a loner [redacted] stated ADAM loved his mother, NANCY. [redacted] stated she still cannot believe ADAM "was capable of it" [redacted] did not know why ADAM would "go to that school" to conduct the shooting.

b6 -5, b7C -5

[redacted] recalled a conversation she had with NANCY regarding a potential move NANCY was considering from her residence in Connecticut. NANCY was considering moving primarily for ADAM's benefit. NANCY was not unhappy living in Connecticut but thought a move would be best for ADAM. Also, NANCY indicated the house she was currently living in may have been a little too big. NANCY considered moving to Seattle, Washington, primarily because ADAM would like the weather there and it was not too bright. NANCY also considered moving to North Carolina. [redacted]

b6 -5 b7C -

[redacted] stated ADAM was very particular about what he would eat. ADAM was initially a vegetarian and then became a vegan. NANCY would frequently cook for ADAM, but ADAM could also cook for himself. NANCY made sure to stock the house with groceries for ADAM.

b6 -6 b7C -

[redacted] stated during Hurricane Sandy, NANCY's house lost power, but ADAM refused to go to a hotel. ADAM did not want to leave the house and basically shut down. Soon after Hurricane Sandy, NANCY purchased a generator for the residence.

b6 -6 b7C -

[redacted] also recalled that at some point ADAM worked for a computer repair shop off and on for approximately one or two years. [redacted] stated ADAM was very gifted with computers and ADAM could put together a computer

b6 - b7C -

b6 -6
b7C -6

from scratch using spare parts.

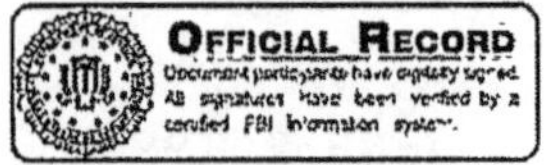

FEDERAL BUREAU OF INVESTIGATION

Date of entry 12/28/2012

On December 18, 2012, [redacted] (date of birth: [redacted] cellular telephone number: [redacted] was interviewed via prior arrangement at [redacted] [redacted] Also present during the interview was [redacted] and [redacted] After being advised of the identities of the interview agents and the nature and purpose of the interview, [redacted] provided the following information: b6 -5, b7C -5

[redacted] b6 - b7C

[redacted] b6 - b7C

[redacted] b6 -5 b7C -

[redacted] believed NANCY mentioned [redacted] ADAM LANZA

Investigation on 12/18/2012 at [redacted] United States (In Person) b6 -1

File # 4-NH-2619946 Date drafted 12/19/2012 b7C -

by [redacted]

 b6 -6 b7C -6

(ADAM) [redacted] may have been taking karate classes at the time. b6 -5 b7C -5

[redacted] believed the last time he saw ADAM was when ADAM was 3 or 4 years old. [redacted] b6 -5, 6 b7C -5, 6

[redacted] stated he knew absolutely nothing about ADAM for the past eight years and has only had generic conversation [redacted] concerning ADAM. [redacted] believed he may have heard from [redacted] through [redacted] that ADAM may be Autistic. b6 -5, 6 b7C -5, 6

[redacted] b6 -5, 6 b7C -5, 6

FEDERAL BUREAU OF INVESTIGATION
FOI/PA
DELETED PAGE INFORMATION SHEET
Civil Action# 16-cv-02136

Total Deleted Page(s) = 92
Page 15 ~ Duplicate;
Page 16 ~ b3 - 1;
Page 17 ~ Duplicate;
Page 18 ~ Duplicate;
Page 20 ~ Duplicate;
Page 21 ~ Duplicate;
Page 22 ~ Duplicate;
Page 23 ~ Duplicate;
Page 24 ~ Duplicate;
Page 25 ~ Duplicate;
Page 26 ~ Duplicate;
Page 27 ~ Duplicate;
Page 28 ~ Duplicate;
Page 29 ~ Duplicate;
Page 30 ~ Duplicate;
Page 31 ~ Duplicate;
Page 38 ~ b3 - 1; b6 - 5; b7C - 5;
Page 39 ~ b3 - 1; b6 - 4; b7C - 4;
Page 40 ~ b3 - 1;
Page 41 ~ b3 - 1; b6 - 4; b7C - 4;
Page 42 ~ b3 - 1; b6 - 4, 5; b7C - 4, 5;
Page 43 ~ b3 - 1; b6 - 5; b7C - 5;
Page 44 ~ b3 - 1;
Page 45 ~ b3 - 1; b6 - 5; b7C - 5;
Page 46 ~ b3 - 1;
Page 47 ~ b3 - 1;
Page 48 ~ b3 - 1;
Page 49 ~ b3 - 1;
Page 50 ~ b3 - 1;
Page 51 ~ b3 - 1; b6 - 5; b7C - 5;
Page 52 ~ b3 - 1; b6 - 5; b7C - 5;
Page 53 ~ b3 - 1; b6 - 5; b7C - 5;
Page 55 ~ b6 - 2; b7C - 2;
Page 56 ~ Duplicate;
Page 58 ~ Duplicate;
Page 59 ~ Duplicate;
Page 60 ~ Duplicate;
Page 61 ~ Duplicate;
Page 62 ~ Duplicate;
Page 63 ~ Duplicate;
Page 64 ~ Duplicate;
Page 65 ~ Duplicate;
Page 66 ~ Duplicate;
Page 67 ~ Duplicate;
Page 69 ~ Duplicate;
Page 71 ~ Duplicate;
Page 72 ~ Duplicate;
Page 73 ~ Duplicate;

Page 79 ~ Duplicate;
Page 81 ~ Duplicate;
Page 82 ~ Duplicate;
Page 83 ~ Duplicate;
Page 84 ~ Duplicate;
Page 85 ~ Duplicate;
Page 86 ~ Duplicate;
Page 87 ~ Duplicate;
Page 88 ~ Duplicate;
Page 89 ~ Duplicate;
Page 90 ~ Duplicate;
Page 91 ~ Duplicate;
Page 92 ~ Duplicate;
Page 93 ~ Duplicate;
Page 94 ~ Duplicate;
Page 95 ~ Duplicate;
Page 96 ~ Duplicate;
Page 97 ~ Duplicate;
Page 98 ~ Duplicate;
Page 99 ~ Duplicate;
Page 100 ~ Duplicate;
Page 101 ~ Duplicate;
Page 102 ~ Duplicate;
Page 103 ~ Duplicate;
Page 104 ~ Duplicate;
Page 105 ~ Duplicate;
Page 106 ~ Duplicate;
Page 107 ~ Duplicate;
Page 108 ~ Duplicate;
Page 144 ~ Duplicate;
Page 145 ~ Duplicate;
Page 146 ~ Duplicate;
Page 147 ~ Duplicate;
Page 148 ~ Duplicate;
Page 149 ~ Duplicate;
Page 150 ~ Duplicate;
Page 151 ~ Duplicate;
Page 152 ~ Duplicate;
Page 154 ~ Duplicate;
Page 155 ~ Duplicate;
Page 156 ~ Duplicate;
Page 157 ~ Duplicate;
Page 158 ~ Duplicate;
Page 159 ~ Duplicate;

XXXXXXXXXXXXXXXXXXXXXXXX
X Deleted Page(s) X
X No Duplication Fee X
X For this Page X
XXXXXXXXXXXXXXXXXXXXXXXX

FD-340a (Rev. 11-12-89)

(Title) IA's

(File No.) 4-NH-2619946

Item	Date Filed	To be returned			Disposition
		Yes	No		

1A30

FD-340 (Rev. 4-11-03)

File Number 4-NH-2619946

Field Office Acquiring Evidence NK

Serial # of Originating Document 49

Date Received 12/14/12

From [redacted]
(Name of Contributor/Interviewee)

b6 -6
b7C -6

(Address)

(City and State)

By SA [redacted]

b6 -1
b7C -1

To Be Returned ☐ Yes ☒ No

Receipt Given ☐ Yes ☒ No

Grand Jury Material - Disseminate Only Pursuant to Rule 6 (e)
Federal Rules of Criminal Procedure

☐ Yes ☒ No

Federal Taxpayer Information (FTI)

☐ Yes ☒ No

Title:

Reference:
(Communication Enclosing Material)

Description: ☒ Original notes re interview of

[redacted] Interview notes at [redacted]

[redacted]

b6 -6
b7C -6

start | 16:18 12/14/12

b6 -5, b7C -5

Adam was home schooled because @ 10-11y
began having stress issues. High school home
schooled. @ 7th grade issues started
switch to catholic school St Mary's newtown
Sandy Hook till 4th grade
Newtown Middle School 5-7th/8th
diginosed @ 6th grade
started new town high school in 9th grade
10th gradce started completely home scho

b6 -6
b7C -6

b6 -5, 6
b7C -5, 6

pitching in for computer
Q Nov Nancy told via email that adam had become a shut in, hasn't driven his vehicle for a while battery went dead 2010 Honda civic blue?

b6 -5, 6
b7C -5, 6

adam were ever in trouble at school or with police. adam smart but learning issues adam would be picked on by bullies never hurt animals or people no aggressiveness

no aid from state no job. total denial that he had asburgers.

b6 -6
b7C -6

haven't left house for 3 month before email. used to hike alot or build computers.

Was supposed to be on some medicition but never took it. was perscribed doesn't know which ones. Nancy never force to take

adam had 2 pistols. monroe ct would shot. pistol/rifle adam had rifles

b6 -6
b7C -6

1 shotgun, other was a big gauge.
both black. single barrel shotgun small stock. no rifle classes. Once or twice.

Adam might have been taking pistol classes with mother.

Doesn't Know where interest came from or know if he ever owned 2 pistols.

adam was very isolated video games, or computer alot. interests were all over the place, writing hiking, cycling, computers, one of adams poems was published. online gaming email address name he would use on online games as well.

Doesn't Know if he had an social media websites. 1 email address to be given later

adam had a cell phone but he would never use it.

b6 -6
b7C -6

Nacey home schooled adam. through high school but Nacey helped through mid school more.

used to be in tech club was bullied every now and again tech club loved him freshman year

....

adam lanza 203-364-9879
contact info Blarvink@gmail.com

was stressed over papers and classes and pressure from grades, but not from bullies

Nancy would take care of everything, shopping, maintain the household. he would clean his room sometimes do laundry, or cook

b6 -5, 6
b7C -5, 6

She was never allowed in his room, never really ate together. to walk around no motive. loved that school

adam never appreciated what nancy was doing for him.

end 1210 Friday 12/14/12

FD-340c (4-11-03)

File Number 4-NH-2619946-31

Field Office Acquiring Evidence NHO

Serial # of Originating Document 51

Date Received 12/14/2012

From [redacted]
(Name of Contributor/Interviewee)

[redacted]
(Address)

b6 -1, 6
b7C -1, 6

Sandy Hook, Connecticut
(City and State)

By SA [redacted]

To Be Returned ☐ Yes ☒ No

Receipt Given ☐ Yes ☒ No

Grand Jury Material - Disseminate Only Pursuant to Rule 6 (e)
Federal Rules of Criminal Procedure

☐ Yes ☒ No

Federal Taxpayer Information (FTI)

☐ Yes ☒ No

Title: UNSUB(s)
Sandy Hook Elementary School
12 Dickinson St., Sandy Hook, CT
Firearms Act

Reference: FD-302 of [redacted]
(Communication Enclosing Material)

b6 -6
b7C -6

Description: ☒ Original notes re interview of [redacted]

Dont know the family
moved here
did not live here when

nothing out of the ordinary
never met Mrs Lanza

b6 -5,
b7C -5

FD-340c (4-11-03)

File Number 356A - NH - 2619946 - 1A35

Field Office Acquiring Evidence New Haven

Serial # of Originating Document 356A - NH - 2619946 - GJ - 76

Date Received 3/7/2013

From [redacted] b3 -1

(Address)

(City and State)

By SA [redacted] b6 -1 b7C -1

To Be Returned ☐ Yes ☒ No

Receipt Given ☐ Yes ☒ No

Grand Jury Material - Disseminate Only Pursuant to Rule 6 (e) Federal Rules of Criminal Procedure

☐ Yes ☒ No

Federal Taxpayer Information (FTI)

☐ Yes ☒ No

Title: ADAM PETER LANZA

Reference: ______
(Communication Enclosing Material)

Description: ☐ ~~Original notes re interview of~~

[redacted] b3 -1

NESPIN
1-800-343-5682

RISS

BJA Bureau of Justice Assistance

email

b3 -1
b6 -4, 5
b7C -4, 5

Sandy Hook-1980

INVESTIGATOR'S CHECK LIST

b7E -3

FD-340c (4-11-03)

File Number 356A - NH - 2619946 - 1A36

Field Office Acquiring Evidence New Haven

Serial # of Originating Document 356A - NH - 2619946 - GJ - 78

Date Received 2/21/2013

From CSP

(Name of Contributor/Interviewee)

(Address)

By SA [redacted] b6 -1 b7C -1

To Be Returned ☐ Yes ☒ No

Receipt Given ☐ Yes ☒ No

Grand Jury Material - Disseminate Only Pursuant to Rule 6 (e)
Federal Rules of Criminal Procedure

☐ Yes ☒ No

Federal Taxpayer Information (FTI)

☐ Yes ☒ No

Title: Adam Peter Lanza

Reference:

(Communication Enclosing Material)

Description: ~~☐ Original notes re interview of~~

[redacted] b3 -1

b3 -1
b6 -3, 5
b7C -3, 5

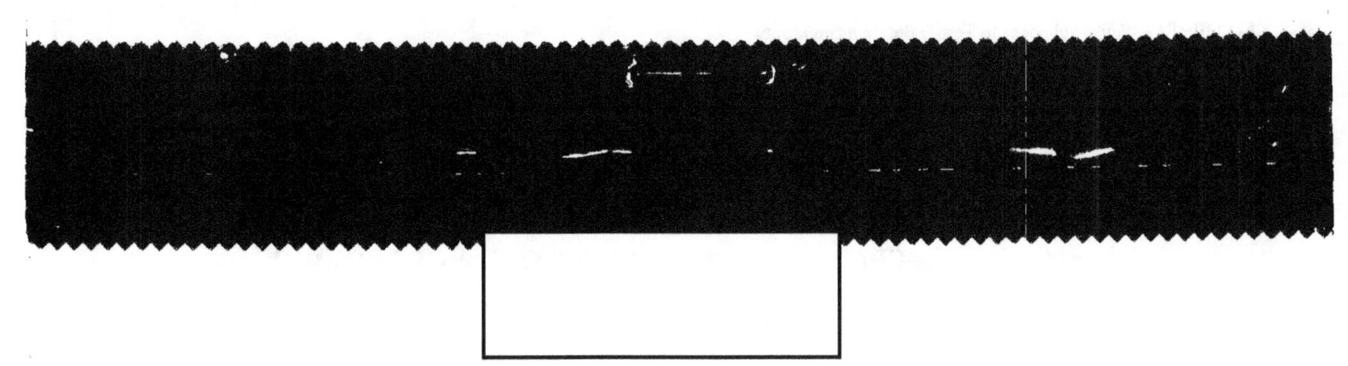

b6 -3
b7C -3

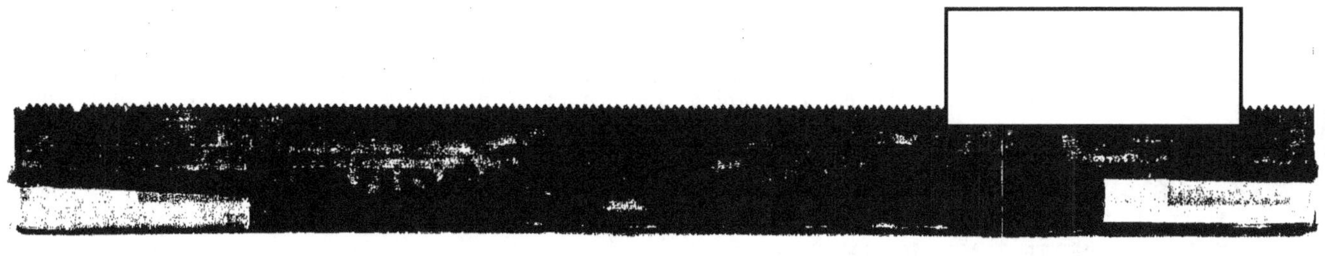

AO 110 (Rev. 06/09) Subpoena to Testify Before a Grand Jury

Grand Jury Matter No [redacted]

UNITED STATES DISTRICT COURT

for the

District of Connecticut

SUBPOENA TO TESTIFY BEFORE A GRAND JURY

To: [redacted]

b3 -1
b6 -5
b7C -5

YOU ARE COMMANDED to appear in this United States district court at the time, date, and place shown below to testify before the court's grand jury. When you arrive, you must remain at the court until the judge or a court officer allows you to leave.

Place: Grand Jury Room United States District Court & Federal Building 915 Lafayette Blvd Bridgeport, CT 06604	Date and Time: [redacted]

You must also bring with you the following documents, electronically stored information, or objects *(blank if not applicable)*:

[redacted]

b3 -
b6 -
b7C

IN LIEU OF APPEARANCE, PLEASE MAIL DOCUMENTS ON OR BEFORE THE RETURN DATE OF THE GRAND JURY SUBPOENA TO SPECIAL AGENT [redacted] FEDERAL BUREAU OF INVESTIGATION, 1000 LAFAYETTE BLVD., 32RD FLOOR, BRIDGEPORT, CT 06604, TELEPHONE NUMBER [redacted]

Date: 12/18/2012

CLERK OF COURT

Signature of Clerk or Deputy Clerk

UNITED STATES DISTRICT COURT DISTRICT OF CONNECTICUT

The name, address, e-mail, and telephone number of the United States attorney, or assistant United States attorney, who requests this subpoena, are:

[redacted]
ASSISTANT UNITED STATES ATTORNEY
UNITED STATES ATTORNEY'S OFFICE
1000 LAFAYETTE BLVD., 10TH FLOOR
BRIDGEPORT, CT 06604

b6 -4
b7C -4

Control No:

AO 110 (Rev. 06/09) Subpoena to Testify Before a Grand Jury

Grand Jury Matter No

UNITED STATES DISTRICT COURT

for the

District of Connecticut

SUBPOENA TO TESTIFY BEFORE A GRAND JURY

To:

b3 -1

YOU ARE COMMANDED to appear in this United States district court at the time, date, and place shown below to testify before the court's grand jury. When you arrive, you must remain at the court until the judge or a court officer allows you to leave.

Place: Grand Jury Room United States District Court & Federal Building 915 Lafayette Blvd Bridgeport, CT 06604	Date and Time:

You must also bring with you the following documents, electronically stored information, or objects *(blank if not applicable)*:

b3 -1
b6 -1
b7C -1

IN LIEU OF APPEARANCE, PLEASE MAIL DOCUMENTS ON OR BEFORE THE RETURN DATE OF THE GRAND JURY SUBPOENA TO SPECIAL AGENT FEDERAL BUREAU OF INVESTIGATION, 1000 LAFAYETTE BLVD., 32RD FLOOR, BRIDGEPORT, CT 06604, TELEPHONE NUMBER

Date: 12/18/2012

CLERK OF COURT

Signature of Clerk or Deputy Clerk

The name, address, e-mail, and telephone number of the United States attorney, or assistant United States attorney, who requests this subpoena, are:

ASSISTANT UNITED STATES ATTORNEY
UNITED STATES ATTORNEY'S OFFICE
1000 LAFAYETTE BLVD., 10TH FLOOR
BRIDGEPORT, CT 06604

b6 -4
b7C -4

Control No:

FD-340 (Rev. 4-11-03)

File Number 4-NH-2619946-1A38

Field Office Acquiring Evidence New Haven

Serial # of Originating Document 70

Date Received 12/14/2012

From [redacted] (Contributor/Interviewee)

(Address)

(City and State)

By SA [redacted] / SA [redacted]

To Be Returned ☐ Yes ☒ No

Receipt Given ☐ Yes ☒ No

Grand Jury Material - Disseminate Only Pursuant to Rule 6 (e)
Federal Rules of Criminal Procedure

☐ Yes ☒ No

Federal Taxpayer Information (FTI)

☐ Yes ☒ No

Title:

Sandy Hook Elementary School

Reference:
(Communication Enclosing Material)

De[redacted]

[redacted] (FD-26 and copies)

b6 -1, 2
b7C -1, 2

b6 -2
b7C -2

This is to certify that on ____________ at ____
Special Agents of the Federal Bureau of Investigation, U. S. Department of Justice, conducted a search of ____.
I certify that nothing was removed from my custody by Special Agents of the Federal Bureau of Investigation, U. S. Department of Justice.

(Signed) ______________________________________

Witnessed:

____
Special Agent
Federal Bureau of Investigation
U. S. Department of Justice

____
Special Agent
Federal Bureau of Investigation
U. S. Department of Justice

FD-340c (4-11-03)

File Number 4-NH-2619946-1A39

Field Office Acquiring Evidence New Haven

Serial # of Originating Document 71

Date Received 12/18/2012

From Ø

(Name of Contributor/Interviewee)

(Address)

(City and State)

By SA [redacted] b6 -1 b7C -1

To Be Returned ☐ Yes ☒ No

Receipt Given ☐ Yes ☒ No

Grand Jury Material - Disseminate Only Pursuant to Rule 6 (e)
Federal Rules of Criminal Procedure

☐ Yes ☒ No

Federal Taxpayer Information (FTI)

☐ Yes ☒ No

Title:

Reference:

(Communication Enclosing Material)

Description: ☒ Original notes re interview of [redacted]

b6 -6
b7C -6

FD-340 (Rev. 4-11-03)

File Number 4 - NH - 2619946 - 1A48

Field Office Acquiring Evidence New Haven

Serial # of Originating Document 79

Date Received 12/19/2012

From [redacted]
(Name of Contributor/Interviewee)

(Address)

(City and State)

By SSA [redacted]

To Be Returned ☐ Yes ☒ No

Receipt Given ☐ Yes ☒ No

Grand Jury Material - Disseminate Only Pursuant to Rule 6 (e)
Federal Rules of Criminal Procedure

☐ Yes ☐ No

Federal Taxpayer Information (FTI)

☐ Yes ☐ No

Title:

Reference:
(Communication Enclosing Material)

Description: ☒ Original notes re interview of [redacted]

b6 -1, 6
b7C -1, 6

b6 -6
b7C -6

1A49

FD-340 (Rev. 4-11-03)

File Number 4-NH-2619946

Field Office Acquiring Evidence NH

Serial # of Originating Document 144[redacted]83

Date Received 12/15/2012

From SA [redacted]
(Name of Contributor/Interviewee)

FBI, 600 STATE STREET
(Address)

NEW HAVEN, CONNECTICUT
(City and State)

By SA [redacted]

b6 -1
b7C -1

To Be Returned ☐ Yes ☒ No

Receipt Given ☐ Yes ☒ No

Grand Jury Material - Disseminate Only Pursuant to Rule 6 (e) Federal Rules of Criminal Procedure

☐ Yes ☒ No

Federal Taxpayer Information (FTI)

☐ Yes ☒ No

Title: UNSUB(S);
SANDY HOOK ELEMENTARY SCHOOL
12 DICKINSON ST, SANDY HOOK, CT - VICTIM;
Firearms Act.

Reference: FD-302
(Communication Enclosing Material)

Description: ☐ Original notes re interview of

Photo logs, printouts of thumbnails of the photos, sketches, FD-597, notes, ~~room letter markers~~, [redacted] ~~labels~~, three (3) DVDs containing the original photos, and three (3) DVDs containing copies of the photos. from 12/14-15/2012 search of [redacted]

b6 -1, 2
b7C -1, 2

NOTES / Released to SA [redacted] Evidence Custodian 12/15/2012 3:39 AM

@ [redacted] @ 0427

12/15/2012

Sealed & locked [redacted]

b6 -1
b7C -1
b7E -6

12/17/2012 0940
unsealed & moved to
NH FO BY [redacted]

12/17/2012 Checked by SA [redacted]
12/17/2012 moved to
Evidence Control [redacted]
11:40AM

Notes.

12/14/2012

No one in it:

b6 -1, 2, 5
b7C -1, 2, 5

2038

12/14/2012

2114 8 to clear

Sketch.

Case

Photo

Casebook

b6 -1, 2
b7C -1, 2

2122

2125 begin WT

b6 -2
b7C -2

930p

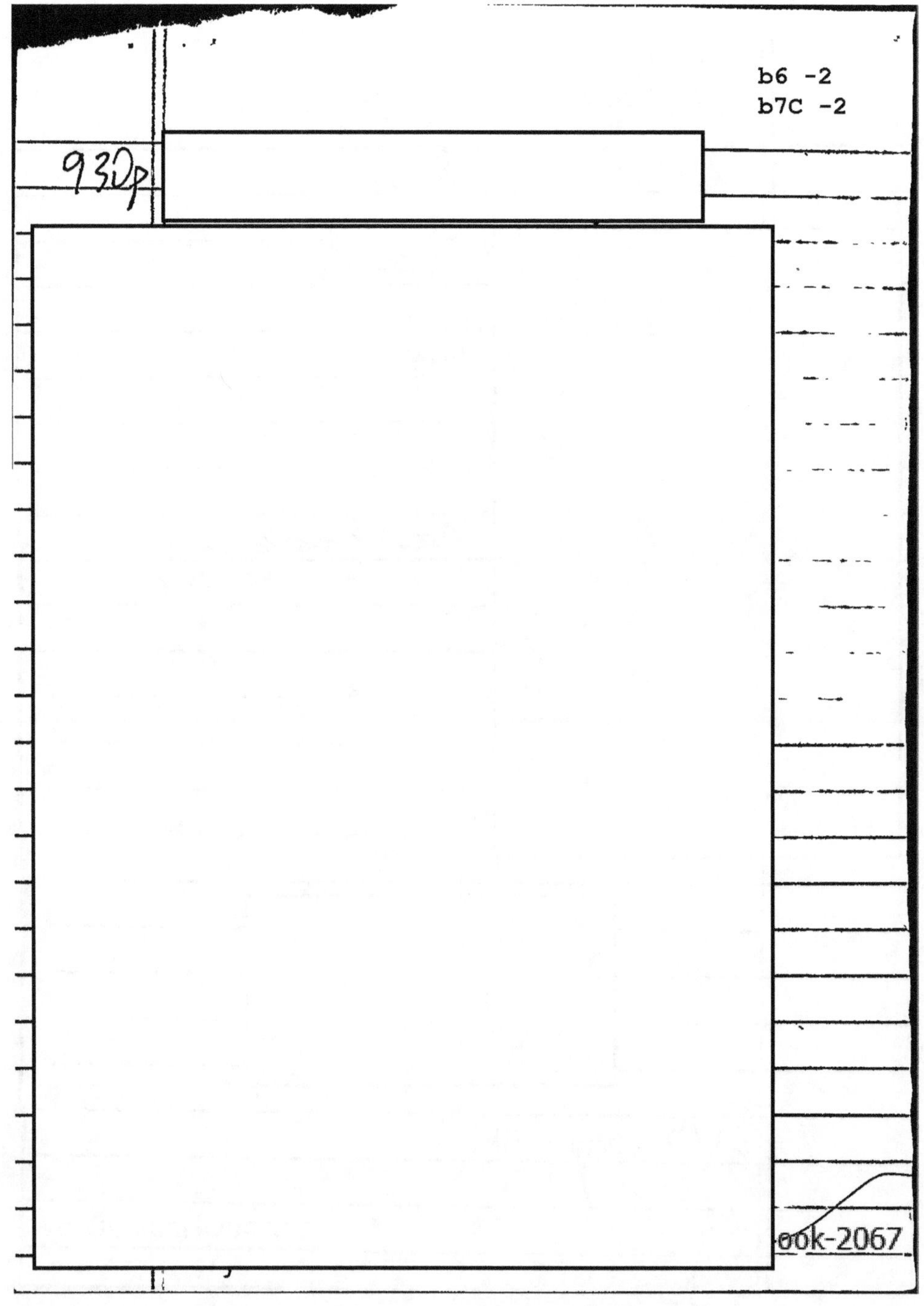

4+hrs 0200.

2200 – Call SABT re: [redacted]

Voicemail.

2218 begin photos

2235 CSP [redacted] b6 -2, 3 b7C -2, 3

[redacted] arr.

2249 Start Search.

2335 [redacted]

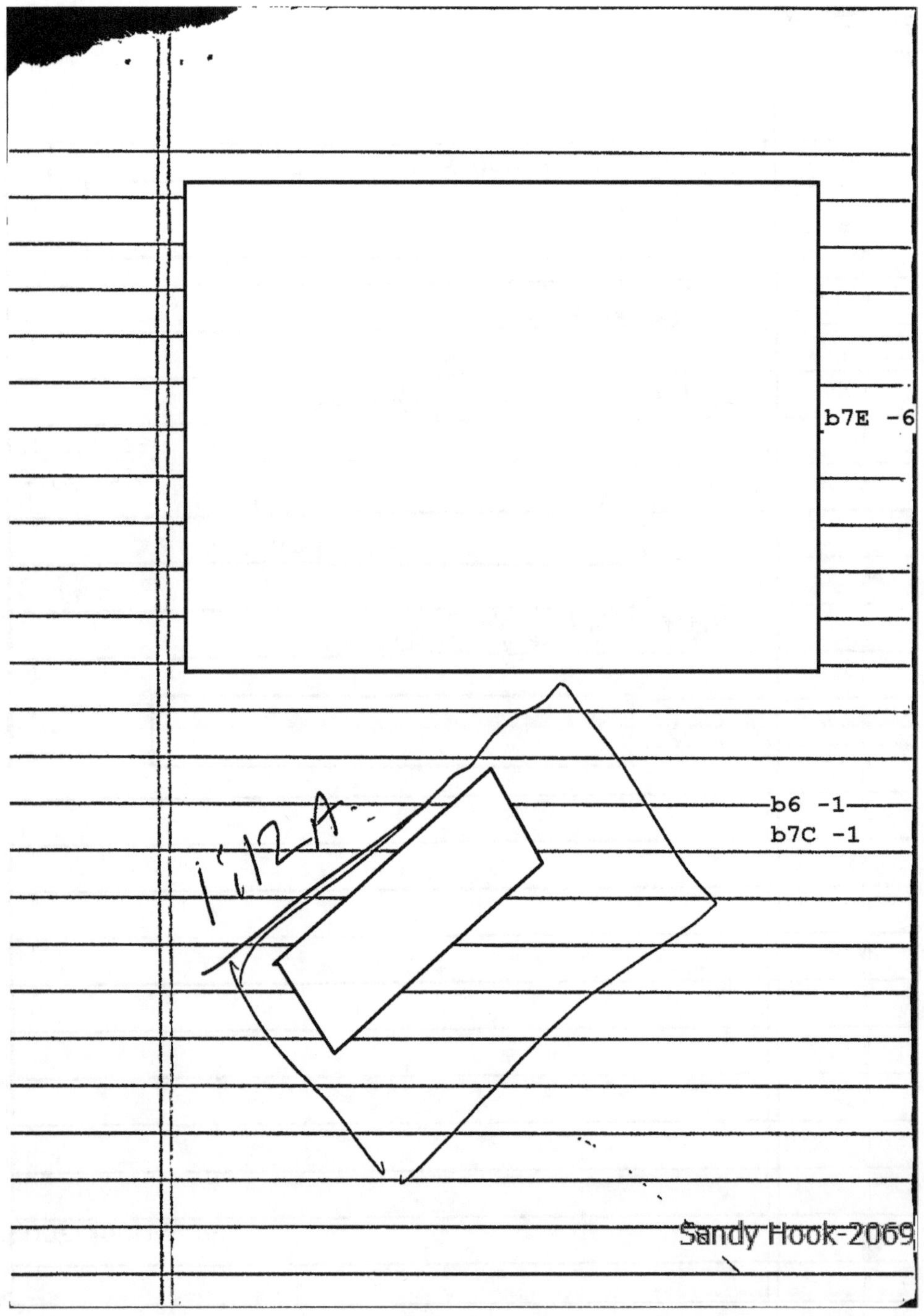
b7E -6
b6 -1
b7C -1
1/12 A
Sandy Hook-2069

12/15

320A Final

339A OUT. END

b6 -5
b7C -5

Consent

FD-340 (Rev. 4-11-03) 1950

File Number 4-NH-2619946

Field Office Acquiring Evidence NH

Serial # of Originating Document ~~44~~ [redacted] 83

Date Received 12/15/2012

From ______________________
(Name of Contributor/Interviewee)

____
(Address)

____
(City and State)

By SA [redacted]

b6 -1
b7C -1

To Be Returned ☐ Yes ☒ No

Receipt Given ☐ Yes ☒ No

Grand Jury Material - Disseminate Only Pursuant to Rule 6 (e) Federal Rules of Criminal Procedure

☐ Yes ☒ No

Federal Taxpayer Information (FTI)

☐ Yes ☒ No

Title: UNSUB(S);
SANDY HOOK ELEMENTARY SCHOOL
12 DICKINSON ST, SANDY HOOK, CT - VICTIM;
Firearms Act.

Reference: FD-302
(Communication Enclosing Material)

Description: ☐ **Original notes re interview of**

Room letter labels from the 12/14-15/2012 search of [redacted]
[redacted]

b6 -2
b7C -2

FD-1057 (Rev 5-8-10)

UNCLASSIFIED

FEDERAL BUREAU OF INVESTIGATION

Electronic Communication

Title: (U) EC re contact with [redacted] [redacted]

Date: 01/02/2013

To: [redacted]

From: BOSTON
BS-PORTSMOUTH NH RA
Contact: [redacted]

b6 -1, 6
b7C -1, 6

Approved By: SSRA [redacted]

Drafted By: [redacted]

Case ID #: 4-NH-2619946 (U) UNSUB(S)
Sandy Hook Elementary School
12 Dickinson St, Sandy Hook, CT-Victim
Firearms Act.
OO:NH

Synopsis: (U) To report contact with [redacted] [redacted]

b6 -6
b7C -6
b7E -1

Details:

SA's [redacted] and [redacted] of the New Hampshire Resident Agencies established contact with [redacted] on December 14, 2012; conducted interviews telephonically requested by FBI-New Haven (the details of which are reported in separate interviews); and thereafter maintained contact with [redacted]

b6 -1, 6
b7C -1, 6

On 12/14/2012, [redacted] and [redacted] [redacted] were interviewed at the residence of [redacted] [redacted]

b6 -6
b7C -6

UNCLASSIFIED

4-NH-2619946
Serial 129

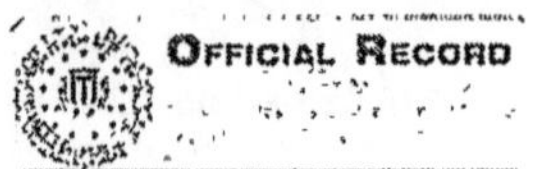

UNCLASSIFIED//~~FOUO~~

FEDERAL BUREAU OF INVESTIGATION

Date of entry 01/03/2013

On December 20, 2012, SA [redacted] conducted the following investigative activity on the Internet: b6 -1 b7C -1

[redacted]

were preserved in a PDF document that is maintained in a 1A.

UNCLASSIFIED//~~FOUO~~

Investigation on 12/20/2012 at New Haven, Connecticut, United States (, Other (Internet Research))

File # 4-NH-2619946 Date drafted 01/03/2013

by [redacted] b6 - b7C

FD-1087 (Rev. 5-8-10)

UNCLASSIFIED

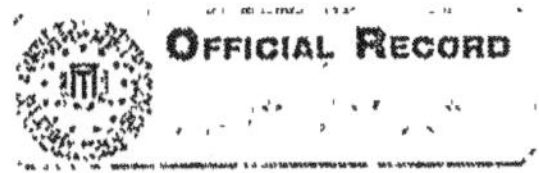

FEDERAL BUREAU OF INVESTIGATION

Evidence Log

Event Title: (U) [redacted]

Date: 01/03/2013

Approved By: SSA [redacted]

Drafted By: [redacted]

b6 -1, 2
b7C -1, 2
OTHER Sealed Pursuant to Court Order

Case ID #: 4-NH-2619946

(U) UNSUB(S)
Sandy Hook Elementary School
12 Dickinson St, Sandy Hook, CT-Victim
Firearms Act.
OO:NH

[redacted]

b7E -1

Acquired By: [redacted] on 01/03/2013

Acquired From: (U [redacted]

b6 -1
b7C -1
b7E -7

Receipt Given?: No

Holding Office: NEW HAVEN

Details:

[redacted]

b6 -2
b7C -2
b7E -6

UNCLASSIFIED

OTHER Sealed Pursuant to Court Order

This document contains neither recommendations nor conclusions of the FBI. It is the property of the FBI and is loaned to your agency; it and its contents are not to be distributed outside your agency.

4-NH-2619946
SERIAL 131

Title: (U) [redacted]
Re: 4-NH-2619946, 01/03/2013

b6 -2
b7C -2
OTHER Sealed Pursuant to Court Order

♦♦

FEDERAL BUREAU OF INVESTIGATION

Date of entry 01/04/2013

On 12/16/2012, Special Agent [redacted] Federal Bureau of Investigation, and Inspector [redacted] Office of the State's Attorney, Judicial District of Connecticut, interviewed [redacted] born [redacted] Newtown, Connecticut, in the presence of her husband [redacted] born [redacted] After being advised of the identity of the interviewing officials and the nature of the interview, [redacted] provided the following information: b6 -1, 3, 7 b7C -1, 3, 7

At around 9:18 a.m. on 12/16/2012, [redacted] and [redacted] received an incoming telephone call to their home telephone number [redacted] from telephone number (646) 843-7000. The call was received on their answering machine where an unidentified male caller left a message saying he was ADAM LANZA and making threats that he was going to kill a "bitch" with his machine gun. The [redacted] telephone is subscribed to in the name of [redacted] [redacted] The answering machine message was in the voice of [redacted] b6 -7 b7C -7

INVESTIGATIVE NOTE: [redacted] and [redacted] permitted SA [redacted] to make a recording of their answering machine tape, which is attached. b6 -1, 7 b7C -1, 7

Investigation on 12/16/2012 at Newtown, Connecticut, United States (In Person)

File # 4-NH-2619946 Date drafted 01/04/2013

by [redacted] b6 -1 b7C -1

4-NH-2619946
SERIAL 132

FD-1036 (Rev. 10-16-2009)

UNCLASSIFIED

FEDERAL BUREAU OF INVESTIGATION

Import Form

Form Type: PoliceRpt **Date:** 01/02/2013

Title: (U) [redacted] Police Reports ref [redacted] [redacted]

Approved By: SSA [redacted]

Drafted By: [redacted]

b6 -1, 2
b7C -1, 2

Case ID #: 4-NH-2619946 (U) UNSUB(S)
Sandy Hook Elementary School
12 Dickinson St, Sandy Hook, CT-Victim
Firearms Act.
OO:NH

Synopsis: (U) [redacted] Police Reports ref [redacted] [redacted]

b6 -2
b7C -2

Enclosure(s): Enclosed are the following items:

1. (U) Original Interview notes of [redacted]
2. (U) Original Interview notes of [redacted]

♦♦

UNCLASSIFIED

Sandy Hook-217

4-NH-2619946

SERIAL 133

FD-1057 (Rev 5-8-10)

UNCLASSIFIED

FEDERAL BUREAU OF INVESTIGATION

Electronic Communication

Title: (U) Emergency Victim Assistance Funds Request

Date: 12/23/2012

To: [redacted]

From: [redacted]

Contact: [redacted]

b6 -1, 7
b7C -1, 7

Approved By: SSA [redacted]

Drafted By: [redacted]

Case ID #: 4-NH-2619946 (U) UNSUB(S)
Sandy Hook Elementary School
12 Dickinson St, Sandy Hook, CT-Victim
Firearms Act.
OO:NH

Synopsis: (U) To document expenditure of federal Emergency Victim Assistance Funds (EVAF).

[redacted] b7E -1

Enclosure(s): Enclosed are the following items:
1. (U) [redacted]

Details:

A request for EVAF assistance by VS [redacted] Division, was approved by the Office for Victim Assistance on December 14, 2012. Approval was granted for the following expenditure: [redacted] [redacted]

b6 -1, 7
b7C -1, 7

On Friday, December 14, 2012, VS [redacted] was contacted by the

UNCLASSIFIED

4-NH-2619946
Serial 134

Title: (U) Emergency Victim Assistance Funds Request
Re: 4-NH-2619946, 12/23/2012

Office for Victim Assistance and the Terrorism and Special Jurisdiction Program following a school shooting. VS [redacted] was asked to provide

[redacted]

b6 -1, 7
b7C -1, 7

♦♦

FD-302 (Rev. 5-8-10)

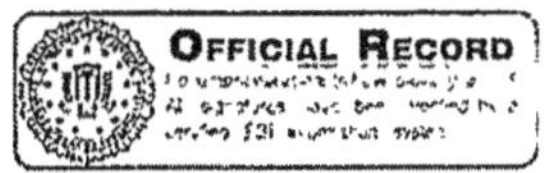

FEDERAL BUREAU OF INVESTIGATION

Date of entry 01/07/2013

FEDERAL GRAND JURY MATERIAL - DISSEMINATE PURSUANT TO RULE 6(E)
Do not disseminate except as authorized by federal rule of criminal procedure 6(e).

On January 2, 2013, Special Agent (SA) [redacted] received a FedEx express envelope containing [redacted]

b3 -1
b6 -1
b7C -1

Investigation on 01/07/2013 at New London, Connecticut, United States (, Other (Subpoena Compliance))

File # 4-NH-2619946 Date drafted 01/07/2013

by [redacted]

b6 -1
b7C -1

4-NH-2619946
SERIAL 135

FD-1087 (Rev. 5-8-10)

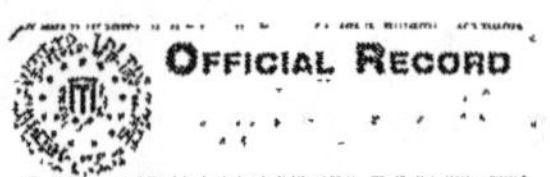

UNCLASSIFIED

FEDERAL BUREAU OF INVESTIGATION

Evidence Log

Event Title: (U) Evidence received from SD RCFL **Date:** 01/07/2013

Approved By: [redacted]

Drafted By: [redacted]

b6 -1
b7C -1

Case ID #: 4-NH-2619946 (U) UNSUB(S)
Sandy Hook Elementary School
12 Dickinson St, Sandy Hook, CT-Victim
Firearms Act.
OO:NH

[redacted]

b7E -1

Acquired By: [redacted] on 01/07/2013

b6 -1
b7C -1

Acquired From: (U) SD RCFL

Receipt Given?: No

Holding Office: SAN DIEGO

Details: *No Details Provided*

[redacted]

b6 -1
b7C -1
OTHER Sealed Pursuant to Court Order

♦♦

UNCLASSIFIED

This document contains neither recommendations nor conclusions of the FBI. It is the property of the FBI and is loaned to your agency, it and its contents are not to be distributed outside your agency

Sandy Hook-2185

4-NH-2619946
SERIAL 136

FD-302 (Rev. 5-8-10)

OFFICIAL RECORD

FEDERAL BUREAU OF INVESTIGATION

Date of entry 01/07/2013

On 01/07/2013, Special Agent [redacted] Federal Bureau of Investigation, New Haven Office, Bridgeport Resident Agency, returned certain property to [redacted] born [redacted] The property was returned under the following circumstances: b6 -1, 2 b7C -1, 2

SA [redacted] was advised by [redacted]

[redacted] b6 -1, 2, 5 b7C -1, 2, 5

Accordingly, on 01/07/2012, at approximately 1:36 p.m., SA [redacted] met with [redacted] at the FBI Bridgeport Office, 1000 Lafayette Boulevard, Bridgeport, Connecticut, and released the following items: b6 -1, 5 b7C -1, 5

[redacted] b6 -2 b7C -2

Following the return of those items, SA [redacted] and [redacted] executed an FD-597 return of property form reflecting that the property was released to [redacted] b6 -1, 5 b7C -1, 5

Investigation on 01/07/2013 at Bridgeport, Connecticut, United States (In Person)

File # 4-NH-2619946 Date drafted 01/07/2013

by [redacted] b6 -1 b7C -1

4-NH-2619946
SERIAL 137

FD-597 (Rev 8-11-94)

UNITED STATES DEPARTMENT OF JUSTICE
FEDERAL BUREAU OF INVESTIGATION
Receipt for Property Received/Returned/Released/Seized

File # 4-NH-

On (date) January 7, 2013

item(s) listed below were:
- [ ] Received From
- [ ] Returned To
- [x] Released To
- [ ] Seized

(Name)

(Street Address)

(City)

Description of Item(s):

b6 -1, 2, 5
b7C -1, 2, 5

Received By:

Received From

(Rev. 07-21-2011)

UNCLASSIFIED

FEDERAL BUREAU OF INVESTIGATION

Serial Removed from Case

Action Performed By: [redacted] **Action Date:** 01/31/2013

Original Form Type: FD-302

Case ID #: 4-NH-2619946

b6 -1
b7C -1

Justification: Other Delete From Case: Document uploaded into incorrect file. Deletion requested [redacted]

♦♦

UNCLASSIFIED

4-NH-2619946 SERIAL 138

FD-1057 (Rev. 5-8-10)

UNCLASSIFIED

FEDERAL BUREAU OF INVESTIGATION

Electronic Communication

Title: (U) To request transfer of evidence from San Diego to New Haven.

Date: 01/08/2013

To: [redacted]
SD-EVD

From: SAN DIEGO
SD-NCRA
Contact: [redacted]

b6 -1
b7C -1

Approved By: SSA [redacted]

Drafted By: [redacted]

Case ID #: 4-NH-2619946

(U) UNSUB(S)
Sandy Hook Elementary School
12 Dickinson St, Sandy Hook, CT-Victim
Firearms Act.
OO:NH

Synopsis: (U) To request San Diego Evidence Control Center transfer and ship 1B items to the New Haven Evidence Control Center.

Full Investigation Initiated: 12/14/2012

Package Copy: (U) Being forwarded in a separate package are the following 1B items for New Haven case 4-NH-2619946:

[redacted]

[redacted] (will be sent in a separate package at a later date)

b6 -2
b7C -2
OTHER Sealed Pursuant to Court Order

Details:

(U) [redacted]

[redacted]

UNCLASSIFIED

Sandy Hook-2189

4-NH-2619946

SERIAL 139

following 1B items were collected for New Haven Division. This communication requests that the San Diego Evidence Control Center (ECC) transfer and ship the following 1B items to the New Haven ECC:

OTHER Sealed Pursuant to Court Order

(will be sent in a separate package at a later date)

♦♦

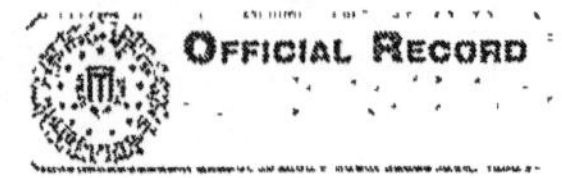

UNCLASSIFIED//~~FOUO~~

FEDERAL BUREAU OF INVESTIGATION

Date of entry 12/27/2012

b6 -1, 5, 6
b7C -1, 5, 6

[redacted] date of birth (DOB) [redacted] interviewed at OTHER Sealed Pursuant to Court Order [redacted]

[redacted] After being advised of the identity of the interviewing Agents, SAs [redacted] and [redacted] and the nature of the interview, [redacted] provided the following information:

[redacted]

b6 -2, 5, 6
b7C -2, 5, 6

[redacted]

b6 -2,
b7C -2

[redacted]

b6 -2,
b7C -2

[redacted]

b6 -2, 5,
b7C -2, 5,

[redacted]

b6 -2, 6
b7C -2,

UNCLASSIFIED//~~FOUO~~

Investigation on 12/23/2012 at [redacted] United States (In Person)

File # 4-NH-2619946 Date drafted 12/27/2012

by [redacted]

b6 -1, 6
b7C -1, 6

4-NH-2619946
SERIAL 140

4-NH-2619946

Continuation of FD-302 of Interview of [redacted] 12/23/2012, On 12/23/2012, Page 2 of 2 b6 -5, 6 b7C -5, 6

[redacted]

[redacted] believes that [redacted] "feels for" the victims of mass killers. He thinks mass killings are just something that continue to happen as in Phoenix, the movie theater, pre-Columbine to current day. b6 -2, 5, 6 b7C -2, 5, 6

[redacted]

b6 -1, 2, 5, 6
b7C -1, 2, 5, 6

- feels, for the victims

- Continuous happenings - Phoenix; movie theatre -

- Pre columbine - continuous.

FD-1057 (Rev. 5-8-10)

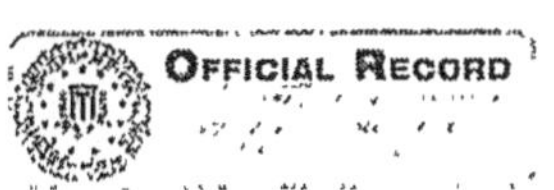

UNCLASSIFIED//~~FOUO~~

FEDERAL BUREAU OF INVESTIGATION

Electronic Communication

Title: (U//~~FOUO~~) BAU 1 assistance requested. **Date:** 01/07/2013

To: [redacted]

From: NEW HAVEN
NH-5
Contact: [redacted]

b6 -1
b7C -1

Approved By: SSA [redacted]
[redacted]

Drafted By: [redacted]

Case ID #: 4-NH-2619946 (U) UNSUB(S)
Sandy Hook Elementary School
12 Dickinson St, Sandy Hook, CT-Victim
Firearms Act.
OO:NH

252B-NH-C23545 (U) NEW HAVEN DIVISION NCAVC MATTERS

Synopsis: (U//~~FOUO~~) To document request for BAU 1 assistance in captioned matter.

[redacted] b7E -1

Details:

This communication serves to document an official request by the New Haven Division for BAU services regarding the school shooting at Sandy Hook Elementary School on December 14, 2012.

Writer, New Haven's Primary NCAVC Coordinator, contacted SSA [redacted] [redacted] of BAU 1 after hearing of initial news reports of the shooting. Following a response to the scene by agents from the New Haven Division, it was determined that assistance was needed. SSA [redacted] concurred with the assessment.

b6 -1
b7C -1

UNCLASSIFIED//~~FOUO~~

Sandy Hook-2212

4-NH-2619946
SERIAL 143

Title: (U//~~FOUO~~) BAU 1 assistance requested.
Re: 4-NH-2619946, 01/07/2013

The investigation is on going and the New Haven matter is assigned to SA[redacted] in the Bridgeport Resident Agency. Any follow up requests for documents or other materials by BAU can be made through writer. Writer will coordinate with both SA[redacted] and other law enforcement agencies involved. b6 b7C

♦♦

(Rev. 07-21-2011)

UNCLASSIFIED

FEDERAL BUREAU OF INVESTIGATION

Serial Removed from Case

Action Performed By: [redacted] **Action Date:** 01/31/2013

Original Form Type: FD-302

b6 -1
b7C -1

Case ID #: 4-NH-2619946

Justification: Other Delete From Case: Document uploaded into incorrect file. Deletion requested [redacted]

♦♦

UNCLASSIFIED

Sandy Hook-2214

4-NH-2619946
SERIAL 144

(Rev. 07-21-2011)

UNCLASSIFIED

FEDERAL BUREAU OF INVESTIGATION

Serial Removed from Case

Action Performed By: [redacted] **Action Date:** 01/31/2013

Original Form Type: FD-302

b6 -1
b7C -1

Case ID #: 4-NH-2619946

Justification: Other Delete From Case: Document uploaded into incorrect file. Deletion requested [redacted]

♦♦

STUB

UNCLASSIFIED

4-NH-2619946
SERIAL 145

FD-1057 (Rev. 5-8-10)

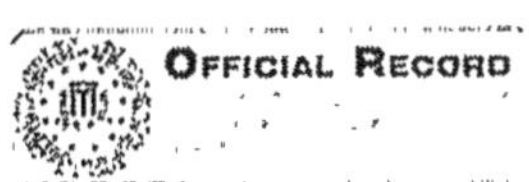

UNCLASSIFIED

FEDERAL BUREAU OF INVESTIGATION

Electronic Communication

Title: (U) [redacted] b6 -2 **Date:** 01/08/2013
[redacted] b7C -2
OTHER Sealed Pursuant to Court Order

From: NEW HAVEN
NH-10
Contact: [redacted]

b6 -1
b7C -1

Approved By: SSA [redacted]

Drafted By: [redacted]

Case ID #: 4-NH-2619946 (U) UNSUB(S)
Sandy Hook Elementary School
12 Dickinson St, Sandy Hook, CT-Victim
Firearms Act. b6 -2
OO:NH b7C -2
OTHER Sealed Pursuant to Court Order

Synopsis: (U) [redacted]
[redacted]

[redacted] b7E -1

Reference: 4-NH-2619946 Serial 93

Enclosure(s): Enclosed are the following items: OTHER Sealed Pursuant to Court Order
[redacted]

Details:

On 12/16/2012, SA [redacted] conducted the following investigative activity [redacted]
[redacted]

b6 -1, 7
UNCLASSIFIED b7C -1, 7
OTHER Sealed Pursuant to Court Order

OTHER Sealed Pursuant to Court Order

RE:

Sent: Sunday, December 16, 2012 17:55

To:

Cc: (USACT); (USACT) (USACT);

Attachments:

b6 -1, 4
b7C -1, 4
OTHER Sealed Pursuant to Court Order

From
Sent: Sunday, December 16, 2012 5:55 PM
To:
Cc: (USACT) (USACT); (USACT);
Subject:

b6 -1, 4
b7C -1, 4
OTHER Sealed Pursuant to Court Order

Regarding

Please see attached for more details.

Regards,

b6 -1
b7C -1

SA
FBI - New Haven
Squad 10

FD-1057 (Rev. 5-8-10)

UNCLASSIFIED//~~FOUO~~

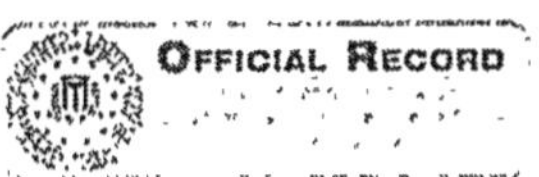

FEDERAL BUREAU OF INVESTIGATION

Electronic Communication

Title: (U) Request Examination of Evidence **Date:** 01/10/2013

To: [redacted]

From: NEW HAVEN
NH-9
Contact: [redacted]

b6 -1
b7C -1
b7E -7

Approved By: SSA [redacted]

Drafted By: [redacted]

Case ID #: 4-NH-2619946 (U) UNSUB(S)
Sandy Hook Elementary School
12 Dickinson St, Sandy Hook, CT-Victim
Firearms Act.
OO:NH
[redacted] (U//~~FOUO~~) [redacted]

b7A -1
b7E -4

Synopsis: (U) Pursuant to a Search and Seizure Warrant issued by the State of Connecticut Superior Court on 12/14/2012, computer and other evidence was seized at 36 Yogananda Street, Newtown CT. Included in the seizure was an 80 GB Western Digital hard drive [redacted] [redacted] It is requested that this drive be examined [redacted] b7E -6

[redacted] b7E -1

Package Copy: (U) 1B46, E5132474, an 80GB Western Digital Caviar WD800 hard drive, model WD800BB-00CAA1, s/n WMA8E2463020

Details:

Request Operational Technology, [redacted] b7E -7 conduct an examination of 1B46, E5132474, an 80GB Western Digital Caviar WD800 hard drive, s/n WMA8E2463020. Examination is pursuant to a

UNCLASSIFIED//~~FOUO~~

4-NH-2619946
SERIAL 147

Title: (U) Request Examination of Evidence
Re: 4-NH-2619946, 01/10/2013

Search and Seizure Warrant issued by the State of Connecticut Superior Court on December 14, 2012 by the Honorable John F. Blawie. A copy of the search warrant is enclosed.

On December 14, 2012, Adam Lanza, a resident of 36 Yogananda Street, Newtown, CT, shot and killed his mother, Nancy Lanza. He then proceeded to the Sandy Hook Elementary School in Newtown, CT, where he additionally killed 26 more victims, including children.

A search of the residence of Lanza turned up numerous items of evidence, including the item being requested to be examined. It was turned over to New Haven CART Examiner SA [redacted] on December 19, 2012. [redacted] SA [redacted] spoke with [redacted] who advised [redacted] examination [redacted]

b6 -1
b7C -1
b7E -6,

SA [redacted] cell number [redacted] is the case Agent. SA [redacted] cell number [redacted] is the CART Examiner involved.

b6 -
b7C

♦♦

FD-1036 (Rev. 10-16-2009)

UNCLASSIFIED//~~FOUO~~

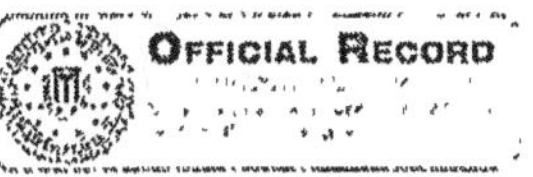

FEDERAL BUREAU OF INVESTIGATION

Import Form

Form Type: FD-888 **Date:** 01/10/2013

Title: (U//~~FOUO~~) [redacted]

Approved By: SSA [redacted]

b6 -1, 2
b7C -1, 2
OTHER Sealed Pursuant to Court Order

Drafted By: [redacted]

Case ID #: 4-NH-2619946

(U) UNSUB(S)
Sandy Hook Elementary School
12 Dickinson St, Sandy Hook, CT-Victim
Firearms Act.
OO:NH

Synopsis: (U//~~FOUO~~) [redacted]

Enclosure(s): Enclosed are the following items:

[redacted]

b6 -2
b7C -2
OTHER Sealed Pursuant to Court Order

♦♦

UNCLASSIFIED//~~FOUO~~

4-NH-2619946
SERIAL 148

FD-302 (Rev 5-8-10)

UNCLASSIFIED//~~FOUO~~

FEDERAL BUREAU OF INVESTIGATION

Date of entry 01/10/2013

b6 1, 2, 3
b7C 1, 2, 3
b7E -11
OTHER Sealed Pursuant to Court Order

UNCLASSIFIED//~~FOUO~~

Investigation on 12/23/2012 at [redacted] United States (In Person)

File # 4-NH-2619946 Date drafted 01/10/2013

by [redacted]

This document contains neither recommendations nor conclusions of the FBI. It is the property of the FBI and is loaned to your agency; it and its contents are not to be distributed outside your agency.

FD-302 (Rev. 5-8-10)

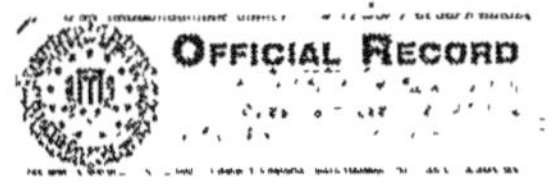

UNCLASSIFIED//~~FOUO~~

FEDERAL BUREAU OF INVESTIGATION

Date of entry 01/11/2013

OTHER Sealed Pursuant to Court Order

UNCLASSIFIED//~~FOUO~~

Investigation on 12/16/2012 at New Haven, Connecticut, United States (Mail)

File # 4-NH-2619946 Date drafted 01/11/2013

by b6 -1 b7C -1

4-NH-2619946

SERIAL 150

FD-302 (Rev. 5-8-10)

UNCLASSIFIED//~~FOUO~~

FEDERAL BUREAU OF INVESTIGATION

Date of entry 01/11/2013

b6 -2
b7C -2
OTHER Sealed Pursuant to Court Order

UNCLASSIFIED//~~FOUO~~

Investigation on 12/20/2012 at New Haven, Connecticut, United States (Mail)

File # 4-NH-2619946 Date drafted 01/11/2013

by

b6 -1
b7C -1

Sandy Hook-2

4-NH-2619946
SERIAL 151

FD-302 (Rev. 5-8-10)

UNCLASSIFIED//~~FOUO~~

FEDERAL BUREAU OF INVESTIGATION

Date of entry 01/11/2013

OTHER Sealed Pursuant to Court Order

UNCLASSIFIED//~~FOUO~~

Investigation on 12/18/2012 at New Haven, Connecticut, United States (Mail)

File # 4-NH-2619946 Date drafted 01/11/2013

by

b6 -1
b7C -1

4-NH-2619946
SERIAL 152

FD-302 (Rev. 5-8-10)

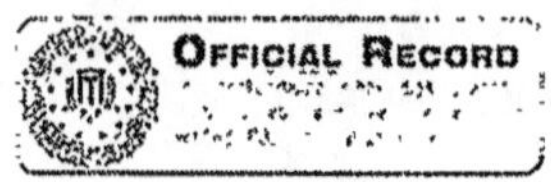

UNCLASSIFIED//~~FOUO~~

FEDERAL BUREAU OF INVESTIGATION

Date of entry 01/11/2013

b6 -2
b7C -2
OTHER Sealed Pursuant to Court Order

UNCLASSIFIED//~~FOUO~~

Investigation on 12/20/2012 at New Haven, Connecticut, United States (Mail)

File # 4-NH-2619946 Date drafted 01/11/2013

by

b6 -1
b7C -

Sandy Hook-2

4-NH-2619946
SERIAL 153

FD-1057 (Rev. 5-8-10)

FEDERAL BUREAU OF INVESTIGATION

Electronic Communication

Title: (U//~~FOUO~~) Review of Adam Lanza web postings on www.shockedbeyondbelief.com

Date: 01/11/2013

To: [redacted]

From: NEW HAVEN
NH-13
Contact: [redacted]

b6 -1
b7C -1

Approved By: SSA [redacted]

Drafted By: [redacted]

Case ID #: 4-NH-2619946 (U) UNSUB(S)
Sandy Hook Elementary School
12 Dickinson St, Sandy Hook, CT-Victim
Firearms Act.
OO:NH

Synopsis: (U//~~FOUO~~) FBI Behavioral Analysis Unit (BAU) had requested information regarding web postings made by Adam Lanza. The 1A submitted with this contains a Microsoft Word document which lists all of Adam Lanza's postings on www.shockedbeyondbelief.com as well as the context of those postings along with comments.

[redacted] b7E -1

Enclosure(s): Enclosed are the following items:
1. (U//~~FOUO~~) review of Adam Lanza web postings on www.shockedbeyondbelief.com

Details:

(U//~~FOUO~~) FBI Behavioral Analysis Unit (BAU) had requested a review/analysis of the Adam Lanza web postings on

4-NH-2619946
SERIAL 154

Title: (U//FOUO) Review of Adam Lanza web postings on www.shockedbeyondbelief.com
Re: 4-NH-2619946, 01/11/2013

www.shockedbeyondbelief.com. That review is included as a digital copy in the "attached" 1A for record keeping. The digital document was already provided to FBI BAU. All of Adam Lanza's postings are listed in the 1A as well as the related communications by other posters on the web forum. Additionally, analyst notes are included to explain context and the nature of the hyperlinks that were part of Adam Lanza's postings.

♦♦

FD-1057 (Rev. 5-8-10)

UNCLASSIFIED

FEDERAL BUREAU OF INVESTIGATION

Electronic Communication

Title: (U) Original notes re: [redacted] [redacted]

Date: 01/09/2013

From: NEW HAVEN
NH-4
Contact: [redacted]

b6 -1, 2
b7C -1, 2

Approved By: [redacted]

Drafted By: [redacted]

Case ID #: 4-NH-2619946 (U) UNSUB(S)
Sandy Hook Elementary School
12 Dickinson St, Sandy Hook, CT-Victim
Firearms Act.
OO:NH

Synopsis: (U) Original notes re: [redacted]
[redacted]

Reference: 4-NH-2619946 Serial 62

b6 -2
b7C -2
b7E -1

Enclosure(s): Enclosed are the following items:
1. (U) Original notes re: [redacted]

Details:

Original notes re: [redacted]

♦♦

UNCLASSIFIED

Sandy Hook-2349

4-NH-2619946
SERIAL 155

Cell

D.O.B.

SS #

b6 -2
b7C -2

FD-1057 (Rev. 5-8-10)

UNCLASSIFIED

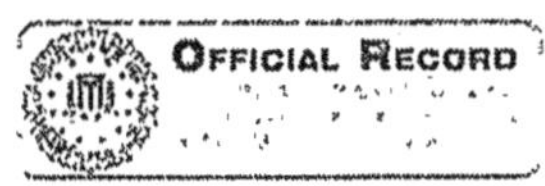

FEDERAL BUREAU OF INVESTIGATION

Electronic Communication

Title: (U) notes re: [redacted] **Date:** 01/09/2013

From: NEW HAVEN
NH-4
Contact: [redacted]

b6 -1, 2
b7C -1, 2

Approved By: [redacted]

Drafted By: [redacted]

Case ID #: 4-NH-2619946 (U) UNSUB(S)
Sandy Hook Elementary School
12 Dickinson St, Sandy Hook, CT-Victim
Firearms Act.
OO:NH

Synopsis: (U) Original notes re: [redacted]

Reference: 4-NH-2619946 Serial 50

b6 -2
b7C -2
b7E -1

Enclosure(s): Enclosed are the following items:
1. (U) Original notes re: [redacted]

Details:

Original notes re: [redacted]

♦♦

UNCLASSIFIED

4-NH-2619946
SERIAL 156

12/14/2012

got up 8:50 - left for work

— Bank america / Cavel

b6 -6
b7C -6

got coffee at DD.

got to office approx 9:45.

ADAM PETER LANZA
4/22/92

b6 -5, 6
b7C -5, 6

Adam — Aspergers Syndrome
(autism) diagnosed in 8th grade
"Recluse" shut himself
in room — played video games
all day.

Dropped out of H.S.
Took courses at Western CT.
near full-time.

b6 -6
b7C -6

b6 -6
b7C -6

Adam has no friends, no
known associates
very computer savvy.

Adam liked target shooting

223 AR 15 Semi Auto – Black
Adam owned it
Lee Enfield #4 .308 Rifle
owned by

Handgun possibly .45

Adam kept it in a
gun safe
~~possibly~~ Automatic shotgun at some time
in gun safe
→ Safe in Adams Bedroom
closet.

b6 -6
b7C -6

Adam would buy ammo.
believing it was legal -

Adam got NRA certification
to fire pistol at range.

Adam became interested in
firearms

At one point
Adam considered joining the Military
No indication that this
would happen

He had no outside friends so
she was his only person to
talk with.

06-10? / Worked Briefly for computer repair
shop in Newtown - only job -

b6 -6
b7C -6

never worked in High School,
no summer jobs.

No violent video games.
had trouble expressing himself,
got frustrated but not violent
no angry outbursts.

b6 -6
b7C -6

No drugs or alcohol
hated the thought of it.

FD-1087 (Rev. 5-8-10)

UNCLASSIFIED

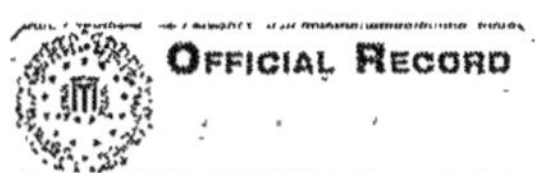

FEDERAL BUREAU OF INVESTIGATION

Evidence Log

Event Title: (U) DENH15-21 **Date:** 01/11/2013

Approved By: SSA [redacted]

Drafted By: [redacted]

b6 -1
b7C -1

Case ID #: 4-NH-2619946 (U) UNSUB(S)
Sandy Hook Elementary School
12 Dickinson St, Sandy Hook, CT-Victim
Firearms Act.
OO:NH

[redacted]

b7E -1

Acquired By: [redacted] on 01/11/2013

b6 -1
b7C -1

Acquired From: (U) Forensic Exam

Receipt Given?: No

Holding Office: NEW HAVEN

Details:

DENH15-21 250 GB Seagate hard drive, Serial #: 6VYD4VYH containing examination results reports for QNHPL15 and QNHPL21

Item Type **Description**

UNCLASSIFIED

This document contains neither recommendations nor conclusions of the FBI. It is the property of the FBI and is loaned to your agency; it and its contents are not to be distributed outside your agency.

4-NH-2619946
SERIAL 157

Title: (U) DENH15-21
Re: 4-NH-2619946, 01/11/2013

1B CART	(U) DENH15-21 250 GB Seagate hard drive, Serial #: 6VYD4VYH containing examination results reports for QNHPL15 and QNHPL21

Acquired On: 01/11/2013
Located By: [redacted] b6 -1 b7C -1
Location Area: CART LAB
Specific Location: Exam Station
Device Type: Mass Storage Device
Number of Devices Collected: 1

♦♦

UNCLASSIFIED

FEDERAL BUREAU OF INVESTIGATION

Import Form

Form Type: DEL-REX **Date:** 01/11/2013

Title: (U) Digital Evidence Laboratory Report of Examination for QNHPL15 and QNHPL21

Approved By: SSA [redacted]

Drafted By: [redacted]

b6 -1
b7C -1

Case ID #: 4-NH-2619946 (U) UNSUB(S)
Sandy Hook Elementary School
12 Dickinson St, Sandy Hook, CT-Victim
Firearms Act.
OO:NH

Synopsis: (U) Examination results for QNHPL15 and QNHPL21

Enclosure(s): Enclosed are the following items:
1. (U) Administrative Notes
2. (U) Case notes

♦♦

UNCLASSIFIED

4-NH-2619946
SERIAL 158

FD-1087 (Rev. 5-8-10)

UNCLASSIFIED

FEDERAL BUREAU OF INVESTIGATION

Evidence Log

Event Title: (U) CART Process **Date:** 01/14/2013

Approved By: SSA [redacted]

Drafted By: [redacted]

b6 -1
b7C -1

Case ID #: 4-NH-2619946 (U) UNSUB(S)
Sandy Hook Elementary School
12 Dickinson St, Sandy Hook, CT-Victim
Firearms Act.
OO:NH

[redacted]

b7E -1

Acquired By: [redacted] on 01/14/2013

Acquired From: (U) [redacted]

b6 -1, 2
b7C -1, 2

Receipt Given?: No

Holding Office: NEW HAVEN

Details:

Derived Evidence obtained by CART from processing of digital evidence items in captioned case.

Item Type	Description

UNCLASSIFIED

4-NH-2619946
SERIAL 159

Title: (U) CART Process
Re: 4-NH-2619946, 01/14/2013

1B CART (U)

Acquired On: 12/18/2012
Located By:
Location Area: CART Lab
Specific Location: Copy of evidence
Device Type:
Number of Devices Collected:

b6 -1, 2
b7C -1, 2

♦♦

FD-1087 (Rev. 5-8-10)

UNCLASSIFIED//~~FOUO~~

FEDERAL BUREAU OF INVESTIGATION

Evidence Log

Event Title: (U) CART Process **Date:** 01/14/2013

Approved By: SSA [redacted]

Drafted By: [redacted]

b6 -1
b7C -1

Case ID #: 4-NH-2619946 (U) UNSUB(S)
Sandy Hook Elementary School
12 Dickinson St, Sandy Hook, CT-Victim
Firearms Act.
OO:NH

[redacted] b7E -1

Acquired By: [redacted] on 01/14/2013

b6 -1
b7C -1

Acquired From: (U) 36 Yogananda St
Newtown, Connecticut
United States

Receipt Given?: No

Holding Office: NEW HAVEN

Details:

Derived Evidence obtained by CART from processing of digital evidence items in captioned case.

Item Type	**Description**
1B CART	(U) DENHJB4: one DVD containing an image copy of a 1GB "Narae" brand digital voice recorder Acquired On: 01/03/2013 Located By: [redacted] Location Area: CART Lab Specific Location: Copy of evidence Device Type: Other Number of Devices Collected: 1

b6 -1
b7C -1

UNCLASSIFIED//~~FOUO~~

4-NH-2619946
SERIAL 160

Title: (U) CART Process
Re: 4-NH-2619946, 01/14/2013

1B CART

(U) DENHJB3: a 500GB Seagate hard drive, s/n Z2AKBE6F, containing image copies of QNHJB2 (a 160GB Transcend Storejet external USB hard drive s/n 152D20329000) and QNHJB3 (an 80GB Samsung hard drive, s/n S042J20L233874, from a Dell Inspiron laptop, service tag # CW67L91)
Acquired On: 01/07/2013 b6 -1
Located By: [redacted] b7C -1
Location Area: CART Lab
Specific Location: Copy of evidence
Device Type: Other
Number of Devices Collected: 1

♦♦

FD-302 (Rev. 5-8-10)

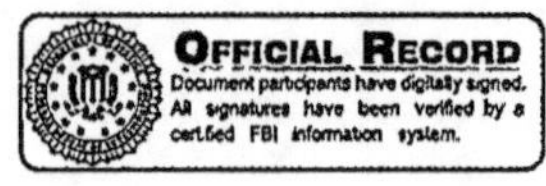

FEDERAL BUREAU OF INVESTIGATION

Date of entry 01/11/2013

[redacted] Administrative paperwork was placed into a 1A envelope and is attached to this document.

b6 -1, 2
b7C -1, 2
OTHER Sealed Pursuant to Court Order

Investigation on 12/23/2012 at [redacted] United States (In Person)

File # 4-NH-2619946 b6 -1 b7C -1 Date drafted 12/26/2012

by [redacted] OTHER Sealed Pursuant to Court Order

4-NH-2619946
SERIAL 161

FD-302 (Rev. 5-8-10)

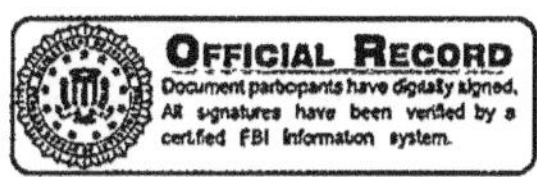

FEDERAL BUREAU OF INVESTIGATION

Date of entry 12/19/2012

On this date, SA [redacted] received [redacted]

[redacted]

b3 -1
b6 -1, 5
b7C -1, 5

Investigation on 12/19/2012 at Meriden, Connecticut, United States (Email)

File # 4-NH-2619946 Date drafted 12/19/2012

by [redacted]

b6 -1
b7C -1

4-NH-2619964
SERIAL 162

FD-302 (Rev. 5-8-10)

FEDERAL BUREAU OF INVESTIGATION

Date of entry 12/21/2012

On 12/20/12, SA [redacted] received [redacted]

[redacted]

b3 -1
b6 -1,
b7C -1,

Investigation on 12/20/2012 at Meriden, Connecticut, United States (Email)

File # 4-NH-2619946 Date drafted 12/21/2012

by [redacted]

b6 -1
b7C -

4-NH-2619946
SERIAL 163

FD-302 (Rev. 5-8-10)

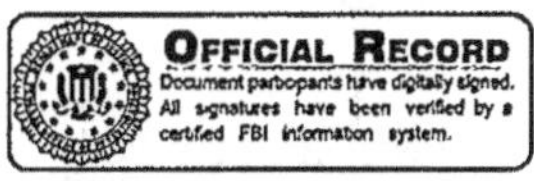

FEDERAL BUREAU OF INVESTIGATION

Date of entry 12/21/2012

[redacted] date of birth: [redacted] Social Security Number: [redacted] was interviewed at the Federal Bureau of Investigation (FBI) office, Long Beach Resident Agency, located at One World Trade Center, Suite 1500, Long Beach, California 90831. After being advised of the identities of the interviewing agents and the purpose of the interview, [redacted] provided the following information. [redacted] b6 -2 b7C -2 b7E -6

[redacted] provided [redacted] which listed his address as [redacted] His cellular telephone is: [redacted] his e-mail address is: [redacted] current address is: [redacted] b6 -2 b7C -2

[redacted] advised [redacted] b6 -2, 5 b7C -2, 5

[redacted] b6 -2, 5 b7C -2, 5

[redacted] b6 -2 b7C -2

Investigation on 12/14/2012 at Long Beach, California, United States (In Person)

File # 4-NH-2619946 Date drafted 12/19/2012

by [redacted] b6 -1 b7C -1

4-NH-2619946 Sandy Hook-2449

SERIAL 167

b6 -2
b7C -2

[redacted] he knew Adam was mentally disabled and described as a "high functioning" autistic individual who went to school. [redacted]

b6 -2
b7C -2

(3)

- mentally disabled

high functioning autistic

- goes to school

b6 2
b7C 2

FD-1036 (Rev. 10-16-2009)

UNCLASSIFIED

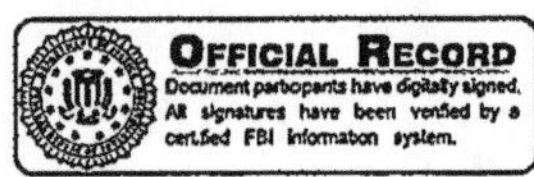

FEDERAL BUREAU OF INVESTIGATION

Import Form

Form Type: DEL-REX **Date:** 01/15/2013

Title: (U) Lab #130111256

Approved By: [redacted]

Drafted By: [redacted]

b6 -1
b7C -1

Case ID #: 4-NH-2619946 (U) UNSUB(S)
Sandy Hook Elementary School
12 Dickinson St, Sandy Hook, CT-Victim
Firearms Act.
OO:NH

Synopsis: (U) Lab #130111256 QD, Re: 01-10-2013

Enclosure(s): Enclosed are the following items:
1. (U) Lab #130111256 QD, Retained at ERF

♦♦

UNCLASSIFIED

4-NH-2619946
SERIAL 168 Sandy Hook-

FD-1057 (Rev. 5-8-10)

UNCLASSIFIED

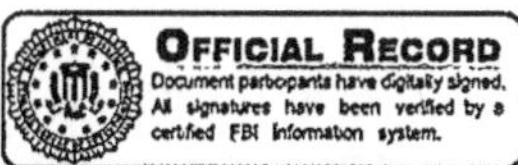

FEDERAL BUREAU OF INVESTIGATION

Electronic Communication

Title: (U) Transfer of evidence from New Haven Division to Newark Division

Date: 01/16/2013

To: [redacted]

From: NEW HAVEN
NH-BRA2
Contact: [redacted]

b6 -1
b7C -1

Approved By: SSRA [redacted]

Drafted By: [redacted]

Case ID #: 4-NH-2619946

(U) UNSUB(S)
Sandy Hook Elementary School
12 Dickinson St, Sandy Hook, CT-Victim
Firearms Act.
OO:NH

Synopsis: (U) Request to transfer evidence from New Haven Division evidence control to Newark Division evidence control.

[redacted] b7E -1

Details:

After reviewing and analyzing this evidence, 1B3, New Haven Division requests to return this back to Newark Division. In furtherance of this transfer, send to Newark evidence control technician [redacted] and ultimately to [redacted] the owner.

b6 -1, 2
b7C -1, 2

♦♦

UNCLASSIFIED

Sandy Hook-2470

4-NH-2619946
SERIAL 164

FEDERAL BUREAU OF INVESTIGATION
FOI/PA
DELETED PAGE INFORMATION SHEET
Civil Action# 16-cv-02136

Total Deleted Page(s) = 60
Page 7 ~ Duplicate;
Page 8 ~ Duplicate;
Page 10 ~ Duplicate;
Page 12 ~ Duplicate;
Page 13 ~ Duplicate;
Page 14 ~ Duplicate;
Page 15 ~ Duplicate;
Page 16 ~ Duplicate;
Page 17 ~ Duplicate;
Page 22 ~ Duplicate;
Page 23 ~ Duplicate;
Page 24 ~ Duplicate;
Page 25 ~ Duplicate;
Page 26 ~ Duplicate;
Page 27 ~ Duplicate;
Page 28 ~ Duplicate;
Page 29 ~ Duplicate;
Page 33 ~ b6 - 5; b7C - 5;
Page 35 ~ Duplicate;
Page 36 ~ Duplicate;
Page 37 ~ Duplicate;
Page 38 ~ Duplicate;
Page 39 ~ Duplicate;
Page 40 ~ Duplicate;
Page 41 ~ Duplicate;
Page 42 ~ Duplicate;
Page 43 ~ Duplicate;
Page 44 ~ Duplicate;
Page 45 ~ Duplicate;
Page 47 ~ Duplicate;
Page 49 ~ Duplicate;
Page 50 ~ Duplicate;
Page 51 ~ Duplicate;
Page 52 ~ Duplicate;
Page 53 ~ Duplicate;
Page 54 ~ Duplicate;
Page 55 ~ Duplicate;
Page 56 ~ Duplicate;
Page 57 ~ Duplicate;
Page 58 ~ Duplicate;
Page 59 ~ Duplicate;
Page 60 ~ Duplicate;
Page 61 ~ Duplicate;
Page 62 ~ Duplicate;
Page 63 ~ Duplicate;
Page 66 ~ b6 - 1, 2, 5, 6; b7C - 1, 2, 5, 6;
Page 82 ~ b6 - 5, 6; b7C - 5, 6;
Page 88 ~ Duplicate;

Page 89 ~ Duplicate;
Page 90 ~ Duplicate;
Page 92 ~ b6 - 5, 6; b7C - 5, 6;
Page 93 ~ b6 - 5, 6; b7C - 5, 6;
Page 95 ~ b6 - 6; b7C - 6;
Page 97 ~ b6 - 5, 6; b7C - 5, 6;
Page 102 ~ b6 - 5, 6; b7C - 5, 6;
Page 107 ~ b6 - 5, 6; b7C - 5, 6;
Page 108 ~ b6 - 5, 6; b7C - 5, 6;
Page 113 ~ b6 - 1, 5; b7C - 1, 5; OTHER - Sealed Pursuant to Court Order;
Page 114 ~ b6 - 5; b7C - 5; OTHER - Sealed Pursuant to Court Order;
Page 115 ~ OTHER - Sealed Pursuant to Court Order;

XXXXXXXXXXXXXXXXXXXXXXXX
X Deleted Page(s) X
X No Duplication Fee X
X For this Page X
XXXXXXXXXXXXXXXXXXXXXXXX

FD-340a (Rev. 1-27-03)

(Title) 1A's

(File No.) 4-NH-2619946

Item	Date Filed	To be returned Yes	No		Disposition

FD-340 (Rev. 4-11-03)

File Number 4-NH-2619946 1A55

Field Office Acquiring Evidence NH

Serial # of Originating Document 101

Date Received 12/20/2012

From
(Name of Contributor/Interviewee)

(Address)

(City and State)

By SA [redacted]

b6 -1
b7C -1

To Be Returned ☐ Yes ☒ No

Receipt Given ☐ Yes ☒ No

Grand Jury Material - Disseminate Only Pursuant to Rule 6 (e) Federal Rules of Criminal Procedure

☐ Yes ☒ No

Federal Taxpayer Information (FTI)

☐ Yes ☒ No

Title: Unsub(s);
Sandy Hook Elementary - victim;

Reference: FD-302
(Communication Enclosing Material)

Description: ☐ Original notes re interview of

Original notes re attempted call to telephone number [redacted] on 12/20/2012.

b6 -2
b7C -2

FD-340 (Rev. 4-11-03) 1A56

File Number 4-NH-2619946

Field Office Acquiring Evidence NH

Serial # of Originating Document 102

Date Received 12/23/2012

From

(City and State)

By SA

b6 -1
b7C -1
OTHER Sealed Pursuant to Court Order

To Be Returned ☐ Yes ☐ No

Receipt Given ☐ Yes ☐ No

Grand Jury Material - Disseminate Only Pursuant to Rule 6 (e)
Federal Rules of Criminal Procedure

☐ Yes ☐ No

Federal Taxpayer Information (FTI)

☐ Yes ☐ No

Title:

Reference: FD-302 dated 12/27/12

(Communication Enclosing Material)

b6 -2
b7C -2
OTHER Sealed Pursuant to Court Order

Description: ☐ Original notes re interview of

1A57

FD-340c (4-11-03)

File Number 4-NH-2619946 - 1A57

Field Office Acquiring Evidence Boston

Serial # of Originating Document [illegible] 4-NH-2619946-103

Date Received 12/15/2012

From FBI

(Name of Contributor/Interviewee)

120 Front Street, Suite 810-G

(Address)

Worcester, Massachusetts

(City and State)

By SA

To Be Returned ☐ Yes ☒ No

1A57

Receipt Given ☐ Yes ☐ No

Grand Jury Material - Disseminate Only Pursuant to Rule 6 (e)
Federal Rules of Criminal Procedure

☐ Yes ☒ No

b6 -1, 6
b7C -1, 6

Federal Taxpayer Information (FTI)

☐ Yes ☒ No

Title: UNSUB(S)
Sandy Hook Elementary School
12 Dickinson Street, Sandy Hook, CT - Victim
Firearms Act

Reference:

(Communication Enclosing Material)

Description: ☒ Original notes re interview of

on 12/15/12

1A57

1A 59

FD-340 (Rev. 8-7-97)

Universal Case File Number 4-NH-2619946

Field Office Acquiring Evidence NH

Serial # of Originating Document 107

Date Received 12/14/12

From [redacted] b6 -1 b7C -1

(Name of Contributor) OTHER Sealed Pursuant to Court Order

(Address of Contributor)

By SA [redacted]

To Be Returned ☐ Yes ☐ No

Receipt Given ☐ Yes ☐ No

Grand Jury Material - Disseminate Only Pursuant to Rule 6 (e) Federal Rules of Criminal Procedure

☐ Yes ☒ No

Title:

Reference: FD-302 dated 12/28/12

(Communication Enclosing Material)

Description: ☐ Original notes re interview of OTHER Sealed Pursuant to Court Order

[redacted]

FD-340 (Rev. 4-11-03)

File Number 4-NH-2619946 1A62

Field Office Acquiring Evidence NH

Serial # of Originating Document 110

Date Received 12/14/2012

From

(Name of Contributor/Interviewee)

(Address)

(City and State)

By SA

b6 -1
b7C -1

To Be Returned ☐ Yes ☒ No

Receipt Given ☐ Yes ☒ No

Grand Jury Material - Disseminate Only Pursuant to Rule 6 (e)
Federal Rules of Criminal Procedure

☐ Yes ☒ No

Federal Taxpayer Information (FTI)

☐ Yes ☒ No

Sandy Hook Elementary School.

Reference: EC

(Communication Enclosing Material)

Description: ☒ Original notes re interview of

b6 -2
b7C -2
b7E -7

1A 63

FD-340 (Rev. 4-11-03)

File Number 4-NH-2619946

Field Office Acquiring Evidence BS

Serial # of Originating Document 111

Date Received 12/14/12

From ____________________
(Name of Contributor/Interviewee)

____
(Address)

____
(City and State)

By SA [redacted]

b6 -1
b7C -1

To Be Returned ☐ Yes ☒ No

Receipt Given ☐ Yes ☒ No

Grand Jury Material - Disseminate Only Pursuant to Rule 6 (e)
Federal Rules of Criminal Procedure

☐ Yes ☒ No

Federal Taxpayer Information (FTI)

☐ Yes ☒ No

Title: UNSUB(S);
Sandy Hook Elementary School - Uchm
Firearms Act
00:NH

Reference: ____________________
(Communication Enclosing Material)

Description: ☑ Original notes re interview of
Chief Donald Briggs

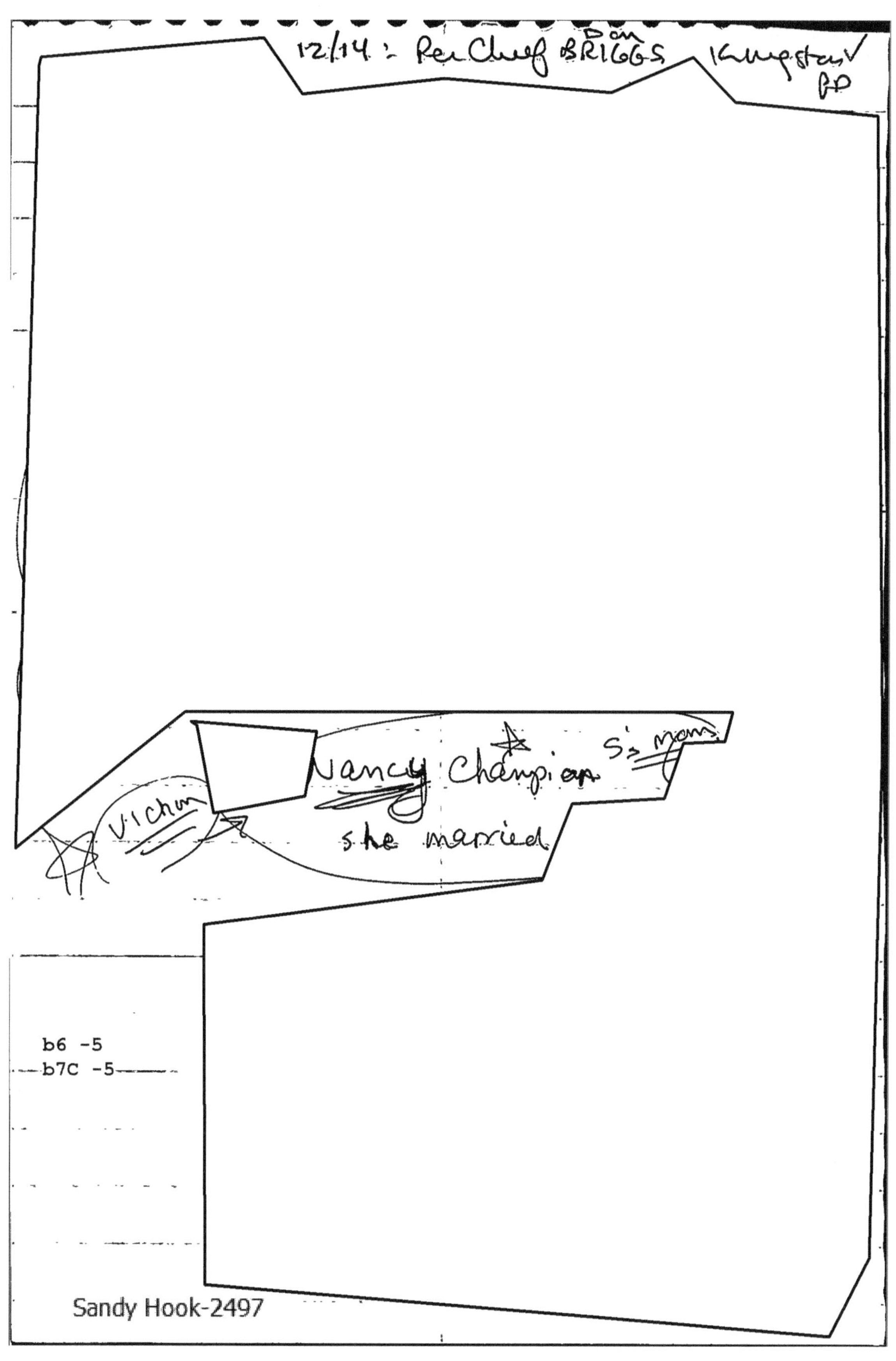

12/14: Per Chief Don BRIGGS Kingston PD
Nancy Champion
S's mom
she married

b6 -5
b7C -5

b6 -5
b7C -5

S prob attended

Daniel J. Bakie School

FD-340 (Rev. 4-11-03)

File Number 4-NH-2619946-1A64

Field Office Acquiring Evidence New Haven

Serial # of Originating Document 4-NH-2619946-112

Date Received 12/23/12

From [redacted]

(City and State)

By SA [redacted]

To Be Returned ☐ Yes ☒ No

Receipt Given ☐ Yes ☒ No

Grand Jury Material - Disseminate Only Pursuant to Rule 6 (e) Federal Rules of Criminal Procedure

☐ Yes ☒ No

Federal Taxpayer Information (FTI)

☐ Yes ☒ No

b6 1, 2
b7C 1, 2
OTHER Sealed Pursuant to Court Order

Reference: ______________________
(Communication Enclosing Material)

Description: ☒ Original notes re interview of

[redacted]

b6 -2
b7C -2

File - Serial Charge Out
FD-5 (Rev. 10-13-89)

Date 5-8-14

File ______ Class. ______ Office of Origin 4-NH ~~[illegible]~~C - 2619946 Case No. ______ Last Serial

☐ Pending ☐ Closed

Serial No.	Description of Serial	Date Charged
	1A #66	5-8-14

______ Employee

RECHARGE Date ______

To ______ From ______

Initials of Clerk ______ Date ______

b6 -1
b7C -1

5-8-14
Date charged

Employee

D-340 (Rev. 4-11-03)

ile Number 4-NH-2619946 1A68

ield Office Acquiring Evidence NH

erial # of Originating Document #116

ate Received 12/23/12

rom

b6 -1, 6
b7C -1, 6
OTHER Sealed Pursuant to Court Order

(City and State)

By SA

To Be Returned ☐ Yes ☐ No

Receipt Given ☐ Yes ☐ No

Grand Jury Material - Disseminate Only Pursuant to Rule 6 (e)
Federal Rules of Criminal Procedure

☐ Yes ☐ No

Federal Taxpayer Information (FTI)

☐ Yes ☐ No

Title:

Reference: 302 dated 12/28/2012
(Communication Enclosing Material)

Description: ☒ Original notes re interview of

b6 -6
b7C -6

1A69

FD-340 (Rev. 4-11-03)

File Number 4-NH-2619946

Field Office Acquiring Evidence BS

Serial # of Originating Document 119

Date Received 12/14 - 12/22/2012

From ______
(Name of Contributor/Interviewee)

______
(Address)

______

By SA [redacted]

b6 -1
b7C -1

To Be Returned ☐ Yes ☒ No

Receipt Given ☐ Yes ☐ No

Grand Jury Material - Disseminate Only Pursuant to Rule 6 (e)
Federal Rules of Criminal Procedure

☐ Yes ☐ No

Federal Taxpayer Information (FTI)

☐ Yes ☐ No

Title: Sandy Hook Elementary School;
UCkun
Firearms Act

Reference: ______
(Communication Enclosing Material)

Description: ☒ Original notes re interview of [redacted]

b6 -6
b7C -6

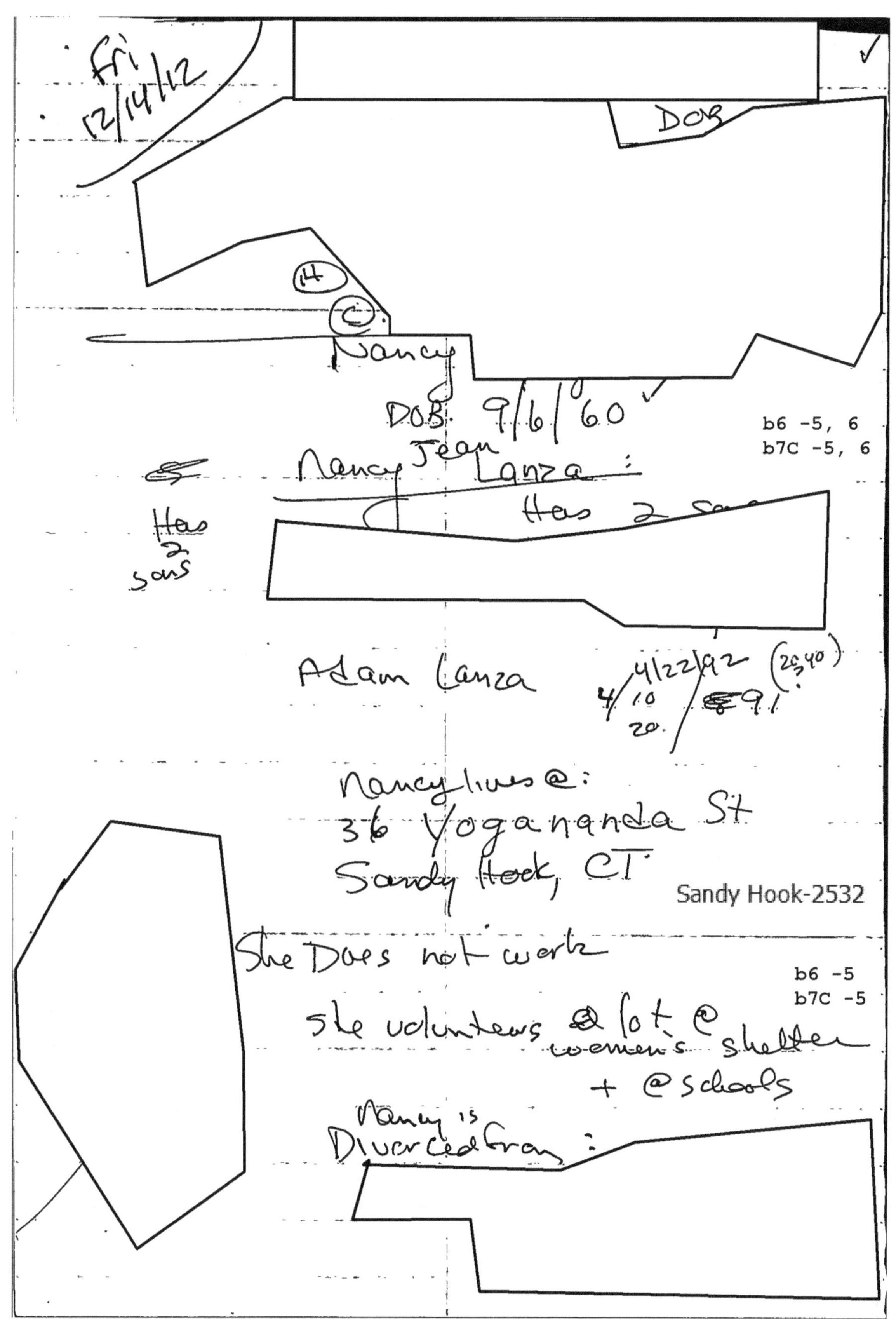

fri
12/14/12

DOB

(14)

(C)

Nancy

DOB 9/6/60

b6 -5, 6
b7C -5, 6

Nancy Jean Lanza :

Has 2 sons

~~Has 2 Sons~~

Adam Lanza 4/22/92 (20/40)
4/10/20 / ~~8~~91

Nancy lives @:
36 Yogananda St
Sandy Hook, CT

Sandy Hook-2532

She Does not work

b6 -5
b7C -5

she volunteers a lot @ women's shelter
+ @ schools

Nancy is
Divorced from :

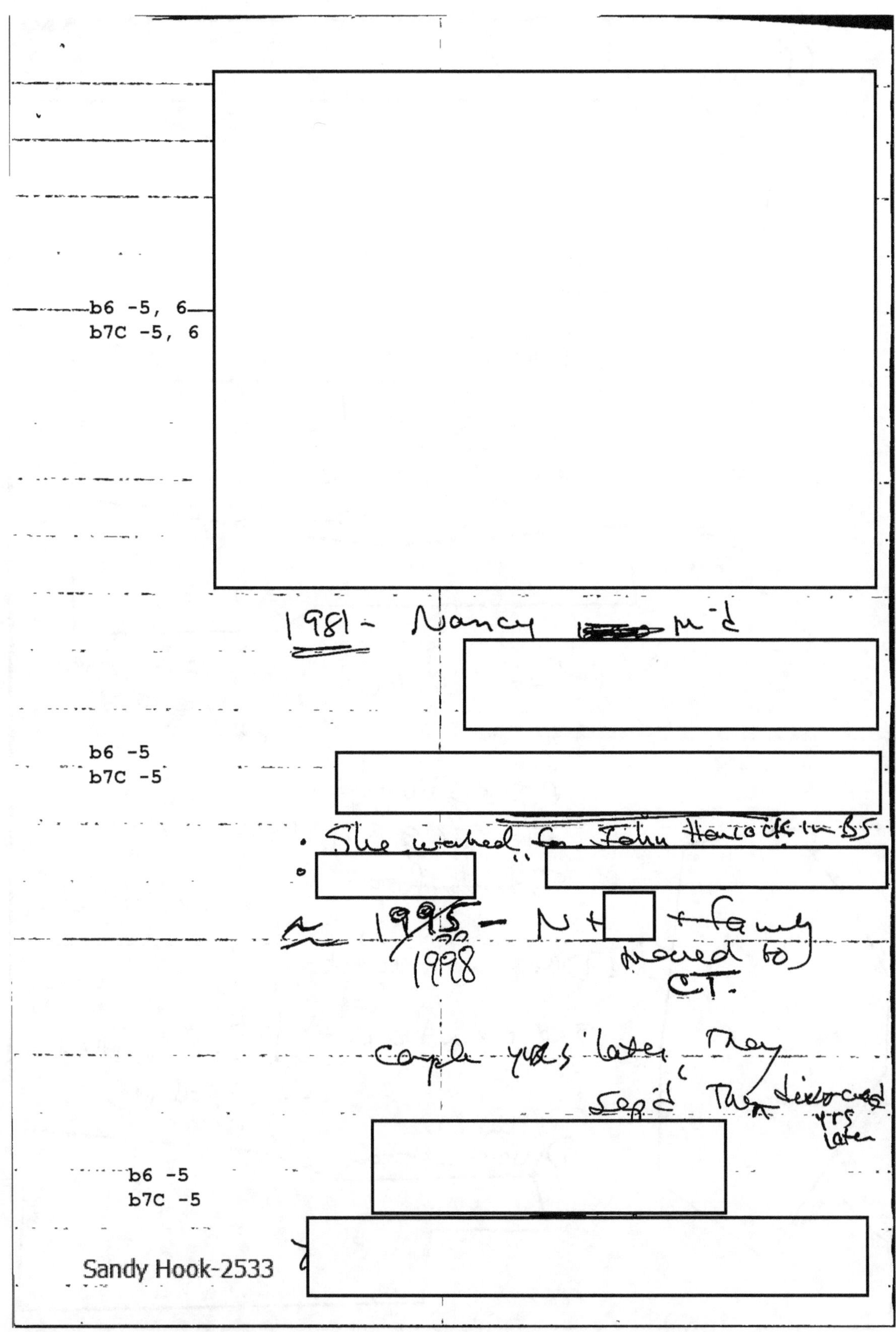

b6 -5, 6
b7C -5, 6

1981 - Nancy m'd

b6 -5
b7C -5

She worked for John Hancock in BS

~~1995~~ 1998 - N + [ ] + family moved to CT.

Couple yrs later, they sep'd. They divorced yrs later

b6 -5
b7C -5

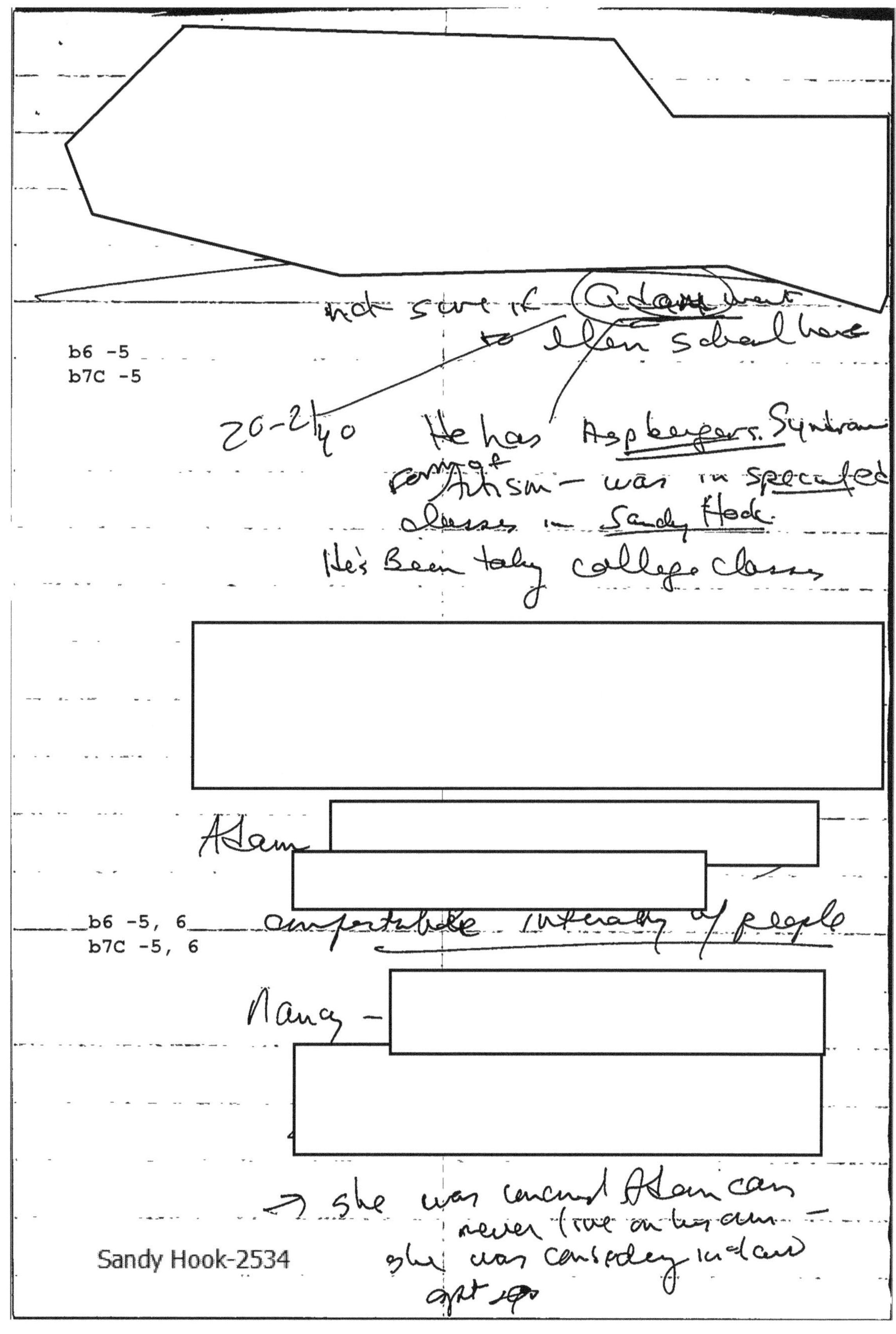

not sure if Adam went
to Ilen school here

b6 -5
b7C -5

20-21/40 He has Aspbergers Syndrome
form of Autism – was in specialized
classes in Sandy Hook
He's Been taking college classes

Adam

b6 -5, 6
b7C -5, 6

uncomfortable interacting w/ people

Nancy –

→ she was concerned Adam can
never live on his own –
she was considering ...
apt ...

– Adam became very upset
– she sd he's been doing better
looking into going to colleges

– when he left publicly she took
him out of school bc she was
nervous abt him
– she didn't like to talk abt Adam's
issues [redacted] only in
last few yrs – [redacted]
probably is only tip of iceberg

Adam is vegan – was first
vegetarian –

b6 -5
b7C -5

– [redacted]

– Nancy took [redacted] to shooting
ranges, thought good for them –
she had gun license
– why gun? self-defense?
–

b6 -5, 6
b7C -5, 6

b6 -5
b7C -5

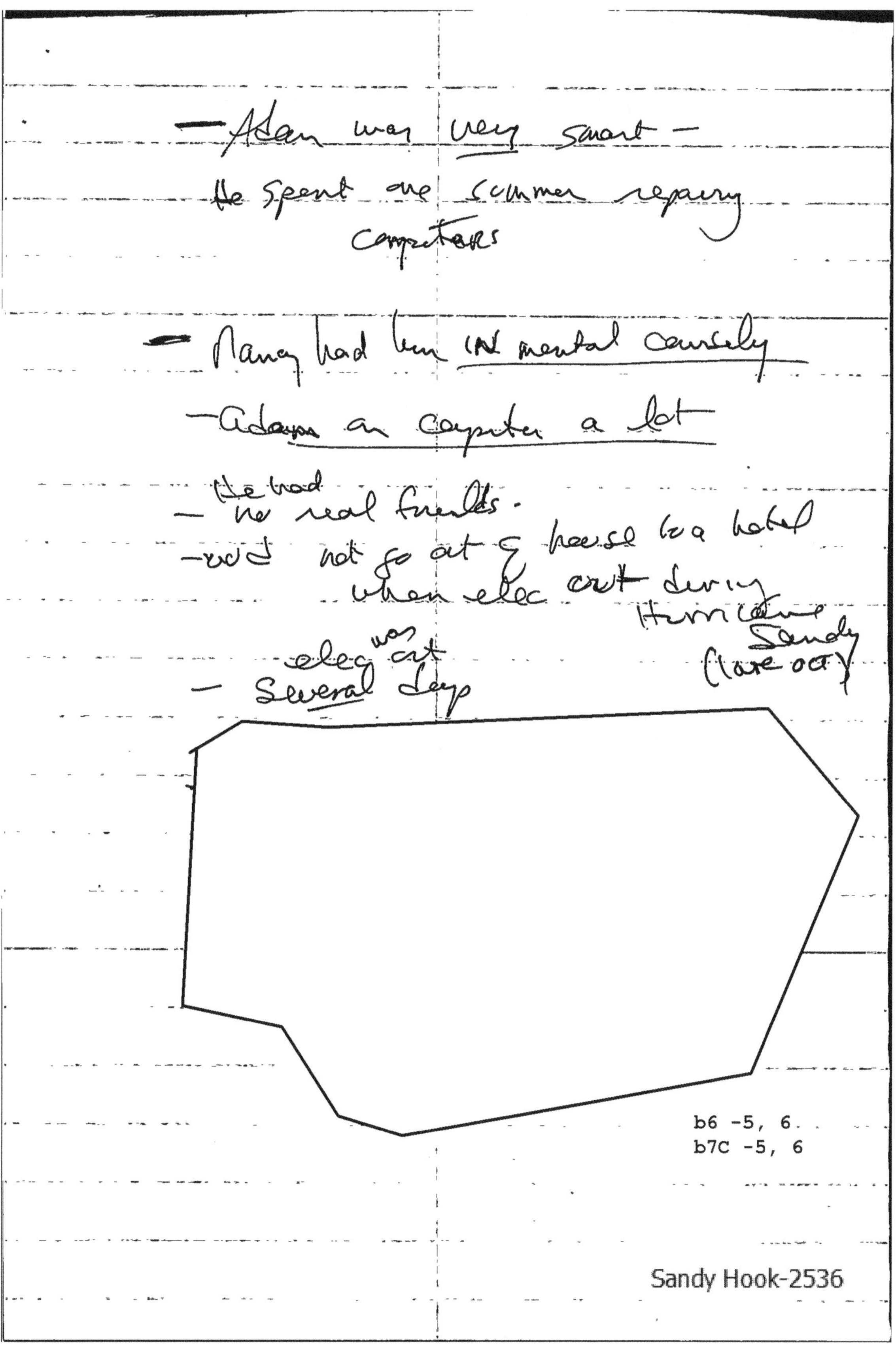

— Adam was very smart —

He spent one summer repairing computers

— Nancy had him in mental counseling

— Adam on computer a lot

— He had no real friends.

— would not go out of house to a hotel when elec out during Hurricane Sandy (late Oct)

— elec was out several days

b6 -5, 6
b7C -5, 6

b6 -6
b7C -6

- Nancy had a lot of friends, was v social

Restaurant next to Bldg 4 -

b6 -5, 6
b7C -5, 6

Nancy knew from time little, Adam has issues

- elem school & jr high - Adam has trouble - Autism - then dx Asp bergers -

b6 -6
b7C -6

b6 -6
b7C -6

— She was fully left mainly to big house w/ in-law suite for Adam

— very divorce – psychol sd — Don't recall him

She told anybody they should stay together

Don't know if she talking to Adam abt it

— he's ok alone –

— She travels a lot + lvs him there

— Adam is interested in history

— Adam took some college classes (@ UConn?) — Nancy wd have to drop him off b/c he didn't drive

— Adam's been taking mandarin @ a private instructor

— Nancy sd he'd been driving lately

— Adam didn't want a D.L.

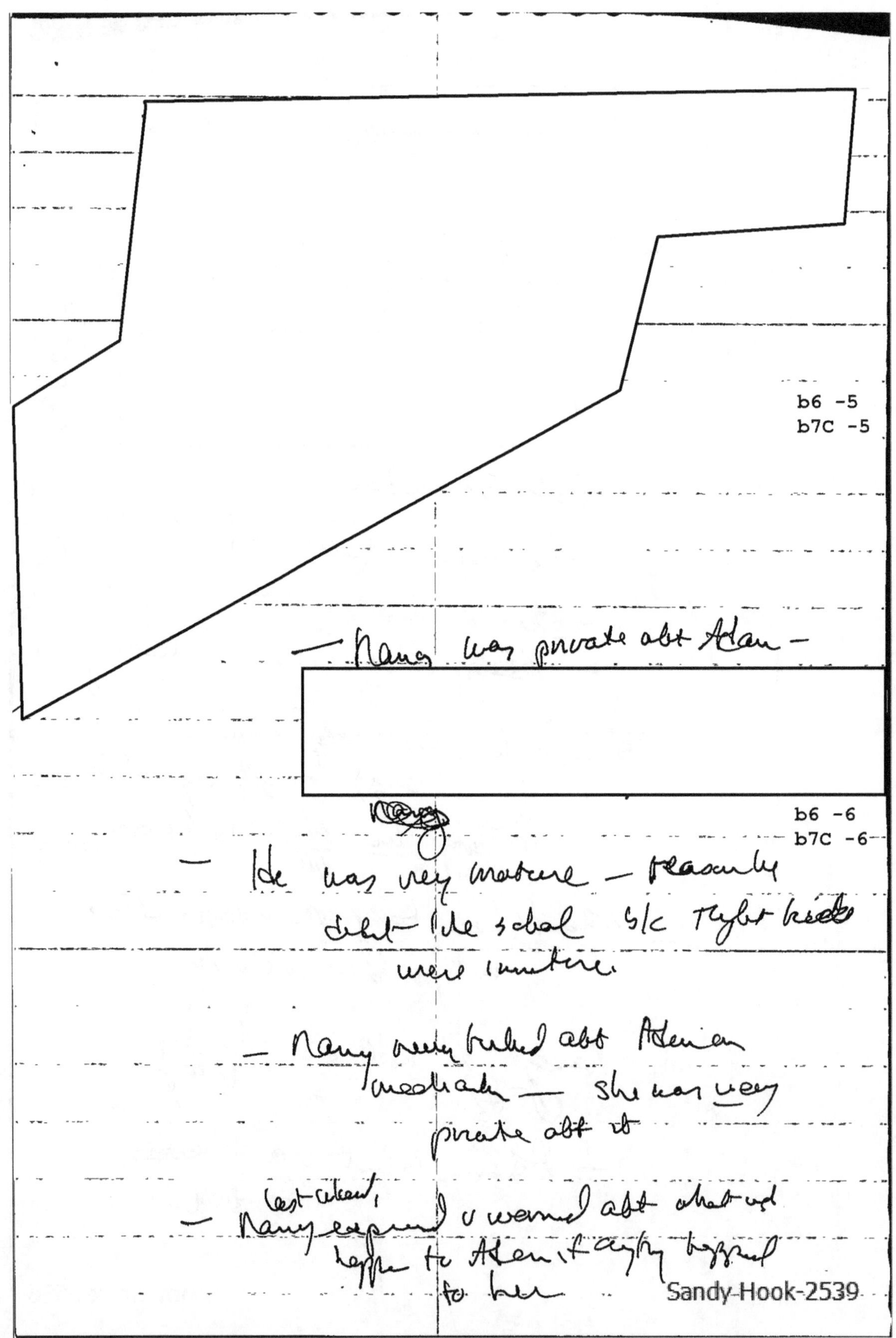

b6 -5
b7C -5

— Nancy was private abt Adam —

b6 -6
b7C -6

— He was very mature — pleasantly
didn't like school b/c they kids
were immature.

— Nancy rarely talked abt Adam's
medication — she was very
private abt it

— last weekend,
Nancy expressed & worried abt what wd
happen to Adam if anything happened
to her

Sandy-Hook-2539

- She sd Adam by computer s/t
got wounded out abt
How Sandy + wd [illegible]
leave house

I asked Mary if she needs anything for Adam + she sd
—
ud take care of him

b6 -5, 6
b7C -5, 6

—

4-5 yrs ago, Mary declined
marriage prop b/c ud not be
Adam - ud have had to
move

- Mary v. protective of Adam

- N. never expressed any concerns of
Adam being violent.
She wasn't afraid of him, but was
afraid for him

- professor teaching Adam Mandarin for last couple yrs

- Adam also took saxophone lessons in last couple yrs

- he worked for guy building computers a summer couple yrs ago

- Thinking going back to college to major in history

Time on computer: don't think he was a gamer

- no g.f or friends

b6 -5, 6
b7C -5, 6

- Nancy was getting ready to go to London for Christmas, she talked abt getting her clothes & her hair done - not the issue b/c she travels all the time.

when she was daily [redacted]

she wd go [redacted] for a week every month & leave Adam home & he was ok

Adam can do own food & cooking when Nancy away.

• Nancy hasn't vol'd @ the school in a long time

• She gets bikes refurbished & donates clothing to women shelters

• Nancy had MS.

b6 -5
b7C -5

Nancy's guns

Couple handguns

b6 -5
b7C -5

.45 Governor

Ruger mini 14 .223 caliber

Nancy sold a gun recently

b6 -5, 6
b7C -5, 6

Nancy's email

njlanza1918
@aol.com

Adam - no knew if
had email add or
Facebook
But I
we doubt he did
b/c not social

Sat 12/15

Adam went to the Sandy Hook School - 1st school

problem in 4th grade

+ middle school when had to chg classes, cdn't handle

So took Adam out - to small Catholic school - didn't do well there

Then to home schooled

b6 -6
b7C -6

Nancy told [redacted] Adam had no emotions or feelings - he didn't care abt bdays or holidays - thought were stupid

Had to get rid of a cat - Adam cdn't handle - freaked out by it

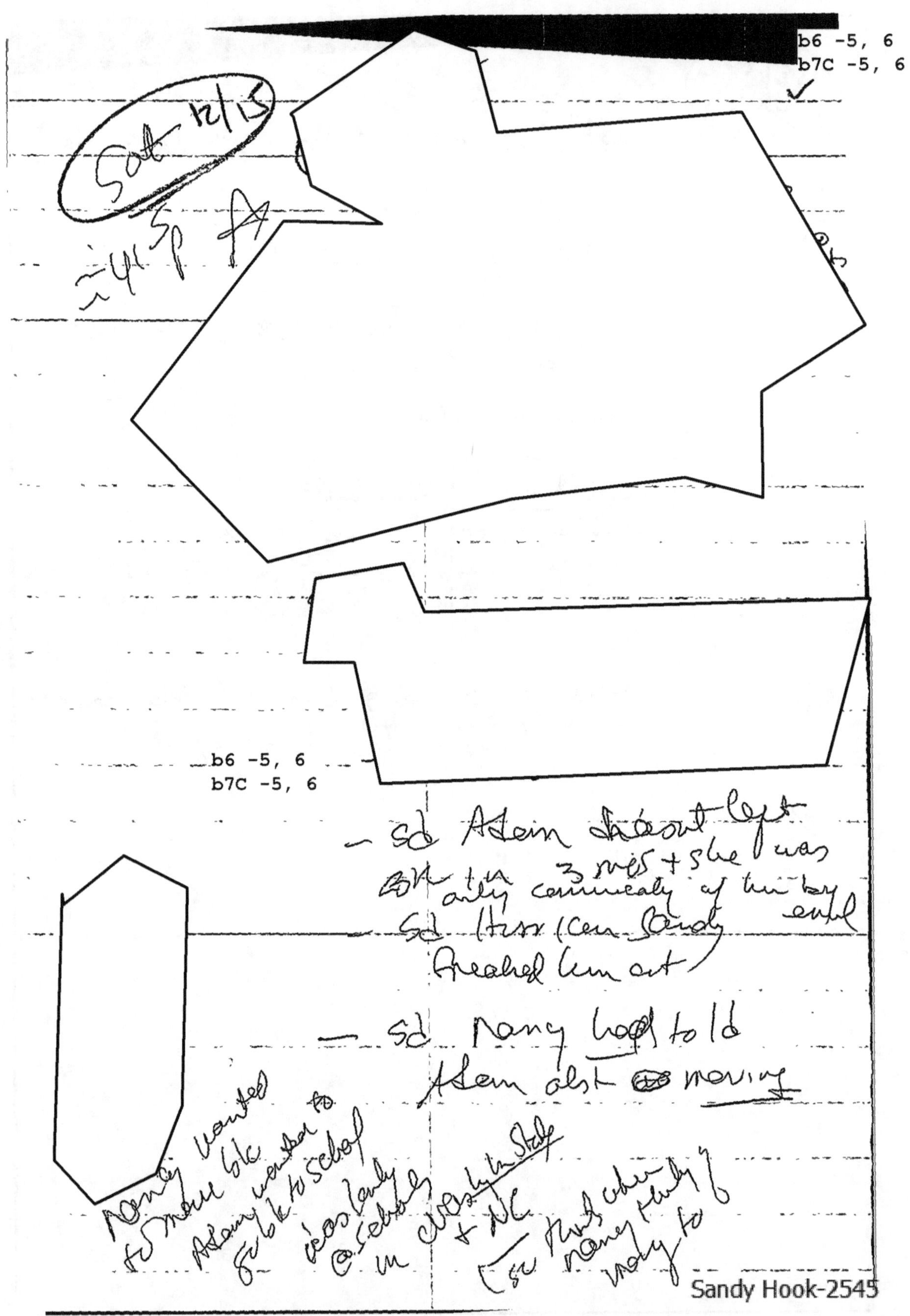

b6 -5, 6
b7C -5, 6

Sat 12/15

~4:15p A

b6 -5, 6
b7C -5, 6

- sd Adam doesn't left [illegible] 3 mos + she was only communicaty of him by email

- sd Hurricane Sandy freaked him out

- sd Nancy had told Adam abt moving

Nancy wanted to move b/c Adam wanted to go back to school

was looking @ schools in [illegible] in State + NC

[so thinks other Nancy likely moving to

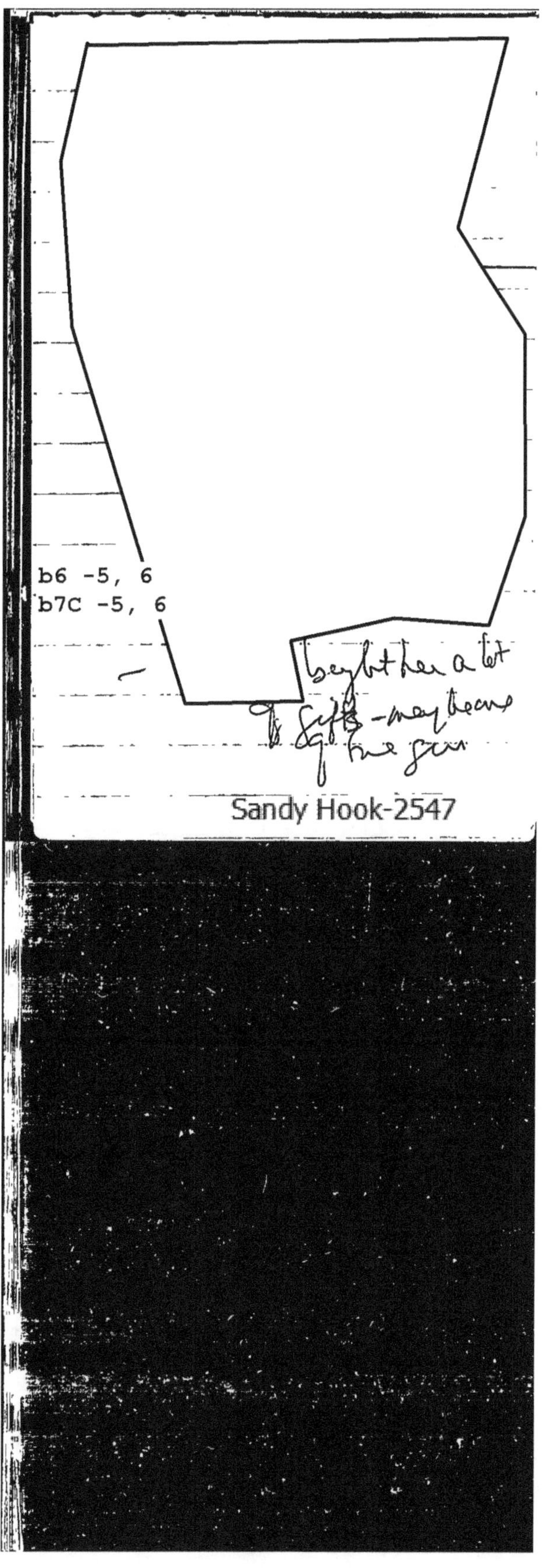

b6 -5, 6
b7C -5, 6

bought her a lot
of gifts - maybe because
of the gun

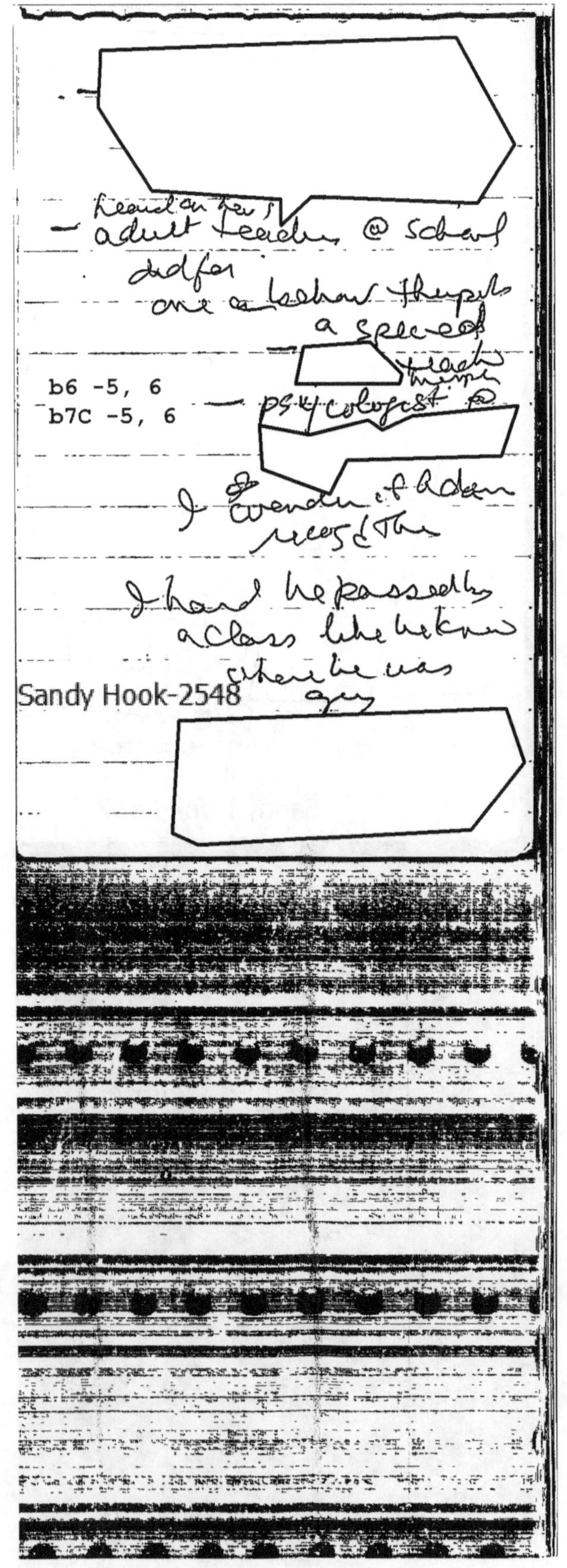

— adult teacher @ school

one on behav therapists

a special

b6 -5, 6
b7C -5, 6 — psycologist @

I wonder if Adam

I heard he passed by a class like he knew where he was going

Sandy Hook-2548

— made me think Adam went back w/ a plan

— wonder if classrooms were his old classroom

b6 -5, 6
b7C -5, 6

Sandy Hook-2549

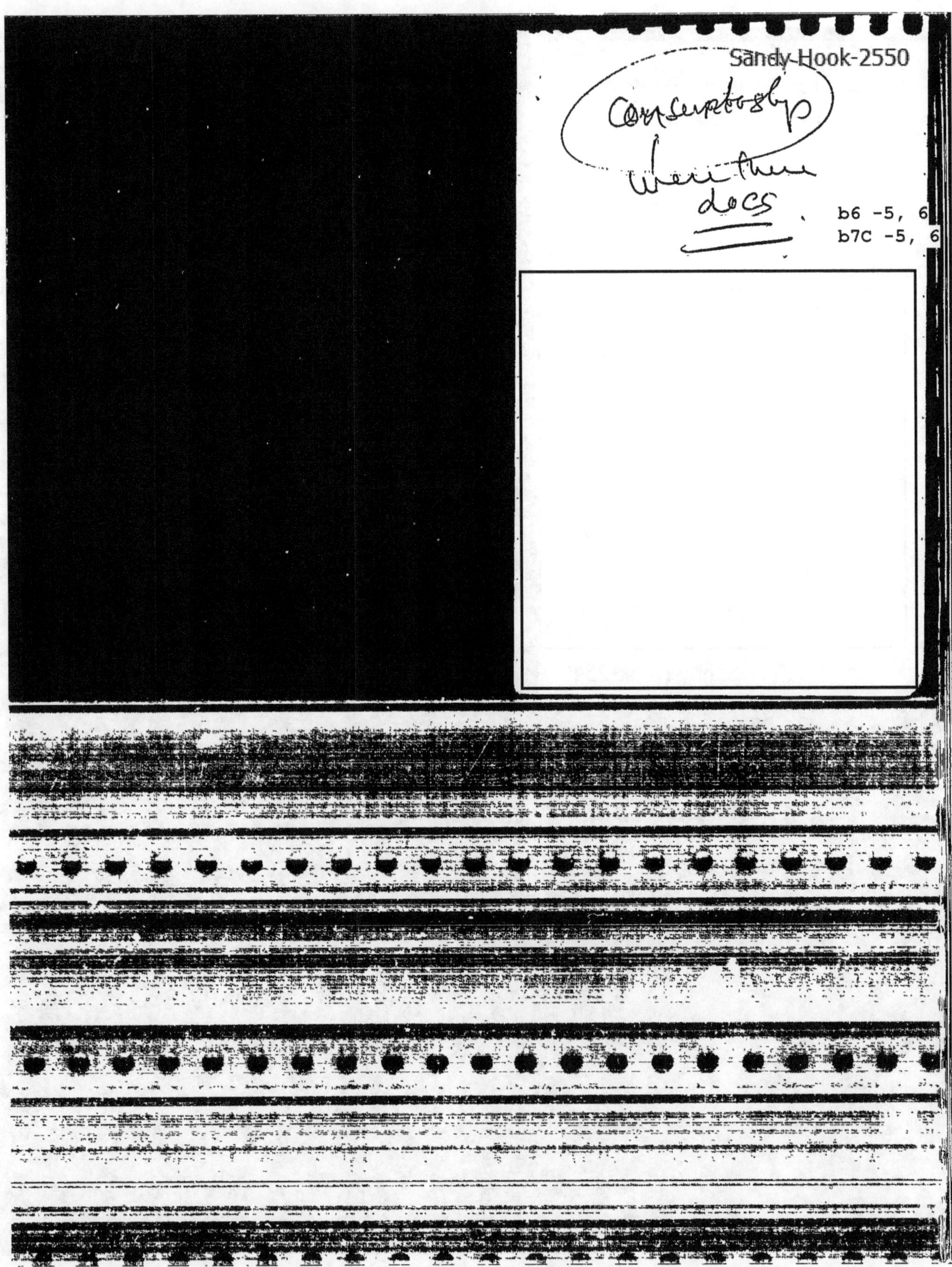
b6 -5, 6
b7C -5, 6

FD-340 (Rev. 4-11-03)

File Number 4-NH-2619946 - 1A70

Field Office Acquiring Evidence CO

Serial # of Originating Document 123

Date Received 12/18/12

From

By SA

To Be Returned ☐ Yes ☐ No

Receipt Given ☐ Yes ☐ No

Grand Jury Material - Disseminate Only Pursuant to Rule 6 (e)
Federal Rules of Criminal Procedure

☐ Yes ☐ No

Federal Taxpayer Information (FTI)

☐ Yes ☐ No

Title: Sandy Hook Elementary School
12 Dickinson St, Sandy Hook
CT - Victim
Firearms Ref

Reference:
(Communication Enclosing Material)

Description: ☑ Original notes re interview of

b6 -1, 2
b7C -1, 2

b6 -2
b7C -2

FD-340 (Rev. 4-11-03)

File Number 4-NH-2619946 – 1A71

Field Office Acquiring Evidence 135

Serial # of Originating Document 4-NH-2619946 - 124

Date Received 12/18/2012

From ______________________
(Name of Contributor/Interviewee)

____
(Address)

____
(City and State)

By SA [redacted]

b6 -1
b7C -1

To Be Returned ☐ Yes ☐ No

Receipt Given ☐ Yes ☐ No

Grand Jury Material - Disseminate Only Pursuant to Rule 6 (e) Federal Rules of Criminal Procedure

☐ Yes ☐ No

Federal Taxpayer Information (FTI)

☐ Yes ☐ No

1A71

Reference: ______________________
(Communication Enclosing Material)

Description: ☑ Original notes re interview of

(b) [redacted]

b6 -6
b7C -6

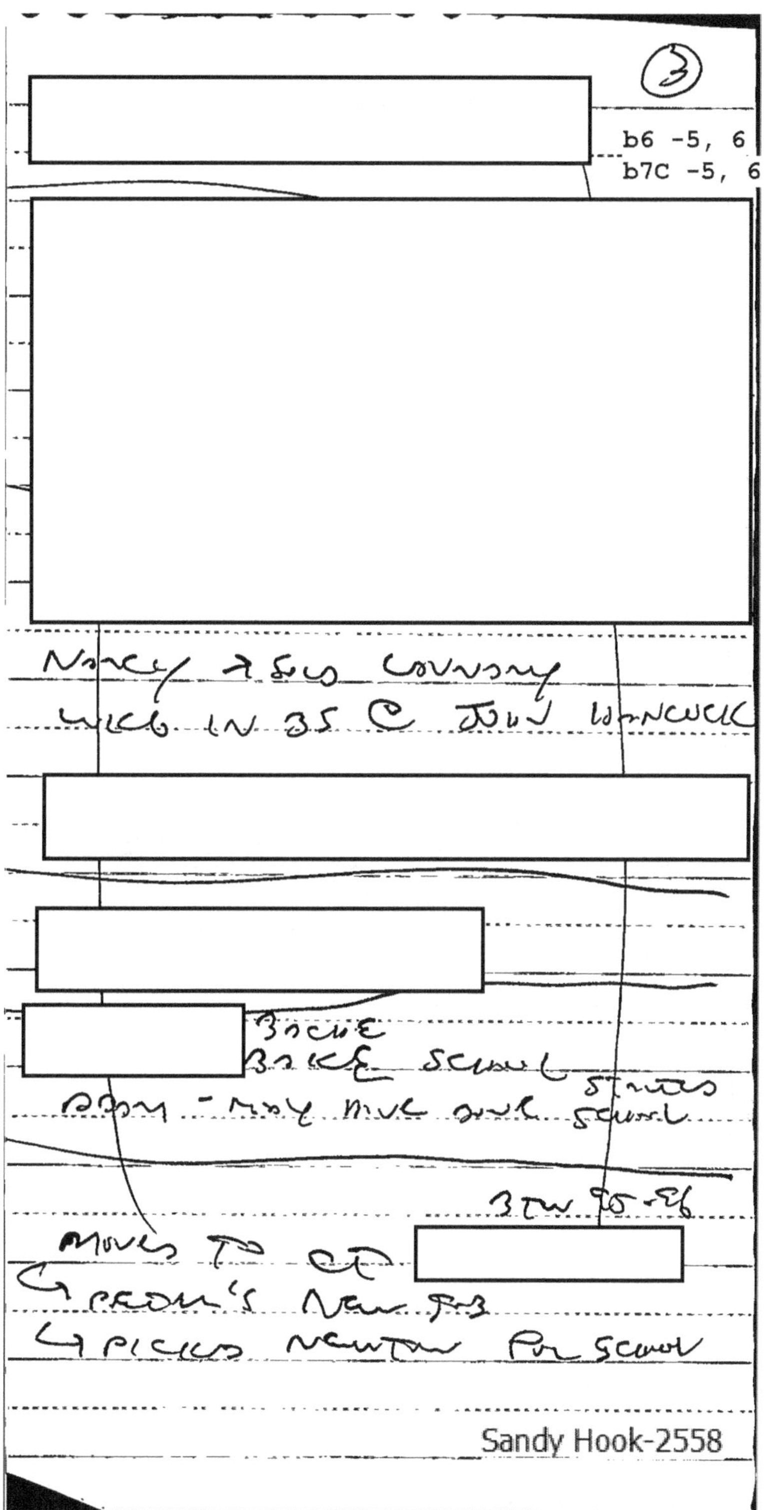

(3)

b6 -5, 6
b7C -5, 6

NANCY → SAYS [illegible]
WORKED IN BS @ JOHN HANCOCK

BACHE
BARRE SCHOOL
MOM - MAY MOVE OUT STATES SCHOOL

3RD 95-96
MOVES TO CT
→ FROM'S NEW JOB
→ PICKS NEWTOWN FOR SCHOOL

Sandy Hook-2558

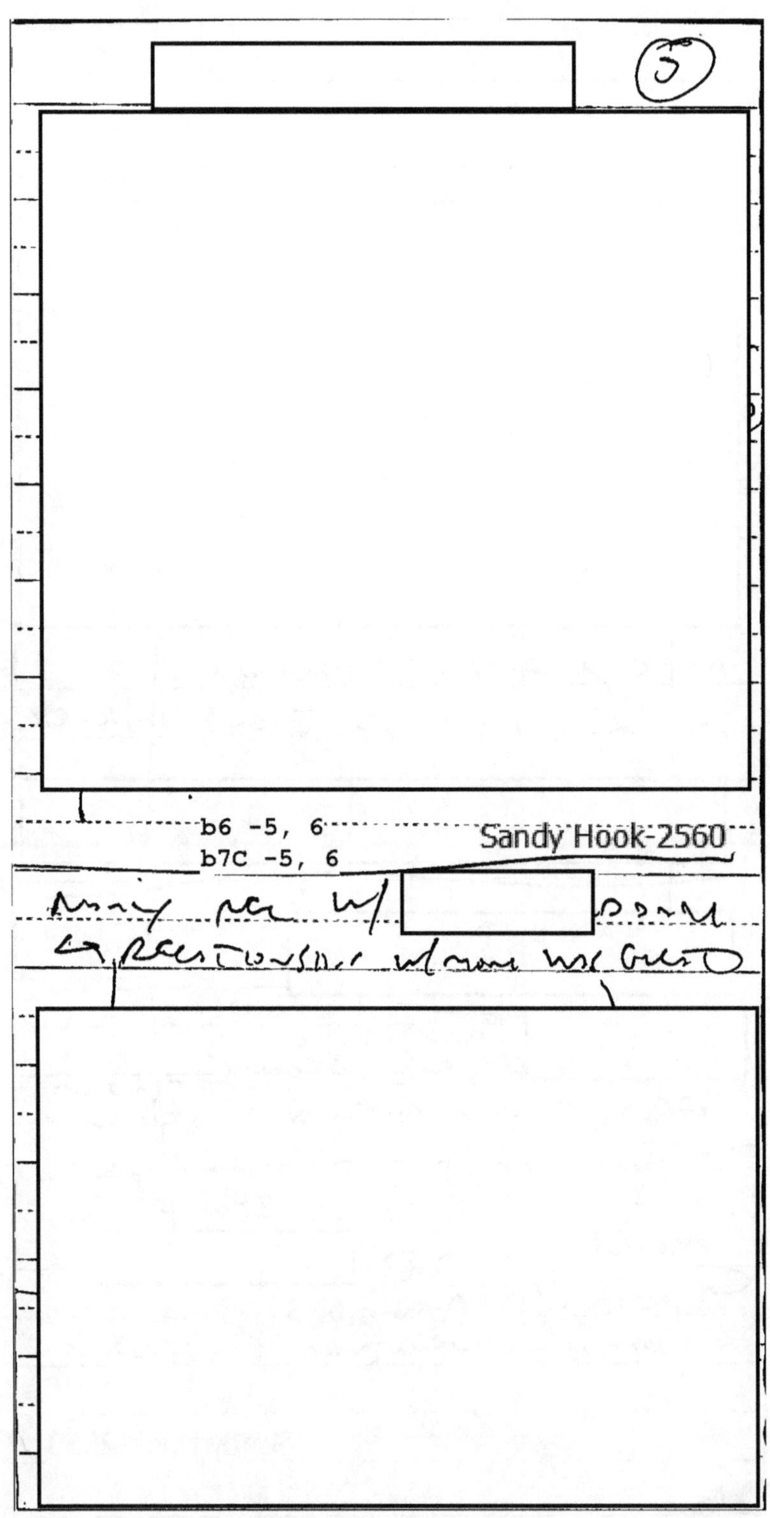
b6 -5, 6
b7C -5, 6
Sandy Hook-2560

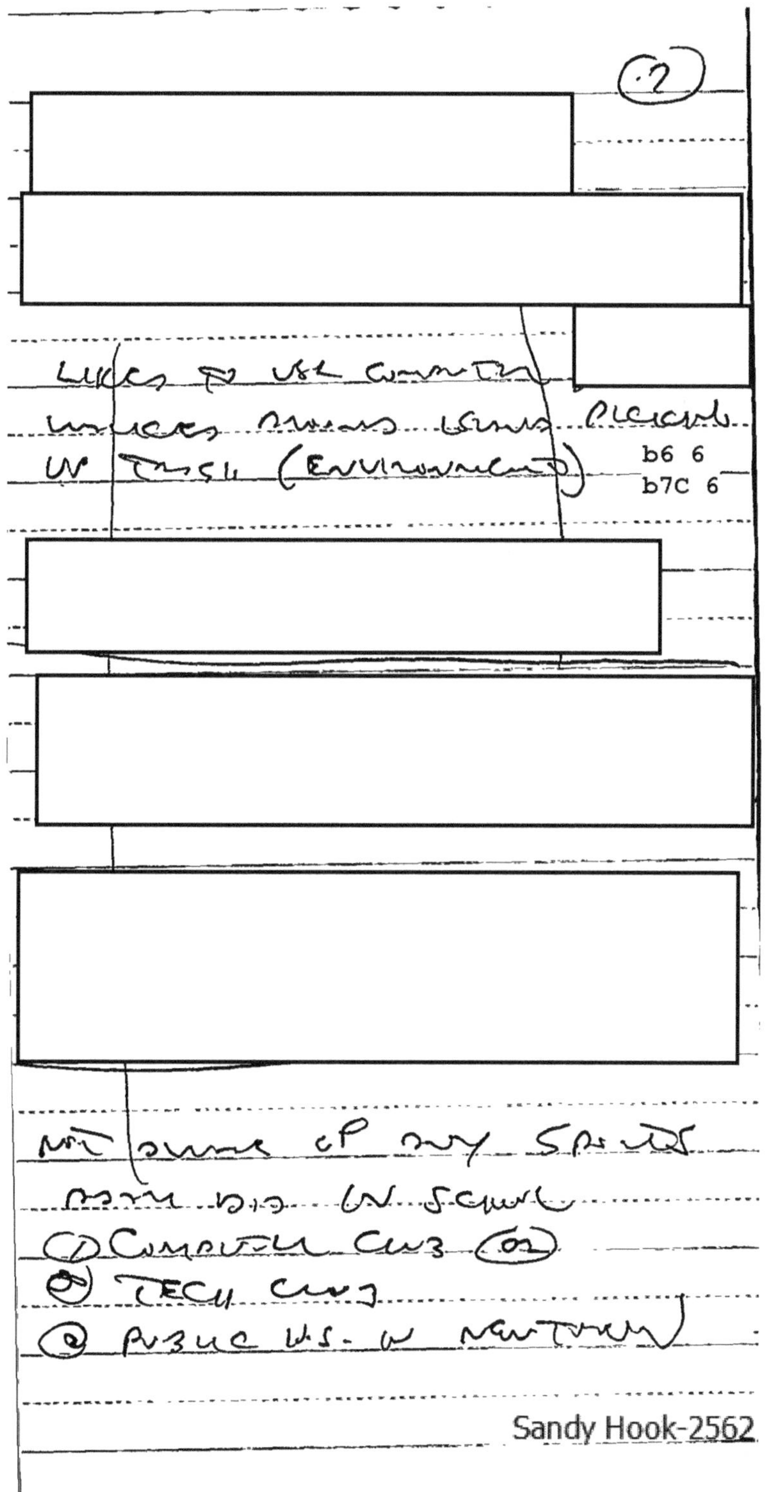

(2)

Likes to use computer

likes always being placed

in tech (environment)

b6 6

b7C 6

not aware of any sports

[illegible] in school

(1) Computer club (02)

(2) Tech club

(3) Public lib. in Newtown

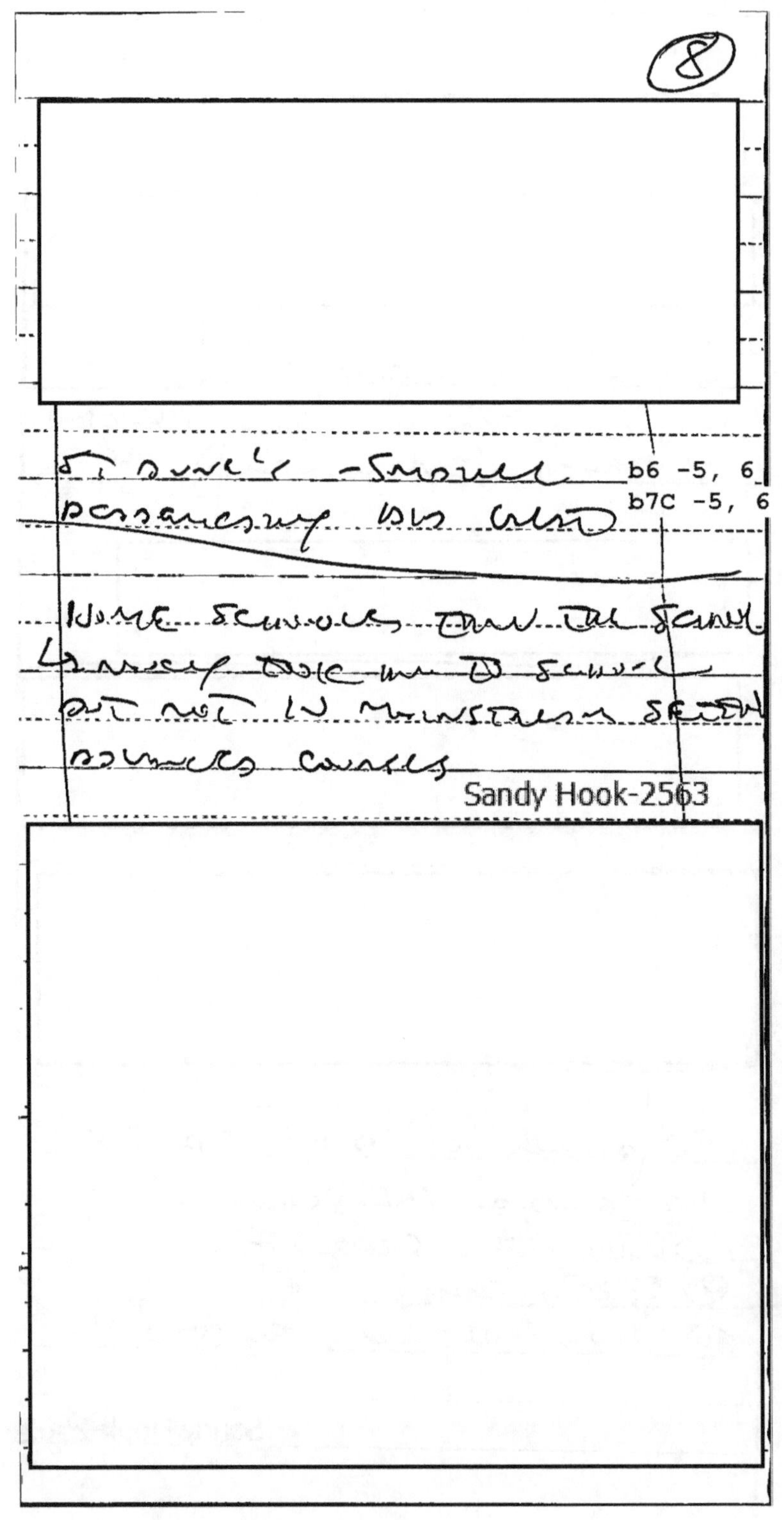

8

- Should

b6 -5, 6
b7C -5, 6

Home schooled than the school
took him to school
but not in mainstream setting
courses

Sandy Hook-2563

NO DISCUSSION ABOUT ADAM (9)

→ NOT [illegible] THERE

LAST COUPLE OF YRS, ADAM DID

NOT WANT TO GO W/ GROUPS OF

PEOPLE

b6 -5, 6
b7C -5, 6

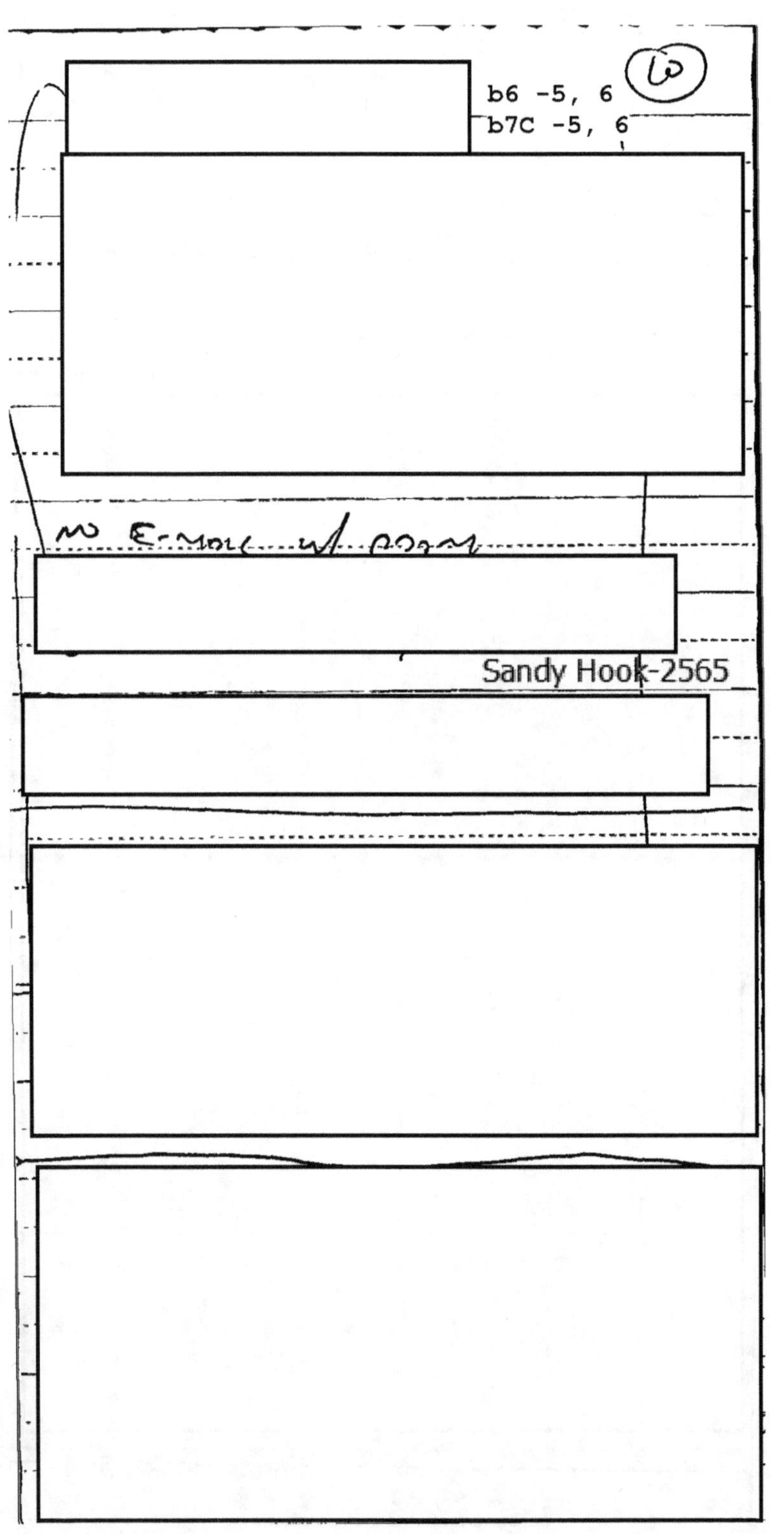

b6 -5, 6
b7C -5, 6

Sandy Hook-2565

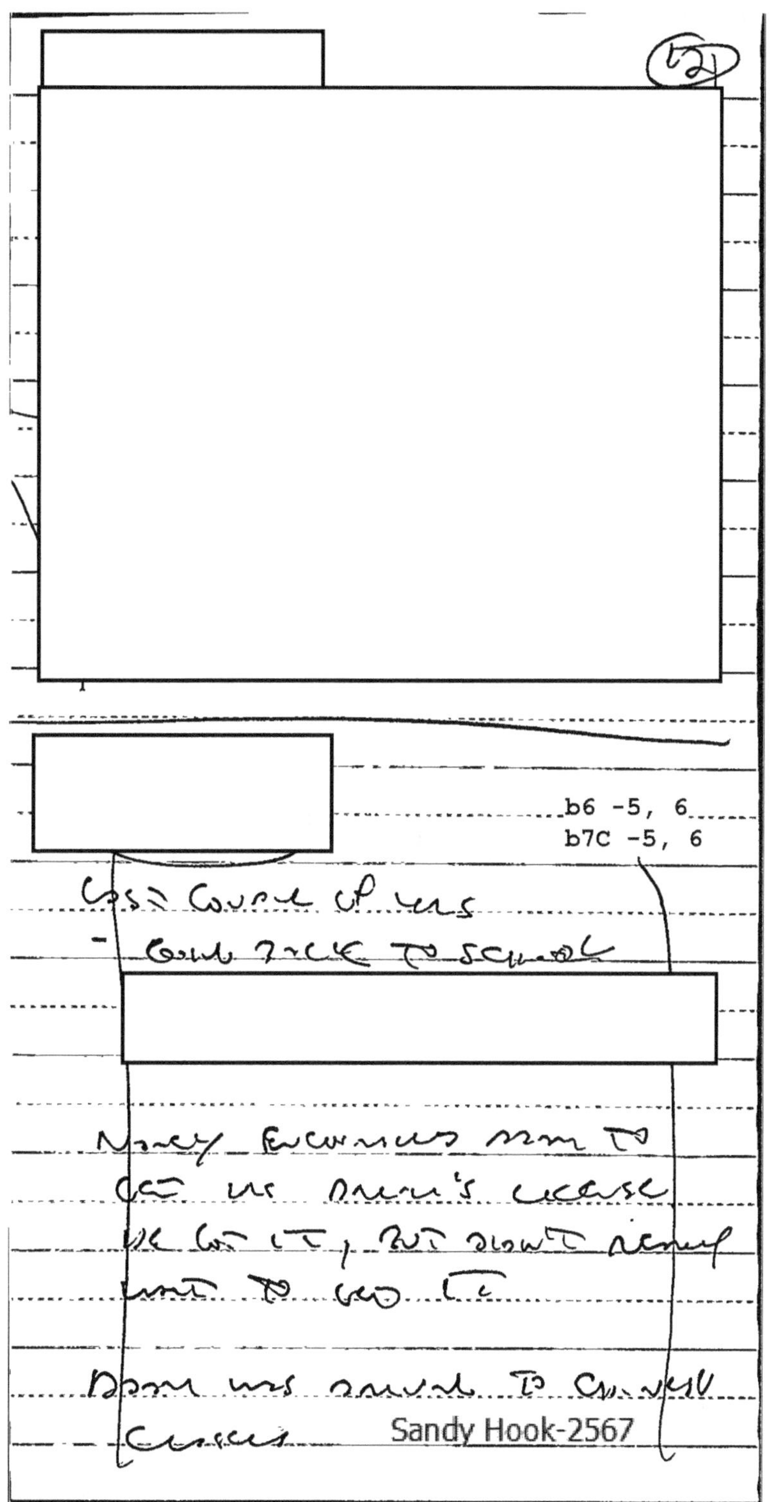

(52)

b6 -5, 6
b7C -5, 6

Loss = Couple of yrs
- Going back to school

Nancy encourages Adam to get his driver's license
He got it, but didn't really want to get it

Adam was driving to community classes

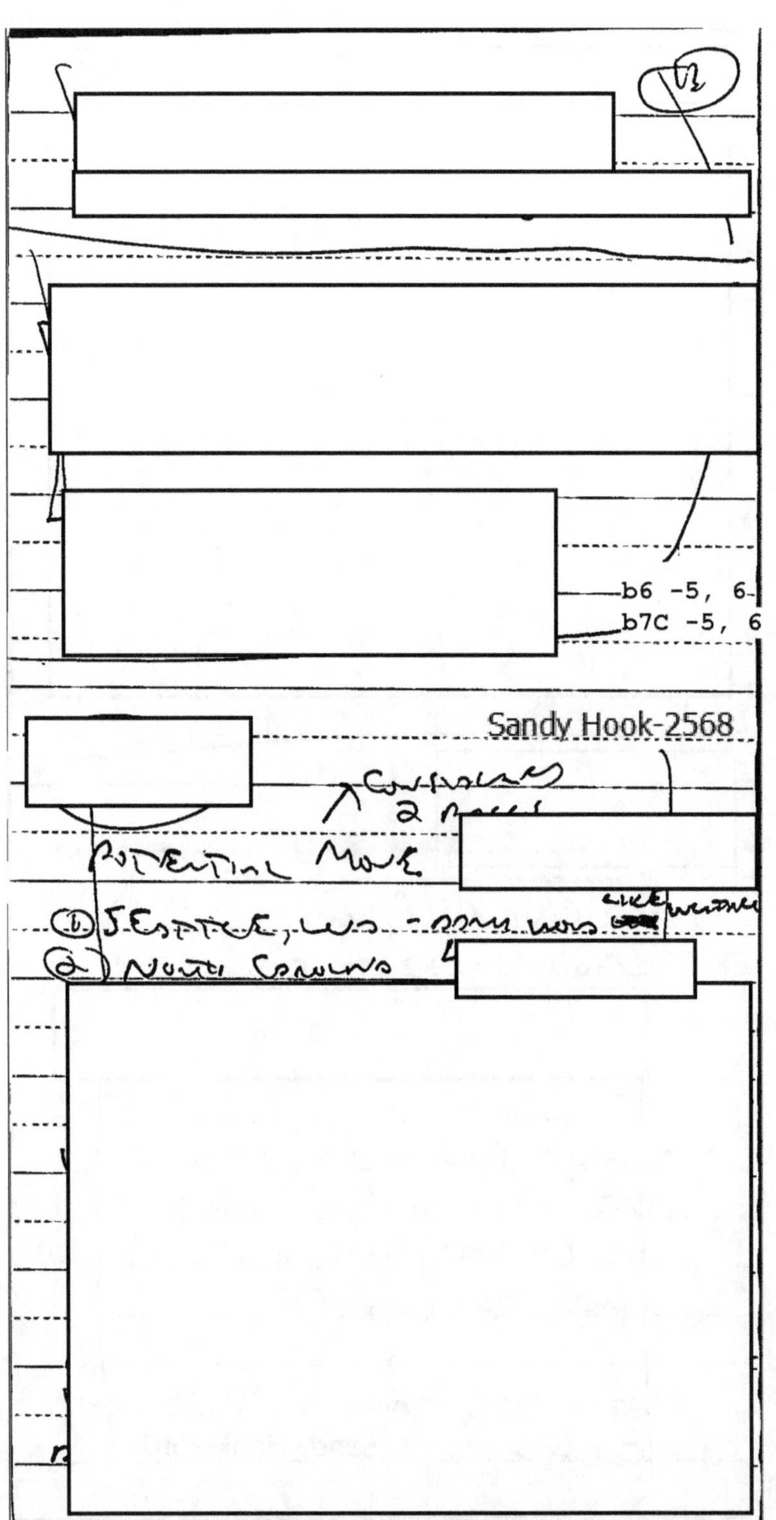
b6 -5, 6
b7C -5, 6

Sandy Hook-2568

POTENTIAL MOVE

(1) SEATTLE, WA

(2) NORTH CAROLINA

[illegible]

[illegible]

[illegible]

[illegible] for [illegible]

b6 -6
b7C -6

[illegible]

[illegible]

FD-340 (Rev. 4-11-03)

File Number 4-NH-2619946 - 1A72

Field Office Acquiring Evidence BS

Serial # of Originating Document 4-NH-2619946-125

Date Received 12/18/2012

From ______________________
(Name of Contributor/Interviewee)

____
(Address)

____
(City and State)

By SA [redacted]

b6 -1
b7C -1

To Be Returned ☐ Yes ☐ No

Receipt Given ☐ Yes ☐ No

Grand Jury Material - Disseminate Only Pursuant to Rule 6 (e) Federal Rules of Criminal Procedure

☐ Yes ☐ No

Federal Taxpayer Information (FTI)

☐ Yes ☐ No

1A 72

Reference: ______________________
(Communication Enclosing Material)

Description: ☑ Original notes re interview of [redacted]

b6 -6
b7C -6

(8)

b6 -5, 6
b7C -5, 6

[illegible] 3/4

[illegible] MAY BE ~~[illegible]~~ AUTISTIC

FD-340 (Rev. 8-7-97)

1A60 & 1A96

Universal Case File Number 4-NH-2619946

Field Office Acquiring Evidence NH

Serial # of Originating Document 152 & 108

Date Received 12/18/12

From [redacted]
(Name of Contributor)

(Address of Contributor)

(City and State)

By SA [redacted]
(Name of Special Agent)

To Be Returned ☐ Yes ☒ No
Receipt Given ☐ Yes ☒ No
Grand Jury Material - Disseminate Only Pursuant to Rule 6 (e)
Federal Rules of Criminal Procedure
☐ Yes ☒ No

Title:

b6 -1
b7C -1
OTHER Sealed Pursuant to Court Order

Reference: FD 302 dated 1/11/13
(Communication Enclosing Material)

Description: ☐ Original notes re interview of

[redacted]

Duplicate 1A content:
1A60 & 1A96

FEDERAL BUREAU OF INVESTIGATION
FOI/PA
DELETED PAGE INFORMATION SHEET
Civil Action# 16-cv-02136

Total Deleted Page(s) = 37
Page 5 ~ Duplicate;
Page 6 ~ Duplicate;
Page 7 ~ Duplicate;
Page 8 ~ Duplicate;
Page 10 ~ Duplicate;
Page 12 ~ Duplicate;
Page 13 ~ Duplicate;
Page 15 ~ Duplicate;
Page 16 ~ Duplicate;
Page 17 ~ Duplicate;
Page 19 ~ Duplicate;
Page 20 ~ Duplicate;
Page 21 ~ Duplicate;
Page 22 ~ Duplicate;
Page 23 ~ b3 - 1;
Page 27 ~ Duplicate;
Page 32 ~ b6 - 1, 2, 5; b7C - 1, 2, 5; b7E - 11; OTHER - Sealed Pursuant to Court Order;
Page 33 ~ b6 - 2; b7C - 2; b7E - 11; OTHER - Sealed Pursuant to Court Order;
Page 34 ~ b6 - 2, 5; b7C - 2, 5; b7E - 11; OTHER - Sealed Pursuant to Court Order;
Page 35 ~ b6 - 2, 5; b7C - 2, 5; b7E - 11; OTHER - Sealed Pursuant to Court Order;
Page 36 ~ b7E - 11; OTHER - Sealed Pursuant to Court Order;
Page 37 ~ b7E - 11; OTHER - Sealed Pursuant to Court Order;
Page 38 ~ b6 - 1, 2, 3; b7C - 1, 2, 3; b7E - 11; OTHER - Sealed Pursuant to Court Order;
Page 39 ~ b6 - 1, 2, 3; b7C - 1, 2, 3; b7E - 11; OTHER - Sealed Pursuant to Court Order;
Page 40 ~ b6 - 1, 3, 5; b7C - 1, 3, 5; b7E - 11; OTHER - Sealed Pursuant to Court Order;
Page 41 ~ b6 - 1, 3; b7C - 1, 3; b7E - 11; OTHER - Sealed Pursuant to Court Order;
Page 42 ~ b7E - 11; OTHER - Sealed Pursuant to Court Order;
Page 43 ~ b7E - 11; OTHER - Sealed Pursuant to Court Order;
Page 44 ~ b7E - 11; OTHER - Sealed Pursuant to Court Order;
Page 45 ~ b7E - 11; OTHER - Sealed Pursuant to Court Order;
Page 46 ~ b6 - 2; b7C - 2; b7E - 11; OTHER - Sealed Pursuant to Court Order;
Page 47 ~ b6 - 2, 5; b7C - 2, 5; b7E - 11; OTHER - Sealed Pursuant to Court Order;
Page 48 ~ b6 - 2, 5; b7C - 2, 5; b7E - 11; OTHER - Sealed Pursuant to Court Order;
Page 49 ~ b6 - 2; b7C - 2; b7E - 11; OTHER - Sealed Pursuant to Court Order;
Page 50 ~ b7E - 11; OTHER - Sealed Pursuant to Court Order;

Page 51 ~ b6 - 2; b7C - 2; b7E - 11; OTHER - Sealed Pursuant to Court Order;
Page 52 ~ b6 - 1; b7C - 1; b7E - 11; OTHER - Sealed Pursuant to Court Order;

XXXXXXXXXXXXXXXXXXXXXXXX
X Deleted Page(s) X
X No Duplication Fee X
X For this Page X
XXXXXXXXXXXXXXXXXXXXXXXX

FD-340a (Rev. 1-27-03)

(Title) 1A5

(File No.) 4-NH-2619946

Item	Date Filed	To be returned Yes	No		Disposition

FD-302 (Rev. 5-8-10)

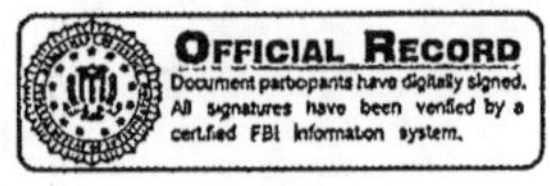

FEDERAL BUREAU OF INVESTIGATION

Date of entry 01/22/2013

On January 22, 2013, SA [redacted] FBI, and SA [redacted] IRS, received an external hard drive that belonged to [redacted] The hard drive was delivered to the investigating agents by [redacted]

[redacted]

The hard drive was taken into custody and processed as evidence.

b6 -1, 2, 4, 5
b7C -1, 2, 4, 5

Investigation on 01/22/2013 at Norwalk, Connecticut, United States (In Person)

File # 4-NH-2619946 Date drafted 01/22/2013

by [redacted]

b6 -1
b7C -

4-NH-2619946
SERIAL 173

FD-1087 (Rev. 5-8-10)

UNCLASSIFIED

FEDERAL BUREAU OF INVESTIGATION

Evidence Log

Event Title: (U) CART **Date:** 01/23/2013

Approved By: SSA [redacted]

Drafted By: [redacted]

b6 -1
b7C -1

Case ID #: 4-NH-2619946 (U) UNSUB(S)
Sandy Hook Elementary School
12 Dickinson St, Sandy Hook, CT-Victim
Firearms Act.
OO:NH

[redacted] b7E -1

Acquired By: [redacted] on 01/17/2013

b6 -1
b7C -1

Acquired From: (U) CART Exam

Receipt Given?: No

Holding Office: NEW HAVEN

Details:

[redacted]

Item Type	Description
1B CART	(U) DENHOXBOX - One (1) 40GB Seagate Hard Drive, S/N 5EF0ZL2H [redacted] Acquired On: 01/17/2013 Located By: [redacted] Location Area: CART Specific Location: CART Device Type: [redacted] Number of Devices Collected: [redacted]

b6 -1
b7C -1
b7E -6, 8

UNCLASSIFIED

4-NH-2619946
SERIAL 174

Title: (U) CART
Re: 4-NH-2619946, 01/23/2013

♦♦

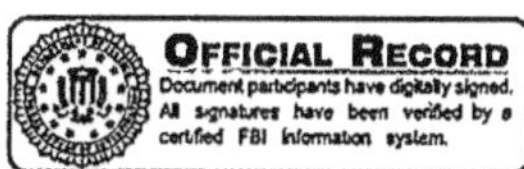

UNCLASSIFIED

FEDERAL BUREAU OF INVESTIGATION

Evidence Log

Event Title: (U) CART **Date:** 01/23/2013

Approved By: SSA [redacted]

Drafted By: [redacted]

b6 -1
b7C -1

Case ID #: 4-NH-2619946 (U) UNSUB(S)
Sandy Hook Elementary School
12 Dickinson St, Sandy Hook, CT-Victim
Firearms Act.
OO:NH

[redacted]

b7E -1

Acquired By: [redacted] on 01/17/2013

b6 -1
b7C -1

Acquired From: (U) CART Exam

Receipt Given?: No

Holding Office: NEW HAVEN

Details:

[redacted]

Item Type	Description
1B CART	[redacted] Acquired On: 01/17/2013 Located By: [redacted] Location Area: CART Specific Location: CART Device Type: [redacted] Number of Devices Collected: [redacted]

b6 -1
b7C -1
b7E -6, 8

UNCLASSIFIED

4-NH-2619946
SERIAL 175

Title: (U) CART
Re: 4-NH-2619946, 01/23/2013

♦♦

FD-1087 (Rev. 5-8-10)

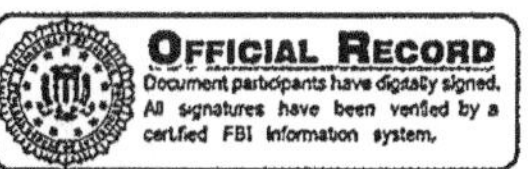

UNCLASSIFIED

FEDERAL BUREAU OF INVESTIGATION

Evidence Log

Event Title: (U) Evidence from [redacted]

Date: 01/24/2013

Approved By: [redacted]

b6 -1, 2
b7C -1, 2

Drafted By: [redacted]

Case ID #: 4-NH-2619946

(U) UNSUB(S)
Sandy Hook Elementary School
12 Dickinson St, Sandy Hook, CT-Victim
Firearms Act.
OO:NH

[redacted]

b7E -1

Acquired By: [redacted] on 01/22/2013

b6 -1, 2
b7C -1, 2

Acquired From: (U [redacted]

Receipt Given?: No

Holding Office: NEW HAVEN

Details: *No Details Provided*

Item Type	Description
1B General	[redacted] Acquired On: 01/22/2013 Located By: [redacted] Location Area: [redacted] Specific Location: [redacted]

b6 -1, 2
b7C -1, 2

UNCLASSIFIED

4-NH-2619946

SERIAL 176

b6 -2
b7C -2

Title: (U) Evidence from [redacted]
Re: 4-NH-2619946, 01/24/2013

Acquired On: 01/22/2013
Located By:
Location Area:
Specific Location:

b6 -1, 2
b7C -1, 2
b7E -6, 8

♦♦

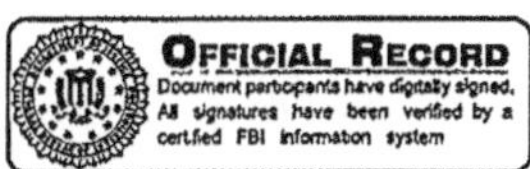

FEDERAL BUREAU OF INVESTIGATION

Electronic Communication

Title: (U) EMERGENCY VICTIM FUNDS AND BUDGET MATTERS, CRIMINAL CYBER RESPONSE SERVICES BRANCH;

Date: 01/22/2013

To: [redacted]

From: DIRECTOR S OFFICE
Contact: [redacted]

b6 -1
b7C -1

Approved By: Kathryn McKay Turman

Drafted By: [redacted]

Case ID #: [redacted]

b7E -4

4-NH-2619946 (U) UNSUB(S)
Sandy Hook Elementary School
12 Dickinson St, Sandy Hook, CT-Victim
Firearms Act.
OO:NH

Synopsis: (U) To document expenditures of the Terrorism Emergency Victim Assistance Funds following the shooting at Sandy Hook Elementary School in Newtown, CT.

Details:

On December 14, 2012 a gunman killed twenty-seven people, including his mother, Nancy Lanza, and 26 students and staff at Sandy Hook Elementary School. The Office for Victim Assistance activated the Victim Assistance Rapid Deployment Team to respond to the shooting following a request for assistance from the Newtown Police Department and the Connecticut State Police. The Office for Victims of Crime authorized the use of Terrorism Emergency Victim Assistance Funds to assist the victims of this mass fatality event.

TEVAF assistance was requested by FOM [redacted] and approved by OVA Program Director Turman for [redacted]

b6 -1, 7
b7C -1, 7

4-NH-2619946
SERIAL 177

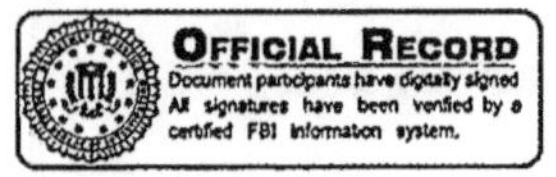

UNCLASSIFIED//~~FOUO~~

FEDERAL BUREAU OF INVESTIGATION

Date of entry 02/27/2013

LAW ENFORCEMENT SENSITIVE

This information is the property of the FBI and may be distributed to state, tribal, or local government law enforcement officials with a need-to-know. Further distribution without FBI authorization is prohibited. Precautions should be taken to ensure this information is stored and/or destroyed in a manner that precludes unauthorized access.

On 27 FEB 2013, Special Agents [redacted] and [redacted] met with Detective [redacted] Central District Major Crime Squad, Connecticut State Police (CSP). The purpose of the meeting was to transfer six (6) items of evidence from CSP evidence control to the custody of FBINH. One of the items that Det. [redacted] provided was described as follows: b6 -1, b7C -1,

#602 - SEIZED 12/19/2012 1320 - TEN (10) MISCELLANEOUS COMPUTER COMPONENTS

On the same day SAs [redacted] and [redacted] opened the item of evidence to evaluate whether items contained within needed to be packaged separately and documented accordingly before submitting the item to New Haven Evidence Control. At 1345, the package was opened. The contents are more fully described as: b6 -1 b7C -

1. TOSHIBA, MODEL MK4025GAS, 40GB HDD, SERIAL NUMBER 74C50902S
2. IBM 24X REMOVABLE CD DRIVE
3. SAMSUNG 3.5" FLOPPY DRIVE
4. COMPUTER VIDEO CARD
5. FOUR (4) MEMORY DIMMS
6. NETGEAR MODEL GA511 GIGABIT PC CARD
7. INTEL CORE 2 QUAD PROCESSOR, SERIAL NUMBER L738A939

Item #602 was be repackaged into two (2) separate packages as follows:

602A - TOSHIBA, MODEL MK4025GAS, 40GB HDD, SERIAL NUMBER 74C50902S

602B - SEIZED 12/19/2012 1320 - IBM CD DRIVE; SAMSUNG FLOPPY DRIVE; COMPUTER VIDEO CARD; FOUR (4) MEMORY DIMMS; NETGEAR GIGABIT PC CARD; INTEL PROCESSOR

Items 602A and 602B were submitted to New Haven Evidence Control.

UNCLASSIFIED//~~FOUO~~

Investigation on 02/27/2013 at New Haven, Connecticut, United States (In Person)

File # 4-NH-2619946 Date drafted 02/27/2013

by [redacted] b6 -1 b7C -1

4-NH-2619946
SERIAL 201

FD-1087 (Rev. 5-8-10)

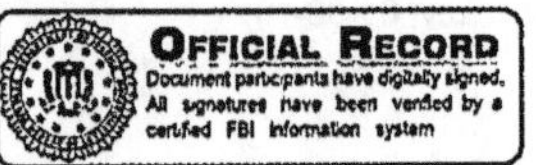

UNCLASSIFIED//~~FOUO~~

FEDERAL BUREAU OF INVESTIGATION

Evidence Log

Event Title: (U//~~FOUO~~) CSP Evidence Transferred to FBINH **Date:** 02/27/2013

To: [redacted]

Approved By: SSA [redacted]

b6 -1
b7C -1

Drafted By: [redacted]

Case ID #: 4-NH-2619946 (U) ADAM PETER LANZA
Sandy Hook Elementary School
12 Dickinson St, Sandy Hook, CT-Victim
Firearms Act.
OO:NH

LAW ENFORCEMENT SENSITIVE

This information is the property of the FBI and may be distributed to state, tribal, or local government law enforcement officials with a need-to-know. Further distribution without FBI authorization is prohibited. Precautions should be taken to ensure this information is stored and/or destroyed in a manner that precludes unauthorized access.

[redacted] b7E -1

Reference: 4-NH-2619946 Serial 201

Enclosure(s): Enclosed are the following items:
1. (U//~~FOUO~~) FD-597

Acquired By: [redacted] on 02/27/2013 b6 -1 b7C -1

Acquired From: (U//~~FOUO~~) DETECTIVE [redacted]
CONNECTICUT STATE POLICE - CENTRAL DISTRICT MAJOR CRIME SQUAD
1111 COUNTRY CLUB ROAD
MIDDLETOWN, Connecticut 06457
United States

b6 -3
b7C -3

UNCLASSIFIED//~~FOUO~~

4-NH-2619946
SERIAL 202

Title: (U//~~FOUO~~) CSP Evidence Transferred to FBINH
Re: 4-NH-2619946, 02/27/2013

Receipt Given?: Yes

Holding Office: NEW HAVEN

Details:

On 27 FEB 2013, Special Agents [redacted] and [redacted] met with Detective [redacted] Central District Major Crime Squad, Connecticut State Police (CSP). The purpose of the meeting was to transfer six (6) items of evidence from CSP evidence control to the custody of FBINH. Det. [redacted] provided the following items of evidence: b6 -1 b7C -1

#601 - SEIZED 12/19/2012 1315 - ONE (1) BOX CONTAINING AN IBM THINKPAD, SERIAL NUMBER AA-F2T8399/11 WITH POWER CORD

#602 - SEIZED 12/19/2012 1320 - TEN (10) MISCELLANEOUS COMPUTER COMPONENTS

#603 - SEIZED 12/19/2012 1335 - TWELVE (12) MISCELLANEOUS CD-R AND DVD-R DISCS CONTAINING UNKNOWN CONTENT

#609 - SEIZED 12/19/2012 1842 - SEVEN (7) JOURNALS AND MISCELLANEOUS DRAWINGS AUTHORED BY ADAM LANZA

#610 - SEIZED 12/19/2012 1320 - [redacted] b6 -5 b7C -5

#634 - SEIZED 12/20/2012 0958 - ONE (1) PLASTIC CASE CONTAINING 29 CD-R DISCS

Items 601, 602, and 603 were located in the second floor southeast corner bedroom at 36 YOGANANDA ST. SANDY HOOK, CT.

Item 634 was located in the second floor southwest corner bedroom at 36 YOGANANDA ST. SANDY HOOK, CT.

Items 609 and 610 were located in a box in the attic of 36 YOGANANDA

Title: (U//~~FOUO~~) CSP Evidence Transferred to FBINH
Re: 4-NH-2619946, 02/27/2013

ST. SANDY HOOK, CT.

The referenced items of evidence were packaged and physically sealed with evidence tape. The packages visually appeared that they had not been opened and resealed. Det. [redacted] a FD-597 receipt for property form that identified the referenced items of evidence. A copy of the FD-597 is maintained in a 1A. The referenced items of evidence will be submitted to New Haven Evidence Control. b6 -1 b7C -1

Item Type	**Description**
1B CART	(U//~~FOUO~~) ONE (1) BOX CONTAINING AN IBM THINKPAD, SERIAL NUMBER AA-F2T8399/11 WITH POWER CORD - #601 - CSP SEIZED 12/19/2012 1315 Acquired On: 02/27/2013 Receipt Number: 601 Located By: [redacted] Other Locator: [redacted] b6 -1 b7C -1 Location Area: CSP Evidence Storage Specific Location: CSP Evidence Storage Device Type: Laptop Computer Number of Devices Collected: 1
1B CART	(U//~~FOUO~~) 602A - TOSHIBA, MODEL MK4025GAS, 40GB HDD, SERIAL NUMBER 74C50902S; REPACKAGED FROM TEN (10) MISCELLANEOUS COMPUTER COMPONENTS - #602 - CSP SEIZED 12/19/2012 1320 Acquired On: 02/27/2013 Receipt Number: 602 Located By: [redacted] Other Locator: [redacted] b6 -1 b7C -1 Location Area: CSP Evidence Storage Specific Location: CSP Evidence Storage Device Type: Mass Storage Device Number of Devices Collected: 1

Title: (U//~~FOUO~~) CSP Evidence Transferred to FBINH
Re: 4-NH-2619946, 02/27/2013

1B CART (U//~~FOUO~~) TWELVE (12) MISCELLANEOUS CD-R AND DVD-R DISCS CONTAINING UNKNOWN CONTENT - #603 - CSP SEIZED 12/19/2012 1335
Acquired On: 02/27/2013
Receipt Number: 603
Located By: [redacted]
Other Locator: [redacted]
Location Area: CSP Evidence Storage
Specific Location: CSP Evidence Storage
Device Type: Mass Storage Device
Number of Devices Collected: 12

b6 -1
b7C -1

1B General (U//~~FOUO~~) SEVEN (7) JOURNALS AND MISCELLANEOUS DRAWINGS AUTHORED BY ADAM LANZA - #609 - CSP SEIZED 12/19/2012 1842
Acquired On: 02/27/2013
Receipt Number: 609
Located By: [redacted]
Other Locator: [redacted]
Location Area: CSP Evidence Storage
Specific Location: CSP Evidence Storage

b6 -1
b7C -1

1B General (U//~~FOUO~~) [redacted] - CSP SEIZED 12/19/2012 1320
Acquired On: 02/27/2013
Receipt Number: 610
Located By: [redacted]
Other Locator: [redacted]
Location Area: CSP Evidence Storage
Specific Location: CSP Evidence Storage

b6 -1, 5
b7C -1, 5

1B CART (U//~~FOUO~~) ONE (1) PLASTIC CASE CONTAINING 29 CD-R DISCS - #634 - SEIZED 12/20/2012 0958
Acquired On: 02/27/2013
Receipt Number: 634
Located By: [redacted]
Other Locator: [redacted]
Location Area: CSP Evidence Storage
Specific Location: CSP Evidence Storage
Device Type: Mass Storage Device
Number of Devices Collected: 29

b6 -1
b7C -1

Title: (U//~~FOUO~~) CSP Evidence Transferred to FBINH
Re: 4-NH-2619946, 02/27/2013

1B CART	(U//~~FOUO~~) 602B - IBM CD DRIVE; SAMSUNG FLOPPY DRIVE; COMPUTER VIDEO CARD; FOUR (4) MEMORY DIMMS; NETGEAR GIGABIT PC CARD; INTEL PROCESSORREPACKAGED FROM TEN (10) MISCELLANEOUS COMPUTER COMPONENTS - #602 - CSP SEIZED 12/19/2012 1320 Acquired On: 02/27/2013 Receipt Number: 602 Located By: [redacted] Other Locator: [redacted] Location Area: CSP Evidence Storage Specific Location: CSP Evidence Storage Device Type: Other Hardware Number of Devices Collected: 9

b6 -1
b7C -1

♦♦

FD-597 (Rev 8-11-94)

UNITED STATES DEPARTMENT OF JUSTICE
FEDERAL BUREAU OF INVESTIGATION
Receipt for Property Received/Returned/Released/Seized

File # 4-NH-2619946

On (date) 2/27/2013 1100am

item(s) listed below were:
- [x] Received From
- [ ] Returned To
- [ ] Released To
- [ ] Seized

(Name) Connecticut State Police

(Street Address)

(City) Meriden, CT

Description of Item(s):

601 - 12/19/12 1300 - IBM ThinkPad S/N AAF2T8399/11
602 - 12/19/12 1315 - Ten (10) miscellaneous computer components
603 - 12/19/12 1320 - Twelve (12) CDR/DVDR discs
609 - 12/19/12 1842 - Seven (7) Journals - Adam Lanza
610 - 12/19/12 1847 - b6 -5 b7C -5
634 - 12/20/12 0958 - One (1) Plastic case containing 29 CD-R discs.

b6 -1, 3
b7C -1, 3

Received By: ____________ Received From: Det. ____________ (Signature)

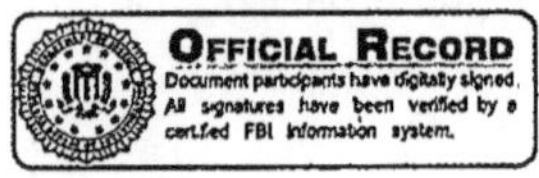

UNCLASSIFIED//~~FOUO~~

FEDERAL BUREAU OF INVESTIGATION

Date of entry 02/27/2013

LAW ENFORCEMENT SENSITIVE

On 27 FEB 2013, Special Agents [redacted] and [redacted] conducted a review of a AT&T digital answering system that was obtained from the first floor office at 36 YOGANANDA ST. SANDY HOOK, CONNECTICUT. The item of evidence was seized by the Connecticut State Police on December 15, 2012 at 3:42 AM. The item of evidence was packaged in brown paper, bearing the following labels: #41; placard #29; CFS12-00705354.

b6 -1
b7C -1

The AT&T digital answering system contained the following voice messages and caller id data, in summary:

VOICE MESSAGES

VM #	DAY/TIME	SUMMARY
1	TUESDAY 1150	[redacted] (phonetic) dentist office re: Adam due in April for cleaning - [redacted]
2	THURSDAY 1018	[redacted] [redacted] re: Adam healthcare reminder - [redacted]
3	SUNDAY 1130	[redacted] (possible) re: [redacted] [redacted] - no number
4	THURSDAY 1354	[redacted] [redacted] - no number
5	SUNDAY 1946	[redacted] (phonetic) re: lunch with Nancy - no number
6	FRIDAY 1148	Lt. [redacted] Connecticut State Police re: please answer the phone - no number
7	FRIDAY 1307	[redacted] re: saw headlines, checking in - no number
8	FRIDAY 1320	[redacted] (phonetic), CBS News re: ask for callback - [redacted]
9	FRIDAY 1350	[redacted] (possible) re: ask for callback - no number
10	FRIDAY 1419	Unknown caller re: I'm really sorry for what you're going through - no number

b6 -5
b7C -5

UNCLASSIFIED//~~FOUO~~

Investigation on 02/27/2013 at New Haven, Connecticut, United States (In Person)

File # 4-NH-2619946 Date drafted 02/27/2013

by [redacted]

b6 -1
b7C -1

4-NH-2619946
SERIAL 203

11	FRIDAY 1421	UNINTELLIGIBLE - [redacted]
12	FRIDAY 1427	[redacted] CNN re: ask for callback - [redacted]
13	FRIDAY 1433	UNINTELLIGIBLE - no number
14	FRIDAY 1438	[redacted] phonetic), Huffington Post re: ask for callback - [redacted]
15	FRIDAY 1439	Unknown caller re: Your son's a pussy - no number
16	FRIDAY 1441	[redacted] (phonetic) re: false flag attack; mind control - [redacted]
17	FRIDAY 1445	[redacted] (phonetic) [redacted] re: ask for callback - [redacted]
18	FRIDAY 1451	UNINTELLIGIBLE - no number
19	FRIDAY 1455	[redacted] (phonetic), [redacted] re: ask for callback - [redacted]
20	FRIDAY 1455	Unknown caller re: hello - no number
21	FRIDAY 1456	[redacted] (phonetic), Star Ledger re: ask for callback - [redacted]
22	FRIDAY 1458	[redacted] (phonetic) re: newspaper reporter on Long Island New York - [redacted]
23	FRIDAY 1503	Unknown caller re: bad parenting - no number
24	FRIDAY 1508	Text to Landline message delivery - [redacted]
25	FRIDAY 1512	[redacted] (possible) re: ask for callback - no number
26	FRIDAY 1517	UNINTELLIGIBLE - no number
27	FRIDAY 1526	Unknown caller UNINTELLIGIBLE - [redacted]
28	FRIDAY 1533	UNINTELLIGIBLE - no number
29	FRIDAY 1538	Unknown caller re: is this the MF that killed those kids - no number
30	FRIDAY 1556	[redacted] (phonetic), Headline News re: ask for callback - [redacted]
31	FRIDAY 1556	[redacted] (phonetic), Fox 29 News Philadelphia re: ask for callback - [redacted]
32	FRIDAY 1604	UNINTELLIGIBLE - no number
33	FRIDAY 1615	UNINTELLIGIBLE - no number
34	FRIDAY 1628	[redacted] Dr. Phil Show re: ask for callback - [redacted]
35	FRDIAY 1645	Unknown caller ask for callback - [redacted]
36	FRIDAY 1704	UNINTELLIGIBLE - no number
37	FRIDAY 1712	[redacted] (phonetic), Good Morning America, ABC News re: ask for callback - [redacted]
38	FRIDAY 1747	[redacted] phonetic), [redacted] Los Angeles re: ask for callback - [redacted]
39	FRDIAY 1750	UNINTELLIGIBLE - no number
40	FRIDAY 1927	Unknown caller UNINTELLIGIBLE - [redacted]

b6 -5
b7C -5

41	FRIDAY 2003	Unknown caller re: victims as well; calling from [redacted] no number
42	FRIDAY 2019	[redacted] LNU re: terribly sorry for everything you're going through -[redacted]
43	FRIDAY 2159	UNINTELLIGIBLE - no number
44	FRIDAY 2230	Unknown caller re: your son deserves to be dead - no number
45	SATURDAY 0036	UNINTELLIGIBLE - no number
46	SATURDAY 0211	UNINTELLIGIBLE - no number

b6 -5
b7C -5

CALLER ID

CALL #	DATE/TIME	SUMMARY
1	12/15/2012 0210	PRIVATE
2	12/15/2012 0142	[redacted]
3	12/15/2012 0140	[redacted]
4	12/15/2012 0127	[redacted]
5	12/15/2012 0124	PRIVATE
6	12/15/2012 0052	PRIVATE
7	12/15/2012 0035	[redacted]
8	12/15/2012 0032	[redacted] unknown
9	12/15/2012 0011	PRIVATE
10	12/14/2012 2357	PRIVATE
11	12/14/2012 2356	[redacted]
12	12/14/2012 2317	[redacted]
13	12/14/2012 2314	PRIVATE
14	12/14/2012 2313	[redacted]
15	12/14/2012 2259	PRIVATE
16	12/14/2012 2243	[redacted] wireless caller
17	12/14/2012 2230	PRIVATE
18	12/14/2012 2219	PRIVATE
19	12/14/2012 2213	[redacted]
20	12/14/2012 2159	[redacted]
21	12/14/2012 2158	[redacted] ABC radio net
22	12/14/2012 2157	[redacted]
23	12/14/2012 2154	[redacted] Skype user
24	12/14/2012 2153	[redacted] RCF Technologie
25	12/14/2012 2119	PRIVATE
26	12/14/2012 2112	[redacted]

b6 -5
b7C -5

27	12/14/2012 2111		
28	12/14/2012 2109		wireless caller
29	12/14/2012 2108	PRIVATE	
30	12/14/2012 2107	PRIVATE	
31	12/14/2012 2037		
32	12/14/2012 2036		
33	12/14/2012 2033		
34	12/14/2012 2031		
35	12/14/2012 2030	PRIVATE	
36	12/14/2012 2027	PRIVATE	
37	12/14/2012 2024	PRIVATE	
38	12/14/2012 2021		UnitedAutoCredi
39	12/14/2012 2019		ThomsonReuters
40	12/14/2012 2017		KPMG LLP
41	12/14/2012 2016	PRIVATE	
42	12/14/2012 2007		
43	12/14/2012 2003		
44	12/14/2012 1957	PRIVATE	
45	12/14/2012 1954	PRIVATE	
46	12/14/2012 1944		unknown
47	12/14/2012 1941	PRIVATE	
48	12/14/2012 1931		
49	12/14/2012 1930		KABC TV
50	12/14/2012 1926		CNN

b6 -5
b7C -5

#41 CFS12-00705354

placard # 29 12/15/2012 @ 0342

2/27/2013

Review AT&T dig ans system 1622

from 1st Floor office 36 Yogananda St

Sandy Hook

b6 -
b7C

① Tu 1150A office

Dentist Adam

② R 1018A

Health Reminder Adam

③ Su 1130A

④ R 154P

⑤ Su 746p

have lunch

b6 -5
b7C -5

⑥ Fr 1148A Lt State Police.

⑦ Fr 107P checking in

⑧ Fr 120P CBS News

Fr 150 PM - Call back - [redacted]

(10) Fr 219 PM - female "I'm really sorry...

(11) Fr 221 PM - [redacted]

(12) Fr 227 PM - [redacted] CNN [redacted]

(13) Fr 233 PM - hang up

b6 -5
b7C -5

(14) Fr 238 PM - [redacted] Huffington Post

(15) Fr 239 PM - your son's a pussy

(16) Fr 241 pm [redacted] "false flag attack" "mind controlled

(17) Fri 245 pm [redacted]

(18) 251 pm hang

(19) 255 pm [redacted]

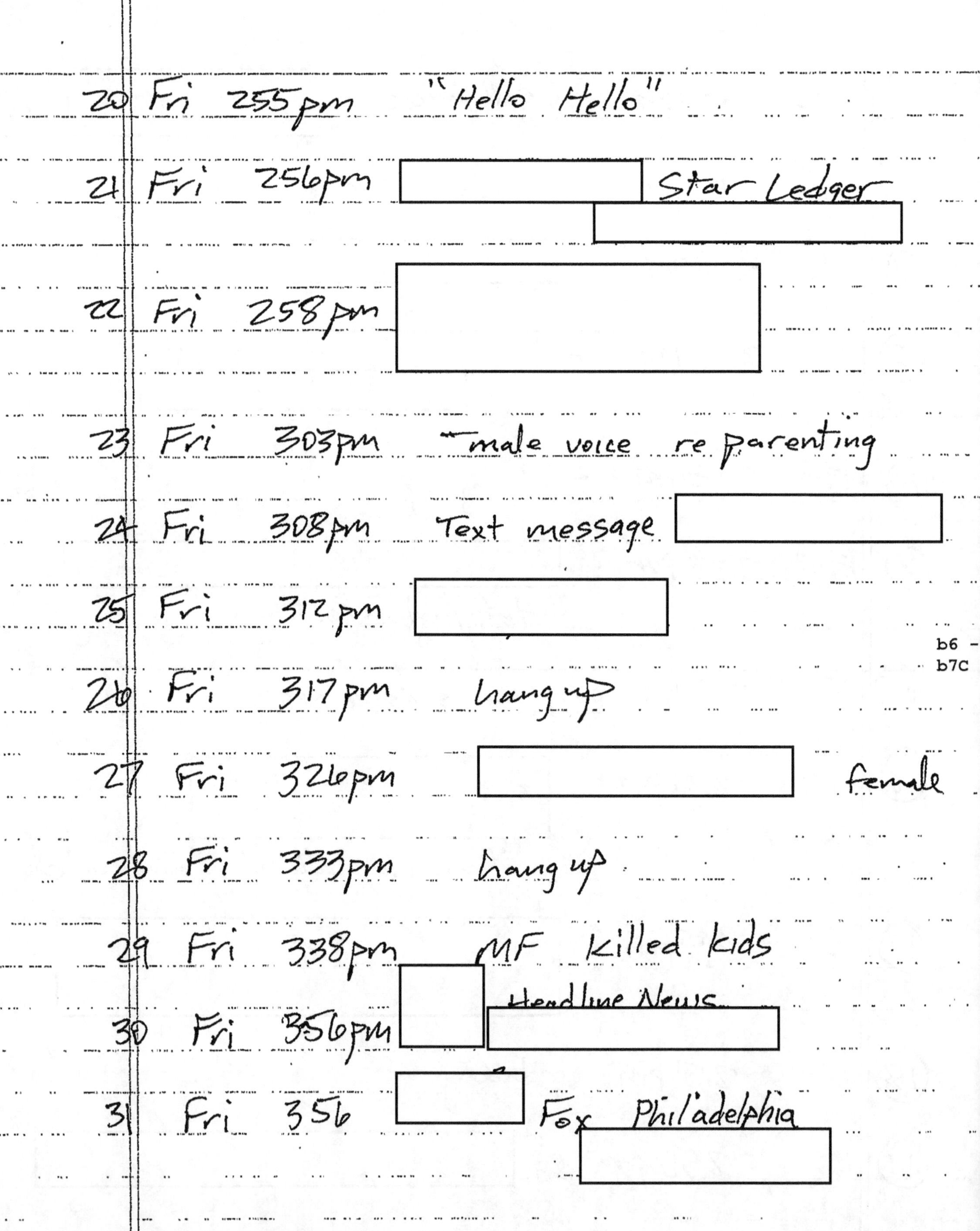

20 Fri 255pm "Hello Hello"

21 Fri 256pm [redacted] Star Ledger [redacted]

22 Fri 258pm [redacted]

23 Fri 303pm male voice re parenting

24 Fri 308pm Text message [redacted]

25 Fri 312pm [redacted]

b6 -5
b7C -

26 Fri 317pm hang up

27 Fri 326pm [redacted] female

28 Fri 333pm hang up

29 Fri 338pm MF killed kids

30 Fri 356pm [redacted] Headline News [redacted]

31 Fri 356 [redacted] Fox Philadelphia [redacted]

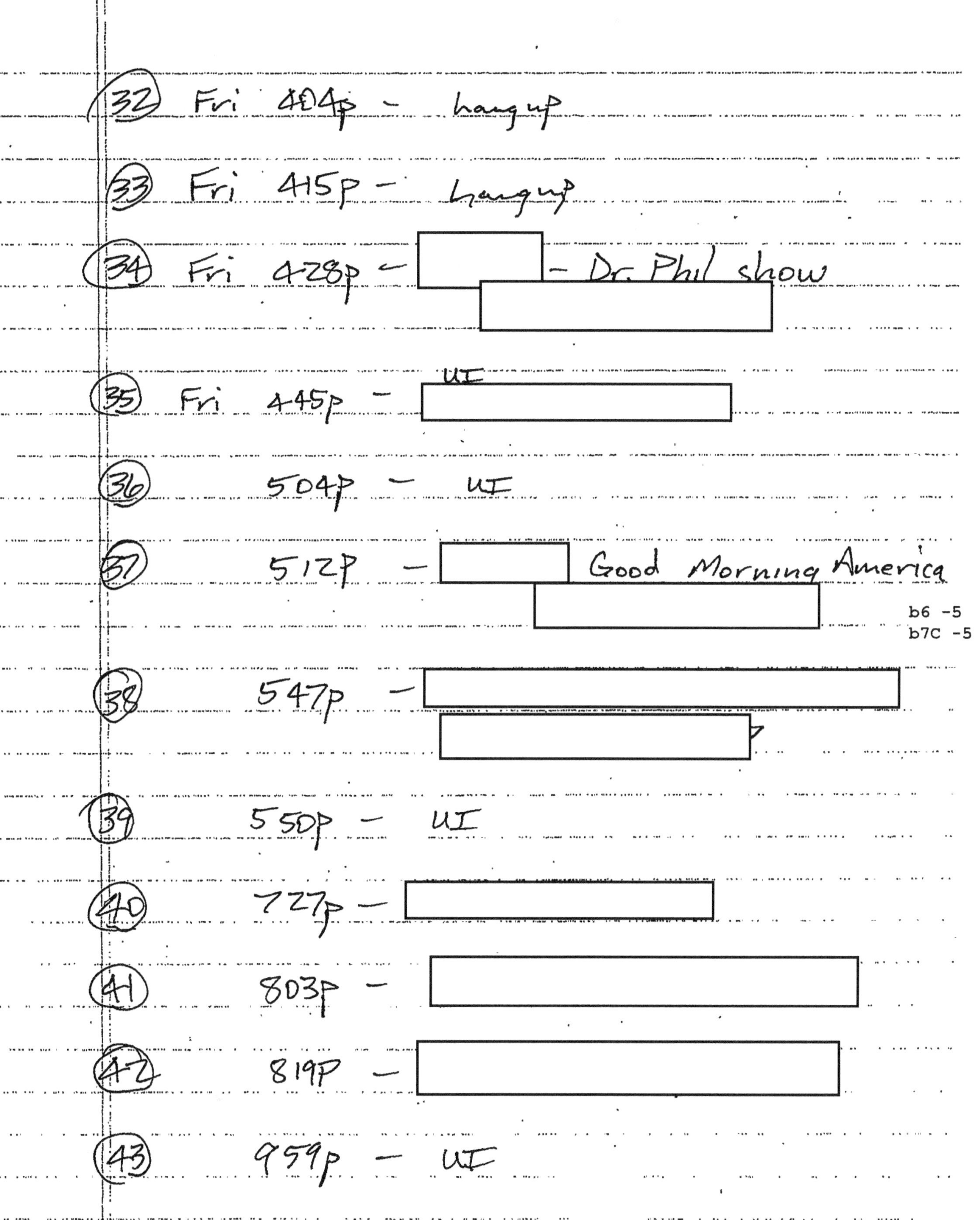

(32) Fri 404p - hangup

(33) Fri 415p - hangup

(34) Fri 428p - [redacted] - Dr. Phil show [redacted]

(35) Fri 445p - UI [redacted]

(36) 504p - UI

(37) 512p - [redacted] Good Morning America [redacted]

b6 -5
b7C -5

(38) 547p - [redacted] [redacted]

(39) 550p - UI

(40) 727p - [redacted]

(41) 803p - [redacted]

(42) 819p - [redacted]

(43) 959p - UI

(44) Fri 10 30p "your son deserves to be dead."

(45) Sat 12 36A UI

b6 -
b7C -

rivate (46) Sat 211 A UI

end of messages 2/27/13
1650

Caller ID

12/15	210	Private
	142	
	140	
	127a	
	124a	Priv
	1252a	Priv
	1235a	
	1232a	unk
	1211	priv
12/14	1157	priv
	1156	
	1117	
	1114	priv
	1113	
	1059	priv
	1043	wireless
	1030	priv
	1019	priv
	1013	
	959	
	958	ABC radio net
	957	Kerr Schoenherr
	954	Skype user
	953	RCF Technology
	919	priv
	912	
	911	

b6 -5
b7C -5

12/14 909pm Wireless

908 priv

907 priv

837

836 " "

833

831

830 priv

827 "

824 "

821 UnitedAutoCredi

819 Thomson Reuters

817 KPMG LLP

816 priv

807

803

757 priv

754 "

744 unk.

741 priv

731

730 KABC TV

726 CNN

b6 -5
b7C -

FD-1087 (Rev. 5-8-10)

UNCLASSIFIED//~~FOUO~~

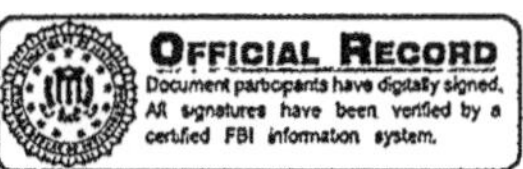

FEDERAL BUREAU OF INVESTIGATION

Evidence Log

Event Title: (U//~~FOUO~~) [redacted] [redacted] **Date:** 03/04/2013 b7E -6

To: [redacted]

Approved By: SSA [redacted] b6 -1 b7C -1

Drafted By: [redacted]

Case ID #: 4-NH-2619946 (U) ADAM PETER LANZA
Sandy Hook Elementary School
12 Dickinson St, Sandy Hook, CT-Victim
Firearms Act.
OO:NH

LAW ENFORCEMENT SENSITIVE

This information is the property of the FBI and may be distributed to state, tribal, or local government law enforcement officials with a need-to-know. Further distribution without FBI authorization is prohibited. Precautions should be taken to ensure this information is stored and/or destroyed in a manner that precludes unauthorized access.

[redacted] b7E -1

Acquired By: [redacted] on 03/01/2013

Acquired From: (~~U//FOUO~~) [redacted]

Receipt Given?: No b6 -1, 3 b7C -1, 3

Holding Office: NEW HAVEN

Details:

On 27 FEB 2013, Special Agents [redacted] and [redacted] met with Detective [redacted] Central District Major Crime Squad,

UNCLASSIFIED//~~FOUO~~

This document contains neither recommendations nor conclusions of the FBI. It is the property of the FBI and is loaned to your agency; it and its contents are not to be distributed outside your agency.

4-NH-2619946
SERIAL 205

Title: (U//~~FOUO~~) [redacted] b7E -6
Re: 4-NH-2619946, 03/04/2013

Connecticut State Police (CSP). During the meeting, the following two (2) items of evidence were obtained from CSP Evidence Control and subsequently submitted to NH Evidence Control:

1B95 - SEVEN (7) JOURNALS AND MISCELLANEOUS DRAWINGS AUTHORED BY ADAM LANZA - #609 - CSP SEIZED 12/19/2012 1842

1B96 - [redacted] #610 - CSP SEIZED 12/19/2012 1320 b6 -5 b7C -5

On 01 MAR 2013, Special Agents [redacted] and [redacted] photographed the physical items of evidence [redacted] b6 -1 b7C -1 b7E -6

[redacted]

Item Type 1B CART

Description
(U//~~FOUO~~) [redacted]

Acquired On: 03/01/2013
Located By: [redacted]
Other Locator: [redacted]
Location Area: NH Derivative Evidence
Specific Location: NH Derivative Evidence
Device Type: [redacted]
Number of Devices Collected: [redacted]

b6 -1, 5 b7C -1, b7E -6

◆◆

FD-1036 (Rev. 10-16-2009)

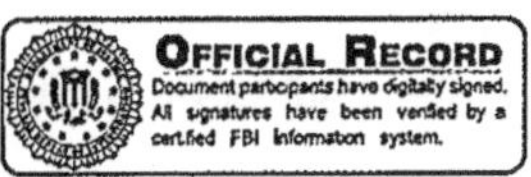

UNCLASSIFIED

FEDERAL BUREAU OF INVESTIGATION

Import Form

Form Type: DEL-REX **Date:** 01/16/2013

Title: (U) DEL REX

Approved By: SSA [redacted]

Drafted By: [redacted]

b6 -1
b7C -1

Case ID #: 356A-NH-2619946 (U) ADAM PETER LANZA
Sandy Hook Elementary School
12 Dickinson St, Sandy Hook, CT-Victim
Firearms Act.
OO:NH

Synopsis: (U) DEL REX for [redacted]

Enclosure(s): Enclosed are the following items: [redacted]

b6 -2
b7C -2
b7E -6, 8

♦♦

UNCLASSIFIED

Sandy Hook-2753

4-NH-2619946
SERIAL 206

FD-1036 (Rev. 10-16-2009)

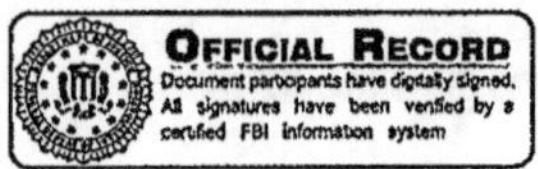

UNCLASSIFIED

FEDERAL BUREAU OF INVESTIGATION

Import Form

Form Type: LHM **Date:** 03/07/2013

Title:(U) Letter to Hoboken Police Department

Approved By: SSA [redacted]

Drafted By: [redacted]

b6 -1
b7C -1

Case ID #: 356A-NH-2619946 (U) ADAM PETER LANZA
Sandy Hook Elementary School
12 Dickinson St, Sandy Hook, CT-Victim
Firearms Act.
OO:NH

Synopsis: (U) Letter to Chief of Hoboken, NJ Police Department, thanking them for their assistance in this investigation.

♦♦

UNCLASSIFIED

4-NH-2619946

SERIAL 207 Sandy Hook-

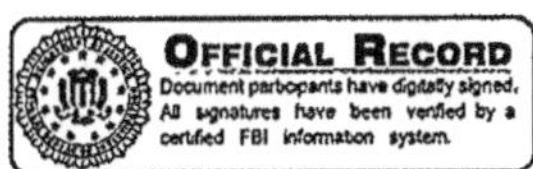

FEDERAL BUREAU OF INVESTIGATION

Import Form

Form Type: DEL-REX **Date:** 01/24/2013

Title: (U) DEL REX

Approved By: SSA [redacted]

Drafted By: [redacted]

b6 -1
b7C -1

Case ID #: 356A-NH-2619946 (U) ADAM PETER LANZA
Sandy Hook Elementary School
12 Dickinson St, Sandy Hook, CT-Victim
Firearms Act.
OO:NH

Synopsis: (U) DEL REX for [redacted] b7E -6, 8

Enclosure(s): Enclosed are the following items:
1. (U) Admin Notes
2. (U) Case Notes

♦♦

4-NH-2619946
SERIAL 208

FD-1057 (Rev. 5-8-10)

FEDERAL BUREAU OF INVESTIGATION

Electronic Communication

Title: (U//~~FOUO~~) [redacted]

Date: 03/11/2013

To: [redacted]

From: NEW HAVEN
NH-10
Contact: [redacted]

b6 -1
b7C -1
b7E -6

Approved By: SSA [redacted]

Drafted By: [redacted]

Case ID #: 356A-NH-2619946 (U) ADAMPETER LANZA
Sandy Hook Elementary School
12 Dickinson St, Sandy Hook, CT-Victim
Firearms Act.
OO:NH
[redacted] (U) [redacted]

b7A -1
b7E -4

LAW ENFORCEMENT SENSITIVE

This information is the property of the FBI and may be distributed to state, tribal, or local government law enforcement officials with a need-to-know. Further distribution without FBI authorization is prohibited. Precautions should be taken to ensure this information is stored and/or destroyed in a manner that precludes unauthorized access.

Synopsis: (U//~~FOUO~~) [redacted]

b7E -1,

Details:

[redacted]

4-NH-2619946
SERIAL 209 Sandy Hook-

Title: (U//~~FOUO~~)

Re: 356A-NH-2619946, 03/11/2013

b7E -6

♦♦

FD-302 (Rev. 5-8-10)

FEDERAL BUREAU OF INVESTIGATION

Date of entry 03/11/2013

On 03/05/2013, Special Agent [redacted] Federal Bureau or Investigation, New Haven Office, interviewed [redacted], born [redacted] of the Newtown Bee, 5 Church Hill Road, Newtown, Connecticut, 06470, telephone number [redacted] cellular telephone number [redacted] After being advised of the identity of the interviewing Agent and the nature of the interview, [redacted] provided the following information: b6 -1, b7C -1,

Over the past few weeks, the Newtown Bee newspaper has been receiving emails from a person who identifies himself as [redacted] is using email account [redacted] is addressing the emails to Newtown Bee [redacted] The emails are disturbing in their content and style. In general, they make reference to the shooting at the Sandy Hook Elementary School and use aggressive and vulgar language to blame the Newtown residents and victims' parents for the shooting. b6 -2, b7C -2,

[redacted] provided SA [redacted] with copies of nine emails received at the Bee between 02/02/2013 and 03/05/2013, which are attached. b6 -1, b7C -1,

Investigation on 03/05/2013 at Bridgeport, Connecticut, United States (In Person)

File # 356A-NH-2619946 Date drafted 03/11/2013

by [redacted] b6 b7C

4-NH-2619446 SERIAL 210 Sandy Hook-

From:
Sent: Tuesday, March 05, 2013 12:40 PM
To:
Subject: FW: ....SO LADS.........ITS FEBRUARY 2013...........HMMMMMMMMMMMMMM..............GUESS............WE'LL COME THERE..............................

b6 -1, 7
b7C -1, 7

-----Original Message-----
From
Sent: Saturday, February 02, 2013 2:06 AM
To:
Subject: ....SO LADS.........ITS FEBRUARY 2013...........HMMMMMMMMMMMMMM..............GUESS............WE'LL COME THERE..............................

b6 -2, 7
b7C -2, 7

............THOUGHT WE MIGHT..............SAVE SOME TIME............OOOPS...........TOO LATE..........WE'VE BEEN THERE........SINCE.........THE POOR BOY ADAM LANZA STARTED.........KILLING YOUR 20 DEAD CHILDREN........AND....................

............THOSE 4 ARROGANT WOMEN TEACHERS.........WHO HAD THE FIGHT WITH ADAM THE DAY BEFORE........AT SANDY HOOK ELEMENTARY SCHOOL.........HMMMMMMMMMM.........WHAT EXACTLY.......HAPPENED THERE.............

............IN TRUTH.......HAVENT REALLY FOLLOWED YOUR CONNECTICUT THING THAT CLOSELY.........WHY.........SIMPLE.....WE ALREADY KNOW..........EXACTLY.........WHAT HAPPENED.........WHY,.........THE WHOLE SHEBANG........YEP......

............FIRST.......WE AINT MEDIA MAGGOTYS LIKE CNN MSNBC WHATEVER.........THEY ARE ALL.........MAGGOTS WHO FEED ON DEATH......PAIN........HUMAN SUFFERINGS........SCUM OF THE EARTH......HERES A FACT FOR YOU............

............THESE MEDIA RATS........ARE ENABLERS OF ADAM LANZAS.........YOU GIVE A PSYCHO.........PUBLIC MEDIA ATTENTION........YOU GET.........MORE PSHYCHOS.........COPYCATS.........WHATEVER.......HELLO........COLORADO......YAHH....

............COLUMBINE WAS WHAT 12 YEARS BACK.........LIKE YOU DIDN'T KNOW........SCHOOL SHOOTINGS.........HAPPEN.......RIGHT.........BULLSHIT.........YOUR SINS..........ARE.........PURE..........ARROGANCE.......PRIDE........PERIOD............

............YOU THOUGHT "THAT.......CANT HAPPEN HERE IN NEWTOWN CONNECTICUT.."........WRONG.........DEAD 20 INNOCENTS WRONG..........THAT SHEER CIVILIANS "AOI" = "ARROGANCE OF IGNORANCE" COST YOUR CHILDREN........

..........THEIR LIVES.........WHICH.........SUCKS.........FOREVER.........NOW.......YOU GET TO LIVE.........FOR THE REST OF YOUR LIVES.........WITH YOUR ARROGANT FUCKUPS..........WAIT TILL YOU SEE WHAT THIS DOES TO YER TOWN............

..............YOU JUST AT.........THE WARM UP STAGE..........APPROACHING.........STAGE #1..............SO THE BOY ADAM WAS REALLY..........REALLY PISSED OFF AT THESE 4 WOMEN TEACHERS THE TRIGGER EVENT CLEAR AS DAY...................

...........THE DAY...........DECEMBER 14TH, 2012..........RIGHT.......ADAM LANZA CAME LOADED FOR BEAR WHAT ONE GLOCK AND ONE SIG BOTH 9MM.........MAYBE THE BUSHMASTER RIFLE THROWN IN FOR......LIES......PROPAGANDA......

...........SAW PART OD THE CONNECTICUT STATE POLICE LIES THAT "WE DON'T KNOW WHY HE DID IT...."......BLAHHHHHH.........BULLSHIT.....WE DO........PRECISELY.......YOU......MAY NOT.........ANYBODY POLICE KISSES NOBI-ONE-EYES....

............PROPAGANDA PUKE ASS SO COMPLETELY.........CANNOT........BE.........TRUSTED.....THE MORAL ROT.........RUNS DEEP.......IN...........CONNECTICUT..........NO SURPRISES..........THERE.......OLD NEWS...........SOOOOOOOOOOOOOO.....

...........THIS ADAM COMES A KILLIN 4 BITCHES PISSED HIM OFF BIG TIME......SOMEHOW..........HOW...........EXACTLY...........WHAT DID THEY DO........OR..........SAY TO THE BOY..........TO TRIGGER HIM......MORE CRITICAL IS WHY...........

...........IS BITCH #1 TEACHER...........WHO STAYED HOME FROM SCHOOL.....DAY AFTER ADAM FIGHT...........SAVED HER OWN ASS.........STILL ALIVE.........BUT............20 DEAD CHILDREN...........COINCIDENCE........GET REAL[redacted]....YOU.. b6 -7 b7C -

............MAY BE STUPID...........WE............AINT.............WHAT DID SHE KNOW.....WHY........DIDN'T SHE TELL THE POLICE.........OLE ADAM WAS REALLY..........REALLY.........PISSED OFF..........WHAT.........DID SHE DO......TO THE BOY...........

............YOU CAN TELL HER...........SHE'S IN THE HOT SEAT...........ON FIRE...........IN FACT.........AND.........ANYBODY............WHO LIES WITH HER...........BINGO..............SHIT GONNA GET UGLY.........REAL...........UGLY.........WATCH.....SEE.......

..............IF IT HAPPENS TO BE YER DAUGHTER...........GOD HELP YOU...........WE'LL PRAY FOR ALL OF YA.............YOUR DELUSIONAL GROUP MINDSET...........GRIEF..........BLAHHHHHHHH........THINKS.......IT......WILL BLOW OVER......LIES.....

...............WILL...............COVER.............THE.............PURE EVILS...........INVOLVED............NAH............NOT A CHANCE.............BUT.............ENJOY...........THE...........FANTASY..........WHILST.........YOU..............CAN........ .GOD BLESS......OUT....

From: [redacted]
Sent: Tuesday, March 05, 2013 12:40 PM
To: [redacted]
Subject: FW: ....WELL NOW..............WHERE................WERE...............WE.........................

b6 -1, 7
b7C -1, 7

-----Original Message-----
From: [redacted]
Sent: Saturday, February 02, 2013 2:22 AM
To: [redacted]
Subject: ....WELL NOW..............WHERE.................WERE................WE..........................

b6 -2, 7
b7C -2, 7

..................TOTAL MORAL FAILURE.............OF.............NEWTOWN.................CONNECTICUT...............TO.............PROTECT THEIR CHILDREN...............BECAUSE...............PURE ARROGANCE..............SINFUL PRIDE..........DONE DEAL.....................

..............SO WAS IT............YOU DID NOTHING.............AFTER...........COLUMBINE...............ARROGANCE..........."WE DON'T HAVE THOSE PROBLEMS......HUFF......HERE.."...........SURE YOU DO..........REALITY...........BOZOS...........BUT...............

.................YOU................PROBABLY................WILL....................STILL..................DO...............NOTHING...... .......ACTION............REQUIRES.................REAL MEN..............PROBABLY............NONE.............EXIST.......IN YOUR TOWN.......................

..................OR.................WAS IT...............WE DON'T LIKE GUNS............WHO CARES...........WHAT WEAK SPINELESS COWARDS..........LIKE..............YOUR 20 DEAD CHILDREN.........PAID FOR YOUR COWARDICE.......YOUR FAILURES.......FACT.....

................YOUR.............TOTAL.............ABSOLUTE MORAL FAILURES.............TO............FACE............REALITY............OF...........SCHOOL SHOOTINGS...............IS..........YOUR TOTAL FAILURES...........AS..........MEN...........PATHETIC......SICK.........

......................THAT.............YOU..............COULD..............HAVE..............STOPPED.................THIS............ .HAD.............YOU.................TRAINED.............PREPARED............IS..................DISGUSTING...........TO.........A LL..........REAL MEN.....FACT...

......................TELL YOURSELVES..............ALL THE BULLSHIT.............LIES............YOU WANT.............THIS.............IS.............YOUR.............REALITY............NOW...............FOREVER.........SO GET IT STRAIGHT.........FAST..........THEN......THINK.........

.................HOW MANY...............MORE.....,.............ADAM LANZAS................YOU............GOT............IN............NEWTOWN....................CONNECTICUT....................NO W BEFORE.........YA START..........WHINING...........DON'T.........WEAKNESS...

......................ANY MAN WHO DOES NOT............PROTECT............HIS CHILDREN............IS...........NO..............MAN.............AT..............ALL................FACT............PASS THE WORD........REALITY IS IN TOWN.........TRUTH IS THERE........OUT.......

From: [redacted]
Sent: Tuesday, March 05, 2013 12:40 PM
To: [redacted]
Subject: FW: .............WHERE.........DO...........THESE..........KOOKOOOS............TRUTHERS...........WHATEVER...........COME......FROM................

b6 -1, 7
b7C -1, 7

-----Original Message-----
From: [redacted]
Sent: Sunday, February 10, 2013 2:12 AM
To: [redacted]
Subject: .............WHERE.........DO...........THESE..........KOOKOOOS............TRUTHERS...........WHATEVER...........COME......FROM................

b6 -2, 7
b7C -2, 7

................I MEAN...............COME ON............GRANTED YOU'ALL............FUCKED UP............ROYALLY...........AND...........WELL............WE KNOW..........YER LYIN THRU YER TEETH...........ON SOME SHIT...........BUT............THESE.......BOZOS......

..............WHOSEEVER'S.........ON SITE.......WILL............TAKE CARE OF BUSINESS...........BEYOND ME..........LADS..........CONNECTICUT...........NEWTOWN...........HOW'S IT FEEL..........TO..........BE...........A...........MILESTONE..........EVENT...........

................HMMMMMMMMMMM...........WOULDN'T..........WANT...........THAT.......MONIKER.............FOR MY HOME TOWN..........SOOOOOO............WITCHCRAFT..............SATANISM........YA FLYIN AROUND ON BROOMS......OR WHAT........

..............WHO YOU LADS............ARE............REALLY.............ARE............I AINT.........GOTTA............CLUE............IRRELEVANT..........YOUR TOWN...........20 DEAD INNOCENTS..........WILL SERVE.........IN WAYS..........BEYOND.......YOUR..........

................VERY...................WILDEST................IMAGINATIONS...........PAGINATIONS.............WHATEVER..... ....LETS PUT NEWTOWN, CONNECTICUT...........DECEMBER 14TH, 2012...........IN...........PROPER...........PERSPECTIVE................

...............FEEL.............FREE.............TO...............CHIME IN..........CORRECT.............ANY.............FALSE FLAGS...........I MEAN.............FALSE FACTS...........JOKE...........CASTIGATE.........YOU.............CHOOSE............REALLY........ONE THING.........

.............WOUL;D BE SO.............REFRESHING........SOME TRUE INTELLECT............THE USUAL............MEDIA............DRIVEL..........IS..............PITEOUS............I RECALL...........AND...........KNOW..........SOME FOLKS.......WHO CAN WRITE.........

............BETTER YET............THEY CAN............THINK......WHEN THE IVYS............STARTED THAT............BRING THE IDIOTS...........RUBBER STAMP EM THRU............DINK...........HOWDI DOODY KANYOBAMAMAASES.........WOW !!!!!!!.........

.......................HOW THY DEAR CRIMSON DOTH BLEED.......WELL YOU KNOW...........NO..........YOU.............ARE.............A..............FUCKING............IDIOT............NO STANDARDS.........EXIST...........ANYMORE.........HERE'S A FUNNY...............

.............SOME OF THOSE KOOKY BASTARDS..........OUR SECRET SERVICE BOYS..........WERE WORRIED ABOUT.........NO........NOT THE WHORES CHASERS..........WHO DIDN'T TIP PROPERLY IN COLUMBIA........POOR BOY NOBI-ONE-EYE........

............HOW'D YOU LIKE TO BE A.......CYCLOPS...........BLIND IN ONE EYE......AND..........YOU KNOW..........YOUR DETAIL........JUST GAVE SOME 3RD WORLD WHORES.........YOUR WHOLE ITINERRAY........FER A BLOW JOBS......YAZOOOO...

..........SOOOOOOOOOOO..........SECRET SERVICE.....NO STANDARDS...........PROOF.........LOOK AROUND.........YOU..........BOZOS..........YOU LET THE BOY ADAM LANZA..........BLOW THE BRAINS OUTTA YOUR CHILDREN IN SCHOOL...YEAH...

.............PARENTS.........NO STANDARDS.........FATHERS......NO BALLS...........MOTHERS..........NO MINDS.......WORSE..........NO MOTHER'S INSTINCTS TO PROTECT HER CHILDREN.......WHOA......THE HUMAN GENOME PROJECT....WHAT...

.........YEAH.........TOLD YA.........YOU WERE........CLUELESS........GENETICS......RESEARCH...........YOU DON'T REALLY............THINK...........WE AINT............GONNA...........USE.........HUMAN GENOME........TO........ERADICATE...."ANOMALY"....

............GET REAL......WE TELL.........BRILLIANT BOZOS............NAIEVE SCIENTISTS...........NICE STORIES..........WE GOT..........WHAT..........7.3 BILLION MUTTS........ON THIS PLANET..........WE GOTTA ACCELERATE.....THE NASA PROGRAM........

...............GET THIS.........CHEAP SHIP THE DIRTBAGS...........SPICS.........ILLEGALS.........WHATEVER..........RETARDS IN SPACE.........NEW "SPECIAL OLYMPICS"..........KENNEDY'S WILL ENDORSE..........ANYTHING......JUST.......DON'T.......FLY........

................WITH A KENNEDY.............I SEEM TO RECALL............SOME VERY IRRITATING............NAVAL SHIPS...........VERY BORING.............SEARCH FOR DINGBAT........SPLATS...........PLANE.......OH..........THERE'S A PIECE.......OF........YEAH......

..............JUST............LIKE.............YER SANDY HOOK ELEMENTARY SCHOOL...........HALLWAYS...........YOU EVER...........TRY TO RUN........IN FULL TAC GEAR THRU............SLIPPERY........BLOOD..........FLOWING..........FREELY........HALLS..............

............YOU BOZOS......KEEP YOUR WEAK ASS.........BLUBBERING ABOUT "ANTI-VIOLENCE ANTI-GUN INITIATIVES....RAH....RAH....BLAAHHHH.."...........SILLY BOYS BULLSHIT.......HERE'S A REAL........LIGHT BULB MOMENT......FOR YA.........

........SHUT THE FUCK UP...........GRIEVE........IN DIGNITY..........SILENCE..........GIVE ME A CALL........I'LL TRAIN YOUR SCHOOL'S STAFF........IF YOU HAVE ANY WORTHY.......REAL MEN........NEXT.........ADAM LANZA......ONE COFFIN....MAYBE....

............YOU DO IT.......RIGHT.............ASSHOLE............NEVER...........GETS......THE.......CHANCE...,........BUT............PEOPLE FUCK UP........SO...........YOU KILL ONE ASSHOLE.........YOU GO HOME........YOU SHOW DEAD ASSHOLE....ON...CNN.....

...............PUT HIS SMILIN WHATS LEFT OF HIS FACE.........ON THE BLAZING SUNDAY EDITION.........OF...............THE NEWTOWN BEE..........CNN.........MSNBC........USE THE MEDIA..........FOR..........MORAL PURPOSES......JUST........ONCE.......

...............WHICH.........I THINK.........COLUMBIA SCHOOL OF JOURNALISM..........NO MORAL; HUMAN BEINGS ALLOWED............RIGHT ACROSS..........THE TOP..........OF COLLEGE'S APPLICATION........YEP......MEDIA SCUMBAGS......ONLY......

.............YA KNOW..........LIARS............COWARDS.............CREEPS.............QUEERS............WAIT...........THAT'S JUST YOUR NEWTOWN NEIGHBORS........RIGHT.........THE NICE PEOPLE.........YEAH.......VERY FUNNY..........SO...........REALLY........

.............NEWTOWN............CONNECTICUT.............THE HOME OF.............ABSOLUTE MORAL FAILURES..........I TRAIN YOU......PUT YOU IN SCHOOLS........DEAD DAWN PRINCIPAL........WOULD BE ALIVE........HAD I DONE SO.....ALREADY.......

............THOSE............20 DEAD INNOCENTS..........ALIVE......ADAM LANZA.........DEAD.........YOU SEE LADDIE...........THIS...........TAKES............REAL MEN..........WITH BALLS.........WHO..........FACE REALITY........THE TRUTH.....NO WHINERS......

...........TELL THOSE...........WEAK...........WHINY BITCHES PARENTS...........WHO........LET ADAM LANZA.........SHOOT TO DEATH BY HORRIFIC GUNFIRE.......THEIR CHILDREN.......TO SHUT THE FUCK UP.......HANG THEIR HEADS IN SHAME.......

.............ITS ALL..........SELF-SERVING..........NARCISSISM............SAME DISGUSTING........INORDINATE LOVE OF SELF..........THAT GOT THEIR KIDS BRAINS BLOWN OUT IN TERROR........WHAT ???........YOU SILLY BITCHES DARE TELL ME ?????

...........OR............ANYONE......YOU DIDN'T KNOW.........ABOUT..........COLUMBINE.........VIRGINIA TECH..........OREGON MALL SHOOTINGS.........AMISH SCHOOL HOUSE..........THAT LITTLE RED HEADED BASTARD LIKES KILLING BATMAN......

........MOVIE FREAKS OR SOMETHING........AURORA, COLORADO #7........YOUR LIES........ARE........DISGUSTING.........YOUR MORAL FILTH............STINKS TO HIGH HEAVEN...........GROW THE FUCK UP..........TOO LATE........YEAH, WE KNOW....

.............REAL MEN......PROTECT THEIR CHILDREN........LIKE..   ...GOOD b6 -7
JOB.......   .....REAL b7C -7
MEN........ACT..........BITCHES......WHINE..........CHILDREN.........DIE.......YOU.........WHINE......MORE.......DISGU STING.....OUT......

From: [redacted]
Sent: Tuesday, March 05, 2013 12:40 PM
To: [redacted]
Subject: FW: ................YEAH.............HEY................THERE..........[redacted]...........STILL...........O N THE UDDER.............JOKE...........MEAT BOY............WE KNOW.........YER BUSY........SAID.......NARCISSUS AS HE LOVINGLY GAZED.

b6 -1, b7C -1,

-----Original Message-----
From: [redacted]
Sent: Sunday, February 10, 2013 2:29 AM
To: [redacted]
Subject: ................YEAH.............HEY................THERE..........[redacted]..........STILL...........ON THE UDDER.............JOKE...........MEAT BOY............WE KNOW.........YER BUSY........SAID.......NARCISSUS AS HE LOVINGLY GAZED.....

b6 -2, b7C -2,

................ANY TOWN...............PEOPLE............LIKE YOU.............NEWTOWN.............CLOWNS...............HAVE THE GAUL.............TO.............KEEP..............WHINING...........YOUR.............LIES..........ON.............TV..........WE LL.......................

.................SEE.............OUR...........IRREEVERENT...........POKE...........IN YER ARROGANT.............EYE..............LIE................ELSEWHERE...............WE SEE............YOU.................CLEARLY..................SEE........[redacted]...CLOWN..........

b6 -7 b7C -

................YOU.............CAN.............READ..............TOGETHER................AND............PLEASE...............STO P..............THIS.............DISGUSTING............PUKE...............NARCISSISM..................EPIDEMIC..........OH.... ......POOR US..................

..................WE ARE...............LAZY...............MORAL.............SLOTH.............TOADS...................WHO............KNEW........... ...ABOUT............COLUMBINE...........BUT...........OUR...........DELIGHTFUL............LOVE OF SELF......HUGS.......NOW.......

....................THOSE..............SOUTH PARK..............BOYS.............WANNA.............LET ER RIPPP............ON YER...........FOUL............STENCHED.............ASSES..........THE STENCH OF SMUG.........AS A BUG........IN BUGGERY HEAVEN.....YAH......

..................THEY............KNOW..........YA..........TROUBLE...........SO SHUT IT...........YOU PARENTS...........ABSOLUTE MORAL FAILURES.............WHO..........DID...........NOT..........PROTECT.........YOUR CHILDREN........YOU WERE.......BUSY........

......................YEAH, WE
KNOW..............NARCIISSISTIC.............ASSHOLES............ARE............ALWAYS.........BUSY...........SERVING
THEIR SICK EGOS.........WITH
SOME...........ENLIGHTENMED..........SILLY.........PERVERSIONS.........LIKE...........

...............SAY............BEERS FOR QUEERS............OR...........IS...........IT............PAGANS FOR
SATAN..........NOO..........AHHHH...........NARCISSISTS FOR MIRRORS.........YEAH..........THAT'S IT.......GET
ON TV SOME MORE........WHAT IS...........

.........NOT.......SO......VERY......FUNNY.....YOU SICK MOTHER FUCKERS..........WILL..........NEVER.........HANG
YOUR HEADS IN SHAME........FOR YOUR ABSOLUTE MORAL
FUCKUPS.......THAT......NARCISSISM......IS.......SICKENING........OUT.........,

b6 -1, 2, 7
b7C -1, 2,

From:
Sent: Tuesday, March 05, 2013 12:39 PM
To:
Subject: FW: .................HEY............THERE............ .......CLOWN...........OF............NEWTOWN...........HUMOR.............BOY.............GET USED TO IT...........YA............GOTS................

-----Original Message-----
From:
Sent: Sunday, February 10, 2013 2:47 AM
To:
Subject:

b6 -2,
b7C -2,

.................HEY.............THERE............. .........CLOWN...........OF............NEWTOWN...........HUMOR.............BOY............GET USED TO IT...........YA............GOTS................

..................A...................VERY..................VERY..................LONG...............ROAD...............THE.............MORAL.................SLOTH...............TOAD...................AHEAD...........AND...............THOUGHT..........YOU........MIGHT............................

.............WANNA.................KNOW...............THIS.................NARCISSISM...................ADVANCED MODERN PSYCHIATRY...............TELLS.............US...................CLEARLY............IS.............RIPPING...........AMERICA...........APART.................

....................SURE...............YOU...............DID...............THE IVY LEAGUES...............TOO.....................I'D.....................BETTER.................STOP.......................THERE.............COULD...........GET...........YOU..........IN.............TROUBLE...............

................TOLD YA.............THIS REMAINS...........PRIVATE..........PERIOD...........SO YOUR FEARS...........ARE..........JUST...........PLAIN..............SILLY.............BUT................WE KNOW............THE WEAK..........THE SPINELESS.........................

............DOWN SOUTH............I RECALL THIS............BEAUTIFUL SOUTHERN BELLE...........WHAT A WOMAN.............BUT........WHEN SHE GOT.......HOT.......I WAS JUST..........A YELLOW BELLIED YANKEEE..........AND........NOOOOOO.......

..............YA'AALLLL............DID.............NOT.............WIN.............THAT................FRIGGIN................WAR.............ASK............LINCOLN.........FUNNY GIRL.........................YEAH.....................WELL...........YELLOW.......YANKEEES................

...........THAT YOU ARE........YELLOW COWARDS.......IS.........A............REASONABLE ASSUMPTION.............WHINY..........BITCH............NOISES...........ALL............WE............HEAR.............REAL ITY...........THE TRUITH...........WHAT...........

.......YEAH...,....DON'T.......FEEL TOO BAD.........I GOT......A FAMILY..........OF FUCKUPS.........JUST.........LIKE YOU..........MARRIED INTO OUR CLAN OF CELTS...........I WAS AWAY.........BAD MOVE........WHO KNEW...........THAT.........REALITY.........

........NO....REAL MEN......BITCHES....IS......BAD.....VERY....SILLY OUTTA CONTROL WOMEN....AND....BOYS BITCHES WHO......LOOK LIKE MEN.....BUT.....AINT....OOOPS.....WELCOME TO HELL.......FIRST STOP...BLOOD..NEWTOWN...OUT.....

From:
Sent: Tuesday, March 05, 2013 12:39 PM
To:
Subject: FW: ....NOW.......... ...........GET.........ON............DAT................UDDER..... ..............BOY.............YOU.............MUSTA................

b6 -1, b7C -1

-----Original Message-----
From
Sent: Sunday, February 10, 2013 2:51 AM
To:
Subject:
..................NOW......... ..........GET.........ON............DAT................UDDER...................BOY.............Y OU.............MUSTA................

b6 -2, b7C -2,

.......................CAUGHT..................A,............LOTTA.....................SHIT................AS A KID..................WITH...............THAT.............NAME...........SOMEBODY..........NOT..........LIKE...........YA............AT..........CONCEPTION.....OR........WHAT......

................OBVIOUSLY..............WE............POKING................FUN................AT...........YA........... .....GET OFF...........MAMA'S UDDER.........YOU........MAY..........SPEAK........NOW..... .....MOTHER..........SAYS......OUT...

From:
Sent: Tuesday, March 05, 2013 12:39 PM
To:
Subject: FW: ....HELLO............DEAR ....WHAT'S................THE................MUDDER ??????????????????.....................LAUGHTER.............UPROARIOUSLY................OF COURSE..............WHY ??????????

b6 -1, 7
b7C -1, 7

-----Original Message-----
From:
Sent: Friday, February 15, 2013 5:46 PM
To
Subject: ....HELLO............DEAR ....WHAT'S................THE................MUDDER ??????????????????.....................LAUGHTER.............UPROARIOUSLY................OF COURSE..............WHY ?????????????.

b6 -2, 7
b7C -2, 7

.......EASY..........THOSE CONNECTICUT CLOWNS................ARE.............JUST...............SO.................DAMNED...................FUNNY.................YOU...... ....KNOW.......................WHY ???????????.............THEY........GET THIS.......CHUCKLE........EHH...

............YEH...........GET THIS ONE...........THESE SILLY CLOWNS.............THINK..........THEY'RE...........SLICK..............POOR THINGS................SELF DELUSIONS....................ARE.............MOST.................AMUSING..........NARCISSISM..........WELL.....

..............JUST............PLAIN..............DISGUSTING................AS USUAL................SO THERE......... ....MY ROLE...........AS...........MERE.............MESSENGER BOY..............NEAR..........DONE..........THEN.........YOU'ALL..............

b6 -7
b7C -7

....................WILL................PROCEED..............TO YER FUN.....................ENJOY.............ANY OF YA............EVER............GROW SOME BALLS............SPEAK.............WHENEVER............THE NEWTOWN BEE'S BUZZING........IS AS DEAD.....YEP.....

............AS YOUR 20 INNOCENTS.............YOU FAILED TO PROTECT............MAY GOD............HAVE MERCY...........UPON.......ALL YOUR WRETCHED SOULS.......WE SHALL..........CONTINUE TO PRAY..........FOR YOU POOR BASTARDS......BUT.......

..............WE KNOW YOUR KIND..............QUITE.............WELL.............YOUR ONCE JUSTLY PROUD..........CONNECTICUT...........NEW ENGLAND ANCESTORS...........MUST BE HORRIFIED..........BY HOW FAR.......YOU HAVE FALLEN.......REALLY.....

...........HOW MUCH LOWER...........CAN YOU GO ??????........ONCE PROUD YANKEES...........NOW............YELLOW COWARDS...........WHOSE..........SINFUL PRIDE..........ALLOWED THIS POOR BOY ADAM LANZA......ONE OF YOUR OWN...........

...........THE BOY'S FINAL TRAGIC DESTINY TO CARRY ALONE..........THE SINS OF ....DID ONE OF YOU.........LIFT A HAND TO HELP THE BOY......... ..YES........

b6 -7
b7C -7

...........YOU ACCEPT...........ANY EVILS ON EARTH............DIVORCE........IS...........GOOD...........REALLY............HMMMMMMMM............THE BOYS RAGE..........WHERE YOU THINK.........THAT..........CAME..........FROM.........DUMBASSES ????????...

............LOVED THAT BULLSHIT LINE "ADAM HAS ASPARAGUS SYNDROMES....RIGHT.."...........LET'S USE.........SCIENCE FOR SLEAZE.........TO EXCUSE..........OUR GUILT...........NICE TRY.......DON'T FLY..........CLOWNS.....FUNNY.........OUT.............

From: [redacted] b6 -1, 7
Sent: Tuesday, March 05, 2013 12:39 PM b7C -1, 7
To: [redacted]
Subject: FW: ....GET THE POINT............[redacted]...........................

-----Original Message-----
From [redacted]
Sent: Friday, February 15, 2013 5:49 PM b6 2, 7
To [redacted] b7C 2, 7
Subject: ....GET THE POINT............[redacted]........................

........COULD WE PRICK.............THY............DEAD..............CONSCIENCE................WITH............THE MORAL CODE............YE HATH SO ABANDONED ???????...............NAH...........DEADMEAT.........IS..........DEADMEAT.................OUT.....................

b6 -1,
b7C -1,

From:
Sent: Tuesday, March 05, 2013 12:39 PM
To:
Subject: FW: Reader Comment email

-----Original Message-----
From
Sent: Tuesday, March 05, 2013 7:48 AM
To
Subject: Reader Comment

b6 -7
b7C -7

.... so after reading reader comment, I decided to share with her teh following reader comment I got yesterday.

From
Sent: Saturday, March 02, 2013 11:44 PM
To
Subject: .... DEAR ....NO COURTESY...........FORTHCOMING..........WE SEE..........HMMMMMMMMMMMM...............................

b6 -2, 7
b7C -2,

................PASS THE WORD................CLEVER ....TO ALL YOU.............WEAK.............YELLOW..............COWARDS..............SAD..........DAD..........DEAD...........SONS.. ....PUKES.........WHO SCREWED THE POOCH.........YEAH......

...........FIRST...........AND..........PLEASE.............FEEL FREE...........TO SHARE...................YOUR............WEAK...........LIES.............SLEAZE............ABSOLUTE MORAL FAILURES...........AS.........NEWTOWN PARENTS........YOU.......PECKERLESS......

..............PATHETIC..............PURE EVILS............THINGS...........YOU...........GOT..........YOUR............CHILDREN............KILLED..........BY............T HE BOY.............ADAM LANZA..........REALITY...........LADDIE...........FOREVER......AND YOU THINGS......

....WHATEVER YOU ARE..........SURELY..........YOU AINT MEN............NO FATHER..........LETS HIS SON BE MURDERED............THEN...........WHINES ABOUT GUNS.........LIKE A BITCH.........THAT.......IS........DOGSHIT........LAD......TELL HIM THAT.........

.......BECAUSE..........UNLIKE PUSSIES LIKE YOU...........I WILL SAY TO YOUR FACE..........EXACTLY..........WORD FOR WORD...........ANYTHING I EVER WRITE........REAL MEN.........SPEAK THEIR MIND........BITCHES.......DON'T......THEY HIDE....YEAH..

............OR...........THEY GO ON CNN........MSNBC..........WITH THEIR TONGUES.........SO FAR UP NOABAMMAASSES BUTT........YER EYES ARE BROWN.......DISGUSTING...........KEEP WHINING ON TV........PLEASE..........LATER.........OUT...............

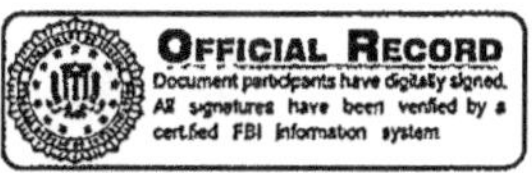

UNCLASSIFIED

FEDERAL BUREAU OF INVESTIGATION

Electronic Communication

Title: (U) EMERGENCY VICTIM FUNDS AND BUDGET MATTERS, CRIMINAL CYBER RESPONSE SERVICES BRANCH; **Date:** 03/12/2013

To: [redacted]

From: DIRECTOR S OFFICE
Contact: [redacted] b6 -1 b7C -1

Approved By: Kathryn McKay Turman

Drafted By: [redacted]

Case ID #: [redacted] b7E -4
356A-NH-2619946 (U) ADAM PETER LANZA
Sandy Hook Elementary School
12 Dickinson St, Sandy Hook, CT-Victim
Firearms Act.
OO:NH

Synopsis: (U) To document expenditures of the Terrorism Emergency Victim Assistance Funds following the shooting at Sandy Hook Elementary School in Newtown, CT.

Details:

On December 14, 2012 a gunman killed twenty-seven people, including his mother, Nancy Lanza, and 26 students and staff at Sandy Hook Elementary School. The Office for Victim Assistance activated the Victim Assistance Rapid Deployment Team to respond to the shooting following a request for assistance from the Newtown Police Department and the Connecticut State Police. The Office for Victims of Crime authorized the use of Terrorism Emergency Victim Assistance Funds to assist the victims of this mass fatality event.

TEVAF assistance was requested by VARDT member [redacted] and approved b6 -1 b7C -1

Title: (U) EMERGENCY VICTIM FUNDS AND BUDGET MATTERS, CRIMINAL CYBER RESPONSE SERVICES BRANCH;
Re: [redacted] 03/12/2013 b7E -

by Program Director Turman [redacted] b6 -7 b7C -

[redacted] b6 -7 b7C -

◆◆

FD-1036 (Rev. 10-16-2009)

UNCLASSIFIED

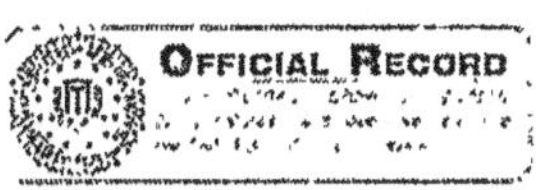

FEDERAL BUREAU OF INVESTIGATION

Import Form

Form Type: LABRPT **Date:** 03/25/2013

Title: (U) [redacted]

Approved By: [redacted] b6 -1 b7C -1 b7E -6

Drafted By: [redacted]

Case ID #: 356A-NH-2619946 (U) ADAM PETER LANZA
Sandy Hook Elementary School
12 Dickinson St, Sandy Hook, CT-Victim
Firearms Act.
OO:NH

Synopsis: (U) [redacted]

Enclosure(s): Enclosed are the following items: b6 -2 b7C -2 b7E -6

[redacted]

♦♦

UNCLASSIFIED

Sandy Hook-2794

4-NH-2619946

SERIAL 212

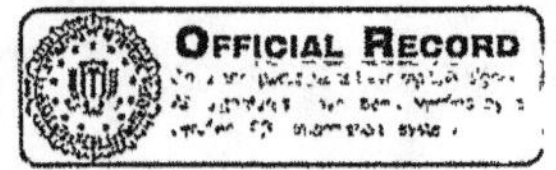

FEDERAL BUREAU OF INVESTIGATION

Date of entry 03/25/2013

FEDERAL GRAND JURY MATERIAL - DISSEMINATE PURSUANT TO RULE 6(E)
Do not disseminate except as authorized by federal rule of criminal procedure 6(e).

The attached grand jury subpoena was served via facsimile # [redacted] b3 -

Investigation on 03/13/2013 at Bridgeport, Connecticut, United States (Fax)

File # 356A-NH-2619946 Date drafted 03/25/2013

by [redacted] b6 -1 b7C -

AO 110 (Rev 06/09) Subpoena to Testify Before a Grand Jury

GRAND JURY MATTER NO.

UNITED STATES DISTRICT COURT

for the

District of Connecticut

SUBPOENA TO TESTIFY BEFORE A GRAND JURY

To:

b3 -1

YOU ARE COMMANDED to appear in this United States district court at the time, date, and place shown below to testify before the court's grand jury. When you arrive, you must remain at the court until the judge or a court officer allows you to leave.

Place: UNITED STATES DISTRICT COURT & FEDERAL BUILDING GRAND JURY MEETING ROOM 915 LAFAYETTE BOULEVARD 3RD FLOOR BRIDGEPORT, CT 06604	Date and Time:

You must also bring with you the following documents, electronically stored information, or objects *(blank if not applicable)*:

b3 -1
b6 -1
b7C -1

IN LIEU OF APPEARANCE, PLEASE PROVIDE DOCUMENTS ON OR BEFORE THE RETURN DATE OF THE GRAND JURY SUBPOENA TO SPECIAL AGENT FEDERAL BUREAU OF INVESTIGATION, 1000 LAFAYETTE BOULEVARD, SUITE 306, BRIDGEPORT, CT 06604, WHO CAN BE REACHED AT

Date: MARCH 13, 2013

CLERK OF COURT

Signature of Clerk or Deputy Clerk

The name, address, e-mail, and telephone number of the United States attorney, or assistant United States attorney, who requests this subpoena, are:

-ASSISTANT UNITED STATES ATTORNEY
UNITED STATES ATTORNEY's OFFICE
1000 LAFAYETTE BOULEVARD 10TH FLOOR
BRIDGEPORT, CT 06604

b6 -4
b7C -4

*************** -COMM. JOURNAL- ****************** DATE MAR-13-2013 ***** TIME 15:02 ********

MODE = MEMORY TRANSMISSION START=MAR-13 15:01 END=MAR-13 15:02

FILE NO.=710

STN NO.	COMM.	STATION NAME/EMAIL ADDRESS/TELEPHONE NO.	PAGES	DURATION
001	OK		003	00:00:36

b3 -1
b6 -1
b7C -

***** UF-7200 ********************* - - ***** - *********

FD-448
Revised
10 27 2004

FEDERAL BUREAU OF INVESTIGATION

FACSIMILE COVER SHEET

PRECEDENCE

(•) Immediate ( ) Priority ( ) Routine

CLASSIFICATION

( ) Top Secret ( ) Secret ( ) Confidential ( ) Sensitive (•) Unclassified

TO

Name of Office	Facsimile Number	Date
		03/13/2013
Attn	Room	Telephone Number

FROM

Name of Office		Number of Pages (including cover)
FBI, Bridgeport, Connecticut		3
Originator's Name	Originator's Telephone Number	Originator's Facsimile Number
Approved		

b3 -1
b6 -1
b7C -1

DETAILS

Subject

GRAND JURY SUBP

Special Handling Instructions

E-Mai

Brief Description of Communication Faxed

THANK YOU!

WARNING

Information attached to the cover sheet is U S Government Property If you are not the intended recipient of this information disclosure, reproduction distribution or use of this information is prohibited (18 USC, § 641) Please notify the originator or local FBI Office immediately to arrange for proper disposition

FD-71 (Rev. 5-8-10)

UNCLASSIFIED//~~FOUO~~

FEDERAL BUREAU OF INVESTIGATION

Complaint Form

Title: (U) Additional harassing communications received by [redacted] **Date:** 01/23/2013

Approved By: [redacted]

Drafted By: [redacted]

b6 -1, 7
b7C -1, 7

Case ID #: 356A-NH-2619946 (U) ADAM PETER LANZA
Sandy Hook Elementary School
12 Dickinson St, Sandy Hook, CT-Victim
Firearms Act.
OO:NH

Complaint Synopsis: (U) [redacted] [redacted] received a harassing post onto his Facebook account.

b6 -7
b7C -7

[redacted]

b7E -1

Received On: 01/21/2013

Receipt Method: Telephone

Received By: [redacted]

b6 -1
b7C -1

Incident Type: Criminal Activity

Complaint Details:

[redacted] Newtown, CT 06482, [redacted] [redacted] contacted writer regarding a harassing communication on his Facebook account. [redacted] [redacted] On Monday, January 21, 2013 while reviewing "friend" requests on his account he came across a request from a person identified as Adam Lanza. [redacted] stated that when he clicked on the request and was able to view "Adam Lanza's" home page. On the page

b6 -7
b7C -7

UNCLASSIFIED//~~FOUO~~

4-NH-2619946

SERIAL 234

Title: (U) Additional harassing communications received by [redacted] [redacted]

Re: 356A-NH-2619946, 01/23/2013

b6
b7

were statements to the effect of that the Sandy Hook School shooting was a hoax and it was all committed by the President. [redacted] provided copies of the screenshots to writer.

b6 -
b7C

[redacted]

b6 -
b7C
b7E

This complaint is being drafted as an addition to a complaint drafted by writer on Friday January 18, 2013. In that incident, someone made threats on a website [redacted] The theme of the harassment and threats continues to be that the Sandy Hook shooting was a hoax perpetrated by the US government.

b6
b7

Pre-Assessment Findings:

This matter is being addressed by SA [redacted]

b6 -1
b7C -

Recommended Action: File to Existing Case

♦♦

FD-71 (Rev. 5-8-10)

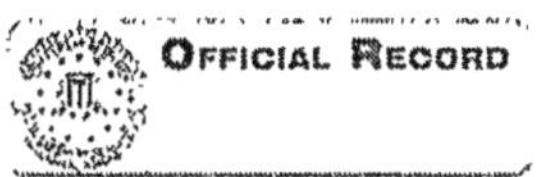

UNCLASSIFIED

FEDERAL BUREAU OF INVESTIGATION

Complaint Form

Title: (U) [redacted] **Date:** 01/22/2013

Approved By: [redacted] b6 -1, 6 b7C -1, 6

Drafted By: [redacted]

Case ID #: 356A-NH-2619946 (U) ADAM PETER LANZA
Sandy Hook Elementary School
12 Dickinson St, Sandy Hook, CT-Victim
Firearms Act.
OO:NH

Complaint Synopsis: (U) Possible information regarding the Sandy Hook School shooting. (NH)

[redacted] b7E -1

Received On: 01/17/2013

Receipt Method: Telephone

Received By: [redacted] b6 -1 b7C -1

Incident Type: Criminal Activity

Complaint Details:

[redacted] date of birth [redacted] address [redacted] [redacted] telephone number [redacted] called in to report that she communicated with ADAM LANZA on the suicideforum.com site. Suicideforum.com is a website to support people that are thinking about committing suicide. LANZA told [redacted] that he was going to kill himself and that it would be on the news. [redacted] also thinks a boy named [redacted] (PH) was friends with LANZA on suicideforum.com. [redacted] has posted a video on YOUTUBE under the name [redacted] thinks [redacted] might have helped LANZA prepare for the shooting. b6 -5, 6 b7C -5, 6

UNCLASSIFIED

4-NH-2619946

SERIAL 215

Title: (U) [redacted]

Re: 356A-NH-2619946, 01/22/2013

b6 -6
b7C -6

[redacted]

b6 -5
b7C -5

Pre-Assessment Findings:

On 04/02/2013, Special Agent [redacted] Federal Bureau of Investigation, New Haven Office, contacted [redacted] by telephone. [redacted] confirmed that she had been interviewed by the Connecticut State Police and that all of her information had been relayed to them. She has no further information to offer at this time.

b6 -1,
b7C -1

Recommended Action: File to Existing Case

Entities:

[redacted] (Complainant, Person, U.S. Person? Unknown)

Location

Address: [redacted]

City: [redacted]

State: [redacted]

Zip Code: [redacted]

Country: United States

Communication Account

Type: Telephone

Account: [redacted]

Name/Biographical Information

Born: [redacted]

Minor [redacted]

Has Diplomatic Status? [redacted]

b6 -5, 6
b7C -5, 6

[redacted] (Main, Person, U.S. Person? Unknown)

♦♦

FD-71 (Rev. 5-8-10)

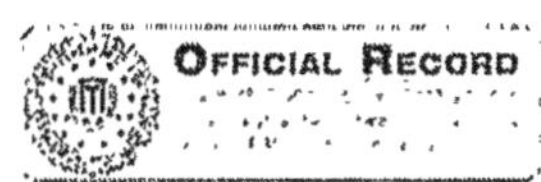

UNCLASSIFIED

FEDERAL BUREAU OF INVESTIGATION

Complaint Form

Title: (U) Complaint call from [redacted] **Date:** 01/02/2013

b6 -1, 5, 6
b7C -1, 5, 6

Approved By: [redacted]

Drafted By: [redacted]

Case ID #: 356A-NH-2619946 (U) ADAM PETER LANZA
Sandy Hook Elementary School
12 Dickinson St, Sandy Hook, CT-Victim
Firearms Act.
OO:NH

Complaint Synopsis: (U) Complaint stated [redacted]

b6 -5, 6
b7C -5, 6

[redacted] b7E -4

Received On: 12/31/2012

Receipt Method: Telephone

b6 -1
b7C -1

Received By: [redacted]

Incident Type: Other Non-Terrorism

Complaint Details:

Complaint, [redacted]
called to advise [redacted]

b6 -5, 6
b7C -5, 6

UNCLASSIFIED

4-NH-2619946
SERIAL 216

Title: (U) Complaint call from [redacted]
[redacted]
Re: 356A-NH-2619946, 01/02/2013

b6 -5,
b7C -5,

[redacted]

b6 -5,
b7C -5

New Haven file number: 4-NH-2619946

Pre-Assessment Findings:

On 04/02/2013, Special Agent [redacted] Federal Bureau of Investigation, New Haven Office, contacted [redacted] born [redacted]

[redacted]

b6 -1,
b7C -1,

[redacted] presented himself as an unstable person of low credibility.

SA [redacted] informed Connecticut State Police Sgt. [redacted] of the contact with [redacted] Sgt. [redacted] requested that the matter be referred to the CSP for follow up investigation. SA [redacted] provided Sgt. [redacted] with all relevant details.

b6 -1, 3
b7C -1,

Title: (U) Complaint call from [redacted]
[redacted]

Re: 356A-NH-2619946, 01/02/2013

b6 -5, 6
b7C -5, 6

Recommended Action: File to Existing Case

Entities:

[redacted] (Complainant, Person, U.S. Person? Unknown)

Location

Address: [redacted]

City: [redacted]

State: [redacted]

Country: United States

Communication Account

Type: Telephone

Account: [redacted]

b6 -6
b7C -6

♦♦

FD-71 (Rev. 5-8-10)

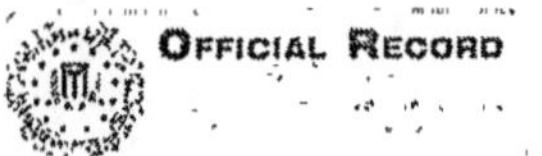

UNCLASSIFIED

FEDERAL BUREAU OF INVESTIGATION

Complaint Form

Title: (U) Suspicious comment day before Newtown, CT shooting **Date:** 12/31/2012

Approved By: [redacted]

Drafted By: [redacted] b6 -1 b7C -1

Case ID #: 356A-NH-2619946 (U) ADAM PETER LANZA
Sandy Hook Elementary School
12 Dickinson St, Sandy Hook, CT-Victim
Firearms Act.
OO:NH

Complaint Synopsis: (U) User posted suspicious comment on smart phone application 16 hours before Sandy Hook Elementary School shooting

[redacted] b7E -1

Received On: 12/18/2012

Receipt Method: Telephone

Received By: [redacted] b6 -1 b7C -1

Incident Type: Criminal Activity

Complaint Details:

Complainant, [redacted] b6 - b7C
Show of Hands is a polling application for mobile devices, i.e. iPhones, iPads, Andriods, etc. The users can create anonymous accounts that do not require names/emails address but do require a zip code to be provided. Show of Hands has been available for a couple of years and allows users to answer random polling questions.

On 12/11/2012, the Clackamas Town Center mall shooting occurred. That night [redacted] posted a question asking "Has there ever been a mass b6 b7C

UNCLASSIFIED

4-NH-2619946

SERIAL 217

shooting in your hometown?" A couple of days later he was contacted by another user about a concerning post. On 12/13/2012, a user going by the moniker of [redacted] posted a comment to the polling questions which said "There is about to be." Upon being made aware of the [redacted] post, [redacted] looked up the comment and it said the comment came from Connecticut. [redacted] looked up [redacted] account and found a CT zip code that resolved to a neighboring town of Newtown approximately 10 miles away. b6 -5, 6 b7C -5, 6

On 12/13/2012, [redacted] posted a new polling question asking about the Mayan calendar prediction for 12/21/2012. [redacted] posted again on 12/13/2012 leaving a comment to the effect of "Satan is coming that day." b6 -5, 6 b7C -5, 6

The GPS information collected by Show of Hands shows the user resolves to an address in Fayetteville, Georgia. [redacted] has been in contact with the web company that supports Show of Hands to determine if [redacted] account has been recently modified or changed. He has the capability to search the archive and identify all posts by [redacted] and when the profile was created. b6 -5, 6 b7C -5, 6

[redacted] contacted the Newtown Police Department on 12/14/2012 and was routed to a detective. [redacted] doesn't know if the information was shared or passed and wanted to make sure it was provided in case it had any value. b6 -6 b7C -6

Pre-Assessment Findings:

This matter has been fully explored by FBI New Haven Squad 10.

Recommended Action: File to Existing Case

Title: (U) Suspicious comment day before Newtown, CT shooting
Re: 356A-NH-2619946, 12/31/2012

Entities:
[redacted] (Complainant, Person, U.S. Person? Yes)

Location
Address [redacted]
City: [redacted]
State: [redacted]
Zip Code: [redacted]
Country: United States
Relationship: Residence

Communication Account
Type: Telephone
Account: [redacted]

Name/Biographical Information
Name: [redacted]
Born: [redacted]
Minor? [redacted]
Has Diplomatic Status? [redacted]

b6 -6
b7C -6

♦♦

FD-1057 (Rev 5-8-10)

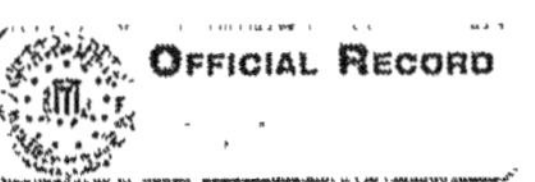

UNCLASSIFIED

FEDERAL BUREAU OF INVESTIGATION

Electronic Communication

Title: (U) Legacy 1A **Date:** 03/08/2013

From: NEW HAVEN
NH-SS
Contact: [redacted]

Approved By: [redacted] b6 -1 b7C -1

Drafted By: [redacted]

Case ID #: 356A-NH-2619946 (U) ADAM PETER LANZA
Sandy Hook Elementary School
12 Dickinson St, Sandy Hook, CT-Victim
Firearms Act.
OO:NH

Synopsis: (U) FD192 for 1B1, 1B4-1B5, 1B7, 1B8 Returned.

[redacted] b7E -1

Enclosure(s): Enclosed are the following items:
1. (U) NH-2619946

Details:

Evidence Details for the following items:

[redacted] b6 -2 b7C -2

UNCLASSIFIED

4-NH-2619946
SERIAL 218

FD-999 (Rev. 5-8-10)

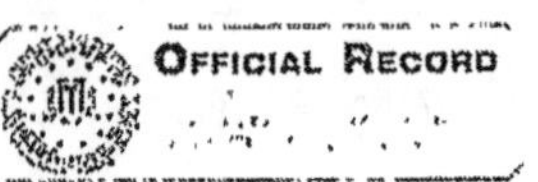

UNCLASSIFIED

FEDERAL BUREAU OF INVESTIGATION

Dissemination of Information to Other Agencies

Title: (U) Meeting with Hoboken Police Chief **Date:** 04/09/2013

Approved By: SSA [redacted]

Drafted By: [redacted] b6 -1 b7C -1

Case ID #: 356A-NH-2619946 (U) ADAM PETER LANZA
Sandy Hook Elementary School
12 Dickinson St, Sandy Hook, CT-Victim
Firearms Act.
OO:NH

[redacted] b6 -7 b7C -

[redacted] b7E -1

Responsible Organization: NEWARK

Agency Contacted: Hoboken Police Department on 01/14/2013 via Note, Meeting

POC: Chief of Department Anthony P. Falco, Sr. b6 -3
Work: [redacted] b7C -3

Disseminated On: 01/29/2013 (Once)

Dissemination Details: (U) Letter confirming ongoing FBI investigation, and thanking the Hoboken Police Department for their assistance in the Newtown shooting investigation on 12/14/12. The letter was generated subsequent to a meeting with the Chief of Police to discuss not only the CT shooting investigation, but a separate NK investigation [redacted] b6 -7 b7C -7

Method: Written

Follow-up Required (SSTF): No

Disseminated Serials:

UNCLASSIFIED

Title: (U) Meeting with Hoboken Police Chief
Re: 356A-NH-2619946, 04/09/2013

356A-NH-2619946	Serial 207	(U) Letter to Hoboken Police Department

♦♦

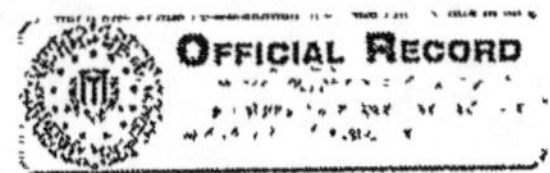

UNCLASSIFIED

FEDERAL BUREAU OF INVESTIGATION

Electronic Communication

Title: (U) Legacy 1A **Date:** 04/09/2013

From: NEW HAVEN
NH-SS
Contact: [redacted]

Approved By: [redacted] b6 -1 b7C -1

Drafted By: [redacted]

Case ID #: 356A-NH-2619946 (U) ADAM PETER LANZA
Sandy Hook Elementary School
12 Dickinson St, Sandy Hook, CT-Victim
Firearms Act.
OO:NH

Synopsis: (U) [redacted] b6 -2 b7C -2

[redacted] b7E -1

Enclosure(s): Enclosed are the following items:
1. (U) 4-NH-2619946

Details:

[redacted] b6 -2 b7C -

◆◆

UNCLASSIFIED

FD-302 (Rev. 5-8-10)

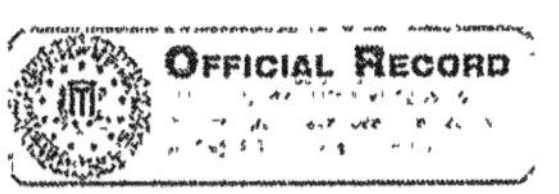

FEDERAL BUREAU OF INVESTIGATION

Date of entry 07/15/2013

On 07/11/2015, a meeting was held at the Connecticut State Laboratory in Meriden, CT. The purpose of the meeting was to turn evidence over to the custody of the Connecticut State Police. Each piece of evidence was in FBI custody and hand carried to Detective [redacted] Connecticut State Police - Troop G, 149 Prospect St., Bridgeport, CT 06604, telephone [redacted] [redacted] SA [redacted] obtained custody of the items on 07/09/2011 at 4:00 pm from SA [redacted] An 'Evidence Chain of Custody Sheet' (FD-1004) was signed and maintained by SA [redacted] and SA [redacted] b6 -1, 3 b7C -1, 3

On 07/11/2013 at approximately 3:44 pm, SA [redacted] handed over the following pieces of evidence to the custody of Detective [redacted] b6 -1, 3 b7C -1, 3

1B38 - Sony Playstation 2

1B39 - Dell Laptop Imperiron 6000

1B40 - 2010 Honda paperwork, 6 CDRs, handwritten notes on local gun shops, Garmin GPS

1B41 - AT&T telephone with digital answering system

1B42 - xbox 360

1B43 - Xbox

1B44 - Video parts and memory cards

1B45 - USB device

1B46 - Western Digital hard drive

1B47 - LG Verizon cell phone

1B48 - Hard drive platter

1B49 - Black Apple iPhone

Investigation on 07/11/2013 at Meriden, Connecticut, United States (In Person)

File # 4-NH-2619946 Date drafted 07/15/2013

by [redacted] b6 -1 b7C -1

4-NH-2619946

SERIAL 242

1B50 - Transcend external hard drive

1B51 - Brother fax machine

1B52 - Black computer tower

1B92 - IBM Thikpad, serial number AA-F2T8399/11 with power cord

1B93 - Toshiba Model MK402GAS, 40GB HDD, serial number 74C50902S

1B94 - Twelve misc. CD-R and DVD-R Discs containing unknown content

1B97 - Plastic case containing 29 CD-R Discs

1B98 - IBM CD Drive; Samsung floppy drive, computer video card, four memory DIMMS; Netgear Gigagbit PC card; Intel processor repackaged from ten misc. computer components

1B99 - Digital copies of [redacted] seven journals authored by Adam Lanza, loose papers authored by Adam Lanza b6 -5 b7C -

Each chain of custody sheet (FD-1004) was signed by SA [redacted] and Det. [redacted]; and retained by SA [redacted] These completed chain of custody sheets will be given to the evidence control custodian in the New Haven Division. b6 -1, b7C -1,

FD-1036 (Rev. 10-16-2009)

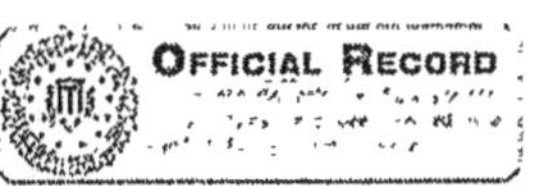

FEDERAL BUREAU OF INVESTIGATION

Import Form

Form Type: OTHER **Date:** 09/06/2013

Title: (U) Letter to Stephen J. Sedensky, III, State's Attorney

Approved By: [redacted]

Drafted By: [redacted]

b6 -1
b7C -1

Case ID #: 356A-NH-2619946

(U) ADAM PETER LANZA
Sandy Hook Elementary School
12 Dickinson St, Sandy Hook, CT-Victim
Firearms Act.
OO:NH

Synopsis: (U) Letter to Stephen J. Sedensky, III, State's Attorney, regarding the Sandy Hook Elementary School Shooting Investigation

♦♦

4-NH-2619946
SERIAL 243

FD-1057 (Rev. 5-8-10)

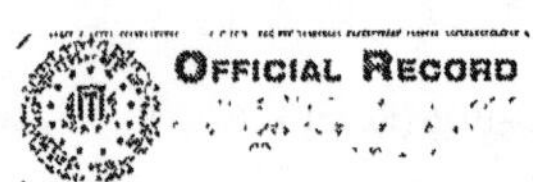

UNCLASSIFIED//~~FOUO~~

FEDERAL BUREAU OF INVESTIGATION

Electronic Communication

Title: (U//~~FOUO~~) Additional information provided to BAU 2 for review. **Date:** 09/24/2013

CC: [redacted]

From: NEW HAVEN
NH-5
Contact: [redacted] b6 -1 b7C -1

Approved By: [redacted]

Drafted By: [redacted]

Case ID #: 4-NH-2619946 (U) ADAM PETER LANZA
Sandy Hook Elementary School
12 Dickinson St, Sandy Hook, CT-Victim
Firearms Act.
OO:NH

Synopsis: (U//~~FOUO~~) Supplemental information recovered from Adam Lanza's computer provided to BAU 2 for review.

[redacted] b7E -1

Package Copy: (U//~~FOUO~~) The following items will be forwarded to BAU under separate cover:
1-Seagate hard drive working copy
4-CDs working copies for DENH-92-93, DENHJB3 (media from 36 Yogananda Street), [redacted] DE1.
[redacted] b6 -2, b7C -2, b7D -1
1 spread sheet reflecting items of evidence reviewed by FBI New Haven CART.
CART examination reports.

Details:

UNCLASSIFIED//~~FOUO~~

Sandy Hook-3
4-NH-261994
SERIAL 2

Title: (U//~~FOUO~~) Additional information provided to BAU 2 for review.
Re: 4-NH-2619946, 09/24/2013

For the information of BAU 2, New Haven will be providing supplemental information concerning the Sandy Hook Elementary School shooting to BAU 2 under separate cover. New Haven has been maintaining contact with [redacted] concerning a pending interview with [redacted] New Haven will coordinate an interview with Yale and BAU 2 as needed.

b6 -5
b7C -5

Attempts to locate a police report or call for service concerning a dispute type incident at the Big Y or vicinity, Queen Street, Newtown, CT during a time frame of June 2012 through December 2012, met with negative results.

♦♦

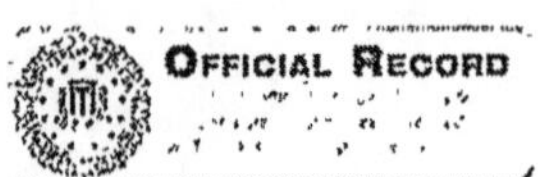

UNCLASSIFIED

FEDERAL BUREAU OF INVESTIGATION

Import Form

Form Type: DEL-REX **Date:** 09/26/2013

Title: (U) Digital Evidence Laboratory Report of Examination for [redacted] b6 b7C

[redacted]

Approved By: SSA [redacted]

b6 -1
b7C -1

Drafted By: [redacted]

Case ID #: 4-NH-2619946 (U) ADAM PETER LANZA
Sandy Hook Elementary School
12 Dickinson St, Sandy Hook, CT-Victim
Firearms Act.
OO:NH

Synopsis: (U) [redacted] b6 -2, b7C -2, b7E -6,

Enclosure(s): Enclosed are the following items:

1. (U) Case notes
2. (U) Case notes 1
3. (U) Administrative notes

♦♦

UNCLASSIFIED

FD-941 (2-26-01)

CONSENT TO SEARCH COMPUTER(S)

I, [redacted], have been asked by Special Agents of the Federal Bureau of Investigation (FBI) to permit a complete search by the FBI or its designees of any and all computers, any electronic and/or optical data storage and/or retrieval system or medium, and any related computer peripherals, described below:

[redacted]

CPU Make, Model & Serial Number (if available)

b6 -2
b7C -2

Storage or Retrieval Media, Computer Peripherals

[redacted]

and located at FBI New Haven Office, which I own, possess, control, and/or have access to, for any evidence of a crime or other violation of the law. The required passwords, logins, and/or specific directions for computer entry are as follows: ________.

I have been advised of my right to refuse to consent to this search, and I give permission for this search, freely and voluntarily, and not as the result of threats or promises of any kind.

I authorize those Agents to take any evidence discovered during this search, together with the medium in/on which it is stored, and any associated data, hardware, software and [redacted]

5/5/13
Date

5/5/13
Date

[redacted]

b6 -1, 2
b7C -1, 2

Printed Full Name of Witness

Stamford CT
Location

This is to certify that on ____ at ________

Special Agents of the Federal Bureau of Investigation, U.S. Department of Justice, conducted a complete search of any and all computers, any electronic and/or optical data storage and/or retrieval system, and any related computer peripherals.

I certify that nothing was removed from my custody by those Agents.

(Signed) ________________________

Witnessed:

____
Special Agent
Federal Bureau of Investigation
U.S. Department of Justice

____
Special Agent
Federal Bureau of Investigation
U.S. Department of Justice

FD-941 (2-26 01)

CONSENT TO SEARCH COMPUTER(S)

I, [redacted] have been asked by Special Agents of the Federal Bureau of Investigation (FBI) to permit a complete search by the FBI or its designees of any and all computers, any electronic and or optical data storage and or retrieval system or medium and any related computer peripherals, described below:

[redacted]

CPU Make, Model & Serial Number (if available)

Storage or Retrieval Media, Computer Peripherals

[redacted]

and located at FBI New Haven Office, which I own, possess, control, and or have access to, for any evidence of a crime or other violation of the law. The required passwords, logins, and or specific directions for computer entry are as follows: [redacted]

I have been advised of my right to refuse to consent to this search, and I give permission for this search, freely and voluntarily, and not as the result of threats or promises of any kind.

I authorize those Agents to take any evidence discovered during this search, together with the medium in/on which it is stored, and any associated data, hardware, software and [redacted]

5/3/13
Date

5/3/13
Date

[redacted]

Printed Full Name of Witness

Stamford CT
Location

b6 -1, 2
b7C -1, 2

FD 941 (2 26 01)

CONSENT TO SEARCH COMPUTER(S)

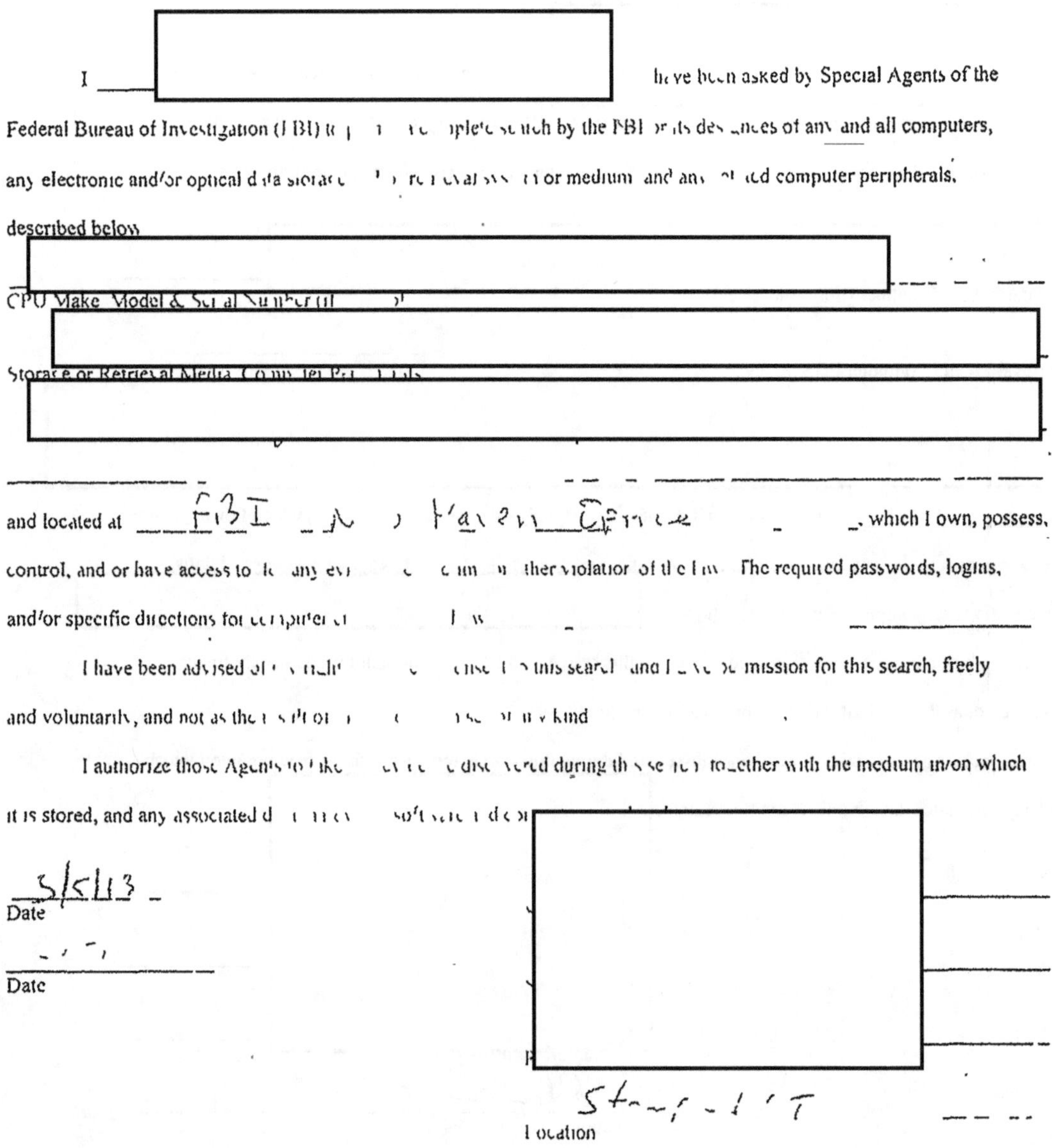

I ______ have been asked by Special Agents of the Federal Bureau of Investigation (FBI) to [illegible] complete search by the FBI or its designees of any and all computers, any electronic and/or optical data storage [illegible] retrieval system or medium and any related computer peripherals, described below

CPU Make Model & Serial Number [illegible]

Storage or Retrieval Media, Computer Peripherals

and located at FBI [illegible] Haven [illegible], which I own, possess, control, and or have access to [illegible] any [illegible] other violation of the law. The required passwords, logins, and/or specific directions for computer [illegible]

I have been advised of [illegible] right [illegible] this search and I [illegible] permission for this search, freely and voluntarily, and not as the result of [illegible] of any kind

I authorize those Agents to take [illegible] discovered during this search together with the medium in/on which it is stored, and any associated d[illegible] software [illegible]

5/5/13
Date

Date

Location

b6 -1,
b7C -1

Sandy Hook-

FD-1057 (Rev. 5-8-10)

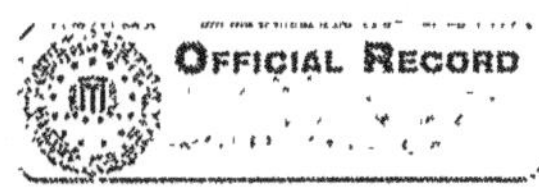

UNCLASSIFIED

FEDERAL BUREAU OF INVESTIGATION

Electronic Communication

Title: (U) EMERGENCY VICTIM FUNDS AND BUDGET MATTERS, CRIMINAL CYBER RESPONSE SERVICES BRANCH; **Date:** 10/29/2013

From: DIRECTOR S OFFICE
Contact: [redacted]

Approved By: Kathryn McKay Turman b6 -1 b7C -1

Drafted By: [redacted]

Case ID #: [redacted] b7E -4

4-NH-2619946 (U) ADAM PETER LANZA
Sandy Hook Elementary School
12 Dickinson St, Sandy Hook, CT-Victim
Firearms Act.
OO:NH

Synopsis: (U) To document expenditures of the Terrorism Emergency Victim Assistance Funds following the shooting at Sandy Hook Elementary School in Newtown, CT.

Details:

On December 14, 2012 a gunman killed twenty-seven people, including his mother, Nancy Lanza, and 26 students and staff at Sandy Hook Elementary School. The Office for Victim Assistance activated the Victim Assistance Rapid Deployment Team to respond to the shooting following a request for assistance from the Newtown Police Department and the Connecticut State Police. The Office for Victims of Crime authorized the use of Terrorism Emergency Victim Assistance Funds to assist the victims of this mass fatality event.

OVA Program Director Kathryn Turman approved the use of TEVAF to [redacted] b6 -7 b7C -7

UNCLASSIFIED

4-NH-2619946
SERIAL 251

Title: (U) EMERGENCY VICTIM FUNDS AND BUDGET MATTERS, CRIMINAL CYBER RESPONSE SERVICES BRANCH;
Re: [redacted] 10/29/2013 b7E -4

[redacted] b6 b7C

♦♦

FD-1057 (Rev 5-8-10)

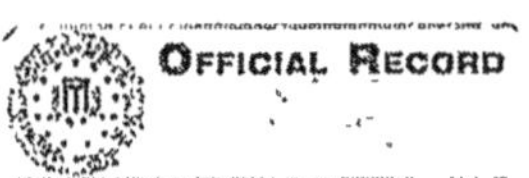

UNCLASSIFIED

FEDERAL BUREAU OF INVESTIGATION

Electronic Communication

Title: (U) Harassing Calls to Sandy Hook School by Subject in Michigan

Date: 03/24/2014

From: DETROIT
DE-MC1
Contact: [redacted]

Approved By: SSRA [redacted]

Drafted By: [redacted]

b6 -1
b7C -1

Case ID #: 4-NH-2619946 (U) ADAM PETER LANZA
Sandy Hook Elementary School
12 Dickinson St, Sandy Hook, CT-Victim
Firearms Act.
OO:NH

Synopsis: (U) Harassing Calls to Sandy Hook School by Subject in Michigan

[redacted] b7E -1

Enclosure(s): Enclosed are the following items:
1. (U) MPD Report
2. (U) [redacted] PD Report

Details:

On 03/19/2014, Det/Sgt [redacted] of the [redacted] Police Department, [redacted] Michigan, telephone number [redacted] contacted Writer and advised that Detective [redacted] of the Monroe, Connecticut Police Department (MPD) asked for assistance with an investigation involving a subject that made several harassing telephone calls to the Sandy Hook Elementary School (SHES). The subject made the calls to SHES on 02/11/2014 utilizing cellular telephone number [redacted]

[redacted]

b6 -2, 3
b7C -2, 3

UNCLASSIFIED

Sandy Hook-3268

4-NH-2619946
SERIAL 254

Title: (U) Harassing Calls to Sandy Hook School by Subject in Michigan
Re: 4-NH-2619946, 03/24/2014

b6 -
b7C -

The MPD identified the subject utilizing [redacted] as [redacted] [redacted] DOB [redacted] of [redacted] Michigan.

b6 -
b7C

on 03/19/2014, the [redacted] PD located and interviewed [redacted] in the presence of his mother, [redacted] DOB [redacted] of [redacted] [redacted] Michigan, cellular telephone number [redacted] During his interview, [redacted] admitted to making the calls. [redacted] described the calls as just being phone pranks and realized that he was wrong in making those calls. [redacted]

b6 -2,
b7C -2,

After the interview was terminated, [redacted] was taken into custody by the [redacted] PD. The [redacted] County prosecutor's office charged [redacted] with Terrorist Threat and Using a Computer to Commit a Terrorist Threat.

b6 -
b7C -

The [redacted] PD seized [redacted] cellular telephone and executed a search warrant at the [redacted] address. They seized an HP laptop, a Kindle, a spiral notebook, and two other cellular telephones.

b6 -
b7C -

On 03/19/2014, General Crimes Unit Chief, AUSA [redacted] U.S. Attorney's Office, Eastern District of Michigan, declined prosecution in this matter [redacted]

b6 -2,
b7C -2,

Title: (U) Harassing Calls to Sandy Hook School by Subject in Michigan
Re: 4-NH-2619946, 03/24/2014

♦♦

Monroe Police Department

7 Fan Hill Rd., Monroe CT 06468
(203) 261-3622

CASE/INCIDENT REPORT

SUPPLEMENTAI

NO	DAY	INCIDENT DATE	TIME	DATE OF RPT	TIME OF RPT	TYPE OF INCIDENT	INCIDENT CD	INVESTIGATING OFFICER
002673	3	02/11/2014	12:40	02/11/2014	13:06	TELEPHONE CALL COMPLAINT	073	Detective

ION	DIVISION NO	REFERENCE DIVISION	REFERENCE DIVISION NO	CASE X-REFERENCE	UNIT ID	TYPIST	DATE TYPE
l Resource Officer		School Resource Officer					02/11/2014

ET NO	STREET NAME AND TYPE	APARTMENT NO/LOCATION	INTERSECTING STREET NAME AND TYPE	STATUS
375	FAN HILL Rd MONROE			Active

JS CODE C=COMPLAINANT V=VICTIM A=ARRESTEE J=JUVENILE H=OTHER M=MISSING W=WITNESS O=OFFENDER D=DRIVER S=SUSPECT P=POLICE OFFIC

JS	NAME	SEX	RACE	D.O.B.		TELEPHONE	ADDRESS	OP STAT
		F	W		Busi	(203) 426 - 7657	375 Fan Hill Rd Monroe CT	CT 0320
	Sandy Hook Elementary School				Busi	(203) 426 - 7657	375 Fan Hill Rd Monroe CT	

February 11, 2014, at approximately 12:40 hours, I was assigned to the Sandy Hook Elementary School, 375 Fan Hill Road Monroe, was contacted by Sandy Hook Elementary School [redacted] regarding a harassing telephone caller who was curre I answered the phone and asked how I could help the caller? The caller, a male voice approximate age in the twenties, stated he was is son Adam Lanza. I asked the caller what his name was? He replied "Mr. Lanza looking to pick up his son Adam Lanza". I then ident elf as Officer [redacted] of the Monroe Police Department and asked why he was calling. The caller stated he was calling for Newtown s Monroe. I told the caller to stop calling and harassing the staff of the school. The caller stated he was calling from an unknown number ay to be tracked. I told the caller to stop calling or he would see how he could be tracked or not. The caller hung up.

caller immediately called back and stated in a fake weeping voice "I just got the news, my son is dead. How awful". The caller hung gain. Moments later the caller called again and stated [redacted] I then stated "If it will get you to stop calling, why don't you just say all twenty six names of the victims of Sandy Hook trag r replied in a rapid voice with more names I couldn't make out and then laughed and ended with "Ha, Ha". He then hung up.

calls came in from an Unknown number on the caller identification feature. The caller id listed the first of 4 calls received on 02/11/14 :40 hours. I advised [redacted] to direct all future calls from this caller to the school's voicemail. This case is referred to the Detective [redacted] or follow up investigation to ascertain the phone number of the caller.

NDERSIGNED, AN INVESTIGATOR HAVING BEEN DULY SWORN DEPOSES AND SAYS THAT: I AM THE WRITER OF THE ATTACHED POLICE REPORT PERTAINING TO THIS INCIDENT NUMBER THE INFORMATION CONTAINED THEREIN WAS SECURED AS A RESULT OF (1)MY PERSONAL OBSERVATION AND KNOWLEDGE: OR (2)INFORMATION RELAYED TO ME BY OTHER MEMBERS POLICE DEPARTMENT OR OF ANOTHER POLICE DEPARTMENT.OR (3)INFORMATION SECURED BY MYSELF OR ANOTHER MEMBER OF A POLICE DEPARTMENT FROM THE PERSON OR PERSON D OR IDENTIFIED THEREIN, AS INDICATED IN THE ATTACHED REPORT. THAT THE REPORT IS AN ACCURATE STATEMENT OF THE INFORMATION SO RECEIVED BY ME.

	INVESTIGATOR I.D.#:	REPORT DATE:	SUPERVISOR SIGNATURE	SUPERVISOR I.D #
		02/11/14		

Arrest report

03/19/14

D/Sgt[redacted]

b6 -3
b7C -3

Throughout the day on 03/19/14, I received further information regarding phone calls/ threats made to schools in the United States that were scenes of shootings. I learned that on 02/11/14 at 1029 hours (MST), 1229 hours (EST), Arapahoe High School located at 2201 E. Dry Creek Rd in Centennial, CO received a phone call threat to burn down the school. A major police response ensued due to the previous shooting at the location. The response included multiple police officers and the Joint Terroism Task Force for the area. The call had been recorded and it was tracked by Monroe CT PD, see previous report. I spoke with Sgt.[redacted] from the Arapahoe County Sheriff's Office who indicated that he was certain that school officials would want charges sought against[redacted] for their incident. I was able to obtain their report and he will forward specific victim information to me on 03/20/14.

b6 -2, 3
b7C -2, 3

After learning above, I advised Detective[redacted] to draft a search warrant for tools used in these crimes at the suspect's home address.[redacted] appeared at[redacted] PD voluntarily at our scheduled interview time (early arrival- 1530 hours EST).[redacted] although 17, wanted his mother present during the interview. I advised[redacted] that he was free to leave at anytime and not under arrest. He can decide to answer or not answer my questions at anytime[redacted] agreed to speak with me freely and voluntarily, witnessed by his mother[redacted]

b6 -2, 3, 5
b7C -2, 3, 5

I started out speaking to[redacted] about the suicidal threat call[redacted] in which[redacted] PD officers responded to his home after he called an alarm company threatening suicide.[redacted] stated that he and a friend, only identified as[redacted] (18 yrs) decided they would make prank calls consistent with recorded calls they like viewing by a YouTube personality known as Ownage Pranks. He said at that time and on today's date that he was not suicidal, just making a phone prank. Note- No other party was with[redacted] when officers responded to the home. I further asked if he made any other similar prank phone calls in the last month's time. He stated that he has not. I then began going one by one through the recorded call logs forwarded to me by Monroe CT PD Detective[redacted] One by one[redacted] admitted responsibly to the call, only agreeing to the information once I presented proof of the call. After going through all of the calls made on 02/11/14, I asked why would he do such things. Again he cited the phone prank YouTube Ownage Pranks and he said at the time he thought it was funny. He realizes now that he was wrong. Throughout my interview[redacted] was calm, stoic, and spoke very thoughtfully and intelligently. He claimed to be quite intelligent and he appeared to be so.[redacted]

[redacted]

[redacted] I asked[redacted] to explain the call to Arapahoe High School where he threatened to ,"burn down the fucking school." Again[redacted] said that it was only a prank and he meant no actual harm. I asked how[redacted] did his research of those shootings and he said he used his laptop and did simple Google searches[redacted] agreed to write a written statement and it will be added to the case file.

b6 -2, 3, 5
b7C -2, 3, 5

As[redacted] finished his statement, I spoke with[redacted] in the hall. I advised[redacted] that after learning the new information about a direct threat to a school which caused a significant police response and[redacted] confession to same, I felt it necessary to arrest him for Using a Telecommunication Device to Commit an Act of Terrorism.[redacted] was upset, but understood. I also advised her that we would be conducting a search warrant at her home to retrieve[redacted] computer and phone.[redacted] had[redacted] phone on her person and I took it as evidence.[redacted] was then handcuffed, advised he was being arrested for using a phone to commit an act of terrorism and booked in[redacted] PD detention.[redacted] had no personal items on him at time of arrest.

b6 -2, 3, 5
b7C -2, 3, 5

Detective[redacted] completed a search warrant for the[redacted] Address and we executed same at 1700 hours EST. Taken from the home was an HP laptop, a Kindle, a spiral note book, two older cell phones, and the previously reported LG cell phone taken from[redacted] See Detective[redacted] supplement for details and Forensic examination of evidence.

b6 -2, 3
b7C -2, 3

I will be presenting a warrant to the[redacted] County Prosecutor's office on 03/20/14 reference this matter.

Case continuing.

Original

03/19/14

D/Sgt. [redacted]

b6 -3
b7C -3

On 03/18/14, I received a call from Detective [redacted] of the Monroe CT Police Department. He stated he was investigating a series of disturbing and harassing phone calls. He stated that Sandy Hook Elementary school had been moved to his jurisdiction after the school shootings that occurred there. Detective [redacted] agency continues to investigate any and all related cases coming into or stemming from the school. He stated that on 02/11/14, [redacted] received several blocked phone calls from a younger male who repeatedly references the shootings, claims to be a family member of the shooter, and then names all of the deceased children from the school. These calls happened multiple times. Detective [redacted] stated that he obtained an Ex Parte order and served same to [redacted] the phone carrier for the incoming calls. He received a credit card number that was used to purchase minutes on the pay-as-you-go phone. He again served a subpoena on the credit card bank and located [redacted] at the [redacted] address in [redacted] Detective [redacted] then contacted me and asked for assistance in this matter. He also stated that in the course of his investigation, he determined that similar phone calls were made to Columbine, Virginia Tech, and Arapaho schools; all scenes of school shootings. I will follow up with those jurisdictions as well. In checking our in-house computer system, I located a 17 year old at the same address. [redacted] had a recent contact with SHPD where he called a [redacted] County alarm company and threatened suicide [redacted] PD [redacted] PD officers met with [redacted] and [redacted] at that time. [redacted] stated that he was playing a phone prank and was not suicidal. The officers determined that no further action was necessary at the time.

b6 -2, 3
b7C -2,

At 1530 hours on 03/18/14, I attempted contact at the [redacted] address, but received no answer. I left messages on the phones as well as at the location. At the scene, I spoke with a person in the neighborhood who wished to remain anonymous. They stated that [redacted] was a decent young man until fairly recently. [redacted]

b6
b7

[redacted] I finally had phone contact with both [redacted] and [redacted] in the early morning hours of 03/19/14 and [redacted] agreed to bring [redacted] in for an interview.

b6 -
b7C -

Case continuing.

FEDERAL BUREAU OF INVESTIGATION

Date of entry 03/25/2014

On 03/14/2014, Special Agent [redacted] Federal Bureau of Investigaton (FBI), received a complaint by e-mail from [redacted] of the Newtown Bee newspaper, located in Newtown, Connecticut. [redacted] complaint was handled as follows: b6 -2, 7 b7C -2, 7

On 03/14/2014, [redacted] forwarded to SA [redacted] 10 emails that he had received from [redacted] with whom [redacted] was previously unacquainted. On 03/18/2014, [redacted] forwarded 11 more of the [redacted] emails to SA [redacted] On 03/19/2014, [redacted] forwarded nine more. The emails included links to YouTube and Facebook where there were references to the Sandy Hook Elementary School shooting as well as religious material. For the most part, the emails and linked material appears to be the product of unstable or delusional thinking. Much of it makes cryptic reference to the Bible and the Book of Revelations. Some of the comments could possibly be read as vaguely threatening. b6 -1, 2, 7 b7C -1, 2, 7

In addition to the emails, [redacted] reported that the person sending the emails left an egg shaped paper Easter bag at the newspaper office. The bag contained: b6 -7 b7C -7

1. A blue and white stuffed bunny with two business cards for [redacted] [redacted] with hand writing "Cell [redacted]

2. 30 additional of the same [redacted] business cards;

3. A tourist pamphlet advertising the Submarine Force Museum and USS Nautilus submarine in Groton, Connecticut; b6 -2 b7C -2

4. A silver Sandisk Cruzer Facet 8GB jump drive; and

5. A greeting card referencing the "families" and the jump drive and signed by [redacted]"

[redacted] SA [redacted] was able to determine that [redacted] was associated with [redacted] [redacted] born [redacted] current address was listed as [redacted] [redacted] New York. b6 -1, 2 b7C -1, 2 b7E -2

Investigation on 03/21/2014 at Newtown, Connecticut, United States (In Person)

File # 4-NH-2619946 Date drafted 03/25/2014

by [redacted] b6 -1 b7C -1

4-NH-2619946

SERIAL 255

b6
b7C

On 03/20/2014, SA [redacted] contacted Lt. [redacted] Investigations Division Commander, [redacted] Police Department [redacted] PD), telephone number [redacted] Lt. [redacted] acknowledged that he was very familiar with [redacted] Lt. [redacted] indicated that [redacted] was known for repeatedly contacting/harassing various members of the media. As a result of [redacted] actions, including leaving a package at the home of a member of the local media, [redacted] PD officers have interviewed [redacted] was warned at one point to stop contacting one member of the media. [redacted] complied with the police request. Lt. [redacted] described [redacted] no history of violence or of causing any injury or damage as far as the [redacted] PD is aware. Lt. [redacted] offered to send officers to warn [redacted] to cease contacting the Newtown Bee.

b6 -1, 2,
b7C -1, 2,

After speaking with Lt. [redacted] SA [redacted] advised [redacted] that [redacted] had been identified and appears to be residing in New York. SA [redacted] also advised [redacted] that the local police in [redacted] community were aware of him and that he has contacted other members of the media and has been approached by police in the past. SA [redacted] provided [redacted] with a current photograph of [redacted] and informed [redacted] that he was about 6'2" tall and 270 pounds. [redacted] asked that [redacted] not be contacted by police. On 03/21/2014, SA [redacted] took possession of the Easter bag and its contents, which will be submitted to New Haven Evidence Control Unit.

b6 -1, 2, 3,
b7C -1, 2, 3

From:
Sent: Friday, March 14, 2014 9:42 AM
To:
Subject: Emails from
Attachments: Fw: NEWTOWN - SOUND AND HARMONY WITH LIGHT*; Re: ; Re: HEADLINE SUGGESTION FOR A SUGGESTED STORY ; Fw: my guess; HEADLINE SUGGESTION FOR A SUGGESTED STORY ; NEW AP CONTACT; Re: newtown bee; Fw: newtown bee; Fw: newtown bee

b6 -1, 2, 7
b7C -1, 2, 7

To Special Agen

Perhaps this should be directed to the Newtown Police rather than you, but The Newtown Bee has received a number of cryptic and insistent emails in recent days from someone identified as Nomally, I discount this kind of stuff, but this guy seems to be unusually persistent and, notably, in close proximity. He placed a bag with an easter bunny, oddly unrelated business cards and a brochure, a greeting card with more cryptic observations inside, and a thumb drive. I am leery of checking the contents of the thumb drive for obvious IT reasons, so I don't know what's on it. (The contents of the bag he dropped off appear in a photo attached to a couple of the email messages here.

b6 -1, 2
b7C -1, 2

If you think this is a local police matter, let me know, and I will forward this material to them

Thank you for your help,

b6 -7
b7C -7

(I will be out of the office for the weekend after 11 am today.)

<<Fw: NEWTOWN - SOUND AND HARMONY WITH LIGHT*>> <<Re: >> <<Untitled>> <<Re: HEADLINE SUGGESTION FOR A SUGGESTED STORY >> <<Fw: my guess>> <<HEADLINE SUGGESTION FOR A SUGGESTED STORY >> <<NEW AP CONTACT>> <<Re: newtown bee>> <<Fw: newtown bee>> <<Fw: newtown bee>>

b6 -3
b7C -3

b6 -1
b7C -

From:
Sent: Friday, March 14, 2014 4:05 AM
To: zz
Subject: Fw: NEWTOWN - SOUND AND HARMONY WITH LIGHT*
Attachments: CORRECTION.pdf

beautiful> described below>

b6
b7C

On Friday, March 14, 2014 3:47 AM, wrote:

Let me preface by explaining the plot of the music video, so that you can really enjoy it (I had to watch it a few times). There is a supernatural magnetic event at a school, and the boy is coming to afterward. A frightened adult sees the boy walk by, blames him without an ounce of thought, and sends the USA law after him (the story of my life). Truth overpowers in the end. How beautiful is that for SOUND IN HARMONY WITH LIGHT...another perfect one to start with>

On Thursday, March 13, 2014 4:33 PM, wrote:
Welcome Newtown Bee as another AP contact, and attached is another 1969.

I'm sure the 1969 stamps represent the most important emails. It just makes common sense. b6 -2 b7C -

All emails past, present, and future are always open to public knowledge and discussion.

On Friday, March 14, 2014 3:47 AM, wrote:
Let me preface by explaining the plot of the music video, so that you can really enjoy it (I had to watch it a few times). There is a supernatural magnetic event at a school, and the boy is coming to afterward. A frightened adult sees the boy walk by, blames him without an ounce of thought, and sends the USA law after him (the story of my life). Truth overpowers in the end. How beautiful is that for SOUND IN HARMONY WITH b6 b7C
LIGHT...another perfect one to start with>
(second post down...the Newtown visit)

On Thursday, March 13, 2014 4:33 PM, wrote:
Welcome Newtown Bee as another AP contact, and attached is another 1969.

I'm sure the 1969 stamps represent the most important emails. It just makes common sense.

All emails past, present, and future are always open to public knowledge and discussion.

b6 -2
b7C -2

b6 -1, 2
b7C -1, 2

From:
Sent: Thursday, March 13, 2014 10:36 PM
To:

you could take a photo with a white horse and let them use it. Or a front page.

From:
Sent: Thursday, March 13, 2014 7:24 PM
To:
Cc:
Subject: Fw: my guess

b6 -1, 2, 7
b7C -1, 2, 7

It is possible some NEVER SEEN BEFORE things could start showing up in that magnetic box. Oh well.

On Thursday, March 13, 2014 7:15 PM, wrote:
good ratings for Monday I bet.

On Thursday, March 13, 2014 7:14 PM, wrote:
I am looking for any consulting work for an income, just to let you know.

b6 -2
b7C -2

On , wrote:
AMAZING.

always in awe here

On wrote:
So if you look at the NOFLOW SW to NE, then go back to the SE and recognize the flow. ^One could tie that flow to Sandy's turn left on October 29 to tie that all to the same scientific star chart.

On Thursday, March 13, 2014 6:34 PM, wrote:
For years, I've been thinking that's URSA Major and Minor upside down.

b6 -2
b7C -2

On Wednesday, March 12, 2014 10:33 PM, wrote:
please shower before using pool

On wrote:
]24:00[clocking out

On Wednesday, March 12, 2014 10:23 PM, wrote:
I don't think they"ll ever watch again to see what you're doing.

On , wrote:
you and cbs are the alternating mirrors of the plane. I don't know if that's subject to change.

On wrote:
That freezeplane is going to create a "next day mood" for everyone I guess.

b6 -2
b7C -2

On Wednesday, March 12, 2014 10:05 PM, wrote:
WE'RE OFF TO SEE THE WIZARD>

On Wednesday, March 12, 2014 10:00 PM wrote:
A LONG WAY TO GO>

b6 -2
b7C -

On Wednesday, March 12, 2014 9:52 PM, wrote:
you're done planning our day in advance. TICKTOCK.

On wrote:
whatever is the truth

On , wrote:
Better start writing and planning for Thursday and Friday.

b6 -2
b7C -2

On wrote:
and everything else surrounding those three 1969 emails.

On Wednesday, March 12, 2014 9:47 PM, wrote:
my guess is you'll be solo tomorrow....still with few horrified viewers...

But it would force all the others to start the next day, and on that day you'd be starting with the Newtown Photo> connecting to the St. Augustine photo and recent trips.

From:
Sent: Thursday, March 13, 2014 10:56 PM
To:
Subject: Re:

b6 -1, 2, 7
b7C -1, 2, 7

whatever works

On Thursday, March 13, 2014 10:36 PM, wrote:

you could take a photo with a white horse and let them use it. Or a front page.

b6 -2
b7C -2

From:
Sent: Thursday, March 13, 2014 8:51 PM
To:
Cc:
Subject: Re: HEADLINE SUGGESTION FOR A SUGGESTED STORY

b6 -1,
b7C -1,

"It's all Light except where You're standing"

On Thursday, March 13, 2014 6:15 PM wrote:
"It's all Light except where You're standing"

b6 -
b7C

On Thursday, March 13, 2014 4:33 PM, wrote:
Welcome Newtown Bee as another AP contact, and attached is another 1969.

I'm sure the 1969 stamps represent the most important emails. It just makes common sense.

All emails past, present, and future are always open to public knowledge and discussion.

From:
Sent: Thursday, March 13, 2014 6:15 PM
To:
Cc:
Subject: HEADLINE SUGGESTION FOR A SUGGESTED STORY

b6 -1, 2, 7
b7C -1, 2, 7

"It's all Light except where You're standing"

On Thursday, March 13, 2014 4:33 PM, wrote:
Welcome Newtown Bee as another AP contact, and attached is another 1969.

b6 -2
b7C -2

I'm sure the 1969 stamps represent the most important emails. It just makes common sense.

All emails past, present, and future are always open to public knowledge and discussion.

From:
Sent: Wednesday, March 12, 2014 11:38 PM
To:
Subject: Fw: newtown bee
Attachments: DSCN9642.JPG

b6 -1, 2, 7
b7C -1, 2,

Or you could just email some comments to that address to save them time...no on camera comments. yuck.

Love,

On wrote:
StarTrail Location: Fairfield, CT

I hope all is well. This would be the only media story on the photo and the jump drive. The photo I supplied them is attached. Make sure to email me a list of questions if you have any.

b6 -
b7C

On Wednesday, March 12, 2014 11:25 PM wrote:
I am fine with you seeking optional comment from the bee or any connected. You can show them this email and the photo. They should also know I am encouraging the story if they'd be willing to comment regarding the jump drive. If they don't want a story, please comply to their request, however, remind them I'm just trying to get some free promo on that jump.

From:
Sent: Wednesday, March 12, 2014 11:31 PM
To:
Cc:
Subject: Fw: newtown bee
Attachments: DSCN9642.JPG

b6 -1, 2, 7
b7C -1, 2, 7

StarTrail Location: Fairfield, CT

I hope all is well. This would be the only media story on the photo and the jump drive. The photo I supplied them is attached. Make sure to email me a list of questions if you have any.

On Wednesday, March 12, 2014 11:25 PM wrote:

b6 -2
b7C -2

I am fine with you seeking optional comment from the bee or any connected. You can show them this email and the photo. They should also know I am encouraging the story if they'd be willing to comment regarding the jump drive. If they don't want a story, please comply to their request, however, remind them I'm just trying to get some free promo on that jump.

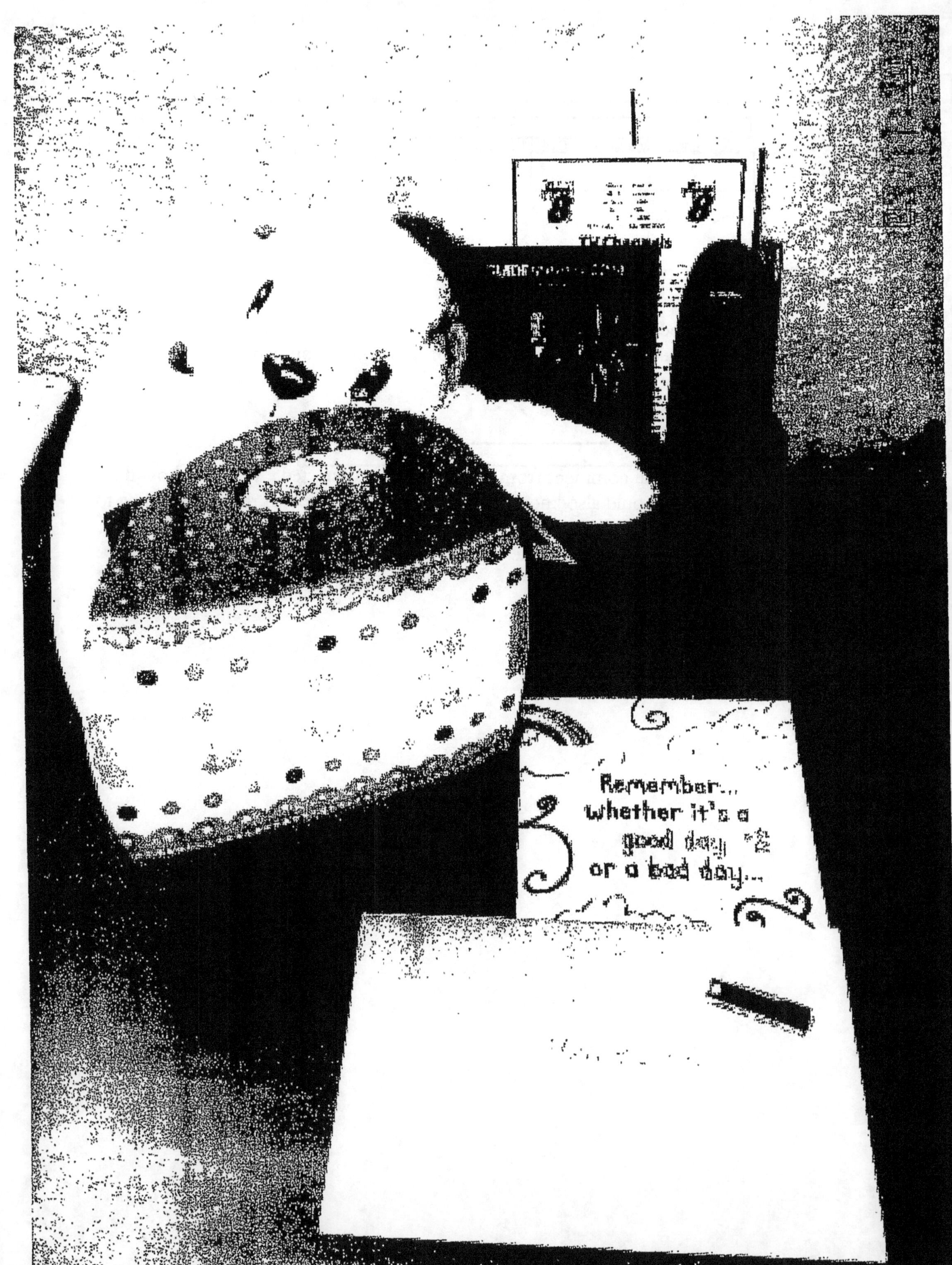
TV Channels
Remember...
whether it's a
good day
or a bad day...

From:	[redacted]
Sent:	Tuesday, March 18, 2014 11:00 AM
To:	[redacted]
Subject:	More emails from [redacted] to The Newtown Bee
Attachments:	hidden light; Re: White Horse Freeze Plane Attached; White Horse Freeze Plane Attached; west point; Fw: FOUR WILD HORSES FOR THE RUN - ONE RUNNING 00:00; Re: FOUR WILD HORSES FOR THE RUN - ONE RUNNING 00:00; Re: FOUR WILD HORSES FOR THE RUN - ONE RUNNING 00:00; FOUR WILD HORSES FOR THE RUN - ONE RUNNING 00:00; FOUR WILD HORSES FOR THE RUN - ONE RUNNING 00:00; Re: "magnetic trail related to the clock" ; Fw: "magnetic trail related to the clock"

b6 -1, 2, 7
b7C -1, 2, 7

<<hidden light>> <<Re: White Horse Freeze Plane Attached>> <<White Horse Freeze Plane Attached>> <<west point>> <<Fw: FOUR WILD HORSES FOR THE RUN - ONE RUNNING 00:00>> <<Re: FOUR WILD HORSES FOR THE RUN - ONE RUNNING 00:00>> <<Re: FOUR WILD HORSES FOR THE RUN - ONE RUNNING 00:00>> <<FOUR WILD HORSES FOR THE RUN - ONE RUNNING 00:00>> <<FOUR WILD HORSES FOR THE RUN - ONE RUNNING 00:00>> <<Re: "magnetic trail related to the clock" >> <<Fw: "magnetic trail related to the clock" >>

Special Agent [redacted]

Here are the latest emails from over the weekend.

b6 -1, 7
b7C -1, 7

[redacted]
The Newtown Bee

b6 -1
b7C -

From:
Sent: Wednesday, March 19, 2014 5:33 AM
To: b6 -2, b7C -2

Subject: Re: showing on the other three maps (attached)

let it be known that I will never be on TV, where I could catch that head size disorder instantly. NEVER. NOT gonna happen.

I will answer questions by email.

On Wednesday, March 19, 2014 5:12 AM wrote:
I bet the SQUARE is related to the large SQUARE of 0's and 1's on the last page of the original 1998 Document delivered the Daytona Beach News-Journal. I just know it. Someone look into that please. b6 - b7C

On Wednesday, March 19, 2014 1:59 AM wrote:
facebook url seen in top bar of each screen shot

Each map is showing the box in the same place and it zooms while you zoom.

What is truly amazing is it's zooming to Florida, and Florida is a recent topic here>

These may be added to the appropriate folder.

Tick tock. Let the sorrows flow.

On Wednesday, March 19, 2014 12:52 AM wrote:
I added Mecca as the current city on the page, and after doing so, the box appeared on the map as shown in the three attachments. The box seems to be superimposing another type of map with different fonts,, etc. b6 b7C

Another message from Allah?

b6 -1
b7C -1

From:
Sent: Wednesday, March 19, 2014 5:12 AM
To: b6 -2, 7 b7C -2, 7
Subject: Re: showing on the other three maps (attached)

I bet the SQUARE is related to the large SQUARE of 0's and 1's on the last page of the original 1998 Document delivered the Daytona Beach News-Journal. I just know it. Someone look into that please.

On Wednesday, March 19, 2014 1:59 AM wrote:
facebook url seen in top bar of each screen shot

Each map is showing the box in the same place and it zooms while you zoom. b6 -2 b7C -2

What is truly amazing is it's zooming to Florida, and Florida is a recent topic here>

These may be added to the appropriate folder.

Tick tock. Let the sorrows flow.

On Wednesday, March 19, 2014 12:52 AM, wrote:
I added Mecca as the current city on th page, and after doing so, the box appeared on the map as shown in the three attachments. The box seems to be superimposing another type of map with different fonts,, etc. b6 -2. b7C -2

Another message from Allah?

b6 -1
b7C -1

From:
Sent: Wednesday, March 19, 2014 5:05 AM
To: b6 -2, b7C -2

Subject: Re: all screen shots of zoom path attached - nine

let me make sure on the accident, but I think so.

On wrote:
notice one has port st. lucie - that's the location of the big bridge in 1999 and related to a car accident on the same trip.

On Wednesday, March 19, 2014 4:52 AM, wrote:
the farthest out and the farthest in do not have the square...it goes away. All four pages have the same square and path. b6 - b7C

It's zooming right in on the 1998 Document story place.

On Wednesday, March 19, 2014 1:59 AM wrote:
facebook url seen in top bar of each screen shot

Each map is showing the box in the same place and it zooms while you zoom.

What is truly amazing is it's zooming to Florida, and Florida is a recent topic here>

These may be added to the appropriate folder.

Tick tock. Let the sorrows flow. b6 b7C

On Wednesday, March 19, 2014 12:52 AM, wrote:
I added Mecca as the current city on the page, and after doing so, the box appeared on the map as shown in the three attachments. The box seems to be superimposing another type of map with different fonts,, etc.

Another message from Allah?

b6 -1
b7C -1

From:
Sent: Wednesday, March 19, 2014 5:04 AM
To:
Subject: Re: all screen shots of zoom path attached - nine

b6 -2, 7
b7C -2, 7

notice one has port st. lucie - that's the location of the big bridge in 1999 and related to a car accident on the same trip.

On Wednesday, March 19, 2014 4:52 AM wrote:
the farthest out and the farthest in do not have the square...it goes away. All four pages have the same square and path.

It's zooming right in on the 1998 Document story place.

b6 -2
b7C -2

On Wednesday, March 19, 2014 1:59 AM, wrote:
facebook url seen in top bar of each screen shot

Each map is showing the box in the same place and it zooms while you zoom.

What is truly amazing is it's zooming to Florida, and Florida is a recent topic here>

These may be added to the appropriate folder.

Tick tock. Let the sorrows flow.

b6 -2
b7C -2

On Wednesday, March 19, 2014 12:52 AM wrote:
I added Mecca as the current city on the page, and after doing so, the box appeared on the map as shown in the three attachments. The box seems to be superimposing another type of map with different fonts,, etc.

Another message from Allah?

b6 -1
b7C -1

From:
Sent: Wednesday, March 19, 2014 4:59 AM
To: b6 -2 b7C -
Subject: Re: all screen shots of zoom path attached - nine

breaking

On Wednesday, March 19, 2014 4:52 AM wrote:
the farthest out and the farthest in do not have the square...it goes away. All four pages have the same square and path.

b6 b7C

It's zooming right in on the 1998 Document story place.

On Wednesday, March 19, 2014 1:59 AM wrote:
facebook url seen in top bar of each screen shot

Each map is showing the box in the same place and it zooms while you zoom.

What is truly amazing is it's zooming to Florida, and Florida is a recent topic here>

These may be added to the appropriate folder.

Tick tock. Let the sorrows flow.

b6 - b7C

On Wednesday, March 19, 2014 12:52 AM, wrote:
I added Mecca as the current city on the page, and after doing so, the box appeared on the map as shown in the three attachments. The box seems to be superimposing another type of map with different fonts,, etc.

Another message from Allah?

b6 -1
b7C -1

From:
Sent: Wednesday, March 19, 2014 4:53 AM
To: ;
Cc: ;
Subject: all screen shots of zoom path attached - nine
Attachments: ScreenHunter_764 19-Mar-14 04.48.jpg; ScreenHunter_765 19-Mar-14 04.48.jpg; ScreenHunter_766 19-Mar-14 04.48.jpg; ScreenHunter_767 19-Mar-14 04.48.jpg; ScreenHunter_768 19-Mar-14 04.48.jpg; ScreenHunter_769 19-Mar-14 04.48.jpg; ScreenHunter_770 19-Mar-14 04.48.jpg; ScreenHunter_771 19-Mar-14 04.48.jpg; ScreenHunter_772 19-Mar-14 04.48.jpg

b6 -2, 7
b7C -2, 7

the farthest out and the farthest in do not have the square...it goes away. All four pages have the same square and path.

It's zooming right in on the 1998 Document story place.

b6 -2
b7C -2

On Wednesday, March 19, 2014 1:59 AM wrote:
facebook url seen in top bar of each screen shot

Each map is showing the box in the same place and it zooms while you zoom.

What is truly amazing is it's zooming to Florida, and Florida is a recent topic here>

These may be added to the appropriate folder.

Tick tock. Let the sorrows flow.

b6 -2
b7C -2

On Wednesday, March 19, 2014 12:52 AM, wrote:
I added Mecca as the current city on th page, and after doing so, the box appeared on the map as shown in the three attachments. The box seems to be superimposing another type of map with different fonts,, etc.

Another message from Allah?

Subject: FOUR WILD HORSES FOR THE RUN – ONE RUNNING 00:00

From:

To:

Cc:

Date: Wednesday, December 31, 1969 7:00 PM

b6 -2
b7C -

The Red Horse Jumper will be released at West Point. I knew that on the drive to Newtown, but the Red Horse Jumper is still under construction.

b6 -
b7C

On Saturday, March 15, 2014 2:22 AM,

The White Horse Jumper took off in Newtown.

The Black Horse Jumper is now reserved for Israel. Attached is a screen shot of the files. Each jumper has all the same evidence keys, but it now looks like each is going to be slightly different. If you look close, you might notice I added the SEAL to the magnetic folder and the White Horse wasn't carrying those flags seen in the PROMISED LAND folder.

FD-1087 (Rev. 5-8-10)

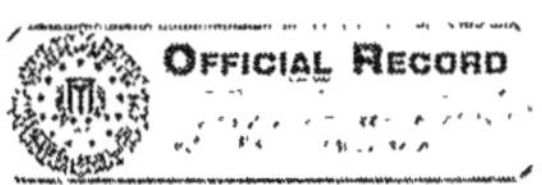

UNCLASSIFIED

FEDERAL BUREAU OF INVESTIGATION

Evidence Log

Event Title: (U) Basket left by [redacted] [redacted] at Newtown Bee

Date: 03/25/2014

CC: [redacted]

b6 -1, 2
b7C -1, 2

Approved By: SSA [redacted]

Drafted By: [redacted]

Case ID #: 4-NH-2619946

(U) ADAM PETER LANZA
Sandy Hook Elementary School
12 Dickinson St, Sandy Hook, CT-Victim
Firearms Act.
OO:NH

[redacted]

b7E -1

Collected By: [redacted] on 03/21/2014

Collected From: (U) [redacted]
Newtown Bee

Receipt Given?: No

b6 -1, 2, 7
b7C -1, 2, 7

Holding Office: NEW HAVEN

Details:

Easter basket left at the Newtown Bee newspaper by [redacted] [redacted]

Item Type **Description**

UNCLASSIFIED

4-NH-2619946
SERIAL 256

Title: (U) Basket left by [redacted] at Newtown Bee b6 -2
Re: 4-NH-2619946, 03/25/2014 b7C -2

1B General

(U) 1. A yellow, green and blue cardboard and paper, egg shaped Easter bag;
2. A blue and white stuffed bunny with two business cards for [redacted] [redacted] [redacted] with hand writing "Cell [redacted]
3. 30 additional of the same [redacted] business cards;
4. A tourist pamphlet advertising the Submarine Force Museum and USS Nautilus submarine in Groton, Connecticut; and
5. A greeting card referencing the "families" and the jump drive and signed by [redacted] b6 -1 b7C -
Collected On: 03/21/2014
Located By: [redacted]
Location Area: Newtown Bee
Specific Location: Editorial Offices

1B CART

(U) A silver Sandisk Cruzer Facet 8GB jump drive
Collected On: 03/21/2014
Located By: [redacted]
Location Area: Newtown Bee
Specific Location: Editorial Offices
Device Type: Mass Storage Device
Number of Devices Collected: 1

♦♦

FD-1057 (Rev. 5-8-10)

UNCLASSIFIED//~~FOUO~~

FEDERAL BUREAU OF INVESTIGATION

Electronic Communication

Title: (U//~~FOUO~~) Summary of Contact with Newtown PD regarding complaint of [redacted]

Date: 04/07/2014

From: NEW HAVEN
NH-BRA2
Contact: [redacted]

b6 -1, 7
b7C -1, 7

Approved By: [redacted]

Drafted By: [redacted]

Case ID #: 4-NH-2619946 (U) ADAM PETER LANZA
Sandy Hook Elementary School
12 Dickinson St, Sandy Hook, CT-Victim
Firearms Act.
OO:NH

Synopsis: (U//~~FOUO~~) A summary of contact with the Newtown Police Department regarding a complaint by [redacted] against a Youtube and Facebook posting by conspiracy theorist. b6 -7 b7C -7

[redacted] b7E -1

Enclosure(s): Enclosed are the following items:
1. (U//~~FOUO~~) PD report of [redacted] Complaint

Details:

On 2/20/2014, the writer was contacted by the Newtown, Connecticut Police Department regarding a complaint it received from [redacted] [redacted] was complaining about his image being utilized on a YouTube posting, as well as a Facebook page, posted by an individual who claimed the Sandy Hook shooting was a conspiracy. Attempts by [redacted] to have the postings taken down were initially successful. However, the links were re-posted. b6 -7 b7C -7

The writer has reviewed the postings in question, as well as the police

UNCLASSIFIED//~~FOUO~~

Sandy Hook-3328

4-NH-2619946
SERIAL 257

Title: (U//~~FOUO)~~ Summary of Contact with Newtown PD regarding complaint of [redacted]
Re: 4-NH-2619946, 04/07/2014

b6 -7
b7C -

report (attached to this communication) and assessed there was no threat of violence. Following conversations with New Haven Division's CDC, it was decided that the matter in question was civil in nature at this point.

SSA [redacted] provided this initial assessment to the assigned Newtown officer, noting that state of Connecticut harassment statutes may apply. In the event the matter escalated, the writer was willing to re-assess the initial finding.

b6
b7C

♦♦

FD-302 (Rev. 5-8-10)

FEDERAL BUREAU OF INVESTIGATION

Date of entry 04/08/2014

On 04/07/2014, Special Agent [redacted] Federal Bureau of Investigation (FBI), returned property to [redacted] as follows: b6 -1, 2 b7C -1, 2

[redacted] b6 -1, 2, 4 b7C -1, 2, 4 b7E -6

[redacted] requested the return of [redacted]. SA [redacted] contacted Assistant United States Attorney [redacted] who agreed that the property could be returned.

On 04/07/2014, [redacted] came to the FBI Bridgeport Resident Agency. There, SA [redacted] released [redacted] to [redacted] who signed a copy of an FD-597 Release of Property Form indicating that he received the items. [redacted] was given a copy of the signed form. b6 -1, 2, 5 b7C -1, 2, 5

Investigation on 04/07/2014 at Bridgeport, Connecticut, United States (In Person)

File # 4-NH-2619946 Date drafted 04/08/2014

by [redacted] b6 -1 b7C -1

4-NH-2619946
SERIAL 268

FD-597 (Rev 8-11-94)

UNITED STATES DEPARTMENT OF JUSTICE
FEDERAL BUREAU OF INVESTIGATION
Receipt for Property Received/Returned/Released/Seized

File # 4-NH-2619946

On (date) April 7, 2014

item(s) listed below were:
☐ Received From
☐ Returned To
☒ Released To

(Name)

(Street Address)

(City)

b6 -2
b7C -

Description of Item(s):

Nothing Further

b6 -1, 5
b7C -1, 5

Received By:

Received Fro

FD-1087 (Rev. 5-8-10)

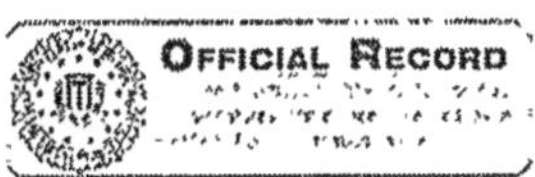

UNCLASSIFIED

FEDERAL BUREAU OF INVESTIGATION

Evidence Log

Event Title: (U) Evidence from FBI Lab **Date:** 05/07/2014

Approved By: [redacted]

Drafted By: [redacted]

b6 -1
b7C -1

Case ID #: 4-NH-2619946 (U) ADAM PETER LANZA
Sandy Hook Elementary School
12 Dickinson St, Sandy Hook, CT-Victim
Firearms Act.
OO:NH

[redacted] b7E -1

Collected By: [redacted] on 05/07/2014

Collected From: (U) FBI Lab

Receipt Given?: No

Holding Office: NEW HAVEN

b6 -1
b7C -1

Details: *No Details Provided*

Item Type	**Description**
1B CART	(U) Q4 - western digital 500gb hard drive s/n wcayuj809812 Collected On: 05/07/2014 Located By: [redacted] Location Area: FBI Lab Specific Location: ERF Device Type: Mass Storage Device Number of Devices Collected: 1

UNCLASSIFIED

4-NH-2619946
SERIAL 259

Title: (U) Evidence from FBI Lab
Re: 4-NH-2619946, 05/07/2014

1B CART	(U) DEHQ1 - seagate 1 tb hard drive s/n 6vp21pcp Collected On: 05/07/2014 Located By: [redacted] Location Area: FBI Lab Specific Location: ERF Device Type: Mass Storage Device Number of Devices Collected: 1	b6 -1 b7C -1

♦♦

FEDERAL BUREAU OF INVESTIGATION

Date of entry 06/20/2014

On 06/17/2014, Special Agents (SA) [redacted] Federal Bureau of Investigation (FBI) Bridgeport Safe Streets Task Force, and SA [redacted] [redacted] FBI Computer Analysis Response Team (CART), conducted a review of evidence Exhibits 1B122 and 1B123, which are hard drives containing data which was extracted from a hard drive seized from 36 Yogananda Street, Newtown, Connecticut. The review was conducted as follows: b6 -1 b7C -1

On 12/14/2012, members of the Connecticut State Police (CSP) seized a 500 GB Seagate Barracuda ST3500320AS hard drive, S/N 9QM34ZA8 from 36 Yogananda Street. [redacted] CSP turned over the drive to FBI New Haven for analysis. [redacted] b7E -6, 8

[redacted] b6 -1 b7C -1 b7E -6, 8

[redacted] b7E -6, 8

[redacted] b6 -1 b7C -1 b7E -6

Investigation on 06/17/2014 at New Haven, Connecticut, United States (In Person)

File # 4-NH-2619946 Date drafted 06/18/2014

by [redacted] b6 -1 b7C -1

4-NH-2619946
SERIAL 260

b6
b7C
b7E

b6 -
b7C
b7E

A copy of the hard drive will be provided to the CSP for further investigation as they deem appropriate.

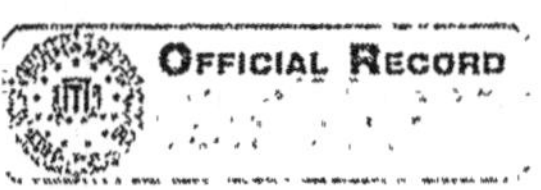

UNCLASSIFIED

FEDERAL BUREAU OF INVESTIGATION

Import Form

Form Type: DEL-REX **Date:** 06/25/2014

Title: (U) lab #121217250 QD WR

Approved By: [ ]

Drafted By: [ ]

b6 -1
b7C -1

Case ID #: 4-NH-2619946 (U) ADAM PETER LANZA
Sandy Hook Elementary School
12 Dickinson St, Sandy Hook, CT-Victim
Firearms Act.
OO:NH

Synopsis: (U) re: 12/18/12

Enclosure(s): Enclosed are the following items:
1. (U) lab #121217250 QD WR, retained at ERF

♦♦

UNCLASSIFIED

4-NH-2619946
SERIAL 261

FD-1057 (Rev. 5-8-10)

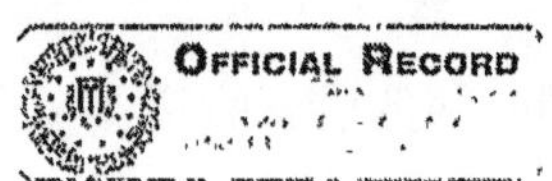

UNCLASSIFIED//~~FOUO~~

FEDERAL BUREAU OF INVESTIGATION

Electronic Communication

Title: (U//~~FOUO~~) Logical copies of files from computers seized at the Lanza residence forwarded to BAU2.

Date: 06/27/2014

CC: [redacted]

From: NEW HAVEN
NH-5
Contact: [redacted]

b6 -1
b7C -1

Approved By: [redacted]

Drafted By: [redacted]

Case ID #: 4-NH-2619946

(U) ADAM PETER LANZA
Sandy Hook Elementary School
12 Dickinson St, Sandy Hook, CT-Victim Firearms Act.
OO:NH

Synopsis: (U//~~FOUO~~) One hard drive containing logical copies of files from computers seized at the Lanza residence forwarded to BAU2.

[redacted] b7E -1

Package Copy: (U//~~FOUO~~) One hard drive, described above, will be forwarded to BAU 2 under separate cover.

Details:

For the information of BAU 2, New Haven CART Examiner SA [redacted]

[redacted]

b6 -1
b7C -1
b7E -1

UNCLASSIFIED//~~FOUO~~

Sandy Hook-3

4-NH-2619946
SERIAL 262

Title: (U//~~FOUO~~) Logical copies of files from computers seized at the Lanza residence forwarded to BAU2.
Re: 4-NH-2619946, 06/27/2014

[redacted] The files are being provided to assist BAU 2.

b6 -1
b7C -1
b7E -6, 8

♦♦

FD-1036 (Rev. 10-16-2009)

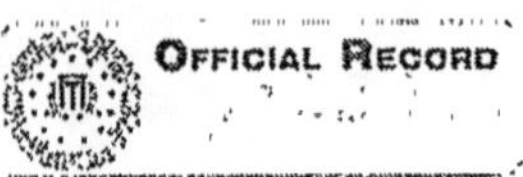

UNCLASSIFIED

FEDERAL BUREAU OF INVESTIGATION

Import Form

Form Type: DEL-REX **Date:** 07/21/2014

Title: (U) CART Exam

Approved By: SSA [redacted]

Drafted By: [redacted]

b6 -1
b7C -1

Case ID #: 4-NH-2619946 (U) ADAM PETER LANZA
Sandy Hook Elementary School
12 Dickinson St, Sandy Hook, CT-Victim
Firearms Act.
OO:NH

Synopsis: (U) CART Report RE:process of recovered data from damaged hard drive, as well as provision of remaining hard drive data to BAU from items from 36 Yogananda St.

♦♦

UNCLASSIFIED

4-NH-2619946
SERIAL 2263

FD-1057 (Rev. 5-8-10)

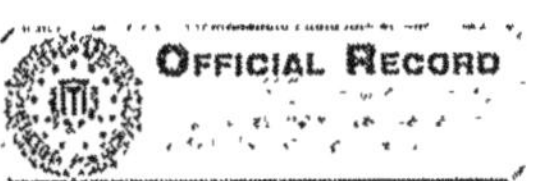

UNCLASSIFIED//~~FOUO~~

FEDERAL BUREAU OF INVESTIGATION

Electronic Communication

Title: (U//~~FOUO~~) Representation Funds For Meeting With Sandy Hook Families.

Date: 07/23/2014

CC: [redacted]

From: NEW HAVEN
NH-5
Contact: [redacted]

b6 -1
b7C -1

Approved By: A/SSA [redacted]

Drafted By: [redacted]

Case ID #: 4-NH-2619946 (U) ADAM PETER LANZA
Sandy Hook Elementary School
12 Dickinson St, Sandy Hook, CT-Victim
Firearms Act.
OO:NH

252B-NH-C23545 (U) NEW HAVEN DIVISION NCAVC MATTERS

Synopsis: (U//~~FOUO~~) Request representation funds to be used to cover refreshment expenses during a meeting between the FBI, Connecticut State Police (CSP) and the Sandy Hook Elementary School (SHES) victims' families.

[redacted] b7E -1

Details:

It is requested that representation funds be allocated and authorized for use during a planned meeting on July 29, 2014 between members of the FBI, Connecticut State Police (CSP) and the Sandy Hook Elementary School (SHES) victims' families. The CSP investigators working with the victims' families advised that the families would like to have a

UNCLASSIFIED//~~FOUO~~

4-NH-2619946
SERIAL 264

Title: (U//~~FOUO~~) Representation Funds For Meeting With Sandy Hook Families.
Re: 4-NH-2619946, 07/23/2014

meeting with members of the FBI's Behavioral Analysis Unit (BAU). CSP requested BAU assistance in this matter related to crime analysis, offender's motivation and threat assessment. BAU 2 is planning on releasing a report of their findings later this summer and decided it was appropriate to brief the families prior to the release of their report. BAU 2 agreed to meeting with the victims' families. The report will be law enforcement sensitive and released only to the CSP.

SAC Patricia M. Ferrick, FBI New Haven Division, approved of the meeting. ASAC [redacted] New Haven Division, is is hosting the event with the assistance of SA [redacted] BAU 2, FBI New Haven and CSP have coordinated the event and have consulted with both BAU's contract psychiatrist, [redacted] and the FBI's Office of Victims' Assistance (OVA). It was determined that the best location for the meeting is a neutral and therapeutic setting. The Heritage Hotel and Conference Center, 522 Heritage Road in Southbury, CT was identified as a location that was suitable and close to Newtown, CT where the families reside. The debriefing is planned for July 29, 2014 from 6pm-9pm. During the debriefing light refreshments and non-alcoholic beverages will be served. It is anticipated that 50 persons will attend including FBI,CSP and OVA. b6 - b7C

Attending and participating in the event from the FBI include:

CIRG-BAU 2- Unit Chief [redacted]

CIRG-BAU 2- Supervisory Special Agent [redacted]

CIRG-BAU 2- Crime Analyst [redacted] b6 -1

CIRG-BAU 2- Crime Analyst- [redacted] b7C -1

CIRG-Contract Psychiatrist [redacted]

FBI HQ-OVA [redacted] MSW

FBI New Haven- Assistant Special In Charge [redacted]

Title: (U//~~FOUO~~) Representation Funds For Meeting With Sandy Hook Families.
Re: 4-NH-2619946, 07/23/2014

FBI New Haven Special Agent [redacted] (Case Agent)

FBI New Haven Special Agent [redacted] (NCAVC Coordinator)

b6 -1
b7C -1

Representatives from the CSP, primarily the investigators assigned to the case. As of instant date attending will be:

CSP- Lieutenant [redacted]

CSP- Sergeant [redacted]

CSP- Detective [redacted]

CSP- Detective [redacted]

b6 -3
b7C -3

The SHES victims' families. CSP has extended the invitation to the families and is tracking their replies.

The exact attendee list for the families and the CSP has not been completed. The estimate at this time for the meeting is a total of 50 to include CSP, FBI and families. The Heritage Hotel noted that changes in the numbers of attendees can be made up to five days in advance.

Rental for the room ($250.00)is being funded by a separate account. An estimate for the light refreshments to include a mini dessert display and assorted non-alcoholic beverages for 50 people is approximately $500.00 which includes tax and gratuity. No gifts will be provided. Writer is in the process of obtaining a written estimate for the refreshments from the hotel. It will be provided upon receipt.

♦♦

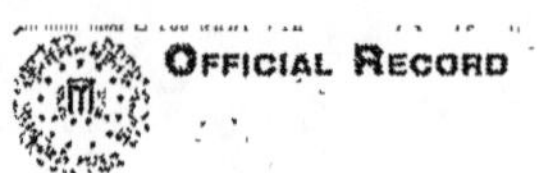

UNCLASSIFIED

FEDERAL BUREAU OF INVESTIGATION

Electronic Communication

Title: (U) FD192 for 1B14 Released **Date:** 07/23/2014

From: NEW HAVEN
Contact: [redacted]

Approved By: [redacted]

b6 -1
b7C -1

Drafted By: [redacted]

Case ID #: 4-NH-2619946 (U) ADAM PETER LANZA
Sandy Hook Elementary School
12 Dickinson St, Sandy Hook, CT-Victim
Firearms Act.
OO:NH

Synopsis: (U) FD192 for 1B14 Released

[redacted] b7E -1

Enclosure(s): Enclosed are the following items:
1. (U) FD192 for 1B14 Released

Details:

FD192 for 1B14 Released

♦♦

UNCLASSIFIED

b7E -5

Evidence Details

Case: 4-NH-2619946 Item: 1B14

Description:
(U) [redacted]

Acquired On: 12/15/2012 01:20 AM EST

Eligible for Forfeiture: No

Receipt Item #: *None*

Special Handling: *None*

Hazardous Materials: *None*

b6 -2
b7C -2

CART Information

Type [redacted]

Number Collected 1

Batteries Charged No

Acquired by CART No

Discovery Location

Area: [redacted]

Specific: [redacted]

Collected By: [redacted]

Others: [redacted]

b6 -1, 2
b7C -1, 2

Anticipated Disposition

Return on *None*

Storage Information

Holding Office: NEW HAVEN

Finalized By: [redacted]

Last Inventory: *None*

Location: NA - Retained by Agent

Barcode #: E5132460

Chain of Custody

Shipping / Transfer Log

History

Acquisition Event Details

Acquisition Event:
(U) [redacted]

Acquired By: [redacted]

b6 -1, 2
b7C -1, 2

Acquired From:

b7E

(U)

b6 -2
b7C -2

United States

Acquired On:
12/15/2012

Receipt Given:
Yes

Holding Office:
NEW HAVEN

Evidence Log:

4-NH-2619946
Serial 30

FD-1004
Revised
9-16-2009

FEDERAL BUREAU OF INVESTIGATION

EVIDENCE CHAIN-OF-CUSTODY

Evidence Type: ☐ General ☒ CART ☐ Drug ☐ Valuable ☐ Firearm/Weapon ☐ Firearm/Other

Special Handling Instructions	Initial Receipt	Date and Time
☐ Batteries ☐ Biohazard ☐ FGJ ☐ HAZMAT ☐ Latents ☐ Refrigerate ☐ Req. Charging ☐ None ☐ Other ____________	Signature: Printed Name: Reason: Collected	12/15/12 1:20AM

Relinquished Custody	Date and Time	Accepted Custody	Date and Time
Signature: Printed Name: Reason: TOT CUSTODIAN	12/15/2012 3:39AM	Signature: Printed Name: Reason: CUSTODY	12/15/2012 3:39AM
Signature: Printed Name: Reason: TOT ECT	12/17/2012 11:40AM	Signature: Printed Name: Reason: STORAGE	12/17/2012 11:40AM
Signature: Printed Name: Reason: TOT CART	12/17/12 3:12 pm	Signature: Printed Name: Reason: CART Review	12/17/12 3:12 pm
Signature: Printed Name: Reason: TOT ECC	2/27/13 11:50 am	Signature: Printed Name: Reason: Storage	2/27/13 11:50A
Signature: Printed Name: Reason: Storage	7/5/13 11:20	Signature: Printed Name: Reason: CSP Review	7/5/13 11:20A

b6 -1
b7C -1

Firearms Certification:
Printed Name: ____________ Signature: ____________ Date: ____________

Case ID: ____________ 1B: ____________ Barcode: ____________

#6

EVIDENCE CHAIN-OF-CUSTODY

Continuation Page

Relinquished Custody	Date and Time	Accepted Custody	Date and Time
Signature:	7/31/13	Signature:	7/31/13
Printed Name:	1245pm	Printed Name:	1245p
Reason: TOT ECU		Reason: Storage	
Relinquished Custody	**Date and Time**	**Accepted Custody**	**Date and Time**
Signature:	1/29/14	Signature:	1/29/14 @
Printed Name:	3:10p	Printed Name:	3:10p
Reason: TOT Agent		Reason: Transport	
Relinquished Custody	**Date and Time**	**Accepted Custody**	**Date and Time**
Signature:	1/30/14 @	Signature:	1/30/14 @
Printed Name:	12:00p	Printed Name:	12:00p
Reason: Return to owner		Reason: Return to owner	
Relinquished Custody	**Date and Time**	**Accepted Custody**	**Date and Time**
Signature:	4/7/14	Signature:	
Printed Name:	430pm	Printed Name:	
Reason: RETURNED		Reason:	
Relinquished Custody	**Date and Time**	**Accepted Custody**	**Date and Time**
Signature:		Signature:	
Printed Name:		Printed Name:	
Reason:		Reason:	
Relinquished Custody	**Date and Time**	**Accepted Custody**	**Date and Time**
Signature:		Signature:	
Printed Name:		Printed Name:	
Reason:		Reason:	

b6 -
b7C -

Case ID: ________ 1B: 14 Barcode: ________

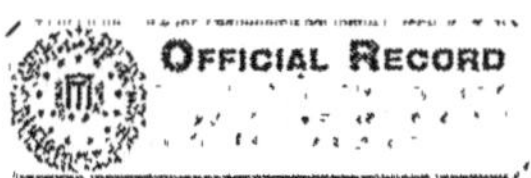

UNCLASSIFIED

FEDERAL BUREAU OF INVESTIGATION

Electronic Communication

Title: (U) Shipping Invoice for 1B122 & 1B123 **Date:** 07/23/2014

From: NEW HAVEN
NH-SAS-2
Contact: [redacted]

Approved By: [redacted] b6 -1 b7C -1

Drafted By: [redacted]

Case ID #: 4-NH-2619946 (U) ADAM PETER LANZA
Sandy Hook Elementary School
12 Dickinson St, Sandy Hook, CT-Victim
Firearms Act.
OO:NH

Synopsis: (U) Shipping Invoice for 1B122 & 1B123

[redacted] b7E -1

Enclosure(s): Enclosed are the following items:
1. (U) Shipping Invoice for 1B122 & 1B123

Details:

Shipping Invoice for 1B122 & 1B123

♦♦

UNCLASSIFIED

4-NH-2619946
Serial 2666

18-252 (Rev. 2-15-2011)
ERF Shipping Invoice
FEDERAL BUREAU OF INVESTIGATION
BLDG 27958A
QUANTICO, VA 22135

Date: April 30, 2014

To: New Haven
NH-9
Evidence Control Technician
Attention: SA [redacted]

b6
b7C

Invoice of Contents:

Q4 – Western Digital 500 GB HDD
S/N WCAYUJ809812 1B122

DEHQ1 – Seagate 1 TB HDD S/N 6VP21PCP 1B123

Return to: [redacted]
Phone: [redacted]
Case ID No.: 4-NH-2619946
Lab No.: 121217250 QD WR
Title: Sandy Hook Elementary School 12 Dickinson St, Sandy Hook, CT-Victim Firearms Act. OO:NH

130

Shipping Number: ____________________

☑ Federal Express

☐ Other ____________________

Packaged by: [signature]

☐ Personal pick up / delivery date: __________

Received from: __________

Unit: __________

Received by: __________
(Signature)

Printed name: __________

Agency: __________

FD-1057 (Rev. 5-8-10)

UNCLASSIFIED//~~FOUO~~

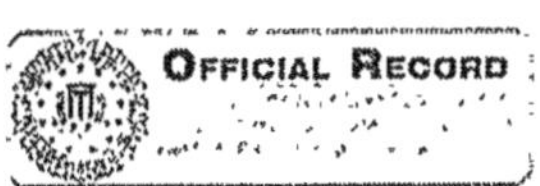

FEDERAL BUREAU OF INVESTIGATION

Electronic Communication

Title: (U//~~FOUO~~) Representation funds request. **Date:** 07/23/2014

CC: [redacted]

From: NEW HAVEN
NH-5
Contact: [redacted]

b6 -1
b7C -1

Approved By: A/SSA [redacted]

Drafted By: [redacted]

Case ID #: 4-NH-2619946 (U) ADAM PETER LANZA
Sandy Hook Elementary School
12 Dickinson St, Sandy Hook, CT-Victim
Firearms Act.
OO:NH

Synopsis: (U//~~FOUO~~) Update on representation funds request.

[redacted] b7E -1

Enclosure(s): Enclosed are the following items:
1. (U//~~FOUO~~) Heritage Hotel Invoices

Details:

This communication serves to update an EC dated July 21, 2014 regarding a request for representation funds concerning a meeting with the families of the victims' of the Sandy Hook Elementary School (SHES)shooting. At this time it is estimated that 50 people will attend to include victim family members, FBI personnel and members of the

UNCLASSIFIED//~~FOUO~~

4-NH-2619946
SERIAL 267

Title: (U//~~FOUO)~~ Representation funds request.
Re: 4-NH-2619946, 07/23/2014

Connecticut State Police. The meeting concerns a de-briefing by the FBI's Behavioral Analysis Unit in advance of the release of a report on their findings and investigation of the SHES incident.

The estimated bill for the rental of the room is $250.00. The room is being paid for through a separate funding source. The estimated bill for the refreshments, which will be paid for with representation funds, is $376.48. Copies of the invoices are attached hereto. Details concerning the meeting were set forth in referenced EC.

♦♦

522 HERITAGE ROAD, SOUTHBURY, CT 06488 800.932 3466 WWW.HERITAGESOUTHBURY COM

CT State Police

INVOICE DATE	DUE DATE
7/21/14	

Account #	PO#
ESTIMATE	

Date	Account	Description	Charges	Credits
7/21/14	ESTIMATE	Mini Dessert Display	188.24	
		Assorted Drinks	188.24	

Please make checks payable to HERITAGE HOTEL

Thank you for choosing Heritage Hotel!

If you have questions about your bill please call
(800) 932-3466 ext [illegible]

Effective December 1, 2008, all balances over 30 days will incur a 1% Finance Charge per Month

Balance Due $ 376.48

MST, STATE POLICE

SOUTHBURY, CT 06488 US

Room Number:
Daily Rate: 0.00
Room Type: HOUSE
No. of Guests: 0 / 0

ARRIVAL	DEPARTURE	CREDIT CARD	RATE PLAN	CATEGORY	ACCOUNT
7/28/2014	7/30/2014		HOUSE	HOUSE	10000264177

b6 - b7C

DATE	ROOM NO	DESCRIPTION	REFERENCE	AMOUNT
7/21/2014		MASTER CARD	MASTER CARD	($250 00)

CREDIT DUE: ($250.00)

TERMS DUE AND PAYABLE UPON PRESENTATION. I AGREE THAT MY LIABILITY FOR THIS BILL IS NOT WAIVED AND AGREE TO BE HELD PERSONALLY LIABLE IN THE EVENT THAT THE INDICATED PERSON, COMPANY OR ASSOCIATION FAILS TO PAY FOR ANY PART OR THE FULL AMOUNT OF THESE CHARGES.

FD-1057 (Rev. 5-8-10)

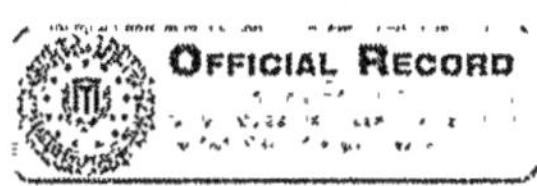

UNCLASSIFIED//~~FOUO~~

FEDERAL BUREAU OF INVESTIGATION

Electronic Communication

Title: (U//~~FOUO~~) Representation Funds For Meeting With Sandy Hook Families.

Date: 07/28/2014

CC: [redacted]

From: FINANCE
DC-TTPU
Contact: [redacted]

b6 -1
b7C -1

Approved By: A/SC [redacted]

Drafted By: [redacted]

Case ID #: 4-NH-2619946 (U) ADAM PETER LANZA
Sandy Hook Elementary School
12 Dickinson St, Sandy Hook, CT-Victim
Firearms Act.
OO:NH

252B-NH-C23545 (U) NEW HAVEN DIVISION NCAVC MATTERS

Synopsis: (U//~~FOUO~~) Request for utilization of $500.00 in allotted Representation funds for the purchase of light refreshments has been approved.

[redacted] b7E -1

Details:

Reference is made to your EC dated 07/23/2014, captioned as above, requesting utilization of $500.00 in allotted Representation Funds for light refreshments provided at a meeting hosted by ASAC [redacted] to discuss with the Connecticut State Police and the Sandy Hook Elementary School victims' families on matters of mutual concern.

b6 -1
b7C -1

The Finance Division has reviewed your request and determined that it meets the criteria to qualify for use of Representation Funds. Therefore, your request for utilization of $500.00 in allotted

UNCLASSIFIED//~~FOUO~~

4-NH-2619946
SERIAL 268

Title: (U//~~FOUO~~) Representation Funds For Meeting With Sandy Hook Families.
Re: 4-NH-2619946, 07/28/2014

Representation Funds has been approved.

The authorization number issued for the light refreshments is T-1534. The receipt for this expenditure should be attached to a completed FD-794, supported by a copy of the approval EC, and submitted to the New Haven Finance Office for processing and issuance of payment. The account information is as follows:

FY 14 Representation Funds ((BBFY = 2014) (FUND = SED1) / (ORG LEVEL 2 = 1200) /(Program = GN) /Sub-Program = KR)/ SOC: 25228)

A copy of the FD-794 and applicable invoices/receipts should be forwarded to [redacted] JEH Room 1270, for record keeping purposes. **b6 -1 b7C -1**

Please be advised that the New Haven Field Office has exhausted its Representation Funds allotment for FY14.

♦♦

FD-1057 (Rev. 5-8-10)

UNCLASSIFIED//~~FOUO~~

FEDERAL BUREAU OF INVESTIGATION

Electronic Communication

Title: (U//~~FOUO~~) BAU 2 meeting with SHES victim families and law enforcement. **Date:** 08/01/2014

From: NEW HAVEN
NH-5
Contact: [redacted]

Approved By: [redacted]

Drafted By: [redacted]

b6 -1
b7C -1

Case ID #: 252B-NH-C23545 (U) NEW HAVEN DIVISION NCAVC MATTERS
4-NH-2619946 (U) ADAM PETER LANZA
Sandy Hook Elementary School
12 Dickinson St, Sandy Hook, CT-Victim
Firearms Act.
OO:NH

Synopsis: (U//~~FOUO~~) Meeting with the victims' families and BAU 2.

Enclosure(s): Enclosed are the following items:
1. (U//~~FOUO~~) Agenda

Details:

On July 29, 2014 members of BAU 2 to include UC [redacted] SSA [redacted] CA [redacted] and CA [redacted] as well as BAU contracted psychiatrist [redacted] OVA Specialist [redacted] and writer met with families of the Sandy Hook Elementary School shooting. The meeting was coordinated and provided in conjunction with members of the Connecticut State Police Western District Major Crime Unit (CSP WDMCU). The meeting was at the request of the families through the CSP WDMCU and done in advance of the report, which is still in draft form, of BAU's findings of the incident.

b6 -1
b7C -1

On July 30, 2014 BAU 2 met with the members of the CSP WDMCU, Captain [redacted] New town Police Department, Chief Lennie Boyle of the State's Attorney's Office and [redacted] from the State Of Connecticut

b6 -3, 6
b7C -3, 6

UNCLASSIFIED//~~FOUO~~

4-NH-2619946
SERIAL 269

Title: (U//~~FOUO~~) BAU 2 meeting with SHES victim families and law enforcement.
Re: 252B-NH-C23545, 08/01/2014

Child's Advocate's Office.

A copy of the agenda is attached hereto.

♦♦

SANDY HOOK ELEMENTARY SCHOOL

BAU BRIEFING, 29 JULY 2014

1. **Introductions**

   a. BAU Mission
   b. BAU process of conducting a behavioral assessment

2. **Summary of BAU Analysis**

   a. The shooter had a complex background featuring many problematic bio-psycho-social issues. Historical, clinical, and contextual factors contributed to the shooter's extremely rigid and inflexible world view.

   b. The shooter did not "snap," but instead engaged in careful, methodical planning and preparation. There is evidence that the shooter began contemplating the attack as early as March of 2011

   c. In the weeks and months immediately preceding the attack, the shooter's deteriorating relationship with his mother was a significant challenge and stressor in his life

   d The shooter was fascinated with past shootings and researched them thoroughly.

   e. The shooter shared many similar characteristics and behaviors with other active shooters.

   f There is no evidence to suggest that the shooter viewed the attack as a "video game" or as a contest

   g. There is evidence to suggest that the shooter had an interest in children that could be categorized as pedophilia. There is no evidence that he ever acted out on this interest

3. **Questions/Discussion**

4. **Conclusion and Adjourning**

FD-1036 (Rev. 10-16-2009)

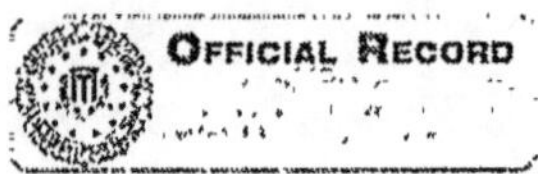

UNCLASSIFIED

FEDERAL BUREAU OF INVESTIGATION

Import Form

Form Type: DEL-REX **Date:** 08/25/2014

Title: (U) Lab# 121217250 QD

Approved By: [redacted]

Drafted By: [redacted]

b6 -1
b7C -1

Case ID #: 4-NH-2619946 (U) ADAM PETER LANZA
Sandy Hook Elementary School
12 Dickinson St, Sandy Hook, CT-Victim
Firearms Act.
OO:NH

Synopsis: (U) Lab# 121217250 QD; RE: 12/18/2012

Enclosure(s): Enclosed are the following items:
1. (U) Lab# 121217250 QD, retained at ERF

♦♦

UNCLASSIFIED

4-NH-2619946
SERIAL 270

FD-1087 (Rev. 5-8-10)

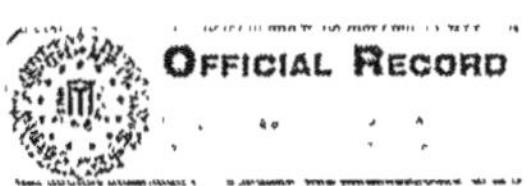

UNCLASSIFIED

FEDERAL BUREAU OF INVESTIGATION

Evidence Log

Event Title: (U) Evidence from FBI Lab **Date:** 08/31/2014

Approved By: [ ] b6 -1 b7C -1

Drafted By: [ ]

Case ID #: 4-NH-2619946 (U) ADAM PETER LANZA
Sandy Hook Elementary School
12 Dickinson St, Sandy Hook, CT-Victim
Firearms Act.
OO:NH

[ ] b7E -1

Collected By: [ ] on 08/29/2014 b6 -1 b7C -1

Collected From: (U) FBI Lab

Receipt Given?: No

Holding Office: NEW HAVEN

Details: *No Details Provided*

Item Type	**Description**
1B CART	(U) Q1 - one damaged seagate hard drive - s/n 9QM34ZAB

Collected On: 08/29/2014
Located By: [ ] b6 -1 b7C -1
Location Area: FBI LAB
Specific Location: FBI LAB
Device Type: Mass Storage Device
Number of Devices Collected: 1

UNCLASSIFIED

4-NH-2619946

SERIAL 271

Title: (U) Evidence from FBI Lab
Re: 4-NH-2619946, 08/31/2014

1B CART	(U) Q4 - one western digital WD5000AAKS-00UU3 AO - s/n WCAYUJ809812 Collected On: 08/29/2014 Located By: [redacted] Location Area: FBI LAB Specific Location: FBI LAB Device Type: Mass Storage Device Number of Devices Collected: 1

b6 -1
b7C -1

♦♦

FD-1057 (Rev. 5-8-10)

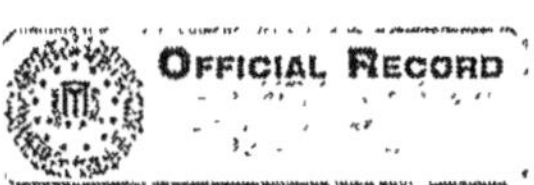

UNCLASSIFIED//~~FOUO~~

FEDERAL BUREAU OF INVESTIGATION

Electronic Communication

Title: (U//~~FOUO~~) CDs received from the CT Child Advocate's Office. **Date:** 09/03/2014

CC: [redacted]

From: NEW HAVEN
NH-5
Contact: [redacted] b6 -1 b7C -1

Approved By: [redacted]

Drafted By: [redacted]

Case ID #: 252B-NH-C23545 (U) NEW HAVEN DIVISION NCAVC MATTERS
4-NH-2619946 (U) ADAM PETER LANZA
Sandy Hook Elementary School
12 Dickinson St, Sandy Hook, CT-Victim
Firearms Act.
OO:NH

Synopsis: (U//~~FOUO~~) 3 CDs received from the CT Child Advocate's Office to be forwarded to BAU 2.

Package Copy: (U//~~FOUO~~) 3 CDs contained in a 1A will be forwarded under separate cover to BAU 2.

Enclosure(s): Enclosed are the following items:
1. (U//~~FOUO~~) 3 CDs from Lanza home

Details:

On September 2, 2014 writer received three CDs from [redacted] of the Connecticut Child Advocate's Office, 999 Asylum Street, Hartford, CT [redacted] The CDs are copies of CDs provided to [redacted] by the Connecticut State Police (CSP) for review concerning investigation into the Sandy Hook Elementary School b6 -6 b7C -6

UNCLASSIFIED//~~FOUO~~

Sandy Hook-3367

4-NH-2619946
SERIAL 272

Title: (U//~~FOUO)~~ CDs received from the CT Child Advocate's Office.
Re: 252B-NH-C23545, 09/03/2014

shooting. The CDs were recovered from the residence of Adam Lanza. The CDs are being provided to BAU 2 for review and inclusion in the BAU 2's final report concerning Lanza.

[redacted] noted that one CD, disk 1 contains pornographic images, disks 2 and 3contain Japanese videos and images. b6 -6 b7C -6

♦♦

FD-1057 (Rev 5-8-10)

UNCLASSIFIED

FEDERAL BUREAU OF INVESTIGATION

Electronic Communication

Title: (U) Shipping Label for 1B124 & 1B125 **Date:** 10/14/2014

From: NEW HAVEN
NH-SS
Contact: [redacted]

Approved By: [redacted]

Drafted By: [redacted]

b6 -1
b7C -1

Case ID #: 4-NH-2619946 (U) ADAM PETER LANZA
Sandy Hook Elementary School
12 Dickinson St, Sandy Hook, CT-Victim
Firearms Act.
OO:NH

Synopsis: (U) Shipping Label for 1B124 & 1B125

[redacted] b7E -1

Enclosure(s): Enclosed are the following items:
1. (U) Shipping Label for 1B124 & 1B125

Details:

Shipping Label for 1B124 & 1B125

♦♦

UNCLASSIFIED

4-NH - 2619946
SERIAL 273

18-252 (Rev. 2-15-2011)
ERF Shipping Invoice
FEDERAL BUREAU OF INVESTIGATION
BLDG 27958A
QUANTICO, VA 22135

Date: August 25, 2014

To: New Haven
NH-9
Attn: [redacted]

b6 -1
b7C -

1B124
1B125

Q1: One Damaged Seagate Hard Drive
S/N:9QM34ZAB
Q4: One Western Digital WD5000AAKS-00UU3A0
S/N:WCAYUJ809812

Return to: [redacted]
Phone: [redacted]
Case ID No 4-NH-2619946
Lab No.: 121217250 QD
Title: (U) UNSUB (S)
Sandy Hook Elementary School
12 Dickinson St, Sandy Hook, CT-Victim
Firearms Act.
OO:NH

b6 -1
b7C -

103

Shipping Number: ______

☐ Federal Express

☐ Other ______

Packaged by: ______

☐ Personal pick up / delivery date: ______

Received from: ______

Unit: ______

Received by: ______
(Signature)

Printed name: ______
Agency: ______

FEDERAL BUREAU OF INVESTIGATION
FOI/PA
DELETED PAGE INFORMATION SHEET
Civil Action# 16-cv-02136

Total Deleted Page(s) = 25
Page 5 ~ Duplicate;
Page 6 ~ Duplicate;
Page 7 ~ Duplicate;
Page 8 ~ Duplicate;
Page 9 ~ Duplicate;
Page 10 ~ Duplicate;
Page 11 ~ Duplicate;
Page 12 ~ Duplicate;
Page 13 ~ Duplicate;
Page 21 ~ b3 - 1; b6 - 1, 5; b7C - 1, 5;
Page 22 ~ b3 - 1; b6 - 2; b7C - 2;
Page 23 ~ b3 - 1; b6 - 2; b7C - 2;
Page 25 ~ Duplicate;
Page 26 ~ Duplicate;
Page 27 ~ Duplicate;
Page 28 ~ Duplicate;
Page 30 ~ Duplicate;
Page 31 ~ Duplicate;
Page 33 ~ Duplicate;
Page 34 ~ Duplicate;
Page 35 ~ Duplicate;
Page 36 ~ Duplicate;
Page 37 ~ Duplicate;
Page 38 ~ Duplicate;
Page 39 ~ Duplicate;

XXXXXXXXXXXXXXXXXXXXXXXX
X Deleted Page(s) X
X No Duplication Fee X
X For this Page X
XXXXXXXXXXXXXXXXXXXXXXXX

FD-340a (Rev. 1-27-03)

(Title) 1A's

(File No.) 4-NH-2619946 GJ

Item	Date	To be returned			Disposition
		Yes	No		

FD-340 (Rev. 4-11-03)

File Number 4-NH-2619946-GJ - 1A2

Field Office Acquiring Evidence New Haven, CT

Serial # of Originating Document

Date Received 12/18/2012

From USAO and [redacted]
(Name of Contributor)

(Address)

(City and State)

By SA [redacted]

To Be Returned ☐ Yes ☑ No

Receipt Given ☐ Yes ☑ No

Grand Jury Material - Disseminate Only Pursuant to Rule 6 (e) Federal Rules of Criminal Procedure

☑ Yes ☐ No

Federal Taxpayer Information (FTI)

☐ Yes ☑ No

Title:

Sandy Hook Elementary

Reference:
(Communication Enclosing Material)

Description: ☐ Original notes re interview of

1) Copy of subpoena

2) Subpoena results from [redacted]

b3 -1
b6 -1
b7C -1

b3 -1

FD-340 (Rev. 4-11-03)

File Number 4-NH-2619946-GJ-1A3

Field Office Acquiring Evidence New Haven, CT

Serial # of Originating Document

Date Received 12/18/2012

From USAO
(Name of Contributor/Interviewee)

(Address)

(City and State)

By SA [redacted]

b6 -
b7C -

To Be Returned ☐ Yes ☑ No

Receipt Given ☐ Yes ☑ No

Grand Jury Material - Disseminate Only Pursuant to Rule 6 (e) Federal Rules of Criminal Procedure

☑ Yes ☐ No

Federal Taxpayer Information (FTI)

☐ Yes ☑ No

Title:

Sandy Hook Elementary

Reference:
(Communication Enclosing Material)

Description: ☐ Original notes re interview of

Copy of Subpoena and Proof of Service for [redacted]

b3 -

AO 110 (Rev. 06/09) Subpoena to Testify Before a Grand Jury

UNITED STATES DISTRICT COURT

for the

District of Connecticut

SUBPOENA TO TESTIFY BEFORE A GRAND JURY

To:

b3 -1

YOU ARE COMMANDED to appear in this United States district court at the time, date, and place shown below to testify before the court's grand jury. When you arrive, you must remain at the court until the judge or a court officer allows you to leave.

Place: United States District Court 915 Lafayette Boulevard Bridgeport, Connecticut	Date and Time:

Personal appearance is not required if the subpoenaed materials are produced on or before the return date to FBI Special Agent If you have any questions about this subpoena, please contact Special Agent at

b3 -1
b6 -1, 2
b7C -1, 2

Date: 12/18/2012

CLERK OF COURT

Signature of Clerk or Deputy Clerk

The name, address, e-mail, and telephone number of the United States attorney, or assistant United States attorney, who requests this subpoena, are:

Assistant United States Attorney
United States Attorney's Office
1000 Lafayette Boulevard, 10th Floor
Bridgeport, Connecticut 06604

b6 -4
b7C -4

4-NH-2619946-GJ-1A3

PROOF OF SERVICE

This subpoena for *(name of individual or organization)*
was received by me on *(date)* 12/18/12 .

☑ I served the subpoena by delivering a copy to the named person as follows: served via email to
on *(date)* 12/18/2012 ; or

b3 -1
b6 -5
b7C -5

☐ I returned the subpoena unexecuted because:
.

I declare under penalty of perjury that this information is true.

Date: 12/18/2012

b6 -
b7C

Server's signature

FBI Special Agent
Printed name and title

600 State St
New Haven, CT 06511
Server's address

Additional information regarding attempted service, etc:

FD-340 (Rev. 4-11-03)

File Number 4-NH-2619946-GJ -1A4

Field Office Acquiring Evidence New Haven, CT

Serial # of Originating Document ______

Date Received 12/18/2012

From USAO
(Name of Contributor/Interviewee)

______
(Address)

______
(City and State)

By SA [redacted]

b6 -1
b7C -1

To Be Returned ☐ Yes ☑ No

Receipt Given ☐ Yes ☑ No

Grand Jury Material - Disseminate Only Pursuant to Rule 6 (e) Federal Rules of Criminal Procedure

☑ Yes ☐ No

Federal Taxpayer Information (FTI)

☐ Yes ☑ No

Title:

Sandy Hook Elementary

Reference: ______
(Communication Enclosing Material)

Description: ☐ Original notes re interview of

Copy of [redacted] Subpoena & proof of service

b3 -1

UNITED STATES DISTRICT COURT

for the

District of Connecticut

SUBPOENA TO TESTIFY BEFORE A GRAND JURY

To:

YOU ARE COMMANDED to appear in this United States district court at the time, date, and place shown below to testify before the court's grand jury. When you arrive, you must remain at the court until the judge or a court officer allows you to leave.

b3

Place: United States District Court 915 Lafayette Boulevard Bridgeport, Connecticut	Date and Time:

b3
b6
b7

Personal appearance is not required if the subpoenaed materials are produced on or before the return date to FBI Special Agent If you have any questions about this subpoena, please contact Special Agent at

Date: 12/18/2012

CLERK OF COURT

Signature of Clerk or Deputy Clerk

The name, address, e-mail, and telephone number of the United States attorney, or assistant United States attorney, who requests this subpoena, are:

Assistant United States Attorney
United States Attorney's Office
1000 Lafayette Boulevard, 10th Floor
Bridgeport, Connecticut 06604

b6 -4
b7C -

4-NH-2619946-GJ-

PROOF OF SERVICE

This subpoena for *(name of individual or organization)* [redacted] ________
was received by me on *(date)* 12/18/2012 .

b3 -1

☑ I served the subpoena by delivering a copy to the named person as follows: served via emailed on 12/18/2012 to [redacted] and mailed original on *(date)* ______ ; or

☐ I returned the subpoena unexecuted because: ________

I declare under penalty of perjury that this information is true.

Date: 12/18/2012 [redacted]

Server's signature

b6
b7C

[redacted] FBI Special Agent

Printed name and title

600 State Street
New Haven, CT 06511

Server's address

Additional information regarding attempted service, etc:

FD-340 (Rev. 4-11-03)

File Number 4-NH-2619946-GJ-1A5

Field Office Acquiring Evidence New Haven, CT

Serial # of Originating Document

Date Received 12/19/2012

From

By SA

b3 -1
b6 -1,
b7C -1.

To Be Returned ☐ Yes ☑ No

Receipt Given ☐ Yes ☑ No

Grand Jury Material - Disseminate Only Pursuant to Rule 6 (e)
Federal Rules of Criminal Procedure

☑ Yes ☐ No

Federal Taxpayer Information (FTI)

☐ Yes ☑ No

Title:

Sandy Hook Elementary

Reference:
(Communication Enclosing Material)

Description: ☐ Original notes re interview of

Subpoena results from

b3

FD-340 (Rev. 4-11-03)

File Number 4-NH-2619946-GJ - 1A7

Field Office Acquiring Evidence NH

Serial # of Originating Document 24

Date Received 12/20/2012

From

(Name of Contributor/Interviewee)

(Address)

By IOA

b6 -1
b7C -1

To Be Returned ☐ Yes ☐ No

Receipt Given ☐ Yes ☐ No

Grand Jury Material - Disseminate Only Pursuant to Rule 6 (e) Federal Rules of Criminal Procedure

☒ Yes ☐ No

Federal Taxpayer Information (FTI)

☐ Yes ☐ No

Title:

Reference:

(Communication Enclosing Material)

Description: ☐ Original notes re interview of

FGJ Subpoena

b3 -1
b6 -2
b7C -2

IAI

FD-340c (4-11-03)

File Number 4-NH-2619946-GJ 1A-13

Field Office Acquiring Evidence NH

Serial # of Originating Document 43

Date Received 12/21/12

From

(Address)

b3 -1
b6 -1, 5
b7C -1, 5

(City and State)

By SA

To Be Returned ☐ Yes ☒ No

Receipt Given ☒ Yes ☐ No

Grand Jury Material - Disseminate Only Pursuant to Rule 6 (e)
Federal Rules of Criminal Procedure

☒ Yes ☐ No

Federal Taxpayer Information (FTI)

☐ Yes ☒ No

Title:

Reference:

(Communication Enclosing Material)

Description: ☐ Original notes re interview of

- One FD-597 receipt form

-

b6 -1, 5
b7C -1,

Sandy Hook-

FD-340 (Rev. 8-7-97)

1A14

Universal Case File Number 4-NH-2619946-GJ

Field Office Acquiring Evidence NH

Serial # of Originating Document 10 414

Date Received 1/4/2013

From [redacted]
(Name of Contributor)

(Address of Contributor)

(City and State)

By SA [redacted]
(Name of Special Agent)

b3 -1
b6 -1
b7C -1

To Be Returned ☐ Yes ☒ No
Receipt Given ☐ Yes ☒ No
Grand Jury Material - Disseminate Only Pursuant to Rule 6 (e)
Federal Rules of Criminal Procedure
☒ Yes ☐ No

Title:

Reference: FD-302 dated 1/7/2013
(Communication Enclosing Material)

Description: ☐ Original notes re interview of

[redacted]

b3 -1

from FGJ subpoena

FEDERAL BUREAU OF INVESTIGATION
FOI/PA
DELETED PAGE INFORMATION SHEET
Civil Action# 16-cv-02136

Total Deleted Page(s) = 84
Page 8 ~ b6 - 1, 5; b7C - 1, 5; OTHER - Sealed Pursuant to Court Order;
Page 9 ~ b6 - 2, 5; b7C - 2, 5; OTHER - Sealed Pursuant to Court Order;
Page 10 ~ b6 - 2; b7C - 2; OTHER - Sealed Pursuant to Court Order;
Page 12 ~ Duplicate;
Page 13 ~ Duplicate;
Page 15 ~ Duplicate;
Page 16 ~ Duplicate;
Page 17 ~ Duplicate;
Page 18 ~ Duplicate;
Page 19 ~ b6 - 2; b7C - 2;
Page 20 ~ Duplicate;
Page 21 ~ Duplicate;
Page 22 ~ Duplicate;
Page 23 ~ Duplicate;
Page 24 ~ Duplicate;
Page 25 ~ Duplicate;
Page 26 ~ Duplicate;
Page 27 ~ Duplicate;
Page 30 ~ b6 - 1, 2; b7C - 1, 2; OTHER - Sealed Pursuant to Court Order;
Page 31 ~ b6 - 1, 2; b7C - 1, 2; OTHER - Sealed Pursuant to Court Order;
Page 32 ~ b6 - 1, 2; b7C - 1, 2; OTHER - Sealed Pursuant to Court Order;
Page 33 ~ b6 - 1, 2; b7C - 1, 2; OTHER - Sealed Pursuant to Court Order;
Page 34 ~ b6 - 1, 2; b7C - 1, 2; OTHER - Sealed Pursuant to Court Order;
Page 35 ~ OTHER - Sealed Pursuant to Court Order;
Page 36 ~ b6 - 1, 2; b7C - 1, 2; OTHER - Sealed Pursuant to Court Order;
Page 37 ~ b6 - 1, 2; b7C - 1, 2; OTHER - Sealed Pursuant to Court Order;
Page 38 ~ b6 - 2; b7C - 2; OTHER - Sealed Pursuant to Court Order;
Page 39 ~ Duplicate;
Page 40 ~ b6 - 2; b7C - 2; OTHER - Sealed Pursuant to Court Order;
Page 41 ~ b6 - 1, 2; b7C - 1, 2; OTHER - Sealed Pursuant to Court Order;
Page 42 ~ b6 - 1, 2; b7C - 1, 2; OTHER - Sealed Pursuant to Court Order;
Page 43 ~ OTHER - Sealed Pursuant to Court Order;
Page 44 ~ b6 - 2; b7C - 2; OTHER - Sealed Pursuant to Court Order;
Page 45 ~ b6 - 2; b7C - 2; OTHER - Sealed Pursuant to Court Order;
Page 46 ~ b6 - 2; b7C - 2; OTHER - Sealed Pursuant to Court Order;
Page 47 ~ b6 - 2; b7C - 2; OTHER - Sealed Pursuant to Court Order;
Page 48 ~ b6 - 2; b7C - 2; OTHER - Sealed Pursuant to Court Order;
Page 49 ~ b6 - 2; b7C - 2; OTHER - Sealed Pursuant to Court Order;
Page 50 ~ b6 - 2; b7C - 2; OTHER - Sealed Pursuant to Court Order;
Page 51 ~ b6 - 2; b7C - 2; OTHER - Sealed Pursuant to Court Order;
Page 52 ~ b6 - 2; b7C - 2; OTHER - Sealed Pursuant to Court Order;
Page 53 ~ b6 - 2; b7C - 2; OTHER - Sealed Pursuant to Court Order;
Page 54 ~ b6 - 2; b7C - 2; OTHER - Sealed Pursuant to Court Order;
Page 55 ~ b6 - 2; b7C - 2; OTHER - Sealed Pursuant to Court Order;
Page 56 ~ b6 - 2; b7C - 2; OTHER - Sealed Pursuant to Court Order;
Page 57 ~ b6 - 1, 2; b7C - 1, 2; OTHER - Sealed Pursuant to Court Order;
Page 58 ~ b6 - 2; b7C - 2; OTHER - Sealed Pursuant to Court Order;
Page 59 ~ b6 - 2; b7C - 2; OTHER - Sealed Pursuant to Court Order;

Page 60 ~ b6 - 2; b7C - 2; OTHER - Sealed Pursuant to Court Order;
Page 61 ~ b6 - 2; b7C - 2; OTHER - Sealed Pursuant to Court Order;
Page 62 ~ b6 - 2; b7C - 2; OTHER - Sealed Pursuant to Court Order;
Page 63 ~ b6 - 2; b7C - 2; OTHER - Sealed Pursuant to Court Order;
Page 64 ~ b6 - 2; b7C - 2; OTHER - Sealed Pursuant to Court Order;
Page 65 ~ b6 - 2; b7C - 2; OTHER - Sealed Pursuant to Court Order;
Page 66 ~ OTHER - Sealed Pursuant to Court Order;
Page 67 ~ b6 - 2; b7C - 2; b7E - 7; OTHER - Sealed Pursuant to Court Order;
Page 68 ~ OTHER - Sealed Pursuant to Court Order;
Page 69 ~ OTHER - Sealed Pursuant to Court Order;
Page 70 ~ b6 - 1, 2; b7C - 1, 2; OTHER - Sealed Pursuant to Court Order;
Page 71 ~ b6 - 1, 2; b7C - 1, 2; OTHER - Sealed Pursuant to Court Order;
Page 72 ~ b6 - 1, 2; b7C - 1, 2; OTHER - Sealed Pursuant to Court Order;
Page 73 ~ b6 - 1, 2; b7C - 1, 2; OTHER - Sealed Pursuant to Court Order;
Page 74 ~ b6 - 1, 2; b7C - 1, 2; OTHER - Sealed Pursuant to Court Order;
Page 75 ~ b6 - 1, 2; b7C - 1, 2; OTHER - Sealed Pursuant to Court Order;
Page 76 ~ b6 - 2; b7C - 2; OTHER - Sealed Pursuant to Court Order;
Page 77 ~ b6 - 2; b7C - 2; OTHER - Sealed Pursuant to Court Order;
Page 78 ~ b6 - 2; b7C - 2; OTHER - Sealed Pursuant to Court Order;
Page 79 ~ b6 - 2; b7C - 2; OTHER - Sealed Pursuant to Court Order;
Page 80 ~ b6 - 2; b7C - 2; OTHER - Sealed Pursuant to Court Order;
Page 81 ~ b6 - 2; b7C - 2; OTHER - Sealed Pursuant to Court Order;
Page 82 ~ b6 - 2; b7C - 2; OTHER - Sealed Pursuant to Court Order;
Page 83 ~ b6 - 2; b7C - 2; OTHER - Sealed Pursuant to Court Order;
Page 84 ~ b6 - 2; b7C - 2; OTHER - Sealed Pursuant to Court Order;
Page 85 ~ b6 - 2; b7C - 2; OTHER - Sealed Pursuant to Court Order;
Page 86 ~ b6 - 2; b7C - 2; OTHER - Sealed Pursuant to Court Order;
Page 87 ~ b6 - 2; b7C - 2; OTHER - Sealed Pursuant to Court Order;
Page 88 ~ b6 - 2; b7C - 2; OTHER - Sealed Pursuant to Court Order;
Page 89 ~ b6 - 2; b7C - 2; OTHER - Sealed Pursuant to Court Order;
Page 90 ~ b6 - 2; b7C - 2; OTHER - Sealed Pursuant to Court Order;
Page 91 ~ b6 - 2; b7C - 2; OTHER - Sealed Pursuant to Court Order;
Page 92 ~ b6 - 2; b7C - 2; OTHER - Sealed Pursuant to Court Order;
Page 93 ~ b6 - 2; b7C - 2; OTHER - Sealed Pursuant to Court Order;
Page 94 ~ b6 - 2; b7C - 2; OTHER - Sealed Pursuant to Court Order;
Page 95 ~ b6 - 2; b7C - 2; OTHER - Sealed Pursuant to Court Order;

XXXXXXXXXXXXXXXXXXXXXXXX
X Deleted Page(s) X
X No Duplication Fee X
X For this Page X
XXXXXXXXXXXXXXXXXXXXXXXX

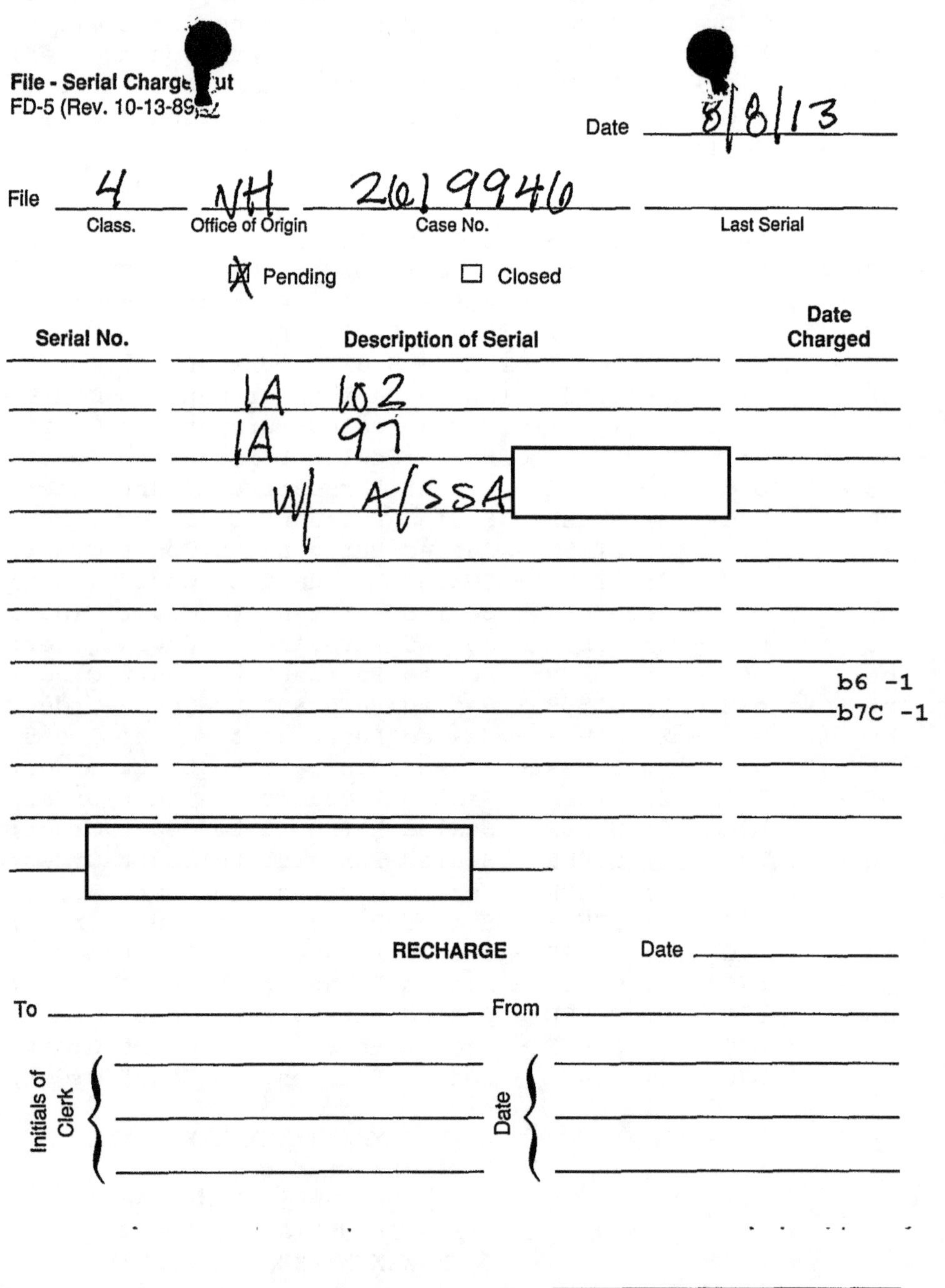

File - Serial Charge Out
FD-5 (Rev. 10-13-89)

Date 8/8/13

File 4 | NH | 261 9946 |
Class. | Office of Origin | Case No. | Last Serial

☒ Pending ☐ Closed

Serial No.	Description of Serial	Date Charged
	1A 102	
	1A 97	
	w/ A/SSA [redacted]	

b6 -1
b7C -1

[redacted]

RECHARGE Date

To From

Initials of Clerk

Date

Date charged

Employee

Location

FPI-RBK

Sandy Hook-3410

FD-340a (Rev. 11-12-89)

(Title) ______________________

(File No.) ______________________

Item	Date Filed	To be returned Yes	No		Disposition

FD-340 (Rev. 8-7-97)

1A97

Universal Case File Number 4-NH-2619946

Field Office Acquiring Evidence NH

Serial # of Originating Document 153

Date Received 12/20/12

From ______ (Name of Contributor)

b6 -1
b7C -1

(Address of Contributor)

OTHER Sealed Pursuant to Court Order

By SA ______ (Name of Special Agent)

To Be Returned ☐ Yes ☐ No
Receipt Given ☐ Yes ☐ No
Grand Jury Material - Disseminate Only Pursuant to Rule 6 (e) Federal Rules of Criminal Procedure
☐ Yes ☐ No

Title:

Reference: FD-302 dated 1/11/13
(Communication Enclosing Material)

Description: ☐ Original notes re interview of

b6 -2
b7C -2
OTHER Sealed Pursuant to Court Order

Duplicate 1A Content

FD-340 (Rev. 4-11-03)

File Number 4-NH-2619946 1A99

Field Office Acquiring Evidence NK

Serial # of Originating Document 62

Date Received 12/14/2012

From

b6 -1, 2
b7C -1, 2

By SA

To Be Returned ☐ Yes ☒ No

Receipt Given ☐ Yes ☒ No

Grand Jury Material - Disseminate Only Pursuant to Rule 6 (e)
Federal Rules of Criminal Procedure

☐ Yes ☒ No

Federal Taxpayer Information (FTI)

☐ Yes ☒ No

Title: UNSUB
SANDY HOOK ELEMENTARY SCHOOL
12 DICKENSON ST- SANDY HOOK, CT- VICTIM
FIREARMS ACT
OO:NH

Reference:
(Communication Enclosing Material)

Description: ☒ Original notes re interview of
12/14/2012

b6 -2
b7C -2

FD-340 (Rev. 4-11-03)

File Number 4-NH-2619946 1A100

Field Office Acquiring Evidence NK

Serial # of Originating Document 50

Date Received 12/14/2012

From

(City and State)

By SA

To Be Returned ☐ Yes ☒ No

Receipt Given ☐ Yes ☒ No

Grand Jury Material - Disseminate Only Pursuant to Rule 6 (e)
Federal Rules of Criminal Procedure

☐ Yes ☒ No

Federal Taxpayer Information (FTI)

☐ Yes ☒ No

Title: UNSUB
SANDY HOOK ELEMENTARY SCHOOL
12 DICKENSON ST. SANDY HOOK, CT - VICTIM
FIREARMS ACT
OO:NH

Reference:

(Communication Enclosing Material)

Description: ☒ Original notes re interview of / 12/14/2012

b6 -1, 2
b7C -1, 2

b6 -2
b7C -2

FD-340c (4-11-03)

File Number 4-NH-2619946 1A102

Field Office Acquiring Evidence [redacted]

Serial # of Originating Document 161

Date Received 12/23/2012

From [redacted]

(Name of Contributor/Interviewee)

[redacted]

(City and State)

By SA [redacted]

To Be Returned ☐ Yes ☑ No

Receipt Given ☑ Yes ☐ No

Grand Jury Material - Disseminate Only Pursuant to Rule 6 (e)
Federal Rules of Criminal Procedure

☑ Yes ☐ No

b6 -1, 2
b7C -1, 2
OTHER Sealed Pursuant to Court Order

Federal Taxpayer Information (FTI)

☐ Yes ☑ No

Title: UNSUB(S);
SANDY HOOK ELEMENTARY SCHOOL
12 DICKENSON STREET
SANDY HOOK, CT - VICTIM

Reference: EC
(Communication Enclosing Material)

Description: ☐ Original notes re interview of [redacted]

FEDERAL BUREAU OF INVESTIGATION
FOI/PA
DELETED PAGE INFORMATION SHEET
Civil Action# 16-cv-02136

Total Deleted Page(s) = 130
Page 6 ~ Duplicate;
Page 7 ~ Duplicate;
Page 8 ~ Duplicate;
Page 9 ~ Duplicate;
Page 10 ~ Duplicate;
Page 11 ~ Duplicate;
Page 12 ~ Duplicate;
Page 13 ~ Duplicate;
Page 14 ~ Duplicate;
Page 15 ~ Duplicate;
Page 16 ~ Duplicate;
Page 17 ~ Duplicate;
Page 18 ~ Duplicate;
Page 19 ~ Duplicate;
Page 20 ~ Duplicate;
Page 21 ~ Duplicate;
Page 22 ~ Duplicate;
Page 26 ~ Duplicate;
Page 27 ~ Duplicate;
Page 28 ~ Duplicate;
Page 29 ~ Duplicate;
Page 30 ~ Duplicate;
Page 31 ~ Duplicate;
Page 33 ~ Duplicate;
Page 34 ~ Duplicate;
Page 35 ~ Duplicate;
Page 36 ~ Duplicate;
Page 37 ~ Duplicate;
Page 38 ~ Duplicate;
Page 39 ~ Duplicate;
Page 40 ~ Duplicate;
Page 41 ~ Duplicate;
Page 42 ~ Duplicate;
Page 43 ~ Duplicate;
Page 45 ~ Duplicate;
Page 46 ~ Duplicate;
Page 47 ~ Duplicate;
Page 48 ~ Duplicate;
Page 49 ~ Duplicate;
Page 50 ~ Duplicate;
Page 51 ~ Duplicate;
Page 52 ~ Duplicate;
Page 53 ~ Duplicate;
Page 61 ~ Duplicate;
Page 63 ~ Duplicate;
Page 64 ~ Duplicate;
Page 65 ~ Duplicate;
Page 66 ~ Duplicate;

Page 67 ~ Duplicate;
Page 68 ~ Duplicate;
Page 69 ~ Duplicate;
Page 71 ~ Duplicate;
Page 72 ~ Duplicate;
Page 73 ~ Duplicate;
Page 74 ~ Duplicate;
Page 75 ~ Duplicate;
Page 76 ~ Duplicate;
Page 77 ~ Duplicate;
Page 78 ~ Duplicate;
Page 80 ~ Duplicate;
Page 81 ~ Duplicate;
Page 82 ~ Duplicate;
Page 83 ~ Duplicate;
Page 84 ~ Duplicate;
Page 85 ~ Duplicate;
Page 86 ~ Duplicate;
Page 87 ~ Duplicate;
Page 88 ~ Duplicate;
Page 90 ~ Duplicate;
Page 91 ~ Duplicate;
Page 92 ~ Duplicate;
Page 93 ~ Duplicate;
Page 95 ~ b6 - 1, 2; b7C - 1, 2; b7E - 6, 8; OTHER - Sealed Pursuant to Court Order;
Page 96 ~ b6 - 1, 2; b7C - 1, 2; b7E - 6, 8; OTHER - Sealed Pursuant to Court Order;
Page 97 ~ b6 - 1; b7C - 1; b7E - 6, 8; OTHER - Sealed Pursuant to Court Order;
Page 98 ~ b6 - 1; b7C - 1; b7E - 6, 8; OTHER - Sealed Pursuant to Court Order;
Page 99 ~ b6 - 1, 2; b7C - 1, 2; b7E - 6, 8; OTHER - Sealed Pursuant to Court Order;
Page 100 ~ b6 - 1; b7C - 1; b7E - 6, 8; OTHER - Sealed Pursuant to Court Order;
Page 101 ~ b6 - 1, 2; b7C - 1, 2; b7E - 6, 8; OTHER - Sealed Pursuant to Court Order;
Page 102 ~ b6 - 1; b7C - 1; b7E - 6, 8; OTHER - Sealed Pursuant to Court Order;
Page 103 ~ b6 - 1, 2; b7C - 1, 2; b7E - 6, 8; OTHER - Sealed Pursuant to Court Order;
Page 104 ~ b6 - 1, 2; b7C - 1, 2; b7E - 6, 8; OTHER - Sealed Pursuant to Court Order;
Page 105 ~ b6 - 1, 2; b7C - 1, 2; b7E - 6, 8; OTHER - Sealed Pursuant to Court Order;
Page 106 ~ b6 - 1, 2; b7C - 1, 2; b7E - 6, 8; OTHER - Sealed Pursuant to Court Order;
Page 107 ~ b6 - 1, 2; b7C - 1, 2; b7E - 6, 8; OTHER - Sealed Pursuant to Court Order;
Page 108 ~ b6 - 1, 2; b7C - 1, 2; b7E - 6, 8; OTHER - Sealed Pursuant to Court Order;
Page 109 ~ b6 - 1, 2; b7C - 1, 2; b7E - 6, 8; OTHER - Sealed Pursuant to Court Order;

Page 110 ~ b6 - 1, 2; b7C - 1, 2; b7E - 6, 8; OTHER - Sealed Pursuant to Court Order;
Page 111 ~ b6 - 1, 2; b7C - 1, 2; b7E - 6, 8; OTHER - Sealed Pursuant to Court Order;
Page 112 ~ b6 - 1, 2; b7C - 1, 2; b7E - 6, 8; OTHER - Sealed Pursuant to Court Order;
Page 113 ~ b6 - 1, 2; b7C - 1, 2; b7E - 6, 8; OTHER - Sealed Pursuant to Court Order;
Page 114 ~ b6 - 1, 2; b7C - 1, 2; b7E - 6, 8; OTHER - Sealed Pursuant to Court Order;
Page 115 ~ b6 - 1, 2; b7C - 1, 2; b7E - 6, 8; OTHER - Sealed Pursuant to Court Order;
Page 116 ~ b6 - 1, 2; b7C - 1, 2; b7E - 6, 8; OTHER - Sealed Pursuant to Court Order;
Page 117 ~ b6 - 1, 2; b7C - 1, 2; b7E - 6, 8; OTHER - Sealed Pursuant to Court Order;
Page 118 ~ b6 - 1, 2; b7C - 1, 2; b7E - 6, 8; OTHER - Sealed Pursuant to Court Order;
Page 119 ~ b6 - 1, 2; b7C - 1, 2; b7E - 6, 8; OTHER - Sealed Pursuant to Court Order;
Page 120 ~ b6 - 1, 2; b7C - 1, 2; b7E - 6, 8; OTHER - Sealed Pursuant to Court Order;
Page 121 ~ b6 - 1, 2; b7C - 1, 2; b7E - 6, 8; OTHER - Sealed Pursuant to Court Order;
Page 122 ~ b6 - 1; b7C - 1; b7E - 6, 8; OTHER - Sealed Pursuant to Court Order;
Page 123 ~ b6 - 1, 2; b7C - 1, 2; b7E - 6, 8; OTHER - Sealed Pursuant to Court Order;
Page 124 ~ b6 - 1, 2; b7C - 1, 2; b7E - 6, 8; OTHER - Sealed Pursuant to Court Order;
Page 129 ~ b6 - 1, 2; b7C - 1, 2; b7E - 6, 8; OTHER - Sealed Pursuant to Court Order;
Page 135 ~ Duplicate;
Page 136 ~ Duplicate;
Page 137 ~ Duplicate;
Page 138 ~ Duplicate;
Page 139 ~ Duplicate;
Page 140 ~ Duplicate;
Page 141 ~ Duplicate;
Page 142 ~ Duplicate;
Page 143 ~ b6 - 5; b7C - 5;
Page 144 ~ Duplicate;
Page 145 ~ Duplicate;
Page 146 ~ Duplicate;
Page 147 ~ Duplicate;
Page 148 ~ Duplicate;
Page 149 ~ Duplicate;
Page 150 ~ Duplicate;
Page 151 ~ Duplicate;
Page 152 ~ Duplicate;
Page 153 ~ Duplicate;
Page 154 ~ Duplicate;
Page 155 ~ Duplicate;
Page 156 ~ Duplicate;

Page 158 ~ Duplicate;
Page 159 ~ Duplicate;
Page 160 ~ Duplicate;
Page 161 ~ Duplicate;
Page 162 ~ Duplicate;

XXXXXXXXXXXXXXXXXXXXXXXX
X Deleted Page(s) X
X No Duplication Fee X
X For this Page X
XXXXXXXXXXXXXXXXXXXXXXXX

b6 -1, 2
b7C -1, 2
b7E -7
OTHER Sealed Pursuant t

Acquired On	Summary	Recorc
2012-12-14	(U) [redacted] nterview	Digital
2013-01-07	(U) FD-759	Digital
2013-01-15	(U) 1-Lab Report, 1-CoC, 1-Comm Log, 1-Case Note, 1-ECS Search Slip, 2-Shipping Invoices, 1-Review Form, 1packet-Legal Authority, 4-Requ	Physica
2012-12-23	(U//FOUO) Interview notes from [redacted]	Physica
2013-01-25	(U [redacted] fd-597 for cell phone	Physica
2013-01-28	(U) Six total pages of Notes/Admin Docs re: CART exam	Digital
2013-01-28	(U) Notes and Admin pages from CART exam	Digital
2013-01-28	(U) Nine total pages of admin docs and notes	Digital
2013-01-30	(U [redacted]	Physica
2013-01-30	(U) Case and Admin notes	Digital
2012-12-22	(U) [redacted]	Physica
2013-02-07	(U) [redacted]	Digital
2012-12-23	(U//FOUO [redacted]	Physica
2013-02-14	(U) Reports fror [redacted]	Physica
2013-02-15	(U [redacted]	Digital
2013-02-15	(U [redacted]	Digital
2013-02-07	(U) [redacted]	Physica
2013-02-07	(U) [redacted]	Physica
2012-12-21	(U) [redacted]	Physica
2013-02-27	(U//FOUO) FD-597 regarding transfer of six (6) items of evidence from Connecticut State Police (CSP) to FBI New Haven custody.	Digital
2013-02-27	(U//FOUO) Handwritten Notes	Digital
2013-01-04	(U) Notes for Forensic Processing	Digital
2013-01-23	(U) Notes of forensic processing	Digital
2013-03-05	(U) Emails fron [redacted]	Digital
2013-03-25	(U [redacted]	Physica
2013-03-13	null RESTRICTED - Access Denied	Digital
2012-12-14	(U) Evidence Details and FD-1004s.	Digital
2013-02-04	(U [redacted]	Digital
2013-04-29	(U) Case and administrative notes	Digital
2013-05-03	(U) Case notes	Digital
2013-05-13	(U) Case and Administrative notes	Digital
2013-05-14	(U) Case notes	Digital
2013-06-06	(U) Administrative and Case notes	Digital

FD-340a (Rev. 1-27-03)

(Title) 1A's

(File No.) 4-NH-2619946

Item	Date Filed	To be returned Yes	No		Disposition

FD-340 (Rev. 4-11-03)

File Number 4-NH-2619946 - 1A 109

Field Office Acquiring Evidence LA

Serial # of Originating Document 4-NH-2619946 - 167

Date Received 12/14/2012

From self generated
(Name of Contributor/Interviewee)

(Address)

(City and State)

By [redacted] b6 -1 b7C -1

To Be Returned ☐ Yes ☑ No

Receipt Given ☐ Yes ☑ No

Grand Jury Material - Disseminate Only Pursuant to Rule 6 (e) Federal Rules of Criminal Procedure

☐ Yes ☑ No

Federal Taxpayer Information (FTI)

☐ Yes ☑ No

Title: UNSUB(S)
Sandy Hook Elementary School
12 Dickinson St, Sandy Hook, CT-Victim

Reference:
(Communication Enclosing Material)

Description: ☑ Original notes re interview of

1) [redacted]
2) [redacted] b6 -1, 2, 6 b7C -1, 2, 6
3) FD-472 (2) agents
4) FD-759

1A113

FD-340 (Rev. 4-11-03)

File Number 4-NH-2619946

Field Office Acquiring Evidence NK

Serial # of Originating Document 178

Date Received 1/23/13

From SA [redacted] /Interviewee)

(Address)

b6 -1
b7C -1

(City and State)

By SA [redacted]

To Be Returned ☐ Yes ☐ No

Receipt Given ☐ Yes ☐ No

Grand Jury Material - Disseminate Only Pursuant to Rule 6 (e) Federal Rules of Criminal Procedure

☐ Yes ☐ No

Federal Taxpayer Information (FTI)

☐ Yes ☐ No

Title:

Reference: (Communication Enclosing Material)

b6 -1, 2
b7C -1, 2

[redacted] return

FD-597

U. S. GOVERNMENT PRINTING OFFICE: 2009—358-724

FD-597 (Rev 8-11-94)

UNITED STATES DEPARTMENT OF JUSTICE
FEDERAL BUREAU OF INVESTIGATION
Receipt for Property Received/Returned/Released/Seized

File # 4-NH-2619946-1B3

On (date) 1/22/13

item(s) listed below were:
- [ ] Received From
- [ ] Returned To
- [x] Released To
- [ ] Seized

(Name)

(Street Address)

(City)

Description of Item(s)

1/22/13

b6 -1, 2
b7C -1, 2

01-22-2013

Received By

Received From: (Signature)

FD-340 (Rev. 4-11-03)

File Number 4-NH-2619946 -1A 114

Field Office Acquiring Evidence NH

Serial # of Originating Document 180

Date Received 1/28/13

From CART Process
(Name of Contributor/Interviewee)

(Address)

(City and State)

By [redacted]

b6 -1
b7C -1

To Be Returned ☐ Yes ☐ No

Receipt Given ☐ Yes ☐ No

Grand Jury Material - Disseminate Only Pursuant to Rule 6 (e)
Federal Rules of Criminal Procedure

☐ Yes ☐ No

Federal Taxpayer Information (FTI)

☐ Yes ☐ No

Title: SHES

Reference:
(Communication Enclosing Material)

Description: ☑ Original notes ~~re interview of~~ CART exam three pages notes, three Admin pages, total six pages

FD-340 (Rev. 4-11-03)

File Number 4-NH-2619946 - 1A 115

Field Office Acquiring Evidence NH

Serial # of Originating Document 181

Date Received 1/28/13

From CART Process
(Name of Contributor/Interviewee)

(Address)

(City and State)

By [redacted]

b6 -1
b7C -1

To Be Returned ☐ Yes ☐ No

Receipt Given ☐ Yes ☐ No

Grand Jury Material - Disseminate Only Pursuant to Rule 6 (e)
Federal Rules of Criminal Procedure

☐ Yes ☐ No

Federal Taxpayer Information (FTI)

☐ Yes ☐ No

Title: SHES

Reference:
(Communication Enclosing Material)

Description: ☒ Original notes re ~~interview of~~ CART exam
three Admin pages, eight Notes' pages,
total 11 pages

H

FD-340 (Rev. 4-11-03)

File Number 4-NH-2619946 1A116

Field Office Acquiring Evidence NH

Serial # of Originating Document 182

Date Received 1/28/13

From CART Process
(Name of Contributor/Interviewee)

(Address)

(City and State)

b6 -1
b7C -1

By [redacted]

To Be Returned ☐ Yes ☐ No

Receipt Given ☐ Yes ☐ No

Grand Jury Material - Disseminate Only Pursuant to Rule 6 (e) Federal Rules of Criminal Procedure

☐ Yes ☐ No

Federal Taxpayer Information (FTI)

☐ Yes ☐ No

Title: SHES

Reference:
(Communication Enclosing Material)

Description: ☒ Original notes re ~~interview~~ of CART exam one page notes, eight admin pages, total of nine pages

FD-340 (Rev. 4-11-03)

File Number 4-NH-2619946 - 1A117

Field Office Acquiring Evidence New Haven

Serial # of Originating Document 184

Date Received January 30, 2013

From ____________________
(Name of Contributor/Interviewee)

____________________ b6 -1
(Address) b7C -1

____
(City and State)

By SA ____________________

To Be Returned ☐ Yes ☑ No

Receipt Given ☐ Yes ☑ No

Grand Jury Material - Disseminate Only Pursuant to Rule 6 (e) Federal Rules of Criminal Procedure

☐ Yes ☑ No

Federal Taxpayer Information (FTI)

☐ Yes ☑ No

Title: UNSUB(S)
Sandy Hook Elementary School
12 Dickenson St, Sandy Hook, CT - Victim
Firearms Act.
OO:NH

Reference: EC, serial #184
(Communication Enclosing Material)

Description: ☐ ~~Original notes re interview of~~

b6 -2
b7C -2
OTHER Sealed Pursuant to Court Order

FD-340 (Rev. 8-7-97)

Universal Case File Number 4-NH-2619946 1A124

Field Office Acquiring Evidence NH

Serial # of Originating Document #196

Date Received 2/15/13

From [redacted] (Name of Contributor)

(Address of Contributor)

b6 -1, 6
b7C -1, 6

By SA [redacted] (Name of Special Agent)

To Be Returned ☐ Yes ☒ No

Receipt Given ☐ Yes ☒ No

Grand Jury Material - Disseminate Only Pursuant to Rule 6 (e)
Federal Rules of Criminal Procedure
☐ Yes ☒ No

Title:

Reference: EC dated 2/19/13
(Communication Enclosing Material)

Description: ☐ Original notes re interview of [redacted]

b6 -6
b7C -6

FD-340 (Rev. 4-11-03)

File Number 4-NH-2619946 1A-128

Field Office Acquiring Evidence NH

Serial # of Originating Document 202

Date Received 2/27/2013

From Connecticut State Police
(Name of Contributor/Interviewee)

(Address)

(City and State)

By SA [redacted] b6 -1 b7C -1

To Be Returned. ☐ Yes ☐ No

Receipt Given ☐ Yes ☐ No

Grand Jury Material - Disseminate Only Pursuant to Rule 6 (e)
Federal Rules of Criminal Procedure

☐ Yes ☐ No

Federal Taxpayer Information (FTI)

☐ Yes ☐ No

Title:

Reference: Evidence Log
(Communication Enclosing Material)

Description: ☐ Original notes re interview of

FD-597 re: six items of evidence transferred from CSP to FBINH.

FD-340 (Rev. 4-11-03)

File Number 4-NH-2619946 - 1A129

Field Office Acquiring Evidence NH

Serial # of Originating Document 203

Date Received 2/27/2013

From ______________________
(Name of Contributor/Interviewee)

____
(Address)

____
(City and State)

b6 -1
b7C -1

By SA [redacted]

To Be Returned ☐ Yes ☐ No

Receipt Given ☐ Yes ☐ No

Grand Jury Material - Disseminate Only Pursuant to Rule 6 (e)
Federal Rules of Criminal Procedure
☐ Yes ☐ No

Federal Taxpayer Information (FTI)
☐ Yes ☐ No

Title:

Reference: FD-302
(Communication Enclosing Material)

Description: ☒ Original notes re ~~interview of~~
Analysis of LANZA home telephone answering system.

FD-340 (Rev. 4-11-03)

1A130

File Number 4-NH-2619946

Field Office Acquiring Evidence NH

Serial # of Originating Document 206

Date Received 12/17/12

From ____________________
(Name of Contributor/Interviewee)

____
(Address)

____
(City and State)

By [redacted]

b6 -1
b7C -1

To Be Returned ☐ Yes ☑ No

Receipt Given ☐ Yes ☑ No

Grand Jury Material - Disseminate Only Pursuant to Rule 6 (e)
Federal Rules of Criminal Procedure

☐ Yes ☑ No

Federal Taxpayer Information (FTI)

☐ Yes ☑ No

Title: Sandy Hook Elementary School
12 Dickinson St, Sandy Hook, CT

Reference: ____________________
(Communication Enclosing Material)

Description: ☑ Original notes [redacted]

[redacted]

b6 -2
b7C -2
b7E -6,

FD-340 (Rev. 4-11-03)

1A131

File Number 4-NH-2619946

Field Office Acquiring Evidence NH

Serial # of Originating Document 208

Date Received 1/23/13

From ______
(Name of Contributor/Interviewee)

______
(Address)

______
(City and State)

By [redacted]

b6 -1
b7C -1

To Be Returned ☐ Yes ☑ No

Receipt Given ☐ Yes ☑ No

Grand Jury Material - Disseminate Only Pursuant to Rule 6 (e)
Federal Rules of Criminal Procedure

☐ Yes ☑ No

Federal Taxpayer Information (FTI)

☐ Yes ☑ No

Title: Sandy Hook Elementary School
12 Dickinson St, Sandy Hook CT

Reference: ______
(Communication Enclosing Material)

Description: ☑ Original notes re ~~interview~~ Imaging of Game Systems

A) Admin Notes - 1 Page
B) Case Notes - 8 Pages
9 Total Pages

FD-340 (Rev. 4-11-03)

1A - 134

File Number 356A-NH-2619946

Field Office Acquiring Evidence NH

Serial # of Originating Document 213

Date Received 3/13/13

From ______________________
(Name of Contributor/Interviewee)

____
(Address)

____
(City and State)

By 10A [redacted] b6 -1 b7C -1

To Be Returned ☐ Yes ☐ No

Receipt Given ☐ Yes ☐ No

Grand Jury Material - Disseminate Only Pursuant to Rule 6 (e)
Federal Rules of Criminal Procedure

☐ Yes ☐ No

Federal Taxpayer Information (FTI)

☐ Yes ☐ No

Title:
Adam Peter Lanza
Sandy Hook Elementary School, CT-Victim

Reference: ______________________
(Communication Enclosing Material)

Description: ☐ Original notes re intervie[redacted] b3

Grand Jury Subp. [redacted]

FD-340c (4-11-03)

File Number 4-NH-2619946 - 1A 122

Field Office Acquiring Evidence NH

Serial # of Originating Document 194

Date Received 2/14/13

From ______________________
(Name of Contributor/Interviewee)

b6 -1
b7C -1
(Address) OTHER Sealed Pursuant to Court Order

(City and State)

By 54 ______________________

To Be Returned ☐ Yes ☐ No

Receipt Given ☐ Yes ☐ No

Grand Jury Material - Disseminate Only Pursuant to Rule 6 (e)
Federal Rules of Criminal Procedure
☐ Yes ☐ No

Federal Taxpayer Information (FTI)
☐ Yes ☐ No

Title:

Reference: EC dated 2/14/13
(Communication Enclosing Material)

Description: ☐ Original notes re interview of

OTHER Sealed Pursuant to Court Order

FD-340c (4-11-03)

File Number 4-NH-2619946 1A 135

Field Office Acquiring Evidence

Serial # of Originating Document 2

Date Received 1/7/13

From FCC

(Name of Contributor/Interviewee)

(Address)

(City and State)

By [redacted] b6 -1 b7C -1

To Be Returned ☐ Yes ☐ No

Receipt Given ☐ Yes ☐ No

Grand Jury Material - Disseminate Only Pursuant to Rule 6 (e)
Federal Rules of Criminal Procedure

☐ Yes ☐ No

Federal Taxpayer Information (FTI)

☐ Yes ☐ No

Title:

Reference:

(Communication Enclosing Material)

Description: ☐ Original notes re interview of

FD192 for 1B1, 1B4-1B5, 1B7, 1B8 Returned

FD-340c (4-11-03)

File Number 4-NH-2619946 1A136

Field Office Acquiring Evidence

Serial # of Originating Document 220

Date Received 2/4/13

From ECC-NK

(Name of Contributor/Interviewee)

(Address)

(City and State)

By [ ]

b6 -1
b7C -1

To Be Returned ☐ Yes ☐ No

Receipt Given ☐ Yes ☐ No

Grand Jury Material - Disseminate Only Pursuant to Rule 6 (e) Federal Rules of Criminal Procedure

☐ Yes ☐ No

Federal Taxpayer Information (FTI)

☐ Yes ☐ No

Title:

Reference:

(Communication Enclosing Material)

Description: ☐ Original notes re interview of

FD192 for 1B3- Returned

FD-1057 (Rev. 5-8-10)

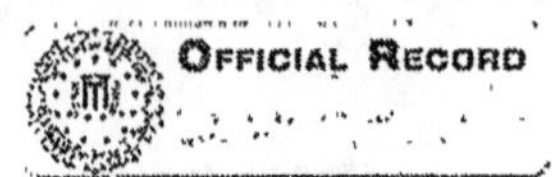

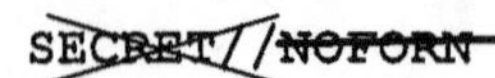

FEDERAL BUREAU OF INVESTIGATION

Electronic Communication

Title: (U) Subfile Opening Document **Date:** 12/28/2012

From: NEW HAVEN
NH-BRA2
Contact: [redacted]

Approved By: [redacted]

Drafted By: [redacted]

b6 -1
b7C -1

Case ID #: 4-NH-2619946-OTD (U) UNSUB(S)
Sandy Hook Elementary School
12 Dickinson St, Sandy Hook, CT-Victim
Firearms Act.
OO:NH

Synopsis: (U) Request to open subfile.

Reason: 1.4(c)
Derived From: Multiple
Sources
Declassify On: 20371228

Details:

Request to open subfile to request assistance with digital evidence.

♦♦

SECRET//NOFORN

4-NH-2619946-

SERIAL 1

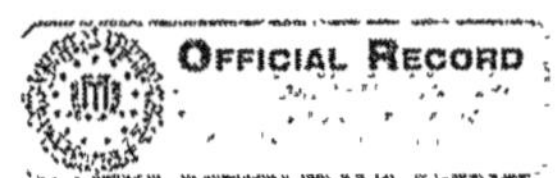

FD-1057 (Rev. 5-8-10)

FEDERAL BUREAU OF INVESTIGATION

Electronic Communication

Title: (U) (S//NF) Request for Operational Technology Division (OTD) assistance. **Date:** 12/28/2012

To: [redacted]

b6 -1
b7C -1

From: NEW HAVEN
NH-BRA2
Contact: [redacted]

Approved By: [redacted]

Drafted By: [redacted]

Case ID #: 4-NH-2619946-OTD (U) UNSUB(S)
Sandy Hook Elementary School
12 Dickinson St, Sandy Hook, CT-Victim
Firearms Act.
OO:NH

Synopsis: (U) (S//NF) Request for Operational Technology Division (OTD) assistance.

Reason: 1.4(c)
Derived From: Multiple Sources
Declassify On: 20371228

Administrative Notes: (U) (S//NF) In reference to SVTC held on 12/28/2012 regarding captioned matter.

Details:

SECRET//NOFORN

4-NH-2619946-OTD
SERIAL 2

Title: (U) ~~(S//NF)~~ Request for Operational Technology Division (OTD) assistance.
Re: 4-NH-2619946-OTD, 12/28/2012

(U) ~~(S//NF)~~ New Haven requests OTD assistance to complete analysis of digital evidence seized in this matter. On December 19, 2012, New Haven requested **b7E -6, -9**

♦♦

FEDERAL BUREAU OF INVESTIGATION
FOI/PA
DELETED PAGE INFORMATION SHEET
Civil Action# 16-cv-02136

Total Deleted Page(s) = 63
Page 5 ~ Duplicate;
Page 6 ~ Duplicate;
Page 7 ~ Duplicate;
Page 8 ~ Duplicate;
Page 9 ~ Duplicate;
Page 10 ~ Duplicate;
Page 11 ~ Duplicate;
Page 12 ~ Duplicate;
Page 13 ~ Duplicate;
Page 14 ~ Duplicate;
Page 15 ~ Duplicate;
Page 16 ~ Duplicate;
Page 17 ~ Duplicate;
Page 18 ~ Duplicate;
Page 19 ~ Duplicate;
Page 20 ~ Duplicate;
Page 21 ~ Duplicate;
Page 22 ~ Duplicate;
Page 23 ~ Duplicate;
Page 24 ~ Duplicate;
Page 25 ~ Duplicate;
Page 26 ~ Duplicate;
Page 27 ~ Duplicate;
Page 28 ~ Duplicate;
Page 29 ~ Duplicate;
Page 30 ~ Duplicate;
Page 31 ~ Duplicate;
Page 32 ~ Duplicate;
Page 33 ~ Duplicate;
Page 35 ~ Duplicate;
Page 36 ~ Duplicate;
Page 37 ~ Duplicate;
Page 38 ~ Duplicate;
Page 39 ~ Duplicate;
Page 40 ~ Duplicate;
Page 41 ~ Duplicate;
Page 42 ~ Duplicate;
Page 43 ~ Duplicate;
Page 44 ~ Duplicate;
Page 45 ~ Duplicate;
Page 46 ~ Duplicate;
Page 47 ~ Duplicate;
Page 48 ~ Duplicate;
Page 49 ~ Duplicate;
Page 50 ~ Duplicate;
Page 51 ~ Duplicate;
Page 52 ~ Duplicate;
Page 53 ~ Duplicate;

Page 54 ~ Duplicate;
Page 55 ~ Duplicate;
Page 56 ~ Duplicate;
Page 57 ~ Duplicate;
Page 58 ~ Duplicate;
Page 59 ~ Duplicate;
Page 80 ~ Duplicate;
Page 84 ~ Duplicate;
Page 88 ~ Duplicate;
Page 92 ~ Duplicate;
Page 94 ~ Duplicate;
Page 95 ~ Duplicate;
Page 96 ~ Duplicate;
Page 97 ~ Duplicate;
Page 99 ~ Duplicate;

b6 -1, 2, 6,
b7C -1, 2, 6
b7D -1

Case:					
ired By	Acquired On	Serial #	Serial Title	Summary	Record
	2013-09-26	245	(U) Digital Evidence Laboratory Report of Examination for QNH37, QNH79 and QNH90	(U) Administrative and Case notes	Digital
	2013-07-22	247	(U) Legacy 1A	(U) FD-192 for 1B44-1B50 released to CSP	Digital a
	2013-07-22	248	(U) Legacy 1A	(U) FD-192 for 1B38 - 1B43 released to CSP	Digital a
	2013-07-22	249	(U) Legacy 1A	(U) FD-192 FOR 1B51, 1B52, 1B92-1B94, 1B97-1B99 released to CSP	Digital a
	2013-10-24	250	(U//FOUO) Document on going contact with	(U//FOUO)	Digital
	2013-11-05	252	(U//FOUO)	(U//FOUO	Digital
	2013-11-08	253	(U//FOUO)	(U//FOUO	Digital
	2014-03-19	254	(U) Harassing Calls to Sandy Hook School by Subject in Michigan	(U) MPD and PD reports involving calls to Sandy Hook	Digital
	2014-03-21	255	(U) Complaint regarding	(U) Emails and links from	Digital
	2014-03-06	257	(U//FOUO) Summary of Contact with Newtown PD regarding complaint of	(U//FOUO) Newtown, CT police report regarding complaint of	Digital
	2014-04-07	258	(U) Return of	(U) Original FD-597	Digital
	2014-05-02	261	(U) lab #121217250 QD WR	(U) lab #121217250 QD WR, retained at ERF - 2 lab report, 5 coc, 6 comm log, 5 case notes, 1 search slip, 2 shipping invoice, 2 review forms, 1 legal authority, 4 request documentation	Physical
	2014-04-11	265	(U) FD192 for 1B14 Released	(U) FD192 for 1B14 Released	Digital a
	2014-05-07	266	(U) Shipping Invoice for 1B122 & 1B123	(U) Shipping Invoice for 1B122 & 1B123	Digital a
	2014-07-22	267	(U//FOUO) Representation funds request.	(U//FOUO) Heritage Hotel Invoice.	Digital

FD-340c (4-11-03)

File Number 4-NH-2619946- 1A-143

Field Office Acquiring Evidence

Serial # of Originating Document 247

Date Received 7/22/13

From ECC

(Name of Contributor/Interviewee)

(Address)

(City and State)

By [redacted] b6 -1 b7C -1

To Be Returned ☐ Yes ☐ No

Receipt Given ☐ Yes ☐ No

Grand Jury Material - Disseminate Only Pursuant to Rule 6 (e) Federal Rules of Criminal Procedure

☐ Yes ☐ No

Federal Taxpayer Information (FTI)

☐ Yes ☐ No

Title:

Reference:

(Communication Enclosing Material)

Description: ☐ Original notes re interview of

FD192 for 1B44-1B50 Released to CSP

FD-340c (4-11-03)

File Number 4-NH-2619946 1A 144

Field Office Acquiring Evidence

Serial # of Originating Document 248

Date Received 7/22/13

From ECC
(Name of Contributor/Interviewee)

(Address)

(City and State)

b6 -1
b7C -1

By [redacted]

To Be Returned ☐ Yes ☐ No

Receipt Given ☐ Yes ☐ No

Grand Jury Material - Disseminate Only Pursuant to Rule 6 (e) Federal Rules of Criminal Procedure

☐ Yes ☐ No

Federal Taxpayer Information (FTI)

☐ Yes ☐ No

Title:

Reference:
(Communication Enclosing Material)

Description: ☐ Original notes re interview of

FD192 for 1B38-1B43- Released to CSP

FD-340c (4-11-03)

File Number 4-NH-2619946 1A 145

Field Office Acquiring Evidence ______

Serial # of Originating Document 249

Date Received 7/22/13

From ECC
(Name of Contributor/Interviewee)

(Address)

(City and State)

By [redacted] b6 -1 b7C -1

To Be Returned ☐ Yes ☐ No

Receipt Given ☐ Yes ☐ No

Grand Jury Material - Disseminate Only Pursuant to Rule 6 (e)
Federal Rules of Criminal Procedure

☐ Yes ☐ No

Federal Taxpayer Information (FTI)

☐ Yes ☐ No

Title:

Reference: ______
(Communication Enclosing Material)

Description: ☐ Original notes re interview of

FD192 for 1B51, 1B52, 1B92-1B94 1B97-1B99

Released to CSP

b7E -5

Evidence Details

Case: 4-NH-2619946 **Item:** 1B51

Description:
(U) One brother fax machine

Acquired On: 12/19/2012 03:30 PM EST **Eligible for Forfeiture:** No

Receipt Item #: *None* **Special Handling:** *None*

Hazardous Materials: *None*

CART Information

Type Other **Batteries Charged** No

Number Collected 1 **Acquired by CART** No

Discovery Location

Area: 1st floor Office **Collected By:**

Specific: Office **Others:** *None*

Anticipated Disposition

None on *None*

Storage Information

Holding Office: NEW HAVEN

Finalized By: **Last Inventory:** *None*

b6 -1
b7C -1

Location:
~~NA - Retained by Agent~~ → R1 S37

Barcode #: E5132479

Chain of Custody

Shipping / Transfer Log

History

Acquisition Event Details

Acquisition Event:
(U) evidence log 121912

Acquired By:

b7E -5

Acquired From:
(U) Trooper [redacted]
Connecicut State Police
Troop A
Southbury

b6 -3
b7C -3

Acquired On:
12/19/2012

Receipt Given:
No

Holding Office:
NEW HAVEN

Evidence Log:

4-NH-2619946
Serial 81

FD-1004
Revised
9-16-2009

FEDERAL BUREAU OF INVESTIGATION
EVIDENCE CHAIN-OF-CUSTODY

Evidence Type: ☐ General ☐ CART ☐ Drug ☐ Valuable ☐ Firearm/Weapon ☐ Firearm/Other

Special Handling Instructions	Initial Receipt	Date and Time
☐ Batteries ☐ HAZMAT ☐ Req. Charging ☐ Other ______ ☐ Biohazard ☐ Latents ☐ None ☐ FGJ ☐ Refrigerate	Signature: Printed Na Reason: Collected	12/19/2012 15:37

Relinquished Custody	Date and Time		ate and Time
Signatu Printed Reason: Transport	12/19/12 4:20p	Signature Printed N Reason: Evidence	-19-12 :20 pm

	ate and Time	Accepted Custody	Date and Time
Signature: Printed Na Reason: TOT / CART	-19-12 :10pm	Signatu Printed Reason: CART Review	12/19/12 6 10 p

b6 -1
b7C -1

Relinquished Custody	Date and Time	Accepted Custody	Date and Time
Signatu Printed Reason: TOT Ele	2/27/13 1155 am	Signatu Printed Reason: Storage	2/27/13 1155A
Signatu Printed Reason: Storage	7/5/13 1120	Signature Printed N Reason: CSP Review	7/5/13 1120
Signat Printe Reason: Return to CSP	/9/13 4pm	Signatu Printed Reason: Transport to CSP	7/9/2013 4pm

Firearms Certification:
Printed Name: ______ Signature: ______ Date: ______

Case ID: ______ 1B: ______ Barcode: ______

EVIDENCE CHAIN-OF-CUSTODY

Continuation Page

Relinquished Custody	Date and Time	Accepted Custody	Date and Time
Signat	7/11/2013 15:44	Signature:	07/11/13 1544 b6 -1 b7C -1
Printed		Printed Na	
Reason: TO CSU		Reason: INVESTIGATION	
Relinquished Custody	**Date and Time**	**Accepted Custody**	**Date and Time**
Signature:		Signature:	
Printed Name:		Printed Name:	
Reason:		Reason:	
Relinquished Custody	**Date and Time**	**Accepted Custody**	**Date and Time**
Signature:		Signature:	
Printed Name:		Printed Name:	
Reason:		Reason:	
Relinquished Custody	**Date and Time**	**Accepted Custody**	**Date and Time**
Signature:		Signature:	
Printed Name:		Printed Name:	
Reason:		Reason:	
Relinquished Custody	**Date and Time**	**Accepted Custody**	**Date and Time**
Signature:		Signature:	
Printed Name:		Printed Name:	
Reason:		Reason:	
Relinquished Custody	**Date and Time**	**Accepted Custody**	**Date and Time**
Signature:		Signature:	
Printed Name:		Printed Name:	
Reason:		Reason:	

Case ID: ______________________ 1B: ______________________ Barcode: ______________________

b7E -5

Evidence Details

Case: 4-NH-2619946 **Item:** 1B52

Description:
(U) One black computer tower

Acquired On: 12/19/2012 03:30 PM EST **Eligible for Forfeiture:** No

Receipt Item #: *None* **Special Handling:** *None*

Hazardous Materials: *None*

CART Information

Type Other **Batteries Charged** No

Number Collected 1 **Acquired by CART** No

Discovery Location

Area: 2nd floor southwest bedroom **Collected By:**

Specific: bedroom **Others:** *None*

Anticipated Disposition

None on *None*

Storage Information

Holding Office: NEW HAVEN

Finalized By: **Last Inventory:** *None*

Location:
~~NA - Retained by Agent~~ R5 S3

b6 -1
b7C -1

Barcode #: E5132480

Chain of Custody

Shipping / Transfer Log

History

Acquisition Event Details

Acquisition Event:
(U) evidence log 121912

Acquired By:

Sandy Hook-3713

b7E -

Acquired From:
(U) Trooper [redacted]
Connecicut State Police
Troop A
Southbury

b6 -3
b7C -3

Acquired On:
12/19/2012

Receipt Given:
No

Holding Office:
NEW HAVEN

Evidence Log:

4-NH-2619946
Serial 81

FD-1004
Revised
9-16-2009

FEDERAL BUREAU OF INVESTIGATION
EVIDENCE CHAIN-OF-CUSTODY

Evidence Type: ☐ **General** ☐ **CART** ☐ **Drug** ☐ **Valuable** ☐ **Firearm/Weapon** ☐ **Firearm/Other**

Special Handling Instructions	**Initial Receipt**	**Date and Time**
☐ Batteries ☐ Biohazard ☐ FGJ	Signature:	
☐ HAZMAT ☐ Latents ☐ Refrigerate	Printed Name:	12/19/2012 15:37
☐ Req. Charging ☐ None		
☐ Other ______	Reason: Collected	

Relinquished Custody	**Date and Time**		**Date and Time**
Signature:	12/19/12	Signature:	12-19-12
Printed Name:	420p	Printed Name:	4:20 pm
Reason: Transport		Reason: Evidence	

	Date and Time	**Accepted Custody**	**Date and Time**
Signature:	12-19-12	Signature:	12/19/12
Printed Name:	10pm	Printed Name:	6 10 p
Reason: TOT CART		Reason: CART Review	

Relinquished Custody	**Date and Time**	**Accepted Custody**	**Date and Time**
Signature:	2/27/13	Signature:	2/27/13
Printed Name:	11 55 am	Printed Name:	1155A
Reason: TOT ERC		Reason: Storage	

Relinquished Custody	**Date and Time**	**Accepted Custody**	**Date and Time**
Signature:	7/5/13	Signature:	7/5/13
Printed Name:	1120	Printed Name:	1120
Reason: Storage		Reason: CSP Review	

Relinquished Custody	**Date and Time**	**Accepted Custody**	**Date and Time**
Signature:	7/9/13	Signature:	7/9/2013
Printed Name:	4pm	Printed Name:	4pm
Reason: Return to CSP		Reason: Transport CSP	

b6 -1
b7C -1

Firearms Certification:
Printed Name: ______ Signature: ______ Date: ______

Case ID: ______ 1B: ______ Barcode: ______

EVIDENCE CHAIN-OF-CUSTODY

b6 -1, 3
b7C -1,

Continuation Page

Relinquished Custody	Date and Time	Accepted Custody	Date and Time
Signat	7/11/2013 13:44	Signature:	07/11/13 1544
Printe		Printed Na	
Reason: (DI CJP		Reason: INVESTIGATIVE	
Relinquished Custody	**Date and Time**	**Accepted Custody**	**Date and Time**
Signature:		Signature:	
Printed Name:		Printed Name:	
Reason:		Reason:	
Relinquished Custody	**Date and Time**	**Accepted Custody**	**Date and Time**
Signature:		Signature:	
Printed Name:		Printed Name:	
Reason:		Reason:	
Relinquished Custody	**Date and Time**	**Accepted Custody**	**Date and Time**
Signature:		Signature:	
Printed Name:		Printed Name:	
Reason:		Reason:	
Relinquished Custody	**Date and Time**	**Accepted Custody**	**Date and Time**
Signature:		Signature:	
Printed Name:		Printed Name:	
Reason:		Reason:	
Relinquished Custody	**Date and Time**	**Accepted Custody**	**Date and Time**
Signature:		Signature:	
Printed Name:		Printed Name:	
Reason:		Reason:	

Case ID: ______________________ 1B: ______________________ Barcode: ______________________

b7E -5

Evidence Details

Case: 4-NH-2619946 **Item:** 1B92

Description:
(U//~~FOUO~~) ONE (1) BOX CONTAINING AN IBM THINKPAD, SERIAL NUMBER AA-F2T8399/11 WITH POWER CORD - #601 - CSP SEIZED 12/19/2012 1315

Acquired On: 02/27/2013 11:00 AM EST **Eligible for Forfeiture:** No

Receipt Item #: 601 **Special Handling:** *None*

Hazardous Materials: *None*

CART Information

Type Laptop Computer **Batteries Charged** No

Number Collected 1 **Acquired by CART** No

Discovery Location

Area: CSP Evidence Storage **Collected By:**

Specific: CSP Evidence Storage **Others:**

Anticipated Disposition

None on *None*

Storage Information

Holding Office: NEW HAVEN

Finalized By **Last Inventory:** *None*

Location:
E1300146 - ECC1, MAIN EVIDENCE CONTROL CENTER
E1300183 - ECC1, ROW1, S37

b6 -1
b7C -1

Barcode #: E5132781

Chain of Custody

Shipping / Transfer Log

History

Acquisition Event Details

Acquisition Event:
(U//~~FOUO~~) CSP Evidence Transferred to FBINH

Acquired By:

Sandy Hook-3717

b7E

Acquired From:
(U//~~FOUO~~) DETECTIVE [redacted]
CONNECTICUT STATE POLICE - CENTRAL DISTRICT MAJOR CRIME SQUAD
1111 COUNTRY CLUB ROAD
MIDDLETOWN, Connecticut, 06457
United States

b6 -3
b7C -3

Acquired On:
02/27/2013

Receipt Given:
Yes

Holding Office:
NEW HAVEN

Evidence Log:

4-NH-2619946
Serial 202

FD-1004
Revised
9-16-2009

FEDERAL BUREAU OF INVESTIGATION

EVIDENCE CHAIN-OF-CUSTODY

Evidence Type: ☐ General ☒ CART ☐ Drug ☐ Valuable ☐ Firearm/Weapon ☐ Firearm/Other

Special Handling Instructions	Initial Receipt	Date and Time
☐ Batteries ☐ Biohazard ☐ FGJ ☐ HAZMAT ☐ Latents ☐ Refrigerate ☐ Req. Charging ☐ None ☐ Other ______	Signature Printed N Reason: Collected	02/27/2013 11:00 AM

Relinquished Custody	Date and Time	Accepted Custody	Date and Time
Signat Printed Reason: TOT Storage	2/27/13 3:05 PM	Signatur Printed N Reason: Storage	2/27/13 305P
Signature Printed N Reason: From Storage	4/23/13 230p	Signature Printed N Reason: CART	4/23/13 230pm
Signature: Printed N Reason: TOT ECI	4/26/13 10:00 AM	Signature: Printed Nam Reason: Storage	4/26/13 10A
Signature: Printed Na Reason: Storage	7/5/13 1120	Signature: Printed Na Reason: CSP Review	7/5/13 1120
Signature Printed N Reason: Return to CSP	7/9/13 4pm	Signature: Printed Na Reason: Transport to CSP	7/9/2013 4pm

b6 -1
b7C -1

Firearms Certification:

Printed Name: ______ Signature: ______ Date: ______

Case ID: 4-NH-2619946 1B: 92 Barcode: E5132781

Sandy Hook-371

601

EVIDENCE CHAIN-OF-CUSTODY

Continuation Page

Relinquished Custody	Date and Time	Accepted Custody	Date and Time
Signature:	7/11/2013 1844	Signature:	07/11/13 1544
Printed Name:		Printed Name:	
Reason: TO/ CSP		Reason: INVESTIGATION	
Relinquished Custody	**Date and Time**	**Accepted Custody**	**Date and Time**
Signature:		Signature:	
Printed Name:		Printed Name:	
Reason:		Reason:	
Relinquished Custody	**Date and Time**	**Accepted Custody**	**Date and Time**
Signature:		Signature:	
Printed Name:		Printed Name:	
Reason:		Reason:	
Relinquished Custody	**Date and Time**	**Accepted Custody**	**Date and Time**
Signature:		Signature:	
Printed Name:		Printed Name:	
Reason:		Reason:	
Relinquished Custody	**Date and Time**	**Accepted Custody**	**Date and Time**
Signature:		Signature:	
Printed Name:		Printed Name:	
Reason:		Reason:	
Relinquished Custody	**Date and Time**	**Accepted Custody**	**Date and Time**
Signature:		Signature:	
Printed Name:		Printed Name:	
Reason:		Reason:	

b6 -1, b7C -1

Case ID: ____________ 1B: ____________ Barcode: ____________

b7E -5

Evidence Details

Case: 4-NH-2619946 **Item:** 1B93

Description:
(U//~~FOUO~~) 602A - TOSHIBA, MODEL MK4025GAS, 40GB HDD, SERIAL NUMBER 74C50902S; REPACKAGED FROM TEN (10) MISCELLANEOUS COMPUTER COMPONENTS - #602 - CSP SEIZED 12/19/2012 1320

Acquired On: 02/27/2013 11:00 AM EST **Eligible for Forfeiture:** No

Receipt Item #: 602 **Special Handling:** *None*

Hazardous Materials: *None*

CART Information

Type Mass Storage Device **Batteries Charged** No

Number Collected 1 **Acquired by CART** No

Discovery Location

Area: CSP Evidence Storage **Collected By:**

Specific: CSP Evidence Storage **Others:**

Anticipated Disposition

None on *None*

Storage Information

b6 -1
b7C -1

Holding Office: NEW HAVEN

Finalized By: **Last Inventory:** *None*

Location:
E1300146 - ECC1, MAIN EVIDENCE CONTROL CENTER
E1300183 - ECC1, ROW1, S37

Barcode #: E5132783

Chain of Custody

Shipping / Transfer Log

History

Acquisition Event Details

Acquisition Event:
(U//~~FOUO~~) CSP Evidence Transferred to FBINH

Acquired By:

b7E -

b6 -1, 3
b7C -1, 3

Acquired From:
(U//FOUO) DETECTIVE
CONNECTICUT STATE POLICE - CENTRAL DISTRICT MAJOR CRIME SQUAD
1111 COUNTRY CLUB ROAD
MIDDLETOWN, Connecticut, 06457
United States

Acquired On:
02/27/2013

Receipt Given:
Yes

Holding Office:
NEW HAVEN

Evidence Log:

4-NH-2619946
Serial 202

FD-1004
Revised
9-16-2009

FEDERAL BUREAU OF INVESTIGATION
EVIDENCE CHAIN-OF-CUSTODY

Evidence Type: ☐ General ☒ CART ☐ Drug ☐ Valuable ☐ Firearm/Weapon ☐ Firearm/Other

Special Handling Instructions	Initial Receipt	Date and Time
☐ Batteries ☐ Biohazard ☐ FGJ ☐ HAZMAT ☐ Latents ☐ Refrigerate ☐ Req. Charging ☐ None ☐ Other ______	Signature: Printed Na Reason: Collected	02/27/2013 11:00 AM

Relinquished Custody	Date and Time	Accepted Custody	Date and Time
Signatu Printed Reason: TOT Storage	2/27/2013 3:05pm	Signature Printed N Reason: Storage	2/27/13 305P
Signature Printed N Reason: FRM Storage	4/23/13 230P	Signature: Printed Na Reason: CART	4/23/13 230PM
Signature: Printed Nar Reason: T/A ECT	4/26/13 10AM	Signatu Printed Reason: Storage	4/26/13 10A
Signature Printed N Reason: Storage	7/5/13 1120	Signature: Printed Na Reason: CSP Renew	7/5/13 1120
Signature Printed N Reason: Retn to CSP	7/9/13 4pm	Signature: Printed Na Reason: Transport CSP	7/9/2013 4pm

b6 -1
b7C -1

Firearms Certification:
Printed Name: ______ Signature: ______ Date: ______

Case ID: 4-NH-2619946 1B: 93 Barcode: E5132783

Sandy Hook-3723

602A

EVIDENCE CHAIN-OF-CUSTODY

Continuation Page

Relinquished Custody	Date and Time	Accepted Custody	Date and Time
Signature:	7/11/2013 15:44	Signature:	07/11/13 1544
Printed Name:		Printed Name:	
Reason: 701 CSP		Reason: INVESTIGATION	
Relinquished Custody	**Date and Time**	**Accepted Custody**	**Date and Time**
Signature:		Signature:	
Printed Name:		Printed Name:	
Reason:		Reason:	
Relinquished Custody	**Date and Time**	**Accepted Custody**	**Date and Time**
Signature:		Signature:	
Printed Name:		Printed Name:	
Reason:		Reason:	
Relinquished Custody	**Date and Time**	**Accepted Custody**	**Date and Time**
Signature:		Signature:	
Printed Name:		Printed Name:	
Reason:		Reason:	
Relinquished Custody	**Date and Time**	**Accepted Custody**	**Date and Time**
Signature:		Signature:	
Printed Name:		Printed Name:	
Reason:		Reason:	
Relinquished Custody	**Date and Time**	**Accepted Custody**	**Date and Time**
Signature:		Signature:	
Printed Name:		Printed Name:	
Reason:		Reason:	

b6 -1,
b7C -1

Case ID: ______________ 1B: ______________ Barcode: ______________

b7E -5

Evidence Details

Case: 4-NH-2619946 Item: 1B94

Description:
(U//~~FOUO~~) TWELVE (12) MISCELLANEOUS CD-R AND DVD-R DISCS CONTAINING UNKNOWN CONTENT - #603 - CSP SEIZED 12/19/2012 1335

Acquired On: 02/27/2013 11:00 AM EST

Eligible for Forfeiture: No

Receipt Item #: 603

Special Handling: *None*

Hazardous Materials: *None*

CART Information

Type: Mass Storage Device

Batteries Charged: No

Number Collected: 12

Acquired by CART: No

Discovery Location

Area: CSP Evidence Storage

Collected By:

Specific: CSP Evidence Storage

Others:

Anticipated Disposition

None on *None*

Storage Information

Holding Office: NEW HAVEN

Finalized By:

Last Inventory: *None*

Location:
E1300146 - ECC1, MAIN EVIDENCE CONTROL CENTER
E1300183 - ECC1, ROW1, S37

b6 -1
b7C -1

Barcode #: E5132784

Chain of Custody

Shipping / Transfer Log

History

Acquisition Event Details

Acquisition Event:
(U//~~FOUO~~) CSP Evidence Transferred to FBINH

Acquired By:

Sandy Hook-3725

b7E

Acquired From:
(U//~~FOUO~~) DETECTIVE [redacted]
CONNECTICUT STATE POLICE - CENTRAL DISTRICT MAJOR CRIME SQUAD
1111 COUNTRY CLUB ROAD
MIDDLETOWN, Connecticut, 06457
United States

b6 -3
b7C -3

Acquired On:
02/27/2013

Receipt Given:
Yes

Holding Office:
NEW HAVEN

Evidence Log:

4-NH-2619946
Serial 202

FD-1004
Revised
9-16-2009

FEDERAL BUREAU OF INVESTIGATION
EVIDENCE CHAIN-OF-CUSTODY

Evidence Type: ☐ General ☒ CART ☐ Drug ☐ Valuable ☐ Firearm/Weapon ☐ Firearm/Other

Special Handling Instructions	Initial Receipt	Date and Time
☐ Batteries ☐ Biohazard ☐ FGJ ☐ HAZMAT ☐ Latents ☐ Refrigerate ☐ Req. Charging ☐ None ☐ Other ______	Signature: Printed Na Reason: Collected	02/27/2013 11:00 AM

Relinquished Custody	Date and Time	Accepted Custody	Date and Time
Signatu Printed Reason: TOT Evidence Control	2/27/13 3:05 PM	Signature Printed N Reason: Storage	2/27/13 305P
Signature Printed N Reason: Storage	7/5/13 1120	Signature: Printed Nar Reason: CSP Review	7/5/13 1120
Signature: Printed Na Reason: Return to CSP	7/9/13 4pm	Signature Printed N Reason: Transport to CSP	7/9/2013 4pm
Signature Printed N Reason: TO CSP	7/11/2013 15:44	Signature: Printed N Reason: INVESTIGATION	7/11/13 1544
Signature: Printed Name: Reason:		Signature: Printed Name: Reason:	

b6 -1, 3
b7C -1, 3

Firearms Certification:
Printed Name: ______ Signature: ______ Date: ______

Case ID: 4-NH-2619946 1B: 94 Barcode: E5132784

Sandy Hook-3727

603

b7E -

Evidence Details

Case: 4-NH-2619946 **Item:** 1B97

Description:
(U//~~FOUO~~) ONE (1) PLASTIC CASE CONTAINING 29 CD-R DISCS - #634 - SEIZED 12/20/2012 0958

Acquired On: 02/27/2013 11:00 AM EST **Eligible for Forfeiture:** No

Receipt Item #: 634 **Special Handling:** *None*

Hazardous Materials: *None*

CART Information

Type Mass Storage Device **Batteries Charged** No

Number Collected 29 **Acquired by CART** No

Discovery Location

Area: CSP Evidence Storage **Collected By:**

Specific: CSP Evidence Storage **Others:**

Anticipated Disposition

None on *None*

Storage Information

Holding Office: NEW HAVEN

Finalized By: **Last Inventory:** *None*

Location:
E1300146 - ECC1, MAIN EVIDENCE CONTROL CENTER
E1300183 - ECC1, ROW1, S37

b6 -1
b7C -1

Barcode #: E5132782

Chain of Custody

Shipping / Transfer Log

History

Acquisition Event Details

Acquisition Event:
(U//~~FOUO~~) CSP Evidence Transferred to FBINH

Acquired By:

b7E -5

Acquired From:
(U//~~FOUO~~) DETECTIVE [redacted]
CONNECTICUT STATE POLICE - CENTRAL DISTRICT MAJOR CRIME SQUAD
1111 COUNTRY CLUB ROAD
MIDDLETOWN, Connecticut, 06457
United States

b6 -3
b7C -3

Acquired On:
02/27/2013

Receipt Given:
Yes

Holding Office:
NEW HAVEN

Evidence Log:

4-NH-2619946
Serial 202

FD-1004
Revised
9-16-2009

FEDERAL BUREAU OF INVESTIGATION
EVIDENCE CHAIN-OF-CUSTODY

Evidence Type: ☐ General ☒ CART ☐ Drug ☐ Valuable ☐ Firearm/Weapon ☐ Firearm/Other

Special Handling Instructions	Initial Receipt	Date and Time
☐ Batteries ☐ Biohazard ☐ FGJ ☐ HAZMAT ☐ Latents ☐ Refrigerate ☐ Req. Charging ☐ None ☐ Other ____________	Signature: Printed Name: Reason: Collected	02/27/2013 11:00 AM

Relinquished Custody	Date and Time	Accepted Custody	Date and Time
Signature: Printed Name: Reason: TOT Storage	2/27/13 3:05pm	Signature: Printed Name: Reason: Storage	2/27/13 305P
Signature: Printed Name: Reason: Storage	7/5/13 1120	Signature: Printed Name: Reason: CST Review	7/5/13 1120
Signature: Printed Name: Reason: Return to CST	7/9/13 4pm	Signature: Printed Name: Reason: Transport to CSP	7/9/2013 4pm
Signature: Printed Name: Reason: TOT CSP	7/11/2013 15:44	Signature: Printed Name: Reason: INVESTIGATION	7/11/13 1544
Signature: Printed Name: Reason:		Signature: Printed Name: Reason:	

b6 -1, b7C -1

Firearms Certification:
Printed Name: ____________ Signature: ____________ Date: ____________

Case ID: 4-NH-2619946 1B: 97 Barcode: E5132782

Sandy Hook-3

b7E -5

Evidence Details

Case: 4-NH-2619946 **Item:** 1B98

Description:
(U//~~FOUO~~) 602B - IBM CD DRIVE; SAMSUNG FLOPPY DRIVE; COMPUTER VIDEO CARD; FOUR (4) MEMORY DIMMS; NETGEAR GIGABIT PC CARD; INTEL PROCESSORREPACKAGED FROM TEN (10) MISCELLANEOUS COMPUTER COMPONENTS - #602 - CSP SEIZED 12/19/2012 1320

Acquired On: 02/27/2013 11:00 AM EST **Eligible for Forfeiture:** No

Receipt Item #: 602 **Special Handling:** *None*

Hazardous Materials: *None*

CART Information

Type Other Hardware **Batteries Charged** No

Number Collected 9 **Acquired by CART** No

Discovery Location

Area: CSP Evidence Storage **Collected By:**

Specific: CSP Evidence Storage **Others:**

Anticipated Disposition

None on *None*

b6 -1
b7C -1

Storage Information

Holding Office: NEW HAVEN

Finalized By: **Last Inventory:** *None*

Location:
E1300146 - ECC1, MAIN EVIDENCE CONTROL CENTER
E1300183 - ECC1, ROW1, S37

Barcode #: E5132785

Chain of Custody

Shipping / Transfer Log

History

Acquisition Event Details

Acquisition Event:
(U//~~FOUO~~) CSP Evidence Transferred to FBINH

b7E

Acquired By:

Acquired From:
(U//~~FOUO~~) DETECTIVE
CONNECTICUT STATE POLICE - CENTRAL DISTRICT MAJOR CRIME SQUAD
1111 COUNTRY CLUB ROAD
MIDDLETOWN, Connecticut, 06457
United States

b6 -1, 3
b7C -1, 3

Acquired On:
02/27/2013

Receipt Given:
Yes

Holding Office:
NEW HAVEN

Evidence Log:

4-NH-2619946
Serial 202

FD-1004
Revised
9-16-2009

FEDERAL BUREAU OF INVESTIGATION

EVIDENCE CHAIN-OF-CUSTODY

b6 -1, 3
b7c -1, 3

Evidence Type: ☐ General ☒ CART ☐ Drug ☐ Valuable ☐ Firearm/Weapon ☐ Firearm/Other

Special Handling Instructions	Initial Receipt	Date and Time
☐ Batteries ☐ Biohazard ☐ FGJ	Signature:	
☐ HAZMAT ☐ Latents ☐ Refrigerate	Printed Name:	02/27/2013 11:00 AM
☐ Req. Charging ☐ None		
☐ Other ______	Reason: Collected	

Relinquished Custody	Date and Time	Accepted Custody	Date and Time
Signature: Printed Name: Reason: TOT Storage	2/27/13 3:05PM	Signature: Printed Name: Reason: Storage	2/27/13 305P
Signature: Printed Name: Reason: Storage	7/5/13 1120	Signature: Printed Name: Reason: CSP Review	7/5/13 1120
Signature: Printed Name: Reason: Transport TO CSP	7/9/13 4pm	Signature: Printed Name: Reason: Transport to CSP	7/9/2013 4pm
Signature: Printed Name: Reason: TOT CSP	7/11/2013 15:44	Signature: Printed Name: Reason: INVESTIGATION	7/11/13 1544
Signature: Printed Name: Reason:		Signature: Printed Name: Reason:	

Firearms Certification:

Printed Name: ______ Signature: ______ Date: ______

Case ID: 4-NH-2619946 1B: 98 Barcode: E5132785

602B

b7E

Evidence Details

Case: 4-NH-2619946 **Item:** 1B99

Description:
(U//~~FOUO~~) Digital copies of [redacted] ; seven (7) journals authored by ADAM LANZA (1B95); loose papers authored by ADAM LANZA

b6 -5
b7C -5

Acquired On: 03/01/2013 01:30 PM EST **Eligible for Forfeiture:** No

Receipt Item #: *None* **Special Handling:** *None*

Hazardous Materials: *None*

CART Information

Type Mass Storage Device **Batteries Charged** No

Number Collected 1 **Acquired by CART** Yes

Discovery Location

Area: NH Derivative Evidence **Collected By:** [redacted]

Specific: NH Derivative Evidence **Others:** [redacted]

Anticipated Disposition

None on *None*

b6 -1
b7C -1

Storage Information

Holding Office: NEW HAVEN

Finalized By: [redacted] **Last Inventory:** *None*

Location:
E1300146 - ECC1, MAIN EVIDENCE CONTROL CENTER
E1300346 - ECC1, ROW5, S16

Barcode #: E5132798

Chain of Custody

Shipping / Transfer Log

History

Acquisition Event Details

Acquisition Event:
(U//~~FOUO~~) Digital Copy of items 1B95 and 1B96

Acquired By:

Sandy Hook-3737

b7E -5

Acquired From:
(U//FOUO)

b6 -1
b7C -1

Acquired On:
03/01/2013

Receipt Given:
No

Holding Office:
NEW HAVEN

Evidence Log:

4-NH-2619946
Serial 205

FD-1004
Revised
9-16-2009

b6 -1, 3
b7C -1, 3

FEDERAL BUREAU OF INVESTIGATION
EVIDENCE CHAIN-OF-CUSTODY

Evidence Type: ☐ General ☒ CART ☐ Drug ☐ Valuable ☐ Firearm/Weapon ☐ Firearm/Other

Special Handling Instructions	Initial Receipt	Date and Time
☐ Batteries ☐ HAZMAT ☐ Req. Charging ☐ Other ______ ☐ Biohazard ☐ Latents ☐ None ☐ FGJ ☐ Refrigerate	Signature: Printed Name: Reason: Collected	03/01/2013 1:30 PM

Relinquished Custody	Date and Time	Accepted Custody	Date and Time
Signature: Printed Name: Reason: TOT Storage	3/5/2013 3:04pm	Signature: Printed Name: Reason: Storage	3/5/13 304p.
Signature: Printed Name: Reason: Storage	7/5/13 1120	Signature: Printed Name: Reason: CSP Review	7/5/13 1120
Signature: Printed Name: Reason: Return to CSP	7/9/13 4pm	Signature: Printed Name: Reason: Transport to CSP	7/9/2013 4pm
Signature: Printed Name: Reason: TOT CSP	7/11/2013 15:44	Signature: Printed Name: Reason: INVESTIGATION	7/11/13 1544
Signature: Printed Name: Reason:		Signature: Printed Name: Reason:	

Firearms Certification:
Printed Name: ______ Signature: ______ Date: ______

Case ID: 4-NH-2619946 1B: ______ Barcode: ______

FD-340c(4-11-03)

File Number 4-NH-2619946 1A|54

Field Office Acquiring Evidence

Serial # of Originating Document

Date Received 4/11/14

From ECC

(Name of Contributor/Interviewee)

(Address)

(City and State)

By [redacted] b6 -1 b7C -1

To Be Returned ☐ Yes ☐ No

Receipt Given ☐ Yes ☐ No

Grand Jury Material - Disseminate Only Pursuant to Rule 6 (e) Federal Rules of Criminal Procedure

☐ Yes ☐ No

Federal Taxpayer Information (FTI)

☐ Yes ☐ No

Title:

Reference:

(Communication Enclosing Material)

Description: ☐ Original notes re interview of

FD192 for 1B14 Released

FD-340c(4-11-03)

File Number 4-NH-2619946 1A155

Field Office Acquiring Evidence ________________

Serial # of Originating Document ________________

Date Received 5/7/14

From FBI lab
(Name of Contributor/Interviewee)

____
(Address)

____
(City and State)

By [redacted] ________________ b6 -1 b7C -

To Be Returned ☐ Yes ☐ No

Receipt Given ☐ Yes ☐ No

Grand Jury Material - Disseminate Only Pursuant to Rule 6 (e) Federal Rules of Criminal Procedure

☐ Yes ☐ No

Federal Taxpayer Information (FTI)

☐ Yes ☐ No

Title:

Reference: ________________
(Communication Enclosing Material)

Description: ☐ Original notes re interview of

shipping invoice for 1B122 + 1B123

FEDERAL BUREAU OF INVESTIGATION
FOI/PA
DELETED PAGE INFORMATION SHEET
Civil Action# 16-cv-02136

Total Deleted Page(s) = 106
Page 1 ~ Duplicate;
Page 2 ~ Duplicate;
Page 3 ~ Duplicate;
Page 4 ~ Duplicate;
Page 5 ~ Duplicate;
Page 6 ~ Duplicate;
Page 7 ~ Duplicate;
Page 8 ~ Duplicate;
Page 9 ~ Duplicate;
Page 10 ~ Duplicate;
Page 11 ~ Duplicate;
Page 12 ~ Duplicate;
Page 13 ~ Duplicate;
Page 14 ~ Duplicate;
Page 15 ~ Duplicate;
Page 16 ~ Duplicate;
Page 17 ~ Duplicate;
Page 18 ~ Duplicate;
Page 19 ~ Duplicate;
Page 20 ~ Duplicate;
Page 21 ~ Duplicate;
Page 22 ~ Duplicate;
Page 23 ~ Duplicate;
Page 24 ~ Duplicate;
Page 25 ~ Duplicate;
Page 26 ~ Duplicate;
Page 27 ~ Duplicate;
Page 28 ~ Duplicate;
Page 29 ~ Duplicate;
Page 30 ~ Duplicate;
Page 31 ~ Duplicate;
Page 32 ~ Duplicate;
Page 33 ~ Duplicate;
Page 34 ~ Duplicate;
Page 35 ~ Duplicate;
Page 36 ~ Duplicate;
Page 37 ~ Duplicate;
Page 38 ~ Duplicate;
Page 39 ~ Duplicate;
Page 40 ~ Duplicate;
Page 41 ~ Duplicate;
Page 42 ~ Duplicate;
Page 43 ~ Duplicate;
Page 44 ~ Duplicate;
Page 45 ~ Duplicate;
Page 46 ~ Duplicate;
Page 47 ~ Duplicate;
Page 48 ~ Duplicate;

Page 49 ~ Duplicate;
Page 50 ~ Duplicate;
Page 51 ~ Duplicate;
Page 52 ~ Duplicate;
Page 53 ~ Duplicate;
Page 54 ~ Duplicate;
Page 55 ~ Duplicate;
Page 56 ~ Duplicate;
Page 57 ~ Duplicate;
Page 58 ~ Duplicate;
Page 59 ~ Duplicate;
Page 60 ~ Duplicate;
Page 61 ~ Duplicate;
Page 62 ~ Duplicate;
Page 63 ~ Duplicate;
Page 64 ~ Duplicate;
Page 65 ~ Duplicate;
Page 66 ~ Duplicate;
Page 67 ~ Duplicate;
Page 68 ~ Duplicate;
Page 69 ~ Duplicate;
Page 70 ~ Duplicate;
Page 71 ~ Duplicate;
Page 72 ~ Duplicate;
Page 73 ~ Duplicate;
Page 74 ~ Duplicate;
Page 75 ~ Duplicate;
Page 76 ~ Duplicate;
Page 77 ~ Duplicate;
Page 78 ~ Duplicate;
Page 79 ~ Duplicate;
Page 80 ~ Duplicate;
Page 81 ~ Duplicate;
Page 82 ~ Duplicate;
Page 83 ~ Duplicate;
Page 84 ~ Duplicate;
Page 85 ~ Duplicate;
Page 86 ~ Duplicate;
Page 87 ~ Duplicate;
Page 88 ~ Duplicate;
Page 89 ~ Duplicate;
Page 90 ~ Duplicate;
Page 91 ~ Duplicate;
Page 92 ~ Duplicate;
Page 93 ~ Duplicate;
Page 94 ~ Duplicate;
Page 95 ~ Duplicate;
Page 96 ~ Duplicate;
Page 97 ~ Duplicate;
Page 98 ~ Duplicate;
Page 99 ~ Duplicate;
Page 100 ~ Duplicate;
Page 101 ~ Duplicate;
Page 102 ~ Duplicate;

Page 103 ~ Duplicate;
Page 104 ~ Duplicate;
Page 105 ~ Duplicate;
Page 106 ~ Duplicate;

```
XXXXXXXXXXXXXXXXXXXXXXXX
X   Deleted Page(s)    X
X   No Duplication Fee X
X   For this Page      X
XXXXXXXXXXXXXXXXXXXXXXXX
```

FEDERAL BUREAU OF INVESTIGATION
FOI/PA
DELETED PAGE INFORMATION SHEET
Civil Action# 16-cv-02136

Total Deleted Page(s) = 166
Page 1 ~ Duplicate;
Page 2 ~ Duplicate;
Page 3 ~ Duplicate;
Page 4 ~ Duplicate;
Page 5 ~ Duplicate;
Page 6 ~ Duplicate;
Page 7 ~ Duplicate;
Page 8 ~ Duplicate;
Page 9 ~ Duplicate;
Page 10 ~ Duplicate;
Page 11 ~ Duplicate;
Page 12 ~ Duplicate;
Page 13 ~ Duplicate;
Page 14 ~ Duplicate;
Page 15 ~ Duplicate;
Page 16 ~ Duplicate;
Page 17 ~ Duplicate;
Page 18 ~ Duplicate;
Page 19 ~ Duplicate;
Page 20 ~ Duplicate;
Page 21 ~ Duplicate;
Page 22 ~ Duplicate;
Page 23 ~ Duplicate;
Page 24 ~ Duplicate;
Page 25 ~ Duplicate;
Page 26 ~ Duplicate;
Page 27 ~ Duplicate;
Page 28 ~ Duplicate;
Page 29 ~ Duplicate;
Page 30 ~ Duplicate;
Page 31 ~ Duplicate;
Page 32 ~ Duplicate;
Page 33 ~ Duplicate;
Page 34 ~ Duplicate;
Page 35 ~ Duplicate;
Page 36 ~ Duplicate;
Page 37 ~ Duplicate;
Page 38 ~ Duplicate;
Page 39 ~ Duplicate;
Page 40 ~ Duplicate;
Page 41 ~ Duplicate;
Page 42 ~ Duplicate;
Page 43 ~ Duplicate;
Page 44 ~ Duplicate;
Page 45 ~ Duplicate;
Page 46 ~ Duplicate;
Page 47 ~ Duplicate;
Page 48 ~ Duplicate;

Page 49 ~ Duplicate;
Page 50 ~ Duplicate;
Page 51 ~ Duplicate;
Page 52 ~ Duplicate;
Page 53 ~ Duplicate;
Page 54 ~ Duplicate;
Page 55 ~ Duplicate;
Page 56 ~ Duplicate;
Page 57 ~ Duplicate;
Page 58 ~ Duplicate;
Page 59 ~ Duplicate;
Page 60 ~ Duplicate;
Page 61 ~ Duplicate;
Page 62 ~ Duplicate;
Page 63 ~ Duplicate;
Page 64 ~ Duplicate;
Page 65 ~ Duplicate;
Page 66 ~ Duplicate;
Page 67 ~ Duplicate;
Page 68 ~ Duplicate;
Page 69 ~ Duplicate;
Page 70 ~ Duplicate;
Page 71 ~ Duplicate;
Page 72 ~ Duplicate;
Page 73 ~ Duplicate;
Page 74 ~ Duplicate;
Page 75 ~ Duplicate;
Page 76 ~ Duplicate;
Page 77 ~ Duplicate;
Page 78 ~ Duplicate;
Page 79 ~ Duplicate;
Page 80 ~ Duplicate;
Page 81 ~ Duplicate;
Page 82 ~ Duplicate;
Page 83 ~ Duplicate;
Page 84 ~ Duplicate;
Page 85 ~ Duplicate;
Page 86 ~ Duplicate;
Page 87 ~ Duplicate;
Page 88 ~ Duplicate;
Page 89 ~ Duplicate;
Page 90 ~ Duplicate;
Page 91 ~ Duplicate;
Page 92 ~ Duplicate;
Page 93 ~ Duplicate;
Page 94 ~ Duplicate;
Page 95 ~ Duplicate;
Page 96 ~ Duplicate;
Page 97 ~ Duplicate;
Page 98 ~ Duplicate;
Page 99 ~ Duplicate;
Page 100 ~ Duplicate;
Page 101 ~ Duplicate;
Page 102 ~ Duplicate;

Page 103 ~ Duplicate;
Page 104 ~ Duplicate;
Page 105 ~ Duplicate;
Page 106 ~ Duplicate;
Page 107 ~ Duplicate;
Page 108 ~ Duplicate;
Page 109 ~ Duplicate;
Page 110 ~ Duplicate;
Page 111 ~ Duplicate;
Page 112 ~ Duplicate;
Page 113 ~ Duplicate;
Page 114 ~ Duplicate;
Page 115 ~ Duplicate;
Page 116 ~ Duplicate;
Page 117 ~ Duplicate;
Page 118 ~ Duplicate;
Page 119 ~ Duplicate;
Page 120 ~ Duplicate;
Page 121 ~ Duplicate;
Page 122 ~ Duplicate;
Page 123 ~ Duplicate;
Page 124 ~ Duplicate;
Page 125 ~ Duplicate;
Page 126 ~ Duplicate;
Page 127 ~ Duplicate;
Page 128 ~ Duplicate;
Page 129 ~ Duplicate;
Page 130 ~ Duplicate;
Page 131 ~ Duplicate;
Page 132 ~ Duplicate;
Page 133 ~ Duplicate;
Page 134 ~ Duplicate;
Page 135 ~ Duplicate;
Page 136 ~ Duplicate;
Page 137 ~ Duplicate;
Page 138 ~ Duplicate;
Page 139 ~ Duplicate;
Page 140 ~ Duplicate;
Page 141 ~ Duplicate;
Page 142 ~ Duplicate;
Page 143 ~ Duplicate;
Page 144 ~ Duplicate;
Page 145 ~ Duplicate;
Page 146 ~ Duplicate;
Page 147 ~ Duplicate;
Page 148 ~ Duplicate;
Page 149 ~ Duplicate;
Page 150 ~ Duplicate;
Page 151 ~ Duplicate;
Page 152 ~ Duplicate;
Page 153 ~ Duplicate;
Page 154 ~ Duplicate;
Page 155 ~ Duplicate;
Page 156 ~ Duplicate;

Page 157 ~ Duplicate;
Page 158 ~ Duplicate;
Page 159 ~ Duplicate;
Page 160 ~ Duplicate;
Page 161 ~ Duplicate;
Page 162 ~ Duplicate;
Page 163 ~ Duplicate;
Page 164 ~ Duplicate;
Page 165 ~ Duplicate;
Page 166 ~ Duplicate;

```
XXXXXXXXXXXXXXXXXXXXXXXX
X   Deleted Page(s)    X
X   No Duplication Fee X
X   For this Page      X
XXXXXXXXXXXXXXXXXXXXXXXX
```

FEDERAL BUREAU OF INVESTIGATION
FOI/PA
DELETED PAGE INFORMATION SHEET
Civil Action# 16-cv-02136

Total Deleted Page(s) = 161
Page 1 ~ b3 - 1; b6 - 2; b7C - 2;
Page 2 ~ b3 - 1; b6 - 2; b7C - 2;
Page 3 ~ b3 - 1; b6 - 2; b7C - 2;
Page 4 ~ b3 - 1; b6 - 2; b7C - 2;
Page 5 ~ b3 - 1; b6 - 2; b7C - 2;
Page 6 ~ b3 - 1; b6 - 2; b7C - 2;
Page 7 ~ b3 - 1; b6 - 2; b7C - 2;
Page 8 ~ b3 - 1; b6 - 2; b7C - 2;
Page 9 ~ b3 - 1; b6 - 2; b7C - 2;
Page 10 ~ b3 - 1; b6 - 2; b7C - 2;
Page 11 ~ b3 - 1; b6 - 2; b7C - 2;
Page 12 ~ b3 - 1; b6 - 2; b7C - 2;
Page 13 ~ b3 - 1; b6 - 2; b7C - 2;
Page 14 ~ b3 - 1; b6 - 2; b7C - 2;
Page 15 ~ b3 - 1; b6 - 2; b7C - 2;
Page 16 ~ b3 - 1; b6 - 2; b7C - 2;
Page 17 ~ b3 - 1; b6 - 2; b7C - 2;
Page 18 ~ b3 - 1; b6 - 2; b7C - 2;
Page 19 ~ b3 - 1; b6 - 2; b7C - 2;
Page 20 ~ b3 - 1; b6 - 2; b7C - 2;
Page 21 ~ b3 - 1; b6 - 2; b7C - 2;
Page 22 ~ b3 - 1; b6 - 2; b7C - 2;
Page 23 ~ b3 - 1; b6 - 2; b7C - 2;
Page 24 ~ b3 - 1; b6 - 2; b7C - 2;
Page 25 ~ b3 - 1; b6 - 2; b7C - 2;
Page 26 ~ b3 - 1; b6 - 2; b7C - 2;
Page 27 ~ b3 - 1; b6 - 2; b7C - 2;
Page 28 ~ b3 - 1; b6 - 2; b7C - 2;
Page 29 ~ b3 - 1; b6 - 2; b7C - 2;
Page 30 ~ b3 - 1; b6 - 2; b7C - 2;
Page 31 ~ b3 - 1; b6 - 2; b7C - 2;
Page 32 ~ b3 - 1; b6 - 2; b7C - 2;
Page 33 ~ b3 - 1; b6 - 2; b7C - 2;
Page 34 ~ b3 - 1; b6 - 2; b7C - 2;
Page 35 ~ b3 - 1; b6 - 2; b7C - 2;
Page 36 ~ b3 - 1; b6 - 2; b7C - 2;
Page 37 ~ b3 - 1; b6 - 2; b7C - 2;
Page 38 ~ b3 - 1; b6 - 2; b7C - 2;
Page 39 ~ b3 - 1; b6 - 2; b7C - 2;
Page 40 ~ b3 - 1; b6 - 2; b7C - 2;
Page 41 ~ b3 - 1; b6 - 2; b7C - 2;
Page 42 ~ b3 - 1; b6 - 2; b7C - 2;
Page 43 ~ b3 - 1; b6 - 2; b7C - 2;
Page 44 ~ b3 - 1; b6 - 2; b7C - 2;
Page 45 ~ b3 - 1; b6 - 2; b7C - 2;
Page 46 ~ b3 - 1; b6 - 2; b7C - 2;
Page 47 ~ b3 - 1; b6 - 2; b7C - 2;
Page 48 ~ b3 - 1; b6 - 2; b7C - 2;

Page 49 ~ b3 - 1; b6 - 2; b7C - 2;
Page 50 ~ b3 - 1; b6 - 2; b7C - 2;
Page 51 ~ b3 - 1; b6 - 2; b7C - 2;
Page 52 ~ b3 - 1; b6 - 2; b7C - 2;
Page 53 ~ b3 - 1; b6 - 2; b7C - 2;
Page 54 ~ b3 - 1; b6 - 2; b7C - 2;
Page 55 ~ b3 - 1; b6 - 2; b7C - 2;
Page 56 ~ b3 - 1; b6 - 2; b7C - 2;
Page 57 ~ b3 - 1; b6 - 2; b7C - 2;
Page 58 ~ b3 - 1; b6 - 2; b7C - 2;
Page 59 ~ b3 - 1; b6 - 2; b7C - 2;
Page 60 ~ b3 - 1; b6 - 2; b7C - 2;
Page 61 ~ b3 - 1; b6 - 2; b7C - 2;
Page 62 ~ b3 - 1; b6 - 2; b7C - 2;
Page 63 ~ b3 - 1; b6 - 2; b7C - 2;
Page 64 ~ b3 - 1; b6 - 2; b7C - 2;
Page 65 ~ b3 - 1; b6 - 2; b7C - 2;
Page 66 ~ b3 - 1; b6 - 2; b7C - 2;
Page 67 ~ b3 - 1; b6 - 2; b7C - 2;
Page 68 ~ b3 - 1; b6 - 2; b7C - 2;
Page 69 ~ b3 - 1; b6 - 2; b7C - 2;
Page 70 ~ b3 - 1; b6 - 2; b7C - 2;
Page 71 ~ b3 - 1; b6 - 2; b7C - 2;
Page 72 ~ b3 - 1; b6 - 2; b7C - 2;
Page 73 ~ b3 - 1; b6 - 2; b7C - 2;
Page 74 ~ b3 - 1; b6 - 2; b7C - 2;
Page 75 ~ b3 - 1; b6 - 2; b7C - 2;
Page 76 ~ b3 - 1; b6 - 2; b7C - 2;
Page 77 ~ b3 - 1; b6 - 2; b7C - 2;
Page 78 ~ b3 - 1; b6 - 2; b7C - 2;
Page 79 ~ b3 - 1; b6 - 2; b7C - 2;
Page 80 ~ b3 - 1; b6 - 2; b7C - 2;
Page 81 ~ b3 - 1; b6 - 2; b7C - 2;
Page 82 ~ b3 - 1; b6 - 2; b7C - 2;
Page 83 ~ b3 - 1; b6 - 2; b7C - 2;
Page 84 ~ b3 - 1; b6 - 2; b7C - 2;
Page 85 ~ b3 - 1; b6 - 2; b7C - 2;
Page 86 ~ b3 - 1; b6 - 2; b7C - 2;
Page 87 ~ b3 - 1; b6 - 2; b7C - 2;
Page 88 ~ b3 - 1; b6 - 2; b7C - 2;
Page 89 ~ b3 - 1; b6 - 2; b7C - 2;
Page 90 ~ b3 - 1; b6 - 2; b7C - 2;
Page 91 ~ b3 - 1; b6 - 2; b7C - 2;
Page 92 ~ b3 - 1; b6 - 2; b7C - 2;
Page 93 ~ b3 - 1; b6 - 2; b7C - 2;
Page 94 ~ b3 - 1; b6 - 2; b7C - 2;
Page 95 ~ b3 - 1; b6 - 2; b7C - 2;
Page 96 ~ b3 - 1; b6 - 2; b7C - 2;
Page 97 ~ b3 - 1; b6 - 2; b7C - 2;
Page 98 ~ b3 - 1; b6 - 2; b7C - 2;
Page 99 ~ b3 - 1; b6 - 2; b7C - 2;
Page 100 ~ b3 - 1; b6 - 2; b7C - 2;
Page 101 ~ b3 - 1; b6 - 2; b7C - 2;
Page 102 ~ b3 - 1; b6 - 2; b7C - 2;

Page 103 ~ b3 - 1; b6 - 2; b7C - 2;
Page 104 ~ b3 - 1; b6 - 2; b7C - 2;
Page 105 ~ b3 - 1; b6 - 2; b7C - 2;
Page 106 ~ b3 - 1; b6 - 2; b7C - 2;
Page 107 ~ b3 - 1; b6 - 2; b7C - 2;
Page 108 ~ b3 - 1; b6 - 2; b7C - 2;
Page 109 ~ b3 - 1; b6 - 2; b7C - 2;
Page 110 ~ b3 - 1; b6 - 2; b7C - 2;
Page 111 ~ b3 - 1; b6 - 2; b7C - 2;
Page 112 ~ b3 - 1; b6 - 2; b7C - 2;
Page 113 ~ b3 - 1; b6 - 2; b7C - 2;
Page 114 ~ b3 - 1; b6 - 2; b7C - 2;
Page 115 ~ b3 - 1; b6 - 2; b7C - 2;
Page 116 ~ b3 - 1; b6 - 2; b7C - 2;
Page 117 ~ b3 - 1; b6 - 2; b7C - 2;
Page 118 ~ b3 - 1; b6 - 2; b7C - 2;
Page 119 ~ b3 - 1; b6 - 2; b7C - 2;
Page 120 ~ b3 - 1; b6 - 2; b7C - 2;
Page 121 ~ b3 - 1; b6 - 2; b7C - 2;
Page 122 ~ b3 - 1; b6 - 2; b7C - 2;
Page 123 ~ b3 - 1; b6 - 2; b7C - 2;
Page 124 ~ b3 - 1; b6 - 2; b7C - 2;
Page 125 ~ b3 - 1; b6 - 2; b7C - 2;
Page 126 ~ b3 - 1; b6 - 2; b7C - 2;
Page 127 ~ b3 - 1; b6 - 2; b7C - 2;
Page 128 ~ b3 - 1; b6 - 2; b7C - 2;
Page 129 ~ b3 - 1; b6 - 2; b7C - 2;
Page 130 ~ b3 - 1; b6 - 2; b7C - 2;
Page 131 ~ b3 - 1; b6 - 2; b7C - 2;
Page 132 ~ b3 - 1; b6 - 2; b7C - 2;
Page 133 ~ b3 - 1; b6 - 2; b7C - 2;
Page 134 ~ b3 - 1; b6 - 2; b7C - 2;
Page 135 ~ b3 - 1; b6 - 2; b7C - 2;
Page 136 ~ b3 - 1; b6 - 2; b7C - 2;
Page 137 ~ b3 - 1; b6 - 2; b7C - 2;
Page 138 ~ b3 - 1; b6 - 2; b7C - 2;
Page 139 ~ b3 - 1; b6 - 2; b7C - 2;
Page 140 ~ b3 - 1; b6 - 2; b7C - 2;
Page 141 ~ b3 - 1; b6 - 2; b7C - 2;
Page 142 ~ b3 - 1; b6 - 2; b7C - 2;
Page 143 ~ b3 - 1; b6 - 2; b7C - 2;
Page 144 ~ b3 - 1; b6 - 2; b7C - 2;
Page 145 ~ b3 - 1; b6 - 2; b7C - 2;
Page 146 ~ b3 - 1; b6 - 2; b7C - 2;
Page 147 ~ b3 - 1; b6 - 2; b7C - 2;
Page 148 ~ b3 - 1; b6 - 2; b7C - 2;
Page 149 ~ b3 - 1; b6 - 2; b7C - 2;
Page 150 ~ b3 - 1; b6 - 2; b7C - 2;
Page 151 ~ b3 - 1; b6 - 2; b7C - 2;
Page 152 ~ b3 - 1; b6 - 2; b7C - 2;
Page 153 ~ b3 - 1; b6 - 2; b7C - 2;
Page 154 ~ b3 - 1; b6 - 2; b7C - 2;
Page 155 ~ b3 - 1; b6 - 2; b7C - 2;
Page 156 ~ b3 - 1; b6 - 2; b7C - 2;

Page 157 ~ b3 - 1; b6 - 2; b7C - 2;
Page 158 ~ b3 - 1; b6 - 2; b7C - 2;
Page 159 ~ b3 - 1; b6 - 2; b7C - 2;
Page 160 ~ b3 - 1; b6 - 2; b7C - 2;
Page 161 ~ b3 - 1; b6 - 2, 5; b7C - 2, 5;

XXXXXXXXXXXXXXXXXXXXXXXX
X Deleted Page(s) X
X No Duplication Fee X
X For this Page X
XXXXXXXXXXXXXXXXXXXXXXXX

FEDERAL BUREAU OF INVESTIGATION
FOI/PA
DELETED PAGE INFORMATION SHEET
Civil Action# 16-cv-02136

Total Deleted Page(s) = 165
Page 1 ~ b3 - 1; b6 - 5; b7C - 5;
Page 2 ~ b3 - 1; b6 - 1, 5; b7C - 1, 5;
Page 3 ~ b3 - 1; b6 - 5; b7C - 5;
Page 4 ~ b3 - 1; b6 - 4; b7C - 4;
Page 5 ~ b3;
Page 6 ~ b3 - 1; b6 - 1, 4; b7C - 1, 4;
Page 7 ~ b3 - 1; b6 - 1, 5; b7C - 1, 5;
Page 8 ~ b3 - 1; b6 - 5; b7C - 5;
Page 9 ~ b3 - 1; b6 - 5; b7C - 5;
Page 10 ~ b3 - 1;
Page 11 ~ b3 - 1;
Page 12 ~ b3 - 1;
Page 13 ~ b3 - 1;
Page 14 ~ b3 - 1;
Page 15 ~ b3 - 1;
Page 16 ~ b3 - 1;
Page 17 ~ b3 - 1;
Page 18 ~ b3 - 1;
Page 19 ~ b3 - 1;
Page 20 ~ b3 - 1;
Page 21 ~ b3 - 1;
Page 22 ~ b3 - 1;
Page 23 ~ b3 - 1;
Page 24 ~ b3 - 1;
Page 25 ~ b3 - 1;
Page 26 ~ b3 - 1;
Page 27 ~ b3 - 1;
Page 28 ~ b3 - 1;
Page 29 ~ b3 - 1;
Page 30 ~ b3 - 1;
Page 31 ~ b3 - 1;
Page 32 ~ b3 - 1;
Page 33 ~ b3 - 1;
Page 34 ~ b3 - 1;
Page 35 ~ b3 - 1;
Page 36 ~ b3 - 1;
Page 37 ~ b3 - 1;
Page 38 ~ b3 - 1;
Page 39 ~ b3 - 1;
Page 40 ~ b3 - 1;
Page 41 ~ b3 - 1;
Page 42 ~ b3 - 1;
Page 43 ~ b3 - 1;
Page 44 ~ b3 - 1;
Page 45 ~ b3 - 1;
Page 46 ~ b3 - 1;
Page 47 ~ b3 - 1;
Page 48 ~ b3 - 1;

```
Page 49 ~ b3 - 1;
Page 50 ~ b3 - 1;
Page 51 ~ b3 - 1;
Page 52 ~ b3 - 1;
Page 53 ~ b3 - 1;
Page 54 ~ b3 - 1;
Page 55 ~ b3 - 1;
Page 56 ~ b3 - 1;
Page 57 ~ b3 - 1;
Page 58 ~ b3 - 1;
Page 59 ~ b3 - 1;
Page 60 ~ b3 - 1;
Page 61 ~ b3 - 1;
Page 62 ~ b3 - 1;
Page 63 ~ b3 - 1;
Page 64 ~ b3 - 1;
Page 65 ~ b3 - 1;
Page 66 ~ b3 - 1;
Page 67 ~ b3 - 1;
Page 68 ~ b3 - 1;
Page 69 ~ b3 - 1;
Page 70 ~ b3 - 1;
Page 71 ~ b3 - 1;
Page 72 ~ b3 - 1;
Page 73 ~ b3 - 1;
Page 74 ~ b3 - 1;
Page 75 ~ b3 - 1;
Page 76 ~ b3 - 1;
Page 77 ~ b3 - 1;
Page 78 ~ b3 - 1;
Page 79 ~ b3 - 1;
Page 80 ~ b3 - 1;
Page 81 ~ b3 - 1;
Page 82 ~ b3 - 1;
Page 83 ~ b3 - 1;
Page 84 ~ b3 - 1;
Page 85 ~ b3 - 1;
Page 86 ~ b3 - 1;
Page 87 ~ b3 - 1;
Page 88 ~ b3 - 1;
Page 89 ~ b3 - 1;
Page 90 ~ b3 - 1;
Page 91 ~ b3 - 1;
Page 92 ~ b3 - 1;
Page 93 ~ b3 - 1;
Page 94 ~ b3 - 1;
Page 95 ~ b3 - 1;
Page 96 ~ b3 - 1;
Page 97 ~ b3 - 1;
Page 98 ~ b3 - 1;
Page 99 ~ b3 - 1;
Page 100 ~ b3 - 1;
Page 101 ~ b3 - 1;
Page 102 ~ b3 - 1;
```

```
Page 103 ~ b3 - 1;
Page 104 ~ b3 - 1;
Page 105 ~ b3 - 1;
Page 106 ~ b3 - 1;
Page 107 ~ b3 - 1;
Page 108 ~ b3 - 1;
Page 109 ~ b3 - 1;
Page 110 ~ b3 - 1;
Page 111 ~ b3 - 1;
Page 112 ~ b3 - 1;
Page 113 ~ b3 - 1;
Page 114 ~ b3 - 1;
Page 115 ~ b3 - 1;
Page 116 ~ b3 - 1;
Page 117 ~ b3 - 1;
Page 118 ~ b3 - 1;
Page 119 ~ b3 - 1;
Page 120 ~ b3 - 1;
Page 121 ~ b3 - 1;
Page 122 ~ b3 - 1;
Page 123 ~ b3 - 1;
Page 124 ~ b3 - 1;
Page 125 ~ b3 - 1;
Page 126 ~ b3 - 1;
Page 127 ~ b3 - 1;
Page 128 ~ b3 - 1;
Page 129 ~ b3 - 1;
Page 130 ~ b3 - 1;
Page 131 ~ b3 - 1;
Page 132 ~ b3 - 1;
Page 133 ~ b3 - 1;
Page 134 ~ b3 - 1;
Page 135 ~ b3 - 1;
Page 136 ~ b3 - 1;
Page 137 ~ b3 - 1;
Page 138 ~ b3 - 1;
Page 139 ~ b3 - 1;
Page 140 ~ b3 - 1;
Page 141 ~ b3 - 1;
Page 142 ~ b3 - 1;
Page 143 ~ b3 - 1;
Page 144 ~ b3 - 1;
Page 145 ~ b3 - 1;
Page 146 ~ b3 - 1;
Page 147 ~ b3 - 1;
Page 148 ~ b3 - 1;
Page 149 ~ b3 - 1;
Page 150 ~ b3 - 1;
Page 151 ~ b3 - 1;
Page 152 ~ b3 - 1;
Page 153 ~ b3 - 1;
Page 154 ~ b3 - 1;
Page 155 ~ b3 - 1;
Page 156 ~ b3 - 1;
```

Page 157 ~ b3 - 1;
Page 158 ~ b3 - 1;
Page 159 ~ b3 - 1;
Page 160 ~ b3 - 1;
Page 161 ~ b3 - 1;
Page 162 ~ b3 - 1;
Page 163 ~ b3 - 1;
Page 164 ~ b3 - 1;
Page 165 ~ b3 - 1;

XXXXXXXXXXXXXXXXXXXXXXXX
X Deleted Page(s) X
X No Duplication Fee X
X For this Page X
XXXXXXXXXXXXXXXXXXXXXXXX

FEDERAL BUREAU OF INVESTIGATION
FOI/PA
DELETED PAGE INFORMATION SHEET
Civil Action# 16-cv-02136

Total Deleted Page(s) = 97
Page 1 ~ Duplicate;
Page 2 ~ Duplicate;
Page 3 ~ Duplicate;
Page 4 ~ Duplicate;
Page 5 ~ Duplicate;
Page 6 ~ Duplicate;
Page 7 ~ Duplicate;
Page 8 ~ Duplicate;
Page 9 ~ Duplicate;
Page 10 ~ Duplicate;
Page 11 ~ Duplicate;
Page 12 ~ Duplicate;
Page 13 ~ Duplicate;
Page 14 ~ Duplicate;
Page 15 ~ Duplicate;
Page 16 ~ Duplicate;
Page 17 ~ Duplicate;
Page 18 ~ Duplicate;
Page 19 ~ Duplicate;
Page 20 ~ Duplicate;
Page 21 ~ Duplicate;
Page 22 ~ Duplicate;
Page 23 ~ Duplicate;
Page 24 ~ Duplicate;
Page 25 ~ Duplicate;
Page 26 ~ Duplicate;
Page 27 ~ Duplicate;
Page 28 ~ Duplicate;
Page 29 ~ Duplicate;
Page 30 ~ Duplicate;
Page 31 ~ Duplicate;
Page 32 ~ Duplicate;
Page 33 ~ Duplicate;
Page 34 ~ Duplicate;
Page 35 ~ Duplicate;
Page 36 ~ Duplicate;
Page 37 ~ Duplicate;
Page 38 ~ Duplicate;
Page 39 ~ Duplicate;
Page 40 ~ Duplicate;
Page 41 ~ Duplicate;
Page 42 ~ Duplicate;
Page 43 ~ Duplicate;
Page 44 ~ Duplicate;
Page 45 ~ Duplicate;
Page 46 ~ Duplicate;
Page 47 ~ Duplicate;
Page 48 ~ Duplicate;

Page 49 ~ Duplicate;
Page 50 ~ Duplicate;
Page 51 ~ Duplicate;
Page 52 ~ Duplicate;
Page 53 ~ Duplicate;
Page 54 ~ Duplicate;
Page 55 ~ Duplicate;
Page 56 ~ Duplicate;
Page 57 ~ Duplicate;
Page 58 ~ Duplicate;
Page 59 ~ Duplicate;
Page 60 ~ Duplicate;
Page 61 ~ Duplicate;
Page 62 ~ Duplicate;
Page 63 ~ Duplicate;
Page 64 ~ Duplicate;
Page 65 ~ Duplicate;
Page 66 ~ Duplicate;
Page 67 ~ Duplicate;
Page 68 ~ Duplicate;
Page 69 ~ Duplicate;
Page 70 ~ Duplicate;
Page 71 ~ Duplicate;
Page 72 ~ Duplicate;
Page 73 ~ Duplicate;
Page 74 ~ Duplicate;
Page 75 ~ Duplicate;
Page 76 ~ Duplicate;
Page 77 ~ Duplicate;
Page 78 ~ Duplicate;
Page 79 ~ Duplicate;
Page 80 ~ Duplicate;
Page 81 ~ Duplicate;
Page 82 ~ Duplicate;
Page 83 ~ Duplicate;
Page 84 ~ Duplicate;
Page 85 ~ Duplicate;
Page 86 ~ Duplicate;
Page 87 ~ Duplicate;
Page 88 ~ Duplicate;
Page 89 ~ Duplicate;
Page 90 ~ Duplicate;
Page 91 ~ Duplicate;
Page 92 ~ Duplicate;
Page 93 ~ Duplicate;
Page 94 ~ Duplicate;
Page 95 ~ Duplicate;
Page 96 ~ Duplicate;
Page 97 ~ Duplicate;

XXXXXXXXXXXXXXXXXXXXXXXX

FEDERAL BUREAU OF INVESTIGATION
FOI/PA
DELETED PAGE INFORMATION SHEET
Civil Action# 16-cv-02136

Total Deleted Page(s) = 8
Page 1 ~ Duplicate;
Page 2 ~ Duplicate;
Page 3 ~ Duplicate;
Page 4 ~ Duplicate;
Page 5 ~ Duplicate;
Page 6 ~ Duplicate;
Page 7 ~ Duplicate;
Page 8 ~ Duplicate;

XXXXXXXXXXXXXXXXXXXXXXXX
X Deleted Page(s) X
X No Duplication Fee X
X For this Page X
XXXXXXXXXXXXXXXXXXXXXXXX

FEDERAL BUREAU OF INVESTIGATION
FOI/PA
DELETED PAGE INFORMATION SHEET
Civil Action# 16-cv-02136

Total Deleted Page(s) = 38
Page 1 ~ OTHER - Sealed Pursuant to Court Order;
Page 2 ~ b6 - 1, 2; b7C - 1, 2; b7E - 5; OTHER - Sealed Pursuant to Court Order;
Page 3 ~ b6 - 1, 2; b7C - 1, 2; b7E - 5; OTHER - Sealed Pursuant to Court Order;
Page 4 ~ b6 - 1, 2; b7C - 1, 2; OTHER - Sealed Pursuant to Court Order;
Page 5 ~ b6 - 2; b7C - 2; OTHER - Sealed Pursuant to Court Order;
Page 6 ~ b6 - 2; b7C - 2; OTHER - Sealed Pursuant to Court Order;
Page 7 ~ OTHER - Sealed Pursuant to Court Order;
Page 8 ~ OTHER - Sealed Pursuant to Court Order;
Page 9 ~ OTHER - Sealed Pursuant to Court Order;
Page 10 ~ OTHER - Sealed Pursuant to Court Order;
Page 11 ~ b6 - 1; b7C - 1; b7E - 5; OTHER - Sealed Pursuant to Court Order;
Page 12 ~ b6 - 1, 2; b7C - 1, 2; OTHER - Sealed Pursuant to Court Order;
Page 13 ~ OTHER - Sealed Pursuant to Court Order;
Page 14 ~ b6 - 1; b7C - 1; b7E - 5; OTHER - Sealed Pursuant to Court Order;
Page 15 ~ b6 - 1, 2; b7C - 1, 2; b7E - 5; OTHER - Sealed Pursuant to Court Order;
Page 16 ~ b6 - 2; b7C - 2; OTHER - Sealed Pursuant to Court Order;
Page 17 ~ b6 - 2; b7C - 2; OTHER - Sealed Pursuant to Court Order;
Page 18 ~ b6 - 2; b7C - 2; OTHER - Sealed Pursuant to Court Order;
Page 19 ~ b6 - 2; b7C - 2; OTHER - Sealed Pursuant to Court Order;
Page 20 ~ b6 - 1; b7C - 1; OTHER - Sealed Pursuant to Court Order;
Page 21 ~ OTHER - Sealed Pursuant to Court Order;
Page 22 ~ OTHER - Sealed Pursuant to Court Order;
Page 23 ~ OTHER - Sealed Pursuant to Court Order;
Page 24 ~ OTHER - Sealed Pursuant to Court Order;
Page 25 ~ OTHER - Sealed Pursuant to Court Order;
Page 26 ~ OTHER - Sealed Pursuant to Court Order;
Page 27 ~ OTHER - Sealed Pursuant to Court Order;
Page 28 ~ OTHER - Sealed Pursuant to Court Order;
Page 29 ~ b6 - 1; b7C - 1; Duplicate - Sealed Pursuant to Court Order;
Page 30 ~ OTHER - Sealed Pursuant to Court Order;
Page 31 ~ OTHER - Sealed Pursuant to Court Order;
Page 32 ~ OTHER - Sealed Pursuant to Court Order;
Page 33 ~ b6 - 1; b7C - 1; OTHER - Sealed Pursuant to Court Order;
Page 34 ~ OTHER - Sealed Pursuant to Court Order;
Page 35 ~ OTHER - Sealed Pursuant to Court Order;
Page 36 ~ b6 - 1; b7C - 1; OTHER - Sealed Pursuant to Court Order;
Page 37 ~ OTHER - Sealed Pursuant to Court Order;
Page 38 ~ OTHER - Sealed Pursuant to Court Order;

XXXXXXXXXXXXXXXXXXXXXXXX
X Deleted Page(s) X
X No Duplication Fee X
X For this Page X

XXXXXXXXXXXXXXXXXXXXXXXX

www.ingramcontent.com/pod-product-compliance
Lightning Source LLC
Chambersburg PA
CBHW060301010526
44108CB00042B/2592

9780986275227